REFERENCE

W9-CEP-740

Notable American Novelists

Revised Edition

MAGILL'S CHOICE

NOTABLE AMERICAN NOVELISTS

REVISED EDITION

Volume 3
John O'Hara — Richard Wright
1015 – 1506
Index

edited by
CARL ROLLYSON
BARUCH COLLEGE, CITY UNIVERSITY OF NEW YORK

SALEM PRESS, INC.
Pasadena, California   Hackensack, New Jersey

1·v.3 (O'HA-Z)
6113554114
2396750

R
813.009
N

Cover photo: ©iStockphoto.com/Stefan Klein

Copyright © 2000, 2008, by Salem Press, Inc.

All rights in this book are reserved. No part of this work may be used or reproduced in any manner whatsoever or transmitted in any form or by any means, electronic or mechanical, including photocopy, recording, or any information storage and retrieval system, without written permission from the copyright owner except in the case of brief quotations embodied in critical articles and reviews. For information address the publisher, Salem Press, Inc., P.O. Box 50062, Pasadena, California 91115.

Some essays in these volumes originally appeared in *Critical Survey of Long Fiction, Revised Edition*, 2000. New material has been added.

∞ The paper used in these volumes conforms to the American National Standard for Permanence of Paper for Printed Library Materials, Z39.48-1992 (R1997).

Library of Congress Cataloging-in-Publication Data

Notable American novelists / edited by Carl Rollyson.
    p. cm. — (Magill's choice)
  Includes bibliographical references and index.
  ISBN 978-1-58765-393-3 (set : alk. paper) — ISBN 978-1-58765-394-0 (vol. 1 : alk. paper) — ISBN 978-1-58765-395-7 (vol. 2 : alk. paper) — ISBN 978-1-58765-396-4 (vol. 3 : alk. paper) 1. Novelists, American—Biography—Dictionaries. 2. American fiction—Bio-bibliography—Dictionaries. 3. American fiction—Dictionaries. I. Rollyson, Carl E. (Carl Edmund)

PS371.N68 2007
813.009'0003—dc22
[B]

                                             2007018542

First printing

Contents—Volume 3

08/31/2012 0147-NLS 12.34

Complete List of Contents

Contents—Volume 1

Contents—Volume 2

Contents—Volume 3

NOTABLE AMERICAN NOVELISTS

NOVELISTS

REVISED EDITION

John O'Hara

Born: Pottsville, Pennsylvania; January 31, 1905
Died: Princeton, New Jersey; April 11, 1970

Principal long fiction • *Appointment in Samarra*, 1934; *Butterfield 8*, 1935; *A Rage to Live*, 1949; *The Farmer's Hotel*, 1951; *Ten North Frederick*, 1955; *A Family Party*, 1956; *From the Terrace*, 1958; *Ourselves to Know*, 1960; *Sermons and Soda Water*, 1960; *The Big Laugh*, 1962; *Elizabeth Appleton*, 1963; *The Lockwood Concern*, 1965; *The Instrument*, 1967; *Lovey Childs: A Philadelphian's Story*, 1969; *The Ewings*, 1972.

Other literary forms • John O'Hara was a prolific writer of short stories, and eleven volumes of stories were published during his lifetime. After O'Hara's death, Random House, his publisher since 1947, brought out two additional collections: *The Time Element, and Other Stories* (1972) and *Good Samaritan, and Other Stories* (1974). Scattered throughout the short-story collections are most of O'Hara's works in the novella form; the only novellas to be separately published are the three in *Sermons and Soda Water*. The play version of the story "Pal Joey" was published in 1952, and in 1961 it was reissued with four others in *Five Plays*. O'Hara's last complete play, *Far from Heaven* (1962), was first published posthumously in 1979, along with an unproduced original screenplay, *The Man Who Could Not Lose* (1959), under the title *Two by O'Hara*. Like many other writers of his period, O'Hara wrote and collaborated on film scripts from the 1930's through the 1950's, and several of his novels were made into films during his lifetime. O'Hara began his writing career as a journalist, and he was several times a newspaper columnist. Two collections of his columns were published: *Sweet and Sour* (1954)—columns written for the Trenton *Sunday Times-Advertiser*—and *My Turn* (1966), a series of syndicated columns written for *Newsday*. A collection of O'Hara's speeches, essays, and interviews, titled *An Artist Is His Own Fault*, was edited by Matthew J. Bruccoli in 1977.

Achievements • Often dismissed as a popular novelist with tendencies toward sensationalism, or as a "social historian," O'Hara nevertheless secured a faithful following among many literary critics for his skill at storytelling and his evocation of times, places, and manners in American society in the first half of the twentieth century. O'Hara himself was equivocal about the label "social historian." In a speech in 1961, he said, "I deny that I am a social historian"; yet he went on to say that "before deciding to write a novel, I consider what opportunities a story offers for my comments on my times." Matthew J. Bruccoli is probably most accurate in calling O'Hara a "novelist of manners," in the sense that he was primarily concerned with the accurate depiction of a social matrix and its effect on human behavior and potential. Like William Faulkner and other twentieth century American novelists, O'Hara turned the realities of his hometown experience into a fictional world; unlike Faulkner, he probed this milieu with a dedication to social realism rather than elevating it to mythic status. In addition to his native eastern Pennsylvania, O'Hara used New York and Hollywood as frequent settings for his fiction. Although he lived and worked in both places, he is most clearly identified with the "Region" of Pennsylvania, on which he could bring to bear an insider's perceptions.

Courtesy, Pennsylvania State University Libraries

The fact that O'Hara was a realistic storyteller rather than an "experimental" novelist was detrimental to his critical reputation during his lifetime. Ironically, the explicit sexuality in much of his work (though restrained by today's standards), which was partially responsible for creating wide popular interest in his novels and which caused *Ten North Frederick* to be suppressed in several cities, overshadowed the depth of his concern with societal mores and pressures. Although he emphasized the role of fate and chance, O'Hara is usually considered a realist rather than a naturalist, largely because he allowed the possibility of moral choice. His long, detailed novels characteristically show people of a privileged socioeconomic level struggling with the realities of social class, personal worth, and complex human relationships.

O'Hara's treatment of his women characters has been overlooked by most critics, yet it may help to account for his enormous contemporary popularity. Long before it was fashionable or even allowable to do so, O'Hara realistically portrayed women as sexual human beings and even dealt openly with lesbianism in some of his novels and stories. Though several of his major female characters (such as Edith Chapin in *Ten North Frederick* and the title character of *Elizabeth Appleton*) are stereotypically manipulative, they are believable, complex people whose motivations are clearly the result of cultural pressures. It would be inaccurate to call O'Hara a feminist novelist, but he acknowledged women's power and their problems in ways that set him apart from most novelists of his period.

Whatever the eventual critical evaluation of O'Hara as a twentieth century American novelist, it is certain that his work will be used as a valuable resource for information about customs, manners, and attitudes in America from the 1920's through the 1950's, much as one consults the work of Theodore Dreiser, Sinclair Lewis, or John Updike. The ear for dialogue, the eye for detail, and the perception of human nature that made him a popular novelist will also ensure his continued importance.

Biography • John Henry O'Hara was born on January 31, 1905, in Pottsville, Pennsylvania. The town of Pottsville became the "Gibbsville" of his fiction, and the surrounding eastern Pennsylvania anthracite coal-mining area, known to residents as the "Region," was the locale of his major novels and stories. The author's father, Patrick O'Hara, was a doctor whose father had settled in the area during the Civil War, and his mother, Katharine Delaney O'Hara, was the daughter of a prosperous businessman in nearby Lykens, which became O'Hara's fictional "Lyons." Dr. Patrick O'Hara was a respected surgeon, necessarily specializing in injuries resulting from mining accidents, and he was seriously disappointed at his firstborn son's refusal to study medicine. Rather than inspiring a dedication to the medical profession, O'Hara's travels with his father to the scenes of medical emergencies provided him with regional lore that found its way into his writing.

Living on Pottsville's "best" street, Mahantongo ("Lantenengo" in the fictional Gibbsville), was a sign of the O'Hara family's relative affluence and provided O'Hara with an awareness of the rigid economic and ethnic stratification of the town. Until his father's early death in 1925, O'Hara led a fairly privileged existence, and his dream of attending Yale was thwarted less by lack of funds than by O'Hara's dismissals from three preparatory schools for low grades and disregard of discipline. The alternative to college was a job as a reporter on the Pottsville *Journal* in 1924, which effectively launched O'Hara's career as a writer.

In 1928, O'Hara left Pottsville for New York, where he worked briefly for the *Herald-Tribune* and *Time* and began to contribute stories to *The New Yorker*, which eventually published more than two hundred of his short stories; accordingly, some have attributed to O'Hara the creation of that subgenre, the *"New Yorker* story." During these early years in New York, O'Hara established friendships with Franklin P. Adams (F. P. A.)—to whose New York *World* column "The Conning Tower" he sometimes contributed—Robert Benchley, Dorothy Parker, and F. Scott Fitzgerald. In 1931, he married Helen Ritchie Petit ("Pet"), but his heavy drinking and frequent unemployment led to a divorce in 1933.

Appointment in Samarra, the first of O'Hara's fifteen novels, was published in 1934, and his first collection of short stories, *The Doctor's Son, and Other Stories*, appeared the following year. Although he was not financially secure for some time, O'Hara's reputation as a fiction writer grew steadily, and for the next twenty years, he lived alternately on the East Coast and in Hollywood, where he wrote film scripts. Although he intermittently aspired to be a playwright, O'Hara's only successful play was *Pal Joey*, based on a series of stories in *The New Yorker*, which ran on Broadway between 1940 and 1941. It was made into a film, starring Frank Sinatra and Rita Hayworth, in 1957. In 1956, O'Hara was given the National Book Award for *Ten North Frederick*, and in 1957 he was inducted into the National Institute of Arts and Letters, from which he resigned in 1961 because he had not been nominated for its Gold Medal for fiction.

In 1937, O'Hara married for the second time, to Belle Mulford Wylie, the mother of his only child, Wylie Delaney O'Hara, born in 1945. The O'Haras moved to Princeton, New Jersey, in 1949, and in 1953, a serious ulcer condition prompted O'Hara to quit drinking permanently. Following Belle's death in 1954, O'Hara married Katharine Barnes Bryan ("Sister") in 1955, and the family moved two years later to Linebrook, a home in Princeton that O'Hara and Sister had designed. O'Hara died at Linebrook April 11, 1970, while working on a sequel to *The Ewings*, his last published novel.

Analysis • In the spring of 1960, John O'Hara wrote as part of his preface to *Sermons and Soda Water:* "The Twenties, the Thirties, and the Forties are already history, but I cannot be content to leave their story in the hands of the historians and the editors of picture books. I want to record the way people talked and thought and felt." Despite his frequent rejection of the seemingly derogatory critical label of "social historian," which seemed to separate him in the minds of critics from more "serious" novelists, O'Hara was committed throughout his career to providing accurate records of the decades and places in which he lived. The novels and novellas that resulted from this commitment are uneven in quality as examples of the art of fiction, but they provide an unmatched portrait of segments of American society in the first half of the century. The central characters of much of his fiction are wealthy, prominent people, whether they are the leading citizens of Gibbsville, Pennsylvania, or Hollywood film stars, yet O'Hara frequently illuminates their circumstances by juxtaposing them with members of other socioeconomic groups: servants, tradesmen, laborers. The result is a panoramic social canvas, consonant with O'Hara's conception of the traditional novel form. Occasionally, as in *From the Terrace*, the realist's attempt at panoramic vision overwhelms artistic control; as Sheldon Grebstein remarks in *John O'Hara* (1966), "the *tranche de vie*... has been cut too thick to be digestible." At his best, however, O'Hara's work reflects the rich diversity of American society, as in his counterpointing of the savvy political boss Mike Slattery and the wealthy, naïve, would-be politician Joe Chapin in *Ten North Frederick*.

As the example of politics suggests, one of O'Hara's major themes is power—not only the power of money, though that is a central metaphor, but also the power inherent in talent, morality, and sexuality. O'Hara shared with F. Scott Fitzgerald a fascination with wealth and social prestige, but his treatment of their influence is far more analytical. His novels typically trace the establishment of a family dynasty, as in *The Lockwood Concern*, or the progress of an individual's aspirations for himself or herself, as in *Ten North Frederick*, and *Elizabeth Appleton*—always within the constraints of a social web rendered palpable by realistic settings and dialogue. O'Hara is concerned particularly with showing the limits of human power, not in the face of an overwhelming fate but as the result of miscalculation, error, or simple human frailty. When Julian English throws a drink in the face of Harry Reilly in *Appointment in Samarra*, or when George Lockwood, in *The Lockwood Concern*, builds a wall around his mansion, neither can foresee the fatal consequences, but both have made choices that dictate almost inevitable results.

As money is a metaphor for power in O'Hara's fiction, sexuality is an ambivalent metaphor for love. Though he was accused of sensationalism and bad taste in his relatively explicit depiction of sexual relationships, O'Hara was primarily interested in showing the potential for manipulation in the human sexual relationship. Women as well as men are portrayed as captive to sexual desire, and both sexes frequently mistake love for possession, or sex for love. From Grace Caldwell Tate's injudicious couplings in *A Rage to Live* to the tender relationship between Jim Malloy and Charlotte Sears in *The Girl on the Baggage Truck* (from *Sermons and Soda Water*), the possibility of true romantic love seems remote in O'Hara's fiction. His realistic approach assumes a basic human egotism and desire for power that renders such love rare.

The structures of O'Hara's novels and novellas reinforce the sense of inevitability of consequence. His novels frequently begin with an apparently small but significant event or action which spins out in mystery-story fashion to create the web that catches the characters and demonstrates their ultimate powerlessness. However, he avoids the predictability of formulaic fiction by using multiple points of view and a wealth of complex, believable characters to play out the drama. In the novellas, the structure is frequently circular, the story beginning at a moment of culmination and then tracing the events that have brought the characters to that point. Common too, especially in the novellas, is O'Hara's use of a narrator, usually Jim Malloy, a journalist whose background and attitudes resemble those of O'Hara. Although these structural devices were not original with O'Hara, he used them skillfully to suit his fictional purposes.

Character is of supreme importance in O'Hara's fiction, and the achievement of adequate characterization determined the form he used. As he said in one of his Rider College lectures, "before I have finished two pages of manuscript my author's instinct has told me how much I want to tell about this character, and thus the length of the story is dictated." The majority of O'Hara's characters inhabit the Pennsylvania "Region" in which he spent his youth, and the fictional canon provides a vivid picture of relationships among people of various social levels over time. The reappearance of certain characters in many works reinforces the sense of a coherent world wherein the codes of morality and propriety dictate the shape of both society and individual human lives.

In its settings, characters, and incidents, O'Hara's fiction is strongly autobiographical, a circumstance that is a natural outgrowth of his desire to be a recorder of his times. Though he did not live in Pottsville, Pennsylvania, after 1930, the town and its people continued to serve as a microcosm of the American culture he dissected throughout his career. Like his autobiographical narrator Jim Malloy, O'Hara returned to Pottsville "only long enough to stand at a grave, to toast a bride, to spend a few minutes beside a sickbed," but the years he spent there left an indelible impression. From his vantage point as the doctor's son, O'Hara observed both the leading citizens and the transients, and later he explored, in his novels and novellas, the lives he imagined to exist behind the placid exterior of the American small town. Part of the autobiographical content of the fiction, however, comes from O'Hara's unfulfilled aspirations rather than from his actual experience. Although his dream of attending an Ivy League college was thwarted by his checkered prep school record and the death of his father, O'Hara's upper-class male characters typically attend prestigious universities and benefit from larger family fortunes than O'Hara's family ever enjoyed. His fiction, like that of Fitzgerald, thus conveys an ambivalent attitude toward the privileged: the wistfulness of the outsider and the realist's desire to reduce them to understandable human terms.

The span of O'Hara's career, from 1934 to 1970, coincided with a period of intense experimentation in literary forms. The fiction of James Joyce and William Faulkner, among others, tested the limits of the novel, and critical opinion during these years favored attempts to break the mold of traditional fiction, to push beyond the bounds of realistic documentation of recognizable human events. Thus, O'Hara's accurate rendition of dialogue lost place to stream of consciousness as an acclaimed technique, and the chronicling of successive generations was less favored than novels spanning a single day, controlled by a single consciousness. O'Hara's novels continue to be appreciated more for their documentary usefulness than for their creative force, yet within the limits of the traditional novel form, O'Hara was a master craftsman who captured and conveyed the human drama and social fabric of a complex period in American life.

Appointment in Samarra • In 1961, O'Hara referred to *Appointment in Samarra* as "a live novel twenty-five years after first publication." O'Hara's first novel would continue to "live," in several senses. It is obviously the work of a professional writer; O'Hara's powers of observation and skill in plot construction are already highly developed in this short novel. Also, *Appointment in Samarra* is set in the "Region" of eastern Pennsylvania, the setting of much of his long fiction throughout his career, and it has strong autobiographical elements. Finally, the novel deals starkly and dramatically with the themes of power and fate and demonstrates O'Hara's understanding of individual human destiny as a delicate balance between necessity and accident. The novel's title derives from a quotation from W. Somerset Maugham; the "appointment in Samarra" is an inescapable appointment with death, yet Julian English, O'Hara's main character, is doomed by his own actions—his tragedy is of his own making.

The story of Julian English is set against a richly detailed social and geographical background. O'Hara takes pains to provide the reader with the flavor of the early Depression years: the names of popular songs, the intricacies of the bootlegger's profession, and the subdued desperation of both rich and poor. To tie the novel even further to an era, there are topical references; Julian English mentions having recently read Ernest Hemingway's *A Farewell to Arms* (1929), and Irma Fleigler counts on President Herbert Hoover's promise that next year will be better for everyone, so that she and her husband can join the country club to which the Englishes belong. The club, and the town and region of which it is the social pinnacle, are treated with the same careful detail. O'Hara devotes several pages to the peculiarities of the anthracite coal region and the social hierarchy of Gibbsville, making clear that no person or action is independent of the social context. Despite the anxieties of what was called in 1930 a "slump," Gibbsville and its inhabitants are filled with self-importance, and none more so than Julian English, the doctor's son.

English and O'Hara share several biographical similarities. Julian, like O'Hara, has refused to adopt his doctor-father's profession, and his refusal has caused a serious rift in the father-son relationship. Julian English admires Franklin P. Adams (F. P. A.), to whom O'Hara dedicated *Appointment in Samarra*, and when a priest asks him whether he is a "frustrated literary man," Julian answers, "I'm not anything. I guess I should have been a doctor." The most important similarity between English and his creator is the sense of insecurity betrayed by this remark, an insecurity that leads both men to heavy drinking and defensive belligerence. The significant difference is that Julian English does not survive his own nature.

To dramatize his perception that the individual is inextricably bound up in his social context, O'Hara deftly shifts the point of view in the novel from interior to exterior views of Julian English, emphasizing the extent to which one person becomes the object of others' scrutiny. The novel covers the last three days of Julian's life, from the moment he throws a drink in Harry Reilly's face at the country club Christmas party until he commits suicide by carbon monoxide poisoning, yet the narrative begins and ends with the observations of Luther and Irma Fleigler, a middle-class couple whose solid respectability and loving relationship contrast sharply with the weakness and manipulation of the far wealthier Julian and Caroline English. Julian's action is, in itself, insignificant—a social error from which all parties could have recovered in time—but it becomes symbolic of Julian's misperception of his own strength and power. With the inevitability of Greek tragedy, social ostracism follows Julian's throwing of the drink; he becomes an outsider to his own group, and he fails in all his efforts to pick up the pieces of his life.

O'Hara presents, one by one, the sources of comfort to which twentieth century men turn in times of personal trouble and shows them all to be ineffective. Family, sex, work, drink, religion, even a simple apology—none provides solace to Julian, who is the isolated twentieth century man, left with nothing in which to believe. If Julian does not understand the motivation for his action, neither does anyone else around him, and neither his father, Dr. English, nor his wife can respond adequately to his anguish. Work fails as an escape because, as the president of a Cadillac dealership, Julian is dependent upon precisely the goodwill of potential customers, which his action has temporarily denied him, and drink leads to either self-pity or further belligerence. Monsignor Creedon, to whom Julian, a Protestant, feels obscurely drawn, confesses that he has sometimes wished he had chosen a different life's work; lacking a true vocation, he cannot provide a spiritual solution to Julian's guilt and loneliness.

Although the major conflict in the novel is that between Julian's personal responsibility for his own actions and fate and the effect of his social surroundings on that fate, O'Hara introduces a third element: heredity. Conscious of his own family heritage, and especially of his forebears' struggle through generations for greater status and respectability in the "Region," O'Hara places great importance on a sense of heritage. His characters are typically aware of where they come from, who their ancestors are, and to what this background entitles them on the social scale. Julian English's grandfather had committed suicide after embezzling money from a bank, and after Julian's suicide, Dr. English consoles himself regarding his own reputation by assuming that people "would see how the suicide strain has skipped one generation to come out in the next."

Dr. English reappears in several of O'Hara's later works, as do several other characters introduced. Jim Malloy, mentioned previously, becomes the narrator of the novellas in *Sermons and Soda Water,* and the relationship between Whit Hofman, here a minor character, and Pat Collins is the basis of the novella *Pat Collins.* In short, *Appointment in Samarra* established O'Hara's major locale, characters, and themes, and much of his fictional canon enlarged upon what was set forth in this novel.

The critical reception of O'Hara's first novel was generally favorable, though some reviewers were disturbed by its relatively explicit sexuality. This reaction was intensified by his next two major novels, *Butterfield 8* and *A Rage to Live,* both of which sold well in part because of the furor, and his collections of short stories were consistently well received. *Appointment in Samarra* had launched its author on a successful career.

Ten North Frederick • Although many of the short stories O'Hara published in the five collections between 1935 and 1947 were set in the "Region," *Ten North Frederick* was the first novel after *Appointment in Samarra* to deal with that locale. *Ten North Frederick* marked the beginning of the major phase of O'Hara's work as well as a new stage in his life. Two years before its publication, he had suffered the bleeding ulcer that persuaded him to give up alcohol permanently, and a few months before, he had married Katharine Barnes Bryan, whom he referred to as "Sister." For the next fifteen years until his death, O'Hara would live a more settled, productive life than ever before. The timing of the novel's publication also began a tradition that continued for the rest of his career. Because O'Hara, always sensitive to reviews, wanted the task of reviewing *Ten North Frederick* to fall to a particular writer for *The New York Times,* the novel was issued on a Thursday in late November. The day was Thanksgiving, and the publication of an O'Hara novel or collection became an annual Thanksgiving event.

Butterfield 8 had been a roman à clef, based on the sensational and tragic story of Starr Faithfull, but despite certain resemblances between the lives of Joe Chapin and Franklin Delano Roosevelt, *Ten North Frederick* is not. Rather, as Matthew Bruccoli suggests, the novel is a "what-if study: what if Roosevelt had been a Gibbsville Republican?" O'Hara undoubtedly had Roosevelt in mind as he created Joe Chapin, and he used some elements of Roosevelt's life—the strong mother with ambitions for her son and a physical crippling in midlife—but his intention was not, as it was in *Butterfield 8,* to write a fictional account of a well-known person. Indeed, whereas

Roosevelt's story is one of triumph over personal adversity, *Ten North Frederick* chronicles the failure of Joe Chapin's ambitions.

Those ambitions are far from modest. Joe Chapin wants nothing less than to leave each of his children a million dollars upon his death and to become president of the United States. The fact that he achieves neither goal is in part the result of circumstances (the Great Depression reduces his financial assets) and in part the result of errors in judgment, such as his attempting to circumvent the local political system managed by Mike Slattery. Despite the magnitude of his hopes, Chapin is neither grasping nor overwhelmingly egotistical. Although he makes some ill-considered decisions about the lives of others—notably his daughter's abortion and the dissolution of her marriage to an Italian musician—he is not a power-hungry schemer. Instead, he is unaware that his own power has limits. Reared to believe in the privileges of wealth and status and trained in the proprieties of social forms, Chapin is merely inflexible. Rules and forms have taken precedence over human responsiveness, and his one extramarital affair, late in his life, seems to be the only spontaneous action of which he is capable.

Joe Chapin's life thus has an opaque surface that prevents even his closest Gibbsville associates from knowing him well. At Chapin's funeral, one of his cousins remarks, "I could never figure Joe out," to which Mike Slattery replies, "We knew exactly what Joe wanted us to know. And believe me, that wasn't much." Coming at the beginning of the novel, this exchange might have foreshadowed the revelation of a secret life that Chapin had hidden carefully from his friends, but O'Hara's intention instead is to show that the reality of Chapin's life is one with its facade. Behind the mask of respectability is a life that is just as sterile as the mask would suggest. With the exception of minor scandals, such as his daughter's elopement and pregnancy, Chapin's experience has been one of single-minded devotion to the accumulation of wealth and status.

Beginning *Ten North Frederick* with the funeral of his main character, O'Hara employed a structural device that attested to his development as a novelist. Both *Appointment in Samarra* and *Ten North Frederick* begin with a moment of crisis or transition, but whereas in *Appointment in Samarra* the rest of the novel traces the almost inevitable results of that moment, *Ten North Frederick* begins with the conclusion—the death of Joe Chapin—and then proceeds to explore the life that has ended. The fact that the major threads of that life are introduced in the conversations at Chapin's funeral and are later developed in all their complexity has caused Sheldon Grebstein to call this a "tapestry novel." Having revealed the significant facts about Joe Chapin's life early in the novel, O'Hara must compel the reader to continue by means other than suspense.

The major strength of *Ten North Frederick*, as of most of O'Hara's fiction, is its characterization. The novel deals with three generations of the Chapin family, beginning with Joe Chapin's parents, though instead of a straight chronological narrative O'Hara uses a flashback technique, weaving past and present together to emphasize the effect of family—especially women—on the formation of character and ambition. Both Joe's mother, Charlotte, and his wife, Edith, have plans for his life; both are women for whom love means power and ownership, and for whom sex is a form of manipulation. Edith Chapin articulates this persistent theme of O'Hara's novels as she thinks, on her wedding night, "It was not Love; Love might easily have very little to do with it; but it was as strong a desire as Love or Hate and it was going to be her life, the owning of this man." As clearly as anywhere in his fiction, O'Hara here portrays women who, because they are denied most masculine forms of power, participate vicariously by requiring their men to succeed in their stead.

Joe Chapin is a failure. If there is a "secret" in his life, it is the depth of his desire for high political office. On the surface a personable, respected pillar of Gibbsville, highly regarded by most of its leading citizens, Chapin nurses the ambition for which his mother has groomed him, but he is not willing to play the political games required to gain the backing of Mike Slattery's organization, nor can money buy him the office he seeks. After he is forced to withdraw from the political arena, only his brief affair with his daughter's friend Kate Drummond gives his life meaning, and when that ends he slowly begins to commit suicide by drinking heavily.

Many of O'Hara's own feelings about accomplishment and aging informed his creation of Joe Chapin. O'Hara was fifty when the novel was completed. Like Chapin, he had gained the respect of many of his contemporaries, but certain measures of "success" had eluded him: in particular, recognition as a first-rate novelist. Both O'Hara and his character had suffered frightening indications of poor health; Chapin ignored the warning that alcohol was killing him, but O'Hara did not. Time had become precious to him, and he reflects on this in the final paragraph of *Ten North Frederick*: "There is always enough to do while the heart keeps pumping. There is never, never enough time to do it all." O'Hara was rewarded for his persistence when *Ten North Frederick* received the National Book Award for 1955. The award citation read in part: "Tough-minded as usual, Mr. O'Hara has written a novel of emotional depth and moral conviction."

Sermons and Soda Water • The swift passing of time to which O'Hara referred in *Ten North Frederick* was one of the reasons he turned to the novella form in the three pieces that make up *Sermons and Soda Water.* The novella took, he said, "a minimum of research," as compared to the "big novel" he was working on simultaneously (probably *The Lockwood Concern*). He wrote these novellas to "get it all down on paper while I can"; "at fifty-five I have no right to waste time." The novella, in other words, could be written quickly, from memory, rather than requiring years of research and writing. This distinction between the novel and the novella suggests that the material for the latter was more likely to be autobiographical, and his use of Jim Malloy as narrator in these three novellas adds to the impression that these are personal narratives.

Although O'Hara never fully defined the terms "novella" and "novelette" as he used them, he suggested in 1968 that the important consideration was character. The form, he said, "tells all that you need to know about certain people in certain circumstances so that those people become figures in the reader's personal library." He had first experimented with a form midway in length between the short story and the novel in the title story of *The Doctor's Son, and Other Stories*, his first collection of short stories, but during the last decade of his career, beginning with *Sermons and Soda Water*, he developed the novella form as a means of disentangling one thread from the usual complex tapestry of his novels. The novella as O'Hara conceived of it has an episodic structure. It follows one conflict, relationship, or problem through a lengthy time span, isolating for dramatic attention only the crucial periods, and briefly summarizing intervening months or years. There are no subplots, and minor characters are functional rather than centers of interest in their own right.

The use of a first-person narrator with a limited consciousness, rather than the omniscient point of view O'Hara employed in most of his novels, helps to ensure the sharp focus required for the novella. Jim Malloy, the narrator of *Sermons and Soda*

Water, tells the reader about the people he has known in his hometown of Gibbsville or those he meets as a journalist in New York. He is a thin mask for O'Hara in the early days of the author's career: the young man from the coal region who begins his career in New York, encounters the wealthy and famous, and keeps up with a few of the people back home. Yet, Malloy has the mature vision of O'Hara at the age of fifty-five, and his perspective on the characters' lives is that of a concerned friend rather than an impressionable young man. Malloy, like O'Hara, is a shrewd observer of human nature, one who finds patterns in life. In *We're Friends Again*, the third novella in *Sermons and Soda Water*, he comments on this ability: "The way things tie up, one with another, is likely to go unnoticed until a lawyer or a writer calls our attention to it." Malloy's function in these novellas is to demonstrate how "things tie up" while remaining more or less removed from the central stories.

In this ultimate detachment from the lives of the characters he describes, Malloy underscores the central theme of *Sermons and Soda Water*: human loneliness and isolation. At the end of *We're Friends Again*, Malloy calls loneliness "the final condition of us all," and O'Hara shows that it affects people at all levels of society—from Charlotte Sears, the film star in *The Girl on the Baggage Truck*, to Pete and Bobbie McCrea of Gibbsville in *Imagine Kissing Pete*. The solution to loneliness is love, but, as O'Hara so often suggests, love is elusive, and one often settles for approximations: attraction, sex, power. As Charlotte Sears says about her relationship with the wealthy, reclusive Thomas Hunterden, "There ought to be another word for love, for people like Hunterden and me." It is left to Malloy, as the controlling consciousness, to find meaning in the lives he relates, and that meaning resides ultimately in his capacity as a writer to discern patterns of inevitability in human life.

The Lockwood Concern • Of the novels written during O'Hara's last decade, *The Lockwood Concern* is particularly interesting as a culmination of many aspects of his career. During this period he used a variety of settings for his fiction—Hollywood in *The Big Laugh*, Philadelphia in *Lovey Childs*—but in *The Lockwood Concern* he returned to the "Region," to the characters and situations that he handled with ease and familiarity. Throughout the early 1960's, O'Hara referred to a "big" novel on which he was working, and at one point he projected that it would be a two-volume work. *The Lockwood Concern* is in fact a one-volume work of average length, but its scope justifies O'Hara's adjective: It is a multigenerational novel, a "century-spanning saga," as the jacket blurb proclaimed.

The theme of *The Lockwood Concern* is consistent with much of O'Hara's other work, and reaches back to *Appointment in Samarra*: the ultimate powerlessness of the individual against the force of circumstance, particularly the folly of attempting to control the destinies of others. The attempts of Abraham and George Lockwood, the second and third generations of the Lockwood family of Swedish Haven (actually Schuylkill Haven, near Pottsville), to establish a family dynasty break down in the fourth generation when George Lockwood's son and daughter reject the town and the family and adopt ways of life antithetical to dynastic responsibilities. The "concern" of the title is a Quaker concept, denoting an overwhelming sense of mission. Abraham Lockwood, in the late nineteenth century, has secularized this religious concept and translated it into a vision of generations of Lockwoods enjoying increasing wealth and prestige, including entrance to the clubs and other bastions of gentility denied him by the uncouth background and behavior of his own father, Moses Lockwood.

The central figure of *The Lockwood Concern* is George Lockwood, who has adopted Abraham's dream and brought it to the point of realization. George Lockwood's children will be the first generation to enjoy full acceptance by elite society, and as an emblem of this progress he has built a family mansion near Swedish Haven. The high, spiked wall around the house testifies to George's sense of exclusivity; it is also the cause of the death of a neighboring farm boy, who becomes impaled while attempting to climb the fence before the house is completed. This tragedy, which George Lockwood hastens to keep quiet, opens the novel, a signal of the crumbling of the erstwhile dynasty. From this point, George struggles to maintain the "concern" against increasing evidence of its demise until he finally falls to his death down a secret staircase he has had built in the still-uninhabited mansion.

O'Hara here used the circular structure that he had perfected in both long and short fiction throughout his career. The novel begins and ends in the mid-1920's but ranges back to the mid-nineteenth century as O'Hara details the history of the "Lockwood concern." It opens with the death of the unnamed farm boy and closes with the death of George Lockwood and, by implication, of the "concern." Simultaneously, the novel has the linear thrust of the historical novel. From the canny, vigorous survival of Moses Lockwood to the effete California existence of George's son Bing, the generations move through historical and cultural change, reflecting shifting values in American society. The novel argues that such change is almost inevitable, and that George Lockwood's attempt at consolidation and stasis is doomed from the start. Social flux is mirrored even in the names of the male Lockwoods over time, from the tradition and authority of "Moses" and "Abraham" to the frivolity of "Bing." Even with such change, however, basic human nature does not alter; George and Bing Lockwood are, in different ways, as conniving and self-interested as their ancestors, though protected by wealth and attorneys against open public disapproval.

The Lockwood Concern is a summation of much that O'Hara had tried and accomplished during thirty years of writing. Though not his best novel, it is one of his most ambitious in subject matter and scope. It provides a history of the "Region" from the time of O'Hara's ancestors until the time when he left it for New York, and it shows the growth of the region from a backwoods settlement to a thriving coal-mining and farming area that sent its sons to Princeton and Harvard. Thematically, the novel shows that O'Hara had come to some conclusions about the interplay of destiny and choice. He had shown in *Appointment in Samarra* that an individual's power over his own life was limited by the influence of society and the intervention of chance. In *Ten North Frederick*, he added great wealth and ambition to the equation and demonstrated their ineffectuality. By the time he wrote *The Lockwood Concern*, O'Hara saw the limits to human power as determined not only by conflicting wills and accidents of fate but also by the very sweep of time and change. Human aspiration pales before the only human certainty—death—which is described as a "secret" known only to those who have experienced it.

By entitling his biography of the author *The O'Hara Concern* (1975), Matthew J. Bruccoli suggests that O'Hara felt a sense of mission similar to that of the Lockwoods. If so, O'Hara's "concern" was not related to a family dynasty but instead to establishing himself among the first rank of American novelists. His lifelong war with literary critics and reviewers over the value of his contribution is evidence that he was never secure in his own reputation. Although he rejected the terms "social realist" and "social historian," these are appropriate characterizations of his best work. O'Hara's sense of history, his precise rendering of detail and dialogue, and his command of narrative technique make him one of the most significant chroniclers of American life in the first half of the twentieth century. The fact that he was a popular novelist during his career, in part because of the more sensational aspects of his work, has detracted from his critical reputation, but his position as an important novelist of manners seems secure.

Nancy Walker

Other major works

SHORT FICTION: *The Doctor's Son, and Other Stories*, 1935; *Hope of Heaven*, 1938; *Files on Parade*, 1939; *Pal Joey*, 1940; *Pipe Night*, 1945; *Hellbox*, 1947; *Assembly*, 1961; *The Cape Code Lighter*, 1962; *The Hat on the Bed*, 1963; *The Horse Knows the Way*, 1964; *Waiting for Winter*, 1966; *And Other Stories*, 1968; *The O'Hara Generation*, 1969; *The Time Element, and Other Stories*, 1972; *Good Samaritan, and Other Stories*, 1974.

PLAYS: *Five Plays*, pb. 1961; *Two by O'Hara*, pb. 1979 (includes *Far from Heaven*, 1962, and the screenplay *The Man Who Could Not Lose*, 1959).

SCREENPLAY: *Moontide*, 1942.

NONFICTION: *Sweet and Sour*, 1954; *My Turn*, 1966; *A Cub Tells His Story*, 1974; *An Artist Is His Own Fault*, 1977.

Bibliography

Bruccoli, Matthew J. *The O'Hara Concern*. New York: Random House, 1975. A carefully researched scholarly biography that reconstructs O'Hara's life and career in scrupulous detail, showing the evolution of his talent and thematic interests. Particularly authoritative in its account of O'Hara's break—and eventual reconciliation—with *The New Yorker*, and the impact of both events on his approach to short fiction. Bruccoli's biography is useful also for its exhaustive primary and secondary bibliographies.

Eppard, Philip B., ed. *Critical Essays on John O'Hara*. New York: G. K. Hall, 1994. Divided into sections on reviews and essays. All of O'Hara's major fiction is discussed, as well as his relationship to naturalism, his view of society, his short stories, and his view of politics, the family, and small towns. Includes a comprehensive introductory chapter on O'Hara's career and the reception of his novels, but no bibliography.

Farr, Finis. *O'Hara*. Boston: Little, Brown, 1973. Written by a journalist of O'Hara's generation, Farr's was the first O'Hara biography and, indeed, the first book to be written about O'Hara after his death, including discussion of novels and stories published during the last five years of his life. Somewhat more anecdotal in tone and scope than Bruccoli's biography, Farr's book, intended for the general reader, nevertheless includes penetrating readings of selected novels and stories, together with a brief but useful bibliography.

Goldleaf, Steven. *John O'Hara: A Study of the Short Fiction*. New York: Twayne, 1999. An excellent introduction to O'Hara's short stories. Includes bibliographical references and an index.

Grebstein, Sheldon Norman. *John O'Hara*. New Haven, Conn.: College and University Press, 1966. The first full-length study of O'Hara's narrative prose, prepared somewhat too soon to take in the full range of the author's later short fiction. Grebstein's volume discusses at length O'Hara's ongoing problems with the critical establishment; although Grebstein strives to achieve objectivity, it is clear that he tends to share the establishment's skeptical view of O'Hara's accomplishments. Grebstein does, however, provide good "readings" of such stories as were then available to him.

Grimes, William. "The John O'Hara Cult, at Least, Is Faithful." *The New York Times*, November 9, 1996, p. 17. An account of a panel discussion on O'Hara by five of his most ardent fans; the group chose O'Hara's *Appointment in Samarra* as the best introduction to O'Hara's work.

MacShane, Frank. *The Life of John O'Hara.* New York: E. P. Dutton, 1980. Looks at O'Hara's life through his work. A thorough study well worth reading for its valuable insights.

_____. Introduction to *Collected Stories of John O'Hara.* New York: Random House, 1984. MacShane, author of a somewhat sensational, if academically sound, biography of O'Hara, is perhaps most notable for his carefully prepared anthology of the author's shorter fiction, preceded by a most perceptive introduction. No small part of MacShane's accomplishment is the selection itself, covering the full length of O'Hara's career, yet subtly—and quite justifiably—weighted toward the stories written after 1960.

Quinn, Joseph L. "A Cold-Weather Journey with John O'Hara." *America* 169 (December 18-25, 1993): 17-21. Points out that throughout his career, O'Hara was preoccupied with the harsh winters and small-town atmosphere of Pottsville, Pennsylvania, the industrial coal-mining community where he was raised; discusses his links to F. Scott Fitzgerald and Ernest Hemingway.

Wolfe, Geoffrey. *The Art of Burning Bridges: A Life of John O'Hara.* New York: Alfred A. Knopf, 2003. Attempt to rehabilitate O'Hara's literary reputation by persuading readers to look past O'Hara's often repellant personal traits and lesser works to see the genius in his finest writings.

Walker Percy

Born: Birmingham, Alabama; May 28, 1916
Died: Covington, Louisiana; May 10, 1990

Principal long fiction • *The Moviegoer*, 1961; *The Last Gentleman*, 1966; *Love in the Ruins: The Adventures of a Bad Catholic at a Time Near the End of the World*, 1971; *Lancelot*, 1977; *The Second Coming*, 1980; *The Thanatos Syndrome*, 1987.

Other literary forms • As a writer of imaginative literature, Walker Percy devoted himself exclusively to the novel. However, he also wrote more than fifty reviews and essays on many of the same topics that inform his novels: existential philosophy, language theory, modern scientific method, contemporary American culture, the South, and literature. With one or two exceptions, the most important of these essays are collected in *The Message in the Bottle* (1975), which has as its peculiarly Percyean subtitle *How Queer Man Is, How Queer Language Is, and What One Has to Do with the Other*. An indispensable book, *The Message in the Bottle* not only clarifies the author's major concerns as well as his commitment to that most basic philosophical question, "What is man?" but also details the formidable intellectual foundation upon which his fiction so unpretentiously rests. That unpretentiousness is especially evident in *Lost in the Cosmos* (1983), ironically subtitled *The Last Self-Help Book*, in which Percy employs satire and semiotics in an effort to clarify the human being's social and more especially spiritual predicament as a uniquely "lost" creature needing the good news of the Gospels but all too often willing to settle for the insights of scientists and talk-show hosts.

Achievements • Walker Percy is perhaps most easily described as a Roman Catholic-existentialist-American-southern novelist, a baggy phrase that at least has the virtue of identifying the various currents that are blended together in his distinctive works. In Percy's fiction, Mark Twain's Huck Finn from the novel *Adventures of Huckleberry Finn* (1884) and Jean-Paul Sartre's Antoine Roquentin from the play *Nausea* (1938) meet in a single character adrift in a world where, despite the formless sprawl of mass society, the possibility of grace still exists. Percy's fiction is readily identifiable by its distinctive narrative voice. That voice—laconic yet disarmingly honest and filled with wonder—gained for Percy both critical respect and a dedicated readership. Percy received the National Book Award for *The Moviegoer*, the *Los Angeles Times* Book Award for *The Second Coming*, and the St. Louis Literary Award for *Lost in the Cosmos*. Among his other literary honors were memberships in the National Institute of Arts and Letters and the American Academy of Arts and Sciences.

Biography • Walker Percy was born in Birmingham, Alabama, on May 28, 1916. When his father, lawyer Leroy Percy, committed suicide in 1929, the widow and her three sons moved to Greenville, Mississippi, where they lived with Leroy's bachelor cousin, William Alexander Percy, who adopted the boys in 1931, following their mother's death in an automobile accident. The Greenville home served as something of a local cultural center; the uncle, the author of several works, including an autobiographical memoir of the South titled *Lanterns on the Levee* (1941), entertained such houseguests as William Faulkner, Carl Sandburg, Langston Hughes, David Cohn, and Harry Stack Sullivan.

During the early 1930's, Percy attended Greenville High School, where he wrote a gossip column and became the close friend of Shelby Foote, who was by then already committed to a literary career. At the University of North Carolina, which was noted for its school of behaviorism, Percy majored in chemistry and received a bachelor's degree in 1937. He then enrolled in Columbia's College of Physicians and Surgeons (M.D., 1941), where, in addition to his studies, he underwent psychoanalysis and became a frequent filmgoer. The turning point in his life came in early 1942 when, as a resident at Bellevue Hospital in New York, Percy contracted tuberculosis. During his two-year convalescence at Saranac Lake, he began reading extensively in philosophy and literature (Sartre, Albert Camus, Søren Kierkegaard, Gabriel Marcel, Fyodor Dostoevski, Nikolai Gogol, Leo Tolstoy, Franz Kafka). What he discovered was that as a medical doctor he knew much about people but had no idea what a human really is.

© Jerry Bauer

Following a relapse and further convalescence in 1944, Percy seemed sure of only two things: He was a doctor who did not wish to practice medicine; he was literally as well as existentially homeless (his uncle having died in 1942). In 1945, he traveled with Shelby Foote to New Mexico and then stayed on alone for a time. On November 7, 1946, he married Mary Bernice Townsend, and less than a year later they both converted to Roman Catholicism. (The decision to convert was, Percy said, in large measure the result of their reading of Kierkegaard's essay, "The Difference Between a Genius and an Apostle.") Soon after, the Percys moved from Sewanee, Tennessee, to New Orleans, Louisiana, where Percy continued his contemplative life, financially secure—thanks to his uncle's estate—and intellectually rich—his landlord, Julius Friend, a professor of philosophy, introduced him to the writings of Charles Saunders Peirce, whose triadic theory of language formed the basis of Percy's own linguistic speculations. (Percy's interest in language had another and more personal source: The younger of his two daughters was born deaf.) In 1950, the Percys moved to Covington, Louisiana, "a pleasant non-place," Percy said, where it is possible to live as a stranger in one's own land; it is neither the "anyplace" that characterizes mass society nor the "someplace" of a New Orleans or a Richmond, where the past haunts the present.

During the 1950's, Percy began publishing essays in such journals as *Thought, Commonweal,* and *Philosophy and Phenomenological Research.* After discarding two early novels, he began writing *The Moviegoer* in 1959, revising it four times before its publication two years later. Until his death on May 10, 1990, Percy lived quietly in Covington, a serious and meditative novelist who was also a Roman Catholic, an existentialist, and a southerner, pondering the world in thought, fiction, and an occasional essay.

Analysis • Walker Percy acknowledged that Kierkegaard's writings provided him with "a theoretical frame of reference," and one of the most important ideas that he adapted from this frame is Kierkegaard's rejection of Hegelian rationalism in favor of a subjective and intensely passionate commitment on the part of the individual. In Percy's view, modern science in general and the social sciences in particular have mistakenly and indiscriminately adopted the behaviorist, or biological, method and have consequently defined the human being reductively and abstractly. Existentialism, including the existential novel, on the other hand, presents an alternative to behaviorism: a "concrete" phenomenological approach whose aim is the recovery of humankind's uniqueness. Percy admits that the behaviorist method is valid to a point; ultimately, however, it must fail, because, in classifying the human as a biological organism acting in accordance with rules applicable to all biological organisms, it fails to deal with what is distinctly human, the nonbiological goals. Concerned solely with sameness, the scientific method cannot account for Fyodor Dostoevski's underground man except as a deviation from the norm. Existentialism, Percy believes, does account for this, as does Christianity, which acknowledges the fall of humanity and his distance from God, and defines existence as "the journey of a wayfarer along life's way." Denying the Fall, modern science makes the Gnostic mistake; it attempts to build Eden, the secular city, where human guilt and anxiety are conditioned away, where all biological needs are met, and where existence is certified by experts.

Percy rejects this "brave new world" and calls instead for a "radical anthropology" that can account for the ontological as well as the biological aspects of human existence. Guilt and anxiety, he points out, are not symptoms of maladjustment to be gotten rid of so that the individual (as human organism) can live the life of the satisfied consumer; rather, these signs of estrangement serve to summon a person not to self-fulfillment but to authentic existence. Humanity is on earth not to have needs met, Percy says, not to surrender sovereignty to the theories of experts (a view raised again by Christopher Lasch in his controversial book, *The Culture of Narcissism*, 1979), but to be saved, and that necessitates consciousness of the human situation.

It is important to realize that Percy's sovereign wayfarer, or castaway, is not entirely identifiable with Kierkegaard's knight of faith. In place of Kierkegaard's extreme subjectivity, Percy posits the intersubjectivity of Gabriel Marcel, a Christian existentialist whose *we are* stands in stark contrast with both Kierkegaard's *I choose* and René Descartes's *I think*. We know we exist, Marcel says, by participating in the world. He does not think of being as experience, however, but as a presence within experience that is to be understood as simultaneously transcendent *and* immanent. To separate the two components of being is to pervert them and to transmogrify the individual as sovereign wayfarer into either angel—the abstract knower, the objective consciousness—or beast—a culture organism satisfying its needs. (The terms are Percy's, borrowed from Blaise Pascal.)

Marcel's quest for being, which is the quest for salvation as well, manifests itself in Percy's theory of language as intersubjective communication, where *we name* implies the same religious affirmation as Marcel's *we are* and Martin Buber's *I-Thou*. Percy originally turned to language theory in order to answer the question "What is man?"

because the answer provided by the behaviorist method was reductive and because the old theological view, along with the words in which it was couched, has been rendered ineffective by the general acceptance of the scientific method, which predisposed modern humanity to view itself as the behaviorists had defined it. Percy then set himself the task of finding "the delta factor": that which makes the human what it is and not something else.

According to the old theological view, humankind's singularity is its "soul," a meaningless word in a scientific age that demands empirical proof. For soul, Percy substitutes language, which he defines not as a sign system (the behaviorist position) but as the uniquely human process of symbolization. At the heart of language (and therefore at the heart of humanity as well) is something mysterious (compare Marcel's "mystery of being"). The mystery is explained by what Percy calls the "coupling process," the intersubjective human context by which people name, or symbolize, the world and in this way come both to know it and to share it. Language is, therefore, an attempt to bridge the gap between self and other, or, considered in the religious context of the fall of humanity, between self and God. What complicates the situation is the fact that in the late twentieth century, Percy believed, language became as meaningless, as clichéd, as the old theology. Before there can be intersubjective communication, humankind must again learn how to speak.

To learn to name and therefore to know and share that knowledge with another is the basic plot of a Percy novel. As Robert Coles has pointed out, Percy's novels trace the protagonist's movement from lofty observation to active participation in the openness of life—its possibilities and the necessity of making choices. Each of his major characters feels estranged "from being, from his own being, from the being of other creatures in the world, from the transcendent being. He has lost something, but what he does not know; he only knows that he is sick to death with the loss of it." Because this quest for being is a quest for God, it involves the hero's progress through Kierkegaard's three stages: the aesthetic (the pursuit of pleasure; the self becomes an uncommitted ironic spectator detached from himself and from others); the ethical (living within a general human code, such as marriage); the religious (requiring an entirely personal and—Kierkegaard would say—absurd leap of faith). The hero's search for being begins only when he or she becomes conscious of his or her despair and tries either to understand it or to alleviate it in one of two ways: rotation or repetition. Rotation—the quest for new experiences to offset "everydayness"—makes up the comic substance of Percy's novels. Repetition—the return to the past—may be rendered comically, but more often it serves a darker purpose, for Percy's heroes are, like William Faulkner's, haunted by the past; as a result, they do not live fully in the present. Only when they confront the past directly and become conscious of it can they break its spell and become sovereign wayfarers.

Frequently, Percy equates the past with the southern stoicism his uncle espoused, which, in Percy's judgment, leads only to pessimism, obsession with death, and "the wintry kingdom of self"; in short, it is the very antithesis of Percy's Christian existentialism. Rotation and repetition provide only temporary relief from the malaise that prevails within the aesthetic stage. The only escape from "aesthetic damnation" is through ordeal, especially the death of a loved one. Ordeal brings heroes face to face with mortality and enables them to see their world and themselves as if for the first time. The search they then begin is in effect a rejection of the absurdist position of aesthetic existentialists such as Albert Camus and Jean-Paul Sartre. The world is not absurd; it is a world to be named, known, and shared by the authentic self and the other in a mode of existence that is not so much religious *or* ethical as a synthesis of the two.

There are analogues for Percy's religious-phenomenological conception of the human search for being in his method of composition and in his prose style. The author's search for narrative form parallels the hero's search for being. Beginning with a situation rather than a plot or set of characters, Percy wrote with no fixed purpose or end in mind. As he explained, the writing, while not "haphazard," involved "many false starts, many blind detours, many blind passages, many goings ahead and backing up. . . . " Stylistically, his elegantly and precisely written novels suggest wonder, humor, and forbearance rather than the ponderous solemnity of other existential novelists such as Sartre. Moreover, his prose is richly and sensuously detailed; like two other converts to Roman Catholicism, Marcel and even more particularly Gerard Manley Hopkins, he took pleasure in a natural and human world that is, although marred by evil, essentially sacramental.

The Moviegoer • John Bickerson Bolling—"Binx"—is the narrator and main character of *The Moviegoer* and the first of Percy's spiritually "sick" protagonists. At the age of twenty-nine, he is a successful broker in a modern world where the church has been replaced by the brokerage house. Although financially secure, Binx feels uneasy; although adept at planning his client's futures, he has trouble living his own life from day to day, fearful that he may at any moment succumb to that worst of all plagues, the malaise of "everydayness." To counter its effects, Binx becomes a moviegoer, partly because films project a "heightened . . . resplendent reality," albeit temporarily, and partly because films provide Binx with accepted role models: thus his impersonations of such canonized figures as Gregory Peck, Clark Gable, Dana Andrews, and Rory Calhoun (who also serves as his confidant). The impersonation can never fully satisfy the moviegoer, however, who must eventually face the fact that the reality of his own life can never attain the heightened illusion of the star's gestural perfection. Moviegoing serves Binx in two additional ways: It enables him to view his world through the perspective of the films he has seen and, more important, to observe the world as if it were itself a film and he the passive audience.

Binx's detachment is both a virtue and a vice. As the detached spectator, he observes those around him closely and accurately, thus exposing the roles they have unknowingly adopted. Appropriately, the novel's temporal setting is the week before Mardi Gras, the period of rehearsals for New Orleans' citywide impersonation. Instead of recognizing their situation as castaways, these others feel serenely at home in the world, whereas in fact they are, as Binx understands, "dead." Neither virtuous nor sinful, they are merely "nice"; they speak, but in clichés; they ask questions, but neither expect nor desire answers. Binx, who fears becoming invisible—losing his identity—is right to keep his distance from these shadowy others. At the same time, however, he longs to be like them, to have his identity certified for him by such spurious means as films, identity cards, *Consumer Reports*, newspaper advice columns, and radio shows such as "This I Believe," which broadcasts the meaningless affirmations of abstracted religionists to a half-believing, half-skeptical Binx.

If it is his ironic detachment that saves Binx from the unreflective life of mass humanity, then it is his "search" that most clearly characterizes his longing for authenticity and being. "To become aware of the possibility of the search is to be onto something," Binx says. "Not to be onto something is to be in despair." Binx distinguishes two kinds of search. The "vertical" leads to abstraction: theories that explain the world but fail to explain what humankind is. (One alternative to such abstraction is the romanticism that killed Binx's father and that the son wisely rejects.) The other is the "horizontal" or phenomenological search that Percy himself counsels in *The Message in the Bottle*. Although Binx is indeed "onto something," his search is different from Percy's; it constitutes a "debased" form of the religious search because, as Percy explained, Binx, like Sartre, "has already ruled God out." His search takes a purely aesthetic form. To ease "the pain of loss," he pursues money and women, but the pursuit leads only to boredom and depression because the novelty of his possessions quickly wears off and everydayness inevitably returns to remind him of his inauthenticity and his position as a castaway.

Binx's yearning has a deeper current. As a college student, he found himself "lost in the mystery of being alive at such a time and place"; upon his return from the Korean War, he began his eight-year "exile" in the New Orleans suburb of Gentilly, which, like Covington, is a "nonplace"; as a broker he has taken to reading *Arabia Deserta*, by the self-styled "God's pilgrim," Charles Montagu Doughty, concealed inside a Standard & Poor binder.

Binx's search begins with the fact of his own "invincible apathy" and eventually leads, after many wrong turns, to authenticity and intersubjective relationships with his fourteen-year-old half-brother, Lonnie Smith, and his twenty-five-year-old cousin Kate Cutrer. There exists a "complicity" between Binx and the dying Lonnie, who faces life with true serenity because he understands it religiously. Like the other dying children in Percy's novels, Lonnie represents the paradox of unmerited suffering in a world ruled by a supposedly benevolent God, a paradox Percy resolves by depicting their spiritual victory in a "world full of God's grace where sorrow and death do not have the final word." Binx attends to the "good news" that Lonnie embodies because, in part, Lonnie's monotonous way of talking makes his words fresh and therefore meaningful, "like a code tapped through a wall."

Kate, unlike Lonnie, lives in pure anxiety, swinging wildly between various extremes, especially the longing to be free and the desire "to be an anyone who is anywhere." Although she lacks Binx's degree of awareness as well as his ironic detachment and is more prone to impersonation than he, Kate, like Binx, is aware of her disease, which others can only understand in psychological terms. (Thus, the novel's epigraph, taken from Kierkegaard: "the specific character of despair is precisely this: it is unaware of being despair.") Binx and Kate neatly complement each other: His childlike "simplemindedness" allows her to feel secure enough to speak honestly, while she correctly points out that in his search Binx may be overlooking something "obvious." Her request that Binx be her God—by which she means he is to tell her what to do—is not at all absurd given Marcel's brand of Christian existentialism. Significantly, her other suitors play the part of intersubjective God rather badly: One wants to send her to a high-priced psychoanalyst; the other promises an interminable vista of "niceness" and everydayness.

Binx's leap from nominal Catholic existing in despair to sovereign wayfarer and authentic being occurs very late in the novel and is effected by what, in a parallel context, Percy calls "some dim dazzling trick of grace." In fact, only a few pages from the end Binx laments that, having but one gift, "a good nose for merde," the only course for him to follow is "to fall prey to desire." There is even some justice to his Aunt Emily's judgment of him: In crucial situations, Binx invariably chooses to "default," to "exit." Yet, in the final pages, it is clear that Binx will do so no longer. Neither, however, will he play the part his aunt has chosen for him—southern stoic. He will go to medical school, not because she wants him to but because now he knows what to do: to observe *and* to serve others. Binx's leap is reflected in the very texture of Percy's prose. Until the epilogue, which takes place one year later, Binx has narrated his tale chiefly in what may be termed his detached, matter-of-fact, moviegoer style, against which the very few lyrical passages, used to underscore Binx's wonder and the gracefulness of his world, stand in vivid contrast. In the epilogue, Binx drops the moviegoer style (and the references to films) entirely; instead, he speaks easily, authentically, authoritatively. The man who earlier had been cousin, half-brother, and ironic impersonator, now is husband, brother, and sovereign wayfarer.

The Last Gentleman • The protagonist of Percy's second novel, *The Last Gentleman*, "Williston Bibb Barrett or Billy Barrett," is a modern-day version of Dostoevski's Prince Myshkin in *The Idiot* (1868). Although far less ironic than Binx Bolling, Barrett is far more disturbed, as his periodic fugue states and bouts of amnesia and déjà vu attest. Existing in a state of pure possibility, he is incapable of making any one decisive act or choice. He has tried and failed both to live the therapeutic life and to "engineer" his own destiny. Knowing something is missing in his life, Barrett seeks to recover reality and find his being in the "gap" between self and other. Specifically, these others are the members of the Vaught family, and his search is a spiritual odyssey, modeled on Mark Twain's *Adventures of Huckleberry Finn* (1884), that takes him from New York to his native Ithaca, then on to Mississippi, and finally to Santa Fe (Holy Faith), New Mexico, and the Sangre de Cristo (Blood of Christ) mountains.

The search begins when Barrett accidentally discovers Kitty Vaught and her sister-in-law, Rita, in Central Park. Rita, a secular humanist and advocate of self-fulfillment, quickly realizes she will not be able either to control or to convert Barrett and tries unsuccessfully to get rid of him. Barrett, however, has already fallen in love with Kitty, a rather pale version of Kate Cutrer—less anxiety-ridden, more successful in her impersonations. Barrett's love affair is both furthered and complicated by Kitty's younger brother, Jamie, whose traveling companion he becomes. The fact that Jamie is dying establishes definite limits to the pure possibility of his and Barrett's lives and causes Barrett to consider his search more profoundly when he meets another sister, Val, and brother, Sutter, the two "absentee experts" (as Barrett calls them) who force him to make his existential choice. Val, a convert to Catholicism and a nun, has dedicated herself to teaching mute children to speak and to believe the Roman Catholic religion. (All people are like her children, she claims; they are waiting to be told what to do.) Whereas she is hopeful and apostolic, Sutter, a diagnostician and pathologist, is suicidal and ironically quixotic. He rejects her belief in the human as wayfarer, claiming "We are doomed to the transcendence of abstraction and I choose the only reentry into the world which remains to us": "lewdness," cynicism, and detachment.

Sutter's mistake, as Barrett well understands, is the positing of extreme alternatives such as God or no God, transcendence or immanence. Moreover, Sutter's concern for Jamie betrays his basically religious nature, and it is this, more than his medical expertise, that has led Barrett to look to him for answers. At Jamie's baptism, it is Sutter who comprehends what is happening. Barrett, although he acts as interpreter between Jamie and the priest, misses the religious significance. He does understand that something has happened, however, and to discover what that something is he tracks down Sutter, who has decided to commit suicide. Barrett's search for an answer is, as Percy noted, a search for a father, ultimately for the Father, God; his own father, Barrett finally realizes, had looked for his answer in all the wrong places—

solitude, "old sad poetry," and the music of Johannes Brahms. The son's "wait" did not keep the father from killing himself, but it does save Sutter, who appears in the final tableau less as an oracle than as Barrett's self-chosen—and therefore sovereign—responsibility.

Love in the Ruins • Subtitled *The Adventures of a Bad Catholic at a Time Near the End of the World*, *Love in the Ruins* is a broad satire on the state of the modern world—in particular, its behaviorist assumptions and political absurdities. The novel may be flawed, as some reviewers have contended, by the author's insistent and at times rather heavy-handed social criticism; there is, however, a comic vitality in this novel that seems to offset such reservations about it as literary art. This comic vitality, quite unlike the irony and understatement that characterize Percy's earlier novels, is appropriate to a work that has the topics of community and reconciliation as two of its major concerns. As Percy explained in an essay titled "Notes for a Novel About the End of the World," the apocalyptic novelist serves two purposes: As prophet, or canary in the coal mine, he cries out in order to avert disaster, and as coupling agent, he connects humankind with reality. It is by means of the coupling process that disaster is averted, as Percy quietly suggests in the novel's closing image of a couple "twined about each other as the ivy twineth," in which what has been a sign of ruin (the ivy) is transformed into a symbol of intersubjective love.

The story, which is spoken into a pocket tape recorder by the hero, Tom More, as he keeps watch for snipers, follows a five-part structure (July Fourth, First, Second, Third, Fourth) that progressively becomes more chaotic until, in the epilogue ("Five Years Later"), peace and order are restored. The time of the novel is a not too distant future that bears a clear, if comically exaggerated, resemblance to the American 1960's: The fifteen-year war in Ecuador continues, racial tensions and Bantu uprisings are increasing, and the Roman Catholic Church has split into three factions. In short, "the center did not hold." The physical setting is just as perverse as the social-political: Paradise Estates, home of the well-to-do and the spiritually impoverished; Fedville, a sprawling compound that includes a Masters and Johnson Love Clinic, where ex-priest Kev Kevin reads *Commonweal* and presides over the vaginal console; Honey Island Swamp, a counterculture retreat; and the golf course, where a banner proclaims "Jesus Christ, the Greatest Pro of Them All."

Percy's hero is as troubled as his society but in a different way. Forty-five years old and a collateral descendent of Sir Thomas More, he is at once a doctor and a mental patient, a diagnostician but also a metaphysician in a world of behaviorists ready and willing to condition away any remaining feelings of guilt he may have. Loving, in descending order of importance, women, music, science, God, and, "hardly at all," his fellow human, he is the type of what Kierkegaard termed aesthetic damnation. He has lost that thread in the world-labyrinth that, until the death of his daughter Samantha, made the world seem sensible and holy. His faith gone, More has his own messianic ambition, a plan to "save" America with More's Qualitative Quantitative Onotological Lapsometer. His invention—"the stethoscope of the spirit . . . the first caliper of the soul"—is designed to measure the "gap" between the outer, social self and true, inner being; he hopes to modify the lapsometer so that it can cure as well as diagnose humankind's "fall" from being, to put together what Descartes tore apart. Like Percy and, to a degree, like Sutter Vaught, More is troubled by the modern world's indifference to being and people's willingness to define themselves in half-measures: the angel that, falling prey to abstraction, is unable to "reenter the lovely ordinary world," or the beast that adapts to its environment and so becomes the organism behaviorists say the human is.

Art Immelmann (Mephistopheles to More's Faust) tempts him with spurious "good news": a multimillion dollar development grant and the Nobel Prize. The price is More's soul—his being, his sense of personal responsibility. More resists the devil and so escapes aesthetic damnation; by not committing the unpardonable sin (refusing God's grace), he puts an end to the "feasting on death" that has preoccupied him since the onset of his daughter's illness and begins to live in the "lovely ordinary world" once again. Instead of an apocalypse, the novel ends with a new beginning, a Christmas morning. Reborn, Tom More no longer loves abstractly or bestially; he has married his former nurse, Ellen Oglethorpe, a Georgia Presbyterian, whose belief takes the form of charity. Equally important, More now knows what it is he wants: not prizes or women, but "just to figure out what I've hit on. Some day a man will walk into my office as ghost or beast or ghost-beast and walk out as a man, which is to say sovereign wayfarer, lordly exile, worker and waiter and watcher."

Lancelot • Percy's fourth novel, *Lancelot*, is by far his most troubling. Structurally, it follows the odd dialogue form of Camus's *The Fall* (1956); until the last two pages, only the voice of the protagonist is heard, addressing a "you" whose responses are not given. More disturbing is the fact that, as Joyce Carol Oates has pointed out, the views of the main character, a self-righteous and unrepentant murderer, are strikingly similar to those of the author. Readers must recognize, as Percy surely does, the nature of the protagonist's grotesque mistake—the sources from which it derives and the ends to which it leads.

Lancelot Andrewes Lamar speaks his Poe-like tale from the Center for Aberrant Behavior in New Orleans, where he has been confined for one year. Although in the course of his apologia/confession Lance identifies his wife Margot's infidelity as the immediate cause of his murdering her and the members of the film company with whom she was involved, the actual causes go much further back and have less to do with Margot than with his own wasted life and his position as the last in a fallen line of southern aristocrats. As a Lamar, Lance has inherited not only the family homestead, Belle Isle, but also a way of judging humankind in absolute terms. His first wife, Lucy, was (or so Lance remembers her) an angel, whereas Margot, who for a time he turned into a goddess, became a beast or devil. Dividing his life into two parts— before he discovered his wife's adultery and after—he proclaims that the past is "absolutely dead" and the future will be "absolutely new." This penchant for absolutes suggests Lance's inability or unwillingness to confront the ambiguity and mystery of human existence and is related to the way the Lamars view human life in terms of individual, historically significant events. Thus, Lance's life is reduced to his 110-yard touchdown run against Alabama and his destruction of Belle Isle and everyone in it. Lance does understand that performing such feats is actually less difficult than living an ordinary life, but when he turns Margot's infidelity into a quest for the "unholy grail," he in effect sidesteps the ordinary life that is far "more complicated and ambiguous" than either the historical events venerated by the Lamars or the clichéd films of Margot and her friends.

Like their film, Lance's quest is superficial and derivative (it is cast in the mold of the Raymond Chandler detective novels he has been reading). Moreover, it leads Lance, as Cleanth Brooks has demonstrated, to commit a modern version of the Gnostic heresy. Claiming that the original sin was something God did to man and judging Christianity as much a failure as southern stoicism, Lance determines to destroy the present age, which he cannot tolerate, and start over in a new Eden with his new Eve, Anna, a fellow patient who, he believes, as the victim of a brutal gang rape, has been restored to innocence. Lance is wrong about Anna, however; she never lost her innocence. He is also wrong about Christianity, if one distinguishes, as Kierkegaard did, between Christianity (as embodied in Percival, Lance's listener to whom the novel is spoken) and Christendom, which Lance is right to reject as a practical alternative to his intolerable age.

Lance's confession, as well as his predicament, brings his friend Percival's spiritual ambivalence into sharp focus; Percival, the "Prince Hal" of their early manhood who has since been ordained Father John, is torn between two roles—priest and psychiatrist—and two approaches to human existence—the religious and the behavioral. It is Percival's fellow psychiatrists who certify Lance as sane, even though both Lance and Percival know there is still something wrong, something missing. As a psychiatrist, Percival cannot help Lance, whose problem is ontological and spiritual rather than psychological, and whose self-righteous ranting masks his deeper uncertainty and longing. When, at the very end of the novel, Lance asks, "Is there anything I can do for you before I leave?," Percival's *"Yes"* identifies him as the apostolic Father John, the bearer of the good news for which Lance has been waiting. Against such grand gestures as blowing up Belle Isle, Percy offers the power of a small, ordinary word freshly heard.

The Second Coming • *The Second Coming* was, as Percy noted, his "first unalienated novel." Instead of the ambiguity that characterizes the endings of his earlier novels, here the author celebrates the unequivocal victory of love over death. Although such a conclusion did not please all reviewers, many of whom found it unconvincing or even sentimental, it is consistent with Percy's religious vision and his flexible aesthetic with its various tones and broad range of narrative structures: the novelist's version of God's plenty.

The novel picks up the life of Will Barrett some twenty years after *The Last Gentleman*. At the age of forty-three, Will is a retired lawyer, a wealthy widower living in Linwood, North Carolina, and recent recipient of the Rotary's man-of-the-year award; yet, he is still a sick man, subject to dizzy spells and tricks of memory. What troubles Will is not the loss of his wife Marion but the sudden realization that he has wasted his life and been "only technically alive." At the brink of the abyss, he sees himself as a total stranger; only 2 percent of himself, he sets out to find the missing 98 percent. His search takes him in a number of directions. One is back to his father, or more specifically to the only "event" in his life. This is a hunting accident that he comes to realize was no accident at all but instead the father's attempt to kill his son and then himself and so free them both from lives not worth living.

Like his father, Will rejects the "death in life" that characterizes modern believers as well as unbelievers; Will also rejects his father's solution, suicide, because it proves nothing. Instead, he devises the "ultimate scientific experiment" that will, he believes, provide conclusive proof of either God's existence or his nonexistence/noninvolvement. As the narrator points out, Will is mad; moreover, his plan (to starve himself and so force God either to save or abandon him) is badly flawed in two important ways. The language Will uses to define his experiment (actually more a "covenant") betrays his egotism as well as his legalistic frame of reference; to his "huge" bequest (his life), he attaches a "huge" condition (God's appearing to him).

Not until much later in the novel does he learn "the economy of giving and getting" and the superiority of ordinary existence to his own ultimate experiments or his father's extraordinary "events." In addition, Will is looking for God in the wrong place. While waiting in the cave for "a clear yes [or] no," he misses the unambiguous beauty of Indian summer; and while he assails God's "unavailability," his own "fade outs," such as the cave experiment, preclude the very intersubjective relationships through which God manifests himself to humankind. The sign he does receive, a toothache, is "a muddy maybe" that cuts short the experiment and sends Will howling in pain out of the wilderness of self and into a world that, while not physically new, can be seen in an original way.

The person who changes Will's angle of vision is Allison Huger (Kitty Vaught's daughter), who has just escaped her own cave, a mental hospital, and begun a new life in an abandoned greenhouse. She resembles Will in that she feels uncomfortable around other people, as well she should, for the Allison they see is the mentally disturbed organism for whom they can imagine nothing better than "the best-structured environment money can buy." Although she wants to live an entirely self-reliant life, each afternoon about four o'clock she experiences a sense of loss or emptiness. What she feels is identical to one of the symptoms of Will's disease (Hausmann's syndrome), which the doctors call "inappropriate longing." There is a pill to control Will's disease, but there is only one way to satisfy the longing, and that is by loving Allison, by finding his being in her just as she finds hers in him. As Allison explains in her characteristically melodic way, "Our lapses are not due to synapses." Percy's love story is not, therefore, simply romantic; rather, it is religious in the Christian existential sense. Their love is, to quote Allison again, "be-all" but not "end-all." When, in the novel's concluding scene, Will Barrett confronts Father Weatherbee, an old priest,

> his heart leapt with joy. What is it I want from her and him, he wondered, not only want but must have? Is she a gift and therefore a sign of the giver? Could it be that the Lord is here, masquerading behind this simple holy face? Am I crazy to want both, her and Him? No, not want, must have. And will have.

Here, as in the four earlier novels, one finds what Sartre called humanity's "useless passion," but for Percy this passionate longing is not useless at all because the world is not absurd. Percy's search is not one of Sartre's purely arbitrary "projects"; rather it is a thoroughly modern and, for many readers, an entirely convincing rendition of John Bunyan's *The Pilgrim's Progress* (1678, 1684) in an age mired in the slough of behaviorism and unbelief.

The Thanatos Syndrome • *The Thanatos Syndrome*, Percy's sixth and last novel, ends a bit differently, which is to say less insistently. Narrator-protagonist Dr. Tom More's "well well well" befits the "smaller scale" of his latter-day desires, yet this fit proves ironic, given the novel's overgrand, at times messianic ambitions (of the kind More himself had in *Love in the Ruins*). Similarities between the two novels are obvious (they share a number of the same characters and the same Futurist-fantasy approach), but both the strengths and the weaknesses of *The Thanatos Syndrome* owe far more to *Lost in the Cosmos* than to *Love in the Ruins*: the satirizing of contemporary absurdities (inauthenticity in some of its craziest manifestations) and the hardening of that spiritual need, which characterizes Will Barrett and Binx Bolling, into religious dogma. What was a translation of Christian belief into psychological, cultural, and semiotic terms in the earlier novels has begun to sound here like a propounding of conservative Roman Catholic teachings, which undermines a novel that otherwise effectively mixes Thomas More's 1516 *Utopia*, medieval romance, Fyodor Dostoevski, and Robin Cook.

The novel picks up the life and times of Tom More in the mid-1990's, a short while after his release from federal prison, where he has served a two-year term for illegally selling drugs. A brilliant diagnostician, More describes himself as "a psyche-iatrist, an old-fashioned physician of the soul" who believes that it is better, psychologically and spiritually speaking, to be sick (anxious, even terrified) than well, for disease is prolapsarian man's natural state. Many of the people around him are, he realizes, anything but anxious. They are, instead, content: without inhibitions, without anxiety, without anything more than rudimentary language skills, and, most important, without a sense of self. With the help of his epidemiologist cousin Lucy Lipscomb, More discovers "Blue Boy," a clandestinely funded pilot project that involves introducing heavy sodium into the local water supply in order to stem the tide of social deterioration (crime, teenage pregnancy, even acquired immunodeficiency syndrome).

Director of Blue Boy and indeed of the entire "Fedville" complex (including an "Equalitarian Center" with facilities for "pedeuthanasia" and "gereuthanasia" and a propensity for obfuscating acronyms) is the ironically "graceful" Bob Comeaux (born Robert D'Angelo Como), who calls Blue Boy "our Manhattan Project." He tries to cajole, seduce, bribe, and threaten More into complicity, all to no avail. Although he remains a lapsed Catholic throughout, the doctor nevertheless sides with the enigmatic, certainly depressed, previously alcoholic, perhaps mad Father Simon (as in Simeon Stylites and Simon Peter) Smith, who spends all of his time up in a fire tower silently triangulating the positions of forest fires, atoning for his sins, and on one notable occasion claiming that all tenderness almost inevitably leads to the gas chamber (or to the Equalitarian Center, which may be the same thing in a different, more socially acceptable, guise). Comeaux would make everyone happy, at the cost of his or her freedom as well as awareness of himself or herself as a distinctly human being: a creature caught in the malaise, lost in the cosmos, in need of something other than heavy sodium, self-help, or Phil Donahue.

Like Saul Bellow's *The Dean's December* (1982), *The Thanatos Syndrome* expresses More's faith (in there being "more" than Comeaux allows) in the form of a doubt concerning the modern belief that the causes and cures of humankind's problems are invariably physical. To the extent that *The Thanatos Syndrome* articulates this doubt, it, like Percy's other novels, succeeds extraordinarily well. To the extent that it propounds Roman Catholic dogma in response to a host of topical issues (abortion, "quality of life," sexual "freedom," child abuse, bio- and behavioral engineering, among others), it fails according to the very terms that Percy himself adopted at the time of his conversion, turning the triadic mystery of Søren Kierkegaard's apostle into dyadic pronouncement, sign into signal, spiritual "predicament" into position paper.

Robert A. Morace

Other major works

NONFICTION: *The Message in the Bottle*, 1975; *Lost in the Cosmos: The Last Self-Help Book*, 1983; *Conversations with Walker Percy*, 1985 (Lewis A. Lawson and Victor A. Kramer, editors); *The State of the Novel: Dying Art or New Science?*, 1987; *Signposts in a*

Strange Land, 1991 (Patrick Samway, editor); *More Conversations with Walker Percy,* 1993 (Lawson and Kramer, editors); *A Thief of Peirce: The Letters of Kenneth Laine Ketner and Walker Percy,* 1995 (Samway, editor); *The Correspondence of Shelby Foote and Walker Percy,* 1997 (Jay Tolson, editor).

Bibliography

Allen, William Rodney. *Walker Percy: A Southern Wayfarer.* Jackson: University Press of Mississippi, 1986. Allen reads Percy as a distinctly American, particularly southern writer, claiming that the formative event in Percy's life was his father's suicide, not his reading of existentialist writers or conversion to Roman Catholicism.

Desmond, John F. *At the Crossroads: Ethical and Religious Themes in the Writings of Walker Percy.* Troy, N.Y.: Whitston, 1997. A useful, accessible introduction to Percy's background in theology and philosophy.

Dupuy, Edward J. *Autobiography in Walker Percy: Repetition, Recovery, and Redemption.* Baton Rouge: Louisiana State University Press, 1996. Discusses Percy's autobiographical novels as psychological fiction. Includes bibliographical references and an index.

Hardy, John Edward. *The Fiction of Walker Percy.* Urbana: University of Illinois Press, 1987. The originality of this book derives from Hardy's choosing to read the novels in terms of internal formal matters rather than (as is usually the case) Percy's essays, existentialism, Catholicism, or southern background.

Kobre, Michael. *Walker Percy's Voices.* Athens: University of Georgia Press, 2000. Analyzes Percy's novels from the theoretical perspective of Russian theorist Mikhail Bakhtin.

Lawson, Lewis A. *Following Percy: Essays on Walker Percy's Work.* Troy, N.Y.: Whitston, 1988. Collects essays originally published between 1969 and 1984 by one of Percy's most dedicated, prolific, and knowledgeable commentators. Discussions of *The Moviegoer* and *Lancelot* predominate.

O'Gorman, Farrell. *Peculiar Crossroads: Flannery O'Connor, Walker Percy, and Catholic Vision in Postwar Southern Fiction.* Baton Rouge: Louisiana State University Press, 2004. Comparative study of O'Connor and Percy as southern writers who were devout Roman Catholics.

Pridgen, Allen. *Walker Percy's Sacramental Landscapes: The Search in the Desert.* Selinsgrove, Pa.: Susquehanna University Press, 2000. A penetrating reading of Percy's novels, focusing on literary technique rather than Percy's southern or Roman Catholic identities.

Quinlan, Kieran. *Walker Percy: The Last Catholic Novelist.* Baton Rouge: Louisiana State University Press, 1996. Chapters on Percy as novelist and philosopher, existentialist, and explorer of modern science. Recommended for the advanced student who has already read Desmond. Includes notes and bibliography.

Samway, Patrick H. *Walker Percy: A Life.* New York: Farrar, Straus and Giroux, 1997. Full biography of Percy.

Sheppard, Beth M., ed. *Signs of the Giver: The Collected Papers of the 2002 Southwestern College Walker Percy Seminar.* New York: Writers Club Press, 2003. Collection of original seminar papers on a variety of subjects relating to Percy.

Wyatt-Brown, Bertram. *The Literary Percys: Family History, Gender, and the Southern Imagination.* Athens: University of Georgia Press, 1994. Explores Percy in the context of his nineteenth century ancestors, including women, who were writers, and analyzes the melancholy that pervades the family.

Katherine Anne Porter

Born: Indian Creek, Texas; May 15, 1890
Died: Silver Spring, Maryland; September 18, 1980

Principal long fiction • *Pale Horse, Pale Rider: Three Short Novels*, 1939; *Ship of Fools*, 1962.

Other literary forms • Katherine Anne Porter is best known for her short fiction. Her stories appear in *Flowering Judas, and Other Stories* (1930), *The Leaning Tower, and Other Stories* (1944), and *The Old Order* (1944) and were gathered in *The Collected Stories of Katherine Anne Porter* (1965). Criticism, essays, and poems were collected in *The Days Before* (1952) and *The Collected Essays and Occasional Writings* (1970).

Achievements • Porter's solid and lasting reputation as a writer is based on a very small output of published work: one novel, a handful of novellas, and fewer than two dozen stories. This slender output, however, represents only a small portion of the fiction she wrote during her lifetime. Exacting and self-critical, she discarded many more stories than she published. By the time her first story appeared in print, she had already developed her fictional techniques to near perfection, and the maturity and craft of her style in *Flowering Judas, and Other Stories*, her first published collection, never was surpassed by her later fiction.

Porter early established her reputation with literary critics and only later became widely known and read. In 1931, one year after the publication of her first volume, she was granted a Guggenheim Fellowship, an award she received again in 1938. The Society of Libraries of New York University awarded her its first gold medal for literature in 1940 upon the publication of *Pale Horse, Pale Rider*. A Modern Library edition of *Flowering Judas, and Other Stories* appeared that same year. In 1943, she was elected a member of the National Institute of Arts and Letters, and in 1949, she accepted her first appointment as writer-in-residence and guest lecturer at Stanford University. In later years, she held similar positions in many other colleges and universities, including the University of Chicago, the University of Michigan, Washington and Lee University, the University of Liège, and the University of Virginia.

By the time she published *Ship of Fools* in 1962, Porter had received three more honors: a Ford Foundation grant in 1959, and in 1962, the O. Henry Memorial Award for her story "Holiday" and the Emerson-Thoreau Bronze medal of the American Academy of Arts and Sciences. *Ship of Fools* became a Book-of-the-Month-Club selection and an immediate best-seller. In the face of its overwhelming popular success, some critics charged that Porter had forsaken her artistic standards in favor of writing a book that would appeal to a large audience. *Ship of Fools* also was criticized for its pessimism and for its failure to conform neatly to the structure of a novel, a supposed flaw especially irksome to those who had admired the formal perfection of Porter's earlier works. Porter herself was surprised by the book's popularity. She had abandoned the form of her earlier work—with its tight plots centered on the fate of a single character—but she had moved deliberately on to something else. She was still writing "honest," she said, a quality that characterized all her fiction. First and last,

Courtesy, Special Collections, University of Maryland Libraries

she was still an artist, a label she applied to herself unhesitatingly.

Though Porter published no new fiction after *Ship of Fools,* her critical and public acclaim grew. It reached its peak when she received both the Pulitzer Prize and the National Book Award for Fiction in 1966.

Biography • Katherine Anne Porter was born Collie Russell Porter in Indian Creek, Texas, on May 15, 1890. She was the third of five children born to Harrison and Mary Alice Jones Porter. When her mother died in 1892, she and her brothers and sisters moved to Kyle, Texas, where they were cared for by their paternal grandmother, Catherine Anne Porter. When Mrs. Porter senior died in 1901, Harrison Porter sold the farm in Kyle and moved with his family to San Antonio.

Facts about Porter's early life and education have been difficult to substantiate, partly because Porter's own accounts were evasive or inconsistent. Although her family apparently was Methodist, Porter attended convent schools, possibly for a time in New Orleans, which may be why later researchers have reported that she was a Roman Catholic from birth. Porter denied this allegation when it appeared in a biographical sketch published by the University of Minnesota series on American writers. Precocious as a child and rebellious as a teenager, she ran away from school at the age of sixteen to marry. The name of her first husband is not known, although the marriage lasted three years.

After the divorce, Porter moved to Chicago, already cherishing the ambition of becoming a professional writer. She worked as a reporter on a Chicago newspaper for a time and signed on as an extra with a motion-picture company for a few months. Passing up the opportunity to travel to Hollywood with the film company, she returned to Texas, where she reported that she made a living as a traveling entertainer, singing Scottish ballads, dressed in a costume she made herself. Thereafter, she wrote drama criticism and society gossip for a Fort Worth weekly, *The Critic.* One year later, she moved to Denver, Colorado, and became a reporter for the *Rocky Mountain News.* In Denver, during the influenza epidemic of 1918, she became severely ill and almost died. This experience, which she fictionalized in *Pale Horse, Pale Rider,* affected her profoundly. "I really had participated in death," she said years later in an interview with Barbara Thompson of the *Paris Review.* She had had "what the Christians call the 'beatific vision'"; she was no longer "like other people."

In 1919 she moved to New York City, where for a brief time she worked as a hack and ghostwriter. The following year she went to study in Mexico. Again she stayed only a short time, but for the next ten years Mexico was to be the center of her intellectual and imaginative life. Returning to Fort Worth, she began to write the stories based on her experiences there. During the next decade she traveled extensively, reviewed books for leading national magazines and newspapers, and worked and reworked the stories that were published in 1930 in *Flowering Judas, and Other Stories.*

Supported by a Guggenheim Fellowship granted that year, she returned to Mexico. In 1931, she sailed aboard a German ship from Veracruz to Bremerhaven. This voyage gave her the setting for *Ship of Fools,* which was not to be published for another thirty years. She lived until the mid-1930's in Paris, marrying and later divorcing Eugene Pressly, a member of the American Foreign Service, and working on her fiction. After her divorce from Pressly, she married Albert Erskine, Jr., of the Louisiana State University faculty. Until her divorce from Erskine in 1942, she lived in Baton Rouge. During this time, she continued to work on her short fiction, but not until the late 1950's did she begin sustained effort on her only full-length novel, *Ship of Fools.* Although by that time many of her acquaintances believed she never would finish it, fragments of the novel appeared in magazines, and, in 1962, *Ship of Fools* was published. Porter wrote no more new fiction after that, although *The Collected Essays and Occasional Writings* appeared in 1970. On September 18, 1980, at the age of of ninety, Porter died in Silver Spring, Maryland.

Analysis • Katherine Anne Porter once suggested that when she sat down to write about her life as accurately as possible, it turned into fiction; indeed, she knew no other way to write fiction. Whether this anecdote is true, it is certain that capturing the past with great detail was an important ingredient in her writing. In a number of the short stories, and in two of the best short novels, Miranda, the central character, is very close to being Porter herself. These stories follow Miranda's life from infancy in her grandmother's house in South Texas, to her scrape with death from influenza in Colorado at the age of twenty-four—her first major step toward maturity.

Concerning the time of her illness, Porter has said that it was as though a line were drawn through her life, separating everything that came before from everything that came after. She had been given up and then had survived, and in some ways all her time after that was borrowed. Perhaps that is why her overtly autobiographical stories deal with the time before that line, the time when she was "alive" and therefore had a life to record. The stories that take place after that incident present her, if at all, as an observer, as someone slightly distant and alienated from life. (It is a question of degree: Miranda is also an acute observer in the stories in which she takes part. Her name, in fact, means "observer" in Spanish.) Porter was in real life a passenger on the ship about which her novel *Ship of Fools* was written, but she speaks of herself as purely an observer, who scarcely spoke a word on the entire voyage. She does not appear directly as a character in the novel.

Old Mortality • The girl, Miranda, in the short novel *Old Mortality,* runs away from school to get married, in part to escape from her family, so suffocatingly steeped in its own past. At the conclusion of the novella, she is determined to free herself once and for all from that past, so that she can begin to consider her own future; but she determines this, the reader is told in the ironic concluding lines, "in her hopefulness, her ignorance." The irony is that Miranda/Porter herself became so obsessed with that past that much of her best work is devoted to it. The explanation for Porter's obsession with the past can perhaps be guessed from the conclusion of *Pale Horse, Pale Rider.* Everything of importance to Miranda has died; only her ravaged body, her spark of a soul somehow survives. She finds that she has no future, only the slow progression to death once again. The past, then, is all she has, yet the past is finally intangible, as the girl in *Old Mortality* discovers as she sifts through all the evidence. At last no truth can be discovered, no objectivity, only the combined and contradictory subjectives: The only truth, once again, is the truth of fiction.

Porter said that in her fiction she is not interested in actions so much as she is interested in the various and subtle results of actions. Certainly, of all her works, *Old Mortality* deals directly with the ramifications of past actions. This short novel spans ten years in the life of the protagonist, Miranda, from the age of eight to the age of eighteen. In that time, the reader learns little of Miranda's life, except that she is bad tempered and that, unlike many of the young women in her widely extended family, she is not going to be a "beauty." She is, rather, the recording center of the novel: The events are brought to her and have their effect on the person she is becoming.

The crucial actions have occurred in the preceding generation. Miranda's family is obsessed by a past event. Miranda's aunt Amy was a great beauty, the measure, in fact, against which all the current crop of beauties are found wanting. She was glamorous, racy, even though tubercular, and for a long time spurned Gabriel's devoted courtship. Gabriel was himself wild, ran a string of racehorses, and was heir to the fortune. Only when he was disinherited and Amy found herself in the terminal stage of her illness did she consent to marry him. The couple went to New Orleans on their honeymoon, and almost immediately Amy died. Miranda tries to sift out the truth of the story. She looks at the photograph of Amy and does not find her so impossibly beautiful and indeed thinks she looks silly in her out-of-fashion dress. Later, she is introduced to Gabriel, and instead of the dashing young man who had once challenged a rival to a duel over Amy, she finds him fat and drunken, down on his luck; the woman whom he married after Amy is bitter and depressed. Later still, Miranda meets Eva, a homely spinster cousin from Gabriel's generation, and Eva says the real truth is that Amy was a lewd woman, who married only because someone else got her pregnant, and took her own life with an overdose of drugs.

After a moment of shock, Miranda realizes that Eva's version, in its negative way, is just as romantic as the others. Miranda does not want to know where the truth lies. By this time, she has left school and has run off to get married. Her father is cool with her, thinking she has deserted the family; indeed she has, and deliberately. She refuses to be trapped in the past, represented by this unknowable woman whose brief life still haunts the family. She wants instead to discover who she—Miranda—is; she wants her own life to exist in the present and future. This is what she determines—in the novel's ironic final line—"in her hopefulness, her ignorance."

In her ignorance, Miranda learns that her past is what she is, the result of those past actions. She has been touched by Amy even more than the others, for she has become Amy, the Amy who refused to live by the others' rules, and at last ran off, married, and never returned—just as Miranda has done. In so doing, Amy and Miranda become separated from the rest of the family, freezing its members in their moment of history just as Porter herself became separated from her family so that she could re-create them forever in her stories.

Noon Wine • *Noon Wine* is set in the rural turn-of-the-century southern Texas of Porter's childhood but does not deal with her family. The characters in this short novel are poor and uneducated farmers, but this does not stop the story from being an intricate and subtle moral allegory. The lingering effect of past actions is not the central theme, as it was in *Old Mortality*, but a sense of the cumulative force of a man's actions gives the story a tragic inevitability. Mr. Thompson is a proud man, and as a result he marries above himself. Instead of a strong woman to help him in the strenuous operation of his farm, he marries a delicate and genteel woman who quickly becomes a near invalid. Further, she insists that they have a dairy, a bit higher class than an ordinary row-crop farm. In the end, Thompson is left with a wife who cannot help him and a kind of farmwork that he does not feel is masculine, and that he therefore shirks. The farm is deteriorating, and the couple are about to go under entirely, when a strange taciturn Swede from North Dakota arrives, asking for work. Instantly there is a revolution. The Swede fixes, paints, repairs everything, and shortly the failing farm becomes productive. As the years go by, the couple are able to buy such luxuries as an icebox, and Mr. Thompson is able to sit on the porch while the work is being done. One day Hatch arrives, a thoroughly evil man. He is a bounty hunter; the Swede, it is revealed, is an escaped homicidal maniac who in a berserk fury stabbed his own brother to death. Thompson refuses to give up the Swede. There is a scuffle; the Swede suddenly appears and steps between them; Thompson, believing he sees Hatch stabbing the Swede in the stomach, smashes Hatch's skull with an ax.

The confrontation is remarkably complex. Hatch, as he is presented in the story, seems a pure manifestation of evil, and so perhaps he should be killed, but ironically he has in fact done nothing. The Swede is a primal murderer, a brother-killer like Cain, and is a threat to murder again. Thompson believes Hatch has stabbed the Swede and acts to defend him, but after he has killed Hatch, the Swede does not have a mark on him, not even, perhaps, the mark of Cain, which has been transferred to Thompson.

Thompson is easily acquitted of the crime in court, but his fundamentalist neighbors in the close-knit community look on him as a murderer. Most important, he must examine his own motives. Was he defending the Swede, or was he defending the success of his farm, which, he must have guiltily realized, was not the result of his work but of the work of another, a sinner, a primal murderer? With his mark of Cain, Thompson goes the rounds of his neighbors, trying to tell his side of the story, believing it less each time himself, until he kills himself, the final consequence of his original pride.

Pale Horse, Pale Rider • Porter has called sleep "that little truce of God between living and dying." If dreams, therefore, take place in a landscape somewhere between life and death, it is appropriate that *Pale Horse, Pale Rider* begins with one of Miranda's many dreams to be recorded. Although the story is set during World War I in a small town in Colorado where Miranda is working for a newspaper, symbolically the story takes place in the dreamlike zone between life and death. In that initial dream, Death rides alongside Miranda, but she tells him to ride on ahead; she is not quite ready to go with him. She wakes up only to be reminded of the war, which is poisoning the lives of many people, who are full of despair because of their inability to control their destinies. The streets are filled with funerals, as the influenza epidemic kills people like a medieval plague. Miranda's work on the paper is hateful, and her only release is when, after work, she meets Adam. Adam, as his name suggests, is the man who should be her companion, her mate in life. He is a soldier, however, on his way to war and committed wholly to death, and so Miranda struggles to withhold her love from him.

The war and the plague, as presented in the novel, are symbols of the struggle of life and its vulnerability. Miranda and Adam differ from others in being existentially aware; all that exists for them is the present tense of their lives. They dance together in a cheap café, knowing that it is all they will ever have. Because they have so little—a brief moment of troubled life, and then death—the integrity of their actions becomes their only value. Miranda tells Adam that he is stupid to fight in a war in which old men send young men to die. He agrees, saying, however, that if he does not go, he can no longer face himself. Miranda has her own costly sense of integrity: As a reporter for the paper, she witnesses a pathetic scandal, and when the victims beg her not to write the story, she does not. The rival papers do, however, and her editor is furious; her colleagues think she is senseless. She is demoted to writing entertainment reviews. Even there, when she writes an unfavorable review of a vaudeville act, she is confronted by the old, broken, has-been actor, and her subsequent compassion struggles against her dedication to her job. Her colleagues counsel her to fake the reviews and make everyone happy, but writing honest reviews is an important value to her.

Miranda gets the flu, and in a long delirious dream comes to the point of death and has a beatific vision. The doctor and nurse fighting to preserve her, working with their own existential integrity, bring her back, but it is so painful being taken away from her vision and back to life, that when life-giving drugs are injected into her, she feels them like "a current of agony."

Miranda had fought, with her tiny spark of consciousness, to survive, to survive for Adam. Then she learns that Adam, perhaps having caught flu from her, has himself died. Her dream of heaven had been so brilliant that the real world seems to her a monochrome, a bleak field in which, with Adam gone, she has nothing. The reader, however, can see beyond this point. Earlier, Miranda and Adam had sung an old spiritual together, of a pale horse with a pale rider, who takes a girl's lover away, leaving her behind to mourn. Miranda is the singer who is left behind to mourn and to record the story for the rest of the world.

Ship of Fools • Porter has described her fiction as an investigation of the "terrible failure of the life of man in the Western World." Her one full-length novel, *Ship of Fools*, is a bleak cross section of modern civilization. It follows the lives of literally dozens of characters, from all levels of the particular society it is observing. More than forty characters of various nationalities are presented in some detail: American, Spanish, Mexican, Cuban, German, Swiss, Swedish. The time is 1931, and chaos is spreading. Soon Adolf Hitler will be in power, the extermination camps will be in operation, and another world war will be under way. The title *Ship of Fools* is a translation of Sebastian Brant's medieval moral allegory, *Das Narrenschiff* (1494). The ship is the world; the time of the journey is the lifetime of the characters. They do not see it that way. They think of it as a temporary voyage. The lies they tell, the treacheries they enact, the hopeless relationships they form, are only temporary, have nothing to do with the course of their real lives, with the objectives they mean to obtain, the moral codes by which they mean to live.

The ship, the *Vera* (truth), leaves Veracruz, Mexico, for the nearly monthlong journey to Bremerhaven. It is a German ship, and the German passengers sit at the captain's table. From the pompous and second-rate captain on down, they are comic grotesques, guzzling their food swinishly and looking suspiciously at everyone who does not eat pork, or who has a slightly large nose, as potentially Jewish. The only seemingly human Germans are Wilhelm Freytag, concealing as long as he can the fact that he has a Jewish wife, and Dr. Schumann, the ship's doctor, the novel's most sympathetic character, urbane, gentle, wise—who, to his own horror, commits perhaps the basest act of anyone on board. The American characters are only slightly less grotesque. William Denny the Texan is pure caricature: To him everyone but a white Texan is a "nigger," "spick," "wop," or "damyankee." He devotes all his time to pursuing sexual pleasure but is fearful that he will be cheated into paying too much for it. The comic result is that he pays out everything and gets nothing in return but a severe drubbing. Mrs. Treadwell, a forty-five-year-old divorcée, is utterly selfish, yet she wonders why she gets nothing from life. David Scott and Jenny Brown, living together, fighting constantly, are, with Dr. Schumann and Wilhelm Freytag, the novel's main characters. David Scott is tied up within himself and will give up nothing to another. Jenny Brown sporadically gives up everything to mere acquaintances yet seems to have nothing of her own within.

One character after another debates humanity's nature: Are all people basically good; are all people naturally depraved; are the pure races good and the mongrel races evil? The characters seem intent on acting out all these possibilities. The most disciplined of them regularly lapse into helpless sentimentality. Freytag thinks that each woman he meets is the beautiful love of his life. One of these women is a Jew, whom he married during a period of extreme romanticism, and now he is déclassé among his German compatriots and cannot admit to himself how regretful he is. David and Jenny, needing everything from each other, have only gone as far as learning each other's weaknesses, of which they take full advantage to lacerate each other. They continue to cling together, always saying they will separate at some later time. Most painful is the folly of the sympathetic Dr. Schumann. He convinces himself that he is in love with a neurotic Spanish countess (he has a wife at home), and under pretense of caring for her as her doctor, he turns her into a hopeless and helpless drug addict in order to keep his power over her.

The most purely evil characters on the ship are the shoddy Spanish dance troupe. Through herculean efforts they almost take control of the ship and certainly take control of the lives of the characters, bringing out their deepest and worst traits, but at the end they sit listless and exhausted, as though the effort were immensely greater than any return they have had from it. This troupe of carnival performers cheats, steals, blackmails, and even kills right before the others, who remark on it but do nothing to stop them, each character feeling it is not his place to do anything. At length, the troupe is sitting confidently at the captain's table, having rearranged everyone's position on the ship. In a kind of Walpurgis Night, they bring the many characters to some sort of climax in an eruption of drunken violence. It is Porter's vision of how World War II began: low thugs and gangsters taking power with the casual, half-intentional connivance of the world.

In the midst of this bleak and pessimistic picture of the Western world, there is one possibility of redemption. The rare positive moments in the novel are when the characters suddenly, often to their own surprise, come together in the act of sex—Porter emphasizing the sensuality of the contact rather than any spiritual qualities. Perhaps Porter is saying that in their fallen state human beings must start at the bottom, with earthly sensuality, in order to slowly acquire a knowledge of spiritual beauty.

Norman Lavers

Other major works

SHORT FICTION: *Flowering Judas, and Other Stories,* 1930; *Hacienda,* 1934; *Noon Wine,* 1937; *The Leaning Tower, and Other Stories,* 1944; *The Old Order,* 1944; *The Collected Stories of Katherine Anne Porter,* 1965.

POETRY: *Katherine Anne Porter's Poetry,* 1996 (Darlene Harbour Unrue, editor).

NONFICTION: *My Chinese Marriage,* 1921; *Outline of Mexican Popular Arts and Crafts,* 1922; *What Price Marriage,* 1927; *The Days Before,* 1952; *A Defence of Circe,* 1954; *A Christmas Story,* 1967; *The Collected Essays and Occasional Writings,* 1970; *The Selected Letters of Katherine Anne Porter,* 1970; *The Never-Ending Wrong,* 1977; *Letters of Katherine Anne Porter,* 1990.

Bibliography

Austenfeld, Thomas Carl. *American Women Writers and the Nazis: Ethics and Politics in Boyle, Porter, Stafford, and Hellman.* Charlottesville: University Press of Virginia, 2001. Comparative study of writings on the era of Adolf Hitler's regime by Porter, Kay Boyle, Jean Stafford, and Lillian Hellman, all of whom saw the rise of the Nazi regime at first hand.

Bloom, Harold, ed. *Katherine Anne Porter: Modern Critical Views.* New York: Chelsea House, 1986. Bloom introduces twelve classic essays, by Robert Penn Warren, Robert B. Heilman, Eudora Welty, and others. The symbolism of "Flowering Judas," the ambiguities of "He," and the dreams in *Pale Horse, Pale Rider* are focuses of attention. Porter is compared with Flannery O'Connor. Includes a chronology, a bibliography, and an index.

Busby, Mark, and Dick Heaberlin, eds. *From Texas to the World and Back: Essays on the Journeys of Katherine Anne Porter.* Fort Worth: TCU Press, 2001. Collection of essays on a variety of subjects pertaining to Porter's life and work.

Fornataro-Neil, M. K. "Constructed Narratives and Writing Identity in the Fiction of Katherine Anne Porter." *Twentieth Century Literature* 44 (Fall, 1998): 349-361. Discusses "Old Mortality," "He," "Noon Wine," and "Holiday" in terms of Porter's fascination with characters who cannot or do not speak; claims that her silent characters are alienated because they communicate by a sign system that others cannot understand.

Graham, Don. "Katherine Anne Porter's Journey from Texas to the World." *Southwest Review* 84 (1998): 140-153. Argues that because the dominant figure in Texas literary mythology was the heroic cowboy, Porter, who had nothing to say about cowboys in her writing, chose instead to identify herself as southerner.

Hartley, Lodwick, and George Core, eds. *Katherine Anne Porter: A Critical Symposium.* Athens: University of Georgia Press, 1969. A collection of seminal essays, this book includes an interview with Porter in 1963, as well as a personal assessment by Porter's friend Glenway Wescott. A group of five essays provide general surveys, and another five focus on particular stories, including "The Grave" and "Holiday." Select bibliography, index.

Spencer, Virginia, ed. *"Flowering Judas": Katherine Anne Porter.* New Brunswick, N.J.: Rutgers University Press, 1993. A volume in the Women Writers: Texts and Contexts series, this collection of critical discussions of Porter's most famous story features background material and important essays, from Ray B. West's influential 1947 discussion of the story to debates about the character of Eugenio as Christ figure.

Stout, Janis. *Katherine Anne Porter: A Sense of the Times.* Charlottesville: University Press of Virginia, 1995. Chapters on Porter's background in Texas, her view of politics and art during the 1920's, her writing and life between the two world wars, and her relationship with the southern agrarians. Also addresses the issue of gender, the problem of genre in *Ship of Fools,* and the quality of Porter's "free, intransigent, dissenting mind." Includes notes and bibliography.

Titus, Mary. *The Ambivalent Art of Katherine Anne Porter.* Athens: University of Georgia Press, 2005. A look at the ways in which Porter confronted issues of gender in her work and her life, including a study of some of her unpublished papers.

Unrue, Darlene Harbour. *Katherine Anne Porter: The Life of an Artist.* Jackson: University Press of Mississippi, 2005. A comprehensive biography of Porter that offers insight into her turbulent personal life and her writing.

Chaim Potok

Born: New York, New York; February 17, 1929
Died: Merion, Pennsylvania; July 23, 2002

Principal long fiction • *The Chosen*, 1967; *The Promise*, 1969; *My Name Is Asher Lev*, 1972; *In the Beginning*, 1975; *The Book of Lights*, 1981; *Davita's Harp*, 1985; *The Gift of Asher Lev*, 1990; *I Am the Clay*, 1992; *Old Men at Midnight*, 2001 (three novellas).

Other literary forms • *Wanderings: Chaim Potok's History of the Jews* (1978) is a personal reconstruction of four thousand years of Jewish history. Potok also wrote essays and book reviews for Jewish and secular periodicals and newspapers. In January, 1988, his stage adaptation of *The Chosen* opened as a short-lived Broadway musical, with music by Philip Springer and lyrics by Mitchell Bernard. Potok wrote two picture books for young children, both illustrated by Tony Auth, *The Tree of Here* (1993) and *The Sky of Now* (1995). He also published essays and stories in various magazines and a collection of short stories about troubled young people, *Zebra, and Other Stories* (1998). In addition, he wrote a few full-length works of nonfiction, including *The Gates of November: Chronicles of the Slepak Family* (1996), the epic story of the families of Solomon Slepak, a Bolshevik and one of the founders of the Soviet Union, who managed to survive all Joseph Stalin's purges without being imprisoned, and his son, Volodya Slepak, a refusenik, one of the Russian Jews who applied for and was for years refused permission by the Soviet government to immigrate to Israel.

Achievements • Critical acceptance and public acclaim greeted Chaim Potok's novelistic explorations of the conflict between Orthodox Judaism and secular American culture. Potok received the Edward Lewis Wallant Award and a National Book Award nomination for *The Chosen*, his first novel. He received the Athenaeum Award for its sequel, *The Promise*. He also received the National Jewish Book Award for Fiction for *The Gift of Asher Lev* and the National Foundation for Jewish Culture Achievement Award for Literature. His sympathetic (critics would say sentimental) portrayal of Jewish fundamentalism and those who choose to leave it highlights the poignancy of an individual's break with tradition. Indeed, Potok's novels test the ability of traditional communities to contribute to the modern world without themselves being assimilated. His evocation of Jewish life in New York in the latter two-thirds of the twentieth century has universal appeal and disturbing implications.

Biography • Born of Orthodox Jewish parents in New York City's Bronx in 1929, Chaim Potok was reared in a fundamentalist culture. Potok's father, Benjamin Potok, was a Polish émigré and no stranger to the pogroms of Eastern Europe. The young Potok was taught that the profound suffering of the Jews would one day transform the world. Yet, as Potok suggests in *Wanderings*, his service as a Jewish chaplain with the U.S. Army in Korea (1956-1957) confronted him with a world of good and evil that had never heard of Judaism. His attempt to come to terms with this larger world led Potok to a critical investigation of his own Jewish heritage and the limitations of the fundamentalist perspective. Though he was ordained a Conservative rabbi in 1954, attracted by doctrines more liberal than those of strict Jewish Orthodoxy, Potok continued his struggle to reconcile fundamental Judaism with the findings of science (as historiography and textual criticism shed new light on ancient traditions). *The Chosen* inaugurated his public search for a voice with which to speak to his heritage as well as to the larger world.

During the early 1960's, Potok taught at the Jewish Theological Seminary in New York, edited *Conservative Judaism*, and in 1965 became editor in chief with the Jewish Publication Society of Philadelphia. In 1975 he became special projects editor. After he married Adena Mosevitzky in 1958, he took up residence in Merion, Pennsylvania. The Potoks had three children: Rena, Naama, and Akiva. Potok served as a visiting professor at the University of Pennsylvania, Bryn Mawr College, and Johns Hopkins University. He died in Merion on July 23, 2002.

© Jerry Bauer

Analysis • In his novels, Chaim Potok returns again and again to the story of a young protagonist coming of age in a culture (usually Jewish) at once mysterious, beautiful, sad, and somehow inadequate. Usually told in the first person, Potok's stories surround the reader with forebodings of the larger, evil world (news of pogroms in Europe, the Holocaust, the first atom bomb) into which his characters are plunged. Potok creates a microcosm of feeling and reaction to events that shake the world. His sentences are simple and reportorial, at times almost a parody of the staccato style of Ernest Hemingway. The stories develop chronologically, though they are frequently invaded by dreams, visions, or voices from the "Other Side."

In each of his stories, Potok sets for himself a question to be answered and reworks his own experiences until he is satisfied with at least a provisional resolution. Controlling metaphors help shape the questions. In *The Chosen*, the baseball game symbolizes the competition between two Jewish cultures, the very strict Hasidic and the more openly assimilationist. What happens to those caught in between those two traditions? The vision of pups being born in *The Book of Lights* represents the entrance of fertile Kabbala mysticism into a world of strict Jewish law. How can Jewish mysticism enrich Orthodoxy? Asher Lev's dreams of his mythical ancestor foreshadow the young artist's confrontation with his own culture. What happens when art brings great hurt? The sound of a little door harp symbolizes the transforming power of the imagination for Ilana Davita Chandal (Potok's first female protagonist) of *Davita's Harp*. What is the place of the imagination in Jewish Orthodoxy? What is the place of women?

The Chosen • *The Chosen* recounts the story of Danny Saunders, brilliant son of a Hasidic rabbi, chosen by tradition to one day succeed his father as leader of the fundamentalist community in Brooklyn, New York. However, Danny is less interested in studying the Talmud (Jewish law) than in probing the works of Sigmund Freud and other secular psychologists. The story closes with the almost inevitable confrontation between Danny and his father, which is mediated by Danny's friend Reuvan Malter. In the climactic scene in Reb Saunders's office, the old rabbi turns to his son and addresses him as a father for the first time. (For years, Danny had been reared in silence, except for times of Talmud study.) With fatherly tears, Reb Saunders explains that the years of silence created a soul of compassion within his brilliant son. Though he may well leave the Hasidic community for secular studies, Danny will always carry with him the legacy of Jewish suffering. That legacy will provide the moral force to change the world.

Reuvan, son of a Talmud scholar of the new school of textual criticism, chooses to become a rabbi. The choices, for Reuvan and for Danny, do not, however, come easily. Reuvan faces ostracism by the Hasidic community for suggesting that some Talmudic texts were of inferior quality and subject to misinterpretation. Danny must seemingly turn against his father if he is to pursue secular studies and abandon his leadership obligations.

The novel is structured almost as a diary, with pages of detailed descriptions of schoolwork in the Jewish high school, visits to the local synagogue, and the ebb and flow of Reuvan's life. Though at times tedious, the very innocence of the language contributes to a certain dramatic intensity. The conflict in the novel is mirrored in the frequent news reports of World War II and in the ensuing controversy over the creation of a Jewish state, Israel, in 1949. The Hasidic community is content to wait for the Messiah to create such a state; Reuvan's father calls for an immediate political settlement. Political questions are present in each of Potok's novels and are of central interest in *Davita's Harp*.

The Promise • Silence is again present in Potok's second novel, *The Promise*, which continues the story of Danny Saunders and Reuvan Malter as they enter their professional lives. The novel begins with shouts of rage from young Michael Gordon, the son of Professor Abraham Gordon, a controversial Jewish philosopher. Michael has been cheated at a carnival booth by an old Jewish man, and both Reuvan and his date, Rachel Gordon, Michael's cousin, stare in horror as Michael angrily denounces Orthodoxy. Michael's father had questioned the supernatural accounts in the Hebrew Bible and, as a result, was excommunicated from the Orthodox community; now Michael is releasing his hate on those who persecuted Professor Gordon. Subsequently, Michael is taken to Danny Saunders, now a psychologist at a residential treatment center. When the boy refuses to speak, Danny isolates him. The agonizing silence breaks Michael's will, and he reveals the hate he feels for his father and his writings, writings that have brought condemnation to them both. Eventually, Michael is finally able to accept his own feelings and reconcile with his parents, and Danny and Rachel are married, the powerful coupling of the brilliant Hasid with the cosmopolitan daughter of a secularist philosopher.

The Promise continues the exploration of Reuvan's choice to receive his rabbinate from an Orthodox seminary and his refusal to become a secular Jew, as Professor Gordon has done. However, Reuvan is uneasy with the traditional method of Talmud study advanced by Rav Kalman, one of his teachers. If the Talmud is the sacred oral tradition of the Jews in written form, contradictory commentaries from rabbis down through the centuries must always be reconciled by newer interpretations, so as not to call God's Word into question. For Reuvan, there is another possibility; a corrupt text could be the source of confusion. Any correction, however, would mean violence to sacred scripture. Reuvan will become a rabbi so that he might debate Rav Kalman and the others from within a common tradition.

Reuvan's father, David Malter, is the voice of quiet wisdom throughout both books. Though a proponent of the new Talmud studies, he is sympathetic toward those whose tightly knit culture is being threatened. As he tells Reuvan in *The Promise*, "We cannot ignore the truth. At the same time, we cannot quite sing and dance as they do. . . . That is the dilemma of our time, Reuvan. I do not know what the answer is." Earlier, Reuvan's father had challenged his son to make his own meaning in the world. Those who had committed themselves to the Hasidic traditions had kept the faith alive through incomprehensible persecution. Now Reuvan must also choose with the greatest seriousness and fervency, for he, too, must make a mark on the world and endure hardship of his own.

My Name Is Asher Lev • Potok picks up this theme in his third novel, *My Name Is Asher Lev*. Covering the period of the late 1940's through the late 1960's, the book is an apologia for the artist. The Orthodox Jewish surroundings are familiar, but this time the controversy is not over textual criticism but rather representational art. Painting is not strictly forbidden to the Orthodox Jew, but it is regarded as useless, as foolishness, as a waste of time better devoted to the study of the Torah, the five books of Moses. Moreover, certain pictures could come close to violating the commandment forbidding graven images. Asher Lev is a born painter, however, and throughout the novel, as he develops his talent, he is increasingly isolated from his family and culture. Asher is born in Crown Heights in Brooklyn in 1943. His father travels extensively for the local Rebbe in an effort to establish Ladover Hasid communities throughout Europe and to aid families immigrating to the United States. Asher's mother must stay with her son in New York because Asher refuses to leave his familiar streets to join his father in Europe. There are long nights of loneliness, waiting for Asher's father to return from some mission or other. Asher's mother suffers a breakdown when her brother, also on a mission for the Rebbe, is killed. She begins to find herself again by plunging into her Russian studies, picking up the work her brother left unfinished. Metaphors of things unfinished and things completed permeate the novel. Asher's father is continually on the move because of the great unfinished work of the Ladover.

Meanwhile, Asher himself finds that he must bring some kind of completeness to the world by painting not only what he sees with his eyes but also what his inner vision reveals to him. Those visions are not always beautiful; his paintings can be like knives, plunging the reality of evil into the soul of the onlooker. The wise Rebbe, sensing Asher's vast talent, entrusts him to Jacob Kahn, himself an artistic genius and a nonobservant Jew. Kahn forces Asher to absorb the work of Pablo Picasso, especially *Guernica* (1937), a painting inspired by the German bombing of the Basque capital during the Spanish Civil War. In time, Asher begins to surpass his teacher.

Asher becomes virtually a stranger to his father. At the end of the novel, Asher's parents stare with mixed rage and amazement at the two crucifixions he has painted. Both are of his mother, looking in abstract fashion at Asher the stranger on one side and at the always-traveling husband on the other. The image of the cross for Asher has become the supreme symbol of suffering, devoid of any Christian preoccupation. The image is too much, however, for his parents, Orthodox Jews. As the Rebbe tells him, "You have crossed a boundary. I cannot help you. You are alone now. I give you my blessings."

There is a marked contrast between Asher's sensitive paintings (an effort to say what must be said about the evil in the world) and his selfish behavior toward his parents. He is one of the least sympathetic of Potok's protagonists because he struggles less with his own anguish than with his need to express his artistic gift at whatever cost. Jacob Kahn's advice, "Be a great painter, Asher Lev. . . . That will be the only justification for all the pain your art will cause," seems too facile. Asher is determined to remain an observant Jew, but he will do so on his own terms. The commandment about honoring one's parents must be radically reinterpreted. The book suffers from the technical difficulty that Asher Lev must be identified as a genius early in the story in order for Potok to create the kind of tension he needs to interest a reader. A mediocre artist who causes pain is merely self-indulgent.

The book reveals something of Potok's larger purpose. Art must be true to itself even if that means surprise or hurt. The artist, painter, or writer must speak from the heart; anything else is mere propaganda. Potok sought to provide a rationale for his novelistic critiques of fundamentalist communities.

Potok introduces something else into Asher's story: Asher often dreams of his "mythic ancestor," a Jew who served a nobleman only to have the nobleman unleash evil upon the world. Just as Asher envisioned that ancient Jew traveling the world, seeking to redress the wrong he had a part in, so must the artist reshape evil into art and so bring a kind of balance to the world. Asher's visions are forerunners of Potok's use of mysticism or imaginative visions themselves as ways of coming to terms with a world gone crazy.

In the Beginning • *In the Beginning* is the story of young David Lurie and his childhood in an Orthodox family in the Bronx during the 1920's. The novel is patterned after the Book of Genesis: David falls from his mother's arms, develops a keen interest in the accounts of the Flood, and learns through the study of the Torah the power of words to shape a world. Potok's fourth novel was his most complex to date, departing from the forthright exposition found in *The Chosen* in favor of a more subtle panoply of impressions of growing up. Like all Potok's protagonists, David is precocious, constantly questioning the world around him, trying to have it make sense. He is sickly, bullied by other boys, and plagued with recurring nightmares.

David functions in the novel as an idealized figure to focus the reader's attention on how Orthodoxy confronts anti-Semitism and growing secularization. David imagines the Golem of Prague crushing those who would harm the Jews like some powerful living robot; as David grows, though, he learns that words can be more powerful than the Golem. Eventually, helped by those who practice textual critique of the Torah, David heads for graduate study at the University of Chicago. Yet, as in Potok's other works, there must also be some kind of reconciliation of the demands of Jewish Orthodoxy with those of secular learning. It is achieved through a vision David has years later as he tours the site of the Bergen-Belsen death camp. David's vision of his dead father, and of his father's brother, David's namesake, is a moving conclusion to the book. David's father despairs that he has lost his son to the evil world, to the very world that took the lives of millions of Jews. He is reassured by David's uncle, however, that the son must journey into that world in order to bring something back to enrich Orthodoxy, which has become moribund. The son must venture out but must never forget his own roots. No anger of humanity can strike evil from the world. Only the patient use of words, with faith in their power to transform creation, can accomplish the task. That will be a new beginning for the world, and for Orthodoxy.

Potok's earlier novels tell the story of those in conflict with their Orthodox heritage. For the first time, *In the Beginning* pictures a reconciliation as a vision or story within the context of the novel. It is a kind of blessing from the beyond; here is the artist at work, crafting the resolution to the story.

The Book of Lights • *The Book of Lights*, narrated in the third person, uses the technique of mystical reconciliation for a more universal purpose. If the Master of the Universe truly exists, how is a believer to accept the death light of the twentieth century, the atomic bomb? Potok's answer is that through the imaginative use of Jewish mysticism, the spark of God can be found in an evil world.

The story departs from Potok's previous novels, which traced the childhood of the protagonist. Only a few pages are devoted to Gershon Loran's early life before his seminary days and subsequent chaplaincy in Korea. Those first pages, however, are significant. Gershon witnesses the birth of some pups on a rooftop in the midst of his rundown neighborhood; he is awed by the presence of life even amid wreckage.

In seminary, Gershon is introduced to the study of the Kabbala and its *Zohar*, a Jewish mystical work from the thirteenth century. The *Zohar* is the book of lights of the novel's title, describing the creation of the world through the emanations of God. There are places where God has withdrawn his light; that has enabled humankind to come on the scene but it has also ushered in great evil. Now the mystic is called to ascend through those emanations to find God.

Such mystical tradition is complex and even contradictory. For Gershon, however, it is the pounding heart of a living faith. Gershon's quiet moments of reverie serve him well during his chaplaincy. Though Potok paints a detailed picture of Gershon's activities in Korea, the crucial story is elsewhere. Gershon's seminary friend, Arthur Leiden, travels with him to Kyoto and Hiroshima. At the Hiroshima monument, Arthur reads from the Psalms and pleads to God in vain for some kind of atonement. Arthur's father had worked with other scientists in developing the atom bomb, and Arthur is haunted by the memory. Later, Arthur is killed in a plane crash; Gershon, visiting Arthur's parents, hears a portion of one of Arthur's letters: "All the world, it seems, is a grayish sea of ambiguity, and we must learn to navigate in it or be drowned." The fact is that Potok's message in the novel; "Loran" is itself a navigational acronym. If Judaism were merely the law, the faith would break on the shoals of the gritty world. Its mystical tradition infuses the faith with the ambiguity of real life. It does not explain but rather affirms the nature of God's creation. The *Zohar* is an imaginative understanding of the nature of God; in it, God enfolds both good and evil. It is a light by which to view a decaying civilization, a light that will survive the death light. In his final mystical vision of his old Kabbala teacher, Gershon learns that the mystical light will help mend the world so that it can be broken again in yet new acts of creation.

Davita's Harp • It is the "mending power" of imagination that is at the heart of *Davita's Harp*. The harp referred to is a small instrument that fits on a door, with little balls that strike piano wires when the door is opened or closed. Here Potok returns to the first-person narrative, tracing the childhood of Ilana Davita Chandal, his first female lead character. She is the daughter of a nonbelieving Jewish mother and a nonbelieving Christian father. Spanning the years from the mid-1930's to 1942, the novel speaks with a new voice yet recapitulates some familiar themes. Davita grows up in the New York area; she remembers frequent moves, strange people coming and going, and the constant singing of the door harp. Her parents are involved in the Communist Party, attempting to fight fascism in Spain and in the United States. Davita is precocious and inquisitive, and her mother intelligent and cool, forever supplying Davita with the meaning of new words: proletariat, strike, idea, magic, war. Davita is spurred in her imaginative development by Aunt Sarah, a devout Episcopalian nurse who tells her Bible stories, and by Jakob Daw, an Austrian writer, now suffering from having been gassed in World War I, who had loved Davita's mother when they were both in Vienna. Daw is sheltered for a time by Davita's parents and spins odd stories for her. There is the story of the little bird, flying to find the source of a beautiful music that soothes the world from the horrors of war. Only if the bird could stop the deceitful music would the world wake to its pain.

Davita's father, Michael Chandal, a journalist with *New Masses*, is killed during the bombing of Guernica during the Spanish Civil War. Soon after, both Jakob Daw and Davita's mother, Channah, become disillusioned with the Stalinists because the communists, too, have committed atrocities. Davita has taken to attending a Jewish high school and becomes an outstanding student. Jakob Daw returns to Europe, where he dies, though his stories live in Davita's heart. Not long afterward, Ezra Dinn, an Orthodox Jew who had loved Davita's mother years before, marries Channah. Slowly, Davita's mother regains her sense of place.

Davita's time of innocence is over. Before Jakob Daw left for Europe, he finished his strange story of the bird. The bird, he said, gave up searching for the music of the world and became very small to fit inside the door harp. There, said Daw, the music was not deceitful but full of innocence. Now, however, Davita encounters something sinister in her adopted tradition. She is the most brilliant student at her yeshiva, but she is passed over for the Akiva Award because, she is told, she is a woman. It is 1942. Another student is selected for the award but learns the truth and refuses it. He is Reuvan Malter, first introduced in *The Chosen*.

Ilana Davita had wanted the prize because it would have given her the opportunity to tell her Jewish community a few words of farewell. "I had made this community my home, and now I felt betrayed by it. . . . I felt suddenly alone. And for the first time I began to understand how a single event could change a person's life." Later, in a vision, Jakob Daw and Davita's father appear, as well as Aunt Sarah. They want to hear her words, and so Davita speaks. She does not understand a world that kills its very best. She had wanted to speak public words of good-bye to her father and Jakob Daw the storyteller. The harp appears in her vision as well, singing in memorial to all the Davitas who would never have an opportunity to "speak their few words to this century."

In the end, Davita will go on to public school, angry with "sacred discontent." In an interview, Potok explained that Davita's experience was based on that of his wife, who was passed over as valedictory speaker because of her sex. *Davita's Harp* is a new exploration for Potok, that of Orthodoxy and feminism. However, the novel also draws from Gershon Loran, David Lurie, and Asher Lev in recognizing the power of the artist's imagination to transform pain and ambiguity into some kind of meaning. A writer is a kind of harp, playing new music that mends the world.

The Gift of Asher Lev • *The Gift of Asher Lev* is framed by death. It begins with the funeral of Yitzchok Lev, Asher's uncle, and the ending of Asher's exile in France to attend the services in Brooklyn. Asher Lev is forty-five; he is joined by his wife, Devorah, their daughter, Rocheleh, eleven, and five-year-old son, Avrumel. Though his family adapts well to the life of the Brooklyn Hasidim, Asher is haunted by the memory of a strange telephone call he received eighteen years earlier, the last time he had visited his parents in New York. It was a voice from the "Other Side," threatening death.

Asher is unable to paint (though he is given to sketching) and he seems to wander aimlessly through the local shops and galleries, as if waiting for a renewal of his gift. In the last year, critics had detected Asher's repetition of old themes, and he feels in danger of losing his gift should he become acclimated to his parents' community. Morose and determined to flee to France again, Asher is asked by the rebbe to stay, at least for a while. Eventually it becomes clear to Asher that he and the aging rebbe are woven inextricably together, as darkness and light. The rebbe has no heir, and it is apparent that the leadership of the Ladover must pass soon to Asher's father; but there can be stability in the community only if there is assurance of the line of succession. If not Asher, then the next heir must be Avrumel, Asher's only son.

By the end of the novel, which takes Asher's story to the late 1980's, the artist has exiled himself again to France, but not without sacrifice. He has left his wife and children in New York, promising to return to them several months hence; yet in his isolation he has begun to paint again. "What kind of God creates such situations?" Asher asks himself as he walks with Devorah. "He gives me a gift and a son, and forces me to choose between them." Later, in France, Asher is visited by the image of the far-away rebbe: "Slowly you begin to unravel the riddle," the vision says. "Your answer may save us and return you to your work. . . . It is sometimes possible for a man to acquire all of the world to come by means of a single act in this world. . . . You will redeem all that you have done and all that you are yet to do." Paradoxically, the sacrifice of Avrumel for the good of the community is a kind of death that redeems that artist himself; a gift on behalf of the world to come in exchange for the gift of the world as it is, in all its ambiguity and horror, and the ability to capture it on canvas.

I Am the Clay • Like *The Book of Lights, I Am the Clay* is a third-person narrative that grew in part from Potok's experiences in Korea. As they flee the North Korean and Chinese armies, a nameless old man and a woman named Gyu find a boy, Kim Sin, who is terribly wounded. The man wants to leave the boy, but the woman insists on taking him with them and heals him of his wounds. Eventually, they return to the village of the old couple to discover that it has not been destroyed. The boy then travels to his village, discovers that it has been razed, and returns to the village of the man and woman. Nearby is an American military installation where the boy gets a job, eventually working for a Jewish chaplain. After the boy reluctantly gets involved with a thief, the chaplain helps him escape by finding him a job in Seoul. By this time, the woman is dead, and the man has learned to love the boy.

The book treats the conflicts between the old, rural way of life and the new, technological way of life as well as between the old religious ideas and the reality of war. When the old man and woman return to their village, they think things will be the same because it has been spared, but they are wrong.

Like the biblical Job, to whom the novel's title alludes, the man, woman, and boy do not understand why they suffer. The woman has learned the words "I am the clay" from a missionary, from whom she has also learned to make the sign of the cross. Blending the sign of the cross into her own ideas about magic, she illustrates Potok's idea of the unity of all people. Although the novel has little to do with Jews, *I Am the Clay* treats one of Potok's central problems: testing one's beliefs in the face of an ambiguous, often harsh, and rapidly changing reality.

Old Men at Midnight • Potok's final work of long fiction pieces together three interconnected novellas that, when taken as a whole, might be viewed as a novel. The narrator for all three stories is Iania Davita Dinn, newly graduated from high school in Brooklyn when the first novella, *The Ark Builder*, unfolds. As interesting as the story is, it is perhaps unfortunate that it is told from the standpoint of the young girl who, as Potok's mouthpiece, is less than convincing. Potok's shadow casts itself over her dialogue and action in this story.

Be that as it may, Noah Stremin, a sixteen-year-old in 1947, to whom Davita gives English lessons, is at first quite reticent and reserved, but as the summer wears on, he eventually tells his tale to Davita. Noah, it turns out, is the only Jew from his Polish village to escape the Holocaust. As he becomes more comfortable with Davita, he tells her of his close friendship with Reb Binyomin, who looks after his village's synagogue.

Davita next appears as a graduate student, in which role she makes a more convincing narrator than she did in *The Ark Builder*. In this second novella, *The War Doctor*, Davita urges a visiting lecturer, Leon Shertov, to record in writing his experiences in Joseph Stalin's Soviet Union. In his youth, when he served in the Russian army during World War I, a Jewish doctor saved his life. Eventually Leon became a KBG interrogator, and as such, he again meets the doctor who saved his life. This time, the doctor is a prisoner, jailed in Stalin's campaign against physicians and, especially, Jewish physicians.

In the third novella, *The Trope Teacher*, Davita has matured into an accomplished woman, an author of some repute, who becomes friends with the renowned historian Benjamin Walter, who needs expert help in writing his memoirs. Davita piques him into dredging the memories of events from his adolescence, when Mr. Zapiski, who served in World War I with Benjamin's father, tutored him. She leads Walter to resurrect long-forgotten memories of his own experiences in World War II, and in so doing, she presents a convincing antiwar argument that borders on pacifism.

The War Doctor is at once the most artistically executed and most disturbing of the stories in this group that, when taken together, present a coherent case for banishing war from the universe. The depths of feeling that Potok brought to his final literary effort is clearly apparent in its execution.

Dan Barnett
Updated by Richard Tuerk

Other major works

NONFICTION: *Wanderings: Chaim Potok's History of the Jews*, 1978; *Tobiasse: Artist in Exile*, 1986; *The Gates of November: Chronicles of the Slepak Family*, 1996; *My First Seventy-nine Years*, 1999 (with Isaac Stern); *Conversations with Chaim Potok*, 2001 (Daniel Walden, editor).

CHILDREN'S LITERATURE: *The Tree of Here*, 1993; *The Sky of Now*, 1995.

Bibliography

Abramson, Edward A. *Chaim Potok*. Boston: Twayne, 1986. The first book-length study of Potok, this volume is the fullest available introduction to his life and works. After a biographical sketch, Abramson discusses each of Potok's novels through *Davita's Harp* and also devotes a chapter to *Wanderings*. Supplemented by a chronology, notes, a good selected bibliography (including a list of secondary sources with brief annotations), and an index.

Kauvar, Elaine M. "An Interview with Chaim Potok." *Contemporary Literature* 28 (Fall, 1986): 290-317. Interview undertaken at the time Potok published his nonfiction book *Tobiasse: Artist in Exile*.

Potok, Chaim. *Conversations with Chaim Potok*. Edited by Daniel Walden. Jackson: University Press of Mississippi, 2001. Collection of interviews with Potok recorded between 1976 and 1999. Many of these pay particular attention to the influence of non-Jewish fiction on Potok's writing. Includes an introduction by the editor, a chronology, and an index.

Shaked, Gershon. "Shadows of Identity: A Comparative Study of German Jewish and American Jewish Literature." In *What Is Jewish Literature?*, edited by Hana Wirth-Nesher. Philadelphia: Jewish Publication Society, 1994. Briefly places *The Chosen* in the context of literature in which Jewish authors and their characters have a dual identity: Jewish as well as that of the country in which they live.

Sternlicht, Sanford. *Chaim Potok: A Critical Companion*. Westport, Conn.: Greenwood Press, 2000. Part of the Critical Companions to Popular Contemporary Writers series. A straightforward guide to the novelist's works through *I Am the Clay*. Also includes two biographical chapters and a bibliography of primary and secondary sources.

Studies in American Jewish Literature 4 (1985). This special issue devoted to Potok includes several valuable critical essays, an interview with Potok conducted in 1981 by S. Lillian Kremer, and an autobiographical essay by Potok, "The First Eighteen Years." An indispensable source.

Reynolds Price

Born: Macon, North Carolina; February 1, 1933

Principal long fiction • *A Long and Happy Life*, 1962; *A Generous Man*, 1966; *Love and Work*, 1968; *The Surface of Earth*, 1975; *The Source of Light*, 1981; *Mustian: Two Novels and a Story, Complete and Unabridged*, 1983; *Kate Vaiden*, 1986; *Good Hearts*, 1988; *The Tongues of Angels*, 1990; *Blue Calhoun*, 1992; *The Honest Account of a Memorable Life: An Apocryphal Gospel*, 1994; *The Promise of Rest*, 1995; *Roxanna Slade*, 1998; *Noble Norfleet*, 2002; *The Good Priest's Son*, 2005.

Other literary forms • Although he is best known as a novelist, Reynolds Price's short fiction is sensitively written and helps to give readers a balanced picture of his writing. His poetry, his retelling of biblical stories, and his dramas, while they are not consistently of the quality of his best novels, are all clearly the work of an author with a strong sense of what he is doing. His collections of essays include some extremely interesting insights into what Price is trying to accomplish philosophically and stylistically in his long fiction. *Late Warning: Four Poems* (1968), *Lessons Learned: Seven Poems* (1977), *Vital Provisions* (1982), and *The Laws of Ice* (1986) are collections of Price's poetry. *The Names and Faces of Heroes* (1963) is an early collection of his short stories; it was followed by *Permanent Errors* (1970). *Things Themselves: Essays and Scenes* (1972) and *A Common Room: Essays 1954-1987* (1987) contain his most salient essays on writing. Among Price's retellings of biblical stories are *Presence and Absence: Versions from the Bible* (1973), *Oracles: Six Versions from the Bible* (1977), and *A Palpable God: Thirty Stories Translated from the Bible with an Essay on the Origins and Life of Narrative* (1978). His dramas include *Early Dark* (1977), *Private Contentment* (1984), and the teleplay *House Snake* (1986). Price's autobiography is *Clear Pictures: First Loves, First Guides* (1989). Price continued to write prolifically into the twenty-first century with the children's book *A Perfect Friend* (2000) and the novels *Noble Norfleet* and *The Good Priest's Son*. During this period, he also published various collections of his stories, poetry, and plays; wrote a number of religious books; and oversaw the publication of *A Great Circle: The Mayfield Trilogy* in 2001, consisting of *The Surface of Earth*, *The Source of Light*, and *The Promise of Rest*.

Achievements • Early in his career Price won the literature award from the National Institute of Arts and Letters, and he has received the Sir Walter Raleigh Award five times. In 1986 *Kate Vaiden* won the National Book Critics Circle Award, and in 1994 Price's *The Collected Stories* (1993) was a finalist for the Pulitzer Prize in fiction. In 1988, in recognition of his achievements, Price was elected to the American Academy of Arts and Letters.

Biography • Born on February 1, 1933, in the rural North Carolina town of Macon, the son of William Solomon and Elizabeth Rodwell Price, Edward Reynolds Price was a child of the Great Depression. Although because of the closeness of his family structure his welfare was not seriously threatened by it, the boy was aware of the social dislocations around him and had what his biographer Constance Rooke calls Dickensian terrors of abandonment and destitution. His parents, hard-pressed economically, lost their house when the father could not raise a fifty-dollar mortgage payment.

Upon graduation from Needham-Broughten High School in Raleigh, Price became an English major at Duke University in 1951, where he came under the influence of William Blackburn, who taught creative writing. Through Blackburn, he met Eudora Welty, who respected his work and ten years later was instrumental in helping to get Price's first book, *A Long and Happy Life*, published.

Upon receiving a bachelor's degree from Duke, Price attended Merton College, University of Oxford, as a Rhodes Scholar; there he received a bachelor of letters degree in 1958. He returned to Duke University in that year as an assistant professor of English and, except for brief intervals, continued to teach there. Beginning in 1977, he served as James B. Duke Professor of English at that institution, where he regularly taught courses in creative writing and on the poetry of John Milton.

Price, who has never been married, burst on the literary scene auspiciously when *Harper's* magazine devoted the whole of its April, 1962, issue to printing *A Long and Happy Life*, which was being released in hardcover at about the same time. The critical reception of this first novel was enthusiastic and brought Price the prestigious William Faulkner Foundation Award for a first novel.

In 1963, he visited England, and in the same year a collection of his short stories, *The Names and Faces of Heroes*, was released. This collection included "Michael Egerton," the short story that had first impressed Welty when she gave a reading at Duke during the early 1950's. The title story, told from the perspective of a young boy, is an especially sensitive study in point of view.

Price's second novel, *A Generous Man*, appeared in 1966 and focused on the Mustian family, as had his first book. The second book is a warm, rollicking story based on a hunt for a python named Death that has escaped from a snake show after being bitten by a dog diagnosed as rabid. The concept is openly allegorical, and Price drives home the allegory well while also presenting an extremely amusing story, with the hydrophobic python constituting the most outrageous phallic symbol in American literature. In 1977, Price produced a play, *Early Dark*, based on the Mustian cycle, and, in 1983, *Mustian: Two Novels and a Story, Complete and Unabridged* was issued, consisting of the first two novels and "The Chain of Love," a short story.

Love and Work and the loosely woven collection *Permanent Errors* both explore matters of heredity and its effect upon people. Neither received overwhelming praise, although they had support among some critics. Price, however, was busy with a much larger project, an ambitious saga of the Kendal-Mayfield family through four generations. The first novel of this story, *The Surface of Earth*, was received with skepticism by some critics when it appeared in 1975, but few could deny the creative zeal it reflected. The second volume of the Kendal-Mayfield story was published in 1981 under the title *The Source of Light*, and it, too, received mixed reviews.

A turning point in Price's life came in 1984, when he was in the middle of writing *Kate Vaiden*. He was stricken with spinal cancer, and the surgery that saved his life also left him a paraplegic. Pain drove Price to seek the help of a psychiatrist, who used hypnosis to control Price's pain. Little did he suspect that through hypnosis he would be put in touch with a distant past that he had not realized existed. Suddenly details of his earliest childhood and of his family surfaced. When *Kate Vaiden* was published in 1986, it was, because of these unexpected insights, a quite different novel from the one Price had originally projected. Price's hypnosis unlocked the memories from which his autobiography, *Clear Pictures: First Loves, First Guides*, published in 1989,

Margaret Sartor

evolved. *The Tongues of Angels*, a novel published in 1990, is also a product of Price's hypnotic communication with his past.

A further literary product of Price's painful illness is his personal narrative *A Whole New Life* (1994). The book not only offers a detailed account of his "mid-life collision with cancer and paralysis" but also celebrates his emergence from that trial into a new and, he affirms, better life. Price's own confrontation with mortality no doubt adds resonance to all his subsequent writings, such as the poignant description of Wade's suffering and death in *The Promise of Rest*. Furthermore, as an affirmation of God's strange grace, *A Whole New Life* displays kinship with Price's numerous retellings of stories from the Bible.

While focusing on long fiction, Price continued to produce notable works in other genres. The plays in his trilogy *New Music* premiered in 1989 and have subsequently been produced throughout the country. Price also wrote a television play, *Private Contentment* (1983), for the American Playhouse series aired by the Public Broadcasting Service (PBS). Along with his lyric poems, Price wrote the lyrics of songs ("Copperline" and "New Hymn") for his fellow North Carolinian James Taylor.

Analysis • Any reading of Reynolds Price's novels quickly demonstrates that Price's work, throughout his career, grapples with puzzling questions. Preeminent among these questions is what effect do families have on communities and on the broader societies outside the isolated communities that provide Price with his microcosms.

Focusing on a single region of North Carolina just south of the Virginia border, Price moved beyond the limitations one sometimes finds in regional writers and in his work deals with universal themes, particularly with those that concern original sin and free choice; biological determinism, particularly as it is reflected in heredity; and the meanings of and relationships between life and death. In Price's novels, children inherit the burden of sin passed on by their parents, and, try as they will, they cannot escape this burden. They have free will, they can make choices, but the choices they make are almost identical to the choices their progenitors have made before them, so they grow up to be like those who have spawned them, no matter how much they struggle to avoid such a resemblance.

Reynolds Price is more than merely the regional author that many people consider him to be. He is regional in the sense that William Faulkner was regional, but his concerns are also as broad as Faulkner's were. Fate plays a strong role in Price's work, and this fate is connected to heredity. Free will enables people to make choices, but in exercising their free will, Price's characters often make the same choices their parents made; therefore, the results are almost identical. Hereditary determinism is stronger in Price's work than in that of almost any other contemporary American author.

Kate Vaiden • Price harbored from his earliest memories questions about his mother and about his parents' relationship with each other. He seldom forgot that his mother almost died in bearing him and that she was left mutilated by his difficult birth. His later relationships with her were always colored by that recollection and by the feeling of guilt it caused him. The guilt of the child is reflected most clearly in *Kate Vaiden*, where Kate blames herself for an act that was as much out of her control as was Elizabeth's difficult confinement out of Reynolds's control.

Despite Kate's innocence of any blame, she continues to blame herself after her father murders her mother and then turns the gun on himself, and her entire adult life—indeed, her life from age eleven onward—is so profoundly affected by that single event, which brought an end to her childhood innocence, that it takes her forty-five years to begin to come to grips with her problems in any effective way. *Kate Vaiden* does not end on any realistic note of hope or promise; rather, it ends with a large question mark. Through writing the novel, however, Price presumably enhanced his understanding of his mother, who, like Kate, was orphaned at an early age.

Love and Work • Price was working toward the solution of problems like those that *Kate Vaiden* poses in his earlier *Love and Work*, in which Thomas Eborn, like Price himself a novelist and a professor, is forced to examine his relationship with his mother and his parents' relationship with each other and to society when his mother dies unexpectedly. Tom has been a dutiful son; he has helped provide for his mother financially. However, he is also a compulsive writer who husbands his time and guards it jealously, organizing his life in such a way that he will always be able to write.

Because of this dedication, he misses his mother's last telephone call; he is busy writing and will not talk with her. Shortly thereafter, she is dead. Price creates in this novel a story that uses place most effectively. Tom Eborn teaches in a southern town not unlike Durham, North Carolina, where Price spent his professional career. Tom has arranged his life to eliminate from it any unnecessary distractions, and in doing this he has excluded from it as well much human contact. Tom's turf—completely his own—is his study, his inviolable space where he can be alone, where he can create. No one dare intrude upon it. His mother's unanticipated death, however, makes Tom realize the wrongness of isolating himself as fully as he has from humankind.

It is clear that one can find much of Reynolds Price in Tom Eborn. To make a simple equation between the two, however, would be fatuous and misleading. *Love and Work* is a novel, and although Price once said that a writer's experience and background have as much to do with writing fiction as has imagination, he also warned that writers slip in and out of autobiography, so that their novels cannot be read as accurate autobiographical statements.

One can profitably read *Love and Work* against Price's consciously constructed autobiography, *Clear Pictures: First Loves, First Guides*, and can find the correspondence between his life and Tom Eborn's. Such a comparison will show Price's departures from autobiographical revelation in this novel. The same caveat must be made for *Kate Vaiden*, which strongly reflects Price's background but which is far from an authentic autobiographical representation.

A Long and Happy Life • Price's consuming interest in the family as the fundamental unit of society is found in his first novel, *A Long and Happy Life*, and pervades his future writing. *A Long and Happy Life* and *A Generous Man*, along with several of Price's short stories and his novel *Good Hearts* have to do with the Mustian family, who live in Macon, North Carolina, the town on the Virginia border in which Price was born and reared. *A Long and Happy Life* revolves around the romance between twenty-year-old Rosacoke Mustian and her boyfriend of six years, Wesley Beavers, two years her senior.

Wesley motorcycles to his native Macon to visit Rosacoke whenever he can take a weekend away from the naval base in Norfolk, 130 miles to the northeast. Wesley is sexually experienced, but Rosacoke is a virgin when the story opens in July. On a scorching day, Rosacoke rides on the back of Wesley's motorcycle to the black church from which her friend Mildred Sutton is to be buried. Mildred has died while giving birth to her child Sledge.

Wesley roars up to the church, deposits Rosacoke, and stays outside polishing his bike. The church moans in ecstasies of religious transport. One woman cries, "Sweet Jesus," and Wesley, hearing her cry, is transported to a sweaty bed in Norfolk, where one of his many women uttered an identical cry at a crucial point in their lovemaking.

Reminded of this, Wesley zooms off in a cloud of red dust so dry and thick that reading about it almost makes one want to wash it off. Wesley has to get ready for the afternoon, for the church picnic that he and Rosacoke will attend. Price's descriptions in this portion of the book are masterful and memorably comic, although the import of what is being communicated is deadly serious and universally significant.

At the church picnic, Wesley tries to seduce Rosacoke, but she resists him, as she always has in the past. The picnic itself is a jolly affair. As the picnickers are about to sit down to their meals, Uncle Simon discovers that his false teeth are missing. Those who have not already begun to consume their barbecued pork and Brunswick stew help Simon look for his teeth. Someone asks him when he last remembers having them.

Simon, after due deliberation, proclaims that he took them out while he was stirring the large kettle of Brunswick stew. With this revelation, all eating comes to an abrupt halt. Simon eventually finds his teeth—they were in his back pocket all along. Nevertheless, the eating never quite gets back to normal, because of the general uncertainty about where the lost dentures were. Vignettes like this help Price to convey a deeply philosophical message to readers without immersing them in specialized terminology or in abstruse and abstract thinking.

A Generous Man • In *A Generous Man*, published four years after *A Long and Happy Life*, Price goes back several years in time and writes about the Mustian family before Wesley Beavers was known to them. Rosacoke is only eleven years old during the action of the later novel. The basic concept of the book is so outrageous that it would have seemed completely ridiculous if not handled delicately and well.

This novel essentially takes up a young boy's coming-of-age. Milo, Rosacoke's fifteen-year-old brother, has just lost his virginity to Lois Provo, the girl who runs the snake show at the Warren County Fair. Years ago, Lois's mother was impregnated by a bounder, who proves to be Milo's cousin. After the truth was known, he abandoned the woman, leaving her only her memories and his eighteen-foot python, Death, who still thrives.

Milo, the morning after his maiden voyage with Lois, wakens to find that his dog, Phillip, is ill. The family gathers for a trip to the alcoholic veterinarian, who promptly diagnoses the dog's illness as rabies. For reasons unrevealed, he neither confines the dog nor destroys it. Instead, he provides a muzzle, and the Mustians leave with their muzzled mutt to go to the fair.

Rato, the mentally disabled son, takes the dog's muzzle off. Despite his retardation, Rato has known all along that the dog does not have rabies but is merely suffering from worms, a bit of information he keeps to himself, not wanting to put his knowledge of dogs and their maladies up against the vet's.

As it turns out, Phillip has a prejudice against snakes, and when he encounters Death, he attacks it. By the time the dust has settled, the dog, the snake, and the mentally disabled Rato have disappeared into the woods. Sheriff Rooster Pomeroy, citing the dangers of having a hydrophobic snake abroad among the loblolly and kudzu, collects a posse, a group of men keen for excitement and camaraderie, to hunt down the missing boy, the dog, and, most urgently, the snake. Spirits are high, and liquor flows freely.

In the course of the hunt, Milo, unaccustomed to alcohol, gets drunk enough to wander out of the woods, straight to Pomeroys' house, where Mrs. Pomeroy has been left alone. Because the sheriff is impotent, Mrs. Pomeroy finds her sexual satisfaction wherever she can, and Milo looks very good to her. They end up in her bed, where, during their pillow talk, Milo learns that Mrs. Pomeroy's first sexual encounter was with his cousin, the same bounder who sired Lois and gave Death to her mother.

Despite his prurient intentions, Milo cannot complete his act because the doorbell rings, prompting him to bolt through the open window, carrying his clothing with him. He rejoins the unlikely search, and it is he who finds Death. The snake wraps itself around Milo, almost choking the life out of him, but ironically Sheriff Pomeroy comes to the rescue and defeats Death with a well-placed gunshot.

Soon Milo wants to resume his lovemaking with Lois, but she is unwilling, because their first encounter left her quite unsatisfied. She classifies Milo among those men who are takers rather than givers in love encounters, and she lets him know it. He promises to reform; in his second encounter with her, his performance is indeed altered. Thus the book's title: Milo has become a man, but, having learned that he must give as well as take, he must mature further to become a generous man.

The Kendal-Mayfield saga • Price's difficulties with the critics when he produced the first volume of the Kendal-Mayfield saga, *The Surface of Earth*, stemmed largely from an inability of many northeastern critics to respond with understanding to a convoluted familial saga that had heavy biblical overtones, that had to do fundamentally with original sin, guilt, conflicted race relations, incestuous feelings, incredibly frequent suicides, and much that is a more common part of rural southern experience than of urban northern experience. Southern families like the two Price writes about in the Kendal-Mayfield novels are smothering families. Their members sometimes try to escape, but the magnetic pull back into the decaying bosom of the family is too strong for them to resist. In that respect, this saga is similar to William Faulkner's *The Sound and the Fury* (1929), in which the Compsons can never escape their heredity and all that it has predestined for them.

It is significant that the family members in the Kendal-Mayfield saga (including those in *The Source of Light* and *The Promise of Rest*, sequels to *The Surface of Earth*) resemble one another so closely. Not only do they sound alike but, more tellingly, they also think alike and act alike from generation to generation. Readers become particularly aware of this because of the compression of the novels: A large time span is telescoped into a few hundred pages.

On a literal level, the events of the saga might seem unlikely; taken symbolically, they assume a broader and deeper meaning and a greater artistic plausibility. Perhaps reflection on the outrageous unreality of parts of *A Generous Man* can help readers to understand some of the quintessential symbolic elements of the Kendal-Mayfield saga. Such comparable sagas as the five novels that make up John Galsworthy's *The Forsyte Saga* (1922) or the three novels of Sigrid Undset's *Kristin Lavransdatter* (1920-1922) suffer from a similar sense of unreality if they are read without conscious consideration of their symbolic contexts.

A considerable amount of the symbolic content of Price's Kendal-Mayfield novels can be found in the dream sequences that are integral to the books. There are more than twenty of them in the first novel, and these sequences serve many purposes beyond suggesting the subconscious state of the characters who have the dreams.

The Surface of Earth • The beginning of the Kendal family history as Price reveals it in *The Surface of Earth* is Bedford Kendal's rendition to his children of their grandparents' tragedy. Their grandmother died while giving birth to their mother. Their grandfather, considering himself responsible for his wife's death, killed himself, leaving his newborn daughter (like Price's own mother) an orphan. Bedford, having married this orphan when she grew to adulthood, soon realized that she was consumed by guilt and that she had a strong aversion to sex, all tied up with the guilt she suffered at the thought of having, through her birth, killed her own mother and driven her father to suicide.

Bedford's children, hearing this story, build up their own guilt feelings and their own aversions to sex. His daughter Eva, the strongest student of thirty-two-year-old Latin teacher Forrest Mayfield, elopes with him. Forrest is looking for family ties and thinks that he has found them among the Kendals, who, on the surface, seem to be an enviable family. However, his marrying Eva disrupts the family's delicate balance, so all that Forrest hopes for in the marriage is not available to him.

The title of book 1 in the novel "Absolute Pleasures," seems to be both an irony and a warning. Eva has her absolute pleasure, her unremitting sexual release on her wedding night, but then guilt possesses her. She dreams an Electra dream of her father stretched out over her body, and she is never able to enjoy sex again. She passes on her sexual aversion to her children, suggesting to her son Rob that he masturbate rather than become ensnared in love relationships with women.

Forrest, meanwhile, has his own hereditary baggage to carry. Forrest and Eva, whose names, as Rooke notes, suggest something primal and essentially sexual, ironically are trapped by their pasts. Price emphasizes another theme on which he has dwelt before: Marriage disrupts the family balance, but guilt over that disruption—at least among the Kendals and the Mayfields—in turn disrupts the marriage. The family and heredity are exacting taskmasters, and they are inescapable.

Eva, like many of Price's women, barely survives the birth of her son Rob, and in this difficult birth, which also severely threatens the life of the infant, one sees an entire cycle recurring. The mother, with her cargo of guilt about sex and about her mother's death in childbirth, has a difficult delivery that will increase her aversion to sex and that will impose upon her newborn child the same guilt with which she has lived. So has it always been with the Kendals; so presumably will it always be.

Eva and Forrest both settle for lives of frequent masturbation, and their masturbation fantasies are tied to their respective father and mother. Forrest, having abjured further sexual encounters with Eva, meditates on a poem by Gaius Valerius Catullus that has to do with ritual castration. He ultimately leaves Eva and makes a ritualized journey back to Bracey, his hometown, to live with his sister Hatt, a widow.

Book 2 of *The Surface of Earth*, the real heart of the novel, is the story of Eva and Forrest's son, Rob Mayfield, named for his paternal grandfather. Rob, now seventeen, is leaving the family nest, but the family surges within him. He has no more hope of leaving it than did any of the Kendals before him. There is no escape from either the biological heredity or the strong pull of memory and custom that families impose.

Rob, obsessed with Oedipal feelings since the onset of puberty, hopes that contact with other women will help him to overcome the shameful feelings that disturb his equilibrium. He tries to seduce his date for the senior prom, but she denies him, whereupon he sheds her. Like Milo in *A Generous Man*, his sexual thoughts are only of his own gratification, and his masturbation gives him an independence when he is rebuffed.

Rob contemplates suicide several times in his period of flight from the nest. He comes closest to it when he sees a clutch of boys shooting at a turtle, trying to kill it. The turtle comes to represent for Rob all the isolation and insensitivity that have plagued his recent life, that have brought him closer to suicide than ever in the past.

Rob seeks to overcome his problems by marrying Rachel, whose father manages a hotel, Panacea Springs, in Goshen. Not in love with Rachel, Rob wavers in his commitment to marry her, and he goes—as his father before him had gone to the first Rob—to his father for counsel. Forrest is now living in a heterodox arrangement with Polly, a woman with whom he makes love only ten times a year, fearing that more frequent contact would jeopardize what they have struggled to achieve. Having seen his father's relationship, Rob can now return to Rachel and marry her.

The dinner on the night before the wedding brings together all the elements of the family that Price needs to show to make his story work. In this evening of premarital celebration, the family history and all that it implies is made clear. That being done, the only task remaining to Price artistically is to kill Rachel off in childbirth, which he promptly does. Rachel dies giving birth to Hutch, whose story becomes the next portion of the saga.

The Source of Light • *The Source of Light* is a more optimistic book than its predecessor. It focuses on Hutch and on the aging and death of his father. In *The Source of Light*, both Hutch and Rob seem to have reached an accord in their lives, to have matured into acceptance of what seems for them inevitable. The pull of the family and the inevitability of their heredity are both still operative, but they are less oppressive than they were in the earlier book.

The Tongues of Angels • Set primarily at a summer camp for boys in western North Carolina, *The Tongues of Angels* is the story of a young man's rite of passage and a commentary on his continuing source of inspiration as a mature artist. Bridge Boatner is now a successful painter, but when his sons ask about the inscription on the back of his first significant landscape, he recounts the circumstances under which he produced it. At the age of twenty-one, Bridge recoiled from the recent death of his father by becoming a counselor at Camp Juniper. There he formed a brief but intense friendship with a troubled but immensely gifted camper, Raphael (Rafe)

Noren, for whom the painting was intended as a gift.

Rafe's angelic name suggests the mysterious nature of his great talents (especially in Native American dancing), but he also exhibits a profound need for love. Having seen his own mother murdered, Rafe is drawn toward Bridge even though he confides little. Bridge enlists Rafe as a model for sketches of angels, and in so doing he, perhaps inadvertently, contributes to the camper's death. In recalling that traumatic event, however, Bridge observes that even now he creates as an artist not merely because of his past errors but by actually using those errors as instruments.

The Promise of Rest • With *The Promise of Rest* Price returns to the Mayfield family saga and completes the trilogy collectively titled A Great Circle. This final novel in the series boldly confronts the twin furies of sexuality and race that have tormented the Mayfields for nine decades.

After more than thirty years of marriage, Ann has left Hutch. Although Hutch has been faithful to her, she feels isolated because of his close friendship with Strawson Stewart, who was once Hutch's student and lover and is still the tenant on the Mayfield homeplace.

Hutch remains a successful poet and teacher at Duke University, but he is devastated by news that his only son, Wade, is suffering from acquired immunodeficiency syndrome (AIDS) in New York City. Wade was estranged from his family, not because of his homosexuality but because his black lover, Wyatt, condemned Hutch and Ann as racists. After Wyatt commits suicide, Hutch brings Wade home to die. At first Hutch tries to exclude Ann from the deathbed watch, but their mutual pain eventually pulls them back together. After Wade's death they learn that he loved not only Wyatt but also Wyatt's sister, Ivory, and with her he fathered a child.

This child, Raven, bears the given name of both Hutch and Wade, and he is proof that the Mayfield clan will not soon become extinct. Raven's link with his grandparents remains tenuous, but in the final scene of the novel he goes with Hutch to visit an aging black cousin and to spread Wade's ashes on the Mayfield farm. Thus, the book affirms racial unity and solace after the pain of death. With a long heritage of sexual confusion and miscegenation, the Mayfields may not readily achieve peaceful rest, but its promise is surely genuine.

Throughout his writing, Price is concerned with showing that people cannot outrun their past. Price's characters are dots on a long, seemingly infinite continuum, and the continuum assumes a life of its own. It is like a steadily flowing river that moves unrelentingly toward the sea. Anything in it that tries to swim upstream is destined to be defeated. Even the strongest of swimmers, the ones who make a little progress against the almost inevitable flow, will be caught ultimately by the flow and swept along with it.

Underlying this theme of the strength of the family and the inability of people to resist their heredities is a pervasive theme of guilt, all of it tied up with pleasure, as manifested by sex, versus death or mutilation, as represented by the childbirth catastrophes of many of Price's characters.

Price's intimate and sensitive knowledge of southern rural life enables him to write some of the most accurate and memorable descriptions in print of the locale in which most of his stories are set. He has grasped the speech rhythms, vocabulary, and syntax of northern North Carolina with an authenticity that remains consistent throughout his novels and stories, as do the unshakably consistent points of view of his characters.

Roxanna Slade • This is Price's first novel since *Kate Vaiden* to be written from a female perspective. Its protagonist, Roxanna Slade, was born in 1900. Readers first meet her when she is twenty and living in a small North Carolina town, and they continue their relationship with her until she is ninety-four, the age at which she unfolds her long, complex story. Roxanna's life has been filled with trials, and, although at ninety-four she is quite removed from them in time, they molded the woman whom Price has created.

The novel's seven chapters are arranged chronologically. Some of them cover an act of such drama that the chapter is confined to one crucial day. Other chapters cover several years as Price telescopes Roxanna's experience. Price structures the chapters to reflect how Roxanna views the patterns of her life.

Some of Roxanna's trials will be familiar to readers of Price's short stories, in which a number of them had their genesis. Roxanna endured a horrible tragedy when the first man she truly loved drowned before her eyes. Having recovered from this catastrophe, Roxanna married, only to suffer the loss of a child. Then she was made aware of her husband's infidelities. While these events are relatively commonplace, and not unlike troubles that may have perplexed Price's readers in their own lives, Roxanna reveals her true strength of character and her fortitude through her rendition of these misfortunes. As the millennium approached, Price chose to comment on American society from the vantage point of a woman who lived through what might be called "the century of women." The suggestion is that in the twenty-first century, women should come into their own quite fully, having made the initial gains they did in the twentieth century.

Price makes it clear that Roxanna has learned to live with disappointment without being embittered by it. She frequently has had cause for anger, but in the wisdom of her years, she has learned to channel this anger to the point that it evaporates. She does not dwell on her regrets and, even at ninety-four, considers life a blessing rather than the curse that many people living through similar experiences might deem it to be. The pervasive theme that emerges from this book is that love is the counterbalancing force in a seemingly chaotic universe.

R. Baird Shuman
Updated by Albert Wilhelm

Other major works

SHORT FICTION: *The Names and Faces of Heroes*, 1963; *Permanent Errors*, 1970; *The Foreseeable Future: Three Long Stories*, 1991; *The Collected Stories*, 1993.

PLAYS: *Early Dark*, pb. 1977; *Private Contentment*, pb. 1984; *New Music: A Trilogy*, pr. 1989, pb. 1990; *Full Moon, and Other Plays*, pb. 1993.

TELEPLAY: *House Snake*, 1986.

POETRY: *Late Warning: Four Poems*, 1968; *Lessons Learned: Seven Poems*, 1977; *Nine Mysteries (Four Joyful, Four Sorrowful, One Glorious)*, 1979; *Vital Provisions*, 1982; *The Laws of Ice*, 1986; *The Use of Fire*, 1990; *The Collected Poems*, 1997.

NONFICTION: *Things Themselves: Essays and Scenes*, 1972; *A Common Room: Essays, 1954-1987*, 1987; *Clear Pictures: First Loves, First Guides*, 1989; *Conversations with Reynolds Price*, 1991 (Jefferson Humphries, editor); *A Whole New Life*, 1994; *Three Gospels*, 1996; *Learning a Trade: A Craftsman's Notebooks, 1955-1997*, 1998; *Letter to a Man in the Fire: Does God Exist and Does He Care?*, 1999; *Feasting the Heart: Fifty-two Essays for the Air*, 2000; *A Serious Way of Wondering: The Ethics of Jesus Imagined*, 2003.

CHILDREN'S LITERATURE: *A Perfect Friend,* 2000.

TRANSLATIONS: *Presence and Absence: Versions from the Bible,* 1973; *Oracles: Six Versions from the Bible,* 1977; *A Palpable God: Thirty Stories Translated from the Bible with an Essay on the Origins and Life of Narrative,* 1978.

Bibliography

Black, James T. "A Conversation with Reynolds Price." *Southern Living* 27 (September, 1992): 38. A brief biographical sketch of Price's life; discusses the ways in which families deal with crisis in his fiction.

Fodor, Sarah J. "Outlaw Christian: An Interview with Reynolds Price." *The Christian Century* 112 (November 22-29, 1995): 1128-1131. Price discusses eroticism in literature, the role of children in his fiction, the women in his novels, the importance of solitude in his life, his views on religion, and the author Flannery O'Connor.

Henry, William A. "The Mind Roams Free." *Time* 143 (May 23, 1994): 66-68. A brief biographical account, focusing on Price's struggle with spinal cancer and the significant amount of work he has written since being told a decade previously he would not survive it.

Powell, Tara. "The Fiction of Mercy: Suffering Delight in Reynolds Price's *The Promise of Rest.*" *Mississippi Quarterly* 53 (Spring, 2000): 251-264. Looks at Price's depiction of suffering and salvation within a Christian context in his novel.

Price, Reynolds. *Conversations with Reynolds Price.* Edited by Jefferson Humphries. Jackson: University Press of Mississippi, 1991. In these fifteen interviews, which originally appeared between 1966 and 1989 in literary quarterlies, student literary journals, newspapers, and magazines, Price speaks articulately and frankly. The collection is indexed and includes a chronology and an informative introduction.

_____. Interview by Wendy Smith. *Publishers Weekly* 241 (May 9, 1994): 51-52. Price discusses his sense of malevolent fate, his troubled family history, his discovery of himself as a writer, his previous works, and the process of writing about his ordeal with cancer.

_____. *Learning a Trade: A Craftman's Notebooks, 1955-1997.* Durham, N.C.: Duke University Press, 1998. This publication of Price's writing journals provides invaluable insights into how he crafted his fiction.

Rooke, Constance. *Reynolds Price.* Boston: Twayne, 1983. Focuses on Price's consistency of vision. After a brief biography and discussion of Price within a literary and geographical context, this study analyzes each of his first seven volumes of fiction—including his first two short-story collections—in detail. Includes a chronology and a select bibliography.

Sadler, Lynn Veach. "Reynolds Price and Religion: The 'Almost Blindlingly Lucid' Palpable World." *Southern Quarterly* 26 (Winter, 1988): 1-11. This article examines religious underpinnings, especially the influence of biblical narrative, in Price's fiction, and also investigates Price's perceptions of the deeper reality of life underlying what is commonly visible.

Schiff, James A., ed. *Critical Essays on Reynolds Price.* New York: G. K. Hall, 1998. A good first stop for the student of Price. Includes a bibliography and an index.

_____. *Understanding Reynolds Price.* Columbia: University of South Carolina Press, 1996. A general introduction to Price's work, focusing primarily on the novels, but also commenting on the relationship of Price's short stories to his longer fiction and memoirs.

Thomas Pynchon

Born: Glen Cove, New York; May 8, 1937

Principal long fiction • *V.*, 1963; *The Crying of Lot 49*, 1966; *Gravity's Rainbow*, 1973; *Vineland*, 1989; *Mason and Dixon*, 1997; *Against the Day*, 2006.

Other literary forms • Before his novels began to come out, Thomas Pynchon published a handful of short stories: "The Small Rain" (1959), "Mortality and Mercy in Vienna" (1959), "Low-Lands" (1960), "Entropy" (1960), and "Under the Rose" (1961—an early version of chapter 3 of *V.*). With the exception of "Mortality and Mercy," these stories appear in the 1984 collection *Slow Learner*, which also includes "The Secret Integration," originally published in 1964. Two magazine publications, "The World (This One), the Flesh (Mrs. Oedipa Maas), and the Testament of Pierce Inverarity" (1965) and "The Shrink Flips" (1966), are excerpts from *The Crying of Lot 49*. Pynchon also published some pieces in *The New York Times Book Review*, including a 1984 meditation on distrust of technology ("Is It O.K. to Be a Luddite?"), a 1988 review of Gabriel García Márquez's *Love in the Time of Cholera*, and a 1993 sketch, "Nearer, My Couch, to Thee," on the sin of sloth (included in the collection *Deadly Sins*, by various hands). He penned introductions to a reissue of Richard Fariña's 1966 novel *Been Down So Long It Looks Like Up to Me* (1983), to a posthumous collection of writings by Donald Barthelme, *The Teachings of Don B.* (1992), and to a reissue of Jim Dodge's 1990 novel *Stone Junction* (1998). Pynchon also wrote liner notes for the albums *Spiked! The Music of Spike Jones* (1994) and *Nobody's Cool* by the rock group Lotion (1995).

Achievements • Among those contemporary novelists who enjoy both a popular and an academic following, Thomas Pynchon stands out as a virtual cult figure. His novels and stories stand up to the most rigorous critical analysis; they prove, like all great works of art, to be the product of a gifted sensibility and careful craftsmanship. At the same time, Dr. Samuel Johnson's "common reader" cheerfully wades through much abstruse matter because this author never fails to entertain—with bizarre plots, incandescent language, anarchic humor, and memorable characters.

Pynchon has an enormous, diverse, and fanatically loyal following. There are more than thirty books on his work, not to mention scholarly journals. Some of the fascination he holds for readers is derived from his reclusive habits. He refused to be interviewed, photographed, or otherwise made into a darling of the media. Thirty years after the publication of his first novel, it finally became known that Pynchon made his home in New York City.

Pynchon was honored with a number of literary awards. He received the William Faulkner Foundation Award for *V.*, the 1967 Rosenthal Foundation Award of the National Institute of Arts and Letters for *The Crying of Lot 49*, and the National Book Award for *Gravity's Rainbow* in 1974. Though the judging committee unanimously voted to award the Pulitzer Prize in fiction to Pynchon for *Gravity's Rainbow*, the committee was overruled by an advisory board that found the novel immoral and "turgid." The William Dean Howells Medal, awarded once every five years, was offered to Pynchon in 1975, but he declined it.

Pynchon occupies a place in the front rank of contemporary American fiction writers, and more than one distinguished critic has declared him America's finest novelist.

Biography • Because of Thomas Ruggles Pynchon, Jr.'s passion for privacy, little is known about his life. His father was an industrial surveyor, and the family lived in Glen Cove, East Norwich, and Oyster Bay—all on Long Island in New York. His father, a Republican, eventually served as town supervisor of Oyster Bay. Pynchon was sixteen when he graduated from Oyster Bay High School in 1953. He was class salutatorian and winner of an award for the senior attaining the highest average in English. With a scholarship at Cornell University, he first majored in engineering physics but, though he was doing well academically, abandoned that curriculum after the first year. A year later, he decided to do a hitch in the Navy before completing his baccalaureate degree. He attended boot camp at Bainbridge, Maryland, and did advanced training as an electrician at Norfolk, Virginia. The two years in the Navy, partly spent in the Mediterranean, provided Pynchon with a number of comic situations and characters, which he has exploited in "Low-Lands," *V., Gravity's Rainbow*, and *Mason and Dixon*. Pynchon finished at Cornell as an English major and graduated in 1959. While at Cornell, Pynchon took a class taught by Vladimir Nabokov; Nabokov's wife, Vera, who did her husband's grading, remembered Pynchon for his distinctive handwriting.

Pynchon lived briefly in Greenwich Village and in uptown Manhattan before taking a job with the Boeing Company and moving to Seattle. With Boeing for two and a half years (until September, 1962), he worked in the Minuteman Logistics Support Program and wrote for such intramural publications as "The Minuteman Field Service News" and *Aerospace Safety*. After leaving Boeing, he lived in California and Mexico and completed *V.*, which was published in 1963 and hailed as a major first novel.

Over the years Pynchon was rumored to be living in various places, including California, Mexico, and Oregon. During the late 1970's, he made a trip to England that mysteriously was noted in the national newsmagazines. For a long time the author eluded his pursuers, but during the 1980's he supplied a few tantalizing autobiographical facts in the introductory essays he wrote for his *Slow Learner* collection and for the 1983 Penguin reprint of *Been Down So Long It Looks Like Up to Me*, the 1966 novel by his Cornell classmate Richard Fariña.

In 1996, Nancy Jo Sales, writing for the magazine *New York*, traced Pynchon to the Manhattan apartment he shared with his wife, Melanie Jackson (also his agent), and their son. The following year a photograph taken by James Bone appeared in the London *Times Magazine*, and a camera crew from CNN taped Pynchon walking down a street. In these instances, Pynchon fought unsuccessfully to suppress publication or broadcast of his likeness.

Analysis • The quest would seem to be the one indispensable element in the fiction of Thomas Pynchon, for each of his novels proves to be a modern-dress version of the search for some grail to revive the wasteland. Pynchon's characters seek knowledge that will make sense of their unanchored lives and their fragmented times; Pynchon hints that questing has a value irrespective of the authenticity of that for which one quests. The quest lends purpose to life, enabling one to function, to see life as worthwhile. At the same time, however, Pynchon invites his more privileged reader to recognize that the ordering principle thus projected is factitious. What is real is the gathering dissolution, the passing of human beings and whole civilizations. All attempts to discover or create order and system are doomed.

Even so, as Pynchon's career developed, one notes what may be a tendency to define some grail of his own, an inclination to search for a way out of the cul-de-sac of a metaphysics perhaps unduly in thrall to the principle of entropy (broadly defined as the gradual deterioriation of the universe caused by irreversible thermodynamic equalization). Pynchon's critics disagree sharply on this point. Some maintain that the intimation of counter-entropic orders in *The Crying of Lot 49* and *Gravity's Rainbow* is merely a hook by which to catch the unwary reader, a means of seducing him or her into system-making as delusive as that of any of Pynchon's characters. Other critics, unwilling to believe that Pynchon's frequently noted affinity with modern science has been frozen at a point attained some time during the 1950's, suspect that Pynchon means to hint at transcendental alternatives implicit in the vast mysteries of contemporary astronomy and particle physics.

Regardless of whether Pynchon is on a grail quest of his own (with all the propensity for mysticism that seems indispensable to such a quester), he continues to create intricate labyrinths in which readers experience the paranoia that also figures as a prominent theme in his work. Paranoia is the conviction that mighty conspiracies exist, that all things are connected "in spheres joyful or threatening about the central pulse of [one]self." Pynchon's protagonists come to believe in this infinite reticulation of conspiracy because it is preferable to the possibility that "nothing is connected to anything." Pynchon's readers, by the same token, encounter fictive structures that formally imitate the paranoid premise: All is connected in great, seamless webs of interdependent detail.

The dialectic between order and disorder is the dialectic between art and life, and it is with reference to this neglected commonplace that one should analyze Pynchon's artifice. In art, traditionally, humanity lays claim—sometimes piously, sometimes impiously—to the divine prerogative of creation, the establishment of order where all before was without form and void. Pynchon gives evidence, since the almost nihilistic *V.*, of a fascination with the religious belief that there are "orders behind the visible," orders analogous to those found beneath the surface in works of art ostensibly reflecting life in all its chaotic aspects. *Gravity's Rainbow*, for example, strikes one at first as a complete mishmash, a welter of all-too-lifelike confusion, but one subsequently discovers it to be as finely crafted as James Joyce's *Ulysses* (1922) or *Finnegans Wake* (1939). Perhaps Pynchon can best be imagined like William Blake, William Butler Yeats, and D. H. Lawrence, as countering the smugness and complacency of a scientific age with a calculated antirationalism.

These remarks adumbrate the last major topoi in Pynchon's work—science and art. Pynchon knows and makes artistic use of science. He has, if nothing else, dispatched legions of humanists in search of information about modern physics, chemistry, engineering, and cartography—disciplines to which they had previously been indifferent. As suggested above, however, science serves vision, not the other way around. Pynchon's work does more than that of any other writer—scientific or literary—to reverse the widening "dissociation of sensibility" that poet T. S. Eliot noted as part of the intellectual landscape since the seventeenth century. In Pynchon, and in his readers to a remarkable extent, C. P. Snow's "two cultures" become one again.

V. • In his first novel, *V.*, Pynchon brilliantly interweaves two narratives, one in the present (mid-1950's), the other in the period 1880 to 1943. The historical narrative, presented obliquely, concerns an extraordinary woman who appears originally as Victoria Wren and subsequently under *noms de guerre* in which the letter *V* of the alphabet figures prominently: Veronica Manganese, Vera Meroving. This is V., who turns up whenever there is bloodshed in the course of the twentieth century. In 1898, for example, she appears at the periphery of the Fashoda crisis in Egypt, and the following year she gravitates to Florence, where the spies of several nations are jockeying for position, engaging in what Pynchon calls "premilitary" activity. In 1913, she is in Paris, involved in a bloody theater riot that, like the crises in Egypt and Florence earlier, proves an earnest of World War I—a kind of fulfillment for V. in her early phase.

When World War I ends with Western civilization intact, though permanently altered, V. begins to be involved with those elements that will figure in the more satisfying carnage of the century's real climacteric, World War II. In 1922, she is in German southwest Africa, where the massacre of the local Herero people reenacts the even greater massacre of two decades earlier and anticipates the really accomplished genocide in Europe between 1933 and 1945. On and off after 1918, she is on Malta, consorting with a group sympathetic to Mussolini and his Fascists. V. dies in an air raid on Malta in 1943—just as the tide turns against the Fascist cause with which she has become increasingly identified.

V.'s affinity with Fascism complements a decadent religiosity, and she comes to personify the drift to extinction of Western culture and of life itself. She gradually loses parts of her body and becomes more and more the sum of inanimate parts: false eye, false hair, false foot, false navel. She is a brilliant metaphor for entropy and the decline of civilization, and her baleful influence is projected in the novel's present in the decadence of the contemporary characters, most of whom are part of a group called the Whole Sick Crew. The Crew is exemplified by its newest member, the winsome schlemiel Benny Profane. Profane is incapable of love and emotional involvement; he is also perennially at war with inanimate objects. His dread of the inanimate suggests that he intuits the cultural situation as the century wanes. Though he is no thinker, he realizes that he and his fellows are Eliot's hollow men, on the way to their whimpering end. His inability to love is presented in comic terms—though fat, he is doted on by various desirable women, including the Maltese Paola Maijstral and the beautiful Rachel Owlglass. The failure is that of his entire circle, for though there is much sex among the Whole Sick Crew, there is no commitment, no love, no hope. The one baby generated by all the sexual freedom is aborted.

The Whole Sick Crew is what Western civilization has become as a result of entropic processes that are utterly random and mindless. The meaninglessness of entropy is something difficult for the human mind to accept, however, and in Herbert Stencil, a marginal member of the Crew, Pynchon presents what becomes his standard character, a person who must discover conspiracy to deal with the fragmentation of life and culture. It is Stencil who does the mythmaking, the elevating of Victoria Wren from mere perverted adventuress to something awesome and as multifaceted as Robert Graves's White Goddess. It is not Stencil alone, for the undeniable desire for connectedness is quintessentially human. It is also shared by the sophisticated reader, who flings himself or herself into the literary puzzle and becomes himself a Stencil, a quester for meaning in the convoluted plot of *V.* and in the identity of the mysterious personage who gives the novel its name. Pynchon's genius manifests itself in his ability to keep his readers suspended between his two mutually exclusive alternatives: that the clues to V.'s identity are the key to meaning and that V. is nothing more than a paranoid fantasy, the product of a mind that cannot deal with very much reality.

The fascination with which readers have responded to *V.* indicates that Pynchon is himself a brilliant mythmaker. Even after one has "solved" the mystery of V. and arrived at an enlightenment that Stencil explicitly rejects as a threat to his emotional and mental stability, one still finds the myth trenchant, moving, even terrifying. The decline of the West is a theme that one has encountered before, but never has one encountered it so cogently as in this woman who loves death and the inanimate. The real conspiracy, then, is an artistic one; the connectedness is that of the novel, the cabal between author and reader.

The Crying of Lot 49 • Pynchon's second novel, *The Crying of Lot 49*, seems slight between *V.* and *Gravity's Rainbow*, and Pynchon himself seems to consider it something of a potboiler. Some readers, however, believe it to be his most perfect work of art. It is the story of Oedipa Maas, who is named "executor, or she supposed executrix" of the estate of an ex-lover, the millionaire Pierce Inverarity. In carrying out her duties, she stumbles upon evidence of a conspiracy to circumvent the United States Postal Service. She discovers Tristero, a *sub rosa* postal system at war for centuries with all officially sanctioned postal services, first in the old world, then in the new. Tristero subsumes an extraordinary number of revolutionary or simply alienated groups. In its new-world phase, it seems to bring together all those within the American system who are disfranchised, disaffected, or disinherited—all those defrauded of the American Dream.

Oedipa, like Herbert Stencil, finds that the harder she looks, the more connections to Tristero she discovers, until the connections start revealing themselves in such number and variety that she begins to doubt her sanity. Oedipa's mental condition, in fact, becomes the book's central conundrum. She first confronts the question in a flashback early in the story. She recalls visiting a Mexico City art gallery with Pierce Inverarity and seeing a disturbing painting by Remedios Varo. In the painting, a group of girls are imprisoned at the top of a circular tower and made to embroider *el Manto Terrestre*—the earth mantle. The tapestry they create, extruded through the tower's windows, contains "all the other buildings and creatures, all the waves, ships and forests of the earth," for "the tapestry was the world." Oedipa recognizes in the painting a representation of the fact that she—like any other human being—is imprisoned mentally and perceptually in the tower of her individual consciousness. External reality, in other words, may be nothing more than what one weaves or embroiders in one's cranial tower. Oedipa weeps at human isolation. Later, tracking down the clues to Tristero (which seems coextensive with Inverarity's estate and enterprises), she cannot free herself from the suspicion that the proliferating connections she is discovering all have their throbbing ganglion in her own mind. She realizes that she is becoming a classic paranoid.

Though Pynchon does not resolve the question of Oedipa's sanity, he hints that becoming sensitized to the problems of twentieth century American culture (and to the horrors of the spiritual void contingent on certain twentieth century habits of mind) involves a necessary sacrifice of sanity or at least serenity. At the end, Oedipa is faced with a harrowing choice: Either she is insane, or Tristero—with its stupendous reticulation—really exists. When Oedipa attempts to rephrase the dilemma, she finds that the paranoia is somehow inescapable:

There was either some Tristero beyond the appearance of the legacy America, or there was just America and if there was just America then it seemed the only way she could continue, and manage to be at all relevant to it, was as an alien, unfurrowed, assumed full circle into some paranoia.

Pynchon implies that Tristero, whatever its status as literal reality, is in effect a necessary fiction, a metaphor for the idea of an alternative to a closed system.

Oedipa's experiences are almost certainly an imaginative version of Pynchon's own. At the time of the novel, 1964, Oedipa is twenty-eight years old—the same age as Pynchon was in that year. Like Pynchon, she has attended Cornell and then gravitated to the West Coast. Like Pynchon, too, she comes to view herself as an "alien," unable to fit into the furrow of American success, prosperity, and complacency. Thus, one can read the novel as Pynchon's account of why he has gone underground. He has made common cause with America's disadvantaged; in all of his fiction, not to mention his article "A Journey into the Mind of Watts," one notes an obvious sympathy with minorities and something like loathing for the mechanisms of corporate greed responsible for the spoilage of the American landscape, both literal and psychic. *The Crying of Lot 49*, then, is a fictional hybrid of the spiritual autobiography—in the same tradition as Saint Augustine's *Confessions* (397-401) and William Wordsworth's *The Prelude* (1850).

These speculations—the need for an alternative to a closed system, the hints of spiritual autobiography—are supported by Edward Mendelson's brilliant essay "The Sacred, the Profane, and *The Crying of Lot 49*" (the single most satisfying reading of the novel, this essay has been reprinted in Mendelson's *Pynchon: A Collection of Critical Essays*, 1978). Mendelson points out the novel's high density of language with religious connotations; he argues that what Oedipa really searches for—and behind her twentieth century humankind—is a new species of revelation, a way out of the agnostic, positivistic cul-de-sac of contemporary rationalism. He also provides an explanation of the novel's odd title. "Lot 49" is a group of stamps—Tristero forgeries—to be sold as part of the settlement of Pierce Inverarity's estate. The novel ends as lot 49 is about to be "cried" or auctioned. Oedipa, present at the auction, expects to confront some representative of the mysterious Tristero, who will attempt to acquire the evidence of the secret organization's existence. Mendelson suggests that the number "49" refers obliquely to the forty-nine-day period between Easter and the descent of the Holy Spirit at Pentecost; the revelation that awaits Oedipa at the crying of lot 49 is symbolically the revelation awaited by the modern world, whose existence so tragically lacks a numinous dimension. Thus, Pynchon ends his novel on a note of expectation, a yearning for some restoration of mystery, some answer to what the narrator calls "the exitlessness, the absence of surprise to life" in the modern age.

Gravity's Rainbow • All of Pynchon's books are filled with bizarre characters and incidents, but *Gravity's Rainbow* is especially dense and demanding. The hero is Tyrone Slothrop, an American Army lieutenant attached to an Allied intelligence unit in World War II. Slothrop's superiors become aware that the map of his sexual conquests (or his sexual fantasies; this is kept ambiguous) coincides with the distribution of German V-2 rockets falling on London. Significantly, the erection *precedes* the arrival of the rocket. This fact, which calls into question the usual mechanism of cause and effect (it complements the fact that the rocket, traveling faster than the speed of sound, is heard falling *after* it has exploded) is of central importance to the novel, for

Pynchon means to pit two scientific models against each other. The older model, still seldom questioned, posits a mechanistic universe that operates according to the laws of cause and effect.

The character associated with this worldview is the sinister Dr. Pointsman, a die-hard Pavlovian threatened by the new model, which posits a universe in which physical phenomena can be plotted and predicted only in terms of uncertainty and probability (Pynchon is on sound theoretical ground here; he is presenting the physics of Werner Heisenberg and Max Planck). The character who embraces the more up-to-date worldview is the sympathetic Roger Mexico, a statistician. Between these two, poor Slothrop—a kind of Everyman—tries to stay alive and, if possible, free. Pointsman and his minions concoct an experiment with Slothrop; they will provide him with the best information they have on the German rocket and then observe him closely for further revelations. Slothrop, aware that he is being used, goes AWOL to embark on a private quest to discover the truth of his personal destiny—and perhaps the destiny of his age as well.

Pynchon picks his historical moment carefully, for World War II was the moment when the technological world came of age. Technology offers humanity complete control of its environment and its destiny; techology offers something very like transcendence—or it offers annihilation. Pynchon's novel is a meditation on the choice, which is seen nowhere more clearly than in the new rocket technology. Will humanity use the rocket transcendentally, to go to the stars, or will people use it to destroy themselves? The answer has been taking shape since the German rocket scientists were sent east and west after World War II, and Pynchon concludes his great narrative with the split second before the ultimate cataclysm: The apocalyptic rocket plunges toward the "theatre" in which the film *Gravity's Rainbow* has unreeled before the reader. Critical opinion is split on the degree of bleakness in this ending. Figuratively, says Pynchon, the world is separated from its end only by "the last delta-t," the last infinitesimal unit of time and space between the rocket and its target. The delta-t, however, is a relative unit of measure. Modern human folly has indeed set in motion the process of his own destruction, but the process might still be arrested by a reordering of priorities, human and technological.

As for Slothrop, he simply fades away. Pynchon says he becomes "scattered," and the word reveals a characteristic aspect of Pynchon's genius. Just as Joyce forced religious and liturgical language to serve his aesthetic ends, Pynchon forces technological language to serve humanistic and spiritual ends. "Scattering," a trope from particle physics, refers to the dispersal of a beam of radiation, but it also evokes *sparagmos*, the ritual dismemberment and dispersal of the divine scapegoat. Slothrop has been associated all along with Orpheus, whose dismemberment became the basis of one of the many fertility cults in the Mediterranean and Near East. In a sense, Slothrop dies for the sins of the modern world, and his scattering coincides with the founding of the Counterforce, a group of enlightened, anarchic men and women devoted to reversing the technology of violence and death. The Counterforce, which has affinities with various countercultural movements waxing at the moment of this novel's composition, is not particularly powerful or effective, but it offers hope for a planet hurtling toward destruction.

After *Gravity's Rainbow*, Pynchon published no new fiction for seventeen years. During this period, the counterculture retreated as the forces of reaction, complacency, and materialism took over, and perhaps it was this frightening and disheartening development that was behind Pynchon's long silence. He may have abandoned a book or books that came to seem unattuned to the post-1960's zeitgeist. However, when the novelistic silence was at last broken, it was with a meditation on the historical polarization of the 1960's and the 1980's.

Vineland • In his long-awaited fourth novel, *Vineland*, Pynchon returns to the California setting of *The Crying of Lot 49*. As in *V.*, Pynchon sets up a dual historical focus. He imagines characters in the present—the portentous year 1984—trying to come to terms with the period, twenty years earlier, when they and the whole country underwent a searing passage. Broadly, then, Pynchon here reflects on the direction the country's history has taken—from anarchic but healthy self-indulgence to neo-Puritan repression. These poles are visible in the People's Republic of Rock and Roll, with its ethic of freedom, pleasure, dope, music, and self-expression, and in the Nixonian and Reaganite reaction that put an end to the polymorphous perversity of the 1960's and ushered in the return to materialism and political conservatism.

The novel is structured—somewhat more loosely than is usual with Pynchon—around the quest of a girl named Prairie for the mother, Frenesi Gates, who abandoned her shortly after her birth. Prairie's father, Zoyd Wheeler, still loves Frenesi, as does the man with whom she was involved before him—the sinister Brock Vond, a federal agent who had used her to infiltrate and subvert PR3 and other radical causes. Zoyd accepts his misery, but Vond will stop at nothing to get Frenesi back in his clutches—not even at kidnapping Prairie, who could be made into an instrument of renewed control. Also involved in the action are female Ninja Darryl Louise—DL—Chastain, an old friend of Frenesi, and DL's companion, the "karmic adjuster" Takeshi Fumimota, a kind of Zen private eye.

The centrality of Prairie, Frenesi, and DL, not to mention the narrational attention to Frenesi's mother and grandmother (Sasha Gates and Eula Traverse), make this essay Pynchon's first in feminist fiction. (Though a woman, *V.*, was central to his first novel, it was really a parody of the kind of matriarchal vision associated with Robert Graves and the White Goddess.) It is in terms of this feminism that he is able in *Vineland* to move beyond the apocalyptic obsession that characterizes all three of his previous novels, as well as the stories "Mortality and Mercy in Vienna" and "Entropy." *Vineland* ends with a vision of familial harmony that is nothing less than mythic—an augury of what an America-wide family might be. Here the reader sees Prairie reunited with her mother and half brother, as Zoyd and others are also integrated. Vond alone is excluded (his surname is an apocope of the Dutch word *vondeling*, a foundling—as if to hint at his inability to be integrated into family wholeness). The reunion of the Traverse-Becker clans, which seem to center in their women, is Pynchon's Kurt Vonnegut-like imagining of the millennium, the era of peace and harmony that ironically succeeds the apocalyptic disruptions everywhere expected in the novel.

Herein, too, is the meaning of Pynchon's setting, the imaginary community of Vineland that provides the novel with its title. Vineland is the name given to the American continent by the Vikings, its first European visitors, at the end of the first millennium. Pynchon's novel reminds American readers that their land has been known to history for one thousand years.

Mason and Dixon • A more proximate past figures in *Mason and Dixon*. In this most massive of his novels, Pynchon ranges over the eighteenth century, with particular attention to the careers of Charles Mason and Jeremiah Dixon, who are sent by the

Royal Society to the far corners of the earth to observe the 1761 and 1769 transits of Venus. Between these two assignments Mason and Dixon accept a commission to establish the much-contested boundary between Pennsylvania and Maryland. The central part of Pynchon's mammoth novel concerns this project, which occupies his protagonists from 1763 to 1767.

The dates are important: Mason and Dixon do their work on the very eve of the American Revolution. Pynchon looks at the America they traverse for the switching points of the great railroad called history. He sees colonial America as a place where Western civilization paused one last time before following its Faustian course toward more rationalism, greater dependence on technology, and the throwing out of spiritual babies with the bathwater of magic and superstition. The religious freedom it offered notwithstanding, America has always, Pynchon suggests, been a place of struggle between the spiritual and material energies of the West. By the latter part of the eighteenth century, with the Revolution in the offing, the secularizing tendencies of the Enlightenment (notably Deism) made America the conservator, merely, of a few "poor fragments of a Magic irreparably broken." No longer the setting of "a third Testament," the New World remained only sporadically the "object of hope that Miracles might yet occur, that God might yet return to Human affairs, that all the wistful Fictions necessary to the childhood of a species might yet come true. . . . " Though aware that popular religion would always figure prominently in the moral economy of the emergent American nation, Pynchon suggests that some more genuine and legitimate spirituality was elbowed aside by the less-than-idealistic interests that fostered revolution (and he offers largely unflattering sketches of figures such as Founders Ben Franklin and George Washington). In the end, America became merely "one more hope in the realm of the Subjunctive, one more grasp at the last radiant whispers of the last bights of Robe-hem, billowing Æther-driven at the back of an ever-departing Deity." Pynchon seems, in *Mason and Dixon*, to reconceptualize the hallowed myth of a quest for religious freedom.

Indeed, he rewrites more than one archetypal American narrative. Thus he intimates, as in *The Crying of Lot 49*, some betrayal of the original American Dream; thus his protagonists, who twin the American Adam, must like so many of their literary predecessors decide whether to reenact the Fall. Pynchon also revisits the captivity narrative, with emphasis not on the godless savagery of the captors but on the nefarious scheming of the Europeans they serve. When American Indians kidnap Eliza Fields of Conestoga, they do so on behalf of evil Jesuits who seek to staff a bizarre convent-brothel called Las Viudas de Cristo: the Widows of Christ. Even more bizarre, perhaps, is Fields's escape with Captain Zhang, a Chinese Feng Shui master who objects to the severely rationalistic mensuration (and cartography) of the arch-Jesuit Padre Zarpazo.

Presently joining the crew of lumberjacks, roustabouts, and hangers-on accompanying Mason and Dixon, Zhang provides an important non-Western perspective on their project. "Boundaries," he declares, should "follow Nature—coast-lines, ridge-tops, river-banks—so honoring the Dragon or *shan* within, from which the Land-Scape ever takes its form. To mark a right Line upon the Earth is to inflict upon the Dragon's very flesh a sword-slash, a long, perfect scar. . . . " Zhang characterizes the Visto (the unnaturally straight ten-yard-wide swath the surveyors cut through the wilderness) as a conductor of *Sha*, the "Bad Energy" that will bring in its train "Bad History." As Zhang subsequently observes,

Nothing will produce Bad History more directly or brutally, than drawing a Line, in particular a Right Line, the very Shape of Contempt, through the midst of a People—to create thus a Distinction betwixt 'em—'tis the first stroke—All else will follow as if predestin'd, unto War and Devastation.

The American Civil War, half a century later, would validate Zhang's remark as prophecy.

Sir Francis Bacon, describing the Idols of the Theater, long ago recognized how received ways of knowing within a given historical period make certain kinds of thinking difficult, if not impossible. Mason, for example, aspires to membership in the Royal Society even as he desperately tries to believe that death—especially the death of his beloved wife Rebekah—is not final. However, the scientific calling that he shares with Dixon affords little latitude for such hope. Pynchon ingeniously imagines his protagonists as imperfectly amphibious men of their age. Each struggles to reconcile a propensity for supernatural or magical thinking with professional obligations to the new, rationalist order. Whether in South Africa, on the island of St. Helena, in America, or at the North Cape, Dixon and Mason sense that they are the inconsequential pawns of forces indifferent or hostile to them. Servants of the powerful and remote Royal Society, the surveyors suffer from a paranoia somewhat different from the usual Pynchon article—or perhaps they simply show us, belatedly, the positive side of a putative psychopathology. Pynchon hints, that is, at something admirable, even redemptive, in the paranoia of his eighteenth century Rosencrantz and Guildenstern. Mason and Dixon resist the coercive intellectual forces of their age.

As brilliantly realized as that age is in these pages, Pynchon delights in anachronistic violation of his historical frame. At a number of points the reader realizes that some piece of elaborately rendered eighteenth century foolery actually mirrors a twentieth century counterpart, for Pynchon frequently circumvents historical constraint to offer droll glimpses of what America and American culture will become. Hilarious, lightly veiled allusions to Popeye, Daffy Duck, the Jolly Green Giant, and *Star Trek* abound, not to mention numerous clever periphrases of a later vernacular. There are no cheap shots here, only the occasional "inexpensive salvo." Characters do not get their backs up—they suffer "Thoracick Indignation." Those hoping to keep costs down are reminded that "*prandium gratis non est*" ("there's no such thing as a free lunch"). The reader smiles, too, at "teton dernier," "aviating swine," "coprophagously agrin," and (of Fenderbelly Bodine exposing his buttocks to a foe) "pygephanous."

Pynchon fills his pages with the imaginative conceits his readers have come to expect. There is, for example, a wonderful talking canine, the Learned English Dog. There is also a character who, at the full moon, turns into a were-beaver. An eighteenth century Valley Girl's every sentence features "as," rather than the "like" that would characterize the speech of her twentieth century sister. A chef with the punning name of Armand Allegre fends off the amorous attentions of a mechanical duck—part Daffy, part Frankenstein's Monster—invented by Jacques de Vaucanson. Such joking has its serious side: De Vaucanson's punch-card technology would be refined in the Jacquard loom and other automated weaving machines that played an important role in the Industrial Revolution, centerpiece of the Enlightenment. Subsequently, punch cards would play their role in the Age of Information.

In *Mason and Dixon*, then, Pynchon characterizes the eighteenth century as the moment in Western history when rationalism became a cultural juggernaut, crushing spiritual alternatives to Enlightenment thinking. As in *V., Gravity's Rainbow,* and the 1984 essay "Is It O.K. to Be a Luddite?" the author focuses on the reification of Faustian appetite in scientific and technological advance, here symbolized in the profoundly unnatural Line that, arrowing its way into the mythic American West, consecrates the new world to reason—and to its abuses.

David Cowart

Other major works

SHORT FICTION: "Mortality and Mercy in Vienna," 1959; "The Small Rain," 1959; "Entropy," 1960; "Low-Lands," 1960; "Under the Rose," 1961; "The Secret Integration," 1964; *Slow Learner: Early Stories,* 1984.

NONFICTION: *Deadly Sins,* 1993.

Bibliography

Berressem, Hanjo. *Pynchon's Poetics: Interfacing Theory and Text.* Urbana: University of Illinois Press, 1993. A theoretically sophisticated treatment of Pynchon.

Birkerts, Sven. "Mapping the New Reality." *The Wilson Quarterly* 16 (Spring, 1992): 102-110. Claims that the American novel has ceased to provide the reader with an encompassing, relevant, challenging picture of life as it is really experienced; suggests the reason is that the texture of contemporary life does not lend itself well to realism; discusses those fiction writers who have adopted strategies for galvanizing the chaos, such as Robert Stone, Thomas Pynchon, Don DeLillo, and Norman Mailer.

Bloom, Harold, ed. *Thomas Pynchon.* New York: Chelsea House, 1986. An extremely useful collection of essays on all aspects of Pynchon's literary works. Contains essays of an introductory nature for first-time readers of Pynchon's prose.

Chambers, Judith. *Thomas Pynchon.* New York: Twayne, 1992. A critical and interpretive examination of Pynchon's work. Includes bibliographical references and an index.

Clerc, Charles. *"Mason and Dixon" and Pynchon.* New York: University Press of America, 2000. Study of Pynchon's most ambitious novel.

Copestake, Ian D. *American Postmodernity: Essays on the Recent Fiction of Thomas Pynchon.* New York: Peter Lang, 2003. Collection of critical essays exploring postmodern aspects of Pynchon's writings.

Dugdale, John. *Thomas Pynchon: Allusive Parables of Power.* New York: St. Martin's Press, 1990. Dugdale provides a critical review and interpretation of Pynchon's work. He includes thorough bibliographical references and an index.

Grant, J. Kerry. *A Companion to "The Crying of Lot 49."* Athens: University of Georgia Press, 1994. Glosses allusions and major themes. Bibliographical references and index.

_____. *A Companion to "V."* Athens: University of Georgia Press, 2001. A chapter-by-chapter close reading of *V.,* explicating Pynchon's allusions, summarizing critical interpretations, and providing a framework for understanding the work.

Green, Geoffrey, Donald J. Greiner, and Larry McCaffery, eds. *The Vineland Papers: Critical Takes on Pynchon's Novel.* Normal, Ill.: Dalkey Archive Press, 1994. First-rate essays and a *Vineland* bibliography by thirteen scholars, including N. Katherine Hayles, David Porush, Molly Hite, and Stacey Olster.

Horvath, Barbara, and Irving Malin, eds. *Pynchon and "Mason and Dixon."* Delaware, 2000. A book-length study of Pynchon's fifth novel.

Hume, Kathryn. *Pynchon's Mythography: An Approach to "Gravity's Rainbow."* Carbondale: Southern Illinois University Press, 1987. This excellent book examines in detail Pynchon's use of myths and legends in *Gravity's Rainbow.* The comments are also applicable to the rest of his prose works. The range of Pynchon's mythography extends from the grail and Faust legends to non-Western myths.

Levine, George, and David Leverenz, eds. *Mindful Pleasures: Essays on Thomas Pynchon.* Boston: Little, Brown, 1976. A useful selection of essays on Pynchon's prose. The essays on Pynchon's use of scientific theories and terminology are particularly valuable in understanding the novel *Gravity's Rainbow* and the short story "Entropy."

Mattessich, Stefan. *Lines of Flight: Discursive Time and Countercultural Desire in the Work of Thomas Pynchon.* Durham, N.C.: Duke University Press, 2003. Explores the ways in which Pynchon's critique of late capitalist society describes the emergence of a new conceptualization of time, which Mattessich calls "subjective displacement."

Sales, Nancy Jo. "Meet Your Neighbor, Thomas Pynchon." *New York* 29 (November 11, 1996): 60-64. Discusses Pynchon's almost mythical status; comments on his popularity during the 1970's and his subsequent reclusiveness.

Weisenburger, S. C. *A "Gravity's Rainbow" Companion: Sources and Contexts for Pynchon's Novel.* Athens: University of Georgia Press, 1988. This volume is an extraordinarily detailed encyclopedia of the sources for the allusions used in Pynchon's novel. Because several of the characters from Pynchon's short stories reappear in *Gravity's Rainbow,* this book is useful in order to trace the influence that Pynchon's short stories have had on his novels.

Ayn Rand

Born: St. Petersburg, Russia; February 2, 1905
Died: New York, New York; March 6, 1982

Principal long fiction • *We the Living*, 1936; *Anthem*, 1938, revised edition 1946; *The Fountainhead*, 1943; *Atlas Shrugged*, 1957; *The Early Ayn Rand: A Selection from Her Unpublished Fiction*, 1984 (Leonard Peikoff, editor).

Other literary forms • In addition to her three novels and one novelette, Ayn Rand published a play and several philosophical disquisitions. An early critique, *Hollywood: American Movie City*, was published in the Soviet Union in 1926 without Rand's permission.

Achievements • Rand won the Volpe Cup at the Venice Film Festival in 1942 for the Italian motion-picture dramatization of *We the Living*, a novel about the failures of the Soviet system. The sole honorary degree, of doctor of humane letters, awarded to Rand by Lewis and Clark College in Portland, Oregon, in 1963 does not reflect the significance of her influence on America's philosophic and political-economic thought.

Biography • Alisa (Alice) Zinovievna Rosenbaum was born the eldest of three children into a Russian Jewish middle-class family in czarist Russia. When her father's pharmacy was nationalized following the Bolshevik Revolution of 1917, Alisa, who had been writing stories since she was nine, found a calling: She turned against collectivism, and she elevated individualism—personal, economic, political, and moral—into a philosophy that eventually attracted a large, occasionally distinguished, following. Early in her career she declared herself to be an atheist.

At the University of Petrograd (now St. Petersburg), Alisa studied philosophy, English, and history, graduating with highest honors in history in 1924. By then the works of French writers Victor Hugo and Edmond Rostand, and of Polish writer Henryk Sienkiewicz, had inspired her passion for the heroic and the ideal. Fyodor Dostoevski and Friedrich Nietzsche also left their marks.

Unhappy because the Soviet system was not moving in the direction of her republican ideals and because she had a dead-end job, Alisa accepted an invitation from relatives and went to Chicago in 1926. In the United States she restyled herself Ayn (the pronunciation rhymes with "mine") Rand and within a few months moved to Hollywood, California.

Working as a film extra, a file clerk, and a waitress and doing other odd jobs from 1926 to 1934, Rand perfected her language skills and became a screenwriter at various motion-picture studios. In 1937, she worked as an unpaid typist for Eli Jacques Kahn, a well-known New York architect, in preparation for her first major novel, *The Fountainhead*. Given her early experience in totalitarian Russia, Rand soon became known as the most driven of American anticommunists. She had acquired U.S. citizenship in 1931. In 1947, she appeared as a "friendly witness" before the House Committee on Un-American Activities (HUAC) during the period of the communist witch-hunts—an action she later admitted regretting. Along the way, in 1929, Rand married Charles Francis (Frank) O'Connor, a minor actor and amateur painter. He died in 1979.

After her major literary successes, Rand devoted herself exclusively to philosophizing, writing, and lecturing. She spoke on numerous Ivy League university campuses. She became a regular at the Ford Hall Forum and a columnist for the *Los Angeles Times*. She was coeditor or contributor to several philosophical publications. Rand was active in the Nathaniel Branden Institute, created to spread her philosophy of "objectivism," until her personal and professional break with Nathaniel and Barbara Branden in 1968. This triangular relationship had played an important part in Rand's life, for the Brandens formed the nucleus of a close group of followers, ironically known as "the collective."

In her seventies Rand, a chain smoker whose loaded cigarette holder had become a symbol of her persona, was diagnosed with lung cancer. She died in March, 1982, in the New York City apartment in which she had lived since 1951. Her wake was attended by hundreds, including Alan Greenspan, an early Rand devotee and later chairman of the Federal Reserve Board Bank. Philosopher Leonard Peikoff, Rand's intellectual and legal heir, was also present.

Rand's publications have sold well over twenty million copies in English and in translation even as literary critics generally dismissed her ideas as reactionary propaganda or pop philosophy. Rand was a paradox. She was a writer of romantic fiction whose ideas were often taken seriously, but she was also a controversial individualist and a contrarian who defied the moral, political, social, and aesthetic norms of her times.

Analysis • In her two major works of fiction, Rand explicated her philosophy of objectivism in dramatic form. Thus, in *The Fountainhead* and especially in *Atlas Shrugged*, Rand argues that reality exists independent of human thought (objectively), that reason is the only workable method for understanding reality, that individuals should seek personal happiness and exist for their own sake and that of no other, and that individuals should not sacrifice themselves or be sacrificed by others. Furthermore, unrestricted laissez-faire capitalism is the political-economic system in which these principles can best flourish. Underlying this essence is the philosophy of unadulterated individualism, personal responsibility, the power of unsullied reason, and the importance of Rand's special kind of morality.

In her long fiction the philosopher-novelist spells out her concept of the exceptional individual as a heroic being and an "ideal man," with his happiness as the highest moral purpose in life, with productive achievement the noblest activity, and reason the only absolute. Rand advocates minimal government intrusion and no initiation of physical force in human interactions. She represents such a system as enshrining the highest degree of morality and justice.

Because Rand also focuses on the denial of self-sacrifice and altruism, a staple of conventional morality and welfarism, she opposes both Christianity and communism. She finds it irrational to place the good of others ahead of one's own rational self-interest. Likewise, she denies mysticism but rather promotes the Aristotelian view that the world that individuals perceive is reality and there is no other. Both her major novels can be considered elitist and antidemocratic in that they extol the virtues of a few innovative, far-thinking individuals over the mediocre majority, which is either ignorant and uncaring or, even worse, actively striving to destroy the brilliant individuals of great ability. Besides disparaging mediocrity, Rand also decried the power of connections, conformity with what has been done before, a trend she found far too evident in the American welfare state, and the intellectual bankruptcy she deemed it to have fostered.

Rand considered herself a practitioner of Romanticism who was concerned with representing individuals "in whom certain human attributes are focused more sharply and consistently than in average human beings." Accordingly, in both these novels the characters of the heroes, sharply drawn, are idealized creations—not depictions of real individuals—who are in control of their own destinies despite major odds.

Library of Congress

The Fountainhead • *The Fountainhead* is the story of Howard Roark, Rand's ideal man, an architect who has a vision of how buildings should really be designed. He is innovative and efficient; he also has a strong aesthetic sense and has integrity—in short, he is a man of principle and artistic individuality. Roark is contrasted with Peter Keating, a former classmate and fellow architect but a "second-hander," constantly replicating conventional styles since he has no originality of his own. He achieves a seeming success by manipulating others. Unlike Roark, whom he envies, Keating does not know who he really is.

Another of Roark's adversaries is Ellsworth Toohey. He writes a column for the *Banner*, arguing that architecture should reflect the art of the people. Gail Wynand is the *Banner*'s owner and newspaper magnate; he appreciates Roark's creativity but buckles under societal pressures, disregards his vision, and thereby engineers his own downfall as a worthy human being.

The love interest is embodied in Dominique Francon, the daughter of Guy Francon, the principal owner of the architectural firm that employs Peter Keating. She is a typical Rand heroine, a self-reliant idealist alienated by the shallow conventions of her day in interwar America and convinced that a life of principle is impossible in a world ruled by mediocrity. Her affair with Roark is motivated not by physical or emotional passion but by the recognition that he is a man of great worth. Along the way, in between and sometimes during other affairs, she marries Keating and then Wynand before finally becoming Mrs. Howard Roark. Dominique seems inconsistent in her ideals, attitudes, and critiques of architectural designs, but the inconsistencies are all part of her effort to spare Roark from ultimate destruction.

Roark, long professionally unsuccessful because he is unwilling to compromise the integrity of his creations, preferring not to work at all or to do menial tasks, eventually overcomes not only financial difficulties but also numerous intrigues by the likes of Keating. For instance, through the mean-spirited Toohey, Roark is assigned to build an interdenominational temple for a patron, Hopton Stoddard, a traditionalist who is abroad at the time. Toohey knows that Stoddard will hate Roark's radically innovative design. Roark makes the building's centerpiece Dominique's nude figure. Toohey incites public condemnation and persuades the patron to sue Roark for breach of contract. Stoddard wins the case, as Roark fails to defend himself in court.

Paradoxically, a friendship develops between Roark and Wynand, attracted to each other for different reasons. Wynand helps Roark in his defense at a second trial, which follows Roark's dynamiting a low-income housing project that Keating had commissioned. The latter had agreed not to alter Roark's design in any way in exchange for Roark's allowing Keating to claim credit for the former's innovative and cost-effective blueprint. When Keating fails to keep his promise and adulterates the design, Roark, with Dominique Francon's assistance, destroys the structure. The trial gives Roark the opportunity to spell out his—that is, Rand's—defense of ethical egoism and opposition to a world perishing from an "orgy of self-sacrifice" and conventional morality. After Roark's exoneration, Wynand commissions him to build the tallest skyscraper in New York City despite Wynand's losing Dominique to Roark.

Ultimately, *The Fountainhead* is a novel of ideas, of heroic characters who are the fountainhead of human progress and of their opposites, who live secondhand, second-rate lives and constantly seek social approval for their beliefs. The philosophy in the novel alternates with the action, and neither can be understood without the other.

Atlas Shrugged • Rand's philosophy extolling the myth of absolute, rugged individualism and its relationship to society is most fully explicated in what proved to be her last work of fiction, several years in the making: the twelve-hundred-page *Atlas Shrugged*. In this novel, Rand tries to answer the question raised by one of her earlier heroes: "What would happen to the world without those who do, think, work, produce?" In this apocalyptic parable, it is John Galt of Twentieth Century Motors, a physicist, engineer, inventor, and philosopher, who is Rand's ideal man and leads the other "men of the mind" on a strike against the exploitation of the genuine creators of wealth by all the leeches and parasites—the nonproducers—whom they had been sustaining.

Rand's philosophy is played out through the stories of the four heroes, the authentic moneymakers. They are the Argentine Francisco d'Anconia, heir to the world's leading copper enterprise; the Scandinavian Ragnar Danneskjold, a onetime philosopher who turns pirate in order to steal wealth back from the looters and return it to the producers of legitimate values; Henry (Hank) Rearden, an American steel magnate and inventor of a metal better than steel; and finally, the other American, John Galt, who, with the others, stops the ideological motor of the world in a strike before rebuilding society. The heroine, railroad heir Dagny Taggart, wonders where the individuals of ability have gone.

Confronting them is an array of villains, manipulative appropriators, enemies of individualism and free enterprise, scabs, and moochers profiting from the achievements of the producers and united by their greed for unearned gains. Especially, there is Dr. Robert Stadler, the counterpart of Gail Wynand in *The Fountainhead*. Stadler, once the greatest physicist of his time, fully cognizant of the value of the human mind, fails to stand up for his principles. The progressive decay of James

Taggart, Dagny's brother and the titular president of Taggart Transcontinental Railroad, parallels that of the society in which he lives.

In the novel, set sometime in the vaguely defined future, America is following Europe down the long, hopeless path of socialism, government regulation, and a predatory state into a new Dark Age. The heroes join forces with other intelligent, freedom-loving leaders of commerce, industry, science, and philosophy to reverse the slide. They do this as Atlas may have done had he grown tired of holding the world on his shoulders without reward.

Eventually, the heroes repair to a secret Colorado mountain citadel, where they wait for their time to rebuild the decaying collectivist society whose end their "strike of the mind" against productive work is hastening. Galt, arrested and tortured by the looters but finally freed by the other heroes, delivers a thirty-five-thousand-word oration via a commandeered radio, epitomizing Rand's objectivism and views of the ideal man. Galt's (Rand's) philosophy then becomes that of the new society: "I swear by my life and my love of it that I will never live for the sake of another man, nor ask another man to live for mine." By the end of the novel, socialism has produced a bankrupt world pleading for the return of the men of the mind, who, after a confrontation with the parasites, start to rebuild society. *Atlas Shrugged* is Rand's most thorough exploration of the social ramifications of politics, economics, psychology, metaphysics, epistemology, aesthetics, religion, and ethics.

Peter B. Heller

Other major works

PLAYS: *Night of January 16th*, pr. 1934, pb. 1936 (also titled *Woman on Trial* and *Penthouse Legend*); *The Unconquered*, pr. 1940 (adaptation of *We the Living*).

SCREENPLAY: *The Fountainhead*, 1949.

NONFICTION: *For the New Intellectual: The Philosophy of Ayn Rand*, 1961; *The Virtue of Selfishness: A New Concept of Egoism*, 1964; *Capitalism: The Unknown Ideal*, 1966; *Introduction to Objectivist Epistemology*, 1967, second enlarged edition, 1990 (Harry Binswanger and Leonard Peikoff, editors); *The Romantic Manifesto*, 1969; *The New Left: The Anti-Industrial Revolution*, 1971; *Philosophy: Who Needs It?*, 1982; *The Ayn Rand Lexicon: Objectivism from A to Z*, 1984 (Peikoff, editor); *The Voice of Reason: Essays in Objectivist Thought*, 1988 (Peikoff, editor); *The Ayn Rand Column*, 1991; *Letters of Ayn Rand*, 1995 (Michael S. Berliner, editor); *Journals of Ayn Rand*, 1997 (David Harriman, editor); *The Art of Fiction: A Guide for Writers and Readers*, 2000 (Tore Boeckmann, editor); *The Art of Nonfiction: A Guide for Writers and Readers*, 2001 (Robert Mayhew, editor).

MISCELLANEOUS: *The Objectivist Newsletter*, 1962-1965 (later *The Objectivist*, 1966-1971, edited by Rand); *The Ayn Rand Letter*, 1971-1976 (published by Rand).

Bibliography

Baker, James T. *Ayn Rand*. Boston: Twayne, 1987. An academic's brief but objective and highly readable treatment of Rand's life and work. Includes a chronology, references, and a bibliography.

Binswanger, Harry. *The Biological Basis of Teleological Concepts*. Los Angeles: Ayn Rand Institute Press, 1990. Written by a philosopher, this is a scholarly work focused on the connection between biology and the concepts at the roots of ethics.

Branden, Nathaniel. *Judgment Day: My Years with Ayn Rand*. Boston: Houghton Mifflin, 1989. A personal account by Rand's disciple, organizer, spokesman, lover, and, ultimately, enemy. Includes photographs.

Britting, Jeff. *Ayn Rand.* Woodstock, N.Y.: Overlook Press, 2005. A readable biography of Rand's literary and personal life but lacking in scholarly analysis.

Gladstein, Mimi Reisel. *The New Ayn Rand Companion.* Westport, Conn.: Greenwood Press, 1999. A compendium of the plots and major characters of Rand's fiction.

Mayhew, Robert. *Ayn Rand's Marginalia.* New Milford, Conn.: Second Renaissance Books, 1995. This volume contains Rand's critical comments on more than twenty thinkers, including Friedrich Hayek, C. S. Lewis, and Immanuel Kant.

Peikoff, Leonard. *Objectivism: The Philosophy of Ayn Rand.* New York: Dutton, 1991. This is the first comprehensive overview of all aspects of Objectivist philosophy, written by the philosopher who was closest to Rand during her lifetime.

Pierpont, Claudia Roth. *Passionate Minds: Women Rewriting the World.* New York: Alfred A. Knopf, 2000. Evocative, interpretive essays on the life paths and works of twelve women, including Rand, connecting the circumstances of their lives with the shapes, styles, subjects, and situations of their art.

Rasmussen, Douglas, and Douglas Den Uyl, eds. *The Philosophic Thought of Ayn Rand.* Urbana: University of Illinois Press, 1984. A collection of scholarly essays by philosophers, defending and criticizing various aspects of Objectivism's metaphysics, epistemology, ethics, and politics.

Reisman, George. *Capitalism: A Treatise on Economics.* Ottawa, Ill.: Jameson Books, 1996. A scholarly work by an economist, developing capitalist economic theory and connecting it to Objectivist philosophy.

Sciabarra, Chris M. *Ayn Rand: The Russian Radical.* University Park: Pennsylvania State University Press, 1995. The evolution of the author as a philosopher, of her dialectics, and of her objectivism, beginning with her early years. Includes a bibliography and photographs.

Torres, Louis, and Michelle Marder Kamhi. *What Art Is: The Esthetic Theory of Ayn Rand.* Chicago: Open Court, 2000. An amusing but respectful application of Rand's definition to the body of twentieth century art.

Marjorie Kinnan Rawlings

Born: Washington, D.C.; August 8, 1896
Died: St. Augustine, Florida; December 14, 1953

Principal long fiction • *Blood of My Blood*, wr. 1928, pb. 2002; *South Moon Under*, 1933; *Golden Apples*, 1935; *The Yearling*, 1938; *The Sojourner*, 1953.

Other literary forms • Although she is best known for one novel, *The Yearling*, Marjorie Kinnan Rawlings produced three other full-length novels and two novellas, the award-winning *Jacob's Ladder* and the undistinguished *Mountain Prelude*, which was serialized in 1947 in *The Saturday Evening Post* but never appeared in book form. She also wrote numerous shorter pieces for periodicals, beginning with a series of sketches about life in Cross Creek, Florida, which were printed in *Scribner's Magazine* under the title "Cracker Chidlings." During her lifetime Rawlings brought out only one book-length volume of short stories, *When the Whippoorwill* (1940). However, virtually all of the short fiction that she published in magazines was collected in Rodger L. Tarr's edition of *Short Stories by Marjorie Kinnan Rawlings* (1994). Rawlings was also the author of a notable autobiographical work, *Cross Creek* (1942), and an anecdotal cookbook, *Cross Creek Cookery* (1942). A children's book, *The Secret River*, was published posthumously in 1955. The author's versatility is evident in *The Marjorie Kinnan Rawlings Reader* (1956), edited by Julia Scribner Bigham. *Selected Letters of Marjorie Kinnan Rawlings* (1983) was edited by Gordon E. Bigelow and Laura V. Monti.

Achievements • During the 1930's and the 1940's, Marjorie Kinnan Rawlings's fiction was popular with the general public and acclaimed by critics. Her novella *Jacob's Ladder* placed second in the 1931 Scribner Prize Contest, and two of her short stories won O. Henry Awards, "Gal Young Un" in 1933 and "Black Secret" in 1946. Her first published novel, *South Moon Under*, was a Book-of-the-Month Club selection, as was *The Yearling*, which brought Rawlings a national reputation, a motion-picture contract, membership in the National Institute of Arts and Letters, and the 1939 Pulitzer Prize for fiction. Her autobiography *Cross Creek* was also a best-seller and a Book-of-the-Month Club selection.

After her death, however, Rawlings was remembered either as a local colorist or as the author of two books for children, *The Secret River*, which in 1956 was selected as a Newbery Honor Book, and *The Yearling*, which in 1963 won the Lewis Carroll Shelf Award. The classification of *The Yearling* as a children's book was ironic, since Rawlings had written it with Mark Twain's *Adventures of Huckleberry Finn* (1884) in mind, intending to appeal at least as much to adults as to children.

The ongoing efforts of a few scholars to call attention to a writer they believed had been both misclassified and unjustly neglected, along with the new emphasis on the relationship between human beings and the natural environment, resulted during the 1980's and the 1990's in an upsurge of interest in Rawlings, her novels, her short stories, and her compelling autobiography. Rawlings is now valued not only for her precision in describing a vanished way of life but also for her lyrical prose, her mystical feelings about nature, and her insistence that there are truly noble people who spend their lives in poverty and obscurity.

Biography • Marjorie Kinnan Rawlings was the older of two children born in Washington, D.C., to Ida May Traphagen Kinnan and Frank R. Kinnan, a patent attorney. Rawlings read widely and began writing early. By the time she was six, she was submitting stories to area newspapers. At the age of eleven, she won a two-dollar prize in a contest sponsored by the *Washington Post*; at the age of fifteen, she placed second in *McCall's* Child Authorship Contest and saw her story published in that magazine.

Rawlings's father died in 1913, and the next year, the family moved to Madison, Wisconsin. That fall, Rawlings entered the University of Wisconsin, where she majored in English and was active in the college publications and in the drama society. As a junior, she was elected to Phi Beta Kappa. After graduation, she moved to New York City and worked for a year for the Young Women's Christian Association. In 1919 she married Charles A. Rawlings, Jr., a journalist whom she had met at the university, and they moved to his hometown, Rochester, New York. During the next nine years, Rawlings wrote features for newspapers, advertising copy, and a syndicated column. However, all the short stories she submitted to magazines were rejected.

After visiting central Florida in 1928, the couple decided to move to the area. Purchasing an orange-grove property at Cross Creek, they settled down in their new home, and Rawlings began using Florida settings for her fiction. Within a year, she was a regular contributor to *Scribner's Magazine*, working closely with the influential editor Maxwell Perkins. Rawlings's first novel, *South Moon Under*, appeared in 1933. During that same year, Charles and Marjorie were divorced.

For the next eight years, Rawlings lived alone at Cross Creek, ran her business and her household, and wrote short stories and two more novels, the disappointing *Golden Apples* and *The Yearling*. She enjoyed cooking and entertaining, going on outdoor expeditions, corresponding with interesting people, and visiting with her neighbors. One of her closest friends was Norton Sanford Baskin. In 1941, she married him and went to live at the Castle Warden Hotel in St. Augustine, which Baskin owned and managed. However, she continued to write stories and books about Cross Creek, including an autobiography titled *Cross Creek* and an anecdotal cookbook, *Cross Creek Cookery*. Ironically, it was this autobiography, which critics consider one of her best, that cost the author four years of constant worry. In 1943, Zelma Cason filed a libel suit against Rawlings, based on the author's description of her in *Cross Creek*. The suit dragged on until 1947, when Rawlings was charged a nominal sum for damages.

Rawlings had decided that her next novel would have a different setting, upstate New York, where she spent her summers, as well as a more "serious" theme. Though it had been ten years in the making, *The Sojourner* lacked the vitality of the Florida works. Despite failing health, Rawlings now began research for a biography of her friend and fellow writer Ellen Glasgow. It would never be completed. On December 10, 1953, while Baskin and Rawlings were at their beach cottage, she suffered a cerebral hemorrhage. She died in the St. Augustine hospital on December 14 and was buried in the Antioch Cemetery at Island Grove, near Cross Creek.

Analysis • Whether they first encounter *The Yearling* as children or as adults, few readers can remain dry-eyed during the scene at the end of the book when the young protagonist, Jody Baxter, is forced to kill his pet deer. However, that memorable episode is just one of many incidents in Rawlings's fiction that illustrate her uncompromisingly realistic view of life. Indeed, it is ironic that for so long Rawlings was thought of as a children's writer, for in fact her rural world is as grim as that of Victorian author Thomas Hardy. Penny Baxter, Jody's father, describes growing up as learning that life is hard, that human beings can be malicious, and that feelings of insecurity and desperate loneliness are just part of being human. Though Rawlings and many of her characters display a mystical appreciation of nature, she never permits one to forget that living in a natural environment means accepting ugliness as well as beauty, suffering as well as joy, and death as a part of the daily routine.

Library of Congress

Jacob's Ladder • The novella *Jacob's Ladder* is a moving story about two poor, young people from the Florida scrub. Florry Leddy and Martin, or Mart, meet one night at a dance and the next day run off together, less troubled about having to travel through a hurricane than by the possibility that Florry's abusive father, Jo, will awake from his drunken stupor and pursue them. Florry is sure that Mart will be kinder to her than Jo has been; her only regret is that she cannot take her dog Sport with her. Sadly, love and loss occur only too often during Florry's life with Mart. Every time she starts to feel secure in a new place, something happens, and they have to move on. Florry cannot stay near her baby's grave; she has to abandon her cat and later her pet raccoon; she even has to let her pet pig be butchered.

Florry knows that Mart is not to blame for what happens to them. After Florry comes down with malaria, the money he has saved from trapping is used for her medical care. His traps are seized by a creditor, who is noted for preying on customers in difficulty. Mart makes enough money fishing in the gulf to buy a boat and nets, but they are lost in a storm. He is doing well at moonshining until a spiteful neighbor informs on him, his still is smashed by revenue agents, and Mart is sentenced to thirty days of hard labor.

As critic Samuel I. Bellman pointed out, Rawlings took the title *Jacob's Ladder* from an old spiritual, which reiterates the idea of laying down one's burdens. When Mart reaches his breaking point, Florry takes up the burden he has carried for so long. The only place to which she has a claim, she tells him, is her old home, and that is where they will go. They make their way through another hurricane and reach the old cabin, which is in a sad state. Jo is made to understand that Mart and Florry are taking over, and the novella ends on a hopeful note.

South Moon Under • In *Jacob's Ladder*, Florry and Mart wandered from the piney woods and the Florida scrub to the Gulf coast and back to the woods. By contrast, *South Moon Under* and *The Yearling* are set entirely in the "Big Scrub," a plateau bounded on the east by the St. John's River and on the west by the Ocklawaha. Before beginning *South Moon Under*, Rawlings spent several weeks in this wilderness area. Piety Fiddia, with whom she stayed, became the model for Piety Jacklin in the novel, and her moonshiner son became the character of Lant Jacklin.

Like Mart and Florry, old Lantry has had difficulty putting down roots, but he is propelled by fear. As he tells his daughter Piety, when he was making moonshine in North Carolina he killed a federal revenue agent, and he has been on the run ever since. However, the scrub is so remote, and his home there so isolated, that Lantry's worst fears are never realized. It is true that every season brings its own problems, drought or rain, insects or blight, but nevertheless Lantry and his family prosper. After his sons move on, Lantry persuades Piety to marry Willy Jacklin, who is a hard worker, if none too bright. Their son Lantry, or Lant, gives his grandfather great pleasure during the old man's last years. However, on his deathbed old Lantry once again succumbs to terror; only in death, it seems, can he escape from fear.

Old Lantry's story could be read simply as a morality tale. However, both in *Jacob's Ladder* and in *South Moon Under*, the author clearly sides with these hardworking, self-sufficient people who do not understand why there should be restrictions on such normal activities as hunting, fishing, whiskey-making, and letting livestock range freely, or why the government should constantly seek to block their efforts to support their families, even send them to prison, leaving those families destitute. As the fence-raising at the beginning of the novel illustrates, those who live in the Big Scrub rely on themselves and on one another, not on the government. One could almost justify Lant's killing his shiftless cousin Cleve as a service to the community, for Cleve is a spy and an informer, but in fact Lant was defending himself. Unlike Cleve's widow, who believes Lant and promptly marries him, outsiders would never understand. Like his grandfather, Lant will always have to live in fear of the law.

The Yearling • Although the setting for *The Yearling* is the same as that of *South Moon Under*, in this novel all of the action takes place within a single year, and instead of focusing on the conflict between two codes and two societies, *The Yearling* describes a boy's initiation into the natural world. It begins one April, with Jody Baxter so overwhelmed by nature's beauty that he cannot sleep; it ends the following April, with a revelation of nature's indifference. In all his hunting and fishing, Jody has never realized that the survival of one creature depends on the death of another. Then Jody's pet fawn Flag destroys the newly planted corn crop, and Penny tells his son the deer must be shot. Jody will never again view nature as he had the previous spring.

Now he knows too much, including the inevitability of loneliness, and only his father's understanding makes his discoveries endurable. Though, like young Jody, Rawlings responded to the breathtaking beauty of the Florida backwoods, she found even more to admire in many of the people who lived there. Her most memorable characters are those who, like Jody and Penny, have the courage to confront life and accept all that it holds for them, even the death of innocence.

Rosemary M. Canfield Reisman

Other major works

SHORT FICTION: *When the Whippoorwill*, 1940; *Short Stories*, 1994 (Rodger L. Tarr, editor).

POETRY: *Poems by Marjorie Kinnan Rawlings: Songs of a Housewife*, 1997 (Rodger L. Tarr, editor).

NONFICTION: *Cross Creek*, 1942 (sketches); *Max and Marjorie: The Correspondence Between Maxwell E. Perkins and Marjorie Kinnan Rawlings*, 1999 (Rodger L. Tarr, editor).

CHILDREN'S LITERATURE: *The Secret River*, 1955.

Bibliography

Acton, Patricia Nassif. *Invasion of Privacy: The Cross Creek Trial of Marjorie Kinnan Rawlings*. Gainesville: University Press of Florida, 1988. A dramatic account of the legal battle between Rawlings and Zelma Cason. Includes notes, index, and illustrations.

Bellman, Samuel I. *Marjorie Kinnan Rawlings*. New York: Twayne, 1974. Stresses the analysis of Rawlings's works. Has copious notes, bibliography, and index.

Morris, Rhonda. "Engendering Fictions: Rawlings and a Female Tradition of Southern Writing." *The Marjorie Kinnan Rawlings Journal of Florida Literature* 7 (1996): 27-39. Argues that though Rawlings used the male voice in order to be "taken seriously" by the establishment, her works reveal a feminist perspective. Well documented.

Parker, Idella, and Mary Keating. *Idella: Marjorie Rawlings' "Perfect Maid."* Gainesville: University Press of Florida, 1992. The employee described by Rawlings in *Cross Creek* as the "perfect maid" recalls her life with Rawlings and comments on the author's feelings about race. Includes photographs and index.

Silverthorne, Elizabeth. *Marjorie Kinnan Rawlings: Sojourner at Cross Creek*. Woodstock, N.Y.: Overlook Press, 1988. The standard biography, based on a close study of the author's papers, her unpublished works, and numerous interviews. Includes helpful list of reviews, illustrations, and index.

Tarr, Rodger L. *Marjorie Kinnan Rawlings: A Descriptive Bibliography*. Pittsburgh: University of Pittsburgh Press, 1996. Lists all of Rawlings's publications but contains very few secondary sources. Includes useful information about her film involvements.

_____, ed. *Max and Marjorie: The Correspondence Between Maxwell E. Perkins and Marjorie Kinnan Rawlings*. Gainesville: University Press of Florida, 1999. Collected correspondence of Rawlings with her editor, Maxwell Perkins, who also worked with such major writers as Ernest Hemingway, F. Scott Fitzgerald, and Thomas Wolfe.

Ishmael Reed

Born: Chattanooga, Tennessee; February 22, 1938

Principal long fiction • *The Free-Lance Pallbearers*, 1967; *Yellow Back Radio Broke-Down*, 1969; *Mumbo Jumbo*, 1972; *The Last Days of Louisiana Red*, 1974; *Flight to Canada*, 1976; *The Terrible Twos*, 1982; *Reckless Eyeballing*, 1986; *The Terrible Threes*, 1989; *Japanese by Spring*, 1993.

Other literary forms • Ishmael Reed may be best known as a satirical novelist, but he also gained a reputation as a respected poet, essayist, and editor. His poetry collections, which include *Catechism of D Neoamerican Hoodoo Church* (1970), *Conjure: Selected Poems 1963-1970* (1972), *Chattanooga* (1973), *A Secretary to the Spirits* (1977), and *New and Collected Poems* (1988), established him as a major African American poet, and his poetry has been included in several important anthologies. In well-received collections of essays, including *Shrovetide in Old New Orleans* (1978), *God Made Alaska for the Indians* (1982), *Writin' Is Fightin'* (1988), and *Another Day at the Front: Dispatches from the Race War* (2002), Reed forcefully presented his aesthetic and political theories. He also proved to be an important editor and publisher. *Nineteen Necromancers from Now* (1970) was a breakthrough anthology for several unknown black writers. *Yardbird Lives!* (1978), which Reed edited with novelist Al Young, includes essays, fiction, and graphics from the pages of the *Yardbird Reader*, an innovative periodical that published the work of minority writers and artists. Reed's most ambitious editing project resulted in *Calafia: The California Poetry* (1979), an effort to gather together the forgotten minority poetry of California's past.

Achievements • Reed earned a place in the first rank of contemporary African American authors, but such recognition did not come immediately. Most established reviewers ignored Reed's first novel, *The Free-Lance Pallbearers*, and many of the reviews that were written dismissed the novel as offensive, childish, or self-absorbed. Although *Yellow Back Radio Broke-Down* was even less traditional than its predecessor, it received much more critical attention and became the center of considerable critical debate. Some reviewers attacked the novel as overly clever, bitter, or obscure, but many praised its imaginative satire and technical innovation. Moreover, the controversy over *Yellow Back Radio Broke-Down* stirred new interest in *The Free-Lance Pallbearers*. Reed's increasing acceptance as a major African American author was demonstrated when his third novel, *Mumbo Jumbo*, was reviewed on the front page of *The New York Times Review of Books*. Both *Mumbo Jumbo* and *Conjure*, a poetry collection published in the same year, were nominated for the National Book Award.

Subsequent novels maintained Reed's position in American letters. In 1975, Reed's *The Last Days of Louisiana Red* received the Rosenthal Foundation Award, and some reviewers viewed *Flight to Canada* as Reed's best novel. However, his work proved consistently controversial. His novels have, for example, been called sexist, a critical accusation that is fueled by comparison of Reed's novels with the contemporary powerful fiction written by African American women such as Alice Walker and Toni Morrison. The charge of sexism is further encouraged by Reed's satirical attack on feminists in *Reckless Eyeballing*. Reed has also been called a reactionary by some critics because of his uncomplimentary portrayals of black revolutionaries. His fiction has been translated into three languages, and his poetry is included in *Poetry of the Negro, New Black Poetry, The Norton Anthology of Poetry*, and other anthologies. In 1998, Reed was awarded the MacArthur "genius" fellowship. This is fitting recognition for a writer who consciously attempted to redefine American and African American literature.

Biography • The jacket notes to *Chattanooga* glibly recount Ishmael Scott Reed's life: "born in Chattanooga, Tennessee, grew up in Buffalo, New York, learned to write in New York City and wised up in Berkeley, California." Each residence played a crucial role in Reed's development.

Reed was born the son of Henry Lenoir and Thelma Coleman, but before he was two years old, his mother remarried, this time to autoworker Bennie Reed. When he was four years old, his mother moved the family to Buffalo, where she found factory work. Reed graduated from Buffalo's East High School in 1956 and began to attend Millard Fillmore College, the night division of the University of Buffalo, supporting himself by working in the Buffalo public library. A satirical short story, "Something Pure," which portrayed Christ's return as an advertising man, brought Reed the praise of an English professor and encouraged him to enroll in day classes. Reed attended the University of Buffalo until 1960, when he withdrew because of money problems and the social pressures that his financial situation created. He married Priscilla Rose Thompson and moved into the notorious Talbert Mall Projects. The two years he spent there provided him with a painful but valuable experience of urban poverty and dependency. His daughter, Timothy Bret Reed, was born there. During his last years in Buffalo, Reed wrote for the *Empire Star Weekly*, moderated a controversial radio program for station WVFO, and acted in several local stage productions.

From 1962 to 1967, Reed lived in New York City. As well as being involved with the Civil Rights movement and the Black Power movement, Reed served as editor of *Advance*, a weekly published in Newark, New Jersey. His work on *Advance* was admired by Walter Bowart, and together they founded the *East Village Other*, one of the first and most successful "underground" newspapers. An early indication of Reed's commitment to encouraging the work of minority artists was his organization in 1965 of the American Festival of Negro Art.

In 1967, Reed moved to Berkeley, and began teaching at the University of California at Berkeley. In 1970, Reed and his first wife divorced (after years of separation), and he married Carla Blank. In 1971, with Al Young, Reed founded the Yardbird Publishing Company, which from 1971 to 1976 produced the *Yardbird Reader*, an innovative journal of ethnic writing and graphics. The Reed, Cannon, and Johnson Communications Company, which later became Ishmael Reed Books, was founded in 1973 and has published the work of William Demby, Bill Gunn, Mei Mei Bressenburge, and other ethnic writers. In 1976, Reed and Victor Cruz began the Before Columbus Foundation. In 1977, Reed's daughter Tennessee was born, and he was denied tenure in the English department at the University of California at Berkeley. He continued to serve as a lecturer at Berkeley, however, and also taught at Yale, Harvard, Columbia, Dartmouth, and a number of other colleges and universities. In 1995, he was awarded an honorary doctorate in letters from the State University of New York at Buffalo.

James Lerager

Reed made important contributions as a poet, novelist, essayist, playwright, and as an editor and publisher. He stated that he considers himself a global writer, and his success at writing poetry in West Africa's Yoruba language and his study of Japanese language and culture for his novel *Japanese by Spring* support this assertion. He also extended his literary range to include plays, such as *The Preacher and the Rapper* (published in 1997), and jazz albums, such as *Conjure I* (1983) and *Conjure II* (1989), and he even completed a libretto and served as the executive producer for a cable television soap opera called *Personal Problems* (1981).

During the early 1990's, Reed was, perhaps, best known for his controversial essays on such issues as the Rodney King and O. J. Simpson trials and the U.S. Justice Clarence Thomas hearings, some of which were collected in *Airing Dirty Laundry* (1993). However, his most important contribution to American letters may well be his work as an editor and publisher for other ethnic writers. In all of his publishing ventures, Reed tries to expose readers to the work of Asian Americans, African Americans, Chicanos, and Native Americans in an effort to help build a truly representative and pluralistic national literature.

Analysis • Ishmael Reed is consciously a part of the African American literary tradition that extends back to the first-person slave narratives, and the central purpose of his novels is to define a means of expressing the complexity of the African American experience in a manner distinct from the dominant literary tradition. Until the middle of the twentieth century, African American fiction, although enriched by the lyricism of Jean Toomer and Zora Neale Hurston, concentrated on realistic portrayals of black life and employed familiar narrative structures. This tendency toward social realism peaked with Richard Wright's *Native Son* (1940) and *Black Boy* (1945), but it was continued into the late twentieth century by authors such as James Baldwin. Reed belongs to a divergent tradition, inspired by Ralph Ellison's *Invisible Man* (1952), a countertradition that includes the work of Leon Forrest, Ernest J. Gaines, James Alan McPherson, Toni Morrison, and Alice Walker.

Believing that the means of expression is as important as the matter, Reed argues that the special qualities of the African American experience cannot be adequately communicated through traditional literary forms. Like Amiri Baraka, Reed believes that African American authors must "be estranged from the dominant culture," but Reed also wants to avoid being stifled by a similarly restrictive countertradition. In *Shrovetide in Old New Orleans*, Reed says that his art and criticism try to combat "the consciousness barrier erected by an alliance of eastern-backed black pseudonationalists and white mundanists." Thus, Reed works against the stylistic limitations of the African American literary tradition as much as he works with them. Henry Louis Gates, Jr., compared Reed's fictional modifications of African American literary traditions to the African American folk custom of "signifying," maintaining that Reed's novels present an ongoing process of "rhetorical self-definition."

Although Reed's novels are primarily efforts to define an appropriate African American aesthetic, his fiction vividly portrays the particular social condition of black Americans. In his foreword to Elizabeth and Thomas Settle's *Ishmael Reed: A Primary and Secondary Bibliography* (1982), Reed expresses his bitterness over persistent racism and argues that the personal experience of racism that informs his art makes his work inaccessible and threatening to many readers:

> I am a member of a class which has been cast to the bottom of the American caste system, and from those depths I write a vision which is still strange, often frightening, 'peculiar' and 'odd' to some, 'ill-considered' and unwelcome to many.

Indeed, Ishmael seems to be an ironically appropriate name for this author of violent and darkly humorous attacks on American institutions and attitudes, for the sharpness and breadth of his satire sometimes make him appear to be a man whose hand is turned against all others. His novels portray corrupt power brokers and their black and white sycophants operating in a dehumanized and materialistic society characterized by its prefabricated and ethnocentric culture. However, Reed's novels are not hopeless explications of injustice, for against the forces of repression and conformity he sets gifted individuals who escape the limitations of their sterile culture by courageously penetrating the illusions that bind them. Moreover, in contrast to many white authors who are engaged in parallel metafictive experiments, Reed voices a confident belief that "print and words are not dead at all."

Reed's narrative technique combines the improvisational qualities of jazz with a documentary impulse to accumulate references and allusions. In his composite narratives, historical and fictional characters coexist in a fluid, anachronistic time. In an effort to translate the vitality and spontaneity of the oral, folk tradition into a literature that can form the basis for an alternative culture, Reed mixes colloquialisms and erudition in novels that are syncretized from a series of subtexts. The literary equivalent of scat singing, his stories-within-stories parody literary formulas and challenge the traditional limits of fiction.

Reed claims that his novels constitute "an art form with its own laws," but he does not mean to imply that his work is private, for these "laws" are founded on a careful but imaginative reinterpretation of the historical and mythological past. The lengthy bibliography appended to *Mumbo Jumbo* satirizes the documentary impulse of social realist authors, but it also underscores Reed's belief that his mature work demands scholarly research in order to be decoded. This artistic process of reinterpretation often requires the services of an interlocutor, a character who explains the events of the narrative in terms of the mythological past. Reed's novels describe a vision of an Osirian/Dionysian consciousness, a sensuous humanism that he presents as an appropriate cultural alternative for nonwhite Americans. His imaginative reconstructions of the American West, the Harlem Renaissance, the American Civil War, and contemporary U.S. politics, interwoven with ancient myths, non-European folk customs, and the formulas of popular culture, are liberating heresies meant to free readers from the intellectual domination of the Judeo-Christian tradition.

The Free-Lance Pallbearers • Reed's first novel, *The Free-Lance Pallbearers*, takes place in a futuristic America called HARRY SAM: "A big not-to-be-believed out-of-sight, sometimes referred to as O-BOP-SHE-BANG or KLANG-A-LANG-A-DING-DONG." This crumbling and corrupt world is tyrannized by Sam himself, a vulgar fat man who lives in Sam's Motel on Sam's Island in the middle of the lethally polluted Black Bay that borders HARRY SAM. Sam, doomed by some terrifying gastrointestinal disorder, spends all of his time on the toilet, his filth pouring into the bay from several large statues of Rutherford B. Hayes.

The bulk of the novel, although framed and periodically informed by a jiving narrative voice, is narrated by Bukka Doopeyduk in a restrained, proper English that identifies his passive faith in the establishment. Doopeyduk is a dedicated adherent to the Nazarene Code, an orderly in a psychiatric hospital, a student at Harry Sam College, and a hapless victim. His comically futile efforts to play by the rules are defeated by the cynics, who manipulate the unjust system to their own advantage. In the end, Doopeyduk is disillusioned: He leads a successful attack on Sam's Island, uncovers the conspiracy that protects Sam's cannibalism, briefly dreams of becoming the black Sam, and is finally crucified.

The Free-Lance Pallbearers is a parody of the African American tradition of first-person, confessional narratives, a book the narrator describes as "growing up in soulsville first of three installments—or what it means to be a backstage darky." Reed's novel challenges the viability of this African American version of the *Bildungsroman*, in which a young protagonist undergoes a painful initiation into the darkness of the white world, a formula exemplified by Wright's *Black Boy* and James Baldwin's *Go Tell It on the Mountain* (1953). In fact, the novel suggests that African American authors' use of this European form is as disabling as Doopeyduk's adherence to the dictates of the Nazarene Code.

The novel is an unrestrained attack on U.S. politics. HARRY SAM, alternately referred to as "Nowhere" or "Now Here," is a dualistic vision of a United States that celebrates vacuous contemporaneity. The novel, an inversion of the Horatio Alger myth in the manner of Nathanael West, mercilessly displays American racism, but its focus is the corruptive potential of power. Sam is a grotesque version of Lyndon B. Johnson, famous for his bathroom interviews, and Sam's cannibalistic taste for children is an attack on Johnson's Vietnam policy. With *The Free-Lance Pallbearers*, Reed assaults of his society, but it is not until his later novels that he attempts to construct an alternative.

Yellow Back Radio Broke-Down • *Yellow Back Radio Broke-Down* is set in a fantastic version of the Wild West of popular literature. Reed's protagonist, the Loop Garoo Kid, is a proponent of artistic freedom and an accomplished Voodoo *houngan* who is in marked contrast to the continually victimized Doopeyduk. Armed with supernatural "connaissance" and aided by a white python and the hip, helicopter-flying Chief Showcase, the Kid battles the forces of realistic mimesis and political corruption. His villainous opponent is Drag Gibson, a degenerate cattle baron given to murdering his wives, who is called upon by the citizens of Yellow Back Radio to crush their rebellious children's effort "to create [their] own fictions."

Although *Yellow Back Radio Broke-Down* satirizes Americans' eagerness to suspend civil rights in response to student protests against the Vietnam War, its focus is literature, specifically the dialogue between realism and modernism. The Loop Garoo Kid matches Reed's description of the African American artist in *Nineteen Necromancers from Now*: "a conjurer who works JuJu upon his oppressors; a witch doctor who frees his fellow victims from the psychic attack launched by demons." Through the Loop Garoo Kid, Reed takes a stand for imagination, intelligence, and fantasy against rhetoric, violence, and sentimentality. This theme is made explicit in a debate with Bo Shmo, a "neo-social realist" who maintains that "all art must be for the end of liberating the masses," for the Kid says that a novel "can be anything it wants to be, a vaudeville show, the six o'clock news, the mumblings of wild men saddled by demons."

Reed exhibits his antirealist theory of fiction in *Yellow Back Radio Broke-Down* through his free use of time, characters, and language. The novel ranges from the eighteenth century to 1969, combining historical events and cowboy myths with modern technology and cultural detritus. Reed's primary characters are comically exaggerated racial types: Drag Gibson represents the whites' depraved materialism, Chief Showcase represents the American Indian's spirituality, and the Loop Garoo Kid represents the African American's artistic soul. Reed explains the novel's title by suggesting that his book is the "dismantling of a genre done in an oral way like radio." "Yellow back" refers to the popular dime novels; "radio" refers to the novel's oral, discontinuous form; and a "broke-down" is a dismantling. Thus, Reed's first two novels assault America in an attempt to "dismantle" its cultural structure.

Mumbo Jumbo • In *Mumbo Jumbo*, Reed expands on the neo-hoodooism of the Loop Garoo Kid in order to create and define an African American aesthetic based on Voodoo, Egyptian mythology, and improvisational musical forms, an aesthetic to challenge the Judeo-Christian tradition, rationalism, and technology. Set in Harlem during the 1920's, *Mumbo Jumbo* is a tragicomical analysis of the Harlem Renaissance's failure to sustain its artistic promise. Reed's protagonist is PaPa LaBas, an aging hoodoo detective and cultural diagnostician, and LaBas's name, meaning "over there" in French, reveals that his purpose is to reconnect African Americans with their cultural heritage by reunifying the Text of Jes Grew, literally the Egyptian Book of Thoth. Reed takes the phrase Jes Grew from Harriet Beecher Stowe's Topsy and James Weldon Johnson's description of African American music's unascribed development, but in the novel, Jes Grew is a contagion, connected with the improvisational spirit of ragtime and jazz, that begins to spread across America during the 1920's. Jes Grew is an irrational force that threatens to overwhelm the dominant, repressive traditions of established culture. LaBas's efforts to unify and direct this unpredictable force are opposed by the Wallflower Order of the Knights Templar, an organization dedicated to neutralizing the power of Jes Grew in order to protect its privileged status. LaBas fails to reunify the text, a parallel to the dissipation of the Harlem Renaissance's artistic potential, but the failure is seen as temporary; the novel's indeterminate conclusion looks forward hopefully to a time when these artistic energies can be reignited.

The novel's title is double-edged. "Mumbo jumbo" is a racist, colonialist phrase used to describe the misunderstood customs and language of dark-skinned people, an approximation of some critics' description of Reed's unorthodox fictional method. However, "mumbo jumbo" also refers to the power of imagination, the cultural alternative that can free African Americans. A text of and about texts, *Mumbo Jumbo* combines the formulas of detective fiction with the documentary paraphernalia of scholarship: footnotes, illustrations, and a bibliography. Thus, in the disclosure scene required of any good detective story, LaBas, acting the part of interlocutor, provides a lengthy and erudite explication of the development of Jes Grew that begins with a reinterpretation of the myth of Osiris. The parodic scholarship of *Mumbo Jumbo* undercuts the assumed primacy of the European tradition and implicitly argues that African American artists should attempt to discover their distinct cultural heritage.

The Last Days of Louisiana Red • In *The Last Days of Louisiana Red*, LaBas returns as Reed's protagonist, but the novel abandons the parodic scholarship and high stylization of *Mumbo Jumbo*. Although LaBas again functions as a connection with a non-European tradition of history and myth, *The Last Days of Louisiana Red* is more traditionally structured than its predecessor. In the novel, LaBas solves the murder of Ed Yellings, the founder of the Solid Gumbo Works. Yellings's business is dedicated to combating the effects of Louisiana Red, literally a popular hot sauce but figuratively an evil state of mind that divides African Americans. Yelling's gumbo, like Reed's fiction, is a mixture of disparate elements, and it has a powerful curative effect. In fact, LaBas discovers that Yellings is murdered when he gets close to developing a gumbo that will cure heroin addiction.

In *The Last Days of Louisiana Red*, Reed is examining the self-destructive forces that divide the African American community so that its members fight one another "while above their heads . . . billionaires flew in custom-made jet planes." Reed shows how individuals' avarice leads them to conspire with the establishment, and he suggests that some of the most vocal and militant leaders are motivated by their egotistical need for power rather than by true concern for oppressed people. Set in Berkeley, California, *The Last Days of Louisiana Red* attacks the credibility of the black revolutionary movements that sprang up during the late 1960's and early 1970's.

Flight to Canada • *Flight to Canada*, Reed's fifth novel, is set in an imaginatively redrawn Civil War South, and it describes the relationship between Arthur Swille, a tremendously wealthy Virginia planter who practices necrophilia, and an assortment of sociologically stereotyped slaves. The novel is presented as the slave narrative of Uncle Robin, the most loyal of Swille's possessions. Uncle Robin repeatedly tells Swille that the plantation is his idea of heaven, and he assures his master that he does not believe that Canada exists. Raven Quickskill, "the first one of Swille's slaves to read, the first to write, and the first to run away," is the author of Uncle Robin's story.

Like much of Reed's work, *Flight to Canada* is about the liberating power of art, but in *Flight to Canada*, Reed concentrates on the question of authorial control. All the characters struggle to maintain control of their stories. After escaping from the plantation, Quickskill writes a poem, "Flight to Canada," and his comical verse denunciation of Swille completes his liberation. In complaining of Quickskill's betrayal to Abraham Lincoln, Swille laments that his former bookkeeper uses literacy "like that old Voodoo." In a final assertion of authorial control and the power of the pen, Uncle Robin refuses to sell his story to Harriet Beecher Stowe, gives the rights to Quickskill, rewrites Swille's will, and inherits the plantation.

The Terrible Twos • In *The Terrible Twos*, Reed uses a contemporary setting to attack Ronald Reagan's administration and the exploitative nature of the American economic system. In the novel, President Dean Clift, a former model, is a mindless figurehead manipulated by an oil cartel that has supplanted the real Santa Claus. Nance Saturday, another of Reed's African American detectives, sets out to discover Saint

Nicholas's place of exile. The novel's title suggests that, in its second century, the United States is acting as selfishly and irrationally as the proverbial two-year-old. The central theme is the manner in which a few avaricious people seek vast wealth at the expense of the majority of Americans.

Reckless Eyeballing • *Reckless Eyeballing* takes place during the 1980's, and Reed employs a string of comically distorted characters to present the idea that the American literary environment is dominated by New York women and Jews. Although *Reckless Eyeballing* has been called sexist and anti-Semitic by some, Reed's target is a cultural establishment that creates and strengthens racial stereotypes, in particular the view of African American men as savage rapists. To make his point, however, he lampoons feminists, using the character Tremonisha Smarts, a female African American author who has written a novel of violence against women. Reed's satire is probably intended to remind readers of Alice Walker's *The Color Purple* (1982).

Because the novel's central subject is art and the limitations that society places on an artist, it is appropriate that Reed once again employs the technique of a story-within-a-story. Ian Ball, an unsuccessful African American playwright, is the novel's protagonist. In the novel, Ball tries to succeed by shamelessly placating the feminists in power. He writes "Reckless Eyeballing," a play in which a lynched man is posthumously tried for "raping" a woman with lecherous stares, but Ball, who often seems to speak for Reed, maintains his private, chauvinistic views throughout.

The Terrible Threes • *The Terrible Threes*, a sequel to *The Terrible Twos*, continues Reed's satirical attack on the contemporary capitalist system, which, he argues, puts the greatest economic burden on the least privileged. (Reed was also planning a third book in the series, *The Terrible Fours*.) In the first book, there appears a character named Black Peter—an assistant to St. Nicholas in European legend. This Black Peter is an imposter, however, a Rastafarian who studied and appropriated the legend for himself. In *The Terrible Threes*, the true Black Peter emerges to battle the false Peter but is distracted from his mission by the need to do good deeds. Black Peter becomes wildly popular because of these deeds, but a jealous St. Nick and concerned toy companies find a way to put Santa Claus back on top. Capitalism wins again.

Japanese by Spring • *Japanese by Spring* is postmodern satire. Like much of Reed's imaginative work, the book mixes fictional characters with "fictionalized" ones. Ishmael Reed himself is a character in the book, with his own name. The protagonist of *Japanese by Spring* is Benjamin "Chappie" Puttbutt, a teacher of English and literature at Oakland's Jack London College. Chappie dabbled in activist politics in the mid-1960's, but his only concern during the 1990's is receiving tenure and the perks that accompany it. He will put up with virtually anything, including racist insults from students, to avoid hurting his chances at tenure. As in many of Reed's books, Chappie is passive in the face of power at the beginning of his story. He is a middle-class black conservative, but only because the climate at Jack London demands it. Chappie is a chameleon who always matches his behavior to the ideology of his environment. However, when he is denied tenure and is about to be replaced by a feminist poet who is more flash than substance, Chappie's hidden anger begins to surface. Chappie has also been studying Japanese with a tutor named Dr. Yamato. This proves fortuitous when the Japanese buy Jack London and Dr. Yamato becomes the college president. Chappie suddenly finds himself in a position of power and gloats over those who denied him tenure. He soon finds, however, that his new bosses are the same as the old ones. Dr. Yamato is a tyrant and is eventually arrested by a group that includes Chappie's father, a two-star Air Force general. Dr. Yamato is released, though, and a surprised Chappie learns that there is an "invisible government" that truly controls the United States. Chappie has pierced some of his illusions, but there are others that he never penetrates, such as his blindness to his own opportunism.

The novel's conclusion moves away from Chappie's point of view to that of a fictionalized Ishmael Reed. This Reed skewers political correctness but also shows that the people who complain the most about it are often its greatest purveyors. Reed also lampoons American xenophobia, particularly toward Japan, but he does so in a balanced manner that does not gloss over Japanese faults. Ultimately, though, Reed uses *Japanese by Spring* as he used other novels before, to explore art and politics and the contradictions of America and race.

Carl Brucker
Updated by Charles A. Gramlich

Other major works

POETRY: *Catechism of D Neoamerican Hoodoo Church*, 1970; *Conjure: Selected Poems, 1963-1970*, 1972; *Chattanooga*, 1973; *A Secretary to the Spirits*, 1977; *Cab Calloway Stands in for the Moon*, 1986; *New and Collected Poems*, 1988; *New and Collected Poems, 1964-2006*, 2006.

NONFICTION: *Shrovetide in Old New Orleans*, 1978; *God Made Alaska for the Indians*, 1982; *Writin' Is Fightin': Thirty-seven Years of Boxing on Paper*, 1988; *Airing Dirty Laundry*, 1993; *Conversations with Ishmael Reed*, 1995; *Another Day at the Front: Dispatches from the Race War*, 2002 (essays); *Blues City: A Walk in Oakland*, 2003.

EDITED TEXTS: *Nineteen Necromancers from Now*, 1970; *Yardbird Lives!*, 1978 (with Al Young); *Calafia: An Anthology of California Poets*, 1979 (with Young and Shawn Hsu Wong); *The Before Columbus Foundation Fiction Anthology: Selections from the American Book Awards, 1980-1990*, 1992 (with Kathryn Trueblood and Shawn Wong); *MultiAmerica: Essays on Cultural Wars and Cultural Peace*, 1997; *From Totems to Hip-Hop*, 2003.

MISCELLANEOUS: *The Reed Reader*, 2000.

Bibliography

Boyer, Jay. *Ishmael Reed*. Boise, Idaho: Boise State University Press, 1993. A brief (fifty-two-page) installment in the publisher's Western Writers series.

Dick, Bruce Allen, ed. *The Critical Response to Ishmael Reed*. Westport, Conn.: Greenwood Press, 1999. Collection of reviews and critical essays on Reed's writings.

Dick, Bruce Allen, and Pavel Zemliansky, eds. *The Critical Response to Ishmael Reed*. Westport, Conn.: Greenwood Press, 1999. Discusses Reed's novels in chronological order; contains book reviews, essays, an interview in which Reed discusses works in progress, a chronology of his life, and bibliographical information.

Fox, Robert Elliot. *Conscientious Sorcerers: The Black Post-Modern Fiction of LeRoi Jones/ Amiri Baraka, Ishmael Reed, and Samuel R. Delaney*. New York: Greenwood Press, 1987. Situates Reed within both the tradition of black fiction and the self-conscious style of contemporary postmodernist fiction.

Gates, Henry Louis, Jr. *The Signifying Monkey: A Theory of Afro-American Literary Criti-*

cism. New York: Oxford University Press, 1988. The section on Reed examines his fiction, especially the novel *Mumbo Jumbo*, as an extension of the tendency of black English to play deliberately with language.

Harde, Roxanne. "'We Will Make Our Own Future Text': Allegory, Iconoclasm, and Reverence in Ishmael Reed's *Mumbo Jumbo*." *Critique: Studies in Contemporary Fiction* 43 (Summer, 2002): 361-377. Interesting critique of Reed's satirical third novel.

McGee, Patrick. *Ishmael Reed and the Ends of Race.* New York: St. Martin's Press, 1997. Looks at Reed's refusal to meet expectations associated traditionally with African American writers, and examines his use of satire and his antagonism toward political correctness.

Mvuyekure, Pierre-Damien. "American Neo-HooDooism: The Novels of Ishmael Reed." In *The Cambridge Companion to the African American Novel*, edited by Maryemma Graham. New York: Cambridge University Press, 2004. Concise overview of Reed's long fiction.

_____, ed. *A Casebook Study of Ishmael Reed's "Yellow Back Radio Broke-Down."* Normal, Ill.: Dalkey Archive, 2003. Collection of critical essays on Reed's novel *Yellow Back Radio Broke-Down.*

Nicholls, David G. "Ishmael Reed." In *Postmodernism: The Key Figures*, edited by Hans Bertens and Joseph Natoli. Malden, Mass.: Blackwell, 2002. Attempt to view Reed as a postmodernist.

Reed, Ishmael. *Conversations with Ishmael Reed.* Edited by Bruce Dick and Amritjit Singh. Jackson: University Press of Mississippi, 1995. A collection of twenty-six interviews with Ishmael Reed, which cover the years 1968-1995. Includes one self-interview and a chronology of Reed's life.

Weisenburger, Steven. *Fables of Subversion: Satire and the American Novel, 1930-1980.* Athens: University of Georgia Press, 1995. Discusses Reed's use of encyclopedic Menippean satire in *Mumbo Jumbo.*

Anne Rice

Born: New Orleans, Louisiana; October 4, 1941

Principal long fiction • *Interview with the Vampire*, 1976; *The Feast of All Saints*, 1979; *Cry to Heaven*, 1982; *The Claiming of Sleeping Beauty*, 1983 (erotic novel; as A. N. Roquelaure); *Beauty's Punishment*, 1984 (erotic novel; as A. N. Roquelaure); *Beauty's Release: The Continued Erotic Adventures of Sleeping Beauty*, 1985 (erotic novel; as A. N. Roquelaure; collective title for this volume and the previous two, *Sleeping Beauty Trilogy*); *Exit to Eden*, 1985 (as Anne Rampling); *The Vampire Lestat*, 1985; *Belinda*, 1986 (as Anne Rampling); *The Queen of the Damned*, 1988; *The Mummy: Or, Ramses the Damned*, 1989; *The Witching Hour*, 1990; *The Tale of the Body Thief*, 1992; *Lasher: A Novel*, 1993; *Taltos: Lives of the Mayfair Witches*, 1994; *Memnoch the Devil*, 1995; *Servant of the Bones*, 1996; *Violin*, 1997; *Pandora: New Tales of the Vampires*, 1998; *The Vampire Armand*, 1998; *Vittorio the Vampire: New Tales of the Vampires*, 1999; *Merrick*, 2000; *Blood and Gold: Or, The Story of Marius*, 2001; *Blackwood Farm*, 2002; *Blood Canticle*, 2003 (together with *Interview with the Vampire, The Vampire Lestat, The Queen of the Damned, The Tale of the Body Thief, Memnoch the Devil, The Vampire Armand, Merrick, Blood and Gold: Or, The Story of Marius*, and *Blackwood Farm* also known collectively as The Vampire Chronicles); *Christ the Lord: Out of Egypt*, 2005.

Other literary forms • Anne Rice is known primarily for her novels. In addition to her historical fiction and her well-known vampire and witch novel series, Rice published erotic novels. *The Claiming of Sleeping Beauty, Beauty's Punishment*, and *Beauty's Release: The Continued Erotic Adventures of Sleeping Beauty* appeared under the pseudonym A. N. Roquelaure, while Rice used the pen name Anne Rampling for *Exit to Eden* and *Belinda*. Rice also penned the screenplay for the film *Interview with the Vampire* (1994), based on her novel.

Achievements • Anne Rice has experimented with several different literary genres and acquitted herself well in each: gothic horror, historical fiction, erotica, romance. The conventions of gothic fiction, however, best conform to Rice's obsessions with eroticism, androgyny, myth, and the nature of evil. Clearly, for critics and fans alike, the novels that constitute The Vampire Chronicles are her greatest achievement. Gothic horror, like all popular fiction, is customarily slighted by commentators, who peg it as nothing more than a barometer of its own time, devoid of resonance. Paradoxically perhaps, Rice's success grows out of her ability to revamp the vampire, to update the hoary edifice first built by Horace Walpole in 1765 in *The Castle of Otranto*. However, she does more than merely put her archetypal hero, the vampire Lestat, in black leather on a motorcycle; she makes him, in all his selfishness and soul searching, emblematic of the waning days of the twentieth century. If horror can be defined as the sense that the world is on the verge of primeval chaos, Rice might be considered the novelist for the millennium.

Biography • Anne Rice—then named Howard Allen Frances O'Brien—was born on October 4, 1941, in New Orleans, Louisiana, to Howard O'Brien and Katherine Allen

O'Brien. Howard O'Brien's reasons for bestowing his own name on his daughter remain obscure, but bearing a masculine name clearly had a profound effect on her. When she entered first grade, the little girl christened herself Anne. The name stuck, as did a lifelong obsession with androgyny.

The exotic, decadent, intoxicating atmosphere of her hometown must also be counted among Anne Rice's early influences—as must her mother's alcoholism. As she approached puberty, Anne devoted much of her time to reading in a darkened bedroom to the increasingly incapacitated Katherine. It was there, perhaps, that Anne acquired an affinity for vampires. She would later recall how her mother first explained alcoholism as a "craving in the blood" and then asked her to say the rosary. Anne watched her mother alternate between wild exhilaration and collapse and finally waste away, her body drained by addiction and an inability to eat.

Christine Bocchiaro

When Katherine died in 1956, the nexus between blood, religion, and death must have taken root in her young daughter's psyche.

Anne's father remarried when she was sixteen, and, after Anne's sophomore year in high school, he moved the family to Richardson, Texas, where Anne met Stan Rice. Stan was a year younger than Anne, and at first he did not seem to share her romantic feelings about their relationship. It was not until after Anne graduated and moved away to San Francisco that Stan finally realized his feelings. They were married on October 14, 1961, when Anne was twenty.

The couple took up residence in the San Francisco Bay Area, where they would remain for the next twenty-seven years. Stan, a poet, completed his undergraduate education and began teaching creative writing. Anne, too, completed her bachelor's degree, majoring in political science. After receiving a master's degree in creative writing in 1972, she devoted herself full-time to her writing career.

In the meanwhile, however, a momentous event had occurred in the Rices' lives. Their daughter, Michele, who was born in 1966, developed a rare form of leukemia and died two weeks before her sixth birthday. The trauma of this loss seems to have plunged Anne into depression. The old association between blood and death had returned to haunt her, but Rice fought off her demons by submersing herself in her writing. The result was her first published novel, *Interview with the Vampire*.

In 1978, the Rices had a son, Christopher, and a decade later they moved to New Orleans. With the proceeds of many best-selling books and the lucrative sale of film rights, Anne Rice purchased a mansion in the Garden District, which later became the setting of one of her novels and the scene of such memorable parties as the 1995 Memnoch Ball.

Analysis • Rice discovered her strong suit early. Written in five weeks, *Interview with the Vampire* introduced the themes of compulsion, exoticism, and eroticism that would inform all her later works. Although she explored these themes against a wide variety of backdrops, it is her revival of the gothic—and of the vampire, in particular—that both brought her critical attention and transformed her into a popular cultural icon.

The Vampire Chronicles • *Interview with the Vampire* is the first of the books Anne Rice produced in her Vampire Chronicles series. The Vampire Chronicles shift back and forth in time, from the prevampire life of Lestat in eighteenth century rural France to his escapades in twentieth century New Orleans and, then, in *Memnoch the Devil,* to the time of the creation of heaven and hell.

Interview with the Vampire introduces Lestat through the narrative of Louis, a vampire Lestat has "made." Louis relates his story to Daniel, a young reporter. Even as Louis grieves for his mortal life, Daniel craves Louis's power and immortality. Daniel has to overcome his initial horror and skepticism before accepting the truth of what Louis says, but by the end of Louis's long story, Daniel is begging to be made a vampire, too. In *The Vampire Lestat,* Lestat relates his own version of his life. Lestat's narrative, like Louis's, is published as a book. (Indeed, Lestat has written his in order to correct several of Louis's errors.) Lestat, always a show-off, revels in publicity, and he uses the book to launch his career as a rock star. Like so many of Lestat's grand schemes, however, this plan crashes, ending when Lestat barely escapes his fellow vampires' murderous attack as they seek revenge for his unpardonable publication of a book that reveals their secrets.

In *The Queen of the Damned,* Lestat becomes the consort of Akasha, the Egyptian ruler who became the mother of all vampires when a demon wounded and invaded her body, giving her immortal life. Marius, an old Roman sage and vampire, has kept Akasha intact for over two thousand years, but it is Lestat's energetic wooing that brings her out of her long stupor. She revives determined to rid the world of men, whose violence has made them unfit to survive. Only a remnant will endure for breeding purposes, she declares. Having partaken of her blood and fallen deliriously in love with her, Lestat nevertheless struggles against her insane project. He is finally saved from Akasha's wrath by Maharet and Mekare, witches who are also twin sisters and who destroy Akasha.

In *The Tale of the Body Thief,* Lestat, suffering from ennui, succumbs to the temptations of a body thief, Raglan James. The body thief offers Lestat a day of adventure in a mortal body in exchange for his own. Stupidly, Lestat accepts, even paying James twenty million dollars for the privilege of enjoying one day of mortality. James then absconds with both the money and Lestat's body, which Lestat is able to repossess only with the help of David Talbot, head of the Talamasca, a society dedicated to investigating the occult. Lestat, who is in love with David, then makes the resistant David into a vampire.

In *Memnoch the Devil,* a terrified Lestat discovers that he is being stalked by Satan, who calls himself Memnoch because he does not regard himself as a rebel angel or as God's accuser. Memnoch invites Lestat to become his lieutenant—not to gather souls for hell, but to redeem those awaiting enlightenment and salvation. Memnoch's argument is that he is offering God a grander creation, a purer vision of humankind, than God himself has conceived. In the end, Lestat repudiates Memnoch, doubting the devil's word and wondering if what he has "seen" is only what he has imagined.

The Vampire Chronicles rejuvenate the conventions of gothic romance and the horror novel. Like earlier heroes, Lestat is a nobleman of surpassing courage and physical attractiveness. Indeed, the vampire elder, Magnus, makes him into a vampire because he has seen the handsome Lestat on the stage in Paris and admired his indomitable spirit. As in William Godwin's novel, *Caleb Williams* (1794), Lestat is an insatiably curious protagonist attached to an older hero who represents both good and evil. Lestat must know the origins of vampirism, and he must follow his desires regardless of the cost to himself and others.

Lestat's eroticism also partakes of the gothic tradition. Reflecting Anne Rice's abiding interest in androgyny, he finds himself attracted to both men and women, to the goddess Akasha, and to the head of the Talamasca, David Talbot. Deeply devoted to his mother, Gabrielle, he takes her as his vampire lover. Incestuous and homoerotic elements that are veiled or only hinted at in earlier gothic fiction explode in Rice's chronicles. Rice also succeeds in making gothicism contemporary by making Lestat into a rock star, thus underscoring parallels between the cult of celebrity and the allure of the vampire.

The Mayfair Witches series • Rice conceived the first installment of the Mayfair Witches cycle, *The Witching Hour,* in 1985 after concluding *The Vampire Lestat.* She had generated some new characters that she at first envisioned as playing parts in the next Vampire Chronicle. She soon reached the conclusion, however, that these characters—a family of witches and their presiding spirit—deserved an entirely separate book, one set in New Orleans.

The protagonist of *The Witching Hour,* Michael Curry, is a successful forty-eight-year-old businessman who has his life blighted by a near-death experience. After nearly drowning in San Francisco Bay, he is rescued by a mysterious woman in a passing boat. He then discovers that simply by touching objects and people with his hands he has access to other lives and events. His insights, however, are fragmentary—as is his memory of an encounter with otherworldly beings during his drowning episode, when he promised to fulfill a mission for them.

One of Michael's doctors puts him in touch with his rescuer, who Michael believes will help him understand what he is meant to do. When he meets Dr. Rowan Mayfair, a thirty-year-old blonde beauty and a superb surgeon, Michael falls in love with her. Like Michael, Rowan is searching for answers. She has the power both to hurt and to heal people. She can stop a patient's bleeding simply by a laying on of hands; she can also cause a heart attack or stroke if she does not control her rage. Her obsession with saving people is her effort at self-redemption. Just as Michael hopes that touching Rowan and her boat will bring back his sense of mission, Rowan hopes that Michael will help reveal her past, which remains a mystery to her.

Rowan and Michael realize that their fates are linked to New Orleans, where as a boy Michael developed a fixation on a Garden District mansion that turns out to be Rowan's ancestral home. There he saw a spectral man, the Mayfairs' presiding spirit. Michael's intense memories of his childhood are connected, he is sure, with his near-death experience. When Rowan's birth mother dies, Rowan is visited by a spectral man, and she decides that she must return to the Crescent City.

Hovering around this couple is Aaron Lightner, an agent of the Talamasca. Through Aaron, Michael learns that Rowan is the descendant of a matriarchal family of witches that has fascinated the Talamasca for nearly three hundred years. A strong woman, Rowan believes she can destroy Lasher, the spectral man who has maddened the Mayfairs in an attempt to possess them. Like the others, however, Rowan loses control of Lasher, who invades the cells of the fetus growing within her and emerges as a powerful boy-man.

Rowan is rather like a female Dr. Faustus, determined to conquer the secrets of nature. She wants to heal, but the extremity of her desire cuts her off from her own humanity. Like Faust, she risks damnation. She is in thrall to her Mephistopheles, Lasher. When Michael playfully calls his lover Dr. Mayfair, the epithet suggests not only Dr. Faustus but also Dr. Frankenstein. Indeed, although Rowan finds Lasher's proposal that they create a super-race seductive, once their offspring is born, she plans to submit its cells to laboratory tests, thus reducing it to the status of a research subject.

In *Lasher*, the second installment in the series, Rowan has begun to help Lasher fulfill his desire. Together they have a girl child, Emaleth. The central revelation of the book is that the Mayfairs can, by interbreeding, produce a genetic aberration—a legendary race of nearly immortal giants known as Taltos, of which Lasher is a member. The Talamasca believe that Lasher is possessed of a unique genome, so when at the end of the book Michael Curry destroys him and Rowan does away with her demoniac girl child, it seems that Lasher's kind is no more.

However, *Taltos*, the third installment of the series, features another Taltos, Ashlar Templeton, an eccentric and reclusive billionaire toy maker. Ashlar's profession indicates that his nature is far more benign than Lasher's. Indeed, he more closely resembles Rice's vampires than his own protean kind. Unlike Lasher, he is not devoured by a need to propagate his supernatural breed; instead, he yearns—as much as Louis and, in his weaker moments, Lestat—for integration with humanity.

Lisa Paddock

Other major works

SCREENPLAY: *Interview with the Vampire*, 1994.

Bibliography

Badley, Linda. *Writing Horror and the Body: The Fiction of Stephen King, Clive Barker, and Anne Rice*. Westport, Conn.: Greenwood Press, 1996. Badley examines horror fiction as a fantastic genre that distorts the images of the body and the self. She looks at these three authors and their approach to horror as a dialogue on the anxieties of American culture.

Dickinson, Joy. *Haunted City: An Unauthorized Guide to the Magical, Magnificent New Orleans of Anne Rice*. New York: Citadel Press, 1995. Chapters on the city's Creole history, the French Quarter, the Garden District, the cemeteries and tombs, the churches, swamps, and plantations, and the nineteenth century milieu of Lestat.

Hoppenstand, Gary, and Ray B. Browne, eds. *The Gothic World of Anne Rice*. Bowling Green, Ohio: Bowling Green State University Press, 1996. Essays by the most important Rice critics on all aspects of her fiction: the Vampire Chronicles, the romances, and her stories of the supernatural.

Keller, James R. *Anne Rice and Sexual Politics: The Early Novels*. Jefferson, N.C.:

McFarland, 2000. Addresses early works in terms of gender identity and sexual issues. Includes bibliographical references and index.

Ramsland, Katherine M. *Prism of the Night: A Biography of Anne Rice*. New York: Dutton, 1991. Written with her cooperation, this is the most complete source of information about Rice and the first serious attempt to assess her critically and in a broader context.

_____. *The Roquelaure Reader: A Companion to Anne Rice's Erotica*. New York: Plume, 1996. Handbook for general readers of the erotic stories Rice has written under the pen name A. N. Roquelaure.

_____. *The Vampire Companion: The Official Guide to Anne Rice's The Vampire Chronicles*. New York: Ballantine, 1993. Handbook to Rice's vampire stories for general readers.

_____. *The Witches' Companion: The Official Guide to Anne Rice's Lives of the Mayfair Witches*. New York: Ballantine, 1996. Guide to Rice's Mayfair novels by an author who enjoys close access to Rice.

_____, ed. *The Anne Rice Reader*. New York: Ballantine, 1997. Part 1 concentrates on interviews with Rice, her personal essays, and articles about her life and career. Part 2 focuses on literary critiques, assessing Rice's contribution to the literature about vampires, her relationship to the gothic tradition, the film of *Interview with the Vampire*, and her other horror novels.

Rice, Anne. *Conversations with Anne Rice*. Interviews by Michael Riley. New York: Ballantine Books, 1996. Rice discusses her writing, career, women, and horror, gothic, vampire, and erotic literature.

Roberts, Bette B. *Anne Rice*. New York: Twayne, 1994. A solid introductory study with chapters on Rice's life and art, her relationship to the gothic tradition, her vampire series, her historical novels, and her erotic fiction.

Smith, Jennifer. *Anne Rice: A Critical Companion*. Westport, Conn.: Greenwood Press, 1996. Provides criticism and interpretation of Rice's work in the context of women and literature, fantasy fiction, horror tales, the gothic revival, witchcraft in literature, and vampires in literature. Includes bibliography and index.

Mordecai Richler

Born: Montreal, Quebec, Canada; January 27, 1931
Died: Montreal, Quebec, Canada; July 3, 2001

Principal long fiction • *The Acrobats*, 1954; *Son of a Smaller Hero*, 1955; *A Choice of Enemies*, 1957; *The Apprenticeship of Duddy Kravitz*, 1959; *The Incomparable Atuk*, 1963 (also known as *Stick Your Neck Out*); *Cocksure: A Novel*, 1968; *St. Urbain's Horseman*, 1971; *Joshua Then and Now*, 1980; *Solomon Gursky Was Here*, 1989; *Barney's Version*, 1997.

Other literary forms • As a professional writer, spurning academic life for wider creative possibilities, Mordecai Richler was known for producing short stories, essays, articles, film scripts, television plays, and children's literature. Much of his work first appeared in prestigious magazines such as *The Atlantic Monthly*, *The New Yorker*, the *New Statesman*, and *Encounter*. Some of his individual stories, which would often become chapters in his novels, have been collected in *The Street: Stories* (1969). A children's book, *Jacob Two-Two Meets the Hooded Fang* (1975), and two novels, *Joshua Then and Now* and *The Apprenticeship of Duddy Kravitz*, have been made into motion pictures, the latter winning the Golden Bear Award at the Berlin Film Festival in 1974. Richler's screenplay for this film was also nominated for an Academy Award, and it won a Screenwriter's Guild of America Award.

Achievements • After forsaking his native Canada for the more exciting atmosphere of Paris, France, Richler struggled with his work and lived in poor circumstances, publishing few stories. In Paris, however, he met some significant figures of the new literary set who reacted favorably to his work; among them were Allen Ginsberg, Herbert Gold, and Terry Southern. After returning to Canada for a short while, Richler finished his first novel, *The Acrobats*. As is so often the case with Canadian writers, Richler preferred to publish outside his own country, where he felt more appreciated. His first effort was accepted by André Deutsch in London. In later years, with his reputation secure, he decided to publish with the Canadian house McClelland and Stewart.

To make his living exclusively as a writer, Richler left Canada again. Still using his Canadian experience as the substance of his work, Richler was very productive in England, publishing stories and novels that met with much acclaim. Even his film scripts for *No Love for Johnnie* (1961), *Young and Willing* (1964), and *Life at the Top* (1965), which Richler considered inferior work for an often superficial medium, were positively reviewed. Richler twice won Canada's foremost literary prize, the Governor-General's Award, for *Cocksure* and *St. Urbain's Horseman*. Although he achieved a certain notoriety for his searing portraits of Canadian life, he eventually gained acceptance as one of Canada's most distinguished novelists.

Biography • Mordecai Richler was born in the heart of Montreal's Jewish ghetto in 1931. His father was a junk dealer and his mother a housewife, who later wrote a book about her life. Her father was a rabbi whose influence ensured an Orthodox household. By turning away from Orthodoxy at a young age, however, Richler ran into trouble at home, a fact that may account for some of his perceptive but acerbic reflections on family life. To further compound his problems as a youth, his parents were divorced when he was thirteen. As a response to the breakdown at home, Richler joined a Zionist labor group called Habonim and dreamed of settling in Palestine. Only much later, however, did he first go to Israel, and when he did, it was as a journalist.

During his adolescent years, Richler attended Baron Byng High School, a predominantly Jewish school even though it was part of the Protestant school system. In his stories and novels it is transformed into Fletcher's Field High, and Richler peoples it with characters known to him as a schoolboy. After high school, Richler attended Sir George Williams University in Montreal (now Concordia University), since his grades were not good enough for McGill University. Although he returned to Sir George as writer-in-residence, the academic life did not appeal to him. He once remarked that "academe, like girls, whiskey, and literature, promised better than it paid." Rejecting a life of scholarship, Richler decided on the uncertain life of a freelance writer in Europe, where he could develop his own style and not merely put a stamp of approval on someone else's.

During two years when Richler lived in Paris—where he published his first story in a magazine called *Points*—he got his first taste of expatriate life. He then returned to Montreal. There he joined the Canadian Broadcasting Company for a short time, earning enough money to complete his first novel, *The Acrobats*. The novel aroused more attention in England than in Canada, which perhaps convinced him that the richer literary heritage across the Atlantic would fuel his talents. For the best part of twenty years, Richler lived in England, producing many novels, short stories, and film scripts.

Although Richler needed this geographical and cultural change to gain an ironic and critical distance in his work, he used his Canadian experience as the basis of his fiction; he has said that the first twenty years of a writer's life determine the character of his writing and inform his imaginative vision. Even after many years in England, Richler never felt sufficiently integrated into English society to capture the essence of that particular culture. Feeling himself an outsider in England and cut off from the social context of Canada, Richler returned to his native country in 1972 to settle with his wife and five children in Montreal. He died there in 2001.

Analysis • In an article, "Why I Write," Mordecai Richler repeats the honest answer given by George Orwell to the same question: sheer egotism, aesthetic enthusiasm, political purposes, and historical impulse. These reasons, modified by Richler's unique perception, are clues to the form and content of his work.

Richler's egotistical desire to be talked about has, no doubt, been fulfilled, as he is the victim of attacks from both Jews and Protestants for what they consider to be unjust satirical portraits of their respective communities. He even said that to be a Jew and a Canadian is to emerge from the ghetto twice, as a sense of self-consciousness and envy pervades both societies. His satire, however, even when confined by the geography of Montreal, is more universal than some critics have assumed, and this element has enhanced his status as a significant writer. Although Richler never wanted to acquire the role of writer as personality (avoiding the talk-show circuit as much as possible and loathing being cast as the kind of figure Norman Mailer has become), his fierce attacks on provincialism, pretension, community arrogance, envy, and class economic superiority marked him as a highly visible, eccentric, and often vicious outsider.

Christopher Morris

Although there is a great deal of harshness in Richler's writing, it is not merely personal vindictiveness but a narrative strategy of accurate observation informed by imagination; it is a grotesque comic style designed to emphasize the absurdity of the human condition and to mock those whose misdirected values merely cause suffering. In *The Acrobats*, Richler dissects a generation of hollow men who infest the corrupt world of Spain's festival time, in which a loss of belief is symbolized by *fallas*, empty wood and papier-mâché dolls. It is a nightmare world of confusion and fantasy that culminates in the death of antihero André Bennett. Without capturing the flavor and intensity of Ernest Hemingway's lost generation, Richler, in a limited way, sets the themes for his later novels by attacking all attitudes that he thinks are essentially destructive.

Richler admitted to a certain sense of guilt prompted by the discrepancy between his life at home facing a blank page and the memory of his father going to work in his junkyard in subzero weather. Perhaps this recognition of the severity of ordinary life gave him the focus of his work, the precisely observed but critically and ironically rendered life of the common person fighting circumstances greater than himself.

Richler's intelligence, however, does not allow him to glorify uncritically his protagonists. The tension between what is and what ought to be is always present; the result is a controlled realism balanced by a satirical distance that allows fantasy, nightmare, and a morally grounded sense of the ridiculous. As George Woodcock observed, Richler was influenced by the realism of André Malraux, Albert Camus, and Louis-Ferdinand Céline, but Richler himself praised Evelyn Waugh as the greatest novelist of his time, and there is in Richler's work much of the energy, sensibility, and bawdiness of American writers such as Philip Roth.

When Richler spoke of a political purpose, he followed Orwell's idea that a novelist should push the world in a certain direction, that in fact any serious novelist is therefore a moralist. Although many of his stories end tragically, there is still a sense that his characters exist not as victims of a cruel, impersonal fate but as victims of their own and others' actions. The choices they make are important ones and often lead to disaster when they are not based on a consistent moral viewpoint. Norman Price in *A Choice of Enemies* recognizes that choices are significant but no longer has the courage to make the difficult ones that confront his modern generation. He ends up complacently accepting values from his friends. In *The Apprenticeship of Duddy Kravitz*, Richler succeeds in making Duddy a partially sympathetic character, often a victim of powerful people even more ruthless than he is, but Duddy, blinded by ambition, is the indirect cause of his friend Virgil's paralysis from a motor accident. In his enthusiasm for the direct, specific attack, however, Richler's moral position often seems diffuse or simply confusing. Two of his novels, *St. Urbain's Horseman* and *Joshua Then and Now*, manifest a more coherent intention which makes the satire even more meaningful.

Much of the force of Richler's work comes from his observation and memory of life in the Montreal ghetto of his youth. Even novels such as *Cocksure* and *The Acrobats* are distilled through the experience of the expatriate Canadian trying to make sense of a less provincial foreign world. Richler has said that he feels rooted in Montreal's St. Urbain Street, and because that was his time and place, he has elected to get it right. To this end, Richler often writes about the same characters from Fletcher's Field High School as they experience life at different stages of intellectual and emotional growth. A peripheral character such as Jake Hersh, for example, in *The Apprenticeship of Duddy Kravitz* and *The Street: Stories*, will become the focus of *St. Urbain's Horseman*.

The Apprenticeship of Duddy Kravitz • There is so much comic energy in *The Apprenticeship of Duddy Kravitz* that the reader can easily underestimate the social and moral implications of the work. Richler stated that to a certain extent the reader should sympathize with Duddy, who must rise above the poverty of the St. Urbain ghetto to challenge and defeat powerful manipulators such as Jerry Dingleman, the Boy Wonder. The ambiguity of Duddy's character creates a problem of moral focus, however, in that some of his victories are at the expense of truly kindhearted people, such as Virgil Roseboro and Yvette.

There are certainly many reasons for Duddy's aggressive, almost amoral behavior. His mother died when Duddy was very young, leaving him without the female stability he needed at the time. His father, Max the Hack, who drives a Montreal cab and pimps on the side, lets Duddy fend for himself, as most of his affection and attention went to the older son, Lenny. Duddy remembers that his father wrote many letters to Lenny when he worked at a resort, but Max refuses to write to Duddy. Max also encourages Lenny to go to medical school and is proud of his achievements; he makes it obvious that he expects little from Duddy and does not perceive the extent of Duddy's ambition nor his loyalty to his family. Duddy is also often humiliated by the affluent university students with whom he works as a waiter at the Hotel Lac des Sables. Irwin Shubert, for instance, considers Duddy a social inferior and, using a rigged roulette wheel, cheats him out of three hundred dollars.

Although eliciting sympathy by explaining Duddy's situation, Richler undercuts a completely sympathetic attitude toward Duddy by detailing the results of his actions. His exploitation of the other students of Fletcher's Field High School leads even his friend Jake Hersh to believe that he makes everything dirty. Duddy's schemes to make money are clever enough; he works out a system to steal hockey sticks from the Montreal Canadians, but he does not realize that the blame rests on the stick boy, who is trying to earn money through honest, hard work. More seriously, Duddy, through a cruel practical joke, is responsible for the death of Mrs. Macpherson, the wife of one of his teachers. Later, as he tries to make his dream of owning land come true, Duddy rejects his lover Yvette, causes the paralysis of his friend Virgil, from whom he also steals money, and alienates his grandfather, Simcha, who cares for him more than anyone else.

Duddy's relationship with Simcha provides both the moral tone and the narrative drive of the novel. Simcha, a man trusted but not loved by the elders of the St. Urbain ghetto for his quiet, patient integrity, is loved by his favorite, Duddy. Like many others of his generation, Simcha feels the weight of the immigrant's fear of failure and instills Duddy with the idea that a man without land is a nobody. For Simcha, this cliché is a more complex concept associated with the traditional struggles of the Jews and presupposes a sense of responsibility. Duddy misinterprets the implications of his grandfather's advice and perceives it as being a practical imperative to be gained at any cost, involving himself in many schemes—from importing illegal pinball machines to filming bar mitzvahs with a bizarre, alcoholic documentary director—in order to purchase land for commercial development.

For a short time, Duddy's plans misfire; he goes bankrupt and is unable to pay for the land he wants so badly. Upon hearing that the Boy Wonder, the ghetto "miracle" who has escaped his environment by drug peddling and other corrupt means, covets the same land, Duddy forges checks in Virgil's name to get enough money to make the purchase. In a closing scene, Duddy brings his family to see his property. By coincidence, the Boy Wonder arrives, and Duddy drives him away with verbal abuse. His father is more impressed with this act of defiance than with Duddy's achievement, and later, among his circle of friends, Max begins to create a legend about Duddy in much the same way as he created the legend of the Boy Wonder. Although his victory has been effected by deceit and victimization, Duddy's behavior seems vindicated; he smiles in triumph, unaware that he continues only under the spell of a shared illusion. The reader is left elated to a certain extent at the defeat of the Boy Wonder, yet sobered by the figure of Simcha, crying in the car, after having been informed by Yvette of Duddy's method of acquiring the land.

St. Urbain's Horseman • Unlike Duddy Kravitz, whose life is defined by the wealth he acquires, Jake Hersh of *St. Urbain's Horseman* is defined by the exploits of his cousin Joey, the "Horseman" of the title. In his quest for certainty and identity in a world of confusion and moral ambiguity, Jake chooses a dubious model of behavior that eventually becomes an obsession. Much of the comedy and much of the human drama in the book come from the discrepancy between Jake's illusions of the Horseman and the reality of his own life.

Richler experiments with a cinematic style of flashbacks and flash-forwards, not only to create a sense of suspense but also to show the role memory plays in developing a character. It is obvious that Jake is involved in some sort of sex scandal that threatens his married and professional life and the narrative is punctuated by the events in Jake's life that have led him to this degradation. In his youth, he wanted to escape the St. Urbain ghetto and the provincial nature of Canada itself. Typically, however, he leaves Canada to escape boredom only to find it everywhere.

Although Jake's loving relationship with his wife offers the promise of real stability, Jake seems to believe that only his cousin Joey leads a meaningful life, fighting injustice wherever he can find it. Specifically, he thinks Joey is the lone avenger riding after Joseph Mengele, the feared *Doktor* of the Nazi extermination camps. At first, Joey is simply the black sheep of the Hersh family, leaving home at a young age and returning periodically to disrupt the mundane lives of his relatives. Jake, who is eleven years younger than Joey, perceives him to be a hero and dismisses the accusations that he is just a criminal taking advantage of others for his own gain. Uncle Abe even tells Jake that the famed Horseman is more likely to blackmail Mengele than kill him.

By adulthood, Jake's fantasies and nightmares about his cousin assume mythic proportions, and he incorporates this mythology into his daily concerns, measuring himself against the Horseman he has created. Jake's consequent search for Joey in Israel and Germany uncovers the grim reality of Joey's fraud, drug smuggling, and disastrous love affairs, but Jake only rationalizes his negative impression; he places the Horseman's quest for "justice" beyond the sphere of ordinary moral culpability or human responsibility.

Jake reasons that he is a product of his generation, conceived in the Great Depression. He and others like him lived through the Spanish Civil War, World War II, the Holocaust, Hiroshima, the Israeli War of Independence, McCarthyism, the Korean War, and finally the Vietnam War. They were always the wrong age to be involved; they were merely observers, moral bystanders who could protest and give advice but who were fundamentally impotent. Jake wants answers to his plight but feels even more alienated from the important issues of his time because he is a case history of the Jewish intellectual born into the Canadian working class. He finds his generation and its concerns trivial and peripheral, easily susceptible, in his thinking, to the guilt induced by the "injustice collectors"—the prison-camp survivors and the starvelings of Africa.

These issues, these betrayals of age, are contrasted with the more personal betrayals of life: Jake's father rejects his marriage to a non-Jew; Luke Scott decides to choose a British director instead of Jake, his best friend, for his first major script; Jenny dismisses Jake as a lover because he is too young; and Harry Stein implicates Jake in the rape of a young au pair girl. Jake is no more capable of understanding these events than the historical events of more significant import.

After the trial, in which Jake is found guilty of indecent assault and fined, he receives word that the Horseman has been killed in a plane crash while smuggling cigarettes. He retreats to his attic and finds a gun hidden in the Horseman's saddle. It fires only blanks, its efficacy as illusory as the Horseman's exploits. Upon discovering this, Jake seems to have returned to reality, but later in his nightmare, he dreams that he is the Horseman extracting gold fillings from Mengele's teeth with pliers. He wakes up and changes the Horseman's journal to read "presumed dead." The irony is that Jake will probably continue to search for certitude and will live a tolerable life based on illusion; he does not realize that the love of his wife is the stable point that will exist despite the illusion.

Joshua Then and Now • There are many similarities between *St. Urbain's Horseman* and *Joshua Then and Now.* The time-schemes are not linear but shift backward and forward in a search for meaning that takes precedence over simple historical considerations; the characters are again graduates of Fletcher's Field High School who gain obvious material success but who are not immune to even the minor ravages of time; the major issues of the world are always present, but private and personal issues dominate; and Joshua Shapiro, like Jake Hersh, tries to make sense of his own life in terms of facing the past. The important difference between the two novels is that Richler's attitude toward life in *Joshua Then and Now* is much more humane, and love is seen as the moral imperative that makes all other attitudes seem trivial.

Joshua Then and Now begins close to the present with Joshua in a cottage retreat suffering from multiple fractures incurred in a car accident. Because of hints of a sex scandal, he is guarded from the press by his father, Reuben, and his father-in-law, Senator Stephen Hornby. Joshua reads many letters from his fans and colleagues who have scorned him for what they think is his atrocious behavior, but he is able to put this criticism into perspective. He believes this public display of disapproval is what he deserves for the roguish behavior of his youth. Reflecting on his life, he now is able to see clearly what was of real importance.

Joshua's background seems almost surreal; certainly it is more colorful than the lives of his friends in St. Urbain. Joshua's aspiration to be a sportswriter derived from his father, Reuben, who was a Canadian boxing champion. After his retirement from the ring, Reuben became an enforcer for a gangster named Colucci. As a youngster, Joshua had to suffer both his father's long absences and the resentment of the neighborhood over Reuben's involvement with Colucci. Joshua's mother, Esther, is an eccentric who bewilders him even more than his father. At Joshua's bar mitzvah, Esther has too much to drink and decides to let the young boys see her perform as an exotic dancer. She shocks them with the explicitness of her movements and even lets them fondle her. Later in life, she gets involved in pornographic films and in running a massage parlor. It seems that Joshua's independent and sometimes improbable behavior is the logical result of his upbringing.

In trying to prolong his adolescence, Joshua becomes as ridiculous as his parents, and although his exploits seem harmless, they do have consequences; Joshua's fake letters about the novelist Iris Murdoch's homosexual activities, written to make money at the expense of the University of Texas, end up being made public, to Joshua's disgrace. The pranks that he plays to gain revenge on his enemies—taking labels off Pinsky's valuable wine bottles, defacing Jonathan Coles's original painting, and planting illegal currency at Eli Seligson's house—conclude with Joshua's injuring himself in a high-speed car chase. For Joshua, at least, these episodes are a learning experience; they are stages on his way to maturity.

Joshua has many friends from his youth who still get together as the "Mackenzie King Memorial Society," the name being an ironic comment on a prime minister whom they consider a fraud. As successful as they are, however, in their middle age they are susceptible to lawsuits, tax-evasion inquiries, bypass operations, hair transplants, and cancer. The struggle for material wealth and its attainment now seem inadequate as values. More important is Joshua's involvement with the WASP, country-club circle. After marrying Pauline, Joshua is introduced to Jane and Jack Trimble and Pauline's brother Kevin. Joshua marries above his social class, but he takes a resentful and superior attitude to his wife's friends and relatives. He does as much as he can to sabotage a group that he believes has all the advantages. Through the years, however, he sees the disintegration of the Trimble marriage, the dashed hopes of the senator, and the death of Pauline's dependent brother, which precipitates her madness, and realizes that, even with their pretensions, they were only trying to survive.

The echoes of the past are most vividly sounded when Joshua returns to Ibiza, Spain, to confront Mueller, a German, who had disgraced him more than twenty-five years before. To gain revenge on Mueller, Joshua leaves his wife at a crucial time in her life, when she needs his comfort to fight off impending madness. In Spain, he notices remarkable changes: The friends he had are gone; many of his former haunts have been destroyed; the road to Almeria, the route of the retreating Republican army, is now dotted with hotels, condominiums, and commercial signs; and more significant, Mueller is dead, a victim of cancer. To cleanse himself of the past, however,

Joshua pays a price. His wife is institutionalized; then, after a prolonged stay at the hospital, she disappears. The novel ends with a loving reconciliation which suggests a change in Richler's perspective. Still on crutches as a result of his accident, Joshua recuperates at Hornby's cottage, accompanied by his children, the senator, and Reuben. In the final scene, Pauline returns, and Reuben sees Joshua in the vegetable garden without his cane, being supported by Pauline.

Solomon Gursky Was Here • In *Solomon Gursky Was Here*, Richler created his richest and most complex work, a 150-year chronicle of the ambitious and conniving Gursky family (loosely based on the real-life liquor kings of Montreal, the Bronfmans), weaving back and forth in time from the ill-fated Franklin Expedition to the Arctic to the political uncertainties of modern times. Beneath the surface of what is essentially a mystery story, a search for the elusive but seemingly ubiquitous Solomon Gursky, Richler examines the greed and corruption of society, the nature of the Jewish and Canadian people, mythological forces of the past, and the tenuous but compelling hold of love. Although uncompromising in his satirical portrait of the characters, Richler nevertheless alludes to the positive creative power of those who strive for understanding, however difficult the quest may be.

At the center of the novel stands writer Moses Berger, son of failed poet L. B. Berger, who has sold out to the Gurskys. Because of his father, Moses hears of Solomon Gursky at an early age and becomes obsessed with the almost mythical nature of this character. The alcoholic Moses, more a follower than the leader that his name suggests, investigates stories and documents and uncovers clues about why Solomon decided to resist the purely materialistic interests of his brothers Bernard, the ruthless businessman who has built his fortune by bootlegging, and Morrie, his unctious partner. Moses discovers that Solomon's enigmatic grandfather, Ephraim, was a criminal once imprisoned on Botany Bay, by incredible ingenuity the only survivor of the Franklin Expedition, a shaman of Eskimos who taught them Yiddish, and an energetic profligate perplexing in his moral ambiguity. Ephraim is, however, both a comic manifestation and a serious vital force of Judaism, instilling imagination and realism in Solomon, his spiritual heir.

Moses' search for the "real" Solomon, then, is an attempt to reclaim his past as a Jew and participate in the redemptive value of this figure, who takes on the mythic qualities of the raven that insinuates itself into a diversity of situations to provoke the apathetic and the misguided. Although Moses cannot quite verify all the incarnations of the mysterious Solomon, he suspects that Solomon has influenced many of the nobler acts that occur: the attempt to take over Bernard's McTavish distillery, the creation of the Israeli air force, and the success of the raid on Entebbe. By trying to restore order in his own life, through research and the dogged pursuit of the truth concerning Solomon, Moses begins to understand that honest engagement, not exploitation of life, is a source of value and meaning. No one is spared in Richler's caustic view, but some can glimpse hope, however concealed it may be.

Barney's Version • In some respects, Moses' search for truth extends into *Barney's Version*, published almost a decade after *Solomon Gursky Was Here*. In this novel, though, Richler created a character who risks becoming a parody not only of the author's earlier characters but also of the author himself. Barney Panofsky—"trash" television producer, lifelong Montrealer, and rabid hockey fan—is a man whose passions have often been too strong for his own good. Among other fiascoes, he drinks too much, smokes cigars obsessively, bungled three marriages, and potentially committed murder. His faults become an issue, however, only when he learns that Terry McIver, a friend from his youthful years in Paris, is about to publish an autobiography. Rightfully afraid of what Terry has to say about him, Barney immediately sets to penning his memoirs, his version of past events from which the novel's title is born.

The central action of *Barney's Version* is at turns poignant and hilarious. As expected, Barney recounts history much to his own benefit, including scorching depictions of his first two wives, a "martyred" feminist icon and a stereotypical Jewish princess. He rarely offers conscious insight into his own shortcomings and, in fact, often forgets or revises details of his life at its most crucial moments. Nevertheless, Barney manages to make his audience feel sympathy for him, especially in recalling his third botched marriage, to Miriam, a near-perfect woman, Barney's "heart's desire," and his likely soul mate. What ultimately emerges from Barney's memoir is a credible protagonist—foul-mouthed, hedonistic, sometimes oblivious, infrequently accepting blame—who manages to retain his desire for "true love" and for a creative outlet beyond the shallow commercialism of his television production company. As with Richler's other works, Barney becomes an enigmatic hero, tainted by his world experiences, yet still not devoid of hope.

Nevertheless, Barney's hope feels less substantial than the kind exhibited by characters in Richler's earlier fiction. One wonders if Barney truly longs for a better world, or simply for one in which people like Terry McIver do not threaten to reveal his secrets. This question is reinforced by the vitriol that Barney occasionally heaps on some of Richler's most familiar targets (feminists, Quebecer separatists, pretentious Jews, pseudointellectuals, vegetarians, antismoking zealots, and just about any other standard-bearer of political correctness). Despite the ongoing matter of whether Barney did or did not kill his former friend Boogie, the momentum of the novel sometimes feels less like a well-plotted story than a meandering path between Barney's occasional rants. Though unequivocally humorous, such tirades sometimes feel more like a lecture from Barney (or perhaps straight from Richler himself) in which the protagonist's own foibles are tragically overlooked in his attempt to destroy his targets.

Whether a narrow-minded curmudgeon or a keen social satirist, though, Barney does extend Richler's quirky vision of the world with undeniable force. Perhaps to request moderation from a writer like Richler is a mistake. His work has always been effective because of its raw power, its unsparing depiction of any character type that happened to drift beneath the author's lens. Richler was praised widely for the richness of his comic vision and for his keenly observed, unsentimental portrait of Montreal's inhabitants (Jew and non-Jew alike). Through an imaginative extension of this vision, Richler developed into a novelist of importance, with his message transcending the limited boundaries of St. Urbain Street to assume universal significance.

James C. MacDonald
Updated by J. David Stevens

Other major works

SHORT FICTION: *The Street: Stories*, 1969.

SCREENPLAYS: *No Love for Johnnie*, 1961 (with Nicholas Phipps); *Young and Willing*, 1964 (with Phipps); *Life at the Top*, 1965; *The Apprenticeship of Duddy Kravitz*, 1974 (adaptation of his novel); *Joshua Then and Now*, 1985 (adaptation of his novel).

NONFICTION: *Hunting Tigers Under Glass: Essays and Reports,* 1968; *Shovelling Trouble,* 1972; *Notes on an Endangered Species and Others,* 1974; *The Great Comic Book Heroes, and Other Essays,* 1978; *Home Sweet Home,* 1984; *Broadsides: Reviews and Opinions,* 1990; *Oh Canada! Oh Quebec! Requiem for a Divided Country,* 1992; *This Year in Jerusalem,* 1994; *Belling the Cat: Essays, Reports and Opinions,* 1998; *Dispatches from the Sporting Life,* 2001; *On Snooker: The Game and the Characters Who Play It,* 2001.

CHILDREN'S LITERATURE: *Jacob Two-Two Meets the Hooded Fang,* 1975; *Jacob Two-Two and the Dinosaur,* 1987; *Jacob Two-Two's First Spy Case,* 1997.

EDITED TEXTS: *Canadian Writing Today,* 1970; *Writers on World War II: An Anthology,* 1991.

Bibliography

Arsenault, Michel. "Mordecai Richler Was Here." *World Press Review* 37 (June, 1990): 74-75. A brief biographical sketch, noting how Richler satirized the experiences of the French, the Canadians, Jews, and women; contends that although Richler is often accused of presenting an extremely critical view of Canada, he believes it his right to do so.

Benson, Eugene, and William Toye, eds. *The Oxford Companion to Canadian Literature.* New York: Oxford University Press, 1998. Useful not only for general information on Richler but also for context, with a solid cross-index to related writers and literary movements in Canada.

Brenner, Rachel Feldhay. *Assimilation and Assertion: The Response to the Holocaust in Mordecai Richler's Writings.* New York: P. Lang, 1989. Examines the role of Jewishness in Richler's writing and his portrayal of the Holocaust. Includes a bibliography and an index.

Craniford, Ada. *Fiction and Fact in Mordecai Richler's Novels.* Lewiston, N.Y.: E. Mellen, 1992. A good study of Richler's Jewishness and his identity as a Canadian. Includes a bibliography and an index.

Darling, Michael, ed. *Perspectives on Mordecai Richler.* Toronto: ECW Press, 1986. In eight richly footnoted articles by eight different writers, the reader encounters different analyses of Richler's craft and the especially moral vision expressed in his fiction. Some of the articles provide an illuminating overview of Richler's themes; others, particularly those concentrating on his style, may be too specialized for the student reader.

Iannone, Carol. "The Adventures of Mordecai Richler." *Commentary* 89 (June, 1990): 51-53. Notes that Richler is among those Jewish writers who take an interest in the shadier side of Jewish experience, challenging the stereotype of the "good Jewish boy."

McSweeney, Kerry. "Mordecai Richler." In *Canadian Writers and Their Works,* edited by Robert Lecker, Jack David, and Ellen Quigley. Vol. 6. Toronto: ECW Press, 1985. McSweeney provides an orderly, lucid, and insightful analysis of Richler's fiction through *Joshua Then and Now.* The notes and the select bibliography document a wealth of reference material.

Ramraj, Victor J. *Mordecai Richler.* Boston: Twayne, 1983. This six-chapter study of Richler's fiction to *Joshua Then and Now* is enriched by a preface, a useful chronology of Richler's writing life, and a thorough select bibliography. *The Street,* the only one of Richler's fictional works that can be considered a work of short fiction, is examined in the context of Richler's vision and stance toward the Jewish community that he depicts so vividly in all of his fiction.

Richler, Mordecai. Interview by Sybil S. Steinberg. *Publishers Weekly* 237 (April 27, 1990): 45-46. Richler discusses the difficulty of writing the novel *Solomon Gursky*, partly because it was the first time he had to rely on research to authenticate his story and partly because of the complexity of the time sequences.

Sheps, G. David, ed. *Mordecai Richler.* Toronto: McGraw-Hill Ryerson, 1971. The seventeen articles and essays in this book treat Richler's fictional works both specifically and in more general contexts such as their place in Jewish fiction in English. The authors of the pieces are among the preeminent names in Canadian literary criticism. Includes a thoughtful introduction by Sheps.

Woodcock, George. *Mordecai Richler.* Toronto: McClelland and Stewart, 1970. Woodcock has a talent for presenting analyses in a down-to-earth prose style accessible to student readers. In this early work on Richler's fiction, the concluding seventh chapter includes a short assessment of *The Street.*

Conrad Richter

Born: Pine Grove, Pennsylvania; October 13, 1890
Died: Pottsville, Pennsylvania; October 30, 1968

Principal long fiction • *The Sea of Grass*, 1936; *The Trees*, 1940; *Tacey Cromwell*, 1942; *The Free Man*, 1943; *The Fields*, 1946; *Always Young and Fair*, 1947; *The Town*, 1950; *The Light in the Forest*, 1953; *The Lady*, 1957; *The Waters of Kronos*, 1960; *A Simple Honorable Man*, 1962; *The Grandfathers*, 1964; *A Country of Strangers*, 1966; *The Awakening Land*, 1966 (includes *The Trees*, *The Fields*, and *The Town*); *The Aristocrat*, 1968.

Other literary forms • Conrad Richter wrote fourteen novels, all of which were published by Alfred A. Knopf, but in addition to the longer fiction that Richter produced between 1937 and 1968, he also wrote short stories and a variety of nonfiction. He was nearly as prolific a short-story writer as he was a novelist, his earliest published story appearing in 1913. His first volume of collected short stories includes twelve stories under the title *Brothers of No Kin, and Other Stories* (1924); nine more stories were collected in a volume titled *Early Americana, and Other Stories* (1936). Richter wrote short fiction throughout his career, producing more than thirty-one stories, most of which appeared in *The Saturday Evening Post*. Many of Richter's stories still remain uncollected, but a number were gathered in a collection titled *The Rawhide Knot, and Other Stories* (1978). Richter's nonfiction includes four book-length essays on his eclectic personal philosophy: *Human Vibrations* (1926); *Principles in Bio-Physics* (1927); *The Mountain on the Desert* (1955); and *A Philosophical Journey* (1955). Six of Richter's novels have been adapted for motion pictures and television, and Richter himself worked periodically as a writer for Metro-Goldwyn-Mayer in Hollywood between 1937 and 1950, but found that writing for motion pictures was not his forte. His continuing popularity as a writer is reflected by the fact that long after his death, many of Richter's books were still in print.

Achievements • Richter did not achieve widespread recognition during his long career as a writer despite the fact that he won the Pulitzer Prize in fiction in 1951 for *The Town* and the National Book Award in fiction in 1960 for *The Waters of Kronos*, beating out Harper Lee's *To Kill a Mockingbird* and John Updike's *Rabbit Run* among the competition. A reclusive man who spent much of his life in rural Pennsylvania and in the isolated mountains of New Mexico, Richter was not a colorful figure whose life drew attention to his work. Because much of his work appeared in serial form for popular and pulp magazines, he has been too hastily dismissed by academic critics. At his best, Richter is a historical novelist of the first rank. He re-creates the past, not as a historian would, but rather by reproducing the actualities of frontier experience that are conveyed by fidelity to details and local expression. When Richter's purposes as an artist are more fully understood, it seems certain that critical assessments of his work will acknowledge the judgment of the general reader, with whom Richter continues to be popular.

Biography • Conrad Michael Richter was born in Pine Grove, Pennsylvania, on October 13, 1890. The eldest of three sons of a Lutheran minister, he grew up in several small rural Pennsylvania towns where his father had congregations. He came from mixed German, French, and Scotch-Irish blood. One of his forebears served with George Washington's Continental Army, and another fought as a Hessian mercenary for the British. His grandfather, uncle, and great-uncles were preachers. Richter was brought up in bucolic surroundings. and he passed a happy boyhood in a score of central and northern Pennsylvania villages. In 1906, he graduated from Tremont High School and during the next three years took a number of odd jobs—clerking, driving teams, pitching hay, and working as a bank teller. His first permanent job was as a reporter for the Johnstown, Pennsylvania, *Journal,* which he began at the age of nineteen. His first published story, titled "How Tuck Went Home," was written in 1913 while he was living in Cleveland, Ohio. In 1914, a second story, "Brothers of No Kin," was awarded a twenty-five-dollar prize for being one of the best stories of the year. In 1915, Richter married Harvena Maria Achenbach. Taking his bride West to find his fortune in a silver mine venture at Coeur d'Alene, Idaho, he made a short sojourn as a speculator in the mine fields. After returning East, where a daughter was born in 1917, Richter started writing children's literature and published a periodical for juveniles called *Junior Magazine Book.* Meanwhile, his short stories had been appearing in magazines such as *Ladies' Home Journal* and *Saturday Review.*

Richter's early work as a newspaper reporter and editor influenced his literary style. His sparse method of expression was a product of his journalistic training, and the typical length of his novels is about two hundred pages. In lieu of formal education, Richter, like many self-taught people, became a voracious reader. In an interview, he said, "All my life I have been a reader and one of my joys as a boy and young man was a good book in which I could lose myself." His reading was eclectic, ranging from works by the adventure writer W. H. Hudson to those of scientific authors such as Michael Faraday and G. W. Crele, whose theories of chemistry and physics influence Richter's later philosophical works. Ralph Waldo Emerson, Henry David Thoreau, and John Burroughs also helped shape his idealistic views on nature. The most important influence on his own writing came, however, from Willa Cather, whose pioneer characters and Western backgrounds provided the model for much of Richter's fiction.

In his early short fiction, Richter used the formulas of the popular literature of the period, which still abided by the conventions of the genteel tradition. The typical tale revolved around stock plots such as a case of mistaken identity, a rich youth's rehabilitation through hardships shared with the common people, a city girl coming to terms with country life, and so on. As might be expected, these stories used cardboard characters and were tailored to readers' moral and social assumptions. Richter's first stories were self-admitted "potboilers" from which he only expected to get a bit of money for his family. During the period between 1917 and 1928, when Richter was engaged in hack writing and publishing for a living, he started to develop his ideas on "psychoenergics," as he called his theory of human personality. This theoretical interest led to three works, *Human Vibration, Principles in Bio-Physics*, and a privately printed monograph called "Life Energy." These essays contained the germ of another book-length essay that he published twenty-eight years later as *The Mountain on the Desert*, his fullest attempt to articulate his personal philosophy.

In 1928, Richter's wife's illnesses caused a move to the Southwest, an event that would have a major effect on his career as a writer and mark a turning point in his life. What had started as a misfortune would turn out otherwise. Stimulated by the culture and climate of New Mexico, Richter published a second volume of stories,

Early Americana, and Other Stories, and his first novel, *The Sea of Grass.*

The writer's material was enlarged. He had always taken the ingredients of his fiction from family memories and observations; when he moved to New Mexico, as he later wrote in his unpublished *A Few Personal Notes,* "The backlog of my material still came from first sources, fine old-time men and women, chiefly from New Mexico and Arizona, Texas and Indiana territory, who lived through many of the early days."

In 1940, Richter published *The Trees,* the first volume of a trilogy that would be completed with *The Fields* in 1946 and *The Town* in 1950. After the publication of his southwestern novel *Tacey Cromwell* in 1942, Richter received his first literary award, the gold medal for literature given by the Society of Libraries of New York University. In 1944, an honorary Litt.D. degree was conferred upon him by Susquehanna University in recognition of a native son's attainments. During the decade of the 1940's, Richter also received the Ohio Library Medal Award for Literature.

In 1950, Richter returned to his native heath, Pine Grove, Pennsylvania, where he would remain for the rest of his life except for return trips to the Southwest and winters in Florida. In 1951, Richter won the Pulitzer Prize in fiction for *The Town.* Although he wrote one more novel about the West, *The Lady,* most of Richter's remaining career was given over to the subjects with which he had started as a writer—the people and land of his birthplace. He completed his best-selling novel *The Light in the Forest* after his return home; like his later novel, *A Country of Strangers,* it was inspired by the beauty of the eastern landscape and by the deeper sense of history one feels in the East. At the close of the 1950's, Richter was awarded his second honorary doctorate, this time by the university of his adopted state, New Mexico. During the early 1960's, he completed two volumes of his projected Pennsylvania trilogy—*The Waters of Kronos* and *A Simple Honorable Man.* Richter won the National Book Award for the former; he was at work on the third volume of the trilogy when he died in 1968 at the age of seventy-eight. Since his death, two works have appeared: a novel, *The Aristocrat,* and a book of stories, *The Rawhide Knot, and Other Stories.*

Analysis • Conrad Richter's qualities as a writer are partly described by the title of one of his late novels, *A Simple Honorable Man.* Although the book is about his father, the same terms might be used to characterize Richter's fiction, which is simple, concise, and concerned with basic virtues. Thus, it is something of a paradox that Richter's novels and stories are underpinned by a rather complex theory of human life and history, and that these philosophical, quasi-scientific ideas provide a conceptual framework over which the characters, plots, and settings of his fiction are stretched like a covering fabric. Another major tendency of Richter's fiction is that it is intensely autobiographical, deriving from family traditions and experience. In his youth, Richter heard stories of frontier experiences from relatives who had been pioneers themselves. It was his fascination with the way things had been and his conviction that he could inspire his readers to cope with modern problems by showing how ordinary people in the past had overcome the adversities of their frontier that prompted him to become a historical novelist.

Equally important to Richter's development as a novelist, however, were the quasi-scientific philosophical principles that he developed long before his first novel was published. Thus, Richter is unlike most writers in that his fiction does not represent the developing and unfolding of a philosophy, but rather the extension of a belief system that was essentially static after being established. This being the case, it is important to grasp some of the rudiments of Richter's philosophy before discussing his longer fiction, for his themes as a novelist grow out of his philosophical notions.

It must be pointed out that despite their would-be scientific titles and vocabulary (*Human Vibrations* and *Principles in Bio-Physics*), Richter's book-length essays lack the rigor of scientific methodology. At first glance, his theory of life seems to be based upon an odd merging of materialism and idealism. His first premise is that people function in response to bodily cellular vibrations or "vibes" that are regulated by the reserves of psychic or physical energy. If energy abounds, people are in harmony with life. The ultimate expression of human harmony is compassion for fellow humans. Other signs are charity, fortitude, and the confidence to prevail against hardship, a sense of unity with nature, a tendency toward betterment in history, and a quest for freedom. On the other hand, if energy sources are low, there is a lack of harmony in life. Conflict with nature, with other people, and with oneself all signify a deficiency of energy; other such manifestations are restless wandering, fruitless searching for intangibles, and historic change for the worse. Thus, as Richter explains it, human life and history are governed by mechanical laws.

Richter's second premise is based on what can best be described as quasi-scientific ideas. He holds that people respond in mind and body with "cellular energy" to outside stimuli. Activity causes the cells in one's body to overflow, revitalizing the weak cells. The process is like that of an electrical circuit in which there is a constant reenergizing while the operation continues. Therefore, constant use ensures a steady power source, whereas disuse can cause the source to decline and lose power. In human terms, mental and physical exertion stimulate the release of energy and speed up "energy transfer" through the cell structure.

Like many American autodidacts, Richter combined Yankee know-how and practicality with the visions of the crank philosopher. His "bio-physics" serves as a point of departure for accurate historical fiction about the actualities of pioneer life. By Richter's own admission, much of what he produced before he moved to New Mexico in 1928 was hack writing for the pulp magazines, but there, led to new literary subjects, he launched his career as a serious author with a series of stories and novels; inspired by the grand surroundings of his Western residence and informed by extensive research and the philosophical themes that would run through his subsequent fiction, he produced his first novel.

The Sea of Grass • *The Sea of Grass* was well received on publication and is still highly regarded by readers and critics. The similarities between Richter's story of a strongwilled southwestern pioneer woman and Willa Cather's *A Lost Lady* (1923) were quickly noted. The central idea of *The Sea of Grass* was sounded in a short story titled "Smoke over the Prairie," published two years earlier in *The Saturday Evening Post.* The novel is set in New Mexico during the last decades of the nineteenth century. It revolves around a feud between cattle ranchers, led by Colonel James Brewton, who use the open grasslands for grazing, and growing numbers of farmers, called "nesters" by the cattlemen, who are supported by Brice Chamberlain, a federal judge. A subplot concerns a love triangle between Brewton, his wife, Lutie, and Chamberlain, which ends with the tragic death of the son of Brewton and Lutie, whose paternity is uncertain, since it is implied that Chamberlain might well have been the boy's father.

The major theme is the decline of the grasslands, a historic change for the worse. The story is narrated as a reminiscence by Hal Brewton, a nephew of Colonel Brewton. He tells the story of an era that has already passed and thus conveys an aura of nostalgia that Richter himself apparently felt for these bygone days. In fact, Hal Brewton is actually a persona for the author and reflects his attitudes toward events. For this reason, Hal remains a one-dimensional character, yet his role as narrator serves to create an objective view of the material. Hal is involved in the events he describes but not so closely as to have his judgment obscured. He is a boy when the story starts and is the town doctor when the story ends twenty-five years later. The first part of the book is devoted to Lutie, a lively and lovely belle from St. Louis, who comes to Salt Fork, New Mexico, to marry the cattle baron Jim Brewton. The "Colonel," as he is called, has a battle going on with the nesters because he believes that the dry lands are doomed to be blown away if they are plowed. The marriage results in three children, but Lutie grows tired of her life as a rancher's wife and simply walks out, staying away for fifteen years. She had left thinking that her lover Brice Chamberlain would come with her, but he remains to support the cause of the farmers.

The title of the book implies that it is a story about the land, and it is indeed, for the basic conflict of the novel arises from how the land will be used. However, *The Sea of Grass* also introduces the typical Richter hero and heroine in Colonel and Lutie Brewton. The Colonel embodies the best combination of idealism and pragmatism, but he is not complex. He reflects the virtues Richter admires—integrity and courage; he exercises his control over his world with sure authority. Lutie, on the other hand, is the first in a line of female characters in Richter's fiction who are not in harmony with their existence, and who achieve maturity only through hardship and suffering. When she returns to the Southwest, she has finally learned that she needs the sense of fulfillment that comes from the exertion required to survive on the sea of grass. *The Sea of Grass* is ultimately a novel in which the triumph belongs to the earth, for it is the land itself that finally, through a drought, defeats the persistent nesters and subdues Lutie's willful romanticism when her son is destroyed by the violence of the Southwest. Although *The Sea of Grass* is a lasting achievement, it has some of Richter's characteristic flaws as well. There is a thinness to the writing that gives the impression of a screenplay or an extended short story rather than a fully realized novel, a charge leveled with even more justification against Richter's next novel, *Tacey Cromwell.*

Tacey Cromwell • *Tacey Cromwell* was generally not as well received as *The Sea of Grass,* perhaps because the heroine is a prostitute and the hero a gambler. Recalling his Idaho experience, Richter sets the plot of *Tacey Cromwell* in the mining town of Bisbee; his treatment of this setting reflects extensive research concerning life in early Western mining towns. He shows the ethnic diversity of the miners and the pretensions of the leading townsmen, who have risen from humble origins to positions of wealth and power. The plot of the novel is built around the conflict between the rough-and-ready immigrants and the new rich ruling class in town. The narrator is again a small boy, Wickers Covington, who is both an observer and a partial participant in the action, about which he reminisces as he tells the story after the fact.

The book begins with the runaway boy Wickers escaping from an uncle in Kansas who has mistreated him. Changing his name to Nugget Oldaker, he heads to Socarro, New Mexico, where his half brother Gaye Oldaker is living. He finds his kinsman in a house called the White Palace, which is ironically named, for it is a place of prostitution. His brother's mistress is a prostitute named Tacey Cromwell. Fearing that an upbringing in a bordello would prejudice the lad's morals, the couple moves away to give Nugget a decent home. They relocate in a mining town in Arizona, where they settle down and start the climb to success. Tacey and Gaye never marry, but they remain something of a team. She shows incredible altruism toward her former lover, even after he leaves her and takes the richest woman in town as his wife. Tacey's conversion to respectability is hastened by the adoption of two children of a neighbor killed in a mine accident. The good women of the town, however, take umbrage at the children being reared by even a reformed prostitute, and they bring legal action against Tacey, which results in her losing the children.

Undaunted by disappointment in love, community treachery, and sickness, Tacey starts a business as a dressmaker. At first she is boycotted by the priggish ladies, but one of her creations is worn at an annual ball by a lady who did not know or care about Tacey's reputation. The dress is a sensation, and her future as a dressmaker and designer is made overnight. Meanwhile, Gaye has been appointed territorial treasurer, a position he sought after being encouraged by Tacey. His wife, the haughty and puritanical Rudith Watrons, is drenched in a rainstorm that leads to a long illness and finally to her death. Nugget, who has grown up and become a mining engineer, returns to Bisbee, and one of the foster children taken from Tacey is restored to her. Thus, the novel ends with things returned to their original condition, but with the new harmony that hardship always hands to those who accept it in Richter's fictional worlds.

The novel also illustrates the conception of "westering," the process of evolution in which a region goes from frontier to community. Such a process, in Richter's conception, involves more than historical change. On the physiological and psychological levels, *Tacey Cromwell* depicts Richter's theory of altruism. Tacey's selfless assumption of guilt, both hers and her gambler-lover's, so that Gaye and his children might prosper, is close to the formula plot of the prostitute with a heart of gold used by Bret Harte in his Western fiction. Richter, however, has Tacey's sacrifice pay off, and she finally rises to respectability and eventual reunion with her lover and loved ones.

The Lady • *The Lady*, Richter's ninth novel and his third with a southwestern setting, was published fifteen years later in 1957. *The Lady* was better received by the critics and evidences Richter's increased competence as a writer. It is a stronger novel because the central character, Doña Ellen Sessions, is more fully developed than Tacey Cromwell. The plot is partly based on an actual case, an unsolved New Mexico mystery of the frontier period, that involved the disappearance and probable murder of a judge and his young son. The conflict in this book centers on the struggle between

Spanish American sheepherders and Anglo-American cattle ranchers. The story is told by a narrator named Jud, who tells of events that happened sixty years before, when he was a boy of ten. He, like the juvenile narrators of *The Sea of Grass* and *Tacey Cromwell*, is both a participant and a witness. Jud is taken in by his cousin, the Territorial Judge Albert Sessions, after his own father has abandoned him. The judge's wife is the charming and arrogant "Doña Lady Ellen," as she is styled because of her noble Spanish and English bloodlines. She is the mistress of a giant sheep spread, inherited from her parents. In addition to breeding and wealth, she has acquired skills as a horseback rider and markswoman. The villain of the piece is her brother-in-law, a mercenary and unethical lawyer, Snell Beasley. The violent feud that is the focus of the book is begun when Beasley drives a cattle herd through her ranch; there is shooting that results in the death of some of the cattlemen.

The chain of events that leads to the disappearance of Judge Sessions and his young son Wily is set in motion. Thinking Doña Ellen is now vulnerable, Snell Beasley sets out to destroy her. She is forced to sell her once-great ranch, and it seems that her humiliation is complete, yet in the final scene of the novel, poetic justice is served. In a buggy race between Doña Ellen and Snell, there is an accident and her adversary is killed; thus, the heroine gets her revenge in a somewhat melodramatic ending. Her victory underscores Richter's central themes of endurance in the process of "westering" and the mystic bond between people and landscape. It is fitting that Richter's last book about his adopted Southwest should be concluded with a glorification of the land that had inspired him to write the type of fiction that would be his forte—historical romances.

The Trees • While working on his southwestern novels, Richter began during the early 1940's his trilogy, titled *The Awakening Land*, about the Pennsylvania-Ohio frontier, which was conceived from the first as a whole. The first novel of the trilogy, *The Trees*, is set in the late eighteenth and early nineteenth centuries; the novel unfolds the story of a typical pioneer family, the Luckett clan, whose frequent migrations through the great sea of woods that covers the Ohio Valley and the Allegheny Mountains is the basis of the plot. In this novel, Richter vividly depicts the darkness of the forest floor as well as the moral darkness in the heart of people. The protagonist of *The Trees* is a "woods woman" named Sayward Luckett, a larger-than-life figure who is the focal character of the entire trilogy. She is married to Portius Wheeler, who, for reasons never explained, has abandoned his native New England, where he was educated as a lawyer, and has become a loutish and drunken backwoodsman. Although nearly all traces of culture and civilization have been erased from him by the time he is married to Sayward, she nevertheless prevents him from further decline, and he honors her by making a reformation.

In addition, *The Trees* tells how Sayward as a girl had wandered with her nomadic family, breaking away from that way of life to marry Portius and settle down. Richter intended that Sayward's experiences should reflect the whole pioneer experience of movement, settlement, and domestication. Using the span of one woman's life, the process of historical change in the Ohio Valley from hunters to farmers to town dwellers is reflected. Thus, like Richter's southwestern novels, *The Trees* traces social evolution; it also resembles his southwestern novels in being episodic, in having a strong heroine, and in its themes of hardship and endurance, ending in ultimate triumph. It differs most from the earlier books in that there is no boy-narrator; Richter's point of view is omniscient in the trilogy, and he uses more dialect in the dialogue. Further, in an effort to make his depiction of pioneer life more convincing, he uses folktales and superstitions in order to reflect the primitive way of life on the frontier.

The Fields • The final two volumes of the trilogy, *The Fields* and *The Town*, continue the portrait of Sayward and depict the conquering of the land through the process of civilization. *The Fields* tells of Sayward's ten children and her husband's affair with the local schoolmarm, who bears him an illegitimate daughter. Sayward is devastated by Portius's unfaithfulness, yet she recovers from this crushing experience when she hitches a pair of oxen to a plow and begins to till the fields. She sees in the great brutes' tolerance and strength and in the permanence of the earth a prescription for her own survival.

The Town • *The Town*, though not any more successful artistically than the first two parts of the trilogy, was awarded the Pulitzer Prize in 1951, more for the entire series than for its concluding volume. *The Town*, which is set in pre-Civil War Ohio, deals mostly with the romance between Sayward's youngest son, Chancey, and her husband's illegitimate daughter, Rosa Tench. The love between the half brother and sister is marked by tragedy; she commits suicide following a balloon accident. The rest of the book completes Sayward's story. The conflict that fills out the plot is between mother and son: Sayward tries to make a pioneering man out of Chancey, but he refuses to accept her value system and goes off to edit a liberal newspaper in Cincinnati. The newspaper, which is supported by an unknown patron, publishes Chancey's socialist views, which are an affront to his mother. Just before her death, he learns that she was the secret benefactor who had supported his career over the years. Chancey has to reexamine his philosophy in the light of this revelation. He concludes that his mother's doctrine of hard work and self-reliance is a better one than his own. Thus, Sayward dies at the age of eighty having won her last victory, rescuing her baby son from the heresy of socialism; the puritan faith in work of the older generation remains superior to modern liberal social theory.

Thus, in his trilogy, Richter brings full circle the "westering" process in which wilderness gives way to farms and farms become towns—historic change for the better; that is the essence of the American experience. However, as civilization conquers the wilderness, something is lost as well as gained. The frontier's hardships had tested people and honed their character. Modern Americans lack hardiness, vigor, and self-reliance, those qualities of mind and spirit that their ancestors had in abundance, as the heroine of his Ohio trilogy so amply shows.

The Waters of Kronos • Richter produced some half-dozen minor novels on various historical subjects and themes, but the major achievements of his later career are *The Waters of Kronos* and its sequel, *A Simple Honorable Man*, the first two volumes of a projected trilogy that he did not live to complete. The former is regarded as one of Richter's highest artistic successes and won wide critical acclaim, earning the National Book Award for 1960. The book is one of Richter's most autobiographical. His main character, a man named John Donner, resembles Richter himself; the character's parents are very much like his family as well. *The Waters of Kronos* is an almost mystical story in which John Donner, an ill and aged man, returns from the West to his Pennsylvania hometown, which is covered by a human-made lake, to visit the graves of his ancestors. At the cemetery, he meets an old man, who takes Donner down a steep hill where, to his incredulous eyes, he finds his town just as it looked sixty years ago. The remainder of the plot is a reexamination of the scenes of his childhood and a reunion with friends and relatives. The journey into the past enables him to learn that what he has always feared is not true—that the gap between his faith and that of his father is not as wide as he once thought. He discovers that he is his father's spiritual son. His final realization from his return to the past is that they have both worshiped the same god in different ways. Having come to terms with his father's god in his novel, Richter's next book shows how he gains further understanding of his parents as people.

A Simple Honorable Man • *A Simple Honorable Man* describes the life of John Donner's father, Harry, who at the age of forty gives up a career in business for a lifetime of service to the Lutheran Church. Like *The Waters of Kronos*, this book is clearly autobiographical, but it is more than a nostalgic family history, for in this novel as in the previous one, Richter tries to come to grips with a number of philosophical problems. The novel emphasizes that the most important things in life are not social status, or power of office, or money, but altruistic service to others. Harry Donner's greatest satisfaction is not in putting money in the bank but in helping those who are in need.

The third volume of the trilogy, on which Richter was at work when he died, was intended to show, as the first two books had done, his reconciliation with his actual father, his final reconciliation with his spiritual father. The two volumes that he did complete are a fitting capstone to Richter's career as a writer. His personal struggles, reflected through those of the Donners, show him to be a man of spiritual and intellectual integrity. The order and lucidity of the narrative reveal his artistry; the restrained realism that characterizes his fiction mutes the sentimentality inherent in such materials, and even though dealing with personal subject of a moral nature, he never lapses into overt didacticism.

Except for *The Sea of Grass*, Richter's reputation will rest most firmly on the books written in the last stages of his career, especially *The Waters of Kronos*; nevertheless, he will probably continue to attract readers who admire exciting, concise, sometimes lyrical stories and novels about the early history of the United States and the common people who experienced it.

Hallman B. Bryant

Other major works

SHORT FICTION: *Brothers of No Kin, and Other Stories,* 1924; *Early Americana, and Other Stories,* 1936; *The Rawhide Knot, and Other Stories,* 1978.

NONFICTION: *Human Vibrations,* 1926; *Principles in Bio-Physics,* 1927; *A Philosophical Journey,* 1955; *The Mountain on the Desert,* 1955.

Bibliography

Barnes, Robert J. *Conrad Richter.* Austin, Tex.: Steck-Vaughn, 1968. A short and limited approach to Richter the writer. Opens with a brief biography and then follows with a survey of his fiction which used the Southwest as a setting—nine short stories out of seventy and three of his thirteen novels.

Edwards, Clifford D. *Conrad Richter's Ohio Trilogy.* Paris: Mouton, 1970. A good, pene-trating examination of Richter's Ohio Trilogy—*The Trees, The Fields,* and *The Town*—with a detailed analysis of the writer's philosophical and psychological themes.

Gaston, Edwin W., Jr. *Conrad Richter.* Rev. ed. Boston: Twayne, 1989. An excellent in-troduction to Richter, the man and the writer, and his work. Gaston scrutinizes Richter's life and philosophy as they resonate in all of his writings. Includes com-prehensive notes, references, a bibliography, and an index.

Johnson, David R. *Conrad Richter: A Writer's Life.* University Park: Pennsylvania State University Press, 2001. A biography of the novelist, aided by Johnson's access to Richter's private papers.

LaHood, Marvin J. *Conrad Richter's America.* The Hague, Netherlands: Mouton, 1975. LaHood writes an appreciative, if not critical, summary of Richter's literary work. He avoids a chronological approach, devoting separate chapters to discussions of thematic subject matter.

Sinclair Ross

Born: Shellbrook, Saskatchewan, Canada; January 22, 1908
Died: Vancouver, British Columbia, Canada; February 29, 1996

Principal long fiction • *As for Me and My House,* 1941; *The Well,* 1958; *Whir of Gold,* 1970; *Sawbones Memorial,* 1974.

Other literary forms • *The Lamp at Noon, and Other Stories* (1968) is a volume of ten short stories available in a New Canadian Library (McClelland and Stewart) paperback edition. A later collection, *The Race, and Other Stories,* appeared in 1982. In addition to their intrinsic merit, the short stories are important as proving grounds for many of the plots, themes, and characters of Ross's novels.

Achievements • The fact that *As for Me and My House,* Ross's first novel and the one on which his reputation rested for many years, was published in the United States and not in his native land is indicative of his early struggle for recognition in Canada. Previously, he had published several short stories that gained little attention, perhaps because of their rather somber view of the human condition as reflected in the lives of the characters: Canadian prairie dwellers during the Great Depression. A few copies of *As for Me and My House* sold in Canada, but the reading public there was not interested in the Canadian West, a region apart from the rest of the world, and the merits of the novel went largely unappreciated until publication of the New Canadian Library paperback edition in 1957.

As for Me and My House continues to hold a secure place among the classics of Canadian fiction. Like Mark Twain's *Adventures of Huckleberry Finn* (1884) and F. Scott Fitzgerald's *The Great Gatsby* (1925), it is a parable by which a country can measure its imaginative life. In its complex rendering of humans struggling with inner conflict and the psychological effects of landscape and the elements, and in its richly resonant language, it surpasses the best of Frederick Philip Grove, the leading prairie realist before Ross, and it maps a fictional terrain that continued to be explored by Margaret Laurence, Rudy Wiebe, Robert Kroetsch, and others. Though his next two novels, *The Well* and *Whir of Gold,* fail to match the achievement of *As for Me and My House,* a renewing fourth novel, *Sawbones Memorial,* is of high quality.

In his best fiction, a sentence or two of Ross's lean, spare, honest prose can illuminate the life of an entire community. In his best fiction, too, Ross has the ability to identify with his characters and with their time and place. Margaret Laurence once said that "he got his time and place in the prairies exactly right." Ross could not have asked for a more satisfying tribute.

Biography • A very private man, Sinclair Ross was reticent about his personal life and preferred to let his art speak for him. A few articles, interviews, and recollections of friends, however, make it possible to piece together at least the outward facts of his life.

Born January 22, 1908, in northern Saskatchewan, James Sinclair Ross was the third child of Peter and Catherine Ross, who met and married in Prince Albert, Saskatchewan, in 1897. Peter had been born on an Ontario farm to Scottish parents, and Catherine had been born in Scotland. When he was three, Ross's parents separated, his mother taking custody of him and his father taking the two older children. After the separation, Catherine found employment as a housekeeper on several farms. Ross assisted with farm chores and learned the vagaries of horses and men, as well as the daunting effects of landscape and climate on the prairie dwellers. He retained strong memories of his isolation in those years.

After he graduated from high school in 1924, Ross went to work for the Royal Bank of Canada, his sole employer until his retirement in 1968. In 1933, the bank rewarded Ross's stints in several small Saskatchewan towns by sending him to Winnipeg, Manitoba, where he remained until 1946, except for World War II military service, and finally to Montreal. Upon retirement, he lived in Greece for three years and then moved to Spain in 1971. Culture and climate (he suffered from arthritis) influenced Ross's decision to live by the Mediterranean Sea. Competent in Spanish and French, somewhat less so in Greek, Ross read the original versions of the literatures of these languages. Living abroad, he believed, gave him a stronger sense of his Canadian identity. Although the pattern of Ross's life was one of gradual withdrawal eastward from the pioneer prairies toward older, more cosmopolitan cultures, his true subject and setting remained the Canadian prairies, specifically rural Saskatchewan and its people.

Few of Ross's colleagues at the bank knew him as a writer, though he had always been a "compulsive scribbler," he said, despite having had "so little success." Given his isolation from any real literary community, some of Ross's determination to write, mostly at night after long days at the bank, must be credited to his mother, the strongest influence in his life and a model for some of the women in his fiction. Ever conscious of her moral and intellectual refinement (her father had studied theology at the University of Edinburgh, taught at Oberlin College in Ohio, and eventually been ordained a Unitarian minister), Catherine encouraged her young son to take piano lessons, experiment with oil painting, and read widely. In particular, Ross remembered reading the works of Sir Walter Scott, Charles Dickens, and Thomas Hardy, whose *The Return of the Native* (1878) may well have influenced him, he said, though he had never been aware of any literary influences. For many years he had to support his mother as well as himself in the succession of small towns and cities to which she followed him, making it impossible to resign from the bank to devote his full energy to writing.

Ross's most productive period was the 1930's. Many of his best short stories were published then; one of them, "No Other Way," won third prize in a competition for unpublished writers. In 1941, *As for Me and My House* appeared. Ross had already destroyed the manuscripts of two earlier, unsatisfactory novels, and would later destroy another, a possibly autobiographical story of a Canadian soldier from Manitoba written during World War II.

Discouraged by the reception of *As for Me and My House*, Ross did not publish his second novel, *The Well*, until 1958, but it was greeted with even less enthusiasm than his first. *The Well* was influenced by his negative reaction to Montreal, where for twenty-two years the ascetic Ross lived largely within himself, avoiding the "literary swim," as he called it. Much of his third novel, *Whir of Gold*, was also written in Montreal, then completed after retirement. Written in Europe, his fourth novel, *Sawbones Memorial*, is a forgiving reminiscence of the prairies as Ross knew them during the 1930's and 1940's. Bearing an obvious kinship to its predecessors, it is nevertheless a more mellow novel, striking a better balance between humorous detachment and bitterness, rejection, and grudging nostalgia.

Analysis • Despite his relatively small output and rather limited fictional world, Sinclair Ross succeeds in universalizing the human concerns of his novels. Drought, poverty, and the hardship and anxiety they cause are universal concerns, but life on the Canadian prairies during the 1930's and 1940's becomes in Ross's works a paradigm of the human condition everywhere. Moreover, at its most intense there is a characteristic mood in Ross's fiction, a synthesis of human isolation, claustrophobia, and threatening nature, that serves as his trademark, making his writing as distinctive and recognizable as that of his contemporaries Ernest Hemingway and William Faulkner.

"Most writers," Ross said, "have only one or two themes that they constantly develop in their work." Actually, Ross had three: communication, or more often the failure of communication, in human relationships; the struggle to find an authentic self and live a fulfilled existence; and humankind's struggle against the land and the elements. In Ross's novels, man-woman relationships, in particular, are vitiated by a failure to communicate, or even a failure to attempt communication. In *As for Me and My House*, the Bentleys are isolated from each other by their emotional and psychological shortcomings. In *The Well*, a generation gap of attitudes and values separates the old farmer, Larson, and his young wife, Sylvia. In *Whir of Gold*, Sonny McAlpine's emotional immaturity and prairie Calvinist attitudes destroy his chances of happiness with the good-hearted prostitute, Madeleine. Among the prairie homesteaders, poverty, climate, physical toil, pessimism about the future, and a repressive Puritan morality are hardly conducive to romance.

Writing about women in Canadian and American prairie fiction, the novelist Robert Kroetsch asks, "How do you establish any sort of *close* relationship in a landscape—in a physical situation—whose primary characteristic is distance?" Thwarted in their attempts at closeness, Ross's women become domineering and manipulative (Mrs. Bentley), sexually aggressive (Sylvia), or maternal and possessive (Madeleine). Love becomes a power struggle. The women's superior social and intellectual backgrounds, or their emotional needs, cause them to treat their men as sons rather than lovers. As for the men in Ross's novels, Oedipal overtones—their failure in heterosexual love, their need for mothering women, the lack of adequate father figures in their youth, for example—are present in the principal male characters and may conceal a latent homosexuality that Ross does not overtly confront until *Sawbones Memorial*. Indeed, Ross's men seem to have better rapport with animals than with other people, and the best-written passages in his later novels are those involving animals, especially horses. Horses serve as companions or as daring symbols of sexuality, independence, and the imaginative life.

For the artist, a recurrent figure in Ross's world of outsiders and misfits, the failure of communication is especially acute. The aspirations of the artist find little nourishment in prairie society, or—by implication—in Canada and North America as a whole. The failure of Ross's struggling painters and musicians to communicate their vision is symptomatic of the larger failure of the national imagination. In *As for Me and My House*, Philip Bentley's paintings are as stillborn as his first child. In *Whir of Gold*, Sonny McAlpine's musical ambition is blunted by prairie attitudes that burden him even in distant Montreal. In this respect, Sonny, like Philip, is a typical Canadian literary protagonist, incapable of great art or memorable literary heroism on ac-

count of the domination of a persistent puritanism. The failed artist as modern literary hero is a familiar type, best exemplified perhaps by James Joyce's Stephen
Dedalus, but when the Canadian protagonist discovers he is in disagreement with the
dictates of the system, whether religious, social, or other, his peculiar Calvinist-Puri-
tan conditioning causes him to blame himself, internalizing the tension and engaging in painful and destructive soul-searching in an attempt to discover his deficien-
cies.

Philip Bentley's self-absorption and his unfinished pictures of headless figures
and the false fronts of the town are a measure of the frustration of his search for
meaning and significance in life. In this respect, Philip and the other artist-protago-
nists in Ross's fiction represent the human search in modern North America for an
authentic existence, either by coming to terms with a repressive social, cultural, and
natural environment (the Canadian way) or by overthrowing it entirely (formerly the
American way). Ross's characters are locked into themselves and unable to find a
means of escape. This in turn leads to a withholding of emotion and strained relationships devoid of real communication. The trap preventing self-realization in Canada has been called by Northrop Frye the "garrison mentality," the tendency of frontier societies to barricade themselves psychologically and culturally against the alien
wilderness behind the ordered "civilized" propriety of a transported eastern culture,
rather than adapt to the new environment. The superficial Christianity that Bentley
practices, for example, is inadequate to reconcile humankind with nature on the
prairie; there are hints in *As for Me and My House* that a natural, pastoral paganism
would be more helpful. Frozen in its own negations and reinforced in the Great Depression by an overwhelming sense of failure, Christianity engenders guilt and self-
destructive behavior (in the turning to crime of the protagonists of *Whir of Gold* and
The Well, for example), rather than encouraging self-realizing ambition, individualism, and instinct.

Indeed, by the time Ross came to write *The Well* and *Whir of Gold*, he believed that
the real wilderness was in the human chaos of the modern city. The true prairie, as
opposed to the garrison, was regenerative; it was the way to redemption and self-
realization. Completely alienated from society, the criminal is the ultimate outsider,
but in *The Well*, Chris Rowe, the small-time Montreal thug hiding out on a prairie
farm, does find regeneration in nature, the courage to face punishment for his
crimes, and probably an authentic existence within the community of prairie dwellers. Whereas in *The Well* a life in nature regenerates a young criminal, in *Whir of Gold*,
his experience in the city almost destroys Sonny McAlpine. The keys to survival are
his nostalgic recollections of his prairie upbringing, especially those involving his
horse, which serve as an anchor of self and identity amid the disorientation and ve-
nality of Montreal.

Ross's third major theme, humankind's struggle with the land and the elements,
probably derives from experience and observation as well as from his reading of the
literary naturalists, especially Thomas Hardy. Moods are known to be affected by
climate and geography, but on the prairies of Ross's novels, as on Hardy's moors,
characters and their relationships seem to be deterministically influenced by wind,
heat, drought, dust, rain, snow, and ice. The psychological and emotional toll these
elements exact lead characters to regard nature as part of an indifferent, even hostile
universe. Ross was also, however, the first of the Canadian prairie realists to go beyond this naturalistic treatment of the landscape; not only are his characters psychologically conditioned by the prairie, but they also project their own subjectivity onto

the external environment. In effect, they interact with it, so that not only is character determined by external environment, but environment also becomes an extension of the mind. Its challenge can test and strengthen the endurance of those who survive, uniting them in the common struggle against it; it can be a regenerative sanctuary for an urban fugitive such as Chris Rowe.

The defeated ones find little in religion to sustain the human spirit, at least the version of it preferred by prairie Christianity. One of Philip Bentley's redeeming qualities is precisely that he cannot believe in deliverance through a faith reduced to hollow forms and meaningless rituals that hypocritically ignore the Christian virtues of charity and compassion. In a deeper sense, however, Ross is a religious writer in that the underlying concern of his fiction is the human struggle "with the implacable blunderings of Nature" in an indifferent universe. In the face of this daunting situation, Ross holds up rationalists and humanists, such as Mrs. Bentley and Paul Kirby in *As for Me and My House* and Doc Hunter in *Sawbones Memorial*, who stake their faith on human courage, reason, and idealism, "all the things that really are humanity," in Mrs. Bentley's words. Others, such as Sonny McAlpine and old Larson, find solace in the illusory world of the past, a youthful world of happiness and material and spiritual well-being, unthreatened by darker realities. If Ross's characters are escapist-dreamers, though, their dreams must sometimes be blown away, like the false fronts of Main Street in a windstorm, to reveal the reality in which a new, authentic self can be forged.

As for Me and My House • As a youth in Saskatchewan, Ross was encouraged by a United Church minister to enter the ministry rather than banking. Already skeptical about organized religion, although he taught Sunday school and played the organ in church, Ross "was not tempted in the least. But I began to think, 'Suppose I did, or someone else did who did not really believe in it, and felt trapped in the ministry.' That was the origin of *As for Me and My House*." Ross revealed also that he once knew a minister whose plight resembled Philip Bentley's. Mrs. Bentley appears to have been based, at least in part, on Ross's mother, to judge by his recollections of her.

Like Ross's next two novels, *As for Me and My House* is the story of an inner quest for the authentic self. It thus belongs to a literary genre that includes works as diverse as John Bunyan's *The Pilgrim's Progress* (1678), Johann Wolfgang von Goethe's *Wilhelm Meister's Apprenticeship* (1795-1796), Henry David Thoreau's *Walden* (1854), and Walt Whitman's *Leaves of Grass* (1855). It is also kindred to a large number of Canadian works in which the search for personal and national identity is a dominant theme. Ross's ironic vision is nowhere better illustrated than in the fact that Bentley's search for an authentic self compels him to reject the church's way, which is to follow the teachings of Jesus Christ. Finally, he tears down the facade of his old self, but the new, authentic self must be forged in the secular, humanist crucible of art rather than in the empty chalice of the church. Sandra Djwa's perception of the "latter-day Puritanism of the psychological search for self," in a world where "Christianity has become a meaningless form without spirit, where people must learn to reject the false gods without before it it is possible to find the true God within and an authentic sense of direction," suggests the continuing contemporaneity of the book, if one thinks of the self-realization movements of the 1960's and 1970's.

As for Me and My House is a taut, intense, and bitter record of repressed, static lives in rural Saskatchewan during the 1930's. It deals with the Bentleys' year in Horizon, the fourth small-town prairie residence in twelve years for the thirty-five-year-old minister and his wife. Told in journal form by Mrs. Bentley, the book is an indictment of puritanical moral attitudes and cultural sterility. It is also bleakly pessimistic about the possibility of communication in human relationships, especially marriage. Outsiders by virtue of their position in the community and their parishioners' awareness that to them Horizon is merely a way station in a stultifying series of prairie pastorates, the Bentleys are estranged from the townsfolk as well as from each other. With no real vocation as a minister of the Gospel, Bentley wants to believe he has some talent as a painter, but his daubing shows little evidence of this, mainly because his creativity is frozen by self-lacerating guilt arising from his clerical charade.

Embittered by his failure as a minister and twelve years of entrapment in drought- and depression-ridden prairie towns, Philip seeks consolation through an adopted son whose natural father had abandoned him, but—in keeping with the melancholy pattern of discontinuity between the generations in Ross—societal pressure (the boy's Roman Catholicism is unacceptable, as is his parental background) forces the Bentleys to give up their son. Philip lacks a natural father as well as a son. Having sired Philip illegitimately, his father died before he was born; Philip's own child was stillborn. Despite, or on account of, the scorn to which his illegitimacy subjected him, Philip followed his father's path, first into the ministry and then into art. He saw the church's offer of an education in return for a commitment to the ministry as a means of escaping humiliation, but planned to leave it quickly for a painting career. He is prevented from doing so by an inanition of the soul that arises from marital responsibilities, economic conditions, and guilt over abandoning his flock. Adultery seems briefly to offer a way out for Philip, but Mrs. Bentley soon learns of it, and the other woman dies giving birth to Philip's child. In what can be interpreted as a hopeful conclusion, though, the Bentleys adopt this child, and with the money Mrs. Bentley has saved, they leave Horizon for a city life as owners of a used bookstore. Their hope is that the bookstore will allow Philip time to pursue his painting without the crippling emotional and psychological burdens of the past.

The essence of Ross's achievement in *As for Me and My House* lies in the rich complexity of character and theme realized through brilliant manipulation of point of view and language. For almost three decades after the book's publication, it was assumed that Mrs. Bentley's reporting was accurate and that her point of view was reliable. Certainly, if the reader accepts the point of view of her journal, then the town and her husband both fail her. She is the long-suffering, supportive wife, the superior woman languishing in a cultural and domestic wasteland.

As late as 1957, in his introduction to the New Canadian Library edition of the book, Roy Daniells called Mrs. Bentley "pure gold and wholly credible." If the reader accepts Ross's implicit invitation to read between the lines, however, Mrs. Bentley's self-indulgent meanness, her lonely pride, and her manipulation of Philip to satisfy her own ego are the reasons for her defeat and, to some extent, her husband's. The many inconsistencies and outright contradictions in her journal suggest that her single perspective is actually a source of considerable ambiguity in the book and of ambivalence on the reader's part. Several questions are raised: How accurate are her perceptions and assessments of her husband and the townspeople? How accurate are her perceptions of her own behavior and attitudes? Is the fact that the reader never learns her first name a clue to how *non*-revealing her journal is? In 1969, William H. New argued that the reader's ambivalence toward Mrs. Bentley arises not so much from uncertainty about her credibility as from Ross's ironically pitting the reader's viewpoint against hers in such a way that the reader comes to appreciate the depth and complexity of the narrator's situation, and Ross's control of his material. Through ironic use of symbols such as lamps, moths, Philip's study door, railroad tracks, and the false fronts of Horizon's main street, and through imagery involving gardens, horses, heat, dust, rain, snow and the prairie itself, Ross reveals Mrs. Bentley's journal to be an exercise in self-deception and evasiveness. In the final analysis, this book about communication and its failure informs the reader of the impossibility of taking sides, despite the human inclination to do so.

The Well • When *The Well* was published in 1958, Ross had been living in Montreal for twelve years. The new urban environment awakened an interest in the motivations of the criminal mind, while remoteness from the prairie prompted a realization of its regenerative potential. In *As for Me and My House*, Philip Bentley leaves the prairie to seek an authentic self in the city; in *The Well*, Chris Rowe flees the city and achieves authentic selfhood through his moral regeneration on the prairie. Apart from this about-face, the two novels bear a close kinship. Once more the setting is rural Saskatchewan; once more the characters fail to communicate and are claustrophobically trapped by the past as well as the present; once more they are psychologically conditioned by the prairie environment, while projecting their own subjectivity onto it; and once more there is discontinuity between the generations.

The Well is a story of three barren misfits whose lives converge in the little prairie community of Campkin during the 1940's. The central character, Chris Rowe, is a fatherless twenty-year-old criminal from Montreal whose petty larcenies have culminated in the shooting of an intended robbery victim whose fate the novel leaves in doubt. Handsome, tough, and arrogant, Chris nevertheless has a potentially sensitive, gentle, nature that has been brutalized by his urban upbringing. Fleeing on westbound trains to escape arrest, Chris accepts an offer of farmwork in Campkin, his intention being to maintain a low profile for a while before resuming his westward flight. He soon finds himself enmeshed, however, in a conflict for domination over him between Larson, his employer, and Larson's wife, Sylvia.

Like Chris, Larson is pursued by the past. Ten years before, Larson's first wife had died; his son, also named Chris, died soon after. Grief has warped Larson's mind several degrees beyond eccentricity, despite outward symbols of material success such as his Cadillac and new young wife. Pathetically trying to relive the past, Larson makes a virtual shrine of the old homestead he began with his first wife. Its chief icon is the well they dug together, a symbol of their shared achievement and happy union. Larson also keeps a horse with the same name as his dead son's horse, and he even imagines that Chris Rowe is the dead son returned. He treats Chris as a surrogate son, assuming he will take over the farm eventually and reestablish continuity with the Edenic past. To the extent that Larson's aversion to the present stems from his longing for the pretechnological past when farming offered pride of individual accomplishment and close identity with the soil, Ross is sounding a theme found in other prairie realists such as Frederick Philip Grove and Margaret Laurence: the human costs of increasing technology on the prairie farms. As usual, Ross's focus is on the dynamics of one or two human relationships, but *The Well* can be read as a work of social criticism that probes, as Robert Chambers, in his *Sinclair Ross and Ernest Ruckler* (1975), states, "some neglected side effects of that new prairie trinity: mechanization, mobility, and money."

Larson's wife, the voluptuous, ambitious Sylvia, had married Larson five years earlier to escape the poverty and drudgery of life as a waitress in Campkin. Partly because of a thirty-year age difference, there is neither love nor communication between them; in fact, Sylvia's plan is to kill Larson and abscond with his money. If Mrs. Bentley's designs for Philip are manipulative, those of Sylvia for Chris are evil and predatory. Her fantasy is that the adulterous relationship that quickly develops between them will make it easier to coerce Chris into helping her murder Larson, stuff his body down the well, and persuade the townspeople that he suddenly left on a train, as he often talked of doing. After a judicious interval, the two would marry and retire to California. In a lurid climax, Sylvia shoots her husband after wresting the gun from Chris, whose loyalty to his new surrogate father prevents him from doing so. Sylvia is eventually forced out of the house, never to be seen again. Larson expires, but not before he has written a note indicting Sylvia, exculpating Chris, and leaving the farm to him as well. Chris still faces uncertain punishment for the Montreal shooting, but the important thing is that he now has the courage to do so. His refusal to be further tempted into crime by Sylvia, coupled with his loyalty to Larson, is redemptive. After becoming free of the entramelling past, his best instincts released by the regenerative powers of nature and the rhythms of farm life, Chris will have a chance to achieve authentic selfhood, an end to alienation, and even community with the prairie dwellers.

If *As for Me and My House* is Ross's best novel, *The Well* is in many ways his weakest. Ross admitted his failure to "get inside" the criminal mind to make Chris Rowe a sympathetic character. The ending is wildly melodramatic, as Ross also acknowledged. "I would like to do it again and give it a different ending," he said. "I see now how it should be done." The book suffers also from a thinness of texture, a lack of intensity and power, attributable to Ross's decision to substitute the flat, banal language of barely literate characters for the richly metaphorical prose of *As for Me and My House*, and to the general lack of complexity of character, theme, and point of view. In view of these flaws, the book's cool reception seems justified.

Whir of Gold • In two important ways, *Whir of Gold*, Ross's third novel, is a reverse image of *The Well*. The latter is a Rousseauistic study of a victim of urban corruption in Montreal whose innate goodness is brought out by the morally regenerative life in nature; the former is a Hobbesian study of the nasty and brutish life of a prairie youth in the same city. Again, a man and a woman compete for domination of the young hero, but whereas in *The Well* the man is basically decent, despite his misfortunes in life, and the woman grotesquely evil, in *Whir of Gold* the reverse is true. In other ways, *Whir of Gold* resembles *The Well* quite closely. Like Chris Rowe, Sonny McAlpine is arrogant, alienated, and female-dominated. Like Chris, Sonny is drawn into crime. In common with both of the earlier novels, *Whir of Gold* is concerned with entrapment, the failure of communication, and the baneful influence of the past. Its conclusion is more pessimistic than those of Ross's previous novels. Indeed, Sonny McAlpine's struggle and eventual defeat as a musician may represent Ross's pessimistic answer to the question of whether Philip Bentley's move to the city will really enable him to develop an authentic self. In the thirty years between *As for Me and My House* and *Whir of Gold*, Ross seems to have concluded that neither the rural nor urban environment in Canada is capable of nourishing the artistic imagination.

The plot is simple and familiar, sometimes to the point of cliché. Determined to prove his superior musical talent and plagued by guilt over his sensible choice of a career in popular rather than classical music in the Saskatchewan farm community where he was reared, the young, innocent Sonny takes his clarinet to Montreal, but competition and commercialism in the wicked city combine to thwart his ambitions. Out of money and hope, he is contemplating retreat to the West when he meets Madelaine, a good-hearted nightclub floozie as lonely as he. Mad, as she is called, is from Nova Scotia, a place as remote in spirit from Montreal as is Saskatchewan. Comrades in alienation, the two decide to live together in Sonny's skid-row rooming house immediately after a first-night sexual encounter. More spontaneous and generous than other female characters in Ross's works, Mad nevertheless had comparable plans for her man. After he is sexually involved with her, her idea is to return with him to Nova Scotia, where they will manage a restaurant, and live a simple, healthy life far from the psychological rat race and moral wasteland of Montreal. In effect, she tries to trap Sonny into domesticity, as Sylvia tried to trap Chris Rowe through her plot to kill Larson.

As Mad sees it, the chief obstacle to this scheme is Sonny's neighbor Charlie, the only other character of consequence in the small, claustrophobic world of the novel. A small-time, street-mean crook, Charlie exploits Sonny's weaknesses (primarily, a self-destructive urge arising from the guilt he feels about wasting his musical talent) to involve him, against the vehement opposition of Mad, in robbing a jewelry store. In the robbery, Sonny is shot and is himself robbed of his share of the loot by Charlie. The relationship between Sonny and Mad is likewise doomed, as are most male-female relationships in Ross's novels. The protagonist's emotional immaturity causes him unconsciously to seek an Oedipal relationship, which Mad's need to mother conveniently satisfies. Because of his insecurity, however, Sonny is unwilling to risk commitment, treating Mad's mothering as a smothering possessiveness, and her praise of his sexual prowess as proof of his limited talent. Ross implies that Sonny's past background, specifically his repressive prairie puritanism, is largely responsible for both his lack of feeling for Mad and his guilt over his shabby treatment of her.

Sonny, it appears, was Mad's "whir of gold," a fleeting vision of happiness, beauty, and self-fulfillment. The book's title and central symbol derives from an incident in Sonny's childhood. Out of curiosity and cruelty, he once pursued and killed a flicker bird in an attempt to capture it. The bird's wings "flashed like a whir of gold, a gust of feathered light," before it died. Years later, his pursuit of a musical career leads to the deathly alienation of the criminal world, and his aborted relationship with Mad to the bleak realization, once she leaves, that he has rejected probably the best chance for happiness he will ever have. The whir of gold is a fragile thing, impossible to capture. To attempt to do so is to destroy it, and also to destroy oneself through its false promise of permanence.

Ross's deep pessimism about human relationships in *Whir of Gold* is presaged in much of his earlier fiction, where Puritan constraints conflict with the human instinct for beauty, imagination, freedom, and daring. Sonny has an innate predilection for these, but his farm upbringing and moral background have indoctrinated him with practicality, restraint, discipine, and caution, values dictated also by a prudent regard for the often hostile natural elements of the prairie. Not that beauty, imagination, freedom, and daring flourish in Montreal, but Sonny's failure there is partly a deterministic result of his projection of prairie attitudes onto the city, just as earlier Ross characters projected their fears onto the external prairie environment.

Whir of Gold is not a powerfully realized novel. It does not make a profound or relevant statement about psychological repression and cultural alienation. In deferring to trends in popular fiction—inarticulate characters, limited lives, disjointed language, sordid settings—Ross denies it depth of meaning. Referring to the novel's "desperate brand of naturalism," Robert Chambers points out that "Ross's pages are covered with mundane and trivial things, as though the endless plates of bacon and eggs and all those nice hot cups of coffee will somehow cohere to underpin a work of art." The use of Sonny's first-person point of view weakens the novel further. Sonny is a vapid Candide, a vacuous Ulysses, and the other characters mere literary extensions of his personality. Ross professed an interest in the motivations of the criminal mind (though he admitted he probably lacked sufficient insight), but Sonny is incapable of understanding Charlie's character or his own drift toward crime. Similarly, the forays into metaphorical language, so successful in *As for Me and My House*, seem artificially literary because they are inappropriate to Sonny's character. Again, *As for Me and My House* is rich in symbols, but the present novel has only two of any significance: the whir of gold and Sonny's horse, Isobel. Finally, the structure of the book is poorly balanced, with the central Sonny-Mad relationship starved for development in the second half because of Ross's increasing preoccupation with the robbery.

Apart from its successful interweaving of several perspectives in time, *Whir of Gold* did not advance Ross's reputation as a novelist any more than did *The Well*. In fact, it confirmed the uneasy doubts of some that Ross was a one-book author who had reached his peak in his first novel. Perhaps he was essentially a short-story writer, albeit a good one, lacking the technical resources or sustaining vision required of the novelist.

Sawbones Memorial • *Sawbones Memorial* reassured the doubters by proving convincingly that Ross was more than a one-book novelist, though its success is attributable in part to a form that utilizes the economy and precision of the short story. It succeeds also because in it Ross returns to the time and place he knew best, the Canadian prairies during the 1930's. Like *As for Me and My House*, it has a central intelligence who is perceptive and ironically detached. Unlike the two-or-three-person relationships he minutely dissects in earlier novels, Ross creates a large, diverse cast of thirty characters in *Sawbones Memorial*; and while the townspeople seem no less petty and narrow-minded than before, those on the side of life, a generous and enlightened few, dominate the action in his fourth novel. If, as Ronald Sutherland insists, a new Canadian literary hero has replaced the old, Doc Hunter must be counted a member of the new breed. Certainly his self-reliance, independence, and acceptance of life are preferable to Philip Bentley's intense struggle with his demons of guilt and self-doubt. Perhaps, as one reviewer stated, Ross himself "has stopped fighting life and come to terms with it." Perhaps the fact that the book was written in retirement in Europe, at several removes in time and space from Ross's Saskatchewan of the 1930's, explains the mellow, often humorous tone. In any case, the book is more hopeful than any of its predecessors, despite its return to some of Ross's familiar, depressing themes.

Sawbones Memorial is actually a collection of reminiscent vignettes depicting life in Upward, the small town that Doc Hunter has ministered to through forty-five years of pioneering, drought, and depression. The raison d'être of the vignettes is a ceremony held in April, 1948, to mark the doctor's retirement and the opening of the new Hunter Memorial Hospital. Accordingly, both reminiscing and looking to the future are in order. Though the action is limited to a few hours of the present, by the end of the novel Ross has roamed back and forth through four generations and several decades to lay bare the attitudes and preoccupations, the tensions and antagonisms, and the hypocrisies and prejudices of Upward's citizens.

Representing the full diversity of the community, the characters include farmers, storekeepers, teachers, ministers, and housewives, people old and young, living and dead, absent and present. They do not develop psychologically so much as they show the effects of time. Through the episodes in which they appear and reappear, they comment on the action, on Doc Hunter, and on one another. Occasionally, the same incident is retold by different characters, the contrasting viewpoints giving rise to comic or tragic irony. Little by little, the reader comes to know the characters. Doc Hunter's is the unifying point of view for those of the thirty characters whose stories constitute the book; conversely, the reader comes to know him through his shamanlike role in the lives of the other characters. The central character and intelligence, Doc is also the focus of attention at the gathering, as he has been the focus of the town's hopes and fears for over four decades. His own suffering, it is implied, broadens and deepens the efficacy of his mission as a doctor. It seems he was married too long to a frigid wife, and thus shares with other Ross protagonists an unfulfilled emotional life, though his experience has neither embittered him nor lessened his philosophical tolerance of human imperfection, of which there is God's plenty in Upward.

As with many fictional studies of small towns, from Winesburg, Ohio, to Peyton Place and beyond, Upward's appearance of respectability, especially its straitlaced attitudes concerning sexual morality, conceals a closetful of skeletons: rape, abortion, incest, murder, euthanasia, to name only a few. As the town's sole physician for almost half a century, Doc Hunter knows the contents of the closet better than anyone, a fact that gives pause to those who would prefer to forget their past in order to gossip more self-righteously. The more admirable characters, on the other hand, are often outsiders, defined as anyone who deviates from Upward's conventional standards of moral and social behavior. More so than Ross's earlier outsider-protagonist, these are very human characters whose struggles and triumphs the readers can share.

Sawbones Memorial is also more ambitious in form and conception than Ross's earlier novels. The large number of characters, the experimentation with multiple points of view, the reliance on dialogue, monologue, speeches, and flashbacks to convey information, reveal personality, and establish mood (much as in drama and film), are all new. The dialogue is especially remarkable in that each character is individuated through diction, idiom, intonation, or rhythm. (Ross said that the idea of using nothing but the speech of his characters to construct a novel came to him as he overheard fragments of reminiscences at the opening of the Royal Bank's new head office in Montreal.) It is true that the book turns against two familiar themes, the failure of communication and the stultification of the spirit in the small prairie towns of Ross's time. The roots of human alienation, whether personal or social, are still to be found in his agonized confusion over sexuality, but Ross deals with a larger range of human experience than before, including such timeless concerns as the nature of human evil and the evil of human nature, birth and death, youth and age, courage and cowardice, cruelty and compassion. For one day in time, at least, in the spring of 1948, these are reconciled as Doc Hunter speaks of retirement and the continuity symbolized by the new doctor's arrival. It is all beginning again, "just as it was all beginning that day" when he first arrived.

John H. Ferres

Other major works

SHORT FICTION: *The Lamp at Noon, and Other Stories*, 1968; *The Race, and Other Stories*, 1982.

NONFICTION: *Just Wind and Horses*, 1988 (memoir).

Bibliography

Chambers, Robert D. *Sinclair Ross and Ernest Buckler.* Montreal: Copp Clark and McGill-Queen's University Press, 1975. A joint study of two of Canada's finest authors that features close textual analyses of their respective styles.

Fraser, Keith. *As for Me and My Body: A Memoir of Sinclair Ross.* Toronto: ECW Press, 1997. Fraser's revelatory reading of *As for Me and My House* emphasizes the novel's biographical basis, and in particular its veiled acknowledgment of Ross's repressed homosexuality. The book also includes a frank portrait of its subject's later years, when the onset of Parkinson's disease and a growing sense of failure as a writer made Ross's life very difficult.

Mitchell, Ken. *Sinclair Ross: A Reader's Guide.* Moose Jaw, Sask.: Coteau, 1980. Aimed at the general reader, this insightful overview presents an experienced author's response to the work of an older peer.

Moss, John, ed. *From the Heart of the Heartland: The Fiction of Sinclair Ross.* Ottawa: University of Ottawa Press, 1992. A gathering of scholarly essays that includes feminist, postmodernist, semiotic, and narratological studies of Ross's major works. Although some of the contributors tend to wander off into the farther reaches of literary theory, the variety of viewpoints presented makes this a stimulating and thought-provoking collection.

Stouck, David. *As for Sinclair Ross.* Toronto: University of Toronto Press, 2005. Full and thoroughly researched biography of Ross.

Stouck, David, ed. *Sinclair Ross's "As for Me and My House": Five Decades of Criticism.* Toronto: University of Toronto Press, 1991. A useful anthology that includes journalistic as well as academic responses to Ross's most accomplished novel.

Woodcock, George. *Introducing Sinclair Ross's "As for Me and My House": A Reader's Guide.* Toronto: ECW Press, 1990. A somewhat old-fashioned but nonetheless cogent and readable introduction in a series intended for first- and second-year university students.

Henry Roth

Born: Tysmenica, Galicia, Austro-Hungarian Empire (now in Ukranine);
February 8, 1906
Died: Albuquerque, New Mexico; October 13, 1995

Principal long fiction • *Call It Sleep*, 1934; *Mercy of a Rude Stream*, 1994-1996 (includes *A Star Shines over Mt. Morris Park*, 1994; *A Diving Rock on the Hudson*, 1995; *From Bondage*, 1996; and *Requiem for Harlem*, 1998).

Other literary forms • In addition to his novels, Henry Roth wrote a number of essays, short stories, and fragments that editor Mario Materassi collected and published in 1987 as *Shifting Landscape: A Composite, 1925-1987.*

Achievements • With *Call It Sleep*, Roth created a masterpiece of American Jewish fiction and a classic novel of immigration, one that brilliantly adapts the insights associated with Austrian psychoanalyst Sigmund Freud and the techniques associated with Irish writer James Joyce in order to recount the traumatic experiences of an impressionable young foreigner in New York City. However, it was not until thirty years after its publication that the book began to be widely read, studied, and admired. Discouraged by neglect of his first novel, Roth abandoned the literary life and did not return to writing novels until a prodigious burst of creativity in his final years yielded 3,200 manuscript pages of disturbing autobiographical fiction, the tetralogy titled *Mercy of a Rude Stream*, half of which appeared after the author's death at the age of eighty-nine. The sixty-year gap between publication of *Call It Sleep*, in 1934, and *A Star Shines over Mt. Morris Park*, the first volume of the tetralogy, in 1994, represents the most remarkable instance in American literary history of writer's block and late artistic renewal.

Biography • Like David Schearl, the young protagonist of *Call It Sleep*, Henry Roth was born in the Galician region of the Austro-Hungarian Empire but was brought to New York City when only two. Like many other working-class Jewish immigrants, the Roths settled on the lower East Side of Manhattan but later relocated to Harlem. Roth manifested talent with a story in the student magazine of New York's public City College. Eda Lou Walton, a professor at New York University who befriended Roth and encouraged him to write, became his mentor and lover. Eventually, Roth moved into her Greenwich Village apartment, where he wrote *Call It Sleep*. Though Walton helped him find a publisher, the Great Depression year 1934 was not propitious for a literary debut, and, though the book received favorable reviews, its publisher, Robert O. Ballou, was forced into bankruptcy.

Roth began a second novel but, convinced that it was unworthy of the Marxist ideals he then set for himself, he abandoned both it and the cosmopolitan ferment of New York. He married Muriel Parker, a composer he had met at the Yaddo artists' colony, and moved with her to rural Maine. Abandoning her own musical aspirations, Muriel supported him and their two sons by teaching school, while Roth helped by chopping wood, selling maple syrup, fighting forest fires, tutoring stu-

Harvey Wang

dents in Latin and math, and serving as an attendant at a mental hospital. For most of a decade, he raised and slaughtered geese and ducks.

In 1964, *Call It Sleep* was rediscovered, and, at the age of fifty-eight, its obscure author suddenly found himself famous. Roth was plagued by persistent questions about his current projects. In 1968, after an abortive effort to write a novel set during the Spanish Inquisition, he and Muriel moved to Albuquerque, New Mexico. After Muriel's death in 1990, Roth attempted suicide but survived to complete his last great literary task at the age of eighty-nine. Despite agonizing rheumatoid arthritis, he managed to produce an enormous autobiographical fictional sequence, one that revisited its author's strained relationship with his abusive, embittered father and incestuous relationships with his sister and his cousin. Upon Roth's death in 1995, two of the four volumes of *Mercy of a Rude Stream* had been published, while the final two appeared posthumously, in 1996 and 1998, respectively. Enough material remained for two additional volumes, but Roth's publisher, St. Martin's Press, determined that they fell outside the *Mercy of a Rude Stream* cycle and remained uncertain about when or whether they would be published.

Analysis • Through much of the twentieth century, Roth, the novelist who vanished for sixty years after a stunning debut, seemed a gloss on writer F. Scott Fitzgerald's quip that American lives lack second acts. However, his long life offers enough acts to please the most garrulous of playwrights and challenge the most assiduous of biographers. He is at once salutatorian and valedictorian of twentieth century America, a contemporary of both William Faulkner and Don DeLillo. His pioneering use of stream of consciousness captured a newly urbanized, industrialized society undergoing massive transformation, but Roth survived into a very different era to write his own requiem.

In retrospect, *Call It Sleep* seems so unequivocally a major artistic achievement that it is difficult to understand why it was neglected for thirty years. However, in 1934 American culture lacked a category for American Jewish literature. By 1964, Roth fulfilled the need to anoint a worthy ancestor to Saul Bellow, Bernard Malamud, and Philip Roth, to legitimate a newly canonized tradition. It was only after ethnicity became a crucial issue in American society that Roth's novel could be appreciated for its pioneering embodiment of multiculturalism and multilingualism.

Mercy of a Rude Stream is of a different order of accomplishment than *Call It Sleep*. The fictional sequence that Roth created in his final years is of compelling interest to those fascinated by a tormented author's representation of his own compulsions and his desperate attempt to find closure. If Roth's virtuosic first novel appeared ahead of its time, his parting tetralogy was a throwback—a fictional sequence that not only is set during the 1920's but also employs the naturalistic style common to that era.

From *Call It Sleep* to *Requiem for Harlem*, Roth's frustrated literary career is itself the most remarkable narrative he created.

Call It Sleep • *Call It Sleep* begins in May, 1907, with the arrival by ship from Europe of two-year-old David Schearl and his mother Genya. They are met at Ellis Island by David's father, Albert, a surly, abusive man who is embittered by disappointment. Albert is forever falling out with fellow workers and forced to seek new employment, as a printer and then as a milkman. The family moves from modest lodgings in Brooklyn's Brownsville neighborhood to a crowded tenement on the lower East Side of Manhattan. Roth's book focuses on young David's troubling experiences during the years 1911-1913, as a stranger in a strange land. *Call It Sleep* is a coming-of-age novel about a hypersensitive Jewish boy who is forced to cope alone with the mysteries of sex, religion, and love.

After a brief prologue recounting David's arrival in America, Roth organizes his story into four sections, each defined by a dominant image: "The Cellar," "The Picture," "The Coal," and "The Rail." What might otherwise seem casual details are magnified by refraction through the mind of an anxious child. Roth's use of stream of consciousness intensifies the sense of an unformed mind trying to assimilate the varied sensations that assault it. The family apartment is a haven for David, as long as his father, who even doubts his paternity of the boy, is not home and his doting mother can lavish her affections on him. When David ventures out into the clamorous streets, he encounters threats, from both rats and humans.

At the cheder, the drab religious school where Jewish boys are given rote instruction in a Hebrew Bible they cannot understand, David is confused and inspired by Isaiah's account of the angel with a burning coal. Eavesdropping on a conversation between his mother and her sister Bertha, he misconstrues an explanation for why Genya, disgraced after being jilted by a Gentile, married Albert. When Leo, an older Polish boy, persuades David to introduce him to his cousin Esther, David is overwhelmed by incredulity and guilt over the sexual liberties that Leo takes. Fleeing his brutal father, David is shocked into unconsciousness after touching the live rail of a street car. Faced, like the reader, with sensory overload, David might as well call it sleep, embracing temporary oblivion as restoration after a long, disorienting day.

To explore the tensions among Albert, Genya, and David, a clanging family triangle rife with resentments and recriminations, Roth appropriates the theories of Sigmund Freud, particularly in describing the powerful Oedipal bond between mother and son as well as the almost patricidal strife between Albert and David. The authority of James Joyce asserts itself, not only in the fact that Roth's account of David Schearl, a surrogate for the author himself, is in effect another portrait of the artist as a young man but also in his lavish use of stream of consciousness and his meticulous deployment of recurrent imagery.

During the two decades surrounding the turn of the twentieth century, massive, unprecedented migration from eastern and southern Europe was radically reshaping American society, and, more effectively than any other novel, *Call It Sleep* records the traumas experienced when the Old World met the New. Many of Roth's immigrants are inspired by the American Dream of enlarged opportunity, while others are repulsed by an urban nightmare. Call *it*, too, sleep. Though the Schearls are Polish Jews, the eclectic slum in which they live also serves as home to immigrants and natives from many other backgrounds. Not the least of Roth's accomplishments is his success at rendering the diversity of David's environs. Yiddish is the first language of the Schearls, but English, German, Hebrew, Italian, and Polish are also spoken, in varying registers, by characters in the story. In a novel designed for an anglophonic reader, it would be misleading and demeaning to put fractured English into the mouths or minds of fluent Yiddish speakers when they are assumed to be using their native language. Instead, Roth fashions English prose supple enough to represent the varying speech and thoughts of those who speak and think in other tongues.

Call It Sleep is significant for reflecting a momentous phenomenon that transformed the United States but was ignored by many of Roth's literary contemporaries. In its vivid rendition of a child's-eye view, its dramatic exposure of family tensions, and its creation of a rich linguistic texture, Roth's first novel is an artistic triumph.

Mercy of a Rude Stream • Though they were published separately and can be read independently and autonomously, the four novels that constitute *Mercy of a Rude Stream* are best understood together, as a single narrative sequence. The entire tetralogy follows the coming of age of Ira Stigman, a Jewish emigrant to New York, from 1914, when he is eight years old, until 1927, when he is twenty-one and a senior at City College. Despite the change in names and the addition of a younger sister, Minnie, Ira seems largely an extension of David Schearl from *Call It Sleep*. He is also a thinly disguised version of Roth himself. The autobiographical basis of the books is made even more apparent by interpolated sections in which an older Ira, an ailing octogenarian author living in Albuquerque, addresses his word processor, calling it "Ecclesias." He comments on his own renewed, belated efforts at writing fiction. Ira as author poses the question that most readers will raise about Roth himself—why, approaching death, does he struggle to record such lacerating memories?

In narrating his story, Ira forces himself to revisit an unhappy childhood and adolescence, in which he and his mother Leah are terrorized by his psychotic father Chaim. When the family moves from the lower East Side to a largely Irish neighborhood in East Harlem, Ira feels rudely wrenched out of an organic, nurturing Jewish community. He recalls the painful details of broken friendships and of his public disgrace when he was expelled from high school for stealing fountain pens. The most agonizing recollections—and the element that has drawn the most attention to Roth's final books—concern Ira's sexual transgressions. The second volume, *A Diving Rock on the Hudson*, offers the startling revelation that, beginning when he was sixteen and she was fourteen, Ira regularly, furtively committed incest with his sister Minnie. He also maintained covert sexual relations with his younger cousin Stella. Recollections of incest continue through volumes 3 and 4 and fuel the author's suicidal self-loathing. The older Ira longs to die but feels compelled to tell his story first, as though narration might bring purgation and even redemption.

Unlike the bravura *Call It Sleep*, much of *Mercy of a Rude Stream* is written in undistinguished prose that is at best serviceable in evoking working-class, urban life during and after World War I. Ira offers details of jobs he held, including stock boy in an upscale food store, soda peddler in Yankee Stadium and the Polo Grounds, and salesman in a candy shop. His sentimental education is very much connected to his intellectual one, and, though his grades are mediocre, Ira thrives in college. Publication of a short story in the student magazine awakens literary ambitions; his friendship with affluent Larry Gordon enlarges Ira's life beyond his own squalid situation. He begins to acquire social graces and to strike on ideas. Ira becomes inebriated with reading, particularly after Edith Welles, the professor who was Larry's lover, becomes Ira's mentor and lover. Edith, who is modeled after Roth's own Eda Lou Walton, introduces Ira to the most influential books and people of New York's bohemian culture. In the final pages of the cycle's final book, *Requiem for Harlem,* Ira bids farewell to his dysfunctional, debilitating family and his loathsome sexual compulsions by moving down to Greenwich Village to live with Edith. The apprentice artist is finally ready to write a novel very much like *Call It Sleep.* Finally, after disburdening himself of excruciating secrets, the eighty-nine-year-old Roth finished writing and prepared at last to call it sleep.

Steven G. Kellman

Other major works

SHORT FICTION: "Broker," 1938; "Somebody Always Grabs the Purple," 1940; "Petey and Yorsee and Mario," 1956; "At Times in Flight," 1959 (parable); "The Dun Dakotas," 1960 (parable).

MISCELLANEOUS: *Shifting Landscape: A Composite, 1925-1987,* 1987 (Mario Materassi, editor).

Bibliography

Adams, Stephen J. "'The Noisiest Novel Ever Written': The Soundscape of Henry Roth's *Call It Sleep.*" *Twentieth Century Literature* 35 (Spring, 1989). Analyzes the power and integral role of sound in the novel.

Buelens, Gert. "The Multi-Voiced Basis of Henry Roth's Literary Success in *Call It Sleep.*" In *Cultural Difference and the Literary Text: Pluralism and the Limits of Authenticity in North American Literatures,* edited by Winfried Siemerling and Katrin Schwenk. Iowa City: University of Iowa Press, 1996. A study of Roth's first novel, particularly the ways in which he represents different languages and voices.

Halkin, Hillel. "Henry Roth's Secret." *Commentary* 97 (May, 1994). A study of *Mercy of a Rude Stream* and Roth's homosexual experiences.

Kellman, Steven G. *Redemption: The Life of Henry Roth.* New York: W. W. Norton, 2005. An engaging, readable account of the writer's life, particularly examining the long interim between Roth's novels.

Lyons, Bonnie. *Henry Roth: The Man and His Work.* New York: Cooper Square, 1976. The first book-length study to address Roth's early work. Includes an interview, some biographical information, and a detailed reading of *Call It Sleep.*

Sokoloff, Naomi B. *Imagining the Child in Modern Jewish Fiction.* Baltimore: Johns Hopkins University Press, 1992. Roth's David Schearl is linked to representations of the child by other Jewish writers, including Sholom Aleichem, Hayim Nachman Bialik, Jerzy Kosinski, Aharon Appelfeld, David Grossman, A. B. Yehoshua, and Cynthia Ozick.

Walden, Daniel, ed. *Studies in American Jewish Literature* 5, no. 1 (Spring, 1979). A special issue of this journal devoted to essays on Roth. Includes a bibliography and an interview.

Wirth-Nesher, Hana, ed. *New Essays on "Call It Sleep."* New York: Cambridge University Press, 1996. A collection of some of the most engaging and useful analyses of Roth's first novel.

Philip Roth

Born: Newark, New Jersey; March 19, 1933

Principal long fiction • *Letting Go*, 1962; *When She Was Good*, 1967; *Portnoy's Complaint*, 1969; *Our Gang*, 1971; *The Breast*, 1972, revised 1980; *The Great American Novel*, 1973; *My Life as a Man*, 1974; *The Professor of Desire*, 1977; *The Ghost Writer*, 1979; *Zuckerman Unbound*, 1981; *The Anatomy Lesson*, 1983; *Zuckerman Bound*, 1985 (includes *The Ghost Writer*, *Zuckerman Unbound*, *The Anatomy Lesson*, and *Epilogue: The Prague Orgy*); *The Counterlife*, 1986; *Deception*, 1990; *Operation Shylock: A Confession*, 1993; *Sabbath's Theater*, 1995; *American Pastoral*, 1997; *I Married a Communist*, 1998; *The Human Stain*, 2000; *The Dying Animal*, 2001; *The Plot Against America*, 2004; *Everyman*, 2006.

Other literary forms • Five of Philip Roth's short stories are collected along with his novella *Goodbye, Columbus* in a volume bearing that title (1959). A number of his essays, interviews, and autobiographical pieces appear in *Reading Myself and Others* (1975). An unproduced screenplay, *The Great American Pastime*, was anthologized in 1968, and two of his works, *Goodbye, Columbus* and *Portnoy's Complaint*, have been made into films by others. In 1975, Roth began editing a series called Writers from the Other Europe for Penguin Books, to which he contributed several introductions. *The Facts: A Novelist's Autobiography* appeared in 1988. *Patrimony*, a memoir of his father's life, was published in 1991.

Achievements • Roth emerged as a leading Jewish American writer when his first published book, *Goodbye, Columbus*, won the National Book Award in 1960. Many of his subsequent works involved Jewish characters and specifically Jewish American dilemmas; novels such as *Portnoy's Complaint*, *The Counterlife*, and *Operation Shylock*, in particular, involve characters struggling to reconcile their desires to be fully American during the age of American triumphalism with their deeply ingrained sense of separateness. More than a touch of local color, his depictions of Jewish communities form a base from which to spin—and unspin—national and personal narratives. Along with contemporary writers such as John Barth and Norman Rush, Roth created some of American literature's most memorable and most self-conscious storytellers, the angst-ridden Alexander Portnoy, the irrepressible Nathan Zuckerman, and the outwardly controlled, inwardly crumbling Swede Levov.

Roth's special concern in his work is the relationship between a writer and his subject, which is often closely drawn from his own personal life. His fictional accounts of smothering Jewish mothers, harried Jewish fathers, and illicit love affairs involving Jews in his early work made him notorious among the conservative Jewish establishment during the 1970's. Subsequent depictions of family relationships bearing a close resemblance to his own drew fire from his ex-wife Claire Bloom, among others. In his later work, Roth brilliantly presented the fascinating relationship between fiction and autobiography, using fictional surrogates, such as Nathan Zuckerman, to explore what he called "counterlives," or the proliferation of possible lives one single person might have lived.

Throughout his fiction, Roth exhibits the abilities of a master comedian. His ear is arguably the best of any contemporary writer, capturing the spoken voice in a wide variety of accents, intonations, and cadences, but his facility with dialogue sometimes leads critics to miss the serious undercurrents of his work. Roth's fiction covers a variety of satiric modes, from the social (*Portnoy's Complaint*) to the political (*Our Gang*) to the literary and academic (*The Professor of Desire*). Whatever mode he adopts, he presents the objects of his satire or comedy in vivid and compelling fashion. Once referred to as preeminently a social realist (as in *Goodbye, Columbus*), he has transcended that mode successfully in such works as *The Counterlife* and *Deception*, which show him, as ever, both a consummate craftsman and a tireless experimenter with his medium.

© Nancy Crampton

Roth won numerous prestigious awards for his work, including the National Book Critics Circle Award for *Patrimony*, the PEN/Faulkner Award for *Operation Shylock*, the National Book Award for *Sabbath's Theater*, and the Pulitzer Prize for *American Pastoral*. In 2000, *The Human Stain* earned Roth another PEN/Faulkner Award. In 1998, Roth received the National Medal of Arts from President Bill Clinton at a ceremony in the White House. Roth has been a member of the American Academy of Arts and Letters since 1970.

Biography • Born in the Weequahic section of Newark, New Jersey, on March 19, 1933, Philip Roth learned very early what it was like to grow up Jewish in a lower-middle-class neighborhood of a large metropolitan area. His parents were Beth Finkel and Herman Roth, a salesman for the Metropolitan Life Insurance Company. After he graduated from Weequahic High School in 1950, Roth worked for a while at the Newark Public Library and attended Newark College of Rutgers University. A year later, he transferred to Bucknell University in Pennsylvania. Although the family could ill afford the expense of a private college, Herman Roth determined that if his son wanted to go there, he would go. At Bucknell, Roth began writing stories and edited the school's literary magazine. He also had his first love affairs, from which he drew incidents (fictionally transformed, of course) for his subsequent novels. He received his bachelor's degree in English, magna cum laude, in 1954, and he accepted a teaching fellowship at the University of Chicago for graduate work in English.

After receiving his master's degree in English from Chicago, Roth enlisted in the United States Army, but a back injury suffered during basic training resulted in an early discharge. He returned to Chicago to pursue doctoral studies in English but continued writing short stories, which had begun to get published as early as the fall of 1954 in small literary journals such as the *Chicago Review* and *Epoch*. Several of his stories were anthologized in Martha Foley's *Best American Short Stories* and in *The O. Henry Prize Stories*. These awards, the success of his first published volume, *Goodbye, Columbus*, a Houghton Mifflin Literary Fellowship, and a Guggenheim Fellowship persuaded Roth to abandon graduate work in English for a career as a creative writer.

While a graduate student and instructor at the University of Chicago, Roth met and later married his first wife, Margaret Martinson Williams. The relationship was never a happy one, and after a few years they separated, Margaret steadfastly refusing to agree to a divorce. Meanwhile, they spent one year of their marriage (1960) at the Writers' Workshop at the University of Iowa, where Philip served on the faculty. After his first full-length novel, *Letting Go*, was published in 1962, he became writer-in-residence at Princeton University. He later taught English literature at the University of Pennsylvania. His experiences as an academic provided much material for his novels, many of which have a university setting or are otherwise peopled by academics.

The publication of *Portnoy's Complaint* in 1969, a year after his estranged wife was killed in an automobile accident, launched Roth's greatest notoriety, especially among the conservative Jewish community in America, and assured his fame as a novelist. He became an increasingly prolific writer, spending part of the year in his Connecticut home and part in London in an apartment near his writing studio. For years he shared his life with the British stage and screen actor Claire Bloom, whom he married in April, 1990. Their difficult relationship and 1995 divorce became a subject of Bloom's memoir, *Leaving a Doll's House*, and received fictionalized treatment in Roth's 1998 novel, *I Married a Communist*.

Analysis • Although his early works clearly show the influence of his literary idols— Henry James, Leo Tolstoy, Gustave Flaubert, Thomas Wolfe, and Theodore Dreiser— Roth came into his own as a novelist beginning with *Portnoy's Complaint*, which reveals a unique voice in American literature. His subsequent development parallels his growing interest in other Continental writers, such as Anton Chekhov, Franz Kafka, Fyodor Dostoevski, and particularly contemporary writers such as Milan Kundera, whom Roth assisted in getting his works published in America. Roth's first novels are set squarely in his native land: in Newark, where he was born and reared; in the great Midwest, where he went to graduate school; and in New York and Philadelphia, where he lived, wrote, and taught literature at several universities. The protagonists of his later fiction travel abroad to Western and Eastern Europe and as far as Hong Kong. Roth's development as a novelist is thus the development, in part, of a growing cosmopolitanism along with a deepening interest in basic human concerns and predicaments.

Chief among those predicaments is the endless struggle between the id and the superego or, in less Freudian terms, between the drive for sensual gratification and the drive for moral uprightness. On one hand, pulling at his protagonists (all but one of whom are men) is the powerful desire for sexual conquest; on the other is the almost equally powerful desire to lead a morally self-fulfilling and decent life. These drives, conflicting at almost every turn, nearly tear his protagonists apart. Even when, as at the end of *The Professor of Desire*, David Kepesh believes that he has at least achieved a reasonable equilibrium and found peace, a nagging unease enters the picture, upsetting his contentment and providing a presentiment of doom.

Indeed, Roth's heroes, if one can apply that term to such unlikely characters, all seem doomed in one way or another. Their pervasive sense of disaster, however, does not destroy Roth's comedy; it deepens it. The sense of the absurd, of the incongruities of human experience, also pervades Roth's novels and is the source of much rich humor. Moreover, his protagonists usually are fully self-aware; they understand their predicaments with uncommon self-perception, if (more often than not) they are utterly baffled in trying to find a solution to or resolution of their dilemmas. Again, their awareness and frustration combine to make the reader laugh, though the reader must be careful not to let the laughter obscure or nullify the compassion that is also the character's due.

Letting Go • Roth's first full-length novel, *Letting Go*, sets out all these themes and influences. The principal character, Gabe Wallach, is the educated, sophisticated young son of well-off middle-aged easterners, who after a brief stint in the army pursues graduate studies in the Midwest. His mother has recently died, leaving her son with a heavy moral burden: not to interfere in the lives of others as she, regretfully, has done. It is a legacy Gabe finds almost impossible to live up to, until the very end, after he has nearly ruined the lives of several people close to him. Before that, he succeeds, however, in remaining aloof from his widower father, who is lonely and adrift and tries to persuade Gabe to return home. This is Gabe's only success, however, as eventually his father meets and marries a widow who helps him rediscover life's pleasures.

Meanwhile, Gabe has his affairs, none of which works out happily, and his friendships, especially with Paul and Libby Herz, whom he meets during graduate school in Iowa. Paul is a hardworking, highly principled young man who married Libby while they were still undergraduates at Cornell. Their mixed marriage—Paul is Jewish, Libby Catholic—is mainly the result of Paul's misguided sense of devotion and responsibility. Although the passion has long since gone out of their relationship, owing to Libby's poor health and neurotic disposition, Paul remains loyal. Together, they struggle with financial and other problems, including opposition from both sets of parents.

Gabe's life and the Herzes' intersect at various points, invariably with well-intentioned but almost disastrous consequences. At Iowa, Gabe tries to befriend the couple, offers various forms of assistance to them, and finds an unusual attractiveness in Libby, which culminates in little more than a kiss. Their affair, such as it is, focuses partly on Henry James's novel *The Portrait of a Lady* (1880-1881), which Gabe lends to Paul; Libby reads the book, finding in it the last letter Gabe's mother had written him when she lay dying. Both the novel and the letter help to form a bond between Gabe and Libby that endures. Later, when Gabe is teaching at the University of Chicago, their relationship resumes when Gabe helps Paul get a job in his department.

Through Martha Reganhart, with whom Gabe has begun to live, Gabe finds someone who is willing to let her unborn baby be adopted by the Herzes. Paul and Libby have wanted a child and nearly had one, but poverty-stricken as they were, Paul persuaded Libby to have an abortion. The incidents surrounding that event are both comical and dreadful. Afterward, Libby's health never becomes robust enough for her to risk conceiving another child; hence, they hope to adopt one. The circumstances of trying to adopt a baby involve episodes best referred to as "deadly farce," including several in which Gabe intervenes on their behalf. At the same time, Gabe's relationship with Martha, a divorcée with two young children, deepens and then falls apart, largely the result of his inability to make a full and lasting commitment.

Gabe and Paul thus represent contrasting studies in personality. At the end, Gabe finally learns to "let go," the lesson his mother tried to teach him from her deathbed, but letting go for him means abandoning lover, friends, family, and career to become a wanderer in Europe, whence he writes Libby a final letter. Forwarded many times, an invitation to her adopted daughter's first birthday party arrives with no other message in it. This Gabe takes as "an invitation to be forgiven" for his nearly catastrophic interference in their lives. Gabe, however, feels unable to accept forgiveness—not yet, anyway. He is not "off the hook," he says, and does not want to be let off it, not until he can make some sense of the "larger hook" he feels he is still on.

Portnoy's Complaint • The larger hook on which Roth's later protagonists wriggle is precisely the dilemma between commitment and freedom that they all experience. Thus, the protagonist of *Portnoy's Complaint*, Alexander Portnoy, finds himself torn between his desire to maintain his position as New York's Assistant Commissioner for Human Opportunity, a job of considerable responsibility as well as prestige, and his desire to enjoy the full sexual freedoms heralded by the 1960's. For a while he seems to manage both, until his affair with Mary Jane Reed develops into something else— Mary Jane's wish to get married. Her sexual adroitness—she is called "the Monkey"—has kept them together for more than a year, but this demand for full commitment proves too much for Alex, who abandons her in Athens during a trip to Europe in which they have experienced the ultimate of their sexual adventures. Alex flees to Israel, the land of his forefathers, only to find that when he tries to make love there he is impotent. The experience drives him to seek help from Dr. Otto Spielvogel, a New York psychiatrist.

The novel, in fact, is told as a series of confessions, or therapy sessions, and derives its title from the name Dr. Spielvogel gives to his patient's illness. "Portnoy's Complaint" is "a disorder in which strongly felt ethical and altruistic impulses are perpetually warring with extreme sexual longings, often of a perverse nature." The symptoms of the illness, Spielvogel believes, can be traced to the mother-child relationship, and indeed Portnoy's boyhood has been fraught with problems, often hilarious ones as he recounts them, occasioned by his stereotypical Jewish mother. Sophie Portnoy is a domineering, overprotective mother who frequently drives her young son to distraction, as he tries in vain to understand her demands upon him and her suffocating affection. Jack Portnoy, his father, long-suffering (mostly from constipation) and hardworking, seems unable to mitigate the family relationship, exacerbating Alex's quandary. No wonder he grows up as he does, afflicted with the dilemma, or the condition, Dr. Spielvogel describes. By the end of the novel, after the long unfolding of his tales of woe, all Alex hears from his therapist is, "Now vee may perhaps to begin. Yes?"

In a sense, that *is* just the beginning. Roth tried hard to progress further in his next "family" novel, *My Life as a Man*, which took him years to write. Meanwhile, he wrote the pre-Watergate Nixon satire *Our Gang* and the satirical burlesque of American culture *The Great American Novel*, which takes the great American pastime, baseball, as its focus and its vehicle. However, it was the fictionalized account of his marriage—or rather, the affair that turned into marriage through a masterful trick—that really preoccupied Roth in the years following *Portnoy's Complaint.* Roth invents not one fictional surrogate but two: Peter Tarnopol, a writer, and Tarnopol's own fictional surrogate, Nathan Zuckerman. The two "useful fictions" that precede "My True Story," or the novel proper, are Roth's early experiments with "counterlives" developed at greater length and complexity in his finest novel, *The Counterlife.* They provide alternative, "possible" accounts of Peter Tarnopol's early life—and, through Tarnopol's, Roth's.

Peter's problem is trying to discover how he ever got involved with Maureen, his wife of ten years, from whom he is finally separated but who refuses to grant him a divorce. Related to this problem is the current one he experiences with his beautiful and dutiful lover, Susan Seabury McCall, a young widow who provides Peter with apparently everything he wants; however, she is essentially too submissive, too dull. One part of Tarnopol misses the excitement—no, the frenzy—that Maureen brought into his life, while another part hates it. Though it does not follow a strict chronological sequence, the novel becomes an account of his experience first with Maureen, then with Susan, whom he finally also leaves and determines to give up, despite her attempted suicide. Writing the novel in guarded solitude at an artist's colony called Quahsay, Tarnopol retrospectively tries to understand his plight.

The Breast • *The Breast* is another novel written during the period when Roth was trying to compose *My Life as a Man.* This book is the sequel to *The Professor of Desire,* written a few years later. Like Portnoy, Zuckerman, and Tarnopol, Kepesh is a nice Jewish young man brought up by caring parents in a sheltered Jewish environment, who early in life experiences the pleasures of emancipation and of the flesh, first as a Fulbright scholar living in London, then as a graduate student at Stanford University. Like Tarnopol, he becomes the victim of a femme fatale, a woman who, like Maureen, has "lived." Helen Baird is a striking beauty, but more than her beauty, her experience living abroad as the lover of a Hong Kong millionaire attracts Kepesh. They become lovers and later, disastrously, husband and wife. Gradually, Kepesh sinks into the condition of becoming Helen's servant, if not slave, until she flees once more to Hong Kong, hoping to reunite with her erstwhile lover. He will not have her, and David must rescue her, but in the process he becomes aware that their life together is over, and they get divorced.

David now moves back to New York, where he gets a job teaching comparative literature, meets Claire, a young schoolteacher, and falls in love with her. During this period he undergoes psychotherapy to "demythologize" his marriage to Helen; Dr. Klinger becomes Claire's advocate against David's brooding over Helen. During this period also, David's mother dies, and like Gabe Wallach in *Letting Go,* Kepesh has a widowed father on his hands. However, the elder Mr. Kepesh is by no means as demanding as Dr. Wallach; on the contrary, he is delighted with his son's liaison with Claire (as he was not with the marriage to Helen) and hopes that they will marry. The novel ends as the young couple along with the elder Mr. Kepesh and a friend of his, a concentration camp survivor, spend a weekend in a bungalow in the Catskills, not far from where David grew up, and where he now ponders his future. He seems to have everything he wants or needs, but somehow he feels dissatisfied, anxious, afraid that ennui will set in and destroy everything or that some other disaster will overtake them.

It does, but the disaster is hardly anything that David Allen Kepesh anticipates. About a year later, as his lovemaking with Claire has almost ceased, he turns into a six-foot, 155-pound breast. In *The Breast,* Roth partly follows Franz Kafka's "The Metamorphosis" (1915), an obvious, but not exact, source for this novella. Unlike Kafka, Roth tells the story from Kepesh's point of view, using the first-person narrator to convey something of the real anguish Kepesh feels and his amazement at his condition. If he was beset by a dilemma at the end of *The Professor of Desire*, his bafflement there is nothing to what he experiences now. Despite the aid and comfort that everyone—Claire, his father, Dr. Klinger—tries to give him, he remains at the end as bitterly confused and disturbed as ever, thoroughly unreconciled to his lot except as he vainly tries to persuade everyone that what has happened has not happened, that it is all a bad dream from which eventually he will awake, or that he has simply gone mad.

Zuckerman Bound trilogy • Roth's next novels form a trilogy to which he appends an epilogue, all under the title of *Zuckerman Bound*. Again, Roth borrows from autobiography to write his fiction, his own "counterlife." In *The Ghost Writer*, the first of the series that make up this portrait novel, Nathan Zuckerman is at the beginning of a promising career as a writer. He has published a few short stories and is now staying at an artist's colony (Quahsay again), trying to write more. Because he is not far from the home of E. I. Lonoff, a writer he much admires, he visits and is welcomed by the older writer and his wife. Zuckerman is surprised by them in many ways: first by Lonoff's austere life as a writer, spent endlessly turning his sentences around, and then by Hope Lonoff's conviction that her husband would be better off without her. By birth and upbringing far different from him—she is a New England Yankee as opposed to his immigrant origins—she is temperamentally unsuited to the kind of life they have led for many years. She is convinced, moreover, that Lonoff would be better off living with a younger woman, like Amy Bellette, a former student from the nearby women's college where Lonoff teaches, who obviously adores him. Lonoff refuses, however, to entertain any such thoughts of abandoning Hope or realizing his fantasy of living abroad in a villa in Italy with a younger woman.

Nathan is persuaded to stay the night, especially after meeting Amy Bellette, who is also staying there on a brief visit. Nathan has his own fantasy that evening, that Amy is really Anne Frank, author of the famous diary, who has miraculously survived death camps. They fall in love, get married, and thus show his parents and other relatives that, despite what they may think from some of his stories, he is a good Jewish man, the worthy husband of the famous Jewish heroine. As a tribute to Roth's skill as a writer, the account of Amy's survival is quite credible; moreover, it shows Roth's understanding of compassion for the suffering in the death camps. At the same time, it supports Nathan Zuckerman's qualifications as a writer, justifying Lonoff's praise and encouragement of the young man.

Lonoff's belief in Nathan is borne out in *Zuckerman Unbound*, the second novel in the trilogy. By now Zuckerman is the author of several novels, including the notorious *Carnovsky*. This novel is to Zuckerman what *Portnoy's Complaint* was to Philip Roth, and *Zuckerman Bound* recounts experiences similar to those Roth must have had, such as the notoriety that involved mistaking his fictional characters for his real mother and father. Zuckerman is accosted in the streets, on the telephone, and apparently everywhere he goes by people who think they know him because they mistake his confessional novel for actual autobiography. However, fiction and autobiography are at best distant relatives; for example, unlike Zuckerman's father, who is extremely upset by his son's novel and turns on him at his death, Roth's parents remained proud of their son's accomplishments and never took offense at what he wrote, notwithstanding the uproar in the Jewish community.

Zuckerman is beset by would-be hangers-on, such as Alvin Pepler, the Jewish marine, once a quiz-show winner but deprived of full fame by a scam reminiscent of the Charles Van Doren scandal. Zuckerman's brief affair (actually, no more than a one-night stand) with the Irish actor Caesara O'Shea is a comic treatment of the adventures attributed to Roth by columnists such as Leonard Lyons, who insisted he was romantically involved with Barbra Streisand, though actually Roth at that time had not so much as met her. Finally, Zuckerman's trip to Miami with his brother, Henry, which ends with their estrangement on the way home after their father dies of a stroke, is totally different from actual events in Roth's life. All these incidents are, after all, "counterlives," imaginative renderings of what might have or could have happened, not what did.

Similarly, in *The Anatomy Lesson*, the third novel in the series, Roth borrows from incidents in his own life but fictionalizes them so that no one-to-one equivalence can be made. Now, some years later, Zuckerman is afflicted with a strange ailment that causes him intense pain, from which he gets temporary relief only from vodka or Percodan. He can no longer write, but four different women tend to his other needs, including his sexual ones. Among them are a young Finch College student, who also works as his secretary; his financial adviser's wife; an artist in Vermont who occasionally descends from her mountaintop to visit; and a Polish émigré, whom Zuckerman meets at a trichological clinic (in addition to everything else, Zuckerman is losing his hair).

In despair of his life and his calling, Zuckerman decides to give up writing and become a doctor. He flies to Chicago, where he hopes his old friend and classmate, Bobby Freytag, will help him get admitted to medical school. En route on the plane and later from the airport, Zuckerman impersonates Milton Appel, a literary critic modeled on Irving Howe, who early praised Roth's work and then turned against it. In this impersonation, however, Zuckerman pretends that Appel is a pornography king, editor and publisher of *Lickety Split* and an impresario of houses of pleasure. The impersonation is triggered by Appel's appeal, delivered through an intermediary, to Zuckerman to write an op ed article on behalf of Israel.

Zuckerman as the porn king Appel provides plenty of material for those who like to see Roth as antifeminist but who thereby miss the point of his fiction. It is a tour de force, a persona adopting a persona—miles away from the real Roth. At his office in the hospital, Bobby Freytag reminisces with Zuckerman for a bit and then tries to talk him out of his scheme. Only the next day when, under the influence of too much Percodan and vodka, Zuckerman falls and fractures his jaw, does the healing begin, in soul as well as body. Zuckerman learns what real pain and loss are, as he walks the corridors of the hospital watched over by his friend, who also weans him from his drug addiction. At the end, Zuckerman is a chastened and more altruistic individual, though still deluded into thinking he could change into a radically different person.

Zuckerman Bound's epilogue, *The Prague Orgy*, shows Zuckerman not as a doctor but as a famous novelist undertaking an altruistic mission on behalf of an émigré Czech writer whose father had written some excellent, unpublished stories in Yiddish. Unfortunately, the Czech's estranged wife holds the stories but will not release them. Zuckerman manages to fetch them without having to sleep with her, despite her pleas, but the stories are immediately confiscated by the police, who then escort him out of the country (this is pre-1989 Czechoslovakia). Zuckerman thus learns to accept his limitations and to become reconciled to them. He accepts that he will not become "transformed into a cultural eminence elevated by the literary deeds he performs."

The Counterlife • In *The Counterlife*, Nathan and his brother are briefly reunited, mainly so that Roth can explore alternative versions of a fate that first befalls one and then the other. The plot thus doubles back on itself more than once and is too complex for summary treatment. Despite its complexity, the novel is not difficult to follow and is full of surprises that intellectually stimulate as they also amuse the reader. Particularly interesting are the episodes in Israel, where Henry has fled to start a new life, bringing Nathan after him to discover what is going on. Much is going on, including a considerable amount of discussion from characters on the political left and right, with Nathan clearly in the middle. The latter part of the novel finds Nathan in London, married to an English divorcée with a child and trying to come to grips with British anti-Semitism, including some in his wife's family. Throughout the novel, Roth implicitly and sometimes explicitly raises questions about the nature of fiction and the characters that inhabit it.

Roth does so, too, in *Deception*, though in that novel, written almost entirely in dialogue, the experiment takes on a different form. Here, Roth drops his surrogate, Nathan Zuckerman; his main character, present in all the dialogue, is called Philip, who also happens to be a novelist who has written about a character named Zuckerman. Thus Roth seems here to speak in his own voice, though of course he does not, quite: He merely makes the partition separating him from his characters that much thinner, almost to the point of transparency, as when he takes on the critics who claim that when he writes fiction, he does autobiography, and vice versa. The novel is filled with discussions between "Philip" and his lover, who proves to be the woman Nathan married in *The Counterlife*; thus, much of the talk is naturally about fiction.

Sabbath's Theater • Roth turned away briefly from his various author personas to write the wickedly funny *Sabbath's Theater*, a novel about an aging pornographic puppeteer obsessed with death and socially proscribed forms of sex. Mickey Sabbath's perverse confessions and the absurd situations Sabbath creates for himself may remind some of Roth's early novel *Portnoy's Complaint*. However, whereas Alexander Portnoy was tortured by his conflicting desires to be a model American and to satisfy his sexual longings, there is no such conflict in Sabbath. He revels in his capacity to break bourgeois mores, becoming a cause célèbre for First Amendment defenders during the 1950's, when running his randy street theater resulted in his arrest. Since that time, he has lived in a small New England town teaching college drama, until he is forced to resign for sexually harassing female students. Now he is locked in an acrimonious marriage with his wife Roseanna, a recovering alcoholic, and mourning the death of his sexually adventurous mistress, Drenka. If *Portnoy's Complaint* revolved around Portnoy's confessions, *Sabbath's Theater* revolves around Sabbath's unapologetic reveling in nastiness. Through Sabbath's repellent diatribes against the Japanese, women, and self-help groups, Roth draws a figure for whom readers will find little sympathy. Because Sabbath himself seems so thoroughly jaded, many critics have decried the novel's sentimental turn toward Sabbath's past, into the death of his much admired brother in World War II and the resulting demise of his mother, to contextualize Sabbath's bitterness.

American Pastoral • Roth portrays another bitter and obsessed character in *American Pastoral*, but in this novel the stakes are higher and the perspective a degree removed. Merry Levov is the stuttering teenage daughter of a beauty queen and a successful assimilated American Jew. She grows up in a prosperous New Jersey suburb in a loving home, the center of her father Swede's ideal, his "American pastoral." Then life changes. Merry's protests against the Vietnam War turn into ever more violent, clichéd complaints against American imperialism, capitalism, bourgeois complacency, and, finally, her family's own success story. She bombs the town's post office, killing a well-loved doctor and challenging her father's understanding of his life and his country. The story is told through her father's tortured pursuit of both his daughter and the reasons for her rage. Roth deftly weaves social criticism into this compelling story for an insightful depiction of an entire generation blindsided by the great upheavals of the 1960's. Zuckerman reappears to interpret Swede Levov's story as an epic clash between the American innocent pursuing upward mobility and the return of the repressed violence inherent in that American Dream. Merry Levov, Zuckerman says, "transports him out of the longed-for American pastoral and into everything that is its antithesis and its enemy, into the fury, the violence, and the desperation of the counterpastoral—into the indigenous American berserk."

I Married a Communist • Just as ambitious as *American Pastoral*, Roth's next book, *I Married a Communist*, takes the 1950's as its historical backdrop. Nathan Zuckerman again acts partly as interpreter and partly as scribe, this time to his former high school teacher, Murray Ringold. Murray tells the story of his brother Ira, a radio actor who was blacklisted during the era of McCarthyism. Ira becomes a populist hero to many, including young Nathan, until his actor wife, exasperated by Ira's repeated betrayals with other women, exposes him by publishing a tell-all book, *I Married a Communist*. The book destroys not only Ira's heroic profile but also his career, for he becomes blacklisted. The plot once again alludes to events in Roth's own life, particularly to his divorce from Claire Bloom. Like the character Eve Frame, Bloom had a talented teenage daughter who caused friction in the marriage. Also like Eve Frame, Bloom published a memoir in which she, like Roth in several of his novels, exposed intimate details of their personal life. Ira's unthinking acceptance of the Communist Party and his subsequent devolution into an angry, bitter cynic give this political novel a decidedly conservative overtone.

Surveying the corpus of Roth's longer fiction, one may conclude that he is a novelist who rarely repeats himself, even as he reworks ideas, issues, and dilemmas or reintroduces characters and locales. This is the essence of the "counterlife" motif that was present in Roth's work from the start but became explicit only later on.

The Human Stain • Apparently inspired by the life and career of Anatole Broyard, the late, well-known literary critic of *The New York Times*, *The Human Stain* is the story of Coleman Silk, a Newark-born African American whose fair complexion allows him in his adult life to pass as a white man. Determined not to be held back by his black heritage, Coleman renounces his family after the disastrous occasion when he brings his blond sweetheart to meet his mother and she decides to break off their relationship. They had met at college in New York, where he is studying classics after serving in the Navy during World War II. Silk later marries Iris Gittelman, the daughter of atheistic Russian American Jews, and declares himself to be a secular Jew as well. Neither Iris nor any of their children ever learn the secret that Coleman harbors for the rest of his life.

While Silk manages to keep his secret from everyone else, Roth reveals it to the reader by chapter 2 as a means of developing some of the many ironies that pervade the novel. The most significant irony occurs when Silk is accused of bigotry: One day while lecturing, he quite innocently asks his class about the identity of two students who have never shown up, wondering if they are real or "spooks." He does not know that the two students in question are black, and they accuse him of racism for using a derogatory term. Enraged by the accusation and even more by his colleagues' refusal to support him against the charge, he resigns in high dudgeon. He is especially offended when one of his colleagues, himself an African American—the first one ever to be hired at Athena College and by none other than Coleman Silk when he became dean—refuses to stand by him. The turmoil that the controversy occasions becomes too much for Iris Silk, who soon dies of a heart attack, which Coleman blames on the college.

Two years later, Coleman Silk visits the writer Nathan Zuckerman, who lives and works nearby. They scarcely know each other but become close friends when Coleman asks Nathan to write the book about the affair that he has been unable to write himself. In the months that follow, they spend a good deal of time together, until Silk begins his affair with Faunia Farley, a thirty-four-year-old woman who works as a janitor at the college and pretends to be ignorant and illiterate. She is divorced from Les Farley, a half-crazed Vietnam veteran who haunts her and blames her for the death of their two small children when their house caught fire.

The passionate affair in which Coleman and Faunia engage is based firmly but not exclusively on sex, and it affronts not only Les Farley but the college community as well. It especially infuriates Delphine Roux, the young Frenchwoman and Yale Ph.D. who was Coleman's department chair at the time of his resignation. An ardent feminist and an ambitious academic, Delphine nevertheless is lonely and wants a man. When she tries to write an ad for the personals in *The New York Review of Books*, she has problems with both her biography and the description of the kind of man she wants. She realizes only too late—after she accidentally hits the "send" key instead of the "delete" key on her computer—that the man whom she has been describing closely resembles none other than Coleman Silk, and that the message she has been composing has gone out to her entire department and eventually to the entire community.

In this manner, Roth manages to inject some farce into what is otherwise a very serious novel that attacks the kinds of political correctness that had taken over college campuses and much else in American life in the 1990's, when many Americans seemed to be obsessed with the scandal caused by Monica Lewinsky's affair with President Clinton. The "stain" in the title may, in fact, allude to the notorious stain on Lewinsky's blue dress, although it has deeper significance—alluding for example, among other possible interpretations, to the stain of racism that marks human nature.

Only after Silk is killed together with Faunia, deliberately driven off the road by Les Farley in his pickup truck, does Nathan learn the secret that his friend has so carefully guarded all those years. Only then, too, is he able to begin writing the book that Coleman had earlier asked him to write. In the process, he portrays both the racial intolerance that led Coleman Silk to pass as a white man and the pious hypocrisies that culminated in President Clinton's impeachment. Throughout the novel, which brings to a fitting conclusion Roth's "American Trilogy" of *American Pastoral, I Married a Communist*, and *The Human Stain*, Roth offers a portrait of post-World War II life, with a startling mixture of successes and failures that encourages readers to examine closely who and what the United States truly has become.

The Plot Against America • In the 1940 of Philip Roth's reimagined history in this 2004 novel, many Americans are so afraid that President Franklin D. Roosevelt is leading the country into the war in Europe that the Republican Party nominates not Wendell Wilkie but Charles A. Lindbergh, the hero who was the first to fly across the Atlantic Ocean solo. To the great consternation of American Jews, Lindbergh wins the election. Jews are concerned because Lindbergh not only has admired the German *Luftwaffe* but also has accepted a medal from Adolf Hitler himself, a clear sign of his pro-German sympathies.

As nine-year-old Philip Roth narrates events, the Roth family—including Philip's father and mother and his older brother, Sandy—and their friends in the Jewish section of Newark, New Jersey, are terribly upset by this turn of events and fear the worst. They suspect that the kinds of anti-Semitism that Hitler has propounded and is rapidly carrying out in Germany and in the parts of Europe that he has conquered will, under Lindbergh's administration, begin to happen in the United States. The first experience that they have of this intolerance comes during a trip to Washington, D.C., where they are expelled from their hotel despite their confirmed reservations. This outrage is followed by a scene in a cafeteria where the family experiences anti-Semitic slurs. Worse events are still to follow.

Not all Jews believe as Herman Roth believes. A rabbi, Lionel Bengelsdorf, supports the new administration and soon becomes head of the Office of American Absorption. This new office is established to promote Lindbergh's plan to disperse Jews from enclaves, such as the one in which the Roths live in Newark, to other parts of the country, thereby promoting their assimilation into the American mainstream. After years of working for an insurance company, Herman Roth is reassigned to Louisville under this plan, but rather than accept the assignment, he resigns and goes to work instead for his brother's produce business. Sandy Roth, meanwhile, is enticed into a program called "Just Folks," another attempt to foster Jewish assimilation, and spends the summer on a farm in Kentucky with a typical "American" family. He comes back with a southern accent and views quite opposed to those of his father. A neighbor's family, the Wishnows, is forced to accept the reassignment and goes to Danville, Kentucky, a town near Louisville. Later, Mrs. Wishnow is killed in a violent attack against Jews as she tries to drive home one night.

Roth brings in many historical characters: Father Coughlin, the extremist Catholic priest who fulminates against Jews; Walter Winchell, the Jewish newspaper reporter whose Sunday night radio broadcasts the Roth family and their friends dutifully listen to each week, and who at one point runs for president against Lindbergh, only to be assassinated for his efforts; the German foreign minister Joachim von Ribbentrop, who is honored by a state dinner at the White House by President and Mrs. Lindbergh; Fiorello La Guardia, the mayor of New York City, who is an eloquent spokesperson and a champion of civil rights; and many others. The picture of the United States under the Lindbergh administration is a very grim, even terrifying one. Although Roth insists he intended no allusion to politics in the twenty-first century, his novel clearly posts a warning for what might happen should American civil liberties suffer increased depredations, using the Iraq War as a pretext or an excuse.

Roth even brings into *The Plot Against America* the notorious kidnapping case of the 1930's, in which the Lindberghs' infant son was stolen. In this imagined reconstruction of events, the baby is not killed (as he was in actual fact) but taken by the Nazis and brought up in Germany as a good member of the *Hitler Jugend*. Events at the end of the novel culminate with the disappearance of Lindbergh himself and subsequent anti-Jewish riots in many cities across the United States in which 122 Jews lose their lives. Lindbergh, however, has not been kidnapped but has fled to Germany, using the *Spirit of St. Louis* for his escape, and is never seen again. Eventually, law and order are restored (thanks in part to the efforts of Mrs. Lindbergh), the Democrats take over Congress, and Roosevelt wins his unprecedented third term as president.

Jay L. Halio
Updated by Julie Husband

Other major works

SHORT FICTION: *Goodbye, Columbus, and Five Short Stories,* 1959; "Novotny's Pain," 1962, revised 1980; "The Psychoanalytic Special," 1963; "On the Air," 1970; "'I Always Wanted You to Admire My Fasting': Or, Looking at Kafka," 1973.

NONFICTION: *Reading Myself and Others,* 1975, expanded 1985; *The Facts: A Novelist's Autobiography,* 1988; *Patrimony: A True Story,* 1991; *Shop Talk: A Writer and His Colleagues and Their Work,* 2001.

Bibliography

Baumgarten, Murray, and Barbara Gottfried. *Understanding Philip Roth.* Columbia: University of South Carolina Press, 1990. Interpretation and discussion of Roth's fiction. Includes a bibliography and an index.

Cooper, Alan. *Philip Roth and the Jews.* Albany: State University of New York Press, 1996. A carefully researched examination and consideration of Roth's work, his biography, and Roth's political views that are evident in his writing.

Halio, Jay L. *Philip Roth Revisited.* New York: Twayne, 1992. Discusses the critical response to Roth's fiction. Includes a bibliography and an index.

Halio, Jay L., and Ben Siegel, eds. *"Turning Up the Flame": Philip Roth's Later Novels.* Newark: University of Delaware Press, 2004. Collection of critical essays focusing on novels that Roth wrote after 1992.

Milbauer, Asher Z., and Donald G. Watson, eds. *Reading Philip Roth.* New York: St. Martin's Press, 1988. This collection of essays is consistently insightful, examining Roth as a social critic and an exemplar of Jewish alienation. Also compares him to some prominent American novelists, as well as to Franz Kafka.

Milowitz, Steven. *Philip Roth Considered: The Concentrationary Universe of the American Writer.* New York: Taylor & Francis, 2000. Explores Roth's writings on the "concentrationary" world of the "camps" of the Holocaust, how this world keeps revealing itself through memories and other reminders, and how the "shadowy presence" of the Holocaust refuses forgetting.

Omer-Sherman, Ranen. *Diaspora and Zionism in Jewish American Literature: Lazarus, Syrkin, Reznikoff, and Roth.* Hanover, N.H.: University Press of New England, 2002. A discussion of how these writers have addressed the issue of Jewish nationalism and the fate of the Jewish diaspora.

Rand, Naomi R. *Silko, Morrison, and Roth: Studies in Survival.* New York: Peter Lang, 1999. A study of how Leslie Marmon Silko, Toni Morrison, and Roth each use a "survival narrative motif" as a way of defining their ethnic stance.

Roth, Philip. *Conversations with Philip Roth.* Edited by George J. Searles. Jackson: University Press of Mississippi, 1992. Roth talks about his life and the influences on his fiction. Includes a bibliography and an index.

Shechner, Mark. *"Up Society's Ass, Copper": Rereading Philip Roth.* Madison: University of Wisconsin Press, 2003. Lively collection of essays, reviews, and other brief pieces that Shechner wrote over a period of three decades.

Shostak, Debra. *Philip Roth: Countertexts, Counterlives.* Columbia: University of South Carolina Press, 2004. Fascinating attempt to examine recurrent self-revelatory themes in Roth's novels. Draws extensively on Roth's unpublished papers.

Wade, Stephen. *The Imagination in Transit: The Fiction of Philip Roth.* Sheffield: Sheffield Academic Press, 1996. Wade details Roth's growth as a novelist through a study of his fiction, relates the connection of Roth's work to American Jewish literary style, and lists influences on Roth's work.

J. D. Salinger

Born: New York, New York; January 1, 1919

Principal long fiction • *The Catcher in the Rye*, 1951.

Other literary forms • Little, Brown and Company has published three collections of J. D. Salinger's short fiction: *Nine Stories* (1953), *Franny and Zooey* (1961), and *Raise High the Roof Beam, Carpenters, and Seymour: An Introduction* (1963). An unauthorized paperback collection of his stories in two volumes, apparently published by an unidentified source in Berkeley, California, *The Complete Uncollected Short Stories of J. D. Salinger*, was issued in 1974. It provoked Salinger's first public statement in some years, denouncing the collection, which was suppressed by the copyright holders. There has been one film adaptation of his work, produced by Samuel Goldwyn and adapted by Julius J. and Phillip G. Epstein from Salinger's "Uncle Wiggily in Connecticut," renamed *My Foolish Heart* (1950) and starring Susan Hayward and Dana Andrews. Salinger was so upset by the screen version that he banned all further adaptations of his work into any other medium.

Achievements • In the post-World War II years, Salinger was unanimously acclaimed by both literate American youth and the critical establishment. His only novel has sold steadily since its publication, and it not only still generates high sales but also generates intense discussion as to its appropriateness for classroom use. Although he is not a prolific writer, Salinger's popularity in terms of both sales and critical articles and books written about him has continued unabated since the early 1950's.

The Catcher in the Rye is one of the most widely read and influential postwar novels, and it entered the culture as a statement of youth's view of the complex world. The novel has been translated into German, Italian, Japanese, Norwegian, Swedish, French, Dutch, Danish, Hebrew, Czechoslovakian, Yugoslavian, and Russian, and has been highly successful. In Russia, possession of a copy of *The Catcher in the Rye* became something of a status symbol for young intellectuals. Although there have been problems in translating the particularly American idiom into foreign languages, the story touches a nerve that cuts across cultural and global lines. The novel has also been favorably compared to Mark Twain's *Adventures of Huckleberry Finn* (1884) in terms of its portrayal of the "phoniness" of society, the coming of age of a young man, and its use of colloquial language.

Salinger's reputation, paradoxically, has been aided by his refusal to give interviews or to be seen in public. Critics and magazine writers have pursued him relentlessly, trying to discover his thoughts, concerns, and approaches to literature and writing.

Biography • Jerome David Salinger was born in New York, New York, on January 1, 1919, the second child and only son of Sol and Miriam (Jillich) Salinger, although details on Salinger and his parents' life is clouded. Salinger's father was born in Cleveland, Ohio, and has been noted as being the son of a rabbi, but he drifted far enough away from orthodox Judaism to become a successful importer of hams and to marry a

Gentile, the Scotch Irish Marie Jillich, who changed her name soon after to Miriam to fit in better with her husband's family. During J. D.'s early years the Salingers moved several times, to increasingly affluent neighborhoods.

Salinger attended schools on Manhattan's upper West Side, doing satisfactory work in all subjects except arithmetic. He probably spent most of his summers in New England camps like most sons of upper-middle-class New York families; he was voted the "most popular actor" in the summer of 1930 at Camp Wigwam in Harrison, Maine. When he reached high school age, he was placed in Manhattan's famed McBurney School, a private institution, where he was manager of the fencing team, a reporter on the *McBurnean*, and an actor in two plays; however, he flunked out after one year. In September of 1934, his father enrolled him at Valley Forge Military Academy in Pennsylvania.

During his two years at Valley Forge, Salinger did satisfactory, but undistinguished, work. He belonged to the Glee Club, the Aviation Club, the French Club, the Non-Commissioned Officers' Club, and the Mask and Spur, a dramatic organization. He also served as literary editor of the yearbook, *Crossed Sabres*, during his senior year. He is credited with writing a three-stanza poetic tribute to the academy that has since been set to music and is sung by the cadets at their last formation before graduation. Although not yet the recluse that he would later become, Salinger began to write short stories at that time, usually working by flashlight under his blankets after "lights out." Astonishingly, he also appeared interested in a career in the motion-picture business, as either a producer or a supplier of story material. He graduated in June of 1936.

It is unclear what Salinger did after graduation, but he enrolled at least for the summer session of 1937 at Washington Square College in New York. Salinger, in one of his rare interviews, mentioned that he spent some time in Vienna, Austria, and Poland learning German and the details of the ham importing business; it is not clear if his father accompanied him or not, but his trip probably occurred before Adolf Hitler's Anschluss, possibly in the fall of 1937.

On his return, Salinger enrolled at Ursinus College, a coeducational institution sponsored by the Evangelical and Reformed Church at Collegeville, Pennsylvania, not far from Valley Forge. Although he remained only one semester, he wrote a humorous and critical column, "The Skipped Diploma," for the *Ursinus Weekly*. He returned to New York and enrolled in Whit Burnett's famous course in short-story writing at Columbia University. It has been noted that Burnett was not at first impressed with the quiet boy who made no comments in class and seemed more interested in playwriting. However, Salinger's first story, "The Young Folks," was impressive enough to be published in the March, 1940, issue of *Story*, edited by Burnett.

After publishing in a magazine famous for discovering new talent, Salinger spent another year writing without success until, at the age of twenty-two, he broke into the well-paying mass circulation magazines with a "short, short story" in *Collier's* and a "satire" in *Esquire*; he even had a story accepted by *The New Yorker*, which delayed publication of "Slight Rebellion off Madison," until after the war. This story proved to be one of the forerunners to *The Catcher in the Rye*.

During 1941, he worked as an entertainer on the Swedish liner MS *Kungsholm*. Upon his return to the United States, he wrote to the military adjunct at Valley Forge, Colonel Milton G. Baker, to see if there was some way that he could get into the service, even though he had been classified as 1-B because of a slight cardiac condition. After Selective Service standards were lowered in 1942, Salinger was inducted and at-

National Archives

tended the Officers, First Sergeants, and Instructors School of the Signal Corps. He also reportedly corrected papers in a ground school for aviation cadets. He applied for Officers' Candidate School but was transferred to the Air Service Command in Dayton, Ohio, and wrote publicity releases. Finally, at the end of 1943, he was transferred to the Counter-Intelligence Corps. He also conducted a long correspondence with Eugene O'Neill's daughter Oona, who married actor Charles Chaplin.

Salinger continued to write whenever he found the opportunity, publishing again in *Collier's*, *Story*, and at last in the well-paying and highly celebrated *Saturday Evening Post*. One of the *Saturday Evening Post* stories marks the first mention of the character Holden Caulfield. Salinger also sent Whit Burnett two hundred dollars from his earnings from the "slicks" to be used to encourage young writers and be applied to future writing contests for college undergraduates, such

as the one won by Norman Mailer in 1941.

After training in Tiverton, Devonshire, he joined the American Fourth Division and landed on Utah Beach five hours after the initial assault wave on D-Day. He served with the Division through five European campaigns as a special agent responsible for security of the Twelfth Infantry Regiment. There is an unsupported story that Salinger had an audience with author and war correspondent Ernest Hemingway, who shot off the head of a chicken either to impress Salinger or to demonstrate the effectiveness of a German Luger. This incident has been used to explain why Salinger has written about Hemingway in a bad light in his stories and has Holden Caulfield in *The Catcher in the Rye* detest Hemingway's *A Farewell to Arms* (1929). There are also reports that during the war Salinger married a French woman, Sylvia, who was a doctor, possibly a psychiatrist. The two returned together to the United States after the war, according to biographer Ian Hamilton, but the marriage, which took place in September, 1945, lasted only eight months.

After the war, Salinger decided to make a living by selling stories to the so-called "slicks," publishing again in the *Saturday Evening Post* and *Collier's*, which issued "I'm Crazy" in its Christmas issue. "I'm Crazy" featured the long-delayed debut of Holden Caulfield, who had been mentioned as missing in action in several of Salinger's wartime stories. *Mademoiselle*, *Good Housekeeping*, and *Cosmopolitan* also published Salinger's work. *Cosmopolitan* featured a short novelette, "The Inverted Forest," an involved, obscure allegory of an artist, his possible muses, and his fate. During part of this period, Salinger lived with his parents but also kept a Greenwich Village apartment to entertain various young women. He also, supposedly, began to develop an interest in Zen Buddhism that is illustrated in his stories following publication of *The Catcher in the Rye*, especially the Glass family saga, but there is no suggestion that he actually converted to Buddhism.

After the disastrous film version of "Uncle Wiggily in Connecticut" and stories in *Harper's* and *World Review*, Salinger settled down with a contract to produce stories solely for *The New Yorker* and thereafter published exclusively for that magazine. At that time, Salinger was also his most public: He lived in Tarrytown, New York, and even visited a short-story class at Sarah Lawrence College. Although he seemed to enjoy the conversation and interaction, he never repeated it. It was during that period that he decided to avoid all public appearances and concentrate his efforts on writing.

The Catcher in the Rye finally made its appearance on July 16, 1951, although years earlier Salinger submitted, had accepted, and then withdrew a much shorter version. It was not the immediate hit that time suggests, but it did gain Salinger enormous critical praise and respect. The novel was successful enough to cause Salinger to have his picture removed from the dust jacket of the third edition and all subsequent editions; annoyed by the letters, autograph seekers, and interviewers that sought him, he apparently sailed to Europe to keep his composure and avoid publicity.

In 1952 Salinger settled in Cornish, New Hampshire, a small town across the Connecticut River from Windsor, Vermont. His first house in Cornish was a small saltbox on ninety acres with no furnace, no electricity, and no running water. In 1953, Salinger met his future wife, Claire Douglas, in Manchester, Vermont. The daughter of a well-known British art critic, she was then a nineteen-year-old Radcliffe student. During his first two years in Cornish, Salinger fraternized with high school students in the area, attended their basketball games, and entertained them in his home. In November of 1953 he granted Shirley Blaney an interview for the high school page of the Claremont, New Hampshire, *Daily Eagle*. He became upset when the interview was printed prominently on the editorial page of the paper instead. Thereafter he ceased entertaining area students and built a fence around his home.

In January, 1955, he returned to print in *The New Yorker* with the publication of "Franny," the first of the Glass Family series that occupied all of his forthcoming stories. He supposedly dedicated it to his new bride, whom he married in Barnard, Vermont, on February 17, 1955. On December 10 of that year, the Salingers became the parents of their first child, Margaret Ann; on February 13, 1960, his only son, Matthew, was born. Afterward, Salinger concentrated his efforts on rearing his family and documenting the Glass family. Little was heard or read from Salinger after the 1965 publication of "Hapworth 16, 1924" in *The New Yorker.* He was divorced from his wife in November, 1967.

The reclusive Salinger, dubbed "the Greta Garbo of American letters" by *People Weekly* in reference to another famous but hermitic figure, was thrust into the media limelight in the mid-1980's because of disputes over the content of a biography being published by Ian Hamilton. Thwarted in his quest for an interview with Salinger, Hamilton had nevertheless found two valuable, and hitherto untapped, research sources: collections of Salinger letters in Princeton University's Firestone Library and the library of the University of Texas. Galleys of Hamilton's book were slipped to Salinger by a book dealer in 1986, and Salinger immediately protested the use of his unpublished letters. Attempts at compromise failed, and Salinger filed suit against Hamilton and his publisher, Random House. Eventually, a U.S. Court of Appeals ruling decreed that the letters were indeed Salinger's property and could not be quoted, or even paraphrased, without his permission. The Supreme Court declined to hear an appeal, and Salinger returned to his seclusion. Hamilton's book *In Search of J. D. Salinger,* minus the content of the letters but filled out with a detailed account of the controversy, was finally published in 1988.

Salinger has continued to be reclusive, refusing all requests for interviews and ignoring correspondence. Against his will, however, his daughter, Margaret Salinger, went public with their family life with *Dream Catcher: A Memoir* in 2000. Salinger also continues to refuse commentary on his published work, saying, "The stuff's all there in the stories; there's no use talking about it."

Analysis • Salinger's characters are always extremely sensitive young people who are trapped between two dimensions of the world: love and "squalor." The central problem in most of his fiction is not finding a bridge between these two worlds but bringing some sort of indiscriminate love into the world of squalor: to find a haven where love can triumph and flourish. Some characters, such as the young, mixed-up Holden Caulfield, adopt indiscriminate love to aid them in their journey through the world of squalor, while others, such as Seymour Glass, achieve a sort of perfect love, or satori, and are destroyed, in Seymour's case by a bullet through his head. Each of these characters is metropolitan in outlook and situation and is introverted: Their battles are private wars of spirit, not outward conflicts with society. The characters' minds struggle to make sense of the dichotomy between love and squalor, often reaching a quiet peace and transcending their situation through a small act.

Frederick L. Gwynn and Joseph L. Blotner, in *The Fiction of J. D. Salinger* (1958), offer an analysis of Salinger that claims he is the first writer in Western fiction to present transcendental mysticism in a satiric mode, or simply to present religious ideas satirically. Although much has been made of Salinger's Zen Buddhism, the stories do not seem to be about applying Buddhist principles to modern life, nor do they present a clear and coherent statement of what these principles entail or signify. Holden Caulfield does not react as a Buddhist would, nor does he seek consolation from Buddhism. The Glass family may mention Buddhism, but because of their acquaintance with all religions and their high intelligence and hyperkinetic thirst for knowledge, Salinger suggests that they have picked and chosen aspects from various religions and created a composite of them all. If anything, Salinger's characters seem to move toward a "perfect" Christian ideology—indiscriminate love.

The normality of the characters in Salinger's stories is a primary attraction for readers. Holden Caulfield is no better or no worse than any young high school boy; he is merely a bit more articulate and honest in his appraisals, more open with his feelings. Even though the Glasses are brilliant, they are not cerebral or distanced from the reader because of their brilliance; and all the characters live in the same world and environment as the readers do. Their moments of pain and delight are the same as the readers', but Salinger's characters articulate these moments more naturally and completely.

Another element that draws readers into Salinger's world is his use of satire. The satire not only touches upon the characters' descriptions and reactions to the world but also touches on the characters themselves. Holden Caulfield's confrontation with Maurice, the brawny Edmont Hotel elevator operator/pimp, shows not only the ridiculousness of the antagonist but also Holden's stupidity for attempting to reason with him. Even if he does not realize it, Holden does many of the things that he tells readers he hates. He is critical enough, however, to realize that these things are wrong.

All of Salinger's work has also a strong focus on the family; it is held as an ideal, a refuge, and a raft of love amid a sea of squalor. Although the family does not provide the haven that Salinger suggests it might, it is through coming home that the characters flourish, not by running away. Holden Caulfield, in *The Catcher in the Rye*, never realistically considers running away, for he realizes that flight cannot help him. At the critical moment his family may not be ready to grant him the salvation that he needs, but it is his only security. If the world is a place of squalor, perhaps it is only through perfect love within the family unit that an individual can find some kind of salvation. It is important to notice that the family unit is never satirized in Salinger's fiction.

The Catcher in the Rye • The basic story of *The Catcher in the Rye* follows the adventures of sixteen-year-old Holden Caulfield, an independent, self-indulgent, idealistic, and sentimental figure of adolescent rebellion, during a forty-eight-hour period after he has been expelled from Pencey Prep, the latest of three expulsions for Holden. After confrontations with some fellow students at Pencey, Holden goes to New York City, his hometown, to rest before facing his parents. During the trip he tries to renew some old acquaintances, attempts to woo three out-of-towners, hires a prostitute named Sunny, and copes with recurring headaches. Eventually, after two meetings with his younger sister, Phoebe, he returns home. At the beginning of the novel he has told us that he is in California recovering from an illness and that he is reconciled with his family. The entire story of Holden's exploits comes to us through a first-person narration, one that contains youthful phrasing and profanity and has many digressions, but one that has a mesmerizing flow to it.

Holden Caulfield is a confused sixteen-year-old, no better and no worse than his peers, except that he is slightly introverted, a little sensitive, and willing to express his feelings openly. His story can be seen as a typical growing process. As he approaches and is ready to cross the threshold into adulthood, he begins to get nervous and worried. His body has grown, but his emotional state has not. He is gawky, clumsy, and not totally in control of his body. He seeks to find some consolation, some help during this difficult time but finds no one. The school cannot help him, his peers seem oblivious to his plight, his parents are too concerned with other problems (his mother's nerves and his father's business activities as a corporate lawyer). His girlfriend, Sally Hayes, who has a penchant for using the word "grand" and whom Holden calls the "queen of the phonies," is no help, and his favorite teacher, Mr. Antolini, merely lectures him drunkenly. The only people with whom he can communicate are the two young boys at the museum, the girl with the skates at the park, and his younger sister Phoebe: All of them are children, who cannot help him in his growing pains but remind him of a simpler time, one to which he wishes he could return. Eventually, he does cross the threshold (his fainting in the museum) and realizes that his worries were unfounded. He has survived. At the end of the book, Holden seems ready to reintegrate himself into society and accept the responsibilities of adulthood.

Through Holden's picaresque journeys through New York City, he grows spiritually. He slowly begins to recognize the "phoniness" around him and the squalor that constantly presses down on him. Although he castigates himself for doing some of the phony things, lying especially, Holden does realize that what he is doing is incorrect: This understanding sets him above his fellows; he knows what he is doing.

Holden never hurts anyone in any significant way; his lies are small and harmless. Conversely, the phony world also spins lies, but they are dangerous since they harm people. For example, Holden mentions that Pencey advertises that it molds youth, but it does not. He is angry with motion pictures because they offer false ideals and hopes. Yet, his lies help a mother think better of her son. Like Huck Finn, he lies to get along, but not to hurt, and also like Huck, he tries to do good. Near the end of the novel Holden dreams of fleeing civilization and building a cabin out west, something that belies his earlier man-about-town conduct.

By the end of the book, Holden has accepted a new position—an undiscriminating love for all humanity. He even expresses that he misses all the people who did wrong to him. Although not a Christ figure, Holden does acquire a Christlike position—perfect love of all humankind, good and evil. He is not mature enough to know what to do with this love, but he is mature enough to accept it. In this world, realizing what is squalor and what is good and loving it all is the first step in achieving identity and humanity: Compassion is what Holden learns.

Recalling all the suffering and pain that he has witnessed, Holden develops a profound sense of the human condition and accepts Christ's ultimate commandment. In the passage regarding Holden's argument with his Quaker friend Arthur Childs, Holden argues that Judas is not in hell because Jesus would have had the compassion and love not to condemn Judas to hell. Also, Jesus did not have time to analyze who would be perfect for his disciples; thus, they were not perfect and would have condemned Judas if they had had the chance. In this discussion, Holden points out his own dilemma, not having time to analyze his decisions, and his belief in the perfect love that he embraces at the end of the book. Although not a would-be saint, Holden does become a fuller human being through his experiences.

The title symbol of the novel comes from Holden's misreading of a line from a song of Robert Burns. Holden's wish, as expressed to his sister, is to be a catcher in the rye, one standing beneath a cliff waiting to catch any child who falls over it: He seeks to spare children the pain of growing up and facing the world of squalor. He also hopes to provide some useful, sincere activity in the world. The catcher-in-the-rye job is one that Holden realizes is impractical in the world as it is. Only by facing the world and loving it indiscriminately can anyone live fully within it and have any hope of changing it.

In the novel, Holden is also constantly preoccupied with death. He worries about the ducks in Central Park's lagoon freezing in the winter, about Egyptian mummies, and about his dead brother Allie. He cries to Allie not to let him disappear. This symbolizes Holden's wish not to disappear into society as another cog in the great machine, and his desire not to lose what little of himself he feels that he has. To Holden, the change from childhood to adulthood is a kind of death, a death he fears because of his conviction that he will become other than he is. This fear proves groundless by the end of the book. His name also provides a clue: Holden—hold on. His quest is to hold on to his adolescent self and to save other children from the pain of growth. His quest fails, but his compassion and the growth of his humanity provide him with better alternatives.

Regarding sex, Holden tends to be puritanical. His trouble lies in the fact that he begins to feel sorry for the girls he dates, and he has too much compassion for them to defile their supposed virtue. This problem ties in with his compassion: He tries to see people as they are and not as types. He looks quickly and may make rash judgments, but once he talks to or acquaints himself with someone, he sees him or her as an individual. His mentioning of the boring boy he knew in school who could whistle better than anyone is the perfect example: Holden cannot help but confront people as individuals. Again, this shows his growing compassion and indiscriminate love. He sympathizes with the girl's position, which is a very mature quality for a teenager. At Pencey, for example, he wants to protect a childhood friend named Jane Gallagher from Ward Stradlater, remembering that she always kept her kings in the back row in checker games and never used them.

The Catcher in the Rye also reflects the art of a maturing author. Although there is no indication that Holden will become a novelist, there are clues scattered throughout the novel that he has an artistic sensibility. His sensitivity, his compassion, his powers of observation, and his references to himself as an exhibitionist are several such clues.

Later, Salinger more fully develops the contrast between squalor and love in the world and reintroduces various elements of his Caulfield family saga in his grand design of charting the story of the Glass family. The compassion, the satire, the heights of perfect love, the love of the family unit, and the use of brilliant conversational language that characterized Salinger's great novel, *The Catcher in the Rye*, will continue to set his fiction apart.

Domenic Bruni
Updated by James Norman O'Neill

Other major works

SHORT FICTION: *Nine Stories*, 1953; *Franny and Zooey*, 1961; *Raise High the Roof Beam, Carpenters, and Seymour: An Introduction*, 1963.

Bibliography

Alexander, Paul. *Salinger: A Biography*. New York: Renaissance Books, 2000. An attempt to explain Salinger's reclusiveness, which the author relates to themes in Salinger's fiction.

Alsen, Eberhard. *A Reader's Guide to J. D. Salinger*. Westport, Conn.: Greenwood Press, 2003. Offers an insightful analysis of *The Catcher in the Rye*, as well as useful indexes and appendixes covering all of Salinger's fiction.

French, Warren. *J. D. Salinger, Revisited*. Boston: Twayne, 1988. One of the most helpful and informative books on Salinger. French, who has written an earlier book on Salinger, explains here how he changed his perspective on some of Salinger's works. In addition to offering a useful chronology and bibliography, French discusses the New Hampshire area, where Salinger and French have lived. French also makes enlightening comparisons of the stories to films. Notes, references, index.

Gardner, James. "J. D. Salinger, Fashion Victim." *National Review* 49 (April 7, 1997): 51-52. Contends that Salinger is intensely different from what American culture has become since he was last heard from; the adolescent challenge to the falsity of one's elders that inspired *The Catcher in the Rye* has become the most established kind of conformity; analyzes the reasons for the outdatedness of Salinger's last story, "Hapworth 16, 1924."

Kotzen, Kip, and Thomas Beller, eds. *With Love and Squalor: Fourteen Writers Respond to the Work of J. D. Salinger*. New York: Broadway, 2001. A collection of essays by contemporary writers on their personal first impressions of Salinger's work.

Laser, Marvin, and Norman Furman, eds. *Studies in J. D. Salinger: Reviews, Essays, and Critiques of "The Catcher in the Rye" and Other Fiction.* New York: Odyssey Press, 1963. This volume, in addition to discussing the publishing history and early reviews of *The Catcher in the Rye,* also provides a collection of some of the most important criticism of the shorter fiction. A bibliographical apparatus has been supplied for the convenience of teachers and students, as well as suggested topics for writing.

Maynard, Joyce. *At Home in the World: A Memoir.* New York: Picador USA, 1998. This memoir reveals many details of Salinger's private life, which he struggled to suppress. Best source for biographical information.

Pinsker, Sanford. *"The Catcher in the Rye": Innocence Under Pressure.* New York: Twayne, 1993. Argues that *The Catcher in the Rye* has affinities with several great American novels told by a retrospective first-person narrator and that it is perhaps the best portrait of a sixteen-year-old American boy ever written.

Salinger, Margaret A. *Dream Catcher: A Memoir.* New York: Washington Square Press, 2000. Salinger's daughter describes her experience growing up in the shadow of her famous yet reclusive father.

Salzman, Jack, ed. *New Essays on "The Catcher in the Rye."* New York: Cambridge University Press, 1991. Provides an overview of the history of the writing and publication of *The Catcher in the Rye,* its critical reception, attempts at censorship, and its position in a postmodernist literary world. Individual essays examine the novel's ideology in the context of the Cold War, the subculture the book depicts, its treatment of adolescent crisis, and its narrative structure.

Silverberg, Mark. "A Bouquet of Empty Brackets: Author-Function and the Search for J. D. Salinger." *Dalhousie Review* 75 (Summer/Fall, 1995): 222-246. Examines the consequences of J. D. Salinger's "disappearance" from the literary scene and looks at the obsessive desire to find him; explores how Salinger's characters and name have been freed from his person and re-created in various fictional and nonfictional contexts, concluding that while Salinger may have disappeared, his name and creations remain.

Steinle, Pamela Hunt. *In Cold Fear: "The Catcher in the Rye" Censorship Controversies and Postwar American Character.* Columbus: Ohio State University Press, 2000. A study of the impact of the novel on its release during a nervous period in American social history.

William Saroyan

Born: Fresno, California; August 31, 1908
Died: Fresno, California; May 18, 1981

Principal long fiction • *The Human Comedy,* 1943; *The Adventures of Wesley Jackson,* 1946; *Rock Wagram,* 1951; *Tracy's Tiger,* 1951; *The Laughing Matter,* 1953 (reprinted as *The Secret Story,* 1954); *Mama I Love You,* 1956; *Papa You're Crazy,* 1957; *Boys and Girls Together,* 1963; *One Day in the Afternoon of the World,* 1964.

Other literary forms • Despite his many novels, William Saroyan is more famous for his work in the short story, the drama, and autobiography. Each of these areas received emphasis at different stages in his career. During the 1930's, he made a spectacular literary debut with an avalanche of brilliant, exuberant, and unorthodox short stories. Major early collections were *The Daring Young Man on the Flying Trapeze, and Other Stories* (1934), *Inhale and Exhale* (1936), *Three Times Three* (1936), and *Love, Here Is My Hat, and Other Short Romances* (1938). *My Name Is Aram* (1940), a group of stories detailing the experiences of Aram Garoghlanian growing up in a small California town, marks the culmination of his short-story artistry.

Most of Saroyan's plays and his productions on Broadway were concentrated in the years between 1939 and 1942. *My Heart's in the Highlands* was produced by the Group Theatre in April, 1939. His second major production, *The Time of Your Life* (1939), was awarded both the Pulitzer Prize and the New York Drama Critics Circle Award and is still considered Saroyan's best play. *Hello Out There* (1941), a one-act play, is also regarded as a fine drama.

In 1951, Saroyan and Ross Bagdasarian published a popular song, "Come On-a My House." Saroyan also wrote several television plays, including an adaptation of *The Time of Your Life.* Starting with *The Bicycle Rider in Beverly Hills* (1952), Saroyan composed extensive memoirs, including *Here Comes, There Goes, You Know Who* (1961), *Not Dying* (1963), *Days of Life and Death and Escape to the Moon* (1970), *Places Where I've Done Time* (1972), *Sons Come and Go, Mothers Hang in Forever* (1976), *Chance Meetings* (1978), and *Obituaries* (1979).

Achievements • A thorough evaluation of Saroyan's achievement as a writer has yet to be made. By the age of twenty, he had already decided his role in life was to be that of a professional writer, and throughout his remaining fifty years he dedicated himself to that vocation, publishing voluminously in all literary forms, with the exception of poetry. The sheer bulk of his work and his admission that much of it was done merely to earn money have worked against him. Further, his frequent arguments with his critics and his increasingly difficult personality left him with few strong critical advocates.

Saroyan's lasting literary achievement is in the area of the short story, where he expanded the genre by linking narrative form to the essay and infusing his work with a highly individual vision of poetic intensity. Many of his stories feature a character modeled on Saroyan, a writer-persona who, though often obsessed with his own ideas and feelings, is vitally alive to the world of his immediate experience. Several of

Courtesy, D.C. Public Library

the most successful stories concern childhood experiences in an ethnic, small-town environment modeled on Saroyan's Fresno. Saroyan impressed his early readers with his rediscovery of the wondrous in the texture of ordinary American life. *The Saroyan Special: Selected Stories* (1948) is a collection of his best stories. *My Name Is Aram* delineates with some beautiful character portraits Saroyan's sense of the poetic interplay of values in the ethnic community.

Saroyan's plays oppose the vitality of personality and individual dreams to the force of social institutions and the threats of war. In their sense of improvised movement, his plays were a deliberate challenge to the strictly plotted productions of the commercial theater.

Starting in the mid-1940's, Saroyan turned his attention to longer fiction, writing over the next two decades a series of novels concerned with marriage and divorce. Apparently inspired by his own experiences, the books become increasingly skeptical about romantic love and reflect Saroyan's growing cynicism about the man-woman relationship while retaining his fondness for the charm of childhood.

Saroyan's longer fiction grows gradually out of those short stories concerned with growing up in a small town. *My Name Is Aram*, a story collection moving toward novelistic unity, leads directly to *The Human Comedy*, where Saroyan finally succeeds in making a novel out of his childhood material. Although *The Adventures of Wesley Jackson* must be regarded as a failed attempt to write in the picaresque mode, *Rock Wagram* is a surprisingly mature handling of the thematic scope provided by the novel form. Whereas *The Adventures of Wesley Jackson* presents marriage as an idyllic goal for the solitary man, *Rock Wagram* focuses on the crushing effect of the title character's failed marriage. Several shorter book-length works—*Tracy's Tiger, Mama I Love You*, and *Papa You're Crazy*—seem more tied to Saroyan's earlier material in their confinement to the perspectives of childhood and youth and, for the most part, are limited in theme and story situations. Saroyan's other novels—*The Laughing Matter, Boys and Girls Together*, and *One Day in the Afternoon of the World*—are deliberate forays into social areas where relationships are often intense and events are somber in their finality. Like *Rock Wagram*, each of these books centers on a male's struggle with marriage, death, and divorce. The last novel, *One Day in the Afternoon of the World*, features a character who at last seems to have acquired the wisdom to deal with such personal crises. Though his longer fictions are professionally wrought, Saroyan's achievements in the novel form are limited.

The mood of the later novels is picked up and carried to greater extremes in Saroyan's memoirs, a series whose loose formats encourage the author to reveal, often in free associations, his deep anxiety about his relationship to his society. Saroyan's memoirs, generally his weakest works, become increasingly preoccupied with death, the significance of his literary achievements, and with his struggle to ward off a bitterness that he occasionally admits but wants to deny.

Biography • So much of William Saroyan's work—especially his fiction—is drawn from the circumstances of his life that it has a biographical dimension. He was born in 1908, in Fresno, California, the city where he died on May 18, 1981. The child of Armenian immigrants, he faced his first hardship when, at his father's death in 1911, he was placed for four years in the Fred Finch orphanage in Oakland. During these years, his mother worked in San Francisco as a maid, finally gathering the money to move back to a house in Fresno with her four children. Here Saroyan lived from age seven to seventeen, learning Armenian, acquiring an irreverence for the town's chief social institutions, the church and the school, and working as a newspaper boy and as a telegraph messenger to help support the family. At the age of fifteen, he left school permanently to work at his Uncle Aram's vineyards.

In 1926, Saroyan left Fresno, first to go to Los Angeles, then, after a brief time in the National Guard, to move to San Francisco, where he tried a number of jobs, eventually becoming at the age of nineteen, the manager of a Postal Telegraph branch office. In 1928, determined to make his fortune as a writer, he made his first trip to New York. He returned to San Francisco the following year, somewhat discouraged by his lack of success. During the early 1930's, however, he began to write story after story, culminating with his decision in January, 1934, to write one story a day for the whole month. During that year, *Story* published "The Daring Young Man on the Flying Trapeze," and suddenly Saroyan stories were appearing in many of the top periodicals. His first book of stories was published that year, and the following year he had enough money to make an ethnic return, a trip to Soviet Armenia.

Except for a few months in 1936 spent working on motion pictures at the Paramount lot, Saroyan spent the majority of the 1930's in San Francisco. By 1939, he had shifted his activities to drama, writing and producing plays on Broadway. After winning the New York Drama Critics Circle Award for the best play of 1939 to 1940 and the Pulitzer Prize, Saroyan made headlines by rejecting the Pulitzer on the grounds that he was opposed to prizes in the arts and to patronage. More controversy followed when he wrote *The Human Comedy* as a screenplay for Metro-Goldwin-Mayer, then argued about directing the film and tried to buy his work back for twenty thousand dollars, more than he was paid for it. At that time he was also, in a letter to *The New York Times*, publicly denouncing the Broadway theater.

Even though he had pacifist sympathies, Saroyan was inducted into the U.S. Army in October, 1942, serving until 1945. His most traumatic experience during the 1940's, however, was his marriage to Carol Marcus, which lasted from 1943 to 1949, and that was resumed briefly from 1951 to 1953, before a final divorce. The couple had two children, Aram and Lucy.

During the 1950's, Saroyan began to write more long fiction, much of it dealing with marital difficulties. In addition, in 1951, he was the coauthor of a hit song, "Come On-a My House," and during the late 1950's, he began writing television plays. From 1952 to 1959, he lived in a Malibu beach house, an environment that encouraged him to work very steadily. During this time, he lived a less public existence and, feeling monetary pressure because of his gambling and his huge income tax debt, he increasingly developed a reputation as a difficult personality.

In 1960, after some travel about the world, he settled in a modest apartment at 74 Rue Taitbout, Paris. The following year he was briefly a writer-in-residence at Purdue University. By 1962, he had arranged to buy two adjacent houses in Fresno and thereafter alternated living between Fresno and Paris. He spent most of the last fifteen years of his life working on various volumes of memoirs. Five days before his death he called the Associated Press to give this statement: "Everybody has got to die, but I have always believed an exception would be made in my case. Now what?" After much success (much money earned by writing, much money lost by gambling), much international travel, much controversy, much fame, and much obscurity, William Saroyan died of cancer in his hometown, Fresno, in 1981.

Analysis • Saroyan's work habits were a major determinant (for better or worse) of his unique literary effects. He regarded writing as work, something that required disciplined effort, but also as an activity whose chief characteristic was the free play of the mind. As he explained his practice, Saroyan would often give himself assignments, a story or a chapter a day (or so many hours of writing), but would seldom work from a detailed organizational plan. Uncomfortable with mulling over possible styles, attitudes, narrative directions, he would often prefer to plunge into writing, fueled by coffee and cigarettes, hoping that whatever got down on paper would inspire the story to "take off on its own." Whatever relationships would be worked out would be those of deep structure, drawn from his inner being rather than from rhetoric. At times he would begin with a "theory" or abstract idea. (For example, the theory stated at the end of "War" is that hatred and ugliness exist in the heart of everyone.) The act of writing itself was to clarify and refine the idea for the writer. In "Myself upon the Earth," the writer's own situation, his dead father, and his attitudes toward the world begin to weave into the free connections that substitute for a conventional plot. Thematically, the apparently undisciplined becomes the true discipline as the dedication expressed in an attitude toward life—toward humanity—is transformed through the narration into a dedication to art.

There are obvious difficulties with this method of composition. "The Man with His Heart in the Highlands" begins in the course of its improvisation to split in two; when Saroyan puts it into the form of a full-length play, the theme of the importance of acceptance in forming the new American community is finally seen as a basic articulation in the material. Saroyan also acknowledged revision as an important stage in the writing process, but much of his work suffers from a lack of objectivity, the ability to see his own work clearly and revise it accordingly.

Although the act of writing was for Saroyan both a kind of thinking and a performance, the materials of his art were usually the materials of his life. Much in the manner of Thomas Wolfe (an early influence), Saroyan's fiction was often drawn directly from his experience. A letter to Calouste Gulbenkian (in *Letters from 74 Rue Taitbout*, 1969) shows how Saroyan drew in detail on his external experience and his frame of mind for most of the content of "The Assyrian." Writing, he came to believe, was connected with "noticing" life and with the sense that life itself was theatrical. Although Saroyan acknowledged that the process of writing had to discover form in its materials and that the writer had to be transformed into a character framed by his art, the sense of witnessed scene and character in his best work lends a necessary solidity to his creative exuberance.

The favorite writer-personas in Saroyan's early fiction were poet-philosophers in the manner of Walt Whitman; American wiseguys (the young grown suddenly smarter about the ways of the world than their elders); or combinations of the two. His later long fiction featured the writer as a veteran of life, sometimes bitter but with his own philosophic resignation, a mode of stoic humility about what he might be able to accomplish. Saroyan's typical themes—the advocacy of love and a condemnation of war and violence—are less important than the way in which he plays the narrator (usually a writer) against the narrator's circumstances. In the most deep-seated manifestation of this paradigm—the ethnic boy responding to his American environment—Saroyan associates the ethnic self in the ethnic community with naturalness, lack of self-consciousness, true being, and dignity of person. The American environment, while it promises opportunity with its training and its competitive games, also has institutions that seem to specialize in modes of restriction, punishment, and prejudice.

The ethnic responds to his environment with a complex involvement and detachment. On one hand, he is willing, even eager, to be assimilated; on the other hand, however, he is always aware of a kind of existence that has no adequately defined relationship to the American world of conventional social fact. The ethnic's psychological relationship to the world recalls Whitman's democratic paradox of people being intensely individual and at the same time like everyone else. In Saroyan's fiction, there is at times an emphasis on the individual's alienation—as when the protagonist in "The Daring Young Man on the Flying Trapeze" feels "somehow he had ventured upon the wrong earth" and the central character in "1,2,3,4,5,6,7,8" feels the room he is living in is not a part of him and wants a home, "a place in which to return to himself." Invariably, however, the ethnic family and its small-town environment expand quite naturally for Saroyan into a version of the democratic family of people.

This sense of communal home, however, is not easily preserved—as Saroyan's novels with their marital catastrophes and lonely protagonists repeatedly demonstrate. From the beginning, the fate of Saroyan's ethnic was complicated by the fact that his deepest allegiance was to a national community that no longer existed. In an early story, "Seventy Thousand Assyrians," the Assyrian states, "I was born in the old country, but I want to get over it . . . everything is washed up over there." Though Saroyan could be sympathetic to such practicality, he tried to achieve, often with a deliberate naïveté, a poetic point of view that would embrace both existence in the old community of family values (which was a basic part of his being) and existence in the practical new world (which offered the only opportunity for becoming).

From the perspective of Saroyan's writer-persona, the world outside is continually new, funny, sometimes strange, often wonderful, a place of innocent relationships and suspended judgments. A recurring situation in his work has someone who is apprehended for theft trying to explain that he is not guilty because his value system is different from that of his accusers. On one hand, Saroyan believes in an attitude of joyful acceptance: Here he sees man "on the threshold of an order of himself that must find human reality a very simple unavoidable majesty and joy, with all its complications and failures." On the other hand, he imagines, like Whitman, a more somber mystic vision based on "the joyous sameness of life and death." In this mysterious crucible, life is fate, perhaps only glimpsed fully when "drawing to the edge of full death every person is restored to innocence—to have lived was not his fault." Saroyan's basic impulse is to preserve, recapture, and restore the innocence that the world has lost that state of being that sees experience only as a fantastic fate that serves ultimately to redeem the primal self.

My Name Is Aram • Like Sherwood Anderson's *Winesburg, Ohio* (1919) and William Faulkner's *The Unvanquished* (1938), *My Name Is Aram* is a book that falls midway between short-story collection and novel. The stories are separate and distinct, but they all concern the small-town experiences of the same boy, Aram, with his Armenian relatives. There is little sense of sequence but rather an accumulated manifestation of the potential wisdom in this world. Saroyan emphasizes the preservation of innocence, the warding off of the absolute element in the values of the adult culture. Aram and his friends turn social rituals into human games, and in the course of their experiences demonstrate that the many social failures in these stories have really two constituents, the innocent immediacy of the experience (its essential value) and the cultural "truths" and judgments applied to it. Through vital participation in their world, Aram and his friends begin to negotiate its preconceived ideas.

The Human Comedy • The setting, the characters, and the young man's perspective that predominate in *The Human Comedy* all have their sources in Saroyan short stories. The background is World War II, and the California small town has accordingly become "the home front." In the book's basic drama, the innocence in this environment—its vulnerable children, young people, and women and its emotional closeness—must come to terms with death and its finalities.

Within the context of the small-town milieu, the novel focuses primarily on the Macauley family and most often on Homer Macauley, a fourteen-year-old telegraph messenger boy. As Homer delivers telegrams announcing the deaths of soldiers, he finds himself getting caught up psychologically in the shock of the family reactions. On his first such delivery, to Rosa Sandoval, the woman responds with an eerie, calm hysteria in which she confuses Homer with her dead son and begins to think of both as little boys. Feeling at first both compassion and an urge to flee, Homer gradually arrives at an awareness of the meaning of death. With the help of his mother (whose husband has recently died), he fights through feelings of loneliness and isolation toward the idea that death and change afford perspectives for redeeming the values of innocence, love, and life itself.

The ideal of the community dominates the book. The novel implies in its moments of crisis and healing—Homer becoming briefly transformed into the son of another woman; Tobey taking the place of the dead Marcus in the Macauley family—that humankind is a single family. Though the fact of death and the awareness of death are constant threats to the individual, the book, as the allusions to Homer's *Odyssey* (c. 800 B.C.E.) imply, is about to return home, the coming back from the ugly realities of the outside world to the love and security that humankind can provide.

The book seems intent on assuring its readers that despite economic tribulations, the discontent of restless desire, the anxiety connected with competition, and the confining tendency of its institutions, the community is an active, positive force. A working out in the rhythms of experience of the differences between people—age, sex, degrees of formality—invariably shows positive contrasts. The many relationships Homer has with older people are all thematically active ingredients for dramatizing the closeness of the community. *The Human Comedy* insists—perhaps too facilely at times—on the capacity of the American community to regulate the experience of life and the encounter with death.

The Adventures of Wesley Jackson • *The Adventures of Wesley Jackson* may be Saroyan's worst novel. It is marred by two closely related problems, an uncertain grasp of form and a confusion about its issues. Saroyan's indiscriminate use of his own military experience takes the novel hopelessly out of control. Evidently attempting to give himself ample latitude with the novel form, Saroyan chose to employ the picaresque form, referring in his comments on the novel to Mark Twain's *Adventures of Huckleberry Finn* (1884). Unfortunately, Wesley is much too introverted to be an effective picaro of any kind. He is intended to be a nonconformist, but, except for a few anti-Army establishment opinions, his personal idealism and prosaic earnestness only serve to make him seem as remote from the realities of Army life as from the realities of war. Lacking a feeling for the actual operations of the Army, the book meanders haphazardly from the bureaucratic to the personal, from one location to another, from family concerns to writing ambitions, succeeding finally in giving the impression of an Army journal rather than a picaresque novel.

At times the book develops an antiwar theme; at times the theme seems to be the pettiness of the Army bureaucracy. No one theme, however, is developed consistently. Wesley's self-absorbed narration does provide some shaping by turning the officers into bad fathers (cruel figures of authority), the women into sympathetic (though vague) images, and his fellow soldiers into boys, sometimes naughty but basically innocent. In sporadic, almost desultory, fashion the first part of the book features Wesley's search for his father, the essentially good man who has been displaced and ignored by organized society. The last part of the book becomes concerned with Wesley's search for a son (actually a search for a woman to bear him a son). Were Wesley's narration less limited, less egotistical, these thematic threads might have made firmer connections.

Rock Wagram • The split structure of *Rock Wagram*—approximately half the novel taking place in September, 1942, and half in February, 1950—emphasizes the drive of Rock Wagram (pronounced Vah-GRAM) to marry Ann Ford and his resultant puzzled desperation when that marriage fails. The chronological gap, by omitting the marriage and Rock's military experience, accents the negative quality of this part of his life. However, by leaving out the specific difficulties that are so much a part of his later depression, the novel makes Rock's psychology a problematic frame for understanding events instead of using the events of the past to put his psychology in an understandable perspective. At times, the failure of the marriage seems explained by Ann's frivolous, lying character. At other times, the failure seems to grow out of Rock's ethnic assumption that people must become involved in a family existence.

Rock Wagram explores the tensions between people as individuals and people as social animals. In his motion-picture career, Rock has become successful as an individual star, but his acquaintance with Ann kindles his memories of certain values from his Armenian background, particularly the notion that a man is not complete until he had founded his own family, been husband to his wife, father to his children. Unhappily for him, Ann turns out to be like so many other characters whose departures from their true natures disturb him; her lies signify to him that she is refusing to be herself, hoping for something better. Earlier Rock has met a series of men rebelling against their heritage: Paul Key, the Hollywood producer who hates being a Jew; Sam Schwartz, Paul's nephew, who devotes himself to becoming the image of success; and Craig Adams, the completely assimilated Armenian. Although these men are denying both their heritage and their own individuality, they are better adapted to the world of casual social relationships than he, and the book raises doubts about the possibilities of a deeply authentic existence.

Rock chooses to see his life—and the life of man—as involving continual adjustment to a Shavian life force, a power that, once he begins to perceive it through his Armenian ethnic environment, becomes his ultimate guide to true being. To get in tune with this force, he tries to be uninhibited in his social relationships, to go with the flow of events, to pay attention to his circumstances and to the people he is with, and to be, as he puts it, "a good witness" to his own experience and to his world.

Part of Rock's effort to live in terms of true being is a half-conscious cultivation of strategies toward death. His reaction to the death of his brother Haig is rage; at the death of his friend Paul Key, he affects a Hemingwayesque stoicism; and to his mother's death, he responds by plunging deeply and intensely into his subjective nature. In spite of all attempts to come to terms with the reality of death, he seems at last depressed, left with a sense of being part not only of a dying culture but also of a dying world. As he goes back to acting at the end of the narrative, his feeling for his art is one of obligation rather than enthusiasm for an individualized expression of himself. Yet, as the humor in his last statement indicates, he is finally not without hope in probing his lonely situation for its satisfactions.

The Laughing Matter • The laughter of *The Laughing Matter* is that of black comedy. From the time Swan Nazarenus announces to her husband that she is pregnant with another man's child, *The Laughing Matter* moves powerfully but erratically toward what seems an almost self-indulgently gruesome ending. The story line is captive to the emotional tensions and explosions of Evan Nazarenus as he attempts to sort out a future direction for himself, Swan, and their two children, Red and Eva. As he resorts successively to drink, violence, a return to family harmony, an abortion, and more violence, the problem-pregnancy tends to be obscured by his confusing attempts at solution. Because his personality is never clarified in the characterization, and because he often gives the impression of running aimlessly about the countryside, Evan becomes progressively less sympathetic in his shifting relationship to people and events.

The accompaniment to the mad rhapsody of his behavior is more carefully controlled. The children are innocent victims, becoming increasingly aware that something is wrong and even acting out some of the tensions themselves. The Walzes, a neighbor couple, have their own fights, and Evan's brother, Dade, who has, after years of domestic turbulence, lost his family entirely, conveniently defines one possible outcome.

Complicating the question of what to do is the issue of who is to blame. In one scene between Evan and Dade, the two brothers—who often speak in an old-country tongue—review their ethnic fate as heads of families, Evan wondering what they as men have done wrong. Evan debates whether he ought to be more feminine, more kindly, or strive to retain his masculine pride in the face of what may be an essential challenge to his person. His solution, the abortion, is less an act of harsh morality (as he later views it) than the result of a desire to begin again, to regain a kind of innocence by reversing events.

The ironies and the deaths pile up so rapidly at the conclusion that they achieve only a blurred effect. The fact that so much violence results from simple ignorance begins to make the characters comic rather than tragic, and this may have been the prompting behind Saroyan's title. When Evan accuses the wrong man as the adulterer (pushing the poor lonely man toward suicide), and when he shoots and kills his brother Dade under the mistaken notion that they have been responsible for Swan's death from abortion, Evan seems more the incompetent than the grief-stricken victim.

His own death in an auto accident may have been meant to suggest that the whole chain of events was merely a series of accidents, but this must be weighed against the remarks of the doctor who explains to Dade that Swan committed suicide and that she had evidently had a strong death wish for several years. For all its masculine madness, this book begins and ends by pointing an accusing finger at the woman.

Boys and Girls Together • *Boys and Girls Together* is a realistic study of a husband-wife relationship that moves with an understated satire toward black humor. The husband, Dick, is a writer who finds that his current domestic relationship has made it impossible for him to work, thus heaping financial strain upon his already turbulent marriage to Daisy. In the course of their sporadic fighting, the couple discovers greater and greater depths of incompatibility. Dick comes to the conclusion that she is ignorant, trivial, and selfish; Daisy accuses him of being egotistical and immature. Were it not for the two children (Johnny, five, and Rosey, two and a half), the writer, who is a family man, would undoubtedly leave.

As this account of a few days in their lives demonstrates, what keeps the marriage together is their socializing with other couples. The slight story line follows the meeting of Dick and Daisy with two other couples for a few days of fun in San Francisco. Though only casual friends, all the couples have common characteristics: In each instance, the husband has achieved prominence in the arts; in each case, the husband is many years older than the wife; and in each instance, the difference in age seems part of the strain on the marriage. Before all six can get together, the oldest husband, Leander, dies of a heart attack, an episode witnessed by Oscar Bard (the actor) and his wife, and by Leander's wife Lucretia. Dick and Daisy arrive soon after the attack and seem generally ineffective in preventing the scene from sliding from seriousness to farce. Dick eventually begins to act as satiric observer, commenting on Oscar's egotistical discomfort and on Lucretia's performance as grieving widow. The scene has its climax in Oscar's long speech on the difficulties of their kind of marriage. Although he begins by pointing out realistically that the women they have married are not for them, he finally comes to the conclusion that it is sexual attraction that gives the necessary life to all partners in such marriages and that makes them continue to put up with each other. Dick does not disagree. Soon the survivors are planning a trip to Reno as another distraction from the harsh realities around them. Earlier, Dick had resented it when his wife teased him about being a fool for sex. In the last part of the novel, his understated satiric vision outlines them all as characters in a sexual farce.

If all of William Saroyan's writing can be regarded as his attempt to understand and define his position in the world, his long fiction must be seen as his deliberate recognition of the crueler circumstances in that world—death, the failure of love, divorce, the recalcitrant details of life itself. His own marital troubles undoubtedly inspired the novels of the 1950's and 1960's with their fragmented families, and while the intently masculine perspective in these books reveals a serious but virtually unexamined reverence for love and marriage, it also demonstrates the author's own very personal irritation with wives. In nearly all of his novels, the formal problem tends to be the male protagonist's varied reactions to his situation. In *Rock Wagram* and *The Laughing Matter,* Saroyan is successful in focusing these reactions by means of intense emotional pressures, but his confusion about final blame for the marital breakdown makes a fictional closure difficult. With *Papa You're Crazy* and *Mama I Love You,* he moves to the detachment of the child's point of view but is still uncertain about the extent to which the world's facts ought to—and must—impinge on the individual family member. (To what degree, for example, does the particular existence of the parent doom or mold the life of the child?) In *Boys and Girls Together* and *One Day in the Afternoon of the World*, Saroyan gets mixed results from mining the attitudes of his male protagonists for a perspective that would be both a consistent and legitimate interpretation of their marital situations. In Saroyan's long fiction, as well as in his other writing, both his strengths and his weaknesses derive from his insistent emotional presence.

Walter Shear

Other major works

SHORT FICTION: *The Daring Young Man on the Flying Trapeze, and Other Stories*, 1934; *Inhale and Exhale*, 1936; *Three Times Three*, 1936; *Little Children*, 1937; *The Gay and Melancholy Flux: Short Stories*, 1937; *Love, Here Is My Hat, and Other Short Romances*, 1938; *The Trouble with Tigers*, 1938; *Peace, It's Wonderful*, 1939; *Three Fragments and a Story*, 1939; *My Name Is Aram*, 1940; *Saroyan's Fables*, 1941; *The Insurance Salesman, and Other Stories*, 1941; *Forty-eight Saroyan Stories*, 1942; *Dear Baby*, 1944; *Some Day I'll Be a Millionaire: Thirty-four More Great Stories*, 1944; *The Saroyan Special: Selected Stories*, 1948; *The Fiscal Hoboes*, 1949; *The Assyrian, and Other Stories*, 1950; *The Whole Voyald, and Other Stories*, 1956; *William Saroyan Reader*, 1958; *Love*, 1959; *After Thirty Years: The Daring Young Man on the Flying Trapeze*, 1964; *Best Stories of William Saroyan*, 1964; *The Tooth and My Father*, 1974; *The Man with the Heart in the Highlands, and Other Early Stories*, 1989.

PLAYS: *My Heart's in the Highlands*, pr., pb. 1939; *The Hungerers: A Short Play*, pb. 1939, pr. 1945; *The Time of Your Life*, pr., pb. 1939; *Love's Old Sweet Song*, pr., pb. 1940; *Subway Circus*, pb. 1940; *The Beautiful People*, pr. 1940, pb. 1941; *The Great American Goof*, pr. 1940, pb. 1942; *The Ping-Pong Game*, pb. 1940 (one act); *Three Plays: My Heart's in the Highlands, The Time of Your Life, Love's Old Sweet Song*, pb. 1940; *Across the Board on Tomorrow Morning*, pr., pb. 1941; *Hello Out There*, pr. 1941, pb. 1942 (one act); *Jim Dandy*, pr., pb. 1941; *Three Plays: The Beautiful People, Sweeney in the Trees, Across the Board on Tomorrow Morning*, pb. 1941; *Razzle Dazzle*, pb. 1942 (collection); *Talking to You*, pr., pb. 1942; *Get Away Old Man*, pr. 1943, pb. 1944; *Sam Ego's House*, pr. 1947, pb. 1949; *A Decent Birth, a Happy Funeral*, pb. 1949; *Don't Go Away Mad*, pr., pb. 1949; *The Slaughter of the Innocents*, pb. 1952, pr. 1957; *The Cave Dwellers*, pr. 1957, pb. 1958; *Once Around the Block*, pb. 1959; *Sam the Highest Jumper of Them All: Or, The London Comedy*, pr. 1960, pb. 1961; *Settled Out of Court*, pr. 1960, pb. 1962; *The Dogs: Or, The Paris Comedy, and Two Other Plays*, pb. 1969; *An Armenian Trilogy*, pb. 1986 (includes *Armenians, Bitlis*, and *Haratch*); *Warsaw Visitor and Tales from the Vienna Streets: The Last Two Plays of William Saroyan*, pb. 1991.

SCREENPLAY: *The Human Comedy*, 1943.

NONFICTION: *Harlem as Seen by Hirschfield*, 1941; *Hilltop Russians in San Francisco*, 1941; *Why Abstract?*, 1945 (with Henry Miller and Hilaire Hiler); *The Twin Adventures: The Adventures of William Saroyan*, 1950; *The Bicycle Rider in Beverly Hills*, 1952; *Here Comes, There Goes, You Know Who*, 1961; *A Note on Hilaire Hiler*, 1962; *Not Dying*, 1963; *Short Drive, Sweet Chariot*, 1966; *Look at Us*, 1967; *I Used to Believe I Had Forever: Now I'm Not So Sure*, 1968; *Letters from 74 Rue Taitbout*, 1969; *Days of Life and Death and Escape to the Moon*, 1970; *Places Where I've Done Time*, 1972; *Sons Come and Go, Mothers Hang in Forever*, 1976; *Chance Meetings*, 1978; *Obituaries*, 1979; *Births*, 1983.

CHILDREN'S LITERATURE: *Me*, 1963; *Horsey Gorsey and the Frog*, 1968; *The Circus*, 1986.

MISCELLANEOUS: *My Name Is Saroyan,* 1983 (stories, verse, play fragments, and memoirs); *The New Saroyan Reader,* 1984 (Brian Darwent, editor).

Bibliography

Balakian, Nona. *The World of William Saroyan.* Lewisburg, Pa.: Bucknell University Press, 1998. Balakian, formerly a staff writer for *The New York Times Book Review,* knew Saroyan personally in his last years, and her observations of him color her assessment of his later works. She viewed it as her mission to resurrect his reputation and restore him to his place among the finest of twentieth century American writers. Traces his evolution from ethnic writer to master of the short story, to playwright, and finally to existentialist.

Floan, Howard R. *William Saroyan.* New York: Twayne, 1966. Floan's study remains one of the best extensive critical monographs on Saroyan's work. It focuses on Saroyan's early literature, glossing over the post-World War II period as less productive and durable. Contains a valuable annotated bibliography through 1964.

Foster, Edward Halsey. *William Saroyan.* Boise, Idaho: Boise State University Press, 1984. A condensed but helpful survey stressing Saroyan's unique voice. This work draws parallels between his work and that of the Beat generation.

_____. *William Saroyan: A Study of the Short Fiction.* New York: Twayne, 1991. An introduction to Saroyan's short stories that discusses his use of the oral tradition, his Armenian heritage, and his usual themes and experimental techniques. Includes Saroyan's own comments on his fiction as well as previously published essays by other critics.

Haslam, Gerald W. "William Saroyan." In *A Literary History of the American West,* edited by Thomas J. Lyon et al. Fort Worth: Texas Christian University, 1987. A good introductory essay. Haslam focuses on Saroyan's post-World War II decline in popularity and its cause. Includes a select bibliography.

_____. "William Saroyan and San Francisco: Emergence of a Genius (Self-Proclaimed)." In *San Francisco in Fiction: Essays in a Regional Literature,* edited by David Fine and Paul Skenazy. Albuquerque: University of New Mexico Press, 1995. Discusses the influence of San Francisco in a number of Saroyan's stories. Suggests that his stylistic triumph in "The Daring Young Man on the Flying Trapeze" is to force the readers to become co-creators in the story.

Keyishian, Harry, ed. *Critical Essays on William Saroyan.* New York: G. K. Hall, 1995. A collection of essays on Saroyan, from early reviews to critical articles. Helpful essays to a study of Saroyan's short stories are Edward Halsey Foster's discussion of Saroyan's relationship to Gertrude Stein and Walter Shear's essay on Saroyan's ethnicity.

Kherdian, David. *A Bibliography of William Saroyan, 1934-1964.* San Francisco: R. Beachman, 1965. Although in need of updating, this volume is a thorough and indispensable bibliographical guide to both primary and secondary works.

Lee, Lawrence, and Barry Gifford. *Saroyan: A Biography.* New York: Harper and Row, 1984. Lee and Gifford's study is rich with anecdotes and segments of interviews with Saroyan's family, friends, and associates. Supplemented by a chronology and a bibliography.

Leggett, John. *A Daring Young Man.* New York: Alfred A. Knopf, 2003. Leggett relies heavily on Saroyan's journals to produce a sustained glimpse of the author that is neither admiring nor forgiving.

Leslie Marmon Silko

Born: Albuquerque, New Mexico; March 5, 1948

Principal long fiction • *Ceremony*, 1977; *Almanac of the Dead*, 1991; *Gardens in the Dunes*, 1999.

Other literary forms • Leslie Marmon Silko's first published book, *Laguna Woman: Poems* (1974), is a collection of poems. Her earliest published works were short stories, published in magazines, most of which were later included in *Storyteller* (1981). This book defies genre classification by including short fiction, poetry, retellings of traditional stories, and family photographs, all linked by passages of commentary and memoir. Her interest in images interacting with words led Silko to produce a film in 1980 with Dennis Carr titled *Estoyehmuut and the Gunnadeyah* (Arrowboy and the Destroyers). In shooting the film at Laguna, New Mexico, using pueblo residents and elders instead of professional actors, Silko documented a time and place that no longer exist.

Silko's nonfiction works include *The Delicacy and Strength of Lace: Letters Between Leslie Marmon Silko and James Wright* (1986; edited by Ann Wright), and *Yellow Woman and a Beauty of the Spirit: Essays on Native American Life Today* (1996), a collection of essays. In *Sacred Water: Narratives and Pictures* (1993), she self-published her essay on water interwoven with her Polaroid photographs. The first edition was hand sewn and glued by Silko; a subsequent edition was conventionally bound.

Achievements • The publication of Silko's first novel, *Ceremony*, along with N. Scott Momaday's winning of the 1969 Pulitzer Prize for *House Made of Dawn*, marked the beginning of a surge in publishing by Native American authors—the "Native American renaissance" of the late 1960's and early 1970's. However, just as her works defy genre classification, Silko transcends the category of Native American writer. Her earlier works draw heavily on her own experiences and the traditional stories of Laguna Pueblo; later works move beyond the pueblo while maintaining a strong connection with the Southwest and with traditional and autobiographical materials. Her first two novels, *Ceremony* and *Almanac of the Dead*, are experimental in form, testing the limits of the novel as a genre and format. Indeed, Silko once said that she loves working in the novel form because its flexibility imposes so few limitations on the writer. Her third novel, *Gardens in the Dunes*, adheres more closely to conventional novel form, but like the previous two, it is highly political, reflecting Silko's activism.

Her books, particularly *Ceremony* and *Storyteller,* are widely taught in colleges and universities; her short fiction and poetry are widely anthologized. Her works have been translated into Italian and German and are popular internationally, both in translation and in the original English.

Silko's works in fiction, nonfiction, and poetry earned her a National Endowment for the Arts (NEA) Discover Grant (1971), *The Chicago Review* Poetry Award (1974), the Pushcart Prize for Poetry (1977); a MacArthur Prize Fellowship (1981); the *Boston Globe* prize for nonfiction (1986); a New Mexico Endowment for the Humanities "Living Cultural Treasure" Award (1988); and a Lila Wallace *Reader's Digest* Fund

Writers Award (1991). Her story "Lullaby" was selected as one of twenty
best short stories of 1975.

Biography • Leslie Marmon Silko
was born to Leland (Lee) Howard
Marmon and Mary Virginia Leslie in
1948. Her extended mixed-heritage
family (Laguna, Mexican, white)
had a rich history of tribal leadership
and a rich tradition of storytelling.
Growing up at Laguna Pueblo, Silko
rode horses, hunted, and was free
to explore the land of her ancestors,
land that was inextricably tied to the
traditional stories told by her aunts
and grandmother.

In 1964 she entered the University
of New Mexico. In 1966, she married
Richard Chapman and gave birth to
Robert William Chapman. During her
sophomore year, she took a creative
writing class. Despite the success of a
short story written for that class, "The
Man to Send Rainclouds," which was published first in *New Mexico Quarterly* and then
in Kenneth Rosen's anthology of Native American writing as the title piece, Silko did
not yet see herself primarily as a writer. After receiving her bachelor's degree in 1969,
she entered the University of New Mexico law school in the American Indian Law Fellowship program. During the same year, she separated from and eventually divorced
Chapman.

Courtesy, University Press of Mississippi

In 1971, she left law school. Convinced that the American justice system was inherently unjust, and believing that her own role was to call attention to this injustice by
telling stories, she entered graduate school in English at the University of New Mexico. She soon left to teach at Navajo Community College. During the same year, she
married John Silko (whom she would also later divorce) and gave birth to her second
child, Cazimir Silko.

Leaving the Southwest for the first time, Silko moved with her husband and children to Ketchikan, Alaska, in 1973. The impact of the Alaskan landscape and climate
can be seen in her short story "Storyteller," written during this time, and it resurfaces
in *Almanac of the Dead.* She also began writing *Ceremony* while in Alaska, re-creating
her beloved southwestern landscape.

Silko returned to Laguna for a short time before moving to Tucson in 1978, where
she taught at the University of Arizona. She eventually settled on a ranch outside Tucson, enjoying the physical labor of ranch life. In 1981, the year in which *Storyteller* was
published, Silko was awarded the MacArthur Prize Fellowship. Sometimes called the
"genius award," the MacArthur Prize provided five years of financial support, allowing her, for the first time, to devote all of her efforts to writing. While writing *Almanac
of the Dead*, she became incensed about Arizona politics, leading her to paint a mural
of a snake with political graffiti on the outside wall of her Stone Avenue office.

Though later owners painted over the mural, it was well received by the people of the neighborhood and was important both in helping Silko (who describes herself as a "frustrated painter") to overcome writer's block and to develop further her technique of combining images with words. After the publication of *Almanac of the Dead* in 1991, Silko's desire for independence from the publishing world and her experiments with photography (in part inspired by her father, a professional photographer) led her to self-publish *Sacred Water: Narratives and Pictures*.

Analysis • Silko once stated that she tries to write a very different book every time. Indeed, her novels are as different from one another as they are from her books in other genres. Despite such diversity, however, Silko's novels share certain common traits. All draw heavily on her personal experiences, but they are not conventionally autobiographical. Although only *Ceremony* deals exclusively with Native American themes and characters, Native American themes and characters are central in the other two novels as well.

Silko was so attuned to the political situation in northern Mexico that, in *Almanac of the Dead*, published two years before the Zapatista uprising in Chiapas, her description of an uprising in northern Mexico seems prophetic. Silko's work makes use of her eclectic reading on topics as diverse as the Gnostic gospels and orchid collecting.

Silko uses very little dialogue, yet her characters are richly drawn through the use of an omniscient narrator who reveals their inner thoughts and reactions. Her descriptions are vivid and detailed. Though predominantly serious, all of Silko's novels display her wry, ironic sense of humor. An important recurring theme in all of Silko's novels is the conflict between the "destroyers," those whose disregard for the land leads them to exploit it and its people for profit, and those who are in touch with and respect the land. Although those in touch with the land are usually the indigenous people who have not separated themselves from nature, indigenous people can be destroyers, and whites can be in touch with the land.

Ceremony • In *Ceremony*, Tayo, a young veteran of mixed Laguna and white ancestry, returns from World War II with what would now be called post-traumatic stress syndrome. When the Veterans Administration (VA) hospital sends him home to the pueblo uncured, his family asks the tribal healer, old Ku'oosh, to perform the traditional ceremony for reincorporating warriors into the community. The ceremony is only partially successful; Tayo is still deeply disturbed, blaming himself for his cousin and friend Rocky's death and turning to alcohol along with a group of friends who are also veterans. After a fight with his friend Emo, Tayo is sent back to the VA hospital, but his treatment is no more successful than it was the first time.

Betonie, a Navajo medicine man who uses unconventional methods, is more successful. He conducts a Navajo healing ceremony for Tayo that sets him on the road to recovery. When Tayo leaves, Betonie says that to complete the ceremony Tayo must recover the spotted cattle that Tayo and his Uncle Josiah had planned to raise but that had presumably wandered off in Tayo's absence after Josiah died. Tayo discovers that the cattle were stolen by white ranchers and realizes that he had believed the lie that only Indians and Mexicans stole because whites did not need to steal. With the help of Ts'eh, a mysterious woman who turns out to be the spirit of the sacred mountain, Tayo takes the cattle home.

Meanwhile, Emo has become one of the destroyers, a participant in witchery, and he persuades the rest of the group to cooperate in his plan to kill Tayo. Warned by

Ts'eh, Tayo is able to resist the witchery. He returns home and tells his story to the elders in the kiva, who recognize Ts'eh as the spirit who brings rain and healing to their drought-stricken land. Tayo's separation from his community, in part caused by the war but also caused by his rejection as an illegitimate "half-breed," was symptomatic of a larger rift in the community. His healing demonstrates that things must change, that the new must be incorporated into the old, and that the "half-breed" can act as a mediator between the old traditions and the new world. Much of *Ceremony* is told in flashbacks. Traditional Laguna stories are woven throughout, set off from the text. The language is lyrical, and the message is of healing and conciliation.

Almanac of the Dead • When Silko read from this novel at the time of its publication, she announced, "This book attempts to crush linear time." It succeeds by repeatedly shifting time frames. Silko interweaves an enormous cast of characters involved in multiple subplots. They tell the story, in an indeterminate time in the not-too-distant future, of a spontaneous uprising across the Americas of dispossessed indigenous people who move throughout the novel toward an apocalyptic convergence on Tucson, Arizona.

Lecha and Zeta are twins, mixed-blood Yaquis, who have been given pieces of an old Mayan book (the almanac of the title). Unlike the Mayan codices, this book has stayed in the hands of the people. As they work to transcribe the pieces, they discover that the Mayans foretold the coming of the white European invaders—and foretold their demise as well. Seese, a young white woman whose baby has been kidnapped, consults Lecha, who is a psychic, and stays to work for her. Sterling, an old man who is exiled for revealing tribal secrets, also comes to work at the twins' ranch.

Other characters include Allegria, a mercenary architect, and her husband, Menardo, who live near Mexico City; the Tucson branch of the Blue family, mafiosi who dominate the Tucson real estate market; the Indian twin brothers Tacho and Wacah, who embody the mysterious power of twins and lead the people north toward Tucson; and Marxist Mexican revolutionaries Angelita (La Escapia) and El Feo. Their stories intertwine as they converge on Tucson, where the Barefoot Hopi warns that the familiar way of life on earth will end unless the destroyers change their ways and respect the earth. "Eco-warriors" to the north threaten a suicide bombing of a dam. The novel ends as all are poised on the brink of revolution.

Gardens in the Dunes • In an unpublished interview, Silko described her third novel as "full of flowers and light." Set in the time immediately following the stock market crash of 1893, *Gardens in the Dunes* tells the story of Indigo and Sister Salt. The young sisters are the last of the Sand Lizards, a fictional tribe based loosely on the Colorado River tribes that were wiped out around the beginning of the twentieth century. After a Ghost Dance they are attending is raided by the police, the girls are separated from their mother as they flee. Later, their grandmother dies and Indigo is captured by the police. She is sent to boarding school in Riverside.

There she is befriended by Hattie and Edward, a wealthy couple who live near the school. Before marrying Edward, Hattie attended Harvard University until her unconventional thesis proposal on the Gnostic gospels was rejected. Edward is a professional plant collector who sells rare specimens to wealthy buyers. They take Indigo along on their European trip during the school's summer break. Indigo sees the Jesus of the European churches as another manifestation of Wovoka, the prophet of the Ghost Dance. Edward's scheme to steal citron cuttings fails; Hattie, disgusted by his greed, divorces him and vows to help Indigo find her family.

Meanwhile, Sister Salt is befriended by Big Candy, who fathers her baby, the "little black grandfather." When Big Candy's preoccupation with wealth causes him to neglect Sister Salt and the baby, she and the Chemehuevi twins leave to farm land that the twins acquired from an aunt. The sisters are reunited, returning to the old gardens. Indigo plants the seeds and bulbs she collected on her journey, mixing the impractical but beautiful flowers with the traditional food crops. As in earlier works, Silko emphasizes the need to live in harmony with the land, the dangers of capitalism, and the need to use the new along with the old.

Robin Payne Cohen

Other major works

SHORT FICTION: *Yellow Woman*, 1993.

PLAY: *Lullaby*, pr. 1976 (with Frank Chin).

POETRY: *Laguna Woman: Poems*, 1974.

NONFICTION: *The Delicacy and Strength of Lace: Letters Between Leslie Marmon Silko and James Wright*, 1986; *Sacred Water: Narratives and Pictures*, 1993; *Yellow Woman and a Beauty of the Spirit: Essays on Native American Life Today*, 1996; *Conversations with Leslie Marmon Silko*, 2000 (Ellen L. Arnold, editor).

MISCELLANEOUS: *Storyteller*, 1981 (includes poetry and prose).

Bibliography

Allen, Paula Gunn. "The Feminine Landscape of Leslie Marmon Silko's *Ceremony*." In *Studies in American Indian Literature: Critical Essays and Course Design*. New York: Modern Language Association of America, 1983. Interprets Silko's novel from a feminist perspective and sees it as divided into two kinds of characters: earth spirits in harmony with the earth and spirit destroyers. Allen says that this is a novel of feminine life forces and the mechanistic death force of witchery. The women are equable with the land, the life force, a thesis that is central to Native American culture. Analyzes the main characters and the causes for Tayo's illness from a Jungian perspective. Gives a brief and helpful bibliography of Silko's work and of criticism about her fiction. Also discusses her poetry and the storyteller tradition that underpins her fiction.

Barnett, Louise K., and James L. Thorson, eds. *Leslie Marmon Silko*. Albuquerque: University of New Mexico Press, 1999. A collection of critical essays on the entire range of Silko's work through *Almanac of the Dead*, this text offers biographical information on Silko as well as an extensive bibliography of primary and secondary sources complete with a helpful bibliographical essay.

Chavkin, Allan, ed. *Leslie Marmon Silko's "Ceremony": A Casebook*. New York: Oxford University Press, 2002. Fourteen essays offer readings of Silko's novel from a variety of theoretical perspectives and provide background information on Native American culture.

Fitz, Brewster E. *Silko: Writing Storyteller and Medicine Woman*. Norman: University of Oklahoma Press, 2004. An interesting discussion of Silko as a traditional storyteller in a writing, rather than oral, mode.

Graulich, Melody, ed. *"Yellow Woman": Leslie Marmon Silko*. New Brunswick, N.J.:

Rutgers University Press, 1993. An important addition to Silko scholarship, this collection of critical essays contains a great deal of useful background information on the Yellow Woman myth so central to Silko's *Storyteller* collection. In addition, it gathers some of the most influential Silko scholarship.

Owens, Louis. *Other Destinies: Understanding the American Indian Novel.* Norman: University of Oklahoma Press, 1992. In the chapter titled "The Very Essence of Our Lives: Leslie Silko's Webs of Identity," Owens analyzes *Ceremony* as a search for identity through memory and returning home.

Ronnow, Gretchen. "Tayo, Death, and Desire: A Lacanian Reading of *Ceremony*." In *Narrative Chance: Postmodern Discourse in Native American Indian Literatures,* edited by Gerald Vizenor. Albuquerque: University of New Mexico Press, 1989. Provides a detailed reading of *Ceremony*, applying the perspectives of Lacanian psychology and poststructuralist literary criticism.

Salyer, Gregory. *Leslie Marmon Silko.* New York: Twayne, 1997. A critical study; subjects include women and the Laguna Indians in Silko's fiction. Includes a bibliography and an index.

Seyersted, Per. *Leslie Marmon Silko.* Boise, Idaho: Boise State University, 1980. A good critical study of Silko's work; includes a bibliography.

Silko, Leslie Marmon. "Interview." *Short Story,* n.s. 2 (Fall, 1994): 91-95. Discusses the process by which Silko writes her fiction, its sources in the storytelling traditions of her ethnic background, how she began writing and why.

Studies in American Indian Literatures (SAIL) 2, no. 10 (Fall, 1998). Special issue on *Almanac of the Dead.* Includes excellent essays as well as Ellen Arnold's interview, in which Silko discusses *Gardens in the Dunes.*

Wiget, Andrew. *Native American Literature.* Boston: Twayne, 1985. Offers an overview analysis of *Ceremony* and compares the novel to N. Scott Momaday's *House Made of Dawn.* Says the book explores the death of, or threats to, traditional Native American values and ways. *Ceremony* sets the human struggle against mythic Native American legends. Examines *Storyteller.* Says that Silko successfully uses the possibilities afforded her by Native American myths and the persona of the storyteller figure to do more than provide local color: Instead Silko uses these references to develop her characters and plot. Provides a useful but brief bibliography.

Upton Sinclair

Born: Baltimore, Maryland; September 20, 1878
Died: Bound Brook, New Jersey; November 25, 1968

Principal long fiction • *Springtime and Harvest*, 1901; *Prince Hagen*, 1903; *The Journal of Arthur Stirling*, 1903; *Manassas*, 1904 (revised as *Theirs Be the Guilt*, 1959); *A Captain of Industry*, 1906; *The Jungle*, 1906; *The Overman*, 1907; *The Metropolis*, 1908; *The Moneychangers*, 1908; *Samuel the Seeker*, 1910; *Love's Pilgrimage*, 1911; *Sylvia*, 1913; *Sylvia's Marriage*, 1914; *King Coal*, 1917; *Jimmie Higgins*, 1919; *100%*, 1920; *They Call Me Carpenter*, 1922; *Oil! A Novel*, 1927; *Boston*, 1928; *Mountain City*, 1930; *Roman Holiday*, 1931; *The Wet Parade*, 1931; *Co-op*, 1936; *No Pasaran!*, 1937; *The Flivver King*, 1937; *Little Steel*, 1938; *Our Lady*, 1938; *World's End*, 1940; *Between Two Worlds*, 1941; *Dragon's Teeth*, 1942; *Wide Is the Gate*, 1943; *Presidential Agent*, 1944; *Dragon Harvest*, 1945; *A World to Win*, 1946; *Presidential Mission*, 1947; *One Clear Call*, 1948; *O Shepherd, Speak!*, 1949; *Another Pamela: Or, Virtue Still Rewarded*, 1950; *The Return of Lanny Budd*, 1953; *What Didymus Did*, 1954; *It Happened to Didymus*, 1958; *Affectionately Eve*, 1961.

Other literary forms • Between 1901 and 1961, Upton Sinclair wrote or rewrote more than forty novels, but in addition to his longer fiction, Sinclair also wrote and published a massive amount of nonfiction, including pamphlets, analyses of diverse subjects, memoirs, twelve plays, and letters by the thousands. The bibliography of his works is testimony to his amazing fluency, but no one who is so prolific can escape being uneven, and this is indeed the case with Sinclair. His career, which spanned more than six decades, was unified in one respect, however, for both his fiction and his nonfiction were devoted to a single aim—the achievement of social justice.

Everything that Sinclair wrote was written primarily as a means to attain the end he sought, bettering the conditions of life for all people. Thus, much of what Sinclair produced is not belletristic in any full sense, but propaganda to spread his ideas about politics and economics. In books such as *The Industrial Republic* (1907), he tries to explain how socialism will be arrived at by a natural process in America; the theory is based on the premise that social revolutions are bound to be benevolent. During the period following World War I to the onset of the Great Depression, most of Sinclair's writing was nonfiction. In a number of books, which he called his Dead Hand series, an ironic allusion to Adam Smith's "Invisible Hand" of laissez-faire economics, Sinclair deals with the destructive influence of capitalism on numerous American institutions: *The Profits of Religion* (1918) treats the abuses of institutional religions, showing how the established church supports the ruling classes in exchange for economic advantages; *The Brass Check: A Study in American Journalism* (1919) details the operation of class bias in American journalism; *The Goose-Step: A Study of American Education* (1923) reveals higher education's lackeylike relationship to capitalism, fostered by grants and endowments made to the universities by wealthy families and industry. In *The Goslings: A Study of the American Schools* (1924), the same kind of servile relationship with the capitalist status quo is exposed as existing in elementary and high schools, and in *Mammonart* (1925), Sinclair shows how artists and writers down through history have been duped into serving oppressive economic and political power structures. Not even William Shakespeare, Fyodor Dostoevski, or Joseph Conrad were their own men according to Sinclair's ideological criticism. Although the Dead Hand series is flawed by an excess of socialist polemics, Sinclair did an extensive amount of research to produce each book, and though the case is overstated, there is a grain of truth in his analysis of the all-pervasive influence of the economic and political structure of America on those areas that should be most independent of such pressure—the Church, the press, the educational system, the arts.

Of more interest to the general reader are Sinclair's autobiographical works *American Outpost: A Book of Reminiscences* (1932) and *The Autobiography of Upton Sinclair* (1962), which updates his life for the thirty years intervening between the two books. In his accounts of his life, Sinclair reveals himself to be an honest but self-centered idealist. He chronicles his victories and defeats through childhood, youth, and marriage as the educational experiences of a genius; he offers in generally positive and optimistic terms his lifelong belief in progress and his hatred of social inequality and social exploitation.

Achievements • Sinclair's literary remains weighed in at eight tons when being collected for donation to Indiana University Library. Of modern American writers, he is among the most widely translated, his works having been translated into forty-seven languages in thirty-nine countries, yet his literary reputation steadily declined after the 1940's, despite the fact that *The Jungle* was still widely read in high school and college classrooms. Moreover, Sinclair himself has historical importance for the role he played in the American radical movement.

Sinclair's recurring theme as a novelist was class conflict, the exploitation of the poor by the rich, of labor by management, of the have-nots by the haves. With few exceptions, the rich are depicted as useless, extravagant, and unprincipled, while the poor are essentially noble characters who are the victims of capitalistic society. Sinclair's literary method, which came to be called "muckraking," was intended to expose the evils of such a society.

Apart from *The Jungle*, which is the best-known example of this genre, there is the Lanny Budd series—ten historical novels that trace the history of the world from 1913 to 1946. *Dragon's Teeth*, the third in the series, won the Pulitzer Prize for Fiction in 1943 by virtue of its vivid portrayal of conditions in Nazi-dominated Europe. In addition to these, the most widely read of Sinclair's novels, he produced novels on almost every topic of then-current social history, including coal strikes in Colorado in *King Coal*, exploitation by the oil industry in California in *The Wet Parade*, and the legal injustices of the Sacco-Vanzetti case in *Boston*. All of Sinclair's fiction was aimed at the middle-class liberal, whom he hoped to convert to his idealistic vision of a fellowship of labor. Sinclair was thus a spokesman for the progressive era of American history; a chronic protester and iconoclast, he tried to stir the conscience of his nation and to cause change. In only one case, *The Jungle*, was he successful in prompting the desired changes through legislation. As a propagandist writing in the spirit of Thomas Paine and in the idiom of Karl Marx, Sinclair made a permanent impact by what he said, if not by how he wrote, and to this day, he still serves as one of the chief interpreters of American society to other nations.

Biography • Upton Beall Sinclair was born in Baltimore, Maryland, but reared in New York. Finishing high school at the age of twelve, he was too young for college and had to wait until he was fourteen before he could enter the City College of New York

Library of Congress

(CCNY). While an undergraduate, he helped support himself by writing stories and jokes for pulp magazines. In one span of a few weeks, he turned out fifty-six thousand words, an incredible feat even for a prolific prodigy such as Sinclair. In 1898, after taking his bachelor's degree from CCNY, Sinclair enrolled as a special student in the Graduate School of Columbia University, but withdrew after a professor told him, "you don't know anything about writing." In 1900, Sinclair married Meta Fuller and began work on his first novel, *Springtime and Harvest*, which was written in Canada. Soon afterward, in 1902, he joined the Socialist Party. The reception of his early fiction gave him little critical encouragement and no cash of which to speak. His first four novels brought him fewer than one thousand dollars, and the threat of poverty put a strain on his marriage.

In 1905, Sinclair, with Jack London, formed the Intercollegiate Socialist Society, an indication of his growing political radicalism.

Sinclair's first fame came with his fifth novel, *The Jungle*; he was even invited to the White House by President Theodore Roosevelt to discuss the book. With the thirty thousand dollars that *The Jungle* earned for him, Sinclair founded a utopian community, Helicon Colony, in New Jersey. In 1907, an arsonist burned down the colony and Sinclair's fortune with it. This was the first actual persecution that Sinclair had experienced for professing unpopular views. In private life, he faced further difficulties; his wife divorced him in 1911; he remarried in 1913 and moved west with his new wife, Mary Kimbrough, in 1914. Continuing to write at a furious pace, Sinclair became a publisher during World War I with the *Upton Sinclair Magazine*. He also issued a series of tracts on the effects of capitalism, objecting to its effects on education, art, journalism, and literature.

Not all of Sinclair's energies went into writing. He was instrumental in creating The League for Industrial Democracy and the American Civil Liberties Union. Three times he ran for the California state legislature and three times for governor, usually on the Socialist Party ticket but also as a Democrat. In *I, Governor of California and How I Ended Poverty* (1933), he set forth his platform, "End Poverty in California" or "E.P.I.C.," which explained the Depression as a result of private ownership and the economic insanity of limited production. His ideas found a large degree of public acceptance in the early days of the New Deal, and he came close to being elected despite the mudslinging of his opponent. Some critics believe that the chief reason for Sinclair's decline as a novelist was his involvement in electoral politics during the

1930's. His novels of that decade are about specific political situations. *The Flivver King* attacks Ford Motor Company and makes a case for labor unions. "Little Steel" is a story about the organization of steel-mill owners against unions. "Pasaran!" is another short story from the 1930's about the brave fight in the Spanish Civil War against right-wing dictators.

During World War II, Sinclair began the historical record of his times in the Lanny Budd series. The novels in this ten-book series show the metamorphosis of the hero, Lanny, from an espouser of socialist causes to an anticommunist, a change that reflected Sinclair's own changed sympathies.

By the decade of the 1950's, Sinclair had entered semiretirement, during which he nevertheless managed to expand his autobiography and finish six books, including a clever parody of Samuel Richardson's epistolary novel *Pamela* (1740-1741), titled *Another Pamela*, and a biography of Jesus. In these years, Sinclair finally settled his quarrel with the status quo. In his old age, he came to approve of the American establishment's foot-dragging on civil rights and supported American intervention in Vietnam. The old radical had, like so many before him, softened his position.

Analysis • Sinclair was a prodigy as a writer and wrote with great fluency and consequent unevenness. For him, the essential purpose of literature was to expose social evils and promote change; his end as a writer was the improvement of the condition of humankind. Thus, his literary reputation is not really germane to what he was trying to do as a writer. His fiction has more relevance when it is regarded in a political and historical light rather than as literature per se. As the social and economic issues of his time recede into history, so does interest in those books that were simply propaganda.

Although Sinclair was regarded as a literary rebel for his iconoclastic attacks on America's economic, intellectual, and political institutions, he was not in any way an avant-garde writer in terms of style and structure. His subject was society rather than the individual human consciousness. It is necessary in any analysis of Sinclair's fiction to admit at once the defects in his writing. Most of it is journalistic in quality rather than belletristic. In fact, he deliberately wrote against the genteel tradition in American letters. Sinclair employed his rhetoric for practical results rather than to achieve poetic effects. His polemics were couched in fictional form because he believed the novel was a particularly effective medium for his idealistic radicalism.

Sinclair's first four novels were produced between 1900 and 1904. These early works were awkward but full of passionate idealism. In *Prince Hagen* and *The Overman*, which were written before Sinclair discovered socialism, there is already a conflict between the pure-minded and the corrupt oppressors, but no solutions for the problems are proposed. The ideology of socialism provided him with solutions, although Sinclair was not a traditional socialist; to him, socialism was the purest expression of the American Dream. He did not see himself as an overthrower of American values, but as a writer who was helping his fellow citizens return to a vision of human alliance.

Manassas • Prior to *Manassas*, Sinclair's fiction had been based on personal experience. In this novel about the Civil War, a young southerner, Alan Montague, the son of a Mississippi plantation owner, becomes a supporter of abolition. The protagonist is present at many historic moments—the raid at Harper's Ferry, the bombardment of Fort Sumter—and encounters many historical figures, such as Abraham Lincoln, Jefferson Davis, Frederick Douglass, and John Brown. *Manassas* differed from

Sinclair's early books in that it was more realistic and objective. As a work of art, however, *Manassas* is not remarkable. The plot is often an inert review of historical facts, the characterizations are shallow, and the story is too filled with coincidence to be plausible. Despite its flaws, *Manassas* marked a turning point in Sinclair's career. In this novel, he revealed attitudes that pointed toward his development as a writer of exposés.

The Jungle • In 1904, Sinclair was asked by the editor of *The Appeal*, a radical paper, to write a novel about wage slavery and the oppressive conditions of industrial workers that would show that their plight was analogous to that of the black in the Old South. Responding to this offer, Sinclair spent two months in the meatpacking houses of Chicago talking to the workers; he visited the plants also as an official tourist, and in disguise as a worker. The impressions and information Sinclair gathered from this experience were extremely distressing to him. His personal reaction to the corruption he saw was outrage; it is his identification with the exploited workers and his naturalistic descriptions of the oppressive industrial conditions that make *The Jungle* so gripping.

As Sinclair explains in his memoirs, *American Outpost*, he returned to his farm in New Jersey after he had collected his data on the meatpacking industry in Chicago and started writing the novel on Christmas Day, completing it in the summer of 1905 after fewer than six months' work. Although it was published in serial form as it was being written, Sinclair had trouble finding a publisher for the book; it was refused by five houses before Doubleday and Company took it after their lawyers made a careful investigation to avoid any possible libel suits. When *The Jungle* was published in February, 1906, the public was horrified, not by the novel's account of the conditions of the workers as Sinclair and his socialist friends expected, but by the naturalistic descriptions of the slaughterhouses and the evidence of criminal negligence in meat inspection.

The Jungle, like most of Sinclair's fiction, straddles genres; it is partly a novel and partly exposé journalism. Sinclair's purpose in writing the book was to protest the exploitation of the workers and to recommend socialism as a corrective ideology to capitalism; the revelations of unsanitary packing-plant procedures were only a means to those ends. Hardly a dozen pages of this long novel are explicitly concerned with the repugnant details of the slaughterhouse, yet what remains in the reader's mind long after the plot line and thematic intentions fade are the scenes of grinding up poisoned rats, children's fingers, and carcasses of steers condemned as tubercular for canning meats; and the rendering of hogs dead of cholera for a fine grade of lard. Most dramatic of all, however, was Sinclair's report that the men who served in the cooking room occasionally fell into the boiling vats and were returned to the world transubstantiated into Durham's Pure Leaf Lard. The vividness of the author's descriptions had two effects: The first was an immediate drop in meat sales across America and Europe; the second was a summons to the White House to detail the abuses in the meat industry to President Theodore Roosevelt. The outraged public brought pressure to bear on politicians, and Congress enacted the Federal Pure Food and Drug Act of 1906.

The sensational revelations of *The Jungle* have drawn attention from the book's literary qualities. *The Jungle* has been compared to the polemical late works of Leo Tolstoy and to the naturalistic fiction of Émile Zola because of its pessimistic determinism. The setting is the grim slums of Chicago and the gory stockyards. The novel tells the story of a group of recent Lithuanian immigrants who have been lured to America from their old-world villages with the promise of high wages.

Jurgis Rudkus, the novel's principal character, comes to the stockyard district, along with several of his friends and relatives, expecting to realize the American Dream, little aware that they have entered a jungle. Unable to speak English, the immigrants are exploited by almost everyone in power—the politicians, the police, the landlords, and the "Beef Trust" bosses. Jurgis has to pay his foreman part of his low salary to keep his job. He is cheated by a crooked real-estate agent, who sells him a house with a hidden clause that allows the mortgage company to foreclose on Jurgis. After losing his house, Jurgis and his family are afflicted with misery. His job is taken away after he is blacklisted; he serves a jail term for slugging his wife's lascivious boss, who has compromised her honor. In turn, his father dies of disease, his wife and infant son die in childbirth, and finally, he loses his last son in a drowning accident. Jurgis is left without anything; alone and in ill health, he is a broken man. He becomes a hobo, a petty criminal, and a strike-breaking scab—the lowest form of degradation for him.

In his extremity, Jurgis for the first time reflects upon how unjustly he has been treated by society, which he begins to regard as his enemy, but his views are inchoate. One day, by chance he hears a socialist speak. The lecture transforms his conception of the world; socialism is like a revelation, for now there is a way by which the workers of the world can win respect. With Jurgis's conversion, the novel as a narrative ends for all practical purposes. The last chapters are devoted to socialist propaganda and socioeconomic analysis. The optimistic conclusion of the novel contrasts sharply with the pessimistic of the first chapters. Ironically, and to Sinclair's disappointment, the appeal to socialism and the protest against wage slavery did not win the hearts and minds of his audience, but his realistic portrayal of conditions in the meatpacking industry (as he once remarked) surely turned the stomach of the nation.

The Jungle will never be placed in the first rank of American fiction because of its mixture of fictional and journalistic elements, its unresolved contradictions in theme, and its melodramatic plot and bifurcated structure. Sinclair tried to do too many things at once, and he was only partially successful. Most readers think that the true significance of Sinclair's achievement in *The Jungle* lies in the uncensored presentation of the conditions of working-class life. Only Stephen Crane in *Maggie: A Girl of the Streets* (1893) had dealt with slum subjects with such integrity, and Sinclair had no models to follow in depicting this strata of society. In his firsthand observations and deep compassion for the oppressed, he was breaking new ground for literary treatment, which Theodore Dreiser would follow to different purposes.

The Metropolis, The Moneychangers, and Love's Pilgrimage • Following the success of *The Jungle* was difficult for Sinclair. He spent the next eight years trying to repeat what he had done with his first and best "muckraking" book. He produced a number of novels focused on specific problems, but at the other end of the social scale. *The Metropolis* is an exposé of conspicuous consumption among upper-class New York socialites. It is a poor book by Sinclair's own admission and is remarkable only for the absence of socialistic sermons by the author. Sinclair, like F. Scott Fitzgerald, apparently believed that money sets the very wealthy quite apart from the rest of society, but, rather than seeking rapport with his wealthy characters, as Fitzgerald did, Sinclair hoped to reform them. Another novel of this period, *The Moneychangers*, is a story of the machinations of a high financier, obviously patterned on J. P. Morgan; the story tells of the exploits of Dan Waterman, the elderly head of the Steel Trust, who creates a panic on Wall Street purely for personal revenge against a rival steel magnate. Although *The Moneychangers* is not very good fiction, it does have an interesting premise, suggesting a connection between sexual desire and the drive for financial power.

Another novel of this period that deserves mention for its subject is *Love's Pilgrimage*; neofeminist in theme, this work examines the pressures on Sinclair's own marriage because of his male insensitivity to his wife's personal, sexual, and intellectual needs. The novel is also interesting for the insight it offers into Sinclair's personality, for he implies that the divorce his first wife sought was deserved because he prudishly withheld from sexual relations on the theory that it would decrease his creative energy.

King Coal • In 1914, Sinclair was remarried and living in California. The transition in his life resulted in a change in his writing. In the West, Sinclair was drawn back to the problems of the proletariat by labor strife in the Colorado coal mines. As a result of the attempt by the United Mine Workers to organize the miners, the governor of Colorado had called up the state militia to break up strikes. In 1914, in the town of Ludlow, National Guard troops fired into a camp of strikers and their families, killing eleven women and two children. This shocking event outraged Sinclair as nothing had since he had witnessed the brutal conditions of the stockyards.

Following the methods he had used to collect background material for *The Jungle*, he went to Colorado, visited the miners and their families, and talked with the mining officials and labor leaders. His direct contact with the working-class people stirred his emotions and gave him a more realistic point of departure for his next novel, *King Coal*, than any he had employed since *The Jungle*. In fact, *King Coal* was an attempt to repeat the same sort of muckraking performance that had succeeded so well in the former case. However, for Sinclair, *King Coal* did not create the response aroused by *The Jungle*, a fact largely resulting from the lag time in the publication of the novel. When *King Coal* appeared in 1917, the events in Ludlow were three years old and yesterday's news. America had just entered World War I, and the nation's mind was on "doughboys" rather than on coal miners.

The poor reception of *King Coal* was a great disappointment to Sinclair, because he knew he had produced the kind of novel he wrote best. *King Coal*, while not as powerful as *The Jungle*, has the rhetorical strength and the factual validity of the earlier book. Sinclair tells the story of a rich young man named Hal Warner, who impersonates a coal miner in order to investigate working conditions in the western coal camps. He becomes a union sympathizer and labor agitator after he becomes convinced that the mine owners are denying the miners their legal rights and are cheating them out of their wages by rigged scales. After witnessing the futility of getting justice for working men inside the legal system, the miners go on a wildcat strike. Hal persuades his coworkers to join the union, and the novel ends with the lines drawn between labor and management while Hal returns to college, vowing to continue his fight for the working people of America.

Although *King Coal* is not as powerful in its naturalistic details as *The Jungle* and lacks the pessimistic determinism of that novel, it is in the opinion of most critics Sinclair's second-best effort at muckraking. If very few Americans responded to Sinclair's account of the dangers of cave-ins, coal dust, and explosions, this result may be because they were never exposed to such perils, whereas all were subject to health hazards as a result of unsanitary food processing. For this reason, the exposé of negligence in Chicago meatpacking plants had a much more profound and practical effect than the exposé of the inhuman conditions in the coal camps of Colorado.

Oil! A Novel **and** *Boston* • Between World War I and the start of the Depression, Sinclair wrote two remarkable novels based on topical social or political situations. *Oil! A Novel* delves into the Teapot Dome and other oil scandals of the Harding administration, and thus has considerable historical significance as well as being one of Sinclair's most readable books. *Boston,* on the other hand, represents Sinclair's best use of a contemporary event for fictional purposes. This novel enfolds the drama of the Sacco-Vanzetti case, but it also encompasses the whole of Boston's society, suggesting that the city itself was responsible for what happened in this tragic case. The central character is again from the upper classes, an elderly Back Bay aristocrat, Cornelia Thornwell, wife to a governor. Full of vitality and intelligence, she thinks that she has spent her life as an artificial adornment to a great family. She determines late in life to emancipate herself from the mores and manners of the mansion and moves out to board with the Brini family, who are honest Italian mill hands, and starts to earn her own living in a factory.

At this point, Vanzetti enters the story. During a strike in the mill, he plays an important role in keeping up the workers' spirits. He also prevents them from organizing, because as an anarchist, Vanzetti did not support unions. Afterward, Vanzetti and his friend Sacco are marked as "anarchist wops" by the police. They are picked up as suspects in a payroll robbery, and in the midst of the deportation mania of the postwar period, the city's reason and sense of justice are beclouded. The courts, judge, jury, and prosecutor seem determined to make the foreigners pay—if not for the crime, then for their politics. The climax of the novel comes when the cogs of justice bring the proletarian saints, Vanzetti and Sacco, to the electric chair with many doubts about their guilt still lingering.

Through a blending of fact and fiction, Sinclair is able to record a complex and tragic story of social injustice, although the story of the runaway grandmother does get lost in the final pages as the historical facts dominate the plot. As a novel, the two-volume *Boston* is too long except for readers with some special interest in the Sacco-Vanzetti case. As usual, Sinclair was writing for a mass audience, and the novel employs many stock characters and a melodramatic plot; furthermore, a statement of socialist doctrine forms a coda to the novel. Sinclair does, however, create a convincing portrait of Vanzetti. It is in Sinclair's account of the death of this man of dignity and intelligence that the novel gains its greatest power.

The Lanny Budd series • The major literary effort of Sinclair's career was launched just before the outbreak of World War II: a ten-novel series offering a fictionalized history of the Western world in the first half of the twentieth century. The series is unified by its central character, Lanny Budd, and is known collectively by his name. One of the Lanny Budd novels, *Dragon's Teeth,* won for Sinclair a Pulitzer Prize in 1943. A chronicle of Germany's slide into Nazism, *Dragon's Teeth* is a scrupulous study of the fateful years between 1930 and 1934 and reflects an extensive research effort on Sinclair's part. In fact, several critics claimed that if the book were stripped of its fictional ingredient, it might well serve as a history text.

Sinclair creates an air of impending doom as he shows how quickly Europe was led to the abyss. His protagonist, Lanny Budd, is a neutral observer traveling the Continent with his millionaire wife, Irma, who is especially obtuse about economics, politics, and national traits. She is a foil to the sensitive and intelligent Lanny, who is aware of the coming crisis. Irma and her upper-class female friends refuse to believe that their smug routine of bridge and dinner parties will be disrupted. The reader in 1942 received these opinions with a great deal of dramatic irony. Meanwhile, Lanny grows increasingly concerned about the absence of morality in the political climate of Germany. Lanny has rather improbable meetings with the bigwigs of the Nazi regime. He goes hunting with Hermann Göring, has cocktails with Joseph Goebbels, and a discussion with Adolf Hitler about the Jewish question. His interest in this topic is not merely academic, since his sister is married to one of Germany's most prominent Jews. The Jews in Germany, however, are like Irma's circle; they refuse to face the realities of Nazism. The novel ends with Lanny's contriving to help his brother-in-law escape the dragon's teeth of the Nazi menace, closing the story on an exciting climax, somewhat like that of a cliffhanger film of the 1940's.

Sinclair continued the adventures of Lanny Budd, interweaving fiction with fact as he related the sequence of world events in *World's End*, which covers the years 1913 to 1919; *Between Two Worlds* deals with the events between the Versailles Treaty and the stock market crash of 1929; the author then covers the Nazi "Blood Purge" of 1934 to the Spanish Civil War in *Wide Is the Gate*; the annexation of Austria, the invasion of Czechoslovakia, and the Munich pact in *Presidential Agent*; the fall of France in *Dragon Harvest*; and America's entry into the war in *A World to Win*. The years of Allied setbacks, 1941-1943, are covered in *Presidential Mission; One Clear Call* and *O Shepherd, Speak!* deal with the Normandy Invasion and the defeat of the German military machine; and in the sequel to the series, *The Return of Lanny Budd*, Sinclair brings events up to 1949 and the onset of the Cold War between the United States and the Soviet Union.

As a whole, this group of novels is interesting, in part simply because the series surveys a dramatic period of history in considerable detail. Throughout the series, Sinclair's careful research is evident, but the popularity of these novels was also a result of their appeal to patriotism. America's role as the savior of civilization is increasingly emphasized in the later novels in the series. During this period, Sinclair's confidence that progress was represented by socialism and communism was shaken by the example of the Soviet Union. Like so many early twentieth century political radicals, he became an anticommunist during the 1950's.

Sinclair was a propagandist first and a novelist second, if propaganda is defined as an "effort directed systematically toward the gaining of support for an opinion or course of action." He wrote millions of words trying to change, improve, or expose oppressive conditions. Because Sinclair so obviously used literature for ulterior purposes and because he was so prolific, serious critics have unduly neglected him; on the other hand, he has been overrated by those foreign critics who delight in finding indictments of America by an American writer. As time puts Sinclair's contribution to American literature into perspective, it seems certain that he will never be regarded as a great novelist, but he will fairly be judged an honest, courageous, and original writer.

Hallman B. Bryant

Other major works

PLAYS: *Plays of Protest*, pb. 1912; *Hell: A Verse Drama and Photo-Play*, pb. 1923; *Singing Jailbirds*, pb. 1924; *The Millennium*, pb. 1924; *The Pot Boiler*, pb. 1924; *Bill Porter*, pb. 1925; *Wally for Queen!*, pb. 1936; *Marie Antoinette*, pb. 1939; *A Giant's Strength*, pr., pb. 1948.

NONFICTION: *Our Bourgeois Literature*, 1904; *The Industrial Republic*, 1907; *The Fasting Cure*, 1911; *The Profits of Religion*, 1918; *The Brass Check: A Study in American Journalism*, 1919; *The Book of Life, Mind, and Body*, 1921; *The Goose-Step: A Study of American Education*, 1923; *The Goslings: A Study of the American Schools*, 1924; *Letters to Judd*, 1925; *Mammonart*, 1925; *Money Writes!*, 1927; *Mental Radio*, 1930; *American Outpost: A Book of Reminiscences*, 1932; *I, Governor of California and How I Ended Poverty*, 1933; *The Way Out—What Lies Ahead for America?*, 1933; *The EPIC Plan for California*, 1934; *What God Means to Me*, 1936; *Terror in Russia: Two Views*, 1938; *Expect No Peace!*, 1939; *A Personal Jesus*, 1952; *The Cup of Fury*, 1956; *My Lifetime in Letters*, 1960; *The Autobiography of Upton Sinclair*, 1962.

CHILDREN'S LITERATURE: *The Gnomobile: A Gnice Gnew Gnarrative with Gnonsense, but Gnothing Gnaughty*, 1936.

Bibliography

Arthur, Anthony. *Radical Innocent: Upton Sinclair.* New York: Random House, 2006. A well-researched, balanced and thorough portrait of Sinclair that tracks the ups and downs of his career and personal life. Includes 16 pages of black and white photos.

Bloom, Harold. *Upton Sinclair's "The Jungle."* Philadelphia: Chelsea House, 2002. Useful introduction to Sinclair's most famous novel.

Colburn, David R., and George E. Pozzetta, eds. *Reform and Reformers in the Progressive Era.* Westport, Conn.: Greenwood Press, 1983. Examines Sinclair's position as a muckraker and his role in inspiring Progressive reforms. Unlike other journalistic writers, Sinclair was personally and ideologically committed.

Dell, Floyd. *Upton Sinclair: A Study in Social Protest.* New York: AMS Press, 1970. Dell's treatment of Sinclair's career analyzes the apparent discrepancy between his literary position in the United States and throughout the rest of the world. Personal incidents and psychological insights are intertwined with evaluations and interpretations of specific works. Contains a bibliography of out-of-print books and an index.

Harris, Leon. *Upton Sinclair: American Rebel.* New York: Thomas Y. Crowell, 1975. Traces Sinclair's rise from obscurity to fame, with his subsequent decline in popularity. The text provides interesting information regarding source materials for some of his novels. A section of photographs, extensive notes, a list of Sinclair's books, and an index complete the book.

Herms, Dieter, ed. *Upton Sinclair: Literature and Social Reform.* New York: Peter Lang, 1990. This is a collection of papers from the Upton Sinclair World Conference of July, 1988, at the University of Bremen. Includes bibliographical references.

Mitchell, Greg. *The Campaign of the Century.* New York: Random House, 1992. At 665 pages, this excellently researched book details Sinclair's 1934 gubernatorial campaign from August to November, stressing the media's key role in defeating Sinclair and ushering in a new era of media politics. Includes notes.

Mookerjee, R. N. *Art for Social Justice: The Major Novels of Upton Sinclair.* Metuchen, N.J.: Scarecrow Press, 1988. Mookerjee, a critic of writers of the 1930's, provides a reevaluation of *The Jungle, King Coal, Oil! A Novel, Boston,* and the Lanny Budd series. This slender volume is a reminder of the pioneering role of Sinclair in the "documentary novel." Contains a selected bibliography.

Rohde, Stephen R. "Upton Sinclair." In *Great American Writers; Twentieth Century,* edited by R. Baird Shuman. Vol. 10. New York: Marshall Cavendish, 2002. Lavishly illustrated survey of Sinclair's life and writings that pays particular attention to his politics. A prominent civil libertarian, author Stephen Rohde also published a useful guide to collecting Sinclair's books in the May, 2000, issue of *Firsts* magazine.

Scott, Ivan. *Upton Sinclair: The Forgotten Socialist.* Lewiston, N.Y.: Edwin Mellen Press, 1997. See especially chapters 1 and 2, "The Formation of Genius" and "*The Jungle.*" In his introduction, Scott makes a good case for Sinclair's importance. A sound scholarly biography, drawing extensively on the Sinclair collection at Lilly Library, the University of Indiana.

Yoder, Jon A. *Upton Sinclair.* New York: Frederick Ungar, 1975. Like some other critics, Yoder attributes Sinclair's "meager reputation" in part to his socialistic views. Five chapters in this volume examine various facets of the novelist's life and career. Includes a chronology, notes, a bibliography, and an index.

Isaac Bashevis Singer

Born: Leoncin, Poland; July 14 or November 21, 1904
Died: Surfside, Florida; July 24, 1991

Principal long fiction • *Der Sotan in Gorey*, 1935 (*Satan in Goray*, 1955); *Di Familye Mushkat*, 1950 (*The Family Moskat*, 1950); *Der Hoyf*, 1953-1955 (*The Manor*, 1967, and *The Estate*, 1969); *Shotns baym Hodson*, 1957-1958 (*Shadows on the Hudson*, 1998); *Der Kuntsnmakher fun Lublin*, 1958-1959 (*The Magician of Lublin*, 1960); *Der Knekht*, 1961 (*The Slave*, 1962); *Sonim, de Geshichte fun a Liebe*, 1966 (*Enemies: A Love Story*, 1972); *Der Bal-Tshuve*, 1974 (*The Penitent*, 1983); *Neshome Ekspeditsyes*, 1974 (*Shosha*, 1978); *Reaches of Heaven: A Story of the Baal Shem Tov*, 1980; *Der Kenig vun di Felder*, 1988 (*The King of the Fields*, 1988); *Scum*, 1991; *The Certificate*, 1992; *Meshugah*, 1994.

Other literary forms • The first work that Isaac Bashevis Singer published when he moved to the United States was the novel known as "Messiah the Sinner," which was serialized in 1936 but was never published as a book. It was serialized in three Yiddish daily papers: *Der Vorwärts* (the *Jewish Daily Forward*, in New York), the *Warshanahaint* (in Warsaw), and the *Pariser Haint* (in Paris). Singer himself considered this work a "complete failure" and never attempted to translate it. In addition to his novels, Singer wrote memoirs, *Mayn Tatn's Bes-din Shtub* (1956; *In My Father's Court*, 1966), *A Little Boy in Search of God* (1976), *A Young Man in Search of Love* (1978), and *Lost in America* (1980); more than one hundred stories; and numerous books for children. He wrote two works on Hasidism, one in collaboration with the artist Ira Moskowitz titled *The Hasidim* (1973). His Yiddish translations of works by such noted authors as Stefen Zweig, Knut Hamsun, Erich Maria Remarque, and Thomas Mann are well regarded, as are his many literary essays and reviews. Several of Singer's short stories have been adapted as plays; "Yentl der Yeshive Bocher" ("Yentl, the Yeshiva Boy"), which was written in Yiddish during the 1950's, became a Broadway play in 1975 and a film (*Yentl*) in 1983.

Achievements • Singer has been acclaimed by some critics as a genius and referred to by others as one of the greatest writers of the modern world. In the aftermath of the Holocaust, which resulted in the obliteration of central and eastern European Jewry, the works of Isaac Bashevis Singer stand as monuments to a vibrant and vital world. Singer's writing does not idolize this community: He depicts it in its totality, in its full humanity. His people are saints and sinners, believers and heretics, fools and scholars, avaricious merchants and ineffectual rabbis, patient wives and termagants. His imaginative world includes demons, elves, dybbuks, and magicians, mystical figures from a lost folk culture. However, Singer's fiction does more than recall a world destroyed by the Holocaust. The power of his work, while remaining thoroughly Jewish, transcends the boundaries of cultural and religious ethnicity to raise questions about life that have been translatable across the changing contexts of twentieth century thought.

Singer's works are written in Yiddish, the language of the shtetl—the eastern European village or town. For Singer, Yiddish is more than the vernacular of the people of the central and eastern European Jewish community. It is, as he stated in his Nobel Prize lecture, "the wise and humble language of us all, the idiom of a frightened and hopeful humanity." His Yiddish reflects the influence of three languages, Yiddish, Hebrew, and Aramaic, and contains frequent allusions to rabbinic and Talmudic lore. The richness of his prose and its texture, pace, and rhythm are not easy to capture in translation. Singer worked with his translators and participated in the editing. All of his major works first appeared in serial form in the *Forward* (originally a daily, the *Jewish Daily Forward*, then a weekly) prior to their translation and rendition into book form except for his first novel, *Satan in Goray*, which was serialized in the magazine *Globus* in Warsaw in 1933.

One of the outstanding characteristics of Singer's tales is his use of demoniac imagery. This motif does not represent a love of the bizarre, the occult, or the gothic, although Singer is interested in these aspects. His demons figuratively portray the evil side of human nature; moreover, Singer believed that supernatural powers—both good and evil—do exist, and he affirmed his ultimate faith in Providence.

Singer's vision is optimistic when it concerns cosmic matters but pessimistic in dealing with humanity. He differs from his Yiddish literary contemporaries or predecessors in that most have been secularists who relinquished the past in favor of the Enlightenment. Most Yiddish writers after the 1940's portrayed an idealized and sentimental view of the shtetl. Singer could not accept this tradition. He maintains that the greatest gift of God is freedom of choice. Where there is no evil, there is also no freedom. He is aware that good does not always triumph, so his Jews are not all good. His characters share the traits and illusions of all humankind.

Singer is a supreme storyteller. For him, the suspense, the adventure, the age-old pleasures of narrative are paramount. He leaves explanations and interpretations to his readers and critics. Singer achieved a popular success unusual for a writer of his distinction: His works have become best-sellers and have been translated into fifty-eight languages. He won the National Book Award twice and Newberry Awards three times, and he was awarded the Nobel Prize in Literature in 1978. A number of his works have been dramatized and widely performed; some have also been made into motion pictures. He was an engaging and popular figure on the campuses of colleges and universities and a favorite of interviewers; he served as writer-in-residence at Oberlin College, at the University of California, and at Bard College. In 1989, the American Academy and Institute of Arts and Letters bestowed on Singer its highest award, its Gold Medal.

Biography • Isaac Bashevis Singer was born in Leoncin, Poland. There has long been some uncertainty as to the date of his birth; In *Isaac Bashevis Singer: The Magician of West Eighty-sixth Street* (1979), biographer Paul Kresh quotes Singer as stating that November 21 was, as far as he knew, "more or less" the actual date of his birth. For many years, however, he had celebrated July 14 because his parents had told him that was his birthday to cheer him up after they moved.

Singer was the third child in a family of four siblings, who included an older sister, Hinde Esther, an older brother, Israel Joshua, and a younger brother, Moishe. His parents were Pinchas Mendel Singer, a Hasidic rabbi from Tomoszov, and Bathsheba Zylberman, the daughter of the *Mitnagid*—the opposing sect—rabbi of Bilgoray. The couple seemed to be mismatched. Pinchas Mendel, a gentle, pious, spiritual man, was an ardent follower of Hasidism. Bathsheba, a learned, strong-minded woman, was a rationalist and a pragmatist. Israel Joshua, eleven years Singer's senior, inherited his mother's rationalism; Moishe, two years Singer's junior, inherited his father's piety. The confluence of parental legacies—the mysticism of Singer's father and the rationalism of his mother—was Singer's inheritance, reflected in the tensions of his fictive characters: conflicts between the heart and the head, the sacred and the profane, the spiritual and the secular.

Four years after Singer's birth, the family moved to Warsaw, to an apartment on Krochmalna Street. Rabbi Pinchas Mendel became the rabbi of Krochmalna Street, and the Singer home served as its *bet din,* or rabbinic court. Singer's memoirs *In My Father's Court* and *A Day of Pleasure: Stories of a Boy Growing Up in Warsaw* (1969) and the novels *Shosha* and "Yarme and Kayle" (serialized in the *Forward* in 1977 but never published in book form) re-create the intricate

© Nobel Foundation

life that existed on this cobblestoned shtetl street, a "literary goldmine" to which Singer regularly returns.

In 1917, World War I forced Singer, his mother, and his younger brother to flee the city. They went to Bilgoray, where they stayed for four years. The visit was crucial in his development as a writer. The village of Bilgoray, far removed from the bustle of cosmopolitan Warsaw, appeared to be untouched by modernity. Young Singer witnessed old-world spirituality unblemished by the encroaching Enlightenment. This experience remained with him as an eternal reminder of his rootedness—indeed, humankind's rootedness—in the past, in history, in that which transcends human nature. Bilgoray plays an important role in many of his works; Singer once said that he could never have written *Satan in Goray* without having been there. In Bilgoray, he studied the Talmud and modern Hebrew, which in turn he taught in private homes. He also studied the Kabbalah, read the works of philosopher Baruch Spinoza, and studied German and Polish. He became immersed in the rural Hasidic folk culture that would permeate his work.

In 1921, Singer entered a rabbinical seminary in Warsaw. He remained for a year and then went back to Bilgoray and supported himself by teaching Hebrew. Shortly afterward, he joined his parents in Dzikow, a shtetl close to Bilgoray, where his father had accepted a position as a rabbi. He found this village stifling and depressing, and he was delighted when his older brother, who was coeditor of the *Literarische Bleter,* offered him a job as proofreader for the journal. In 1923, Singer moved back to Warsaw to take up this new position. His family was settled in Dzikow, and he never saw his mother or younger brother again.

Singer's brother Israel Joshua was also a writer and served as Singer's mentor. He was the person who exerted the greatest influence on the young Singer, encouraging him when he began to write and instructing him in the rules of good storytelling. Although Isaac was given to mysticism, Israel Joshua was a realist who became part of the Jewish Enlightenment, the *Haskalai*, which was overtaking the shtetl at the beginning of the twentieth century. This situation had caused friction in the Singer home, especially with their father, who was a traditionalist. Joshua—no one called him by his first name—moved out of the house, becoming an artist and then a writer. Singer often visited his brother and discovered, in his studio, a whole new world. He describes the experience of going from his father's house to his brother's studio in *In My Father's Court*, saying: "It is just one step from the study house to sexuality and back again. Both phases of human existence have continued to interest me." Through his brother, he was introduced to secular literature. Singer lived, for the most part, in his brother's literary shadow. He used pseudonyms for his early writings; some stories were signed "Isaac Bashevis" (a form of his mother's first name in Yiddish) to distinguish his works from those of Joshua, while some were signed "Isaac Warshawsky" ("man of Warsaw").

In 1925, Singer made his fiction debut in Yiddish with a short story, "Oyf der elter" (in old age), which won a prize in *Literarishe bleter*'s literary contest. It was published under the pseudonym "Tse." In 1935, it was reprinted in the *Jewish Daily Forward*. His second published story, "Nerot" (candles), appeared in 1925 in *Ha-yon*. In 1932, Singer edited, with Aaron Zeitlin, a magazine called *Globus*, which printed several of Singer's short stories and in 1933 serialized his first novel, *Satan in Goray*, which was published in book form by the Warsaw PEN Club in 1935. In these early years, Singer also began a series of translations into Yiddish, which by 1935 included Hamsun's *Pan* and *Victoria*, Remarque's *All Quiet on the Western Front*, and Mann's *The Magic Mountain*.

Singer fell in love with Runya, the mother of his only child, Israel, who was born in 1929, the year of Singer's father's death. Runya was an avid communist and wanted to live in Russia. She and Singer quarreled heatedly, frequently about political issues. Runya finally took their child and left for Russia in 1934. She was expelled shortly thereafter and went to join her mother in Palestine. After getting settled there, she sent their son to Kibbutz Bet Alpha. He changed his name to Israel Zamir—the Hebrew equivalent of Singer. Singer did not see his son until 1955, when Zamir decided to visit his father; this episode is described in the short story "The Son" in the collection *A Friend of Kafka, and Other Stories* (1970).

Joshua Singer emigrated to the United States with his family in 1933 and found a job on the Yiddish daily, the *Jewish Daily Forward*. He urged his brother to do likewise. With the shadow of Adolf Hitler extending over most of Europe, Singer did not need much coaxing, and in 1935 he followed his brother. He never returned to Poland. Singer's acclimation to America was difficult. English was a strange language to him, and Yiddish, his mother tongue and his literary language, did not seem to have a future in America. *Lost in America* records this transitional period. He reviewed plays for the *Jewish Daily Forward* but could not resume his writing. At the urgings of his Warsaw friend Aaron Zeitlin, he completed a novel, begun in Warsaw, known as "Messiah the Sinner." It was not a success.

In 1937, Singer met Alma Haimann Wasserman at a summer resort in the Catskill Mountains in New York State. She had emigrated from Germany the previous year. Theirs was an attraction with "telepathic qualities," Singer would reminisce in his later years. They married on February 14, 1940. For many years, Alma supported Singer's writing by working in sales positions in New York department stores. She tended to all their financial concerns and served as one of his translators.

The "greatest misfortune" of his life, according to Singer, was the death of his brother Joshua in 1944. In the dedication to the English version of *The Family Moskat*, he extols his brother as his "spiritual father and master." Singer's family sagas, *The Family Moskat*, *The Manor*, and *The Estate*, are efforts to emulate his brother's work; critics agree that they do not represent the best of Isaac Bashevis Singer and are not typical of his work. However, these novels do present a historical overview of Jewish life in Poland, beginning with the Polish uprising of 1863 in *The Manor* and culminating in the catastrophe of the Holocaust during World War II in *The Family Moskat*.

In 1943, *Satan in Goray, and Other Tales* was published in New York in Yiddish, and in the mid-1940's Singer's fiction began appearing regularly. In 1945, "Gimpel Tam" ("Gimpel the Fool"), perhaps Singer's most famous story, was published in *Yidisher kemfe*. During the 1950's a range of Singer's work—long and short novels, a novella, and a collection of short stories—was brought before an English-speaking public. The May, 1953, publication of "Gimpel the Fool," translated by Saul Bellow in the *Partisan Review*, was a crucial breakthrough for Singer. Thereafter, his work appeared widely in English in magazines such as the *Partisan Review*, *Commentary*, *The New Yorker*, *Harper's*, and *Esquire*. In 1960 Singer began his long affiliation with the publishing house of Farrar, Straus and Giroux. With the publication by *The New Yorker* of "The Slaughterer" in 1967, later collected in *The Seance, and Other Stories*, Singer began his exclusive association with that magazine that lasted until his death.

At the suggestion of a friend, Elizabeth Shub, Singer started writing children's books; the first, *Zlateh the Goat, and Other Stories*, appeared in 1966. He published more than fifteen books for children. Singer's books for children are not written with the left hand; indeed, the format is particularly congenial to certain aspects of his genius. His children's books have been extremely popular and have won numerous prizes; they have been translated into a dozen languages in addition to the standard English, French, Spanish, Japanese, and Hebrew. Singer worked with a variety of translators, including his wife, Alma, and his nephew, Joseph.

Analysis • An oft-quoted line from Isaac Bashevis Singer's story "Gimpel Tam" ("Gimpel the Fool") epitomizes his theory of fiction and his worldview: "No doubt the world is entirely an imaginary world, but it is only once removed from the real world." His approach to his material is both imaginative and historical. Sometimes these strains run concurrently; at other times, one is subdued by the other. Through his use of the supernatural, he imaginatively portrays the Jewish community from the seventeenth to the twentieth century.

Singer's concern is not only with Jewish destiny but also with the destiny of any individual. He believes that the soul is a battleground for good and evil impulses. His use of the fantastic suggests the tenuous line between reality and fiction; it also provides what Singer termed a "spiritual stenography" of human behavior. He suggests that the perversions in which humans engage are otherworldly, that people are not always in control of their actions. Although individuals have freedom of choice, this freedom may be illusory because the forces of evil, if allowed to prevail, can be stronger than the forces of good. Ultimately, however, a desire for good can triumph if people can exert all their efforts to that end. The struggle between good and evil, between the spiritual and sensual, supplies the tension in his works. Singer contends that humankind cannot be separated from its passions; they are one and the same. His early novels, especially *Satan in Goray* and *The Magician of Lublin*, illustrate the problem of passions ruling the individual. Singer's solution to human problems is a return to one's ancestral heritage.

Satan in Goray • Singer's first novel, *Satan in Goray*, written while he was still in Poland, is a gothic tale, commingling the historical with the phantasmagoric, the mysticism of Hasidism with the influences of Fyodor Dostoevski and Edgar Allan Poe, the sacred with the profane. The work is historical, contemporary, and prophetic. Its vision is dark, its tone harsh, and it deals with eternal conflicts: between good and evil, between predestination and freedom of choice.

Two historical events constitute the background of this novel: The first is the Cossack rebellion (1648-1649) led by Bogdan Chmielnicki against the Polish landowners, which resulted in the destruction of 100,000 Jews. This was a period of Jewish history remembered for its tremendous loss of life and for its acts of absolute barbarism, surpassed only by the Holocaust of World War II. The second is the messianic movement known as Shabbeteanism, after its originator Shabbetai Zvi (1626-1676). Historically, these movements converged when Shabbetai Zvi, in Smyrna, Turkey, proclaimed himself messiah during the year 1648, the time of the Chmielnicki massacres.

For Singer, however, historical events are important only in their effects upon individuals. His interest, at all times, lies with the passions that govern individuals and engage them in a continuous struggle. In this early work, Singer presents the shtetl of Goray in the aftermath of the Chmielnicki pogrom and indicates how the spiritual decline of the community is related to its physical destruction. The action of the novel takes place during the year 1666, as the survivors of the massacre move back to Goray and attempt to resume their lives. The village, however, cannot be resuscitated. Its people are maimed; its leaders are ineffectual; all are vulnerable. Singer focuses on what happens to people during a time of utmost vulnerability. He presents a good but misguided community, easily led astray by promises of redemption and the cessation of their earthly travails. The community has suffered much, and its prospects for the future are bleak. Its roads and its earth are drenched with the blood of recently murdered people. Life appears meaningless. The inhabitants move about sluggishly. It would seem that the guardian of Israel slumbers, while her adversaries are on the alert.

The work is divided into two parts. The first deals with the struggle between good and evil as represented by the opposing factions within the community. Rabbi Benish Ashkenazi, the spiritual leader of this enervated community, one of its last survivors to return, represents the forces of good within the shtetl. His is the voice of traditionalism. He was a strong leader before the events of 1648. He did not allow the study of the Kabbala, with its promise of messianic redemption and with the asceticism of its adherents. At present, he can resume certain rabbinic functions within the community, he can deal with legal matters, but he cannot handle the spiritual and social problems of the villagers. He cannot control the dissension within his family; likewise, he cannot control the growing dissension in Goray. In both situations, he retreats into his own chambers and ultimately is concerned only with his own salvation. Meanwhile, rumors of the new messiah have filtered into the secluded village, injecting into it a vitality heretofore absent, resurrecting the shtetl as only messianism can. It is, however, a destructive messianism, one that must be preceded by absolute evil, an abrogation of societal restraints, an immersion in sexual perversity and religious heresy. Part 1 ends with the rabbi's leaving town, after being wounded in a battle with Satan, because he does not want to be buried in Goray. He fears that the evil that has overtaken Goray will contaminate even the dead.

Part 2 concerns the spiritual decline of the community through lack of leadership and perversions of the Law in the name of Shabbeteanism. The battle has been lost. After the rabbi leaves, total chaos ensues. Part 2 begins with Rechele's marriage to an impotent ascetic—who is also a believer in Shabbeteanism—and ends with her death, after the dybbuk (a form of Satanic possession) in her body was exorcised. In the interim, the community gets a new leader, Reb Gedaliya, an emissary who proclaims the news of the crowning of the messiah. He is a ritual slaughterer by trade, a charlatan by profession. One of Singer's many perverted religious functionaries, his lust for blood is exceeded only by his lust for Rechele, who is the innocent victim of life's misfortunes. Gedaliya persuades the community that its redemption can take place only upon the abandonment of traditional Jewish life. Singer vividly portrays the manner in which the community loses sight of the relationship between traditional Judaism and redemption and the depths of moral turpitude into which it has plunged. Ultimately, evil—the dybbuk—is exorcised, together with the remaining Shabbeteans, and good returns to Goray. The novel ends in the spirit of a morality tale with these words: "Let none attempt to force the Lord. . . . The Messiah will come in God's own time."

Satan in Goray is a bleak tale in which the forces of good and evil fight for the human soul; humankind, maimed, vulnerable, and misguided, easily succumbs to the passions of lust and perversity. Critics have seen this work as adumbrating events that were soon to take place in Europe. The strength of this early novel lies in its use of demonology and the supernatural, which became a distinctive feature of Singer's fiction.

The Magician of Lublin • Written in 1958, serialized in 1959, and published in English in 1960, *The Magician of Lublin* also deals with human passions, but it is not overcast with the gloom of past events. It reflects an expansiveness often missing in Singer's works. Its focus is not on the Jewish community itself but on the individual in a timeless context. Singer's magician-protagonist is well cast. On a literal level, he is representative of the artist. On a symbolic level, every person may be seen as a magician, living life, like Yasha Mazur, the novel's protagonist, "as if walking the tightrope merely inches from disaster." The variegated personality of the hero, "religious and heretical, good and evil, false and sincere," and the lack of dates in the work lend themselves to a symbolic interpretation. Singer focuses on the single individual and the choices he or she makes. In *Satan in Goray*, historical events negate options. In *The Magician of Lublin*, Singer removes the encumbrances of history and allows his hero to make conscious decisions that determine the progress of his life.

Yasha Mazur is a complex person, vital, exuberant, intense—above all, a man with a personal destiny. Unlike Jacob, the protagonist of *The Slave*, for example, who is a good person, motivated to do right no matter what the circumstances are, Yasha has an intricate personality. It engages him constantly in a struggle of opposing forces. In *Satan in Goray*, the opposing forces are presented as two distinct elements within the community. The triumph of one necessitates the removal of the other. When evil was victorious, Rabbi Benish Ashkenazi had to leave Goray. In *The Magician of Lublin*, however, these forces exist within the individual, enduring aspects of human nature. Yasha Mazur's entire life is a battle. He can never conquer the evil drive. He can only negotiate with it, appease it, or in some other way deal with it, so that it remains dormant. He never knows, however, when it will awaken to begin another round.

Yasha Mazur was reared in a pious Jewish home, studied the Talmud until his father died—his mother died when he was seven—and then joined the circus. He maintains a home in Lublin with his wife, Esther, but roams the Polish countryside as a "circus performer and hypnotist." As an artist or magician, he moves in various worlds, assumes various guises or personalities, and has a different mistress in each world. He aspires to higher things: He is a successful artist and would like to perform in Warsaw, in the summer theater of the prestigious Saxony Gardens. He is barred from doing so because he is Jewish. The closest he comes to achieving this goal is at the apartment of the middle-class Gentile Emilia, located on a street opposite the Saxony Gardens. Yasha's relationship with Emilia focuses the tensions of the work. He thinks he is in love with her, but she refuses the role of mistress. She wants to be his wife. To marry her, Yasha would have to divorce Esther, convert to Christianity, and procure great wealth to maintain the facade he has established in his courting of Emilia. These are formidable decisions that will determine his future.

Singer establishes the dichotomy of predestination and free will early in the work in the contrasting attitudes toward life represented by Yasha and his wife. Esther is a religious woman, married twenty years to Yasha; they have no children. Her entire life consists of making a home for a husband who returns to it only on holidays. She loves him but regrets, at times, not having married someone more stable. The thought of changing her life, however, never crosses her mind. She is a strong believer in Providence and accepts her fate as a lonely woman.

Yasha, although he says that "everything is fate," realizes that he shapes his own destiny in all his choices. He is a magician who consorts with thieves, but he refuses to use his powers for evil purposes. He will not become a thief. When he finally attempts it, out of a desperate need to support Emilia, he fails and injures himself. The man who is so agile that he can walk a tightrope to the awe of his audience becomes a schlemiel and bungles a simple act of burglary. Although he is Jewish by birth, he is a nonbeliever—or says he is—by choice. He does not pray, because God does not answer the prayers of his supplicants: his "gifts" are "plagues, famines, poverty, and pogroms." Nevertheless, to become a Christian for Emilia is a difficult choice for him. He is a libertine, yet he considers the institution of marriage sacred and cannot easily make the decision to break up his home for his new infatuation. He is faced with the dilemma of choosing "between his religion and the cross, between Esther and Emilia, between honesty and crime." These choices will "seal his destiny." He finally chooses to remain with his own religion and decides also that traditionalism is more meaningful than assimilationism.

Yasha is aware that life is the most powerful seductress. He returns to his home and builds for himself a doorless brick prison which frees him from temptation and allows him to meditate on his past actions, yet he discovers that as long as he is alive, he cannot shut out the world. As an artist or a magician, he went out into the world, succumbing to carnal pleasures, drinking, eating, loving unrestrainedly. Having come to the realization that "there must be discipline," he undergoes the transformation from sinner to saint. As an ascetic, in the confines of his self-imposed banishment, considered by all a "holy man," the world comes to him. Even his past love writes him a letter. Yasha's imprisonment has been only partially successful. He has turned his intense feelings in another direction, moving from the sensual to the spiritual. In this work, Singer suggests that people cannot escape their essence: They and their passions are one. *The Magician of Lublin* presents a positive outlook even though it concludes (as does Singer's novel *Shosha*) in a dark cell or room.

Enemies • Singer's novels *Enemies* and *Shosha* directly address the most tragic time of Jewish history, the Holocaust. *Enemies*, ironically subtitled *A Love Story*, is Singer's only novel set in the United States; it deals specifically with survivors of the Holocaust. In *Shosha*, Singer returns for another nostalgic look at the destroyed world in which he grew up and attempts to capture the spirit of his people as the perimeters of death close in on them.

Like *The Magician of Lublin, Enemies* is written on two levels. It fills a gap in Singer's canon. Until this work, Singer's literary aim was to re-create the destroyed world of eastern European Jewry, to present the pulsating life that existed specifically in his native Poland. *Enemies* acknowledges the destruction of his fictive world and deals with problems confronting those who survived. In a note that precedes the work, Singer asserts that although he has lived with survivors for years, this work is in no way typical of the Holocaust experience. The novel presents the "exceptional case," he says, unique to an individual who is a victim both of his own personality and of his persecutors. Certainly, this can be said of all victims, and the novel, despite his abjuration, is a moving depiction of the varied problems many survivors have encountered. Singer's note cautions the reader against a rigorous historical interpretation. The Holocaust serves as a framework within which Singer presents his perennial concern: humankind battling its adversaries in the dark of night, in the fashion of Jacob and the angel. In the biblical narrative, Jacob is not overcome; he walks away, at daybreak, limping but unvanquished. Singer's hero also walks away, but not as a victor.

Enemies bears a similarity to *Satan in Goray* both in its focus on an individual who lives a tormented life, burdened with the knowledge of the tragic destruction of all that is meaningful to him, and in its use of the supernatural. In this work, the spiritual powers that represent the forces of good and evil also reflect a movement away from traditionalism. In addition, they indicate the extent to which the characters, through their previous experiences, have lost touch with reality. *Enemies* also has affinities with *The Magician of Lublin*: The multiple personalities of the protagonist are reflected in his relationships with three strikingly different women.

Enemies is a ghostly story. Herman Broder, the protagonist, is defined through his actions in the Holocaust. He spent those years hiding in a hayloft and has acquired a negative identity in the Holocaust's aftermath. Now, as a survivor, he is psychologically warped and socially maimed. He lacks the courage to commit suicide, hides behind schizophrenia to "deaden" his consciousness, and assumes the guise of a demon. In New York, Broder becomes a ghostwriter for a rabbi. He shuns contact with others to preserve his anonymity and lives a life of haunting duplicity with his second wife and his mistress. The tensions in his spiritual juggling act are intensified by the appearance of his wife from the Old World—he had assumed her to be dead. Ultimately, he disappears, vanishing like a ghost.

The work is divided into three parts. Part 1 establishes the diverse personalities of Broder, "a fraud, a transgressor—a hypocrite," as he sees himself, and the complications they create. Broder's current life in New York is eclipsed by the terrifying experiences of his past. He lives in Brooklyn with his second wife, Yadwiga, the Polish woman who worked for his family before the war and who hid him in a hayloft during the Nazi occupation. He married her in gratitude for saving his life, but his relationship with her is deceitful. She does not know about his professional life or about his mentally disturbed mistress, Masha, who shares with him her experience of the Holocaust. He spends as much time with Masha as he does with Yadwiga, always telling Yadwiga that, as a book salesman, he must go out of town to sell books.

The tangled web of Broder's relationships is further complicated when his first wife, Tamara, who has survived being shot twice—one bullet still lodged within her—comes to New York and seeks him out. Part 1 ends with an additional complication when Masha claims to be pregnant and Broder promises to marry her.

Part 2 attempts a resolution of the problems. Through Broder's conversations with Masha and Tamara, much of the Holocaust experience is re-created. Like Elie Wiesel and other writers of the Holocaust, Singer points out that the full enormity of the Holocaust can never be expressed, because words are inadequate to the task. That which is related, however, is extremely powerful. Singer deals with the theological, social, and philosophical problems, both individual and universal, that confront humankind in coming to terms with the Holocaust. While presenting the myriad issues with which survivors have been faced—equivocal attitudes toward faith, a missing spouse who turns up after the other has remarried, disorientation in a new environment, reestablishing an identity that was nonexistent for a time, relating to people as human beings within a society rather than as individuals competing for survival—Singer indicates that the individual is also his or her own victim, governed by passions he or she cannot or will not control. Broder would not have married Yadwiga if he had thought that Tamara were alive. Now, however, he wants to hold on to all three women. They satisfy different needs: Yadwiga cares for him and worships him with a childlike simplicity; Masha fulfills his sexual desires and fires his imagination with her nightlong storytelling; Tamara is his wife, to whom he feels committed.

When the intricacies of his life seem overwhelming, he resorts to traditionalism as a life-sustaining measure, yet he cannot maintain his resolve to be a good Jew. He is a weak person by nature, and the impact of the Holocaust has left him without a will, without the power to make meaningful choices and decisions. He is, as he tells Tamara, a "corpse." His only alternative is to vanish. Herman Broder joins Singer's other eternal wanderers, the most famous of whom is Gimpel the Fool. The epilogue, in an almost Darwinian statement, attests the insignificance of the individual in the larger scheme of things by confirming Broder's disappearance and suggesting that life nevertheless continues for those who can battle their enemies successfully.

Shosha • *Shosha* is narrated in the first person, unusual in Singer's novels that have been translated into English. Originally appearing in the *Forward* under the title *Neshome Ekspeditsyes* (soul expeditions) in 1974, it is considered a fictionalized and expanded version of the memoir *A Young Man in Search of Love*, which appeared almost simultaneously in 1978. A beautifully wrought work, it is one of the most poignant of all of Singer's novels. Set in Poland during the 1930's, the novel portrays the plight of the Jewish community, overcast with the gloom of the Nazi invasion, yet it brims with the lives, loves, and hopes of its characters. It combines realism with humor and pathos. It is another nostalgic glance at a destroyed world, but it is not a gloomy work. It is, as the Yiddish title indicates, the journey of the author's soul, in an affectionate tribute to the vitality of the shtetl, and stands in defiance of his statement at the end of the work: "Time is a book whose pages you can turn forward, not back." *Shosha* presents a marvelous picture of Warsaw before the war, focusing on its Yiddish cultural and intellectual life, its writers, artists, philosophers, actors, critics, and dilettantes, as well as its simple people. Within this historical framework, Singer presents his protagonist's life in Poland at the time of greatest stress, a time when Jewish life and culture were disintegrating.

In *Shosha*, the conflict between good and evil that animates all of Singer's works takes the form of the relationship between victim and persecutor. All of the characters are concerned with their immediate gratification. They arouse the reader's sympathy because they become victims of their own blindness and naïveté. In their determination to live normally, they love, argue, philosophize, celebrate holidays. They write plays about dybbuks and talk about dybbuks within themselves. They do not recognize the external evil, the phantom that surrounds them or pursues them.

The first part of the novel charts the circular movement of the protagonist as he attempts to reestablish a sense of belonging, transporting the reader to the halcyon days of the narrator's childhood and moving forward to the period preceding the destruction of the shtetl by Hitler. The ancestors of the protagonist, Aaron Greidinger, have lived in Poland for seven hundred years. Krochmalna Street, already familiar to Singer's public through his memoir *In My Father's Court*, not only is a place housing his father's judiciary but also is the scene of the narrator's first love, for Shosha—his neighbor, his playmate, his first audience—who believes and trusts him implicitly and unconditionally.

The work delineates the maturation of the narrator, as the serenity of his youthful universe is quickly replaced by the turmoil of world events with their disquieting effect upon the Jews of Poland. The first twenty years of his life pass rapidly as he moves from Krochmalna Street and attempts to define himself as a writer. In Warsaw, the Writers' Club becomes the focal point for the intellectuals, much as the synagogue was the focal point of the traditional Jewish community. It is through the people whom he meets at the Writers' Club that Aaron Greidinger works out his role as writer and lover.

Greidinger's destiny and identity are intimately bound to his youth on Krochmalna Street, and after twenty years, he returns to the area and visits Shosha and her mother. He is amazed that Shosha has changed only slightly during the years: She and Greidinger are the same age, but she looks like a child. Greidinger falls in love with her immediately. He explains to Betty Slonim, the Yiddish actor from America for whom he is writing a play, that he sees himself in Shosha. Shosha represents the naïveté and gentleness of his childhood, a phase of his life that he wants to recapture and repossess. She is Krochmalna Street. She is the shtetl. She is the traditionalism that refuses to keep in step with modernity but is beautiful nevertheless. She also represents the sources of his creativity, the childlike wonder that Singer the writer still possesses in old age. Part 1 ends with Greidinger's movement back in time, his failure as a playwright, his proposal to Shosha, and his spending most of his time in the small apartment on Krochmalna Street as the political situation worsens for the Jews in Poland.

Part 2 develops the protagonist's affirmation of his unity with his people. It is Yom Kippur, a day of judgment and reckoning for all Jews. The war is getting closer, Poles are more outspoken in their anti-Semitism, and Greidinger spends the day with Shosha, fasting. He marries Shosha two months later during the festival of Hanukkah. By doing so, he forgoes the opportunity to leave Warsaw before the Germans enter. He will not forsake Shosha, knowing that she could not survive by herself during these times. His writing career has improved; he is writing novels that have been accepted by his publisher. Part 2 concludes with the war imminent but with everyone presenting reasons for not leaving Warsaw prior to the German invasion. The epilogue ties the loose ends together. It takes place thirteen years later, during Greidinger's trip to Israel, where he meets his Warsaw friend, Haiml. While seated in the dark, each tells the story of what happened to his family, his friends, and how he escaped. Shosha died, as expected, because in her fragility, she could not keep ahead of the march of malevolence pursuing her and overtaking Europe.

The King of the Fields • Singer's last novel to be published before his death in 1991 was *The King of the Fields*, set in prehistoric Poland, a violent, animalistic place where tribes of cave-dwelling hunters struggle against Poles who cultivate the land. Singer seems to have dipped into a nightmare world so embedded in the past as to be unrelated to the present, yet the hellish qualities of this Stone Age Poland and the brutality of its inhabitants conjure up the Poland of the Holocaust—a wilderness of corruption, a wasteland for humanity.

Scum • *Scum*, written during the late 1960's and published in English the year of Singer's death, re-creates the pre-Holocaust Warsaw at the beginning of the twentieth century. Max Barabander, a thief turned businessman, returns to Singer's famous Krochmalna Street after decades in Argentina. His son has died, and his grieving wife ignores him; he has become impotent. His journey backward to Krochmalna Street is his attempt to journey toward renewed health, or at least toward a new life. He becomes involved both with Shmuel Smetena, the central figure in Krochmalna Street mobster activities, and with a saintly rabbi whose daughter, Tsirele, he wants to marry. He poses as a grieving widower to win Tsirele while working with Shmuel Smetena's mistress on a scheme to seduce unsuspecting young women and ship them off to an Argentinian brothel. The project has a restorative effect on Max's virility, but when the web of lies he must weave begins to unravel, he is exposed as bereft of moral character, one for whom life—his or another's—is devoid of meaning. His only dreams are of "shady deals." *Scum* is Singer's version of the underworld; the literal underworld of gangsters mirrors the underworld of demons and dybbuks that make no appearance in this novel. When human beings are such scum, there seems to be no need for the Evil One.

The Certificate • *The Certificate*, serialized in the *Forward* in 1967, was published posthumously in 1992. Its protagonist, David Bendinger, an eighteen-year-old would-be writer, arrives in Warsaw in 1922 with an unfinished novel, an essay on Spinoza and the Kabbala, and a collection of prose poems. Like so many of Singer's male characters, David soon finds himself involved with three women: Sonya, his old girlfriend; Minna, a woman whom he agrees to marry in order to obtain immigration papers for Palestine; and Edusha, his Marxist landlady. Like the youthful Singer, whom he resembles, David turns every event, no matter how seemingly insignificant, into an occasion for philosophical musing. Unlike Max Barabander of *Scum*, David Bendinger dreams of more than shady deals, and he believes that those around him have worth. No matter how complicated his life becomes, he dreams of writing and he thinks of God.

Meshugah • *Meshugah*, which means crazy, was first called *Lost Souls*, a title that connects this novel with *Shosha*, which was first called *Neshome Ekspeditsyes* (soul expeditions). Serialized in the *Forward* during the early 1980's and appearing in English in 1994, the novel brings Aaron Greidinger, the protagonist of *Shosha*, into a post-

Holocaustal 1950's setting. This most Singer-like character is a Polish exile who serializes novels in Yiddish for the *Forward*. While Aaron has his series of women, his primary mate, Miriam Zalkind, who is writing her dissertation on his work, juggles her own set of men. All are "lost souls" harboring memories of the Holocaust, mourning loved ones, contemplating suicide. Aaron discovers that the real truth of human suffering defies the power of writing—the world is meshugah.

Shadows on the Hudson • *Shadows on the Hudson* was originally serialized in Yiddish twice a week in the *Forward* between January, 1957, and January, 1958. Singer had long wanted this novel to be published in English, but the project was undertaken only years after his death. It is set during the 1940's in Manhattan, and the lives of its characters are, like those in *Meshugah*, overshadowed by the Holocaust. As bleak as *Scum* but without its sordid underworld, *Shadows on the Hudson* deals with characters who strive for some sense and meaning in a world that continuously trips them up. Hertz Dovid Grein rotates between wife, mistress, and lover, always yearning for the one who is not there. His lover, Anna, juggles him along with her first and second husbands. His mistress, Esther, marries another, divorces, flees with Grein, and, in turn, flees him.

In the second part of this three-part novel, these chaotic couplings seem to be headed for resolution in a return to the past and traditional values. Grein returns home to his wife and to orthodoxy, Anna returns to her first husband, Esther marries, and even Anna's long-widowed father marries and has a son. The hope that a retreat from the secular will result in a return to meaning is demolished in part 3, however, when the new couplings are undone and the newborn child is recognized as severely mentally disabled. The shadows of the Holocaust stretch over the Hudson and into the future. What saves this novel, and much of Singer's fiction, from a darkness too intense to bear is his extraordinary ability to create comic situations from the bleakest of moments. Whether caricaturing secondary characters or rendering outlandish a protagonist's rationalization of his or her latest sexual exploit, Singer's comic touch lightens his vision. Except in a few novels such as *Scum* and *The King of the Fields*, there is a redemptive quality in the very need his characters display for meaning and for love.

Singer occupies a unique place in the literary world. His works transcend the barriers of age, education, and culture, and they appeal to all peoples. Singer was a chronicler, historian, spiritualist, and moralist, and his writings are informed by a deep compassion for men and women who are, after all, only human. Singer may admit to a pessimistic view of humankind, but it is a sympathetic rather than a cynical pessimism. Throughout the darkness of his presentation, there flickers a spark of faith in the basic goodness of humankind, the promise of a universal and eternal light.

L. H. Goldman
Updated by Grace Farrell

Other major works

SHORT FICTION: *Gimpel the Fool, and Other Stories*, 1957; *The Spinoza of Market Street*, 1961; *Short Friday, and Other Stories*, 1964; *The Séance, and Other Stories*, 1968; *A Friend of Kafka, and Other Stories*, 1970; *A Crown of Feathers, and Other Stories*, 1973; *Passions, and Other Stories*, 1975; *Old Love*, 1979; *The Collected Stories*, 1982; *The Image, and Other*

Stories, 1985; *The Death of Methuselah, and Other Stories,* 1988.

PLAYS: *The Mirror,* pr. 1973; *Shlemiel the First,* pr. 1974; *Yentl, the Yeshiva Boy,* pr. 1974 (with Leah Napolin); *Teibele and Her Demon,* pr. 1978.

NONFICTION: *Mayn Tatn's Bes-din Shtub,* 1956 (*In My Father's Court,* 1966); *The Hasidim,* 1973 (with Ira Moskowitz); *A Little Boy in Search of God: Mysticism in a Personal Light,* 1976; *A Young Man in Search of Love,* 1978; *Isaac Bashevis Singer on Literature and Life,* 1979 (with Paul Rosenblatt and Gene Koppel); *Lost in America,* 1980; *Love and Exile,* 1984; *Conversations with Isaac Bashevis Singer,* 1985 (with Richard Burgin); *More Stories from My Father's Court,* 2000.

CHILDREN'S LITERATURE: *Zlateh the Goat, and Other Stories,* 1966; *Mazel and Shlimazel: Or, The Milk of a Lioness,* 1967; *The Fearsome Inn,* 1967; *When Shlemiel Went to Warsaw, and Other Stories,* 1968; *A Day of Pleasure: Stories of a Boy Growing Up in Warsaw,* 1969; *Elijah the Slave,* 1970; *Joseph and Koza: Or, The Sacrifice to the Vistula,* 1970; *Alone in the Wild Forest,* 1971; *The Topsy-Turvy Emperor of China,* 1971; *The Wicked City,* 1972; *The Fools of Chelm and Their History,* 1973; *Why Noah Chose the Dove,* 1974; *A Tale of Three Wishes,* 1975; *Naftali the Storyteller and His Horse, Sus, and Other Stories,* 1976; *The Power of Light: Eight Stories,* 1980; *The Golem,* 1982; *Stories for Children,* 1984.

TRANSLATIONS: *Romain Rolland,* 1927 (of Stefan Zweig); *Die Volger,* 1928 (of Knut Hamsun); *Victoria,* 1929 (of Hamsun); *All Quiet on the Western Front,* 1930 (of Erich Remarque); *Pan,* 1931 (of Hamsun); *The Way Back,* 1931 (of Remarque); *The Magic Mountain,* 1932 (of Thomas Mann); *From Moscow to Jerusalem,* 1938 (of Leon Glaser).

Bibliography

Farrell, Grace, ed. *Critical Essays on Isaac Bashevis Singer.* New York: G. K. Hall, 1996. An extensive introduction on Singer's critical reception and the issues that have preoccupied him and his critics. Collects both contemporary reviews and a wide range of essays, including Leslie Fiedler's "I. B. Singer: Or, The American-ness of the American Jewish Writer."

_____. *Isaac Bashevis Singer: Conversations.* Jackson: University Press of Mississippi, 1992. A collection of interviews with Singer that reveal the connections among his philosophy of life, his perspective on literature, and his mode of living.

Guzlowski, John. "Isaac Bashevis Singer's *Satan in Goray* and Bakhtin's Vision of the Carnivalesque." *Critique* 39 (Winter, 1998): 167-175. Argues that Mikhail Bakhtin's notion of the grotesque illuminates Singer's and that Wolfgang Kayser's theories of the grotesque oversimplify his message; concludes, however, that Singer departs from Bakhtin in his less hopeful belief about society's ability to build a new order out of carnival.

Hadda, Janet. "Isaac Bashevis Singer in New York." *Judaism* 46 (Summer, 1997): 346-363. Discusses the transformation of Singer from Bashevis, the sharp-witted, conflicted, occasionally harsh, literary genius, to Isaac Bashevis Singer—and even Isaac Singer—the quaint, pigeon-feeding vegetarian, the serene and gentle embodiment of the timeless values of Eastern European Jews.

_____. *Isaac Bashevis Singer: A Life.* New York: Oxford University Press, 1997. Focusing on both the forces of family and that social environment that influenced Singer, Hadda uncovers the public persona to reveal a more complex man than heretofore understood.

Kresh, Paul. *Isaac Bashevis Singer: The Magician of West Eighty-sixth Street.* New York: Dial Press, 1979. A lively account of Singer's first seventy-five years, told in an often seemingly day-by-day account that creates a delightful sense of intimacy for the reader. Kresh incorporates refreshing quotes and anecdotes and includes thirty-two photographs. His careful attention to facts clarifies the often ambiguous details of Singer's works in terms of creation, translation, publication, and reissue. More than four hundred pages, with a good index and a bibliography.

Mulbauer, Asher Z. *Transcending Exile.* Miami: Florida International University Press, 1985. A thoughtful contemplation of exile in the works of three writers: Joseph Conrad, Vladimir Nabokov, and Singer. The fifty-page chapter on Singer focuses on three novels—*Shosha, The Slave,* and *Enemies: A Love Story*—but is mindful of thematic parallels to the short stories.

Sinclair, Clive. *The Brothers Singer.* London: Allison and Busby, 1983. A fascinating examination of Singer and his work in the context of one of the most important personal and literary relationships of the author's life. Sinclair effectively interweaves biography and literary analysis, conveying a deep understanding of the lives and works of Isaac and Joshua Singer.

Spilka, Mark. "Empathy with the Devil: Isaac Bashevis Singer and the Deadly Pleasures of Misogyny." *Novel* 31 (Summer, 1998): 430-444. Discusses Singer's preoccupation with demonology and sexuality, focusing on his struggles with misogyny; claims the admonitory sequences of Singer's fiction exemplify the risks and hazards of his own personal and fictional struggle to make sense of the pre- and post-Holocaust world he inherited from his parents.

Wolitz, Seth L., ed. *The Hidden Isaac Bashevis Singer.* Austin: University of Texas Press, 2001. A collection of essays focusing on Singer's use of Yiddish language and cultural experience, themes that persist through his writing, his interface with other times and cultures, his autobiographical work, and a translation of a previously unpublished "gangster" novel.

Zamir, Israel. *Journey to My Father, Isaac Bashevis Singer.* New York: Arcade, 1995. A lively memoir by Singer's only child that paints a complex portrait of the writer.

Wallace Stegner

Born: Lake Mills, Iowa; February 18, 1909
Died: Santa Fe, New Mexico; April 13, 1993

Principal long fiction • *Remembering Laughter*, 1937; *The Potter's House*, 1938; *On a Darkling Plain*, 1940; *Fire and Ice*, 1941; *The Big Rock Candy Mountain*, 1943; *Second Growth*, 1947; *The Preacher and the Slave*, 1950; *A Shooting Star*, 1961; *All the Little Live Things*, 1967; *Angle of Repose*, 1971; *The Spectator Bird*, 1976; *Recapitulation*, 1979; *Joe Hill*, 1980; *Crossing to Safety*, 1987.

Other literary forms • Wallace Stegner also published two collections of short fiction, *The Women on the Wall* (1950) and *The City of the Living, and Other Stories* (1956); two biographies, *Beyond the Hundredth Meridian: John Wesley Powell and the Second Opening of the West* (1954) and *The Uneasy Chair: A Biography of Bernard DeVoto* (1974); a collection of critical essays, *The Writer in America* (1951); a historical monograph, *The Gathering of Zion: The Story of the Mormon Trail* (1964); and two volumes of personal essays on the Western experience, *Wolf Willow: A History, a Story, and a Memory of the Last Plains Frontier* (1962) and *The Sound of Mountain Water* (1969). Stegner also published a number of edited works, both nonfiction and fiction.

Achievements • Stegner would have three distinct audiences after the start of his career: the popular magazine audience, readers interested in modern American literature, and a regional audience interested in the culture and history of the American West. From the 1930's, he published seventy-two short stories, with fifty of them appearing in such magazines as *Harper's*, *Mademoiselle*, *Collier's*, *Cosmopolitan*, *Esquire*, *Redbook*, *The Atlantic Monthly*, *The Inter-Mountain Review*, and the *Virginia Quarterly*. Bernard DeVoto, Van Wyck Brooks, and Sinclair Lewis recognized his talent early, and DeVoto was instrumental in encouraging Stegner to continue writing. Stegner enjoyed a solid critical reputation as a regional American writer concerned largely with the problems and themes of the western American experience.

Stegner also won numerous honors throughout his career. He was elected to the American Academy of Arts and Sciences and the National Academy of Arts and Letters, and he was awarded fellowships by Phi Beta Kappa, the Huntington Library, The Center for Advanced Studies in the Behavioral Sciences, and the Guggenheim, Rockefeller, and Wintergreen Foundations. In 1937, he won the Little, Brown Novelette Prize for *Remembering Laughter*. He also won the O. Henry Memorial Award for short stories in 1942, 1948, and 1950, and in 1971 he won the Pulitzer Prize in fiction for his *Angle of Repose*. Other awards for his work include the Houghton Mifflin Life-in-America Award in 1945 and the Commonwealth Club Gold Medal in 1968. In 1981, he became the first recipient of the Robert Kirsch Award for Life Achievement in the *Los Angeles Times* Book Awards.

As a master of narrative technique and a respected literary craftsman, Stegner had the opportunity to influence many young writers associated with the Stanford University Creative Writing Program, where he taught from 1945 to 1971, including Eugene Burdick, one of the authors of *The Ugly American* (1958), Ken Kesey, and

Thomas McGuane. His own theory of literature is rather traditional and appears in his only extended piece of criticism, *The Writer in America.* The creative process, he believed, is basically the imposition of form upon personal experience. The committed writer must discipline himself to the difficult work of creation, choosing significant images from the insignificant and selecting significant actions for his characters. The writer must change the disorderliness of memory into symmetry without violating his readers' sense of what is true to life.

Library of Congress

Biography • Wallace Earle Stegner was born on February 18, 1909, in Lake Mills, Iowa, the second son of George and Hilda Paulson Stegner. He was descended from Norwegian farmers on his mother's side and unknown ancestors on his father's side. His father was a drifter and a resourceful gambler—a searcher for the main chance, the big bonanza. In Stegner's early years, the family moved often, following his father's dream of striking it rich, from Grand Forks, North Dakota, to Bellingham, Washington, to Redmond, Oregon, to East End, Saskatchewan, where they lived from 1914 to 1921. East End left him with memories of people and landscapes that played an important role in *The Big Rock Candy Mountain.* The family moved in 1921 to Salt Lake City, Utah, where Stegner attended high school and began college. Here, Stegner went through the pains of adolescence and, although not himself a Mormon, developed a strong attachment to the land and a sympathy for Mormon culture and values, which are reflected in his later books such as *Mormon Country* (1942), *The Gathering of Zion*, and *Recapitulation.*

From 1925 to 1930, Stegner attended the University of Utah, where he balanced his interest in girls and his studies with a job selling rugs and linoleum in the family business of a close friend. By a fortunate chance, he studied freshman English with Vardis Fisher, then a budding novelist, and Fisher helped stimulate Stegner's growing interest in creative writing. In 1930, he entered the graduate program at the University of Iowa, completing his master's degree in 1932 and completing his doctoral degree in 1935 with a dissertation on the Utah naturalist Clarence Dutton, titled "Clarence Edward Dutton: Geologist and Man of Letters," later revised and published as *Clarence Edward Dutton: An Appraisal* by the University of Utah in 1936. This work fed his interest in the history of the American West and the life of the explorer John Wesley Powell, the subject of his *Beyond the Hundredth Meridian.* Teaching English and creative writing occupied him for several years, beginning with a one-year stint at tiny Augustana College in Illinois in 1934. Next, he went to the University of Utah until 1937, moving from there to teach freshman English at the University of Wisconsin for two years. He also taught at the Bread Loaf School of English in Vermont for several summers and enjoyed the friendship of Robert Frost, Bernard De-Voto, and Theodore Morrison. In 1940, he accepted a part-time position at Harvard University in the English writing program. There, during the Great Depression, he was involved in literary debates between the literary left, led by F. O. Matthiessen, and the conservative DeVoto.

In 1945, Stegner accepted a professorship in creative writing at Stanford University, where he remained for twenty-six years until his retirement in 1971. Stegner's Stanford years were his most productive; he produced a total of thirteen books in this period. In 1950, he made an around-the-world lecture tour, researched his family's past in Saskatchewan and Norway, and spent much of the year as writer-in-residence at the American Academy in Rome. He was also an active environmentalist long before ecology became fashionable. During the Kennedy administration, he served as assistant to the secretary of the interior (1961) and as a member of the National Parks Advisory Board (1962).

Analysis • Stegner was a regional writer in the best sense. His settings, his characters, and his plots derive from the Western experience, but his primary concern is with the meaning of that experience. Geographically, Stegner's region runs from Minnesota and Grand Forks, North Dakota, through Utah and northern Colorado. It is the country where Stegner lived and experienced his youth. Scenes from this region appear frequently in his novels. East End, Saskatchewan, the place of his early boyhood, appears as Whitemud, Saskatchewan, in *The Big Rock Candy Mountain*, along with Grand Forks and Lake Mills, Iowa, his birthplace. Salt Lake City figures prominently in *Recapitulation* and *The Preacher and the Slave*, the story of Joe Hill, a union martyr. *Wolf Willow*, furthermore, is historical fiction, a kind of history of East End, and *On a Darkling Plain* is the story of a much decorated and seriously wounded veteran of World War I who withdraws from society in an isolated shack on the plains outside of East End.

In a much larger sense, Stegner is concerned with the spiritual West—the West as an idea or a consciousness—and with the significance of the Western values and traditions. He is also concerned with the basic American cultural conflict between East and West and with the importance of frontier values in American history. Bo Mason, modeled after Stegner's father, the abusive head of the Mason family in *The Big Rock Candy Mountain*, is an atavism, a character who may have been at home in the early frontier, who searches for the elusive pot of gold—the main chance of the Western myth. Never content with domestic life or with stability, Bo Mason, like George Stegner, moves his family from town to town always looking for an easy fortune. As a man of mixed qualities—fierce pride, resourcefulness, self-reliance, and a short, violent temper—he is ill at ease in the postfrontier West, always chafing at the stability of community and family ties. He continually pursues the old Western myth of isolated individualism that preceded twentieth century domestication of the region. He might have made a good mountain man. Stegner stresses his impact on his family and community and shows the reader the basic tragedy of this frontier type trapped in a patterned world without easy bonanzas.

In *Angle of Repose*, Stegner explores the conflict between the values of self-reliance, impermanence, and Western optimism and the eastern sense of culture, stability, and tradition. In a way, this is the basic conflict between Ralph Waldo Emerson's party of hope (the West) and the party of the past (the East). He also explores the idea of community as a concept alien to the Western myth. Indeed, community as the close-knit cooperation between individuals is shown in Stegner's work as the thing that ended the frontier. In *The Big Rock Candy Mountain* and in *Recapitulation*, there is a longing for community and a pervasive feeling that the Mason family is always outside the culture in which it exists, particularly in Utah, where Mormon culture is portrayed as innocent, solid, stable, and, as a result, attractive. Mormon life is characterized by the absence of frontier individualism and by a belief in permanence and group experience, an anomaly in the Western experience.

The Big Rock Candy Mountain • A third major concern throughout Stegner's work is his own identity and the meaning of Western identity. Bruce Mason in *The Big Rock Candy Mountain* is much concerned with his relationship as an adolescent to the Utah culture and its sense of community.

The Big Rock Candy Mountain, Stegner's fifth novel, is an obviously autobiographical account of his childhood and adolescence. A family saga, the novel follows the history of the rootless Mason family as it follows the dreams of Bo Mason, a thinly disguised version of Stegner's father, as he leads them to Grand Forks, North Dakota, to the lumber camps of Washington, then back to Iowa and up to Whitemud, Saskatchewan, and finally to Salt Lake City and Reno. Family identity problems are played out against the backdrop of an increasingly civilized and domesticated West against which the self-reliant and short-tempered character of Bo Mason stands out in stark relief. His qualities, which might have had virtues in the early settlement of the West, create family tensions and trauma that cause Bruce Mason (Stegner) to develop a hatred for his father only partially tempered by a grudging respect. Bo Mason relentlessly pursues the American Dream and the Western myth of easy success rooted in the early frontier: He endlessly pursues the Big Rock Candy Mountain.

Throughout this odyssey, the family longs for stability and community, for a place to develop roots. Even in Salt Lake City, where Bruce spends his adolescence, Bo keeps the family changing houses to hide his bootlegging business during the Prohibition period. His activities in the midst of puritanical Mormon culture only highlight the contrast between the Masons and the dominant community. Even in his later years, Bo pursues his dream in Reno by operating a gambling house.

Stegner vividly illustrates how this rootless wandering affects family members. Else, Bo's wife, representing the feminine, domesticating impulse, is a saintly character—long-suffering, gentle, and protective of her two sons. She longs for a home with permanence but never finds it. Her initial good nature and mild optimism eventually give way to pessimism as resettlements continue. Three of the family members die: Else is destroyed by cancer; Chet, the other son, who is defeated by both marriage and career, dies young of pneumonia; and Bo, with all his dreams shattered and involved with a cheap whore after Else's death, shoots himself. Only Bruce is left to make sense of his family's experiences, and he attempts to understand his place in the family saga as he strives to generalize his family's history. In the final philosophical and meditative chapters, Stegner tries to link Bruce (and therefore himself) to history, to some sense of continuity and tradition. His family history, with its crudeness and tensions, is made to represent the history of the frontier West with its similar tensions and rough edges. Bruce, who long sought solace and identity in books, excels in school and finally follows the civilized but ironic path of going to law school at the University of Minnesota. He has, finally, reached a higher level of culture than his family ever attained. *The Big Rock Candy Mountain* has achieved a reputation as a classic of American regionalism, while it also deals with broader national themes and myths.

Angle of Repose • *Angle of Repose* is regarded by many critics as Stegner's most finely crafted novel. The metaphoric title is a mining and geological term designating the slope at which rocks cease to fall, the angle of rest. Stegner uses it to apply to the last thirty years of the marriage of Susan Burling and Oliver Ward, two opposite personalities, after their often chaotic early married years. This ambitious work, covering four generations, is a fictionalized biography of the turn-of-the-century writer and illustrator Mary Hallock Foote (1847-1930) and her marriage to Arthur De Wint Foote, an idealistic pioneer and self-educated mining engineer.

Lyman Ward, the narrator, was reared by his grandparents Susan Burling Ward and Oliver Ward, fictionalized versions of the Footes, and is a retired history professor from Berkeley who was disabled in middle age by a progressively arthritic condition. He has been transformed by the disease into a grotesque creature who loses first his leg and then his wife Ellen, who runs off with the surgeon who amputated Lyman's leg. Bitter and disillusioned by his wife's behavior and his son Rodman's radical idealism and contempt for the past, he retires to Grass Valley, California, to write his grandparents' biography. Here, he is assisted by Shelly Hawkes, a Berkeley dropout who shares Rodman's attitude toward history.

As he reads through his grandparents' correspondence, he simultaneously recounts the development of their marriage and discovers the dynamics of their personalities. Susan Ward, cultured, educated in the East, and artistically talented, marries Oliver Ward, an idealistic mining engineer, her second choice for a husband. Without having resolved her disappointment at his lack of culture and appreciation for the arts, she marries him and begins two decades of following him through the West as he looks for professional and financial success in the unstable mining industry. The years in New Almaden, California, Leadville, Colorado, Michoacán, Mexico, and southern Idaho increasingly wear Susan down, despite brief interludes of stability and the frequent company of other eastern scientists and engineers during her Western exile.

In Boise Canyon, Idaho, as Oliver's grand irrigation project falls apart, Susan falls into infidelity with Frank Sargent, Oliver's colorful assistant, and steals away to the countryside under the pretext of taking five-year-old Agnes Ward for a walk. Soon, Agnes's body is found floating in a nearby canal, and the day after her funeral, Frank Sargent commits suicide. Suspecting the worst, Oliver leaves his wife for two years until persuaded to return. For the remaining fifty years of their marriage, Oliver treats her with a kind silence and lack of physical affection, never truly forgiving her. Lyman learns that his grandparents' angle of repose was not the real thing, not a time of harmony but a cold truce full of human weakness. His naïve image of his grandparents based on childhood memories is undercut as he comes to understand them in a more sophisticated way. He learns to respect their strength and complexity.

Lyman's discoveries are all the more poignant because of the similarities between his grandparents' experience and his own relationship with an unfaithful wife who has broken trust, and who, it is implied, will seek a reconciliation. As in *The Big Rock Candy Mountain*, the two main characters symbolize two conflicting impulses in the settlement of the West—Oliver, the dreamer and idealist, pursuing his vision of success in a world with few amenities, and Susan, the finely cultured easterner, yearning for stability and society. Lyman discovers links between his family's past and present and encounters universals of history such as suffering and infidelity that are more poignant to him because he discovers them in his own family history. Finally, the novel suggests that frontier values and the civilizing impulses need their own angle of repose. In essence, American experience had not yet reached its angle of rest; frontier and domestic values lie instead in a kind of uneasy truce.

Recapitulation • A continuation of the family saga played out in *The Big Rock Candy Mountain*, *Recapitulation*, published in 1979, is the moving drama of Bruce Mason's return to Salt Lake City to face his past. Toward the end of a successful career as a diplomat in the United States Foreign Service, Mason returns to the scene of his turbulent adolescence and the death of his family to attend his maiden aunt's funeral. Upon his arrival at the funeral home, the attendant presents him with a message to call Joe Mulder, his best friend in high school and in college at the University of Utah. Bruce was virtually a member of Joe's family for three years during the time when his father's bootlegging business threatened to jeopardize his social life.

Bruce remembers the 1920's and his adolescence before the stock market crash. Trying to find himself, he slowly remembers the time when he was an outsider in Mormon country, a time when he found many of the values that sustained him after the death of his family. Well-liked in high school by his teachers, Bruce was also picked on by the bigger boys and the less able students and acutely embarrassed by the family's house, which doubled as a speakeasy. His first major romance, with Nola, a Mormon country girl who was half American Indian, led to his first sexual encounter. Bruce was infatuated with her but knew her intellectual limits—that ideas put her to sleep and art bored her. Throughout the narrative, he recounts the disintegration of his family during his adolescence.

Stegner stresses Bruce's close relationship with Joe Mulder, but Bruce is emotionally incapable of meeting Joe because he hates being treated as "The Ambassador," a visiting dignitary—a title that would only exaggerate the changes and losses of the past forty-five years. In a sense, he finds that he cannot go home again. He would have nothing in common with Joe except memories of adolescent love affairs and youthful myths. Their past could never be altered or renewed.

A second major theme in *Recapitulation* is the need to belong to some larger community. The Mormon sense of community, whatever its intellectual failings, is viewed nostalgically. Bruce envies the close-knit families of his friends. Nola's family, for example, seems like a tribe, a culture unto itself full of unspoken values and understandings. His decision to attend law school in Minnesota irrevocably removes him from Nola, Utah, and his adolescence, and ultimately from his chance to belong. When he returns to Utah, he is in the later stages of a successful but lonely adult life. His first job out of law school was in Saudi Arabia—a place without available women. He finally becomes a Middle Eastern specialist and a permanent bachelor.

Stegner ends the novel with Bruce, lonely, nostalgic, and emotionally incomplete, unable to make contact with Joe and with his past in a satisfying way. Even though the act of thinking through his past has served him therapeutically, he will continue as a diplomat, making formal contacts with people, living in the surface world of protocol, unable to connect emotionally with people. As the last of his family, he is a solitary figure, a man of deep feelings that he is unable to express. He is, finally, a man who has partially tamed the frontier restlessness and anger of his father and risen above his family's self-destructive tendencies. Nevertheless, Bruce carries on the family's feeling of rootlessness, in a more formal, acceptable way. In the Foreign Service, he never develops roots and is shifted from one diplomatic post to another. In a more formal sense than his father, Bruce is still a drifter. Stegner ends the novel fittingly with Bruce Mason being called back to the diplomatic service as United States Representative to an important OPEC meeting in Caracas, Venezuela, reluctantly pulled away from his efforts to understand his past.

Crossing to Safety • *Crossing to Safety* introduces a new set of characters but also is about coming to terms with the past. Larry and Sally Morgan are a young couple who have moved to Madison, Wisconsin, because Larry has been given a teaching post for a year at the university there. Almost magically, they meet a personable young couple like themselves, Sid and Charity Lang, who also turn out to be very generous. In these Depression days, security is the most sought-after item, and all the young academics vie furiously for tenure. Yet, the Langs (though engaged as furiously in the contest as any) bestow on the Morgans a friendship rare in this backbiting atmosphere— wholehearted, sincere, and giving. Envy and jealousy are not part of their emotional makeup, though they do have their problems. Charity comes from an academic household (her father is a professor), and she wants the same for her family, including a professorship for her husband, who, however, really wants only to write poetry.

Stegner's portrayal of this lifelong friendship is neither idealistic nor blind. He reveals the human sides to his characters, keeping this paragon of *amicitia* from being falsely perfect. The ups and downs of their lives are relayed through flashback: Larry and Sally have come to visit the Langs because Charity is dying from cancer. Larry and Sally's life has not been without tragedy either: The summer after bearing their first child, Sally contracts polio and is permanently disabled.

Ultimately, Larry becomes a successful writer, while Sid never becomes successful either as an academic or as a poet. Belying her name—for she is a strong personality at best, harsh and unyielding at worst—Charity never really forgives Sid for his failure. Yet, Stegner concentrates on the love these people have for one another through thick and thin, creating a compelling story without resorting to tricks of subterfuge or violence to sustain the reader's interest. Stegner's great strength lies in knowing people; he knows their quirks and foibles so well that they come alive on the page without being demeaned or caricatured. In addition, his feeling for mood and setting are twin talents that infuse his writing with life, placing Stegner firmly on the short list of great American novelists.

Richard H. Dillman

Other major works

SHORT FICTION: *The Women on the Wall*, 1950; *The City of the Living, and Other Stories*, 1956; *Collected Stories of Wallace Stegner*, 1990.

NONFICTION: *Mormon Country*, 1942; *One Nation*, 1945 (with the editors of *Look*); *Look at America: The Central Northwest*, 1947; *The Writer in America*, 1951; *Beyond the Hundredth Meridian: John Wesley Powell and the Second Opening of the West*, 1954; *Wolf Willow: A History, a Story, and a Memory of the Last Plains Frontier*, 1962; *The Gathering of Zion: The Story of the Mormon Trail*, 1964; *The Sound of Mountain Water*, 1969; *Ansel Adams: Images 1923-1974*, 1974; *The Uneasy Chair: A Biography of Bernard DeVoto*, 1974; *One Way to Spell Man*, 1982; *American Places*, 1983; *Conversations with Wallace Stegner on Western History and Literature*, 1983; *The American West as Living Space*, 1987; *On the Teaching of Creative Writing: Responses to a Series of Questions*, 1988 (Edward Connery Lathem, editor); *Where the Bluebird Sings to the Lemonade Springs: Living and Writing in the West*,

1992; *Marking the Sparrow's Fall: Wallace Stegner's American West,* 1998 (Page Stegner, editor); *Stealing Glances: Three Interviews with Wallace Stegner,* 1998 (James R. Hepworth, editor); *On Teaching and Writing Fiction,* 2002 (Lynn Stegner, editor).

EDITED TEXTS: *An Exposition Workshop,* 1939; *Readings for Citizens at War,* 1941; *Stanford Short Stories, 1946,* 1947 (with Richard Scowcroft); *The Writer's Art: A Collection of Short Stories,* 1950 (with Scowcroft and Boris Ilyin); *This Is Dinosaur: The Echo Park and Its Magic Rivers,* 1955; *Great American Short Stories,* 1957 (with Mary Stegner); *The Exploration of the Colorado River of the West,* 1957; *Selected American Prose: The Realistic Movement,* 1958; *Report on the Lands of the Arid Region of the United States,* 1962; *Modern Composition,* 1964 (4 volumes); *The American Novel: From Cooper to Faulkner,* 1965; *Twenty Years of Stanford Short Stories,* 1966; *The Letters of Bernard DeVoto,* 1975.

Bibliography

Arthur, Anthony, ed. *Critical Essays on Wallace Stegner.* Boston: G. K. Hall, 1982. Although not an exhaustive discussion of Stegner's works, these essays cover much of his most important writing, including his short fiction. Notes for further reference are included, as are primary and secondary bibliographical information and an index.

Benson, Jackson J. *Down by the Lemonade Springs: Essays on Wallace Stegner.* Reno: University of Nevada Press, 2001. Collection of critical essays on Stegner by his biographer.

_____. *Wallace Stegner: His Life and Work.* New York: Viking Press, 1996. A biography that argues against pigeonholing Stegner as a Western writer. Focuses largely on the people and events that most influenced Stegner's art, including Robert Frost and Bernard DeVoto; covers Stegner's teaching career and his influence on such writers as Ken Kesey, Edward Abbey, Wendell Berry, and Larry McMurty.

Burrows, Russell. "Wallace Stegner's Version of Pastoral: The Topic of Ecology in His Work." *Western American Literature* 25 (May, 1990): 15-25. Stegner's environmentalist stance has had a definite effect on his work, and this article discusses Stegner's use of the pastoral setting in much of his fiction, both long and short. Includes bibliographical information and notes for further reference on points within the article.

Colberg, Nancy. *Wallace Stegner: A Descriptive Bibliography.* Lewiston, Idaho: Confluence Press, 1990. This text contains detailed descriptions of Stegner's works, from his very early writing to *The American West as Living Space.* Colberg also provides sections for other Stegner material, such as contributions to books and edited works. A short appendix that also serves as a secondary bibliography is a good resource for the original publication information for Stegner's individual short stories.

Etulain, Richard W. *Conversations with Wallace Stegner on Western History and Literature.* Rev. ed. Salt Lake City: University of Utah Press, 1990. Collection of interviews with Stegner.

Meine, Curt, ed. *Wallace Stegner and the Continental Vision: Essays on Literature, History, and Landscape.* Washington, D.C.: Island Press, 1997. A collection of papers presented at a 1996 symposium in Madison, Wisconsin. Includes essays on Stegner and the shaping of the modern West, the art of storytelling, history, environmentalism, politics, and bioregionalism.

Rankin, Charles E., ed. *Wallace Stegner: Man and Writer.* Albuquerque: University of New Mexico Press, 1996. A collection of essays by various critics on Stegner's life and art. Most helpful for understanding Stegner's short fiction are the essays by Elliott West on "Storytelling and Western Identity," Jackson J. Benson's "The Story of Wallace Stegner's Fiction," and William Bevis's "The Civic Style."

Robinson, Forrest G. *Wallace Stegner.* Boston: Twayne, 1977. This text is a combination of biographical information on Stegner and interpretation and literary criticism of his work up to the mid-1970's. Robinson provides a chronology of Stegner's life and writings as well as detailed bibliographical information, both primary and secondary. Supplemented by notes and an index.

Stegner, Wallace. "The Art of Fiction: An Interview with Wallace Stegner." Interview by James R. Hepworth. *Paris Review* 115 (Summer, 1990): 58-90. In this interview, Stegner talks about how he became a writer, as well as about writing in general. Although no references are included, this article is useful for the first-hand information it provides about Stegner through the interview process.

Stegner, Wallace, and Richard Etulain. *Conversations with Wallace Stegner.* Rev. ed. Salt Lake City: University of Utah Press, 1990. This edition is an expanded version of a book that first came out in 1983—a later interview section has been added to the first part of the book. In it, Stegner talks about all of his work up to *Crossing to Safety.* Includes biographical information in the form of answers to interview questions and also covers Stegner's view of the American literary West as well as the West—such as Western history and the wilderness areas of the West—in general. References to individual short stories (as well as to the collections) can be found in the index.

Willrich, Patricia Rowe. "A Perspective on Wallace Stegner." *The Virginia Quarterly Review* 67 (Spring, 1991): 240-258. This article covers the high points of Stegner's long career as a writer and scholar, giving both biographical details and information about his work. Good for an overview of, as well as for specifics on, Stegner's literary output.

Gertrude Stein

Born: Allegheny, Pennsylvania; February 3, 1874
Died: Neuilly-sur-Seine, France; July 27, 1946

Principal long fiction • *Three Lives*, 1909; *The Making of Americans*, 1925; *Lucy Church Amiably*, 1930; *A Long Gay Book*, 1932; *Ida, a Novel*, 1941; *Brewsie and Willie*, 1946; *Blood on the Dining-Room Floor*, 1948; *Things as They Are*, 1950 (originally known as *Q.E.D.*); *Mrs. Reynolds and Five Earlier Novelettes, 1931-1942*, 1952; *A Novel of Thank You*, 1958.

Other literary forms • Any attempt to separate Gertrude Stein's novels from her other kinds of writing must be highly arbitrary. Stein thought the novel to be a failed literary form in the twentieth century, claiming that no real novels had been written after Marcel Proust, even including her own novelistic efforts in this assessment. For this and other reasons, it might be claimed that few, if any, of Stein's works are novels in any traditional sense. In fact, very few of Stein's more than six hundred titles in more than forty books can be adequately classified into any traditional literary forms. Her philosophy of composition was so idiosyncratic, her prose style so seemingly nonrational, that her writing bears little resemblance to whatever genre it purports to represent. Depending on one's definition of the novel, Stein wrote anywhere between six and twelve novels, ranging in length from fewer than 100 to 925 pages. The problem is that none of Stein's "novels" has a plot in any conventional sense, that few have conventionally developed and sustained characters, and that several seem almost exclusively autobiographical, more diaries and daybooks than anything else. It is not any easier to categorize her other pieces of writing, most of which are radically sui generis. If references to literary forms are made very loosely, Stein's work can be divided into novels, autobiographies, portraits, poems, lectures, operas, plays, and explanations. Other than her novels, her best-known works are *The Autobiography of Alice B. Toklas* (1933); *Tender Buttons* (1914); *Four Saints in Three Acts* (1934); *Lectures in America* (1935); *Everybody's Autobiography* (1937); and *Portraits and Prayers*, (1934).

Achievements • Whether towering or crouching, Stein is ubiquitous in contemporary literature. A child of the nineteenth century who staunchly adhered to many of its values halfway through the twentieth, she nevertheless dedicated her creative life to the destruction of nineteenth century concepts of artistic order and purpose. In her own words, she set out to do nothing less than to kill a century, to lay the old ways of literary convention to rest. She later boasted that "the most serious thinking about the nature of literature in the twentieth century has been done by a woman," and her claim has great merit. During the course of her career, Stein finally managed to convince almost everyone that there was indeed some point, if not profundity, in her aggressively enigmatic style. The ridicule and parody that frustrated so much of her early work had turned to grudging tolerance or outright lionizing by 1934, when Stein made her triumphant American lecture tour; for the last fifteen or so years of her life, she was published even if her editor had not the vaguest idea of what she was doing (as Bennett Cerf later admitted he had not). On the most concrete level, Stein's distinctive prose style is remarkably significant even when its philosophical dimensions

Library of Congress

are ignored. William H. Gass has observed, Stein "did more with sentences, and understood them better, than any writer ever has."

More important was Stein's influence on other leaders in the development of modernism. As a student of William James and as a friend of Alfred North Whitehead and Pablo Picasso, Stein lived at the center of the philosophical and artistic revolutions of the twentieth century. She was the natural emblem for modernism, and in her person, career, and legend, many of its salient issues converged. In the light of more recent developments in the novel and in literary theory, it has also been argued that Stein was the first postmodernist, the first writer to claim openly that the instance of language is itself as important as the reality to which it refers. Among major writers, Ernest Hemingway was most obviously influenced by his association with her, but her genius was freely acknowledged by F. Scott Fitzgerald, Sherwood Anderson, and Thornton Wilder. William Saroyan explained her influence most directly when he asserted that no American writer could keep from coming under it, a sentiment reluctantly echoed by Edmund Wilson in *Axel's Castle* (1931), even before Stein's great popular success in the mid-1930's.

Biography • Gertrude Stein was born on February 3, 1874, in Allegheny, Pennsylvania, but she was seven before her family settled into permanent residence in Oakland, California, the city she was later to describe as having "no there there." Her birth itself was contingent on the deaths of two of her five brothers and sisters: her parents had decided to have only five children, and only after two children had died in infancy were Gertrude and her older brother, Leo, conceived. Identity was to become one of the central preoccupations of her writing career, and the tenuous nature of her own birth greatly influenced that concern.

Stein's early years were comfortably bourgeois and uneventful. Her father, a vice president of the Union Street Municipal Railway System in San Francisco, was authoritarian, moody, and aggressive, but vacillating, and he may have helped foster her sense of independence, but he undoubtedly left her annoyed by him in particular and by fatherhood in general. Her mother barely figured in her life at all: A pale, withdrawn, ineffectual woman, she left most of the rearing of her children to governesses. By the time Stein was seventeen, both parents had died and she had grown even closer to her immediate older brother, Leo. In 1893, she entered Harvard Annex (renamed Radcliffe College the following year), thus rejoining Leo, who was a student at Harvard. There, Stein studied with William James and Hugo Munsterberg and became involved in research in psychology. Together with the great influence exerted on her thinking by James, this early work in psychology was to provide her with both a subject and a style that would continue in many forms throughout her career. She was awarded her bachelor's degree by Harvard in 1898, almost a year after she had entered medical school at Johns Hopkins University. Her interest in medicine rapidly waned, and she left Johns Hopkins in 1901, failing four courses in her final semester.

After leaving medical school, Stein spent two years moving back and forth between Europe and America. During that time, she was involved in an agonizing love affair with another young woman student at Johns Hopkins, May Bookstaver. The affair was painfully complicated, first by Stein's naïveté, then by the presence of a more sophisticated rival for May's love, Mabel Haynes. The resulting lover's triangle led Stein, in an effort to understand May, to begin formulating the theories of personality that dominated her early writing. The frustration and eventual despair of this lesbian relationship profoundly influenced Stein's view of the psychology of personality and of love. Most directly, Stein's troubled affair with Bookstaver provided her with many, if not most, of the concerns of three of her books, *Quod Erat Demonstrandum,* *The Making of Americans,* and *Three Lives,* the first two of which she began while living in New York in the winter of 1903.

After a brief stay in New York, she lived with Leo, first in Bloomsbury in London, and then, beginning in 1903, in Paris at 27 rue de Fleurus, the address she was to make so well known to the world. In Paris, Gertrude and Leo became more and more interested in painting, buying works by new artists such as Henri Matisse and Picasso. Leo's preference was for works by Matisse, while Gertrude favored the more experimental works of Picasso, marking the beginning of a distancing process that would lead to Leo's complete separation from his sister in 1913. Leo was bright and opinionated, and fancied himself by far the greater creative talent of the two, but his brilliance and energy never produced any creative or significant critical work, and he grew to resent both his sister's independent thinking and her emerging ability to write. Later in his life, he would dismiss Gertrude as "dumb," her writing as "nonsense."

In 1907, Stein met another young American woman in Paris, Alice Toklas, and Alice began to displace Leo as the most important personal influence in Gertrude's life. Alice learned to type so she could transcribe Stein's handwritten manuscripts, beginning with portions of *The Making of Americans* in 1908. In 1909, Alice moved in with Gertrude and Leo at 27 rue de Fleurus, and by 1913, Alice had replaced Leo as Gertrude's companion and as the manager of her household. Stein later referred to her relationship with Alice as a "marriage," and few, if any, personal relationships have ever influenced a literary career so profoundly. Apart from providing Stein with the persona for her best-known work, *The Autobiography of Alice B. Toklas,* Alice typed, criticized, and valiantly worked to publish all of Stein's work for the rest of her career and for the twenty years that Alice lived after Stein's death. Although it is doubtful that Alice was directly responsible for any of Stein's writing, her influence on its composition and on Stein's life was tremendous.

Gertrude and Alice spent the first months of World War I in England as houseguests of Alfred North Whitehead, returning to Paris briefly in 1914, then spending more than a year in Spain. They joined the war effort in 1917 when Stein ordered a Ford motor van from America for use as a supply truck for the American Fund for French Wounded, an acquisition which began Stein's lifelong fascination with automobiles, particularly with Fords. She and Alice drove this van, named "Auntie," until the war ended, work for which she was later awarded the Medaille de la Reconnaissance Française.

Modernism had burst on the American consciousness when the Armory Show opened in New York in 1913, and this show, which had confronted Americans with the first cubist paintings, also led to the association in the public mind of Stein's writing with this shockingly new art, particularly since Stein's first periodical publications had been "Matisse" and "Picasso" in *Camera Work*, the year before. Stein's mammoth, 925-page novel, *The Making of Americans*, was published in 1925, and in 1926, she lectured at Oxford and Cambridge, attempting to explain her idiosyncratic writing style. Her "landscape" novel, *Lucy Church Amiably*, appeared in 1930, but it was in 1933, with the publication of the best-selling *The Autobiography of Alice B. Toklas*, that Stein first captured the public's interest. She became front page news the following year when her opera *Four Saints in Three Acts* was first performed and when she embarked on a nationwide lecture tour, later described in *Everybody's Autobiography* and *Lectures in America*.

Stein and Toklas spent World War II in Bilignin and then in Culoz, France. Although Stein and Toklas were both Jewish, they were never persecuted by occupying forces, owing in part to the influence of Bernard Fay, an early admirer of Stein's work who directed the Bibliothèque Nationale for the Vichy regime. When, after the war, Fay was sentenced to life imprisonment for his Vichy activities, Stein was one of his few defenders. The fact that her art collection survived Nazi occupation virtually intact can only have been through Fay's intercession. During the war, Stein finished another novel, *Mrs. Reynolds* (unpublished), and *Wars I Have Seen* (1945), an autobiographical work. Her novel *Brewsie and Willie*, a series of conversations among American soldiers, was published in 1946.

Stein died following an operation for cancer in the American Hospital in Neuilly-sur-Seine, France, on July 27, 1946. Although Alice Toklas's account of Stein's last words may be apocryphal, it certainly is in keeping with the spirit of her life. As Alice later reconstructed their last conversation, Stein had asked her "What is the answer?" Then, when Alice remained silent, Stein added, "In that case, what is the question?"

Analysis • Although Stein's persistence finally earned her access to readers, it could never guarantee her readers who would or could take her strange writing seriously. As a result, more confusing and contradictory information surrounds her career than that of any other twentieth century writer of comparable reputation. Usually responding in any of four basic ways, readers and critics alike seemed to view her as (1) a literary charlatan of the P. T. Barnum ilk, interested in publicity or money rather than in art; (2) something of a naïve child-woman incapable of comprehending the world around her; (3) a fiery-eyed literary revolutionary, den mother of the avant-garde; or (4) an ageless repository of wisdom and genius. Ultimately, the reader's acceptance or rejection of these various categories will greatly determine his or her response to Stein's writing, which forces the reader to make as many cognitive choices as does that of any major writer.

Stein's many explanations of her writing further complicate its interpretation: Even her "explanations" frustrate as much as they reveal, explicitly setting her up in cognitive competition with her reader, a competition suggested by her favorite cryptogram, which works out to read: "I understand you undertake to overthrow my undertaking." Stein proposes a rhetoric not of misunderstanding, but of antiunderstanding; that is, her "explanations" usually argue precisely against the desirability of explaining.

As Stein bluntly put the matter, "understanding is a very dull occupation." "Understanding" has a special denotation for Stein, sometimes meaning as little as "paying attention to" or "reading." "To understand a thing means to be in contact with that thing," she proclaimed. Central to her mistrust of explanations and interpretations was Stein's often anguished belief that her thoughts could never really be matched to anyone else's. She was deeply troubled by this doubt as she wrote *The Making of Americans*, referring in that work to "the complete realization that no one can believe as you do about anything" as "complete disillusionment in living." Starting from this assumption that no one can ever really understand what someone else says or writes because of the inherent ambiguity of language, Stein not only decided to force her readers to confront that ambiguity but also claimed it as a primary virtue of her writing. She announced triumphantly that

> if you have vitality enough of knowing enough of what you mean, somebody and sometimes a great many will have to realize that you know what you mean and so they will agree that you mean what you know, which is as near as anybody can come to understanding any one.

Stein's focus here is on relationships or process rather than on product—on the act of trying to become one with, rather than focusing on the ultimate result of that act.

Stein's thinking about understanding manifests itself in a number of distinctive ways in her writing, as do her theories of perception and of human psychology. Moreover, during the nearly fifty years of her writing career, her style developed in many related but perceptibly different stages, such as her "cubist" or her "cinema" phases. As a result, no single analysis can do more than describe the primary concerns and features of one of her stylistic periods. There are, however, three central concerns that underlie and at least partially account for all the stages in the development of her style. These concerns are with the value of individual words, with repetition as the basic rhythm of existence, and with the related concept of "movement" in writing. Her articulations of these central concerns all run counter to her reader's expectations about the purpose and function of language and of literature. Her writing surprised her readers in much the same way that her penchant for playing only the black keys on a piano surprised and frustrated all but the most patient of her listeners.

One of Stein's goals was to return full meaning, value, and particularity to the words she used. "I took individual words and thought about them until I got their weight and volume complete and put them next to another word," she explained of seemingly nonsense phrases such as "toasted Susie is my ice cream," or "mouse and mountain and a quiver, a quaint statue and pain in an exterior and silence more silence louder shows salmon a mischief intender." This sort of paratactic juxtaposition of seemingly unrelated words rarely occurs in Stein's novels but represents a problem for her reader in many other ways in her writing. She frequently chose to stress or focus on a part or aspect of the object of her description that the reader normally does not consider. The "things" Stein saw and wrote of were not the "things" with which readers are familiar: Where another observer might see a coin balanced on its edge, Stein might choose either of the descriptive extremes of seeing it literally as a thin rectangle, or figuratively as the essence of money. Characteristically, her most opaque parataxis refers to essences or processes rather than to objects or static concepts.

A related quirk in Stein's style results from her intellectual or emotional attachment to particular words and phrases at certain stages of her career. As she admitted in *The Making of Americans*,

> To be using a new word in my writing is to me a very difficult thing. . . . Using a word I have not yet been using in my writing is to me a very difficult and a peculiar feeling. Sometimes I am using a new one, sometimes I feel a new meaning in an old one, sometimes I like one I am very fond of that one that has many meanings many ways of being used to make different meanings to everyone.

Stein said she had learned from Paul Cézanne that everything in a painting was related to everything else and that each part of the painting was of equal importance—a blade of grass as important to the composition of the painting as a tree. She attempted to apply these two principles to the composition of her sentences, taking special delight in using normally "overlooked" words, arguing that articles, prepositions, and conjunctions—the transitive elements in grammar—are just as important and more interesting than substantives such as nouns and verbs. Her reassessment both of the value of words and of the conventions of description resulted in what Michael J. Hoffman in *The Development of Abstractionism in the Writings of Gertrude Stein* (1965) has described as Stein's "abstractionism." It also resulted in her including in her writing totally unexpected information in perplexingly paratactic word-strings.

A second constant in Stein's style is the pronounced repetition of words, phrases, and sentences, with no change or with only incremental progressions of sounds or associations. Works such as *The Making of Americans* and *Three Lives* contain long passages in which each sentence is a light variation on some core phrase, with great repetition of words even within a single sentence. Stein termed this phenomenon "insistence" rather than repetition, citing her former teacher, William James, as her philosophical authority. James's argument in his *The Principles of Psychology* (1890) that one must think of the identical recurrence of a fact in a fresh manner remarkably resembles Stein's contention that

> in expressing anything there can be no repetition because the essence of that expression is insistence, and if you insist you must each time use emphasis and if you use emphasis it is not possible while anybody is alive that they should use exactly the same emphasis.

Repetition or insistence is perhaps the central aspect of what has been called Stein's "cinema style," based on her claim that in writing *The Making of Americans* she was "doing what the cinema was doing." She added that her writing in that book was "like a cinema picture made up of succession and each moment having its own emphasis that is its own difference and so there was the moving and the existence of each moment as it was in me."

Stein's discussion of "what the cinema was doing" appears in her *Lectures in America* and also suggests the third basic concern of her writing: movement. By "movement," she referred not to the movement of a message to its conclusion or the movement of a plot or narrative, but to "the essence of its going" of her prose, a timeless continuous present in the never-ending motion of consciousness. Stein also credits Cézanne with discovering this concern, "a feeling of movement inside the painting not a painting of a thing moving but the thing painted having inside it the existence of moving." She seemed to understand Cézanne's achievement in terms of James's model of consciousness as an ever-flowing stream of thought. Accordingly, she used her writing not to record a scene or object or idea (products of thought), but to try to capture the sense of the process of perceiving such things. Stein's subject is almost always really two things at once: whatever attracted her attention—caught her eye, entered her ear, or crossed her mind—and the mobile nature of reality, particularly as it is perceived by human consciousness. In fact, Stein was usually more concerned with the nature of her own perception and with that of her reader than she was with its objects. She wanted to escape the conventions of linguistic representation, arbitrary arrangements similar to the "rules" for perspective in painting, and to present "something moving as moving is not as moving should be." As confusing as her resulting efforts sometimes are, her concern with motion makes sense as an attempt to mimic or evoke the nature of consciousness as she understood it.

From James at Harvard and possibly from Henri Bergson in Paris, Stein had learned that the best model for human consciousness was one that stressed the processual, ever-flowing nature of experience. She added to this belief her assumption that the essence of any subject could only be perceived and should only be represented through its motion, echoing Bergson's claim that "reality is mobility." However, this belief led her writing into one of its many paradoxes: She could only attempt to represent the continuous stream of experience through the segmented, inherently sequential nature of language. Streams flow; words do not. Instead, they proceed one by one, like the cars pulled by a train engine. Although James would certainly have objected to Stein's sequential cinema model as an approximation of the stream of consciousness, her motion-obsessed writing probably suggests the flow of consciousness as well as does any literary style.

Things as They Are • Written in 1903 as *Q.E.D.*, but put out of her mind until 1932 and not published until 1950, *Things as They Are* is Stein's most conventional novel. Its sentences employ no unexpected syntax or diction, its central concerns are clear, its time scheme is linear, and its characters are conventionally drawn. If anything, Stein's style in this first novel is markedly old-fashioned, including highly formal sentences that frequently sport balanced serial constructions.

> Adele vehemently and with much picturesque vividness explained her views and theories of manners, people and things, in all of which she was steadily opposed by Helen who differed fundamentally in all her convictions, aspirations and illusions.

Although its conventional style (crudely reminiscent of that of Henry James) is completely unlike that of any other Stein novel, *Things as They Are* is a very significant work for the consideration of Stein's career. Apart from convincingly refuting the suspicion of some of her detractors that Stein was incapable of rational writing, this book establishes her preoccupation with psychological typecasting and vaguely hints at the importance of repetition in her thinking and writing.

Things as They Are charts the growth, turbulence, and eventual dissolution of the relationships among three young women: Adele, the book's central consciousness, an obviously autobiographical figure; Helen Thomas, the object of Adele's love; and Mabel Neathe, Adele's calculating rival for Helen's affection. These three characters closely parallel Stein, May Bookstaver, and Mabel Haynes, and the story of their relationship is the story of Stein's first, agonizing love affair. Although the novel follows these three young women for three years, not much happens. Most of the book relates conversations and correspondence between Adele and Helen, showing Adele's torment first from her not yet understood desire for Helen, then from her growing realization that she is losing Helen to Mabel. Of principal interest to the reader is Stein's self-characterization in her portrayal of Adele.

Three Lives • *Three Lives* is easily Stein's best-known and most respected piece of fiction. Technically three novellas, this work is unified by its three subjects, by its central concern with the nature of consciousness, and by its attempt to blend colloquial idioms with Stein's emerging style, here based largely on her understanding of Cézanne's principles of composition, particularly that "one thing was as important as another thing." "The Good Anna," "Melanctha," and "The Gentle Lena" are the three sections of this work. Anna and Lena are poor German immigrants who patiently work as servants in Bridgepoint, Baltimore; Melanctha is a young black woman who discovers sexuality and love, then turns from a frustrating relationship with a sincere young black doctor to a dissipative affair with a gambler. Because all three women are essentially victimized by their surroundings and die at the end of their stories, this work is deterministic in the naturalist tradition, but *Three Lives* marks the transition from naturalism to modernism as Stein departs from nineteenth century literary conventions. She abandons conventional syntax to try to follow the movement of a consciousness rather than of events, and she develops a new narrative style only partially tied to linear chronology. The result is an interior narrative of consciousness in which Stein's prose style serves as the primary carrier of knowledge. Through the rhythms of her characters' speech and the rhythms of her narration, Stein gives her reader a sense of the basic rhythms of consciousness for these three women—what Stein would elsewhere refer to as their "bottom natures."

Possibly Stein's most widely celebrated piece of writing, "Melanctha" recasts the anguishing love triangle of *Quod Erat Demonstrandum* into the conflict between Melanctha and Jeff Campbell, whose inherently conflicting "bottom natures" or personality types parallel the conflict between Helen and Adele in the earlier work. "Melanctha" has been praised by Richard Wright, among others, as one of the first realistic and sympathetic renderings of black life by a white American author, but Melanctha's race is actually incidental to Stein's central concerns with finding a style to express the rhythms of personality and the frustrating cycles of love.

The Making of Americans • Although it was not published until 1925, Stein's *The Making of Americans* occupied her as early as 1903 and was in fact begun before *Quod Erat Demonstrandum* and *Three Lives*. This mammoth novel began as a description of the creation of Americans from a representative immigrant family: "The old people in a new world, the new people made out of the old, that is the story that I mean to tell, for that is what really is and what I really know." Stein's projected family chronicle soon lost its original focus, becoming first a history of everyone, then a study of character types rather than of characters. Leon Katz, who has worked with this book more than has anyone else, calls it "a massive description of the psychological landscape of human being in its totality." Although the book ostensibly continues to follow events in the lives of two central families, the Herslands and the Dehnings, its real concern is almost always both larger and smaller, ranging from Stein's questions about her own life and identity to questions about the various personality types of all of humanity. As Richard Bridgman suggests, this is "an improvised work of no identifiable genre in which the creator learned by doing," one "full of momentary wonders and botched long-range schemes, lyrical outbursts and anguished confessions." Accordingly, Bridgman concludes that *The Making of Americans* is best thought of "not as a fictional narrative nor a philosophic tract, but as a drama of self-education." In a way, the book chronicles the "making" of Gertrude Stein, presenting a phenomenology of her mind as it works its way through personal problems toward the distinctive "cinema style."

Underlying a great part of the writing in this book is Stein's belief that human personality consists of variations on a few basic "bottom natures" or kinds of identity that can be perceived through a character's repeated actions:

> There are then many things every one has in them that come out of them in the repeating everything living have always in them, repeating with a little changing just enough to make of each one an individual being, to make of each repeating an individual thing that gives to such a one a feeling of themselves inside them.

There are two basic personality types, "dependent independent" and "independent dependent," polarities identified in part by the way the person fights: the first kind by resisting, the second by attacking. Concerns with character-typing dominate the book's first two sections, "The Dehnings and the Herslands" and "Martha Hersland" (the character most closely modeled on Stein's own life), while the third section, "Alfred and Julia Hersland," contains mostly digressions about contemporary matters in Stein's life. The fourth section, "David Hersland," becomes a meditation on the nature of aging and death ("He was dead when he was at the beginning of being in middle living."), and the final section, "History of a Family's Progress," is—even for Stein—an incredibly abstract and repetitive series of reflections on the concerns that had given rise to the novel. This final section contains no names, referring only to "some," "any," "every," or "very many."

Stein later described her efforts in this book as an attempt "to do what the cinema was doing"; that is, to give a sense of motion and life through a series of highly repetitive statements, each statement only an incremental change from the preceding one, like frames in a strip of film. One of the main effects of this technique is to freeze all action into a "continuous present." Not only do Stein's sentences exist in overlapping clusters, depending more for their meaning on their relationships to one another than on individual semantic content, but also her verbs in *The Making of Americans* are almost exclusively present participles, suspending all action in the present progressive tense. "The business of Art," Stein later explained, "is to live in the actual present, that is the complete actual present." As a result, while *The Making of Americans* does ostensibly present a history of four generations of the Hersland family, there exists in it little or no sense of the passage of time. Instead, the book presents a sense of "existence suspended in time," a self-contained world existing quite independently of the "real world," a basic modernist goal that has also become one of the hallmarks of postmodernism.

A 416-page version, abridged by Stein, was published in 1934 but has not been accepted by Stein scholars as adequately representative of the longer work. For all its difficulty, *The Making of Americans* is one of modernism's seminal works and an invaluable key to Stein's literary career.

Lucy Church Amiably • Described by its author as "a novel of Romantic beauty and nature and that Looks Like an Engraving," *Lucy Church Amiably* shares many characteristics with Stein's best-known play, *Four Saints in Three Acts*, and with the several works she called "geographies." The book was Stein's response to the area around Belley, France, where she and Alice spent many summers. Stein's title plays on the existence of the church in a nearby village, Lucey. As Richard Bridgman has observed, Lucy Church refers throughout the book to both that church and to a woman who resembles a relaxed Gertrude Stein. As Bridgman also notes, "the book is essentially a long, lyric diary," with Stein including in it information about the geography, residents, and flora of the surrounding area. This information appears, however, in Stein's distinctive paratactic style:

> In this story there is to be not only white black tea colour and vestiges of their bankruptcy but also well wishing and outlined and melodious and with a will and much of it to be sure with their only arrangement certainly for this for the time of which when by the way what is the difference between fixed.

This novel can perhaps best be thought of as a pastoral and elegiac meditation on the nature of place.

The World Is Round **and *Ida, a Novel*** • In 1939, Stein's novel for children, *The World Is Round*, was published, with illustrations by Clement Hurd. The book focuses on a series of events in the lives of a nine-year-old girl, Rose, and her cousin, Willie. These events are more enigmatic than dramatic but seem to move both children through several kinds of initiations. Identity worries both Rose and Willie ("Would she have been Rose if her name had not been Rose and would she have been Rose if she had been a twin"), as does the contrast between the uncertainties of their lives and the advertised verities of existence, emblemized by the "roundness" of the world. Comprising both the children's meditations and their songs, the book is, for Stein, relatively conventional. Although its sentences are highly repetitive and rhythmic, they present a compelling view of a child's consciousness, and Stein scholars agree on the importance and success of this little-known work.

Originally intended as "a novel about publicity," *Ida, a Novel* expands many of the concerns of *The World Is Round*, extending them from Ida's birth well into her adult life. As is true of all of Stein's novels, there is not anything resembling a plot, and many of the things that happen in Ida's life are surrealistically dreamlike. "Funny things" keep happening to the young Ida, and while the nature of these things is never explained, most of them seem to involve men. Frequently, these men have nothing at all to do with her, or they only glance at her, but Ida sees them as vaguely threatening, and insofar as her novel can be said to have a central concern, it is with certain problems of sexuality. Although Stein later described Ida as having been based on the Duchess of Windsor, this connection is only superficial, and Ida is better seen as another in the long line of Stein's autobiographical characters.

Brewsie and Willie • Stein's novel *Brewsie and Willie* redirected her revolutionary spirit from literary to social and economic problems. In this series of conversations among American soldiers and nurses awaiting redeployment from France to the United States after World War II, Stein pessimistically considered the future of her native land. Stein had long held that the United States was "the oldest country in the world" because it had been the first to enter the twentieth century. By 1945, she believed that America had grown "old like a man of fifty," and that its tired, middle-aged economic system had become stale and repressive. In *Brewsie and Willie,* she describes that economic system as "industrialism," portraying a stultifying cycle of depleting raw materials for overproduction and installment buying. This cycle also locked the worker into "job thinking," making of him a kind of automaton, tied to his job, locked into debt, and, worst of all, robbed of freedom of thought. Through conversations involving Brewsie (Stein's spokesman), Willie, and several other soldiers and nurses, Stein portrays an apprehensive generation of young Americans who see the potential dangers of postwar America but who fear they do not "have the guts to make a noise" about them. These conversations cover a wide range of subjects, from a comparison of French and American baby carriages to the tentative suggestion that the American system must be torn down before "pioneering" will again be possible.

Stein makes little or no effort in this book to differentiate the voices of her speakers, but she does rather amazingly blend her own voice with those of the soldiers. The result is a style that is characteristically Stein's but that also has the rhythm and the randomness of overheard conversation. Often overlooked, *Brewsie and Willie* is one of the most remarkable documents in Stein's writing career.

However idiosyncratic Stein's writing may seem, it must be remembered that a very strong case can be made for its substantial philosophical underpinnings. To her way of thinking, language could refuse few things to Stein, and the limitations of language were exactly what she refused to accept. She bent the language to the very uses that process philosophers such as James and Bergson and Whitehead feared it could not be put. Her stubborn emphasis on the individual word—particularly on transitive elements—her insistent use of repetition, and her ever-present preoccupation with the essential motion of words were all part of Stein's monumental struggle with a language she believed was not accurately used to reflect the way people perceive reality or the motion of reality itself. In a narrow but profound sense, she is the most serious realist in literary history. Stein was not a philosopher—her magpie eclecticism, associational flights, and thundering *ex cathedra* pronouncements ill-suited her for systematic explanation—but in her writing a wealth of philosophy appears.

Brooks Landon

Other major works

SHORT FICTION: *As Fine as Melanctha,* 1954; *Painted Lace, and Other Pieces, 1914-1937,* 1955; *Alphabets and Birthdays,* 1957.

PLAYS: *Geography and Plays,* pb. 1922; *Operas and Plays,* pb. 1932; *Four Saints in Three Acts,* pr., pb. 1934; *In Savoy: Or, Yes Is for a Very Young Man (A Play of the Resistance in France),* pr., pb. 1946; *The Mother of Us All,* pr. 1947; *Last Operas and Plays,* pb. 1949; *In a Garden: An Opera in One Act,* pb. 1951; *Lucretia Borgia,* pb. 1968; *Selected Operas and Plays,* pb. 1970.

POETRY: *Tender Buttons: Objects, Food, Rooms,* 1914; *Before the Flowers of Friendship Faded Friendship Faded,* 1931; *Two (Hitherto Unpublished) Poems,* 1948; *Bee Time Vine, and Other Pieces, 1913-1927,* 1953; *Stanzas in Meditation, and Other Poems, 1929-1933,* 1956.

NONFICTION: *Composition as Explanation,* 1926; *How to Write,* 1931; *Matisse, Picasso, and Gertrude Stein, with Two Shorter Stories,* 1933; *The Autobiography of Alice B. Toklas,* 1933; *Portraits and Prayers,* 1934; *Lectures in America,* 1935; *Narration: Four Lectures,* 1935; *The Geographical History of America,* 1936; *Everybody's Autobiography,* 1937; *Picasso,*

1938; *Paris, France*, 1940; *What Are Masterpieces?*, 1940; *Wars I Have Seen*, 1945; *Four in America*, 1947; *Reflections on the Atomic Bomb*, 1973; *How Writing Is Written*, 1974; *The Letters of Gertrude Stein and Thornton Wilder*, 1996 (Edward Burns and Ulla E. Dydo, editors); *Baby Precious Always Shines: Selected Love Notes Between Gertrude Stein and Alice B. Toklas*, 1999 (Kay Turner, editor).

CHILDREN'S LITERATURE: *The World Is Round*, 1939.

MISCELLANEOUS: *The Gertrude Stein First Reader and Three Plays*, 1946; *The Yale Edition of the Unpublished Writings of Gertrude Stein*, 1951-1958 (8 volumes; Carl Van Vechten, editor); *Selected Writings of Gertrude Stein*, 1962; *The Yale Gertrude Stein*, 1980.

Bibliography

Bowers, Jane Palatini. *Gertrude Stein*. New York: St. Martin's Press, 1993. A succinct, feminist-oriented introduction to Stein, with separate chapters on the short fiction, novels, and plays. Includes notes and bibliography.

Curnutt, Kirk, ed. *The Critical Response to Gertrude Stein*. Westport, Conn.: Greenwood Press, 2000. Although including quintessential pieces on Stein by Carl Van Vechten, William Carlos Williams, and Katherine Anne Porter, this guide to her critical reception also includes previously obscure estimations from contemporaries such as H. L. Mencken, Mina Loy, and Conrad Aiken.

DeKoven, Marianne. *A Different Language: Gertrude Stein's Experimental Writing*. Madison: University of Wisconsin Press, 1983. DeKoven's feminist study focuses on Stein's experimental work published after *Three Lives* and before *The Autobiography of Alice B. Toklas*. She argues that this period of Stein's writing is important not so much because of its influence on other writers but because of its attempt to redefine patriarchal language and provide alternatives to conventional modes of signification.

Dydo, Ulla E., with William Rice. *Gertrude Stein: The Language That Rises, 1923-1934*. Evanston, Ill.: Northwestern University Press, 2003. Dydo, a renowned Stein scholar provides a comprehensive analysis of the letters, manuscripts, and notebooks Stein generated over a twenty year period.

Kellner, Bruce, ed. *A Gertrude Stein Companion*. New York: Greenwood Press, 1988. Kellner supplies a helpful introduction on how to read Stein. The volume includes a study of Stein and literary tradition, her manuscripts, and her various styles, and biographical sketches of her friends and enemies. Provides an annotated bibliography of criticism.

Knapp, Bettina. *Gertrude Stein*. New York: Continuum, 1990. A general introduction to Stein's life and art. Discusses her stylistic breakthrough in the stories in *Three Lives*, focusing on repetition and the use of the continuous present. Devotes a long chapter to *Tender Buttons* as one of Stein's most innovative and esoteric works; discusses the nonreferential nature of language in the fragments.

Mitrano, G. F. *Gertrude Stein: Woman Without Qualities*. Burlington, Vt.: Ashgate, 2005. A study of Stein's writing and a look at why it is relevant today.

Neuman, Shirley, and Ira B. Nadel, eds. *Gertrude Stein and the Making of Literature*. Boston: Northeastern University Press, 1988. A collection of essays on Stein from a variety of theoretical perspectives that attempt to "reread" her work during the 1970's and 1980's. Includes essays on Stein and the modernist canon, her relationship to American art and to Henry James, and her experimental collection of prose fragments, *Tender Buttons*.

Simon, Linda. *Gertrude Stein Remembered.* Lincoln: University of Nebraska Press, 1994. Consists of short memoirs of the modernist writer by her colleagues and contemporaries. Selections include pieces by Daniel-Henri Kahnweiler, Sylvia Beach, Sherwood Anderson, Cecil Beaton, and Eric Sevareid, who offer intimate and often informal views of Stein.

Souhami, Diana. *Gertrude and Alice.* London: Pandora, 1991. The most frank account of Gertrude Stein's long-standing lesbian relationship with Alice B. Toklas, this book shows how strong Alice was and how she dominated many aspects of her forty-year marriage to Stein.

Will, Barbara. *Gertrude Stein, Modernism, and the Problem of "Genius."* Edinburgh: Edinburgh University Press, 2000. A chronological study of Stein's development of her concept of "genius" with much historical context.

John Steinbeck

Born: Salinas, California; February 27, 1902
Died: New York, New York; December 20, 1968

Principal long fiction • *Cup of Gold*, 1929; *The Pastures of Heaven*, 1932; *To a God Unknown*, 1933; *Tortilla Flat*, 1935; *In Dubious Battle*, 1936; *Of Mice and Men*, 1937; *The Red Pony*, 1937, 1945; *The Grapes of Wrath*, 1939; *The Moon Is Down*, 1942; *Cannery Row*, 1945; *The Pearl*, 1945 (serial), 1947 (book); *The Wayward Bus*, 1947; *Burning Bright*, 1950; *East of Eden*, 1952; *Sweet Thursday*, 1954; *The Short Reign of Pippen IV*, 1957; *The Winter of Our Discontent*, 1961.

Other literary forms • In addition to his seventeen novels, John Steinbeck published a story collection, *The Long Valley* (1938), and a few other uncollected or separately printed stories. His modern English translations of Sir Thomas Malory's Arthurian tales were published posthumously in 1976. Three plays he adapted from his novels were published as well as performed on Broadway: *Of Mice and Men* (1937), *The Moon Is Down* (1942), and *Burning Bright* (1951). Three of the six film treatments or screenplays he wrote—*The Forgotten Village* (1941), *A Medal for Benny* (1945), and *Viva Zapata!* (1952)—have been published; the other three also were produced as films—*Lifeboat* (1944), *The Pearl* (1945), and *The Red Pony* (1949), the latter two adapted from his own novels. His nonfiction was voluminous, and much of it remains uncollected. The more important nonfiction books include *Sea of Cortez* (1941, with Edward F. Ricketts), *Bombs Away* (1942), *A Russian Journal* (1948, with Robert Capa), *Once There Was a War* (1958), *Travels with Charley: In Search of America* (1962), *America and Americans* (1966), *Journal of a Novel* (1969), and *Steinbeck: A Life in Letters* (1975; Elaine Steinbeck and Robert Wallsten, editors).

Achievements • From the publication of his first best seller, *Tortilla Flat*, in 1935, Steinbeck was a popular and widely respected American writer. His three earlier novels were virtually ignored, but the five books of fiction published between 1935 and 1939 made him the most important literary spokesman for the Great Depression decade. *In Dubious Battle*, *The Red Pony*, and *Of Mice and Men* established him as a serious writer, and his master work, *The Grapes of Wrath*, confirmed him as a major talent. During these years, his popular and critical success rivaled that of any of his contemporaries.

Although his immense popularity, public recognition, and the impressive sales of his works persisted throughout his career, Steinbeck's critical success waned after *The Grapes of Wrath*, reaching a nadir at his death in 1968, despite his Nobel Prize in Literature in 1962. During World War II, his development as a novelist faltered for many reasons, and Steinbeck never recovered his artistic momentum. Even *East of Eden*, the work he thought his masterpiece, proved a critical failure although a popular success. Since his death, Steinbeck remains widely read, both in America and abroad, while his critical reputation has enjoyed a modest revival. Undoubtedly the appreciation of his considerable talents will continue to develop, as few writers have better celebrated the American Dream or traced the dark lineaments of the American nightmare.

Biography • John Ernst Steinbeck was born on February 27, 1902, in Salinas, California. The time and place of his birth are important because Steinbeck matured as an artist in his early thirties during the darkest days of the Depression, and his most important fictions are set in his beloved Salinas Valley. In one sense, Steinbeck's location in time and place may have made him a particularly American artist. Born just after the closing of the frontier, Steinbeck grew up with a frustrated modern America and witnessed the most notable failure of the American Dream in the Depression. He was a writer who inherited the great tradition of the American Renaissance of the nineteenth century and who was forced to reshape it in terms of the historical and literary imperatives of twentieth century modernism. Steinbeck's family background evidenced this strongly American identity. His paternal grandfather, John Adolph Steinbeck, emigrated from Germany, settling in California after serving in the Civil War.

© The Nobel Foundation

His mother's father, Samuel Hamilton, sailed around Cape Horn from northern Ireland, finally immigrating to the Salinas Valley. John Ernst Steinbeck and Olive Hamilton were the first-generation descendants of sturdy, successful, and Americanized immigrant farm families. They met and married in 1890, settling in Salinas, where the father was prominent in local business and government, and the mother stayed home to rear their four children—three daughters and a son, the third child named for his father. The Steinbecks were refined, intelligent, and ambitious people who lived a quiet middle-class life in the small agricultural service town of Salinas.

Steinbeck seems to have enjoyed a happy childhood, and in fact he often asserted that he did. His father made enough money to indulge him in a small way, even to buy him a red pony. His mother encouraged him to read and to write, providing him with the classics of English and American literature. At school, he proved a popular and successful student and was elected president of his senior class.

After graduation from Salinas High School in 1919, Steinbeck enrolled at Stanford University. His subsequent history belies the picture of the happy, normal young man. He was soon in academic difficulties and dropped out of college several times to work on ranches in the Salinas Valley and observe "real life." His interests were varied, but he settled on novel-writing as his ambition, despite his family's insistence that he prepare for a more prosaic career. This traumatic rejection of middle-class values would prove a major force in shaping Steinbeck's fiction, both his social protest novels and his lighter entertainments such as *Cannery Row.*

Leaving Stanford without a degree in 1925, Steinbeck sojourned in New York for several months, where he worked as a laborer, a newspaper reporter, and a freelance writer. Disillusioned in all his abortive pursuits, Steinbeck returned to California, where a job as winter caretaker of a lodge at Lake Tahoe provided the time to finish his first novel, *Cup of Gold.* The novel, a romance concerned with the Caribbean pirate Henry Morgan, was published by a small press directly before the crash of 1929, and it earned the young writer little recognition and even less money. In 1930, he married Carol Henning and moved with her to Los Angeles and later to Pacific Grove, a seaside resort near Monterey, where he lived in his parents' summer house. Still supported by his family and his wife, the ambitious young writer produced the manuscripts of several novels.

A friend, Edward F. (Ed) Ricketts, a marine biologist trained at the University of Chicago, encouraged Steinbeck to treat his material more objectively. Under Ricketts's influence, Steinbeck modified his earlier commitment to satire, allegory, and Romanticism and turned to modern accounts of the Salinas Valley. Steinbeck's next two novels, *The Pastures of Heaven* and *To a God Unknown*, are both set in the Valley, but both still were marked by excessive sentimentality and symbolism. Both were virtually ignored by the public and the critics. Steinbeck's short fiction, however, began to receive recognition; for example, his story "The Murder" was selected as an O. Henry Prize story in 1934.

Tortilla Flat, a droll tale of Monterey's Mexican quarter, established Steinbeck as a popular and critical success in 1935. (His parents were unfortunate to die just before he achieved his first real success.) The novel's sales provided money to pay his debts, to travel to Mexico, and to continue writing seriously. His next novel, *In Dubious Battle*, established him as a serious literary artist and began the period of his greatest success, both critical and popular. This harshly realistic strike novel followed directions established in stories such as "The Raid," influenced by the realistic impulse of American literature during the 1930's. Succeeding publications quickly confirmed this development in his fiction. His short novels *The Red Pony* and *Of Mice and Men* followed in 1937, his story collection *The Long Valley* in 1938, and his epic of the "Okie" migration to California, *The Grapes of Wrath*, in 1939. His own play version of *Of Mice and Men* won the Drama Critics Circle Award in 1938, and *The Grapes of Wrath* received the Pulitzer Prize in 1940. Steinbeck had become one of the most popular and respected writers in the country, a spokesman for an entire culture.

In 1941, Pearl Harbor changed the direction of American culture and of John Steinbeck's literary development. During the war years, he seemed in a holding pattern, trying to adjust to his phenomenal success while absorbing the cataclysmic events around him. Steinbeck's career stalled for many reasons. He left the California subjects and realistic style of his finest novels, and he was unable to come to terms with a world at war, though he served for a few months as a front-line correspondent. Personal developments paralleled these literary ones. Steinbeck divorced his first wife and married Gwen Conger, a young Hollywood starlet; no doubt she influenced his decision to move from California to New York. Steinbeck began to write with an eye on Broadway and Hollywood.

Steinbeck was forty-three when World War II ended in 1945; he died in 1968 at the age of sixty-six. Over those twenty-three years, he was extremely productive, winning considerable acclaim—most notably, the Nobel Prize in Literature in 1962. However, the most important part of his career was finished. The war had changed the direction of his artistic development, and Steinbeck seemed powerless to reverse his decline.

Again, his personal life mirrored his literary difficulties. Although Gwen Conger presented him with his only children—Tom, born in 1944, and John, born in 1946—they were divorced in 1948. Like his first divorce, this one was bitter and expensive. In the same year, his mentor Ricketts was killed in a car accident. Steinbeck traveled extensively, devoting himself to film and nonfiction projects. In 1950, he married Elaine Scott, establishing a supportive relationship that allowed him to finish his epic Salinas Valley novel *East of Eden*.

Steinbeck tried again and again to write his way back to the artistic success of his earlier years, notably in *The Wayward Bus*, but his commercial success kept getting in the way. *East of Eden*, Steinbeck's major postwar novel, attempted another California epic to match the grandeur of *The Grapes of Wrath*. Although the book was a blockbuster best seller, it was an artistic and critical failure. Steinbeck himself seemed to recognize his own decline, and in his last years he virtually abandoned fiction for journalism.

Of his last novels, only *The Winter of Our Discontent* transcends mere entertainment, and it does not have the literary structures to match its serious themes. Despite the popularity of nonfiction such as *Travels with Charley*, despite awards such as the Nobel Prize and the United States Medal of Freedom, despite his personal friendship with President Lyndon Johnson as a supporter of Vietnam, Steinbeck was only the shell of the great writer of the 1930's. He died in New York City on December 20, 1968.

Analysis • Steinbeck remains a writer of the 1930's, perhaps *the* American writer of the 1930's. Although his first novel, *Cup of Gold*, was published in 1929, its derivative "lost generation" posturing gives little indication of the masterpiece he would publish at the end of the next decade, *The Grapes of Wrath*. Steinbeck developed from a Romantic, imitative, often sentimental apprentice to a realistic, objective, and accomplished novelist in only a decade. The reasons for this change can be found in the interplay between a sensitive writer and his cultural background.

A writer of great talent, sensitivity, and imagination, Steinbeck entered into the mood of the country during the late 1930's with an extraordinary responsiveness. The Depression had elicited a reevaluation of American culture, a reassessment of the American Dream: a harsh realism of observation balanced by a warm emphasis on human dignity. Literature and the other arts joined social, economic, and political thought in contrasting traditional American ideals with the bleak reality of breadlines and shantytowns. Perhaps the major symbol of dislocation was the Dust Bowl; the American garden became a wasteland from which its dispossessed farmers fled. The arts during the 1930's focused on these harsh images and tried to find in them the human dimensions that promised a new beginning.

The proletarian novel, documentary photography, and the documentary film stemmed from similar impulses; the radical novel put more emphasis on the inhuman conditions of the dislocated, while the films made more of the promising possibilities for a new day. Painting, music, and theater all responded to a new humanistic and realistic thrust. The best balance was struck by documentary photographers and filmmakers: Dorothea Lange, Walker Evans, and Arthur Rothstein in photography; Pare Lorentz, Willard Van Dyke, and Herbert Kline in film. As a novelist, Steinbeck shared this documentary impulse, and it refined his art.

In Dubious Battle • *In Dubious Battle* tells the harsh story of a violent agricultural strike in the "Torgas Valley" from the viewpoint of two communist agitators. Careful and objective in his handling of the material, the mature Steinbeck provided almost a factual case study of a strike. In a letter, he indicated that this was his conscious intention:

> I had an idea that I was going to write the autobiography of a Communist. Then Miss McIntosh [his agent] suggested I reduce it to fiction. There lay the trouble. I had planned to write a journalistic account of a strike. But as I thought of it as fiction the thing got bigger and bigger . . . I have used a small strike in an orchard valley as the symbol of man's eternal, bitter warfare with himself.

For the first time, Steinbeck was able to combine his ambition to write great moral literature with his desire to chronicle his time and place.

Significantly, the novel takes its title from John Milton's *Paradise Lost* (1667, 1674) in which the phrase is used to describe the struggle between God and Satan, but it takes its subject from the newspapers and newsreels of the 1930's. The underlying structure demonstrates the universal struggle of good and evil, of human greed and selfishness versus human generosity and idealism. Jim, the protagonist killed at the conclusion, is obviously a Christ figure, an individual who has sacrificed himself for the group. Here, Steinbeck needs no overblown symbolic actions to support his theme. He lets his contemporary story tell itself realistically and in documentary fashion. In a letter, he describes his method in the novel: "I wanted to be merely a recording consciousness, judging nothing, simply putting down the thing." This objective, dispassionate, almost documentary realism separates *In Dubious Battle* from his earlier fiction and announces the beginning of Steinbeck's major period.

Of Mice and Men • *Of Mice and Men* was written in 1935 and 1936 and first published as a novel in 1937 at the height of the Depression. Steinbeck constructed the book around dramatic scenes so that he could easily rewrite it for the stage, which he did with the help of George S. Kaufmann. The play opened late in 1937, with Wallace Ford as George and Broderick Crawford as Lennie. A film version, directed by Lewis Milestone, appeared in 1939. The success of the play and film spurred sales of the novel and created a wide audience for Steinbeck's next book, *The Grapes of Wrath*.

Like his classic story of the "Okie" migration from the Dust Bowl to the promised land of California, *Of Mice and Men* is a dramatic presentation of the persistence of the American Dream and the tragedy of its failure. His characters are the little people, the uncommon "common people," disoriented and dispossessed by modern life yet still yearning for a little piece of land, that little particle of the Jeffersonian ideal. Lennie is the symbol of this visceral, inarticulate land-hunger, while George becomes the poet of this romantic vision. How their dream blossoms and then dies is Steinbeck's dramatic subject; how their fate represents that of America during the 1930's and after becomes his theme. His title, an allusion to the Scottish poet Robert Burns, suggests that the best laid plans "of mice and men often gang a-gley"; so the American vision had gone astray in the Depression decade Steinbeck documented so movingly and realistically.

The Red Pony • *The Red Pony* involves the maturation of Jody Tiflin, a boy of about ten when the action opens. The time is about 1910, and the setting is the Tiflin ranch in the Salinas Valley, where Jody lives with his father, Carl, his mother, Ruth, and the hired hand, a middle-aged cowboy named Billy Buck. From time to time, they are visited by Jody's grandfather, a venerable old man who led one of the first wagon trains to California. "The Gift," the first section of the novel, concerns Jody's red pony, which he names Gabilan, after the nearby mountain range. The pony soon becomes a symbol of the boy's growing maturity and his developing knowledge of the natural world. Later, he carelessly leaves the pony out in the rain, and it takes cold and dies, despite Billy Buck's efforts to save it. Thus Jody learns of nature's cruel indifference to human wishes.

In the second part, "The Great Mountains," the Tiflin ranch is visited by a former resident, Gitano, an aged Chicano laborer reared in the now vanished hacienda. Old Gitano has come home to die. In a debate that recalls Robert Frost's poem "The Death of the Hired Man," Carl persuades Ruth that they cannot take Old Gitano in, but—as in Frost's poem—their dialogue proves pointless. Stealing a broken-down nag significantly named Easter, the old man rides off into the mountains to die in dignity. Again, Jody is faced with the complex, harsh reality of adult life.

In "The Promise," the third section, Jody learns more of nature's ambiguous promises when his father has one of the mares put to stud to give the boy another colt. The birth is complicated, however, and Billy Buck must kill the mare to save the colt, demonstrating that life and death are inextricably intertwined. The final section, "The Leader of the People," ends the sequence with another vision of death and change. Jody's grandfather comes to visit, retelling his time-worn stories of the great wagon crossing. Carl Tiflin cruelly hurts the old man by revealing that none of them except Jody is really interested in these repetitive tales. The grandfather realizes that Carl is right, but later he tells Jody that the adventurous stories were not the point, but that his message was "Westering" itself. For the grandfather, "Westering" was the source of American identity. With the close of the frontier, "Westering" has ended, and the rugged Westerners have been replaced by petty landholders such as Carl Tiflin and aging cowboys such as Billy Buck. In his grandfather's ramblings, Jody discovers a sense of mature purpose, and by the conclusion of the sequence, he too can hope to be a leader of the people.

The Red Pony traces Jody's initiation into adult life with both realism and sensitivity, a balance that Steinbeck did not always achieve. The vision of the characters caught up in the harsh world of nature is balanced by their deep human concerns and commitments. The evocation of the ranch setting in its vital beauty is matched only in the author's finest works, such as *Of Mice and Men*. Steinbeck's symbols grow naturally out of this setting, and nothing in the story-sequence seems forced into a symbolic pattern, as in his later works. In its depiction of an American variation on a universal experience, *The Red Pony* deserves comparison with the finest of modern American fiction, especially with initiation tales such as William Faulkner's *The Bear* (1942) and Ernest Hemingway's Nick Adams stories.

Responding to a variety of social and artistic influences, Steinbeck's writing had evolved toward documentary realism throughout the 1930's. In fiction, this development is especially clear in *In Dubious Battle*, *Of Mice and Men*, and *The Long Valley*. Even more obvious was the movement of his nonfiction toward a committed documentation of the social ills plaguing America during the Depression decade. Steinbeck's newspaper and magazine writing offered detailed accounts of social problems, particularly the plight of migrant agricultural workers in California's fertile valleys. The culmination of this development was *Their Blood Is Strong* (1938), a compilation of reports originally written for the *San Francisco News* and published with additional text by Steinbeck and photographs by Dorothea Lange originally made for the Farm Security Administration.

The Grapes of Wrath • It is significant that Steinbeck first conceived of *The Grapes of Wrath* as just such a documentary book. In March, 1938, Steinbeck went into the California valleys with a *Life* magazine photographer to make a record of the harsh conditions in the migrant camps. The reality he encountered seemed too significant for nonfiction, however, and Steinbeck began to reshape this material as a novel, an epic novel.

Although his first tentative attempts at fictionalizing the situation in the agricultural valleys were heavily satiric, as indicated by the early title *L'Affaire Lettuceberg*, Steinbeck soon realized that the Okie migration was the stuff of an American epic. Reworking his material, adding to it by research in government agency files and by more journeys into the camps and along the migrant routes, Steinbeck evolved his vision. A grand design emerged; he would follow one family from the Oklahoma Dust Bowl to California. Perhaps this methodology was suggested by the sociological case histories of the day, perhaps by the haunted faces of individual families that stared back at him as he researched in Farm Security Administration files.

In discussing his plans for his later documentary film, *The Forgotten Village* (1941), Steinbeck remarked that most documentaries concerned large groups of people but that audiences could identify better with individuals. In *The Grapes of Wrath*, he made one family representative of general conditions. The larger groups and problems he treated in short interchapters that generalized the issues particularized in the Joad family. Perhaps the grand themes of change and movement were suggested by the documentary films of Pare Lorentz (later a personal friend), *The Plow That Broke the Plains* (1936) and *The River* (1938), with their panoramic geographical and historical visions. Drawing an archetypal theme from Sir Thomas Malory, John Bunyan, John Milton, and the Bible—the ultimate source of his pervasive religious symbolism— Steinbeck made the journey of the Joads into an allegorical pilgrimage as well as a desperate race along Route 66. During this journey, the Joad family disintegrates, but the larger human family emerges. Tom Joad makes a pilgrim's progress from a narrow, pessimistic view to a transcendental vision of American possibilities. The novel ends on a note of hope for a new American Dream.

The Grapes of Wrath was a sensational best seller from the beginning. Published to generally favorable reviews in March, 1939, it was selling at the rate of more than twenty-five hundred copies a day two months later. Controversy helped spur sales. As a semidocumentary, its factual basis was subject to close scrutiny, and many critics challenged Steinbeck's material. Oklahomans resented the presentation of the Joads as typical of the state (many still do), while Californians disapproved of the depiction of their state's leading industry. The book was attacked, banned, burned— but everywhere it was read. Even in the migrant camps, it was considered an accurate picture of the conditions experienced there. Some 430,000 copies were sold in a year, and in 1940, the novel received the Pulitzer Prize and the Award of the American Booksellers Association (later the National Book Award). Naturally, all the excitement attracted the attention of Hollywood, in spite of the fact that the controversy over the novel seemed to preclude a film version, or at least a faithful film version. Nevertheless, Darryl F. Zanuck produced and John Ford directed a faithful adaptation starring Henry Fonda in 1940; the film, like the novel, has become a classic, and it gave Steinbeck's vision of America during the 1930's even wider currency.

Indeed, Steinbeck's best work was filmic in the best sense of that word—visual, realistic, objective. These qualities nicely balanced the allegorical and romantic strains inherent in his earlier fiction. During World War II, however, his work, much to its detriment, began to cater to the film industry. In fact, much of his postwar writing seems to have found its inspiration in Hollywood versions of his work. His own screen adaptation of an earlier story, *The Red Pony*, proves a sentimentalized reproduction of the original. Nevertheless, he was occasionally capable of recapturing his earlier vision, particularly in his works about Mexico—*The Pearl* and *Viva Zapata!*

The Pearl • Mexico always had been an important symbolic place for Steinbeck. As a native Californian, he had been aware of his state's Mexican heritage. Even as a boy, he sought out Chicano companions, fascinated by their unconcern for the pieties of WASP culture; he also befriended Mexican field hands at the ranches where he worked during his college summers. Later, his first literary success, *Tortilla Flat*, grew from his involvement with the *paisanos* of Monterey, people who would today be called Chicanos.

For Steinbeck, Mexico was everything modern America was not; it possessed a primitive vitality, a harsh simplicity, and a romantic beauty—all of which are found in *The Pearl*. Mexico exhibits the same qualities in the works of other modern writers such as Malcolm Lowry, Aldous Huxley, Graham Greene, Hart Crane, and Katherine Anne Porter. All of them lived and worked there for some time, contrasting the traditional culture they discovered in Mexico with the emptiness of the modern world. Steinbeck also was fascinated by a Mexico still alive with social concern. The continued extension of the Revolution into the countryside had been his subject in *The Forgotten Village*, and it would be developed further in *Viva Zapata!* For Steinbeck, Mexico represented the purity of artistic and social purposes that he had lost after World War II.

This sense of the writer's personal involvement energizes *The Pearl*, making it Steinbeck's best work of fiction in the years following the success of *The Grapes of Wrath*. At the beginning of the novella, the storyteller states: "If this story is a parable, perhaps everyone takes his own meaning from it and reads his own life into it." The critics have read Steinbeck's short novel in a number of ways, but strangely enough, they have not considered it as a parable of the author's own career in the postwar period. Much like Ernest Hemingway's *The Old Man and the Sea* (1952), *The Pearl* uses the life of a simple fisherman to investigate symbolically an aging artist's difficult maturation.

Steinbeck was presented with the tale during his Sea of Cortez expedition in 1940. In his log, he recounts "an event which happened at La Paz in recent years." The story matches the basic outline of *The Pearl*, though Steinbeck made several major changes, changes significant in an autobiographical sense. In the original, the Mexican fisherman was a devil-may-care bachelor; in *The Pearl*, he becomes the sober young husband and father, Kino. Steinbeck himself had just become a father for the first time when he wrote the novella, and this change provides a clue to the autobiographical nature of the parable. The original bachelor thought the pearl a key to easy living; Kino sees it creating a better way of life for the people through an education for his baby son, Coyotito. If the child could read and write, then he could set his family and his people free from the social and economic bondage in which they toil. Kino is ignorant of the dangers of wealth, and *The Pearl* is the tale of how he matures by coming to understand them. Steinbeck, too, matured from his youthful inno-cence as he felt the pressures of success.

As in his best fiction of the 1930's Steinbeck fuses his universal allegory with docu-mentary realism. Perhaps planning ahead for a screenplay, Steinbeck's prose in the novel often takes a cinematic point of view. Scenes are presented in terms of estab-lishing shots, medium views, and close-ups. In particular, Steinbeck carefully exam-ines the natural setting, often visually contrasting human behavior with natural phe-nomena. As in his best fiction, his naturalistic vision is inherent in the movement of his story; there is no extraneous philosophizing.

Steinbeck's characters in *The Pearl* are real people in a real world, but they are also universal types. Kino, the fisherman named for an early Jesuit explorer, Juana, his wife, and Coyotito, their baby, are almost an archetypal family, like the Holy Family in a medieval morality play. Kino's aspirations are the same universal drives to better himself and his family that took the Okies to the California valleys. Like the Joads, this symbolic family must struggle at once against an indifferent natural order and a corrupt social order. however, aside from the screenplay of *Viva Zapata!*, Steinbeck would never again achieve the fusion of parable and realism that energizes *The Pearl*.

In his Nobel Prize speech of 1962, Steinbeck indicated what he tried to accom-plish in his work:

> The ancient commission of the writer has not changed. He is charged with expos-ing our many grievous faults and failures, with dredging up to the light our dark and dangerous dreams, for the purpose of improvement.

No writer has better exposed the dark underside of the American Dream, but few writers have so successfully celebrated the great hope symbolized in that dream—the hope of human development. Steinbeck's best fictions picture a paradise lost but also posit a future paradise to be regained. In spite of his faults and failures, John Steinbeck's best literary works demonstrate a greatness of heart and mind found only rarely in modern American literature.

Joseph R. Millichap

Other major works

SHORT FICTION: *Saint Katy the Virgin*, 1936; *The Long Valley*, 1938.

PLAYS: *Of Mice and Men*, pr., pb. 1937; *The Moon Is Down*, pr. 1942; *Burning Bright*, pb. 1951.

SCREENPLAYS: *The Forgotten Village*, 1941; *Lifeboat*, 1944; *A Medal for Benny*, 1945; *The Pearl*, 1945; *The Red Pony*, 1949; *Viva Zapata!*, 1952.

NONFICTION: *Their Blood Is Strong*, 1938; *Sea of Cortez*, 1941 (with Edward F. Ricketts); *The Forgotten Village*, 1941; *Bombs Away*, 1942; *A Russian Journal*, 1948 (with Robert Capa); *Once There Was a War*, 1958; *Travels with Charley: In Search of America*, 1962; *Letters to Alicia*, 1965; *America and Americans*, 1966; *Journal of a Novel*, 1969; *Steinbeck: A Life in Letters*, 1975 (Elaine Steinbeck and Robert Wallsten, editors); *Amer-ica and Americans, and Selected Nonfiction*, 2002 (Susan Shillinglaw and Jackson J. Benson, editors).

TRANSLATIONS: *The Acts of King Arthur and His Noble Knights*, 1976.

Bibliography

Astro, Richard, and Tetsumaro Hayashi, eds. *Steinbeck: The Man and His Work.* Corvallis: Oregon State University Press, 1971. One of the first full-length works published after Steinbeck's death, this superb collection of essays presents opinions that regard Steinbeck as everything from a mere proletarian novelist to an artist with a deep vision of humans' essential dignity.

Benson, Jackson J. *The True Adventures of John Steinbeck, Writer.* New York: Viking Press, 1984. This biography emphasizes Steinbeck's rebellion against critical conventions and his attempts to keep his private life separate from his role as public figure. Benson sees Steinbeck as a critical anomaly, embarrassed and frustrated by his growing critical and popular success.

DeMott, Robert J., ed. *Steinbeck's Typewriter: Essays on His Art.* Troy, N.Y.: Whitston, 1996. A good collection of criticism of Steinbeck. Includes bibliographical references and an index.

French, Warren. *John Steinbeck's Fiction Revisited.* New York: Twayne, 1994. This revision of French's earlier Twayne book on Steinbeck provides discussions of all of Steinbeck's major works.

George, Stephen K. *The Moral Philosophy of John Steinbeck.* Lanham, Md.: Scarecrow Press, 2005. Scholarly examination of the philosophical issues running through Steinbeck's writings.

_____, ed. *John Steinbeck: A Centennial Tribute.* New York: Praeger, 2002. A collection of reminiscences from Steinbeck's family and friends as well as wide-ranging critical assessments of his works.

Johnson, Claudia Durst, ed. *Understanding "Of Mice and Men," "The Red Pony," and "The Pearl": A Student Casebook to Issues, Sources, and Historical Documents.* Westport, Conn.: Greenwood Press, 1997. This casebook contains historical, social, and political materials as a context for Steinbeck's three novellas. Contexts included are California and the West, land ownership, the male worker, homelessness, and oppression of the poor in Mexico.

McElrath, Joseph R., Jr., Jesse S. Crisler, and Susan Shillinglaw, eds. *John Steinbeck: The Contemporary Reviews.* New York: Cambridge University Press, 1996. A fine selection of reviews of Steinbeck's work.

Parini, Jay. *John Steinbeck: A Biography.* New York: Henry Holt, 1995. This biography suggests psychological interpretations of the effect of Steinbeck's childhood and sociological interpretations of his fiction. Criticizes Steinbeck for his politically incorrect gender and social views; also takes Steinbeck to task on what he calls his blindness to the political reality of the Vietnam War.

Shillinglaw, Susan, and Kevin Hearle, eds. *Beyond Boundaries: Rereading John Steinbeck.* Tuscaloosa: University of Alabama Press, 2002. Revisionist interpretations of Steinbeck's writings.

Harriet Beecher Stowe

Born: Litchfield, Connecticut; June 14, 1811
Died: Hartford, Connecticut; July 1, 1896

Principal long fiction • *Uncle Tom's Cabin: Or, Life Among the Lowly*, 1851-1852 (serial); 1852 (book); *Dred: A Tale of the Great Dismal Swamp*, 1856; *The Minister's Wooing*, 1859; *Agnes of Sorrento*, 1862; *The Pearl of Orr's Island*, 1862; *Oldtown Folks*, 1869; *My Wife and I*, 1871; *Pink and White Tyranny*, 1871; *We and Our Neighbors*, 1875; *Poganuc People*, 1878.

Other literary forms • In 1843, Harriet Beecher Stowe gathered a number of her sketches and stories into a volume called *The Mayflower: Or, Sketches of Scenes and Characters of the Descendants of the Pilgrims* (1843). For forty years thereafter, she published short fiction and miscellaneous essays in magazines. In *A Key to Uncle Tom's Cabin* (1853), she assembled a mass of sources and analogues for the characters and incidents of her most famous novel. Her 1869 *The Atlantic Monthly* article "The True Story of Lady Byron's Life" and a subsequent elaboration, *Lady Byron Vindicated* (1870), caused a sensation at the time. She also published a geography for children (1833, her earliest publication, issued under her sister Catharine's name), poems, travel books, collections of biographical sketches, and a number of other children's books.

Stowe's stories and sketches remain readable. Her best collection, *Sam Lawson's Oldtown Fireside Stories* (1872), differs from the novel *Oldtown Folks* mainly in degree of plotlessness. Selections from Stowe's frequently long and chatty letters can be found in the *Life of Harriet Beecher Stowe* (1889), written by her son Charles Edward Stowe, and in more recent biographies, but hundreds of her letters remain unpublished and scattered in various archives.

Achievements • Known primarily today for her antislavery novel *Uncle Tom's Cabin*, Stowe also interpreted the life of her native New England in a series of novels, stories, and sketches. Along with Ralph Waldo Emerson and Oliver Wendell Holmes, she contributed to the first issue of the *The Atlantic Monthly* (November, 1857) and for many years thereafter contributed frequently to that Boston-based magazine. As an alert and intelligent member of a famous family of Protestant ministers, she understood the Puritan conscience and outlook as well as anyone in her time, and as a shrewd observer of the commonplace, she deftly registered Yankee habits of mind and speech. All of her novels feature authentic New England characters; after *Uncle Tom's Cabin* and *Dred*, she turned to settings that included all six New England states. Despite a contradictory idealizing tendency, she pioneered in realism.

One of the first American writers to apply a talent for dialect and local color to the purposes of serious narrative, she exerted a strong influence on Sarah Orne Jewett, Mary Wilkins Freeman, and other regionalists of the later nineteenth century. Without a doubt, however, her greatest achievement was the novel that, beginning as an intended short serial in a Washington antislavery weekly, the *National Era*, forced the American reading public to realize for the first time that slaves were not only a national problem but also people with hopes and aspirations as legitimate as their own.

Critics as diverse as Henry Wadsworth Longfellow, Heinrich Heine, William Dean Howells, and Leo Tolstoy in the nineteenth century, and Edmund Wilson and Anthony Burgess in the twentieth, have used superlatives to praise *Uncle Tom's Cabin.*

Biography • When Harriet Elizabeth Beecher was born on June 14, 1811, the seventh child of Lyman and Roxana Beecher, her father's fame as a preacher had spread well beyond the Congregational Church of Litchfield, Connecticut. All seven Beecher sons who lived to maturity became ministers, one becoming more famous than his father. Harriet, after attending Litchfield Academy, a well-regarded school, was sent to the Hartford Female Seminary, which was founded by her sister Catharine—in some respects the substitute mother whom Harriet needed after Roxana died in 1816 but did not discover in the second Mrs. Beecher. In later years, Harriet would consistently idealize motherhood. When Catharine's fiancé, a brilliant young man but one who had not experienced any perceptible religious conversion, died in 1822, the eleven-year-old Harriet felt the tragedy. In 1827, the shy, melancholy girl became a teacher in her sister's school.

In 1832, Lyman Beecher accepted the presidency of Lane Seminary in Cincinnati, Ohio, and soon Catharine and Harriet had established another school there. Four years later, Harriet married a widower named Calvin Stowe, a Lane professor. In the years that followed, she bore seven children. She also became familiar with slavery, as practiced just across the Ohio River in Kentucky; with the abolitionist movement, which boasted several notable champions in Cincinnati, including the future chief justice of the United States, Salmon P. Chase; and with the Underground Railroad. As a way of supplementing her husband's small income, she also contributed to local and religious periodicals.

Not until the Stowes moved to Brunswick, Maine, in 1850, however, did she think of writing about slavery. Then, urged by her brother Henry, by then a prominent minister in Brooklyn, New York, and by other family members in the wake of Congress's enactment of the Fugitive Slave Act, and spurred by a vision she experienced at a church service, she began to construct *Uncle Tom's Cabin.* Even as a weekly serial in the *National Era*, it attracted much attention, and its publication in 1852 as a book made Stowe an instant celebrity. After that year, from her new base in Andover, Massachusetts, where her husband taught, she twice visited Europe; met Harriet Martineau, John Ruskin, the Brownings, and Lady Byron, among others; and saw the scope of her fame increase even further.

Stowe wrote another slavery novel, *Dred*, and then turned her literary attention to New England. The drowning of her son Henry, a Dartmouth student, in the summer of 1857, marred for her the successes of these years. In the fall of 1862, infuriated by the lack of British support for the North in the Civil War and skeptical that President Abraham Lincoln would fulfill his promise to issue a proclamation of emancipation, Stowe visited Lincoln, who is reported to have greeted her with the words, "So this is the little lady who made this big war." She left Washington satisfied that the president would keep his word.

Following Calvin Stowe's retirement from Andover, the family moved to Hartford, the winters usually being spent in northern Florida. Two of the most sensational scandals of the post-Civil War era involved Stowe, the first arising when she published an imprudent and detailed account of Lord Byron's sins as revealed to her some years earlier by the now deceased widow of the poet, the second being an adultery suit brought against her brother Henry in which Stowe characteristically defended him to the hilt. The Byron affair in particular turned many people against her, although her books continued to be commercial successes throughout the 1870's. The most severe personal abuse ever directed at a respectable nineteenth century woman bothered Stowe far less than another personal tragedy: the alcoholism and eventual disappearance of her son Fred in San Francisco, California, in 1870.

In the last twenty-three years of her life, Stowe became the central attraction of the Hartford neighborhood known as Nook Farm, also the home of Charles Dudley Warner and Mark Twain, the latter moving there in part because of its Beecher connections. Her circle of friends included Annie Fields, wife of *The Atlantic Monthly* publisher; George Eliot, with whom she corresponded; and Holmes, always a staunch supporter. In her final years, her mind wandered at times, but she was still writing lucid letters two years before her death on July 1, 1896, at the age of eighty-five.

Analysis • In 1869, after finishing her sixth novel, *Oldtown Folks*, Stowe began a correspondence with George Eliot by sending her a copy. Although an international celebrity, Stowe wanted the approval of this younger and less famous woman who had contributed notably to a movement just beginning to be critically recognized: literary realism. Like Stowe, Eliot came from a deeply religious background and had formed a union with an unromantic and bookish, but supportive, man. Unlike the American novelist, Eliot had rejected religion for rationalism and Romanticism for realism. Had Calvin Stowe's first wife not died, it would have been unthinkable for Harriet Beecher to live with him as Eliot did with George Henry Lewes. In life, the former Miss Beecher cheerfully married the unexciting scholar; in *The Minister's Wooing*, she would not permit her heroine Mary Scudder to marry her scholarly suitor (as Eliot's Dorothea Brooke in *Middlemarch* [1871-1872] was permitted to marry hers, Dr. Casaubon).

Stowe's hope, in a measure fulfilled, that Eliot would like *Oldtown Folks* may be taken as signifying her desire to be recognized as a realist, even though her own realism was strongly tinged with the Romanticism Eliot had come to despise. The young Harriet Beecher had probably learned something from John Bunyan's *The Pilgrim's Progress* (1678, 1684), but most of her other reading—The Arabian Nights, Cotton Mather's *Magnalia Christi Americana* (1702), and the works of Sir Walter Scott and George Gordon, Lord Byron—had little to teach an incipient realist. During the 1830's, when she began to write, American literature did not furnish any likely models. As a result, the reader finds in her works a mingling of realistic and Romantic elements.

Stowe's settings, particularly the New England ones, ring true. She understood her cultural roots, and she proved able to recollect childhood impressions almost photographically. She possessed a keen ear for dialect and a sharp eye for the idiosyncrasies of people she scarcely seemed to have noticed until they turned up in her writing. She used the novel to probe urgent social issues such as slavery and women's rights. Although she liked nature and worked hard at describing it accurately, she disdained her native region's characteristic transcendental interpretations of it. She displayed the realist's aversion to mystery, mysticism, and the legendizing of history.

On the other hand, the Romantic tendencies of Stowe's fiction stand out against its realistic background. Her heroines are invariably saintly, as are certain of her black men such as Uncle Tom and, in *Dred*, Uncle Tiff. Her recalcitrant heroes often undergo rather unconvincing conversions. Occasionally, she introduces a mythic, larger-than-life character such as Dred. In common with most of the generation of

American realists who followed her, she never renounced the heroic but sought to demonstrate its presence among humble and common people. Her heroes differ from those of Twain, William Dean Howells, and Henry James, however, in drawing their strength from a firm Christian commitment: Stowe's piety has been something of an impediment to her modern readers.

The looseness of plotting about which Stowe's critics have complained so much derives in large measure from her inability to develop convincing central characters in most of her novels. Four of her last five novels have plural nouns— words such as *neighbors* and *folks* and *people*—in their titles, but even *Uncle Tom's Cabin* is not about Uncle Tom in the sense that Charles Dickens's *David Copperfield* (1849-1850) or Gustave Flaubert's *Madame Bovary* (1857) is about its title character. In fact, Stowe changed the title of *Dred*

Library of Congress

for a time to *Nina Gordon*, a more central character but one who dies many chapters from the end. *My Wife and I* and *Oldtown Folks* are narrated by relatively colorless central characters.

One of Stowe's most persistent and indeed remarkable narrative traits also works against her realism on occasions. As she confides at the beginning of chapter 44 of *Dred*, "There's no study in human nature more interesting than the aspects of the same subject in the points of view of different characters." The fact that she periodically allowed this interest to distract her from the task at hand is clear. Although she experimented with different points of view—omniscient, first-person, dramatic, and circulating (the last primarily through the use of the epistolary method)—she worked before the time when novelists such as Joseph Conrad, James Joyce, and William Faulkner developed techniques capable of sustaining this kind of interest. It should be pointed out that Stowe uses the expression "points of view" in the sense of "opinions," and she is more likely to present the conflict of opinions through conversations than through living, breathing embodiments of motivating ideas.

It is as a realist before her time that Stowe is most profitably considered. Even where her realism does not serve a socially critical purpose, as it does in *Uncle Tom's Cabin* and *My Wife and I*, she makes her readers aware of the texture, the complexity, of social life—particularly the conflicts, tensions, and joys of New England community life. Understanding how people grow from their geographic, social, religious, and intellectual roots, she is able to convey the reality of isolated Maine coastal villages and the jaunty postwar Manhattan of aspiring journalists. In her best work, she depicts evil not as the product of Mephistophelean schemers or motiveless brutes but of high-minded people incapacitated by a crucial weakness, such as the irreso-lute Augustine St. Clare of *Uncle Tom's Cabin*, the temporizing Judge Clayton of *Dred*, and the imperceptive Dr. Hopkins of *The Minister's Wooing.*

Uncle Tom's Cabin • *Uncle Tom's Cabin: Or, Life Among the Lowly,* remains one of the most controversial of novels. Extravagantly admired and bitterly detested during the 1850's, it still arouses extreme reactions more than a century later. An early barrage of challenges to its authenticity led Stowe to work furiously at the assembling of *A Key to Uncle Tom's Cabin* the next year. In 262 closely printed, double-columned pages, she impressively documented horrors that verified "the truth of the work." This book encouraged the development of an essentially nonliterary mass of criticism, with the result that the novel early gained the reputation of a brilliant piece of propaganda—even President Lincoln supposedly accepting the Civil War as its legacy—but unwor-thy of serious consideration on artistic grounds.

It did not help the novel's cause that the almost inevitable later reaction against this enormously popular story coincided with the effort, spearheaded by Henry James, to establish the novel as a form of art rather than as a mere popular entertain-ment. A writer who strove too singlemindedly for mere verifiability did not merit con-sideration as an artist. In the same year that *Uncle Tom's Cabin* began appearing seri-ally, Nathaniel Hawthorne—James's chief example of the American artist—prefaced his *The House of the Seven Gables* (1851) with a firm declaration of its imaginary basis that contrasted sharply with his attempt to provide a "historical" one for *The Scarlet Letter* one year earlier. Hawthorne's star as a writer of fiction gradually rose; Stowe's sank. Like "Old Ironsides," the vigorous youthful poem of Stowe's staunch friend of later years, *Uncle Tom's Cabin* was relegated to the status of a work that made things happen—important historically but damned by that very fact to the region of the second-rate.

In *A Key to Uncle Tom's Cabin*, Stowe herself called *Uncle Tom's Cabin* "a very inade-quate representation of slavery," but her excuse is significant: "Slavery, in some of its workings, is too dreadful for the purposes of art." She was acknowledging a problem that would continue to bedevil realists for most of the rest of the century. The most prominent spokesman for realism, Howells, agreed with her, and until the 1890's, re-alists would generally exclude things considered "too dreadful." As late as 1891, Thomas Hardy induced mass revulsion by allowing his heroine to be raped in *Tess of the D'Urbervilles* (1891) while referring to her in his subtitle as "a pure woman."

Stowe sandwiched the story of Uncle Tom, the meek Christian capable of turning the other cheek even to the sadistic Simon Legree, between the resolute George and Eliza Harris's escape from slavery and the Harris family's fortuitous reunion at the end of the novel. If the plot is untidy and contrived, a number of the individual char-acters and episodes have remained among the most memorable in fiction. The fa-mous scene in which Eliza crosses the Ohio River ice in early spring is "true" not be-cause the feat had been accomplished (although Stowe knew it had) but because she makes the reader feel Eliza's desperation, the absolute necessity of the attempt, and the likelihood that a person who grew up in her hard school would develop the re-sources to succeed.

The meeting between Miss Ophelia and Topsy illustrates Stowe's talent for drama-tizing the confrontation of stubborn viewpoints. Sold down the river by his first owner, Tom has rescued the angelic daughter of Augustine St. Clare and has been in-stalled to the St. Clare household. Miss Ophelia, a Vermont cousin of St. Clare, has been brought south to take care of Eva, whose mother is languidly incompetent. St. Clare despises slavery but feels powerless to resist it; Ophelia's intransigent New England conscience will not permit her to acquiesce in it. After listening to a considerable amount of her antislavery rhetoric, St. Clare gives his cousin a little black girl rescued from alcoholic parents. Ophelia is revolted by Topsy, so utterly different from the golden, cherubic Eva. Topsy, shrewd and skeptical beyond her years, embodies the insidiousness of slavery itself. Neither was premeditated but simply "grow'd" and now must somehow be dealt with as found. Ophelia must find room in her heart for the little "black spider" or lose face with her cousin. Her struggle with Topsy—and with her own physical aversion—is fierce and richly comical, and its successful outcome believable.

For the modern reader, the death scenes in the novel are more of a problem. Little Eva's protracted illness and beatific death exactly pleased the taste of Stowe's time. Today, her father's senseless and sudden death as a result of his attempt to mediate a tavern brawl seems more like real life—or would if Stowe had not permitted St. Clare to linger long enough to undergo a deathbed religious conversion. Modern reaction to Stowe's climactic scene is complicated by the hostility of writers such as James Baldwin to the character of Uncle Tom, who, in dying at the hands of Legree's henchmen, wins their souls in the process. Whether or not the conversion of Sambo and Quimbo convinces today's reader, Tom's character has been firmly established, and he dies in precisely the spirit the reader expects.

Far less satisfactory is the subsequent escape of two of Legree's slaves from his clutches. Stowe did nothing beforehand to induce belief in a brutal master who could melt into helpless impassivity at the sight of a lock of his dead mother's hair. Finding it expedient to make Legree superstitious, she established this side of his character belatedly and ineptly, and she failed to understand that her conception of the power of motherhood was not universally shared.

In short, the reader's admiration is interrupted by idealistic and sentimental material that does not support Stowe's goal of depicting life as it was. This inconsistency is not surprising. No American had ever written such a novel: realistic in impulse and directed at a current social problem of the greatest magnitude. She had no models and could not, like Twain after her, draw upon experiences as Missourian, journalist, western traveler, and—before he wrote his greatest books—neighbor of Stowe and reader of her work.

Like Twain and Howells after her, Stowe did not banish Romanticism from her novels, but her commitment to realism is clear. Thirty years before Twain's accomplishments with dialect in *Adventures of Huckleberry Finn* (1884), and nearly two decades before Bret Harte popularized the concept of local color, Stowe used dialects—not with perfect consistency but not for the conventional purpose of humor either. For the first time in major American fiction, dialect served the purpose of generating a credible environment for a serious narrative. In the process, she changed the perceptions of hundreds of thousands of readers forever.

Within a year, the book had made Stowe internationally known. When, after several years of minor literary activity, she returned to the subject of slavery, events were unfolding that led inexorably to war. Her brother Henry was outraging North and South alike by holding his own mock slave auction in his Brooklyn church. John Brown was launching his personal civil war in Kansas. In the chamber of the U.S. Senate, abolitionist Charles Sumner was nearly beaten to death by a southern colleague. Stowe herself had been busy with antislavery petitions and appeals.

Dred • From this context emerged *Dred: A Tale of the Great Dismal Swamp*, a more somber novel. As it opens, Nina Gordon has returned to her North Carolina plantation from New York upon the death of her father. She has dallied with several suitors but has sense enough to prefer Edward Clayton, an idealistic young lawyer from another part of her native state. After successfully prosecuting a white man who had hired and then physically abused Nina's domestic slave Milly, Clayton's ambition to counteract such abuses legally is checked when an appeals judge—a man of undoubted probity and, ironically, Clayton's own father—reverses the earlier decision on the grounds that no slave has any rights under state law. Meanwhile, Nina's attempt at benign management of her plantation is set back by the appearance of her wastrel brother Tom, who especially enjoys tormenting her able quadroon steward Harry. Although bearing a strong resemblance to George Harris of *Uncle Tom's Cabin*, Harry is different in two important ways. First, Stowe develops the frustration of this educated and sensitive man much more thoroughly. Second, Harry is, unknown to Nina, the Gordon children's half brother.

When Nina dies in a cholera epidemic, Tom asserts control over the plantation, and Clayton returns home with the resolve to press for changes in a legal code that permits a man to own and mistreat his own brother. Harry is driven to rebel and flee into the nearby swamp, where he falls under the influence of Dred, whom the author styles after the son of the famous black rebel Denmark Vesey, but who resembles even more closely that other noted rebel, Nat Turner.

What happens next exemplifies Stowe's familiarity with the clergy and her talent for controversy. Invited by his uncle to a Presbyterian ministers' conference, Clayton seeks there the moral support for legal reform. Even though he finds one minister passionately committed to rights for slaves, the majority of the brethren turn out to be complacent trimmers, and Clayton learns that he can expect no help in that quarter. Stowe strategically places the conference between two scenes of desperation, both of which illustrate the social system's assault on the family. In the former, Uncle Tiff, the black guardian of two white children whose father is a shiftless squatter on the Gordon plantation, vows to preserve them from the corrupting influence of their slatternly stepmother and takes them to Dred's hidden fastness in the swamp. In the latter, another quadroon Gordon offshoot, Cora, confesses in court to the murder of her own two children to "save" them, as she puts it, from being sold away.

In the swamp, Tiff and the children are succored by Dred, who is one of Stowe's most bizarre creations: half Robin Hood, half self-appointed executioner for the Lord. Too mythic a hero for a realistic novel, Dred unfortunately develops quickly into a very tedious one too, ranting interminably in his guise of Old Testament prophet. Even he is no match, however, for the committed Christian Milly, although she can accomplish no more than the postponement of his planned revenge against the hated whites. When Tom Gordon organizes a party to ransack the swamp for Dred and Harry, the former is killed, and Harry and his wife, along with Tiff and his young charges, escape to the North. In an obviously Pyrrhic victory, Clayton, baffled by his neighbors in his attempt to educate the slaves on his own estate, takes them off to Canada, where they continue to work for him in their freedom.

Tiff is another saintly domestic slave, but he has no power to reclaim any Sambo or Quimbo from degradation. There are no spectacular personal conversions in *Dred* and no hope of any social one. Milly, who has had to endure the loss by death or sale of all her numerous children, seems to win a legal victory over a cruel master and a moral one over the vindictive fugitive Dred, but both turn out to be illusory. Not only the fugitive African Americans but also Clayton the hero must leave the country. If *Uncle Tom's Cabin* stands as a warning to a divided society, *Dred* is a prophecy of disintegration.

The Minister's Wooing • Stowe's next two novels have much in common. Both *The Minister's Wooing* and *The Pearl of Orr's Island* are anchored in New England coastal communities, and both put Yankee manners and speech on display. Each novel boasts a saintly heroine who effects the conversion of a dashing young man with a strong affinity for the sea. Although the former novel paints Newport, Rhode Island, less colorfully than the latter does coastal Maine, *The Minister's Wooing* is a more carefully constructed novel that analyzes New England character more profoundly.

More than any other Stowe novel, *The Minister's Wooing* focuses on its principals: Samuel Hopkins, Congregationalist minister of Newport, and Mary Scudder, daughter of Hopkins's widowed landlady. In several respects, the minister is the historical Dr. Hopkins, learned protégé of the great Jonathan Edwards, eminent theologian in his own right and vigorous opponent of slavery in a town consecrated to the slave trade. During the 1780's, when the novel is set, however, the real Hopkins was in his sixties and possessed a wife and eight children; Stowe makes him middle-aged and a bachelor. Another celebrity of the time plays a significant role: Aaron Burr in the years before he became senator, vice president, and killer of Alexander Hamilton in a duel. Burr is depicted as a charming, unscrupulous seducer of women—a distortion of the historical Burr, no doubt, but one based on the man's reputation.

Stowe's motive for involving these men in her story of pious young Mary Scudder is utterly serious. As friend and student of Edwards, Hopkins represents the stern, uncompromising Puritan past. As Edwards's worldly and skeptical grandson, Burr stands for the repudiation of the past. Mary's choice is not—what would be easy for her—between Hopkins and Burr but between Hopkins and her young lover James Marvyn, who resembles Burr only in his impatience with the hard and incomprehensible doctrines of his forebears. James has grown up with Mary but has gravitated to the sea, and he is not quite engaged to her when he is reported lost in a shipwreck. Mrs. Scudder thereafter nudges Mary toward a union with the unexciting minister, himself an admirer of the young lady's ardent—if for his taste too sunny—Christianity.

Stowe neatly balances the claims of Hopkins's exacting Old Testament theology and Mary's simpler faith in the loving kindness of Jesus. In comforting the lost James's mother, long appalled by the minister's remorseless logic and now driven to near-psychosis by her son's supposed death, Mary's cheerful faith receives its first test. She also befriends an aristocratic young Frenchwoman—Burr's intended victim—and learns of the world of adulterous intrigue. As in her previous novels, Stowe introduces a black servant who has looked on life long and maintained a practical Christianity that is proof against all temptation to despair. Having been freed by her master, Mr. Marvyn, under the minister's influence, Candace works freely for the Marvyns and venerates Dr. Hopkins, not failing, however, to draw Mrs. Marvyn gently from "the fathomless mystery of sin and sorrow" to the "deeper mystery of God's love." Meanwhile, Mary's faith deepens, Stowe probably raising more than a few Protestant eyebrows by likening her explicitly to the Virgin Mary, who "kept all things and pondered them in her heart."

In real life, Catharine Beecher's beloved did not survive his shipwreck, and Stowe's elder sister agonized long over the possibility of his having died unregenerate. In life, Henry Stowe did not miraculously escape drowning. James Marvyn, on the other hand, after a considerable interval in which he inexplicably fails to notify either Mary or his family of his survival, returns a week before Mary's scheduled wedding with the minister. After having promised herself to Hopkins, Mary will not of course renege, so it falls to Miss Prissy, her dressmaker and friend, to approach the formidable theologian with the fact—which he is incapable of divining—that James is Mary's true love. Miss Prissy is one of Stowe's well-conceived realistic characters; an incurable gossip and a hypocrite in her professed admiration for the minister's sermons, she is nevertheless willing to assume the unpleasant initiative on behalf of her friend. Apprised of the true situation, the minister releases Mary and promptly marries her to Marvyn.

As she had in her first *The Atlantic Monthly* short story, Stowe depicts in this novel the psychology of bereavement; what she refuses to present is not death itself but the possibility of a good-hearted lad dying unregenerate. She demonstrates how the rigorous faith of a Hopkins can be a barrier, even a poison, to the unstable, but of the efficacy of Christianity to restore lost lambs, she can conceive no doubt. Even the heterodox Burr nearly succumbs to Mary's entreaties to reform. Stowe's less saintly believers, such as Miss Prissy, and her magnanimous skeptics, like Augustine St. Clare of *Uncle Tom's Cabin*, are more credible. As for Hopkins, willing to jeopardize his church financially and socially by his insistence that the most influential of his parishoners renounce his connections with the slave trade, his final renunciation of Mary is quite consistent with his previous rock-ribbed selflessness.

Oldtown Folks • *Oldtown Folks*, at which Stowe worked in the postwar years and published whole in 1869—for she refused to serialize it in the usual way—repeats many of the concerns of *The Minister's Wooing* and even reintroduces Jonathan Edwards's grandson, here known as Ellery Davenport. Longer, more varied, and much more rambling, this novel contains a considerable amount of Stowe's best writing. In the preface, her narrator, Horace Holyoke, vows to "interpret to the world the New England life and character of the early republic." Today, no one would choose a loose, leisurely narrative to achieve such an ambition, and perhaps no one but Stowe would have attempted it during the 1860's. It is no coincidence that *Oldtown Folks* attracted the attention of Perry Miller, the distinguished twentieth century interpreter of the New England tradition.

The Minister's Wooing had been a theological novel in which no one had very much fun. As if to redress the deficiency, Stowe widens her focus, invests this work with more of the engaging minor characters of *The Pearl of Orr's Island*, and shows her villagers enjoying themselves. Her twenty-seventh chapter, "How We Kept Thanksgiving at Oldtown," which has become an anthology piece in recent years, argues that Oldtown (based on her husband's hometown of Natick, Massachusetts) has fun precisely because the inhabitants take human life seriously enough "to believe they can do much with it." Sam Lawson—Stowe's most famous character outside *Uncle Tom's Cabin*—far from exemplifying the protestant work ethic, is the town idler, universally valued for his skill at "lubricating" with his humorous anecdotes and relaxed manner the "incessant steampower in Yankee life." By contrast, the character most devoted to work, Miss Asphyxia Smith, is easily the most hateful character in the book.

Sam also serves the tenuous plot interest by coming upon two of its three principals (narrator Horace Holyoke is the other) in an abandoned house to which they had fled from Miss Asphyxia's clutches, for, like Uncle Tiff's young charges in *Dred*,

Harry and Tina Percival have been successively deserted by their scalawag father and subjected to the slow death of their mother. Tina, who is adopted by Mehitabel Rossiter, a woman of no physical beauty but much strength of character and intellect, grows into a beautiful and kindhearted but willful woman—exactly the type favored by the unprincipled Davenport. Harry grows up as Horace's companion in the nearby Holyoke household.

Tina, not knowing that Davenport numbers among his previous victims Ellen Rossiter, Mehitabel's younger sister, marries him, and it appears that Stowe will not permit her protagonist the usual eleventh-hour rescue. Tina endures ten years with the erratic Davenport, generously adopting his daughter by Ellen Rossiter, but then, in a switch on the Aaron Burr story, Davenport is killed in a duel. Two years (but only three paragraphs) later, Tina and Horace marry and settle in Boston. At the end of the novel, the Horace Holyokes are discovered back in Oldtown visiting its most durable inhabitant, Sam Lawson.

Any synopsis leaves untouched the merits of *Oldtown Folks*: the interplay of its varied and vital minor characters and the development of its seduction theme. Of the former, Miss Asphyxia, "a great threshing-machine of a woman"; Horace's peppery grandmother, "a valiant old soul, who fearlessly took any bull in life by the horns, and was ready to shake him into decorum"; and Lawson, half nuisance, half good neighbor, are only three of the most memorable. As seducer, Davenport takes advantage of several factors: the intransigence of Calvinism in its death throes, embodied in brilliant but outdated theorizers such as this novel's version of Hopkins, Dr. Stern; the Calvinist legacy of neurosis, skepticism, and rebellion (Miss Rossiter, Tina, and Davenport himself); and the ineffectuality of well-intentioned observers such as Horace and Harry. Thwarted by orthodoxy, which has become a cruel instrument in the hands of its conservative defenders, and averse to the rationalism that played such a large part in the creation of the new republic, the Oldtowners are easily taken in by Davenport, who has turned the passion and intellectual energy inherited from Edwards and the rest of his Puritan forebears to the service of selfish and worldly ends.

My Wife and I* and *We and Our Neighbors • In *My Wife and I* and its sequel, *We and Our Neighbors*, Stowe turns to contemporary Manhattan life, a frivolous and even more worldly existence dotted nevertheless by young men and women of impulses Stowe characterizes as Christian but that may strike today's reader as more generally humanitarian. The full spectrum of views on women's rights is on display, including a conviction, expressed by a young woman struggling for the opportunity to study medicine, that "marriage ought never to be entered on as a means of support." The main business of the two novels, however, is to educate Harry Henderson for marriage and thus to provide a base of operations for his wife, who dedicates herself to neighborliness and charitable offices. Stowe retains her observant eye and spicy descriptive powers, but her narrator cannot "interpret" the Gilded Age as Horace Holyoke in *Oldtown Folks* could interpret post-Revolutionary New England.

Poganuc People • *Pink and White Tyranny*, the story of a man who married and must endure a selfish and demanding woman, must rank, along with the earlier *Agnes of Sorrento*, among Stowe's weakest books. Finally, in *Poganuc People*, she returns to the milieu of *The Minister's Wooing*, *The Pearl of Orr's Island*, and her Oldtown books. Poganuc is the Litchfield of her childhood and Dolly Cushing her closet approximation to an autobiographical heroine. The principal conflict is not between the old religion and the new worldliness but between entrenched Congregationalism and up-start Episcopalianism. The novel begins and ends at Christmas, when the liturgical and social differences between the two denominations stand out most sharply. Like Maggie Tulliver in Eliot's *The Mill on the Floss* (1860), Dolly is precocious, sensitive, and consequently often uncomfortable, but instead of developing the crises of her heroine's maturation, as does Eliot, Stowe whisks her off to a fashionable Boston marriage with a successful merchant, after which the author makes a final survey of the Poganuc people going about their business under the immemorial elms of the village.

Stowe seldom brought her psychological insights to bear on the development of her main characters, with the result that the less important ones invariably seem more convincing. Whether because her most productive years antedated the time of the realistic novel and particularly the psychological novel, or because she felt too strongly the nineteenth century prohibition against a woman exploring the conflicts and repressions of her own life, Stowe left unwritten what might have constituted her richest vein of realism. She never wrote a novel expressing what it felt like to be a vocationless Harriet Beecher approaching womanhood or the second Mrs. Calvin Stowe struggling with sickness, poverty, and the multitudinous demands of husband and children. The woman who wrote of domesticity in her time avoided calling atten-tion to its tensions, exactions, and restrictions. Whatever else family life meant to Stowe, it helped prepare her to do what no American novelist had done before: write powerfully and feelingly about slavery.

Robert P. Ellis

Other major works

SHORT FICTION: *The Mayflower: Or, Sketches of Scenes and Characters of the Descendants of the Pilgrims*, 1843; *Sam Lawson's Oldtown Fireside Stories*, 1872.

POETRY: *Religious Poems*, 1867.

NONFICTION: *A Key to Uncle Tom's Cabin*, 1853; *Sunny Memories of Foreign Lands*, 1854; *Lady Byron Vindicated*, 1870; *Palmetto Leaves*, 1873.

CHILDREN'S LITERATURE: *First Geography for Children*, 1833 (as Catharine Stowe).

MISCELLANEOUS: *The Oxford Harriet Beecher Stowe Reader*, 1999 (Joan D. Hedrick, ed-itor).

Bibliography

Adams, John R. *Harriet Beecher Stowe*. Boston: Twayne, 1989. An introduction to the life and works of Stowe. Includes bibliographical references and an index.

Ammons, Elizabeth, ed. *Critical Essays on Harriet Beecher Stowe*. Boston: G. K. Hall, 1980. This useful collection contains essays on Stowe by literary critics and mod-ern feminist scholars. Dorothy Berkson's essay "Millennial Politics and the Femi-nine Fiction of Harriet Beecher Stowe" is particularly good.

_____. *Harriet Beecher Stowe's Uncle Tom's Cabin: A Casebook*. New York: Oxford University Press, 2007. Collection of critical articles on Stowe's most important work; designed for students. Includes bibliography.

Boydston, Jeanne, Mary Kelley, and Anne Margolis. *The Limits of Sisterhood: The Beecher Sisters on Women's Rights and Woman's Sphere*. Chapel Hill: University of North Caro-lina Press, 1988. A superb study of Stowe and her sisters, Catharine and Isabella. Brief but insightful essays address each woman as an individual and as a sister. Primary documents are appended to each chapter, providing excellent resources. Illustrations, careful documentation, and a detailed index make this an invaluable text.

Brown, Gillian. *Domestic Individualism: Imagining Self in Nineteenth-Century America.* Berkeley: University of California Press, 1990. Examines themes in works by Stowe, Nathaniel Hawthorne, and Herman Melville.

Donovan, Josephine. *"Uncle Tom's Cabin": Evil, Affliction, and Redemptive Love.* Boston: Twayne, 1991. Places *Uncle Tom's Cabin* in literary and historical context. As her subtitle suggests, Donovan views Stowe's masterpiece as a book about evil and its redemption, taking it more or less at face value and reading it with the approach she believes Stowe intended—which has a decidedly feminist bent.

Hedrick, Joan D. *Harriet Beecher Stowe: A Life.* 1994. Reprint. New York: Oxford University Press, 2004. Stowe's family kept a tight rein on her literary remains, and the only previous attempt at a full-scale independent biography, Forrest Wilson's *Crusader in Crinoline* (1941), is now very much out of date. Hedrick's book makes use of new materials, including letters and diaries, and takes fresh approaches to Stowe occasioned by the Civil Rights and women's movements.

Lang, Amy Schrager. *Prophetic Woman: Anne Hutchinson and the Problem of Dissent in the Literature of New England.* Berkeley: University of California Press, 1987. An excellent feminist study, focusing on *Uncle Tom's Cabin* and Stowe's role in the history of Puritan suppression of women who achieve public notice. Stowe's novel constitutes a culmination in this process and presents a model of women as moral superiors who represent the possibility of a future without slavery.

Robbins, Sarah, ed. *The Cambridge Introduction to Harriet Beecher Stowe.* New York: Cambridge University Press, 2007. Brief biography of Stowe with a survey of her writings within the context of nineteenth century American culture and society.

Stowe, Charles Edward, comp. *Life of Harriet Beecher Stowe.* 1889. Reprint. Seattle: University Press of the Pacific, 2004. Compiled by her son, this is the first full-length biography of Stowe, drawn from her letters and her journal. Though not critical, it offers extensive excerpts of her personal writings and of correspondence from other renowned writers. An annotated primary bibliography and a detailed index are included.

Sundquist, Eric J., ed. *New Essays on "Uncle Tom's Cabin."* New York: Cambridge University Press, 1986. A collection of essays on Stowe's most famous novel. The introduction discusses changing literary theories as they relate to *Uncle Tom's Cabin.* The six diverse contributions by notable scholars include analyses of genre and gender issues. A selected bibliography also notes additional criticism.

Tompkins, Jane. *Sensational Designs: The Cultural Work of American Fiction, 1790-1860.* New York: Oxford University Press, 1985. Tompkins addresses *Uncle Tom's Cabin* from the perspective of "the politics of literary history." Nineteenth century popular domestic novels represent attempts to reorganize culture from a woman's perspective, and Stowe's novel is representative of "America's religion of domesticity" as empowerment of women. An excellent and influential study.

Theodore Sturgeon

Born: Staten Island, New York; February 26, 1918
Died: Eugene, Oregon; May 8, 1985

Principal long fiction • *The Dreaming Jewels*, 1950 (also known as *The Synthetic Man*, 1957); *More than Human*, 1953; *I, Libertine*, 1956 (as Frederick R. Ewing; with Jean Shepherd); *The King and Four Queens*, 1956; *The Cosmic Rape*, 1958; *Venus Plus X*, 1960; *Some of Your Blood*, 1961; *Voyage to the Bottom of the Sea*, 1961; *Alien Cargo*, 1984; *Godbody*, 1986.

Other literary forms • Although Theodore Sturgeon was not as prolific as some of the science-fiction fraternity, he wrote more than 190 short stories, 130 articles, and a number of radio and television scripts. His short fiction was assembled in many collections, ranging from *Without Sorcery* (1948) to *The Golden Helix* (1980).

Achievements • Sturgeon's work was once called "the single most important body of science fiction by an American to date." A founder of modern American science fiction, he contributed to the genre's transition from underground to mainstream literature. He was the recipient of Argosy (1947), International Fantasy (1954), Nebula (1970), and Hugo (1971) awards.

Biography • Theodore Sturgeon was born Edward Hamilton Waldo, on February 26, 1918, on Staten Island, New York. His parents were divorced, and, after his mother remarried in 1929, his name was legally changed when he was adopted by his stepfather. After he graduated from high school, where his career as a gymnast was ended by rheumatic fever, he finished a term at Penn State Nautical School and then spent three years at sea. During that time he began to write, producing some forty conventional short stories for McClure's Syndicate before turning to science fiction, which he began to publish in John W. Campbell, Jr.'s *Astounding Science Fiction* in 1939.

Sturgeon recalled that science fiction was "the pornography of its day" and recounted how his stepfather discovered and destroyed his 1935 issues of *Amazing*. When he took up science fiction, Sturgeon was making a commitment to a literary form that promised little prestige and very modest financial returns. He married in the same year he launched his science-fiction career and contributed regularly to *Unknown* and *Astounding Science Fiction* in order to support his family. Although he produced highly regarded stories, such as "It" (1940) and "Microcosmic God" (1941), he had to seek employment outside of writing to earn a living.

After operating a hotel in the British West Indies in 1940, Sturgeon worked as a door-to-door salesman, as assistant chief steward at Fort Simonds, and as a bulldozer operator. In 1942, he pursued the latter occupation in Puerto Rico. Except for *Killdozer!*, a novelette about a machine possessed by a malignant force, his literary output declined sharply between 1942 and 1944, when he returned to the United States and became a copy editor. These were difficult years for Sturgeon, financially and emotionally. Not until 1946, after his marriage ended in divorce, did he fully resume his career under the encouragement of John Campbell.

While continuing to write, Sturgeon tried his hand at running a literary agency and producing advertising copy. The first substantial public recognition for his work came in 1947 when he won a thousand-dollar prize for "Bianca's Hands." (The runner-up in the contest, sponsored by the British magazine *Argosy*, was Graham Greene.) "Bianca's Hands" had been written on Sturgeon's honeymoon years earlier but had found no market because of its bizarre treatment of a "passionate human attachment." Its acceptance marked a turning point for Sturgeon, which was closely followed by the publication of the first of his many anthologies, *Without Sorcery*, with an introduction by Ray Bradbury.

As he entered the period of his greatest creativity, Sturgeon's personal life again underwent change, with a second marriage in 1949 and a third in 1951. His output of fiction was unabated, however, with *The Dreaming Jewels*, his first novel, appearing in 1950, and *More than Human*, published in 1953, winning the 1954 International Fantasy Award, a confirmation of his rank as one of America's foremost writers of science fiction. His stories continued to be anthologized in his own collections and those of others, and he engaged in a broad range of literary activity, from a hoax with Jean Shepherd, *I, Libertine*, published under the name Frederick R. Ewing, to a fictional case history of vampirism, *Some of Your Blood*, and a novel depicting an androgynous utopia, *Venus Plus X*.

As a major author of speculative fiction, he helped to create a climate of acceptance for the genre among the general public. In his book reviews for the *National Review* (1961-1973), for example, he explained and defended his art while introducing some of contemporary science fiction's finest authors to an audience who might otherwise not have learned of them. He was involved in science fiction's growth in other media also, in 1966 moving to Los Angeles to write for the television series *Star Trek*. Late in his life, he published little new fiction, but he continued to compile anthologies of his previous work for new audiences. He married for the fourth time in 1969. Sturgeon was living in Eugene, Oregon, at the time of his death in 1985.

Though Sturgeon deplored the "inexcusable invasions into . . . authors' most intimate motivations" by academic critics, there are nevertheless certain definite biographical influences on his work. Beverly Friend called him "a highly personal writer drawing from his own suffering for his craft." She cites his parents' divorce, his estrangement from his stepfather, his illness in adolescence, and his marital and professional problems as sources for his art.

Analysis • Sturgeon once said, "All great literature is great because it is fable—because it creates typical and archetypical characters and situations that can be applied outside the work to illuminate the human condition." He repeatedly insisted that he did not undervalue the science of science fiction, but he clearly inclined toward minimizing technology as a focus for his work; rather, he concentrated upon fable, often premising his work on occult matters upon which science has had little to say. He said that "in teaching, reviewing, and enjoying science fiction, my emphasis is always on the fiction." This is, he explained, "because I like writers to be read and remembered and (when they can) to move people and shake them; to ignite, to increase their ability to share their visions and their joy and their terror, as well as their knowledge." Sturgeon's criteria for art were more affective than cognitive, and he generally concentrated upon rites of passage rather than technological extrapolation.

Whatever Sturgeon's premise for a story, scientific, psychological, or occult, he wished the work to reflect essential human experiences: "love, and pain, and greed, and laughter, and hope, and above all loneliness." Loneliness is most significant, since he asserted that "what I have been trying to do all these years is to investigate this matter of love, sexual and asexual," and his major fictions are fables of growth toward community and maturity.

The four science-fiction novels that are the heart of Sturgeon's work (*The Dreaming Jewels, More than Human, The Cosmic Rape,* and *Venus Plus X*) develop the idea that "our strange species has two prime motivating forces: sex and worship." Throughout his writing, the latter is the more important, and Sturgeon was unwilling to see the highest self-sacrificial and altruistic acts as having any foundation in sexuality. Sturgeon's center of worship, however, is not to be found outside man but in humanity.

Sturgeon's first novel, *The Dreaming Jewels,* is an exploration of what it means to be human. Its premise is the creation of a "synthetic man" by the action of alien crystals that have a deep collective life of their own, apparently unrelated to the affairs of people. These crystals, seemingly without purpose, "dream" objects into existence, sometimes imperfectly, creating freaks and monsters, and sometimes—when they are mating—perfectly, creating creatures with the power of self-transformation. Such materials are better suited to psychological symbolism than scientific discussion. This is precisely the direction of Sturgeon's art; since he found "more room in inner space than in outer space," his fables are essentially paradigms of psychological growth that begin with the frustrations and alienation of youth and end in maturation and integration. On a number of occasions, he defined science fiction in terms of the derivation of the word "science" from the Latin "to know." "Science fiction is knowledge fiction," he wrote, adding that "by far most of the knowledge is psychological."

In *More than Human,* Sturgeon makes significant use of syzygy, a concept of nonreproductive union signified by a strange word. A collective identity is formed by a group of persons who retain their individuality while contributing to a gestalt that has the ultimate promise of a god. The collective person remains distinctly human, however, and the worship due it is finally worship of humanity. Here the components of the human being, conscience being the highest, are integrated and raised to the highest power. So, too, in a novel that deals directly with sexuality, *Venus Plus X,* the integration of the human personality and worship become paramount, with Sturgeon using androgyny as a symbol of wholeness and providing his utopia's inhabitants with a religion which worships the promise of man.

The form of Sturgeon's novels can present the critical reader with problems. Sturgeon is perhaps most at home as a writer of short stories, and his techniques of composition reflect at times an incomplete transition to the novel's demands. He seemingly pieces together sections that finally form the whole. This is not to say that the structuring of his books is unskillful, for he does finally bring to focus elements that run through them in parallel directions. Also, such a method can be seen as organic to Sturgeon's themes of integration, with loosely related parts finally encompassed in a total vision. Whatever a reader's verdict on form, however, his principal response will probably be to Sturgeon's handling of theme.

Sturgeon's work takes seriously his claim that "the best of science fiction is as good as the best of any modern literature—articulate, poetic, philosophical, provocative, searching, courageous, insightful." He once complained that though the finest science-fiction writers "open their veins into their typewriters, taking their craft and their readers seriously, they seem to be categorically disqualified from the serious attention of mainstream critics and readers." However, this is no longer the case, in part because of Sturgeon's fables of human nature.

The Dreaming Jewels • The revised title of *The Dreaming Jewels* is *The Synthetic Man*, a title that more clearly reflects the subject matter of Sturgeon's first novel but that loses some of the symbolic suggestiveness of the original. Paul Williams has commented that the work is in part based on Sturgeon's resentment of his stepfather and has pointed out the significance of the dream to the creative act of writing science fiction. To this might be added the importance of jewel symbolism in the light of Sturgeon's view of science fiction as "knowledge fiction."

Jewels often symbolize arcane knowledge and spiritual transformation; here they are connected with an unconscious dream-power that can be brought to light for good or ill, and in which reside keys to transformation and regeneration. Contesting for this power are Horty, the "synthetic man"—created by alien crystals that can bring objects, or people, into existence—and Pierre Monetre, a most thoroughgoing misanthrope who would delight in the destruction of humankind. Horty's victory over Monetre (called "maneater" by his subordinates) comes about through his capacity to tap the power of the unconscious, and through the willing sacrifice of Zena, whose education of Horty to human values keeps him from becoming like the alienated Monetre.

Horty's potential alienation comes from abuse by a cruel stepfather, Armand Bluett, a figure Sturgeon has himself identified with "a lot of bitterness and hostility that I wanted to get out." Bluett's viciousness results in the accidental loss of three of Horty's fingers, and the young boy flees after bidding farewell to Kay Hallowell, a girl whose love balances Bluett's hatred. In his flight, Horty is befriended by carnival people, especially Zena, a midget, who notices the boy's sympathetic connection with his only possession, a jack-in-the-box with strange jewels for eyes. These gems prove to have had their effect on the child, gradually transforming him into a creature capable both of communicating with the inner life of the jewels and of transforming himself at will.

Horty's identity is hidden from Monetre, who owns the carnival. Zena disguises him as a girl and warns him never to reveal that he has regenerated his three lost fingers, which Monetre had treated upon his arrival. During his years with the carnival, Horty fails to grow and is only forced to leave when the owner discloses some curiosity about his hand. After leaving, he discovers his gift of transformation, which is useful when he encounters Armand Bluett, now a judge, victimizing Kay Hallowell. Horty cools off the sexually aggressive Bluett by taking Kay's place and slicing off his regenerated fingers, at which sight Bluett passes out. Horty thus becomes the woman who represents love for him so that he might perform a sacrificial mutilation which is both saving and vengeful.

In a series of improbable events, Kay comes under the power of Bluett and Monetre, who is clearly contrasted with Horty. Although both are brilliantly gifted, Horty's mind, under Zena's guidance, has been shaped by "humanity and the extensions of humanity," as against Monetre's, which has been twisted by hatred and desire for power. In the confrontation between Horty and Monetre in a psychic duel, Zena sacrifices herself, instructing Horty to use his power to destroy jewel-created creatures. Because Monetre's character is so inhuman, he is assumed to be one. Ironically, Monetre is biologically human, without possessing any spirit of humanity, while Zena, a synthetic creature, sacrifices herself. In the end, however, Horty kills his adversary, resurrects Zena, who becomes his wife, and assumes Monetre's identity while traveling about trying to undo some of the harm he has done.

Sturgeon has assessed *The Dreaming Jewels* as "a rotten novel." Its chief faults are a contrived plot and a style that lacks the energy of the best of his stories of the 1940's. The use of psychological materials is compelling, however, making it one of Sturgeon's most popular works. Horty's series of transformations are representative of his possession of the secret of the unconscious, the capacity to convert revenge into sacrificial love, whose highest exemplar is Zena. The novel moves from mutilation to regeneration, from revenge to love, with Horty progressing toward wholeness by overcoming alienation and linking the transforming power of the unconscious to positive human values.

More than Human • *More than Human*, Sturgeon's second and best novel, has at the center of its three-part structure a section titled "Baby Is Three," which was published separately a year before the novel appeared. According to Sam Moskowitz, Sturgeon wrote a prologue and epilogue to this section to compose the novel. Like *The Dreaming Jewels*, "Baby Is Three" is about an alienated superman, fifteen-year-old Gerry Thompson, who in a strong first-person narration relates his visit to a psychiatrist, to whom he reveals his murder of his guardian, Miss Alicia Kew. Gerry also explains that he is part of a composite being, *homo gestalt*, a uniting of persons with extraordinary telepathic and telekinetic powers. Gerry has the capacity to probe the minds of others—he does this with the psychiatrist to make sure that he will not remember his visit—but he lacks human sympathy and moral awareness.

Sturgeon once said that "you cannot write stories about ideas—which is why so much hard-core, nuts-and-bolts science fiction fails as literature." In *More than Human*, however, he is fortunate in combining a powerful idea with a sure grasp of style and an effective structure. The first section of the novel, "The Fabulous Idiot," focuses on Lone (a shortened form of *alone*), who is an idiot in the root sense of the word. He is aware of himself alone. He gradually becomes aware of others, first through Miss Kew's sister, Evelyn, who along with Alicia had been the victim of a demonically sexually repressive father, and then through the Prodds, a pathetic couple who take him in, and whose mentally disabled child, "Baby," becomes the center of the gestalt being.

Lone becomes aware of a human community to which he has at least rudimentary obligations and of a more specialized group, composed of abandoned or runaway children, to which Gerry belongs, and that is destined to become a new being. By the end of the novel, this group has become a potential god, "not an exterior force, not an awesome Watcher in the sky, but a laughing thing with a human heart and reverence for its origins." In the book's last section, "Morality," Hip Barrows, the being's final component, its conscience, confronts and converts the ruthless Gerry; Hip sees himself as "an atom and his gestalt as a molecule. He saw these others as cells among cells, and he saw the whole design of what, with joy, humanity would become." His response is a "sense of worship." He participates in a vision not unlike that shared by many Romantic writers of the nineteenth century, what Walt Whitman's follower R. M. Bucke called "Cosmic Consciousness." Sturgeon said that the willingness of science-fiction writers to treat religious themes, "to invent and extrapolate and regroup ideas and concepts in this as in all other areas of human growth and change delights me and is a source of my true love for the mad breed." *More than Human* is Sturgeon's best illustration that such themes can be explored profitably.

More than Human, like *The Dreaming Jewels*, traces the progress of the growth and integration of the person. In each novel, characters move from alienation to wholeness, but in *More than Human*, the key conflict between misanthropy and humanity is handled with greater dramatic skill. In general a more sophisticated work in conception and structure, *More than Human* manages to present the idea of a collective entity without losing sight of individual characters or the dynamics of personality. As a speculative fiction, it deserves the praise and popularity it has enjoyed.

The Cosmic Rape • *The Cosmic Rape* also employs the gestalt theme of *More than Human*, extending the union to all of humankind, which in turn is joined to Medusa, an intergalactic composite creature. Although the underlying theme of the book is essentially the same as that of *More than Human*, it is by no means as successful. Its premises are extrapolated in far less believable fashion, and its structure is not dramatically engaging. Intercut scenes, which range from the United States to Rome to Africa, are skillfully coordinated, but character development suffers in the effort to show individuals becoming a part of the whole.

In *The Cosmic Rape*, Sturgeon attempts to put love into the largest terms, but, ironically, he employs a character most unlikely to initiate cosmic harmony. One Dan Gurlick, a loathsome bum, has become an atom in Medusa by ingesting a sort of seed concealed in a fragment of hamburger. Through him, Medusa seeks to take over the earth telepathically. Medusa is at first thwarted, having dealt only with collective minds elsewhere in the universe. This lack in humanity is repaired, however, as psychic unity among people appears as they cooperate in the destruction of invading machines created by Medusa. In the course of attaining collective consciousness, a variety of characters emerge from sexual repression and exploitation or social alienation to sacrifice themselves. Notable is the metamorphosis of Guido, a misfit who has turned to anarchism because his musical genius has been suppressed by a wicked stepfather.

Ultimately, Medusa is joined to the human collective mind. This connection occurs when Gurlick, himself excluded from the universal intelligence, is permitted to act out the sexual fantasies that Medusa has used to control him. What Gurlick intends as rape is welcomed by a woman now sexually liberated as a part of a larger design; likewise, the joining of humanity to Medusa is transformed from rape to consent. Medusa is in fact possessed by humanity rather than possessing it.

The Cosmic Rape extends the ideas of *More than Human* as far as they can go. However, the extrapolation is ultimately too fanciful and the dramatic power of Sturgeon's myth of human integration is diffused. There is a sense of his recognition of this in his next book, which he calls "a tract"; the social criticism of *Venus Plus X* gives ballast to an imagination which had overextended itself.

Venus Plus X • Sturgeon responded to the charge that "science fiction is characteristically asexual and unaware of love in its larger and largest senses." He believed that this impression had sometimes arisen because writers of science fiction often "work in geological or astronomical time rather than in biographical or historical perspective." Sturgeon had dealt with themes of love in both cosmic and personal perspectives in his earlier novels, but in *Venus Plus X* he turned to utopian fiction to keep the action on a more human scale.

Though Sturgeon had written stories on sex before—"The World Well Lost" (1953) deals with homosexuality, for example—*Venus Plus X* is his most extended statement on sexism and sexual taboos. Although the book has been praised for its pioneering study of sex roles, preceding Ursula K. Le Guin's much discussed *The Left Hand of Darkness* (1969) by nine years, *Venus Plus X* is also notable for its skillfuly ironic employment of science-fiction conventions and for its handling of the symbolism of androgyny.

The novel is structured in alternating chapters of action which are connected only by theme. The first set of chapters deals with suburban life and the questions of sexual identity posed to America during the 1950's. Along with standard problems of sex-role definition for children and general sexism, there are hints of change; Herb Raile comes to realize how Western culture has degraded women and catches glimpses of the significance of androgyny in the style of a rock singer. Contrasted with suburban America is Ledom (*model* inverted), a utopia founded upon the fact that its inhabitants are biologically hermaphrodites. Here, sex-role definition is no problem, and the wholeness of the human being in assuming all social duties is stressed. Against the predatory capitalism and commercialized worship of the suburbs are posed charitable religion and universal sharing.

Androgyny is used by Sturgeon as a symbol of wholeness. Like the universal man of *More than Human*, androgyny can be found in mystical thought as signifying the primordial unity of humankind. In order to stress this aspect of his work, Sturgeon provides the Ledomites with a religion that is an ecstatic celebration of the child. "We keep before us," says the guide to this utopia, "the image of that which is malleable and growing—of that which we have the power to improve. We worship that very power in ourselves, and the sense of responsibility which lives with it." Here again is Sturgeon's drive toward totality, a worship of human potential, yet in order to present this theme, he undercuts a number of science-fiction conventions to make his readers more aware of the symbolic nature of his statement.

The reader discovers that the book's nominal hero, Charlie Johns, is not a time-traveler as he first believes. Ledom does not exist in the distant future as it first appears; rather, it is a society hidden from the eyes of men. The Ledomites wish to test the reaction of the outside world to their culture, and they use Charlie Johns's responses as a gauge. After overcoming his initial bewilderment, Charlie embarks on a course of education, learning that Ledom's technical superiority consists in a machine that can inscribe thought patterns and has revolutionized learning, and a power supply that makes the community self-sufficient. Charlie's approval of technology comes to a screeching halt, however, when he discovers that the hermaphroditism of Ledomites is biologically engineered. His reaction convinces utopian planners that the world is not ready for the revelation of Ledom.

Charlie now regards Ledom as a den of perversion and indicates that it ought to be destroyed. His education, however, has been limited: He has not detected the hints throughout that the whole culture is symbolic, that its essence is "transition." It has been designed to preserve human values while the outside world destroys itself. The novel's disquisition on religion, in fact, suggests that if one human generation could adopt the religion of Ledom, it would be saved. No hermaphroditism would be necessary for a sense of human wholeness.

The final emphasis given Ledom's symbolic nature is the revelation that Charlie Johns is not actually Charlie Johns at all, but merely a collection of his memories, obtained when he was dying after a plane crash and inscribed on the previously blank mind of a biological control. The plot, however, first permits Johns to attempt the standard escape from a dystopia. He finds the one girl who has not been biologically altered, and he tries to leave in what he thinks is a time machine. When he does so, the Ledomites are forced to tell him the truth. He and his girl therefore take up life somewhere between the two worlds, trying to sort out their identities, presumably overcoming the sexism of the man Charlie was, and learning from the wisdom of Ledom. At the same time, on the other side, Herb Raile is working his way slowly and painfully to gain some of Ledom's values.

In spite of some dated writing in the sections on suburbia during the 1950's, this is a book that powerfully anticipates many of the themes taken up by feminists during the 1960's and 1970's. Sturgeon also made fine use of the conventions of utopian fiction only to undercut them, which is most appropriate to his major points about the nature of dynamic evolutionary change throughout his fiction. Utopia, he wrote, "must be life-oriented and recognize that life is change, which is why utopias, be they by Plato or Thomas More, or Joanna Russ, have hidden in them the characteristics of the necropolis." He avoided this by permitting his own utopia to self-destruct, leaving behind the impact of its symbols, and providing in *Venus Plus X* what Sturgeon saw in William Golding's *Lord of the Flies* (1954), "a fable of cultural structures, with a meaning—a 'moral' if you like—far greater than the narrative itself."

Henry J. Lindborg

Other major works

SHORT FICTION: *Without Sorcery: Thirteen Tales*, 1948 (also known as *Not Without Sorcery*); *E Pluribus Unicorn*, 1953; *A Way Home: Stories of Science Fiction and Fantasy*, 1955 (also known as *Thunder and Roses*); *Caviar*, 1955; *A Touch of Strange*, 1958; *Aliens 4*, 1959; *Beyond*, 1960; *Sturgeon in Orbit*, 1964; *. . . And My Fear Is Great/Baby Is Three*, 1965; *The Joyous Invasions*, 1965; *Starshine*, 1966; *Sturgeon Is Alive and Well*, 1971; *The Worlds of Theodore Sturgeon*, 1972; *Sturgeon's West*, 1973 (with Don Ward); *To Here and the Easel*, 1973; *Case and the Dreamer, and Other Stories*, 1974; *Visions and Venturers*, 1978; *Maturity: Three Stories*, 1979; *The Stars Are the Styx*, 1979; *The Golden Helix*, 1980; *Slow Sculpture*, 1982; *Alien Cargo*, 1984; *Pruzy's Pot*, 1986; *A Touch of Sturgeon*, 1987; *To Marry Medusa*, 1987; *The [Widget], the [Wadget], and Boff*, 1989; *The Complete Stories of Theodore Sturgeon*, 1994-2002 (8 volumes).

PLAYS: *It Should Be Beautiful*, pr. 1963; *Psychosis: Unclassified*, pr. 1977 (adaptation of his novel *Some of Your Blood*).

TELEPLAYS: *Mewhu's Jet*, 1950's; *Ordeal in Space*, 1950's; *The Adaptive Ultimate*, 1950's; *The Sound Machine*, 1950's; *They Came to Bagdad*, 1950's; *Dead Dames Don't Dial*, 1959; *Shore Leave*, 1966; *Amok Time*, 1967; *Killdozer!*, 1974; *The Pylon Express*, 1975-1976.

Bibliography

Delany, Samuel. "Sturgeon." In *Starboard Wine: More Notes on the Language of Science Fiction*. Pleasantville, N.Y.: Dragon Press, 1984. Delany is not only one of science fiction's best authors, but also he is one of its best critics, particularly in analysis of style. Here Delany explores some of the nuances of Sturgeon's language and the "realism" of Sturgeon's stories.

Diskin, Lahna. *Theodore Sturgeon*. Mercer Island, Wash.: Starmont House, 1981. The first book-length study of Sturgeon's fiction, this volume focuses primarily on his most famous science fiction.

Gordon, Joan, and Veronica Hollinger, eds. *Blood Read: The Vampire as Metaphor in*

Contemporary Culture. Philadelphia: University of Pennsylvania Press, 1997. Treats *Some of Your Blood* as a harbinger of the more recent sympathetic vampire novels. Includes a bibliography.

Hassler, Donald M. "Images for an Ethos, Images for Change and Style." *Extrapolation* 20 (Summer, 1979): 176-188. An analysis of Sturgeon's themes of love, loneliness, newness, and the nature of change in relation to his ethics and versatile technique. The works discussed include "Microcosmic God," "Slow Sculpture," *More than Human,* and *The Cosmic Rape.*

Kucera, Paul Q. "Intimate Isolation: Sturgeon's *More than Human* and the Power of Privacy." *Extrapolation* 44, no. 4 (December 22, 2003): 437-446. Study of Sturgeon's use of loneliness, with particular attention to his novel *More than Human.*

Malzberg, Barry N. "Grandson of the True and the Terrible." In *The Engines of the Night.* Garden City, N.Y.: Doubleday, 1982. A brief but poignant evaluation of Sturgeon's importance in the history of science fiction.

Moskowitz, Sam. "Theodore Sturgeon." In *Seekers of Tomorrow: Masters of Modern Science Fiction.* Westport, Conn.: Hyperion Press, 1966. This essay is a good general introduction to Sturgeon in terms of his place in science-fiction history and in what makes him "unique."

Pringle, David, ed. *St. James Guide to Horror, Ghost, and Gothic Writers.* Detroit: St. James Press, 1998. Survey of gothic and horror fiction writers that contains a comprehensive bibliography of Sturgeon's works.

Sackmary, Regina. "An Ideal of Three: The Art of Theodore Sturgeon." In *Critical Encounters,* edited by Dick Riley. New York: Frederick Ungar, 1978. Sackmary discusses the motif of threes in Sturgeon's fiction as his symbol for unity.

Stephensen-Payne, Phil, and Gordon Benson, Jr. *Theodore Sturgeon, Sculptor of Love and Hate: A Working Bibliography.* San Bernardino, Calif.: Borgo Press, 1992. Part of the Galactic Central Bibliographies for the Avid Reader series, this is a helpful tool for students of Sturgeon.

Streitfield, David. "Science Fiction and Fantasy." *The Washington Post,* March 7, 1999, p. XO8. Discusses the renaissance of interest in Sturgeon, with the reissue of his *More than Human* and *To Marry Medusa* in paperback, as well as his collected short stories; discusses briefly the story "Scars" and the unfinished "Quietly."

Westfall, Gary. "Sturgeon's Fallacy." *Extrapolation* 38 (Winter, 1997): 255-277. Takes issue with so-called Sturgeon's Law—that 90 percent of everything, especially science fiction, is worthless. Analyzes the output of science fiction in the twentieth century and argues that science fiction is a worthwhile form of writing.

William Styron

Born: Newport News, Virginia; June 11, 1925
Died: Martha's Vineyard, Massachusetts; November 1, 2006

Principal long fiction • *Lie Down in Darkness*, 1951; *The Long March*, 1952 (serial), 1956 (book); *Set This House on Fire*, 1960; *The Confessions of Nat Turner*, 1967; *Sophie's Choice*, 1979.

Other literary forms • Before 1990, William Styron was among the few major modern literary figures discussed within the context of only a single genre—in his case, the novel. Except for a slight and rather odd play, *In the Clap Shack* (1972), and a collection of essays, *This Quiet Dust* (1982), Styron mainly concentrated on novels. In 1990, however, the publication of *Darkness Visible: A Memoir of Madness* was widely hailed. A candid and insightful recounting of Styron's personal battle with severe clinical depression, *Darkness Visible* was an immediate popular success. *A Tidewater Morning: Three Tales from Youth* is a collection of short stories published in 1993.

Achievements • Until the publication of *The Confessions of Nat Turner* in 1967, Styron was well known in literary circles as a young novelist of great talent but largely unrealized potential. *The Confessions of Nat Turner*, riding the crest of a wave of social activism during the late 1960's and capitalizing on a national interest in black literature and history, gave Styron a major popular reputation as well as making him the center of a vitriolic controversy between academic and literary critics on one side, who tended to see the novel as an honest attempt to come to terms with history, and a small group of strident black critics on the other hand, who questioned, often abusively, the ability of any white writer to deal with the black experience and who called Styron's portrait of Nat Turner unflattering and inaccurate. The book and the debate it engendered made Styron a major voice in twentieth century fiction, as well as a rich man.

Despite the twelve-year hiatus between the publication of *The Confessions of Nat Turner* and that of *Sophie's Choice*, Styron's reputation grew, particularly in terms of his role as an interpreter of the South. *Lie Down in Darkness* was recognized as one of the finest presentations in fiction of the modern southern family, haunted by memory, guilt, and time, and *The Confessions of Nat Turner* came to be seen as representative of the concern of southern writers with the burden of history. *The Confessions of Nat Turner* was accepted as a rhetorically beautiful evocation of the past, whatever its historical inaccuracies.

The publication of *Sophie's Choice* in 1979 cemented Styron's position as one of the major figures of contemporary literature. Although several major critics had reservations about the novel, its ambitious confrontation of a moral theme of enormous implication—the Holocaust—and Styron's compelling, lyrical prose made the novel the literary event of the year. With *Sophie's Choice*, some of Styron's lifelong concerns as a novelist become clearer: the unanswerable problem of pain and suffering, the elusive nature of memory, and the ambiguous legacy of history.

Peter Simon

Biography • William Styron was born on June 11, 1925, in Newport News, Virginia, which he later called "a very southern part of the world." His mother, Pauline Margaret Abraham Styron, was from the North, but his father, William Clark Styron, a shipyard engineer, came from an old, if not aristocratic, land-poor Virginia family, and Styron remembers his grandmother telling him as a little boy of the days when the family owned slaves, a memory he was to incorporate years later into *Sophie's Choice*. Styron's father was a "Jeffersonian gentleman," liberal in his views for a southerner, who implanted in his son much of the philosophical curiosity that characterized the young Styron's novels. His mother, a gentling influence, died when Styron was twelve after a long, painful siege with cancer, an experience that was also to leave a mark on his fiction in the form of an almost obsessive concern with physical pain and suffering and the vulnerability of the flesh. After his mother's death, Styron began "going wild," and his father sent him to an Episcopal boys' school in Middlesex County, where he was an indifferent student but a voracious reader. Graduating, he enrolled in Davidson College during World War II but soon dropped out to enlist in the Marines.

Styron's stint in Officers Candidate School marked the beginning of his writing career, for while there, he enrolled in a creative writing course at Duke University under William Blackburn, whom Styron acknowledges as the most powerful formative influence on his work. One of his stories, about a southern lynching, similar in tone and execution to William Faulkner's "Dry September," appeared in a student anthology, Styron's first published fiction. At the tail end of the war, Styron was commissioned and was stationed on a troop ship in the San Francisco Bay, but the Japanese surrendered before he ever left port. Styron was to speak later of his sense of guilt at not having seen action, as well as his feeling of horror at the waste and destruction of the war and the terrible, almost casual way in which life could be lost. Styron condemned the absurdity of Marine Corps life, but he praised the tough training that transformed him physically and mentally. Styron resumed his program at Duke and graduated in 1947. He took a job in New York as an associate editor in the book division at McGraw-Hill. His senior editor and immediate superior was Edward C. Aswell, the august second editor of Thomas Wolfe and an éminence grise to rival editor Maxwell Perkins; Aswell was to appear grotesquely as "The Weasel" in an autobiographical passage in *Sophie's Choice* nearly thirty years later. The callow young Styron found McGraw-Hill humorless and confining, and after six months he was fired.

Living in a Brooklyn boardinghouse on a tiny legacy from his grandmother, Styron took another creative writing course, this time from Hiram Haydn at the New School for Social Research. He began work on his first novel, *Lie Down in Darkness*, the story of a star-crossed upper-middle-class southern family whose failure to find love and meaning in life drives the sensitive daughter, Peyton Loftis, to insanity and suicide. The complex treatment of time in the novel and its high southern rhetoric showed the influence of William Faulkner, whom Styron had been reading intensely, but *Lie Down in Darkness* was manifestly the work of a powerful and original talent. At first, Styron found the writing of the book slow and difficult. Two years after leaving McGraw-Hill, he had written only a few pages that were usable. After he made drastic changes to the novel, dropping the original title ("Inheritance of Night"), eliminating the character Marcus Bonner, shifting the point of view to an omniscient narrator, and withholding the reader's knowledge of Peyton Loftis, Styron found the writing went surprisingly fast—he finished the book and saw it accepted for publication by Bobbs-Merrill before he was recalled by the Marine Corps for service in the Korean War. The novel was published in 1951. Styron was then on active reserve duty, from which he was eventually discharged for an eye problem, but which became the basis for his second novel, *The Long March*.

Lie Down in Darkness was an immediate critical success and a moderate popular one, winning the prestigious Prix de Rome in 1952. At that time, Styron had decamped to Paris and fallen in with a young crowd of American expatriate intellectuals, many of whom would later make names for themselves in literature. George Plimpton and Peter Matthiessen were at the center of a moiling, motley, talented crowd that included Harold Humes, John P. C. Train, Donald Hall, and, on the fringe, writers such as James Baldwin, James Jones, and Irwin Shaw. In 1952 and 1953, the group began compiling a literary magazine, the *Paris Review*, which was to become one of the most influential literary periodicals of the postwar period. Plimpton became the first editor and Matthiessen the fiction editor, and Styron wrote the statement of purpose for the first issue. He also gave the periodical one of the first of its famous "Writers at Work" interviews. It was recorded by Matthiessen and Plimpton at Patrick's, the *Paris Review* crowd's favorite bar, and in it Styron claimed that "this generation . . . will produce literature equal to that of any other generation" and that "a great writer . . . will give substance to and perhaps even explain all the problems of the world." From the start, his ambitions were large.

Although he later said he drank enough brandy in bistros to develop a *crise de foie*, and spent months in the summer of 1952 on a sybaritic "Ovidian idyll" on the Riviera with Humes, Styron was also writing at top speed during this period. In just six weeks, he wrote a novella based on his Marine Corps training-camp experience, *The Long March*, and it was accepted for publication in the fall by *Discovery*, a literary magazine (Knopf would publish it as a book four years later). In 1953, he used the money from his Prix de Rome to travel in Italy, an experience that laid the groundwork for his 1960 novel of expatriates, *Set This House on Fire*, and during this time he met Rose Burgunder, a Jewish poet with some family money from Baltimore, whom he soon married. They returned to America, to Roxbury, Connecticut, which would remain Styron's home, and where he began work on the "big novel" that he planned to follow up the success of *Lie Down in Darkness*.

This was *Set This House on Fire*, a sprawling account of American intellectuals living a life of self-indulgence and self-destruction in postwar Italy. The book contained fine lyrical passages of description, particularly of the physical beauty of Italy and the horrifying squalor and suffering of its people, but as Styron later admitted, the novel was seriously flawed—undisciplined and melodramatic. The reviews were very mixed, and some of them savage. Styron's former friend Norman Mailer called *Set This House on Fire* "a bad, maggoty novel," suggesting that Styron could "write like an angel about landscape, but like an adolescent about people." The novel was better received by Styron's European critics—it is still highly regarded in France—but Styron was wounded by his first really bad press, and he retreated to Roxbury to work on his next book, a novel he resolved to make so thoroughly a work of craftsmanship as to defy criticism.

The Confessions of Nat Turner took years to research and write, and true to Styron's expectations, it was immediately acclaimed as a masterpiece. For years, Styron had had his mind on Nat Turner's 1831 slave rebellion as a subject for fiction. It had taken place close to his own Tidewater Virginia home, and Styron saw the suffering, the violence, and the misunderstanding of the revolt as emblematic both of the South's guilt and pain and of his personal concerns as a writer. Styron claimed that reading Albert Camus's *L'Étranger* (1942; *The Stranger*, 1946) furnished him with the technique he was to use in presenting Nat Turner's story—the narrative persona reflecting from jail—and there is no doubt that much of the novel's perspective on black people and black problems was derived from Styron's friend, the black writer James Baldwin, who was a guest of Styron for months while he himself was writing *Another Country* (1962), his first major novel about black/white relations.

Styron called *The Confessions of Nat Turner* "less a 'historical novel' than a meditation on history," but despite critical accolades, including the praise of Baldwin, who suggested that the novel might be considered the beginning of a black/white "mutual history," Styron became the target of a group of critics who protested vehemently Styron's depiction of Nat Turner. These critics assaulted Styron in print, accused him of racism and of attempting to demean the reputation of a great hero of black history, and hounded him at meetings, readings, and lectures. Ironically, Nat Turner, as Styron presented him, was a strong and sensitive character, unquestionably the hero of the novel, but so volatile was the political climate of America during the late 1960's that for some critics, any black character who was not a warrior saint was unacceptable as a fictional creation.

The critical assaults provoked by *The Confessions of Nat Turner* left Styron bruised, but he was encouraged by the praise for the novel's powerful rhetoric and masterly structure, not to mention its enormous financial success. Of the controversy, he said, "It really had very little effect on me . . . largely because of the fact that I knew that it was politically motivated and hysterical, and that I had not violated any truth that a novelist is capable of doing." He turned to new work, first to a lengthy projected novel, tentatively titled "The Way of the Warrior," a novel that explored the psyche of a career army officer, then to *Sophie's Choice*. While on Martha's Vineyard, Styron dreamed of Sophie, a Polish Catholic survivor of Auschwitz whom he had met in Brooklyn in 1949. He woke with a vision, seeing her name on a door; he decided that the book would focus on a mother who is forced to send her child to death. The book began as an autobiographical reminiscence of his aimless days as a junior editor at McGraw-Hill, when he found himself frustrated artistically, philosophically, and sexually. As he worked through his memories in the character of his narrator, Stingo, whose fictional background is almost identical to Styron's own, he found his real theme: the life and eventual death by suicide of a woman who survived the Nazi concentration camps but emerged terribly scarred emotionally. This woman, the Sophie of the title, becomes the vehicle through which Stingo confronts the potential horror of life, and through her he matures.

Sophie's Choice was five years in the writing, but Styron was richly rewarded when it was finally published in 1979. A few critics, notably John Gardner, raised questions about its structure, and about the sometimes jejune intrusions of the shallow Stingo, but for the most part the novel was accepted as a fine and satisfying offering by a major writer. "It has the feel of permanence," Peter Prescott wrote. The gratifyingly large sales were capped by a spectacular sale of the film rights. In 1983, Meryl Streep won an Academy Award for Best Actress for her portrayal of Sophie in that film.

In 1985, Styron was hospitalized with acute clinical depression. His struggle to overcome his suicidal feelings and to return to health are recounted in his memoir *Darkness Visible*, published five years later. Styron credited the peaceful seclusion of his hospital stay and the loving patience of his wife and grown children (three daughters and a son) as the principal factors in his recovery. After his hospitalization, Styron immediately wrote "A Tidewater Morning," a long short story that fictionalized the death of his mother. After writing *Darkness Visible*, he returned to his work on a novel set during World War II. Styron died of pneumonia at the age of eighty-one after a long period of failing health.

Analysis • The informing patterns of William Styron's fiction are by no means self-evident, and they may not yield themselves readily to the casual critic. Unlike William Faulkner, whom he often resembles in style and technique, his subjects are radically diverse—a doomed southern family, the intellectual jet set of American expatriates, a historical slave revolt, the horror of the Holocaust. He can shift stylistically from the direct "plain style" of *The Long March* to the purple rhetoric of sections in *Set This House on Fire*, and he moves easily from romantic abstraction to concrete objectivity.

Styron is preeminently, almost self-consciously, a writer of "big" novels of weighty moral significance—a fictional *homme sérieux*, as the French say (which may account for some of Styron's great popularity with French critics). The eternal verities embody themselves relentlessly in Styron's writing. Death, suffering, the silence of God—grave truths lumber ponderously and insistently at the reader in each novel, mercifully relieved by flashes of humor and lyrical passages of poetic beauty, which spare Styron the gray fate of being a sort of American Thomas Mann. Nevertheless, the metaphysical predominates in Styron's books.

Strongly underlying all of his novels is a concern with the past, not so much in the form of the passage of time, but rather an awareness that it is either lost or potentially reclaimable. Each of the major novels moves from the present to the past in an attempt to explain or understand how things came to be as they are. *Lie Down in Darkness*, with its relentless burrowing in the Loftis family past, looks backward to explain Peyton's death. In *Set This House on Fire*, Peter Leverett moves very deliberately into the past in pursuit of a piece of himself that is missing, and his whole purpose in dredging up the Italian incidents that form the body of the novel is to reveal the past so that he may deal with the present. Both *The Confessions of Nat Turner* and *Sophie's Choice* are historical novels concerned with the actual past and with what Robert Penn Warren has called "the awful burden of history."

Styron's fiction is historical, but in an intensely personal and psychological way. Each exploration of the past is filtered through the consciousness of a protagonist—Milton Loftis, Cass Kinsolving, Nat Turner, Sophie—and strongly colored by the neuroses of those characters. The alcoholism of Milton and Cass, Nat's brooding rage, and Sophie's aching guilt over her murdered child—at the core of each novel is psychological exploration rather than historical exposition. Historical process is only the context within which individual psychologies grope for resolution. Each of Styron's characters lives on the verge of apocalyptic catastrophe, always on the edge of mental breakdown. Each of his protagonists is close to outright insanity. Two actually commit suicide (Peyton and Sophie); Nat Turner essentially does; and Cass Kinsolving of *Set This House on Fire* is only saved from it by the thinnest of margins. His people may be constantly close to madness, yet Styron makes the reader feel that the madness is legitimate, for his characters search for meaning in a mad world, and only when they fail to find it do they become deranged. Peyton Loftis's loveless family, Nat Turner's unjust world, and the horrors of the concentration camp for Sophie are atmospheres in which genuine sanity is difficult, if not impossible. Perhaps the most representative Styron "hero," though, is Cass Kinsolving of *Set This House on Fire*, the only protagonist who is a philosopher as well as a sufferer. Cass's madness derives from his contemplation of the horror of human life and misery, and he staggers drunkenly around postwar Italy demanding a teleological answer for the chaos of existence in which God is silent; "you can shake the whole universe and just get a snicker up there."

Perhaps it is this tendency to project the struggles of his characters beyond the ordinary world and to magnify them to the borders of melodrama that gives all of Styron's novels powerful religious overtones. Some of this tendency derives from Styron's own Episcopalian background, which is strongly echoed in the style of *Lie Down in Darkness* and *Set This House on Fire* and is particularly evident in the rhetoric of Nat Turner, who is stylistically more Anglican than Baptist. The central problem in these novels is the conspicuous absence of God from human life. Styron's world is one in which, as Cass says in *Set This House on Fire*, "God has locked the door and gone away to leave us to write letters to Him." They are unanswered. By the time Styron comes to reflecting on the horror of the Holocaust in his last book, it seems no answer is possible.

This is Styron's theme—the absence of God and the meaninglessness of life. Consistently, he approaches it through a single technique, the presentation and contemplation of pain and suffering. Styron's novels are a catalog of the slings and arrows of outrageous fortune, some physical, some mental, and some simply the result of an empathic identification with the suffering state of humankind.

On its most elemental level, Styron's depiction of suffering is as pure physical pain. Peyton Loftis is tortured by the ache in her womb, the soldiers of *The Long March* by the agony of their exhausted bodies, Nat Turner by the torments of his imprisonment, and Sophie by the tortures of the concentration camp. In *Set This House on Fire*, physical suffering is Styron's primary metaphor for the pain of humankind's empty relationship with the universe, and the novel is shot through with characters in various stages of suffering from "abuse of the carnal envelope."

Vivid as the physical suffering of Styron's characters is, it is nothing compared to their mental and emotional anguish. Often, this mental anguish derives from their acute sense of alienation—from one another and from God. Milton Loftis, Peyton, Cass Kinsolving, Nat Turner, and Sophie writhe painfully and actively, aware of a pervasive emptiness in their lives.

Lie Down in Darkness • The structural complexities of *Lie Down in Darkness*, combined with the florid rhetoric of the novel, obscure for many readers the essentially simple causality that underlies the book. It is the story of how and why Peyton Loftis becomes insane and kills herself, tracing the roots of her tortured madness to her father's weakness and her mother's inability to love. Peyton's father, Milton, showers her with an excessive adoration that is one facet of his alcoholic self-indulgence; he smothers his daughter with a sloppy, undemanding adulation that counterpoints his wife Helen's psychotic frigidity. Helen is only able to show love in terms of compulsive formal discharge of parental obligations, bitterly resentful of the martyr role she has chosen to play. Eventually, Peyton instinctively rejects both her father's almost unnatural affection and her mother's unnatural lack of it. By the time Peyton cuts herself loose, however, she has been emotionally disabled, unable to accept any genuine love from a series of lovers, including the Jewish artist she marries and who might have brought her peace. She retreats deeper and deeper inside herself, watching first other people and finally the real world recede before her disintegrating mind. The last major section of the novel is her tormented, insane monologue, a brilliant tour de force reminiscent of the Benjy sections of Faulkner's *The Sound and the Fury* (1929).

When *Lie Down in Darkness* was published in 1951, it was widely hailed as a significant addition to the "southern" school of writing led by Faulkner, Ellen Glasgow, Flannery O'Connor, and Thomas Wolfe. Thematically, *Lie Down in Darkness* is not a markedly "southern" novel. Although the Loftis family is from Tidewater, Virginia, and there are mannerisms described in the book that are definitively southern, Milton Loftis's weakness, his wife's cold rage, and their daughter's breakdown are in no way regional. The story could as easily be that of a New England family, such as Eugene O'Neill's Manions. What is actually distinctive about the tragedy of the Loftises is how much it is exclusively their own, rather than a product of the dictates of fate or society. In this respect, the novel differs from Styron's later works, in which he increasingly attributes humanity's sufferings to forces beyond the individual. Although the novel is a tragedy of a single family, Styron is condemning an entire generation that lost its children. In describing her parents' generation as lost, Peyton Loftis says, "They thought they were lost. They were crazy. They weren't lost. What they were doing was losing us."

If Styron traces a source of the Loftis family's deterioration, it is perhaps in their lifestyle. On one level, *Lie Down in Darkness* is almost a novel of manners, for in keeping with the Loftises' "country club" lives, much of the novel delineates social activity—parties, dances, dinners. Emblematic of this are three scenes in which Milton, Helen, and Peyton go through the motions of conventional social rituals while they are torn by violent emotions lying beneath the facade of meaningless behavior. The first of these is a dance at the country club at which Peyton tries to play the role of belle-of-the-ball while her father makes drunken love to his mistress in a cloakroom and Helen seethes at both father and daughter in a jealous rage. Later, a Christmas dinner turns into a grotesque, painful fiasco, as Helen screams insults at her daughter while Milton slobbers drunkenly. Finally, Peyton's wedding becomes a nightmare when Milton again gets drunk and sloppy, and Helen, as always thinly concealing a bitter resentment of Peyton, finally cracks, screaming "Whore!" at her daughter. In a rage, Peyton claws her mother's face with her nails and flees the family forever.

The loss of love, or rather the failure to find it, informs the entire book. The three Loftises grope at one another in despair, reaching out to one another in their separate, psychologically crippled ways for an understanding and affection that will bring them some sort of emotional peace. That peace, though, is impossible because their psychic natures are flawed beyond redemption. Sigmund Freud spins the plot: Milton loves Peyton not wisely, but too well, as she uncomfortably senses, so his love of her must always seem unrequited, and he is destined to be deserted by her at the last; Helen suffers a patent jealous hatred for Peyton, who has a capacity for love that Helen lacks, and who is stranded between the two poles of her parents' emotional inadequacy. The result is endless pain and ultimately annihilation. As Milton wails, "It was awful not to be able to love. It was hell."

It is not hell, though, but obliteration—nothingness—that truly underlies this novel. In the opening scene, Milton meets the train that brings Peyton's body home for burial. The final scene is her throwing herself to her death from a New York City rooftop. Everything between, the whole body of the novel, is an explanation of that death, and the knowledge of Peyton's unavoidable extinction hangs heavily during the entire book. The title is taken from Sir Thomas Browne's gloomy *Hydriotaphia: Or, Urn Burial* (1658), a seventeenth century meditation on the inevitability of death, and the "darkness" of the title is that of the grave. Images of death haunt the dreams of the tortured characters, and the reader is never allowed to forget the ultimate negation implicit in the agony of life.

The Long March • The agony of life, more than the nullity of death, became the focus of Styron's fiction following *Lie Down in Darkness*. His short novel *The Long March* serves almost as a précis for the motif of pain that came to dominate Styron's writing. Not much longer than a substantial short story, *The Long March* stands between the turgid psychological weight of *Lie Down in Darkness* and the ponderous solemnity of *Set This House on Fire* like a breath of fresh air. Short, clean, concise, and plotted without out a wasted word, this unpretentious novella contains some of Styron's most disciplined and readable prose. He trimmed away all the heavy rhetorical and philosophical baggage of his "big" novels, leaving before the reader only his lean and awful central subject—pain and suffering. Appropriately, the pain here is of the most basic and primitive sort—pure physical agony. Stylistically, Styron's writing of the book in 1952 was anomalous in the development of his career, for it was at this period that he was gearing up to write *Set This House on Fire*, and the stylistic and structural complexities of *Lie Down in Darkness* were being inflated to match the ambitious range of the novel to come.

Like the best of Ernest Hemingway, *The Long March* is deceptively simple—a step-by-step account of a thirty-six-mile forced march inflicted on some Marine reserves by their mindless officers and endured by the men with varying degrees of courage or cowardice, acceptance or rejection, but mainly endured with pain. The march itself is relentlessly real for the reader on page after page, the physical pain of the characters becoming a kind of rhythmic pattern in the book. If the novel has a "message," it is embodied in the final lines, in which Captain Mannix, who has undergone the march protesting its sadistic insanity, swollen and aching, confronts a sympathetic barracks maid who asks if it hurts: "His words [were] uttered . . . not with self-pity, but only with the tone of a man who, having endured and lasted, was too weary to tell her anything but what was true. 'Deed it does,' he said."

Set This House on Fire • After the critical success of *Lie Down in Darkness* and the artistic success of *The Long March*, there followed the better part of a decade before the 1960 publication of *Set This House on Fire*. Comfortably ensconced in Roxbury, Connecticut, prosperous, rearing a family, and moving into the center of the New York literary world, Styron's reputation grew steadily, although his literary output did not. His house, along with George Plimpton's New York City apartment, became one of the new camping grounds for the old *Paris Review* crowd, and Peter Matthiessen, James Jones, and James Baldwin were frequent visitors. Throughout the late 1950's, word of his forthcoming "big" novel spread as Styron gave private readings from it, and the publication of *Set This House on Fire* was eagerly awaited.

The novel was indeed big; actually, it sprawled embarrassingly. In place of the personal, family tragedy of *Lie Down in Darkness*, Styron broadened his scope by giving the suffering in this novel a universal dimension and by exploring the metaphysical bases of it. It is not a family that suffers, but the world. The reader sees this world through the eyes of Peter Leverett, a Styron surrogate, but the real protagonist is Cass Kinsolving, a sensitive, drunken American artist in Italy during the 1950's who is aghast by the suffering of humanity. Much of the story is told to Leverett (and the reader) by Cass, who looks for the ultimate implications of every grain of sand. Looking back, he tells Leverett that he remembers Italy as "an infinity of remembered pain," and he finds divine aspects even in his drunkenness: "God surely had clever ways of tormenting a man, putting in his way a substance whereby He might briefly be reached, but that in the end . . . sent Him packing over the horizon trailing clouds of terror." To achieve this broadened projection, Styron enlarges his cast of characters, heightens his rhetoric, and throws the whole show on an enormous stage. A vast parade of people moves through *Set This House on Fire*, many of them poor, sick, or abused, the rest venal and contemptible. The action is lifted from the commonplace to the melodramatic; rape, murder, and mystery dominate. The characters, except for Leverett and Cass's wife, Poppy, are exotic. Mason Flagg is a monstrous idiot typifying Victor Hugo's Quasimodo of *Notre-Dame de Paris* (1831; *The Hunchback of Notre Dame,* 1833). He is the "super bastard" aesthete rich boy, whose cultivated corruption is nauseating but still rich and strange. Cass deteriorates theatrically, staggering about and raving lines from Greek tragedy, a far cry from the humdrum drunkard Milton Loftis.

Heightened rhetoric is Styron's principal method of extending the scope of *Set This House on Fire*. Much of the novel reads like gothic Thomas Wolfe, from Mason's mother's description of "the horror" of her son's expulsion from prep school to Leverett's account of one of the book's several nightmares: "an abomination made of the interlocking black wings of ravens crawling and loathsome with parasites . . . a country in cataclysm and upheaval." Cass spends much of the book in deliberate blasphemy, "raving at that black, baleful, and depraved Deity who seemed coolly-minded to annihilate His creatures," when he is not suffering from delirium tremens and seeing visions of a boiling sea, or giant spiders on Mt. Vesuvius.

This rhetoric not only complements, but makes possible, the projection of much of the novel on a dream level. Styron had done this before, in a Freudian fantasy of Helen Loftis's, in one of Peyton's lover's dreams of babies burning in hell, and in Peyton's entire closing soliloquy. In *Set This House on Fire*, though, the use of dream, vision, and hallucination is so pervasive that much of the novel approaches phantasmagoria. Leverett dreams of a malevolent fiend for several pages, and has recurrent, elaborately described nightmares; Cass is repeatedly haunted, and his drunken ordeal ends with an extended vision of disaster, a passage drawing heavily on Dante and the Book of Revelation. So extensive is Styron's use of dramatic and fantastic imagery that it is often difficult to tell whether he is presenting the reader with a metaphor or a dream, and at one point, when Cass describes himself first making love to a beautiful girl, then suddenly "groping for an answer on some foul black shore," it is impossible to tell whether he is just thinking or hallucinating again. Cass himself probably does not know.

Although they differ in scope and ambition, *Lie Down in Darkness* and *Set This House on Fire* are essentially the same kind of novel. Both are studies in personal alienation and deterioration. Both work through an elevated rhetoric and through psychological revelation. Although *Set This House on Fire* reaches self-consciously for transcendence and philosophical universality, the novel centers on the psychological aberrations of two characters, Cass Kinsolving and Mason Flagg. Similar to the tragedy of the Loftis family in *Lie Down in Darkness*, theirs are individual, not universal, tragedies. In *Lie Down in Darkness*, the tragedies are individual, but they represent the failings of a self-indulgent generation. In *Set This House on Fire*, the tragedies are also individual, yet they represent the tragedies of a hedonistic generation, a generation that was decadent and destructive.

The Confessions of Nat Turner • Styron called *The Confessions of Nat Turner* "a meditation on history." Its subject is not only the character of Nat but also the meaning of slavery itself—what it does to people, and to society. Like Styron's previous novels, the book is a contemplation of horror, with a protagonist who becomes a victim of that horror, but in this case, the horror is not a purely personal one. Significantly, unlike the Loftises and Cass Kinsolving, Nat does not deteriorate but grows through the course of the book as his comprehension of society and life grows. Nat Turner is the richest and most psychologically complex of Styron's characters, and the historical subject matter of the work is filtered through his sensitive consciousness to produce a visionary "meditation" on the world of slavery, dreamlike in quality and poetic in execution. Southern Virginia of the 1830's, the novel's world, is very much a projection of Nat's mind—a mind produced by that world, and savaged by it.

To develop the subtlety of Nat's mind, Styron drew on all his technical and rhetorical resources. His mastery of time shifts and dream sequences, already amply demonstrated, was enhanced in this novel, and he explored a variety of rhetorical styles, varying from rural black dialect to a high Anglican style echoing Joan Didion's *A Book of Common Prayer* (1977) for Nat's more poetic utterances. Nat's mind ranges with astonishing virtuosity over his universe—the natural world, the complexities of human relations, the elusive mysteries of God, and the bitterness of mortality. An enormously sophisticated narrative persona, Nat moves fluidly across time, contemplating the painful mystery of the past, represented by his long-dead African grandmother, and of the future, represented by his own forthcoming death. Nat tells the entire novel in flashback, remembering his abortive slave rebellion and the personal and historical events leading up to it, constantly trying to cipher out the meaning of those events.

The novel is a study of the growth of knowledge and of the growth of Nat's mind. In the introspective isolation of his anguished imprisonment, he reconstructs his lifelong struggle to understand the meaning of existence. He recalls his progression from childhood, when he had no comprehension of what slavery meant, to an early adult period when he accepted his condition either bitterly or philosophically, to a final understanding of slavery in personal, societal, and moral terms. Ironically, as Nat becomes more morally and aesthetically sensitive, he becomes more insensitive in human terms, gravitating toward an acceptance of the violence that finally characterizes his revolt. Only a sudden, visionary conversion to a God of love at the end of the novel saves him from closing the book as an unrepentant apostle of retributory cruelty.

In the process of expanding his knowledge and developing his terrible vision of deliverance from slavery by violence, Nat becomes the spokesman for two familiar Styron themes—the complexity of human psychology and the mystery of human suffering. The most self-searching of Styron's characters, Nat exhaustively explores the ambivalence and ambiguity of his feelings about race, sex, religion, and violence. Although he casts himself convincingly as a Christian prophet, Nat is no simplistic fundamentalist, for he recognizes in his own emotional turmoil personal depths that he can plumb with only partial understanding. His psychology is the battleground of conflicting feelings, symbolized by his powerful attraction to his master's gentle daughter and his vitriolic hatred for all she represents. When he eventually kills her, neither he nor the reader can discriminate his motives. She dies imploring, "Oh, Nat, it hurts so!" and his realization of her pain is the climax of his apprehension of the myriad pains of all humankind, particularly those of his own people. In this concern, he is representative of all Styron's protagonists.

It is almost impossible to deal with *The Confessions of Nat Turner* without mentioning the storm of controversy that followed its publication and success. A number of critics maintained that the novel was historically inaccurate (for example, it portrayed Nat as having homosexual tendencies but never mentioned that there are records indicating that the real Nat Turner had a wife). Styron was also accused of demeaning a black hero, in that his Nat has reservations about his mission and is squeamish about wholesale slaughter. The real complaint against Styron, though, most thoroughly summarized in a casebook edited by John Henrik Clarke, *William Styron's Nat Turner: Ten Black Writers Respond* (1968), was that he was a white man attempting a theme that should be the province of black writers. In answer to the historical criticism, Styron and his defenders point out that *The Confessions of Nat Turner* is a work of fiction which does not pretend to be straight history and that it violates no factual information known to Styron at the time of writing.

The second complaint, that Styron's novel degrades a black hero, is more difficult to understand. Unquestionably, Styron, like any true artist, presents his hero with his neuroses, self-doubts, and weaknesses. In the main, however, Nat is without doubt a positive and even heroic character, arguably the most admirable in all Styron's fiction. Only a critic in search of a black plaster saint *sans peur et sans reproche* could consider the creation of as rich and sensitive a character as Nat a slur. While Styron was researching *The Confessions of Nat Turner*, James Baldwin lived in Styron's cottage, and Baldwin encouraged Styron to write the book. Although Styron never acknowledged Baldwin as the model for his Nat Turner, there are similarities in thinking and speech, and Turner's sexual ambivalence may be based on Baldwin. In any case, Styron's Turner is as much a modern intellectual who ponders the effects of slavery as a historical figure.

Sophie's Choice • Styron's novel *Sophie's Choice* was some twelve years in the works, if somewhat less in the writing, and is in every way as ambitious a novel as *The Confessions of Nat Turner*, although its rank in the Styron canon is still in question. Having dealt in earlier novels with suicide, physical agony, existential despair, and slavery, Styron chose the Holocaust as the logical next state of human misery suitable for artistic contemplation. For a long time, Styron had been moving his narrative personae closer toward the subjects of his novels, introducing clearly autobiographical narrators in *The Long March* and *Set This House on Fire*, and making *The Confessions of Nat Turner* an intensely personal first-person narrative.

For *Sophie's Choice*, Styron turned to the confessional form plied by novelists as various as Saul Bellow and Norman Mailer and poets such as Robert Lowell. The narrator of *Sophie's Choice*, a young southerner named Stingo, is, for all intents and purposes, indistinguishable from the young Styron. A young artist *manqué* in New York, Stingo meets and is fascinated by a beautiful survivor of a Nazi concentration camp, Sophie, who is permanently psychologically scarred by the horror she has undergone, the most ghastly aspect of which was being forced to decide which of her two children would live and which would die. Stingo is the ultimate naïf: sexually, emotionally, morally, and artistically immature. As he comes to know Sophie, he comes to know himself. Stingo is an artist in search of a subject, as Styron evidently felt that he himself had been. Styron's problems with finding subject matter commensurate with his talents as a technician have been pointed out by William Van O'Conner in "John Updike and William Styron: The Burden of Talent" (1964) and by other critics. Styron himself acknowledged his concern with finding a fit subject for his early fiction, but he also believed that a concern with pain had been central to his earlier work. In 1970, he said, "Consciousness of pain and suffering has informed my work. . . . I hope my present work will not be so preoccupied." At that time, he was working on his military novel "The Way of the Warrior," which he eventually abandoned to write a book that returned to the pain motif with a vengeance, along with the other leitmotif of *Sophie's Choice*, that of the artist's finding of himself.

The emotional pain of Peyton Loftis is alienation from family and love. Cass Kinsolving suffers from guilt brought on by self-hatred and contemplation of human suffering. Nat Turner's ultimate pain derives from his isolation from all humankind and God. Sophie and Stingo suffer the pain of guilt. Stingo, the apotheosis of Styron's autobiographical WASP characters, feels he has not "paid his dues," suffered as others have suffered, and he learns of Sophie's anguished life with a guilty voyeurism. Sophie's guilt has a specific origin in her hideous choice to doom one of her children. She also feels ashamed that in Auschwitz she somehow "suffered less" since she was the commandant's mistress and finally survived when others died. Constantly and compulsively her mind plays over the fates of those dead—her little girl, her tortured friends, and the gassed millions whom she never knew. Even memories of her murdered husband and of her father, both of whom she despised, bring her reproach and grief. The knowledge that she did what she had to gives no relief. She says, "I see that it was—beyond my control, but it is still so terrible to wake up these many mornings with the memory of that, having to live with it . . . it makes everything unbearable. Just unbearable." Soon, she will kill herself to stop the pain.

After Sophie's death, the shattered Stingo, who had just become her lover, walks on the beach trying to find some sort of personal resolution and acceptance of a world in which horror and anguish such as Sophie's exist. Her message, though, has been clear: There is no resolution. Madness and suffering of the magnitude represented by the Holocaust can be neither accepted nor understood. Sophie, like Herman Melville's Ishmael, realizes that "there is a wisdom that is woe, and there is a woe that is madness." Stingo has come to know it, too.

With the death of Sophie, Styron seems to have come full circle in his exploration of human suffering and his search for meaning in a flawed and painful world. Both Sophie and Peyton Loftis find death to be the only release from lives so agonizing and painful as to be unbearable. In both his first novel and this one, Styron leads the reader to the edge of the grave and points to it as the goal of life—"therefore it cannot be long before we lie down in darkness, and have our light in ashes." The crucial difference between *Sophie's Choice* and *Lie Down in Darkness*, however, is the character of Stingo, who like Ishmael escapes to tell the tale. The earlier novel leaves the reader in desolation, but the latter, through Stingo, holds forth the possibility of an alternative existence, one not horribly haunted by the knowledge of pain. Stingo's life is hardly one of euphoria, but it is a tenable existence compared to Sophie's untenable one. To some degree, Stingo has paid his dues through her; he has come to know pain and evil through her sacrifice, and therefore he is sadder and wiser, but not destroyed as she is. His survival counterpoints her destruction; the novel that Stingo will write grows out of her ashes and becomes her immortality.

Sophie's Choice is not a cheerful novel, or even an affirmative one, but it is not nihilistic. Perhaps Stingo's optimism at the close is unjustified. A number of critics feel that when Stingo walks on the beach after Sophie's death and finds the morning "excellent and fair," anticipating his own promising career, Styron is simply tacking on an upbeat ending hardly defensible in view of the horror explored by the novel. Similarly, Cass Kinsolving in *Set This House on Fire* never satisfies his thirst for metaphysical answers to terrible questions, but simply decides to stop thirsting and take up fishing. In each of Styron's novels, characters suffer, and some suffer unto death. These tragedies reveal an unjust world, not a nihilistic one—Styron's tragedies are moral pronouncements. As moral pronouncements, the novels point to the possibility of a better way.

John L. Cobbs
Updated by Roark Mulligan

Other major works

SHORT FICTION: *A Tidewater Morning: Three Tales from Youth*, 1993.
PLAY: *In the Clap Shack*, pr. 1972.
NONFICTION: *This Quiet Dust, and Other Writings*, 1982 (expanded, 1993); *Darkness Visible: A Memoir of Madness*, 1990.

Bibliography

Casciato, Arthur D., and James L. W. West III, eds. *Critical Essays on William Styron.* Boston: G. K. Hall, 1982. Collection of critical essays that cover all of Styron's major novels and include bibliographical references.

Coale, Samuel. *William Styron Revisited.* Boston: Twayne, 1991. A brief biography and an analysis of Styron's novels. Coale devotes a chapter to each major work and includes a selected bibliography.

Cologne-Brookes, Gavin. *The Novels of William Styron: From Harmony to History.* Baton Rouge: Louisiana State University Press, 1995. Study of the influence of the modernist movement on Styron, explores Styron's psychological themes, and analyzes his shifting patterns of discourse. Includes analysis of Styron's later work.

Hadaller, David. *Gynicide: Women in the Novels of William Styron.* Madison, N.J.: Fairleigh Dickinson University Press, 1996. Explores women in Styron's fiction, particularly the deaths of women and the meaning of these deaths. Hadaller argues that Styron's depictions force readers to question a society that victimizes women.

Morris, Robert K., and Irving Malin, eds. *The Achievement of William Styron.* Athens: University of Georgia Press, 1975. Provides essays by various critics on Styron's fiction up to *Sophie's Choice*. The essay by Morris and Malin on Styron's career as a visionary novelist is a good introduction to his work.

Vice, Sue. *Holocaust Fiction: From William Styron to Binyamin Wilkomirski*. New York: Routledge, 2000. Survey of fictional works about the Holocaust that helps to put Styron's work in historical perspective.

West, James L. W., III, ed. *Conversations with William Styron*. Jackson: University Press of Mississippi, 1985. Collected interviews with William Styron in which Styron attempts to "restore a little balance," giving his side to the many controversies that his books have caused.

_____. *William Styron: A Life*. New York: Random House, 1998. The first comprehensive biography of Styron, West's extraordinary work lucidly and cogently connects events in Styron's life to his fiction. This is an essential work for anyone who wishes to understand Styron and his writing.

Amy Tan

Born: Oakland, California; February 19, 1952

Principal long fiction • *The Joy Luck Club*, 1989; *The Kitchen God's Wife*, 1991; *The Hundred Secret Senses*, 1995; *The Bonesetter's Daughter*, 2001; *Saving Fish from Drowning*, 2005.

Other literary forms • Amy Tan is best known for her novels, but her work also includes short essays, short stories, and two children's books—*The Moon Lady* (1992) and *The Chinese Siamese Cat* (1994). In addition, Tan wrote the screenplay for the 1993 film version of *The Joy Luck Club*. Her first nonfiction work, *The Opposite of Fate: A Book of Musings* (2003), collects her casual writings that supplement her fiction and her life.

Achievements • Amy Tan is one of the best-known and most popular Asian American writers and, like Maxine Hong Kingston, is considered a guide to the landscape of the Asian American experience. Gracing the best-seller lists, Tan's novels have earned critical and popular acclaim, and *The Joy Luck Club* was made into a major motion picture in 1993 and was adapted for the stage in 1999. Tan won the Commonwealth Gold Award and the Bay Area Book Reviewers Award for *The Joy Luck Club*, which was also nominated for the National Book Award and the National Book Critics Circle Award.

Tan's novels contribute to the dialogue about the meanings of "Asian" and "American" by portraying the intercultural conflict threatening many Asian American immigrant families. Her strong storytelling ability ensures the accessibility of her fiction to general readers; moreover, her work appeals to feminist readers and critics because, as Sau-ling Cynthia Wong points out, Tan's novels belong to significant "discursive traditions" including "mainstream feminist writing; Asian American matrilineal literature; quasi ethnography about the Orient; Chinese American 'tour-guiding' works."

Biography • Amy Tan was born to Daisy and John Tan, both of whom had emigrated from China; they met and married in the United States. As a child, Tan was acutely conscious that she was different from her classmates. She remembers wearing a clothespin on her nose in an effort to reshape that appendage to look more Caucasian. Like most Asian American young people, Tan was American at school and Chinese at home. Although her mother spoke to her in Chinese, Tan answered in English. The tensions in her dual heritage eventually found their way into her novels in her portrayal of the generational conflicts in immigrant families.

At the age of fifteen, Tan lost both her father and her older brother: They died of brain tumors within months of each other. Her mother reacted by leaving California with the remaining children, moving first to the East Coast and then to Europe, where Tan finished high school in Switzerland.

Tan attended three colleges before earning her degree in English and linguistics from San Jose State University. Marrying Louis DeMattei, a tax lawyer, after graduation, Tan began work toward a doctorate in linguistics, but she abandoned her studies for a career before earning her degree. After years as a business writer, Tan realized that, despite a lucrative career, she was unsatisfied, and she decided to attempt a different kind of writing. When she was eight years old, she had won an essay contest, and she cherished dreams of someday writing fiction. Tan set out to fulfill those dreams. Joining a writer's group led by author Molly Giles, she commenced work on the short stories that became the nucleus of her first book.

Tan's first novel, *The Joy Luck Club*, published in 1989, was a critical and popular success, catapulting the author into the ranks of significant American novelists. *The Kitchen God's Wife* followed two years later, garnering high praise and another berth on the best-seller lists. In 1995, Tan published her third novel, *The Hundred Secret Senses*, an exploration of the nature of memory and love.

Analysis • Like the works of many late twentieth century writers, Amy Tan's books are difficult to classify into a single fictional genre. Although Tan's works are indisputably novels, readers and critics agree that her fiction fuses several narrative genres: memoir and autobiography, mythology and folktale, history and biography. Moreover, like Maxine Hong Kingston, Tan appropriates Chinese talk story—a combination of narrative genres from Chinese oral tradition expressed in a local vernacular—to give shape and a distinctive voice to her novels.

Tan's fictional landscape is both geographically vast and spatially confined. The American spaces embrace San Francisco and the Bay Area, while the Chinese locations include a large territory from Guilin to Shanghai and encompass time from feudal China to the twentieth century. Between her protagonists' ancestral homeland and their adopted country lies the Pacific Ocean, symbolically crossed by the woman and the swan in the tale that begins *The Joy Luck Club*. Nonetheless, the crucial events in Tan's novels are contained within definitive boundaries: a circumscribed Chinatown neighborhood, the tiny village of Changmian, one-room accommodations for Chinese pilots and their wives, a stuffy apartment crammed with elderly mah-jongg enthusiasts.

Enclosed by framing narratives set in the late twentieth century, the embedded stories in Tan's novels are set in earlier eras, transporting readers to nineteenth century rural China, war-ravaged Nanking during World War II, or cosmopolitan Shanghai between the wars. Juxtaposing events separated by decades, Tan parallels the dislocations experienced by emigrants from a familiar culture into an alien one with their daughters' painful journeys from cultural confusion to acceptance of their dual heritage.

Tan's protagonists, members of that diaspora community called Asian Americans, represent two groups: Chinese-born immigrants, imperfectly acculturated despite decades of life in America, and American-born women of Chinese ancestry, uncomfortably straddling the border between their ethnic heritage and the American milieu that is their home. Enmeshed by their shared histories in California's ethnic neighborhoods, the women in Tan's novels struggle to create personal identities that reflect their lives, needs, and desires.

Through her fiction, Tan examines identity—its construction, boundaries, and contexts. Indelibly branded by their visible ethnicity, Tan's characters daily negotiate the minefields of cultural disjunction and tensions between Chinese tradition and Americanization, family connections and individual desires. These tensions almost inevitably surface, causing intergenerational conflict and the disintegration of family relationships as members of the older generation look back to China while their daughters remain firmly connected to California.

The Joy Luck Club • *The Joy Luck Club* tells the stories of four mother-daughter pairs: Suyuan and Jing-mei Woo, An-Mei and Rose Hsu Jordan, Lindo and Waverly Jong, and Ying-ying and Lena St. Clair. Implicit in the generational conflicts that erupt between the women is the bicultural angst separating the Chinese-born mothers from their American-born, assimilated daughters. Initially unable to discover common ground, the two groups of women speak different languages, embrace different values, aspire to different ambitions, and lead divergent lives.

The social club of the title binds together the lives of these eight women. As the novel opens, Jing-mei Woo prepares to take her dead mother's place at the mah-jongg table that anchors the club's activities. During Jing-mei's first game, the older women beg her to go to China on her mother's behalf, and their pleas trigger in Jing-mei pain-

Robert Foothorap

ful memories of her Chinatown childhood. Jing-mei's first narrative introduces the other narrators, and except for Suyuan, whose story emerges through Jing-mei's, each woman tells her own story.

Representing the immigrant generation that fled China after World War II, the mothers have had difficult early lives: Suyuan Woo is driven to abandon twins to give them a chance to survive, An-Mei Hsu's mother commits suicide to force her husband to acknowledge An-Mei as his child; Lindo Jong endures an arranged marriage at the age of twelve to an even younger child; and Ying-ying St. Clair, deserted by her first husband, experiences a decade of poverty. In the United States, the mothers must negotiate the traumas of leaving a war-ravaged homeland, starting over in an alien country, and trying to learn a strange language. Through their vicissitudes, they cling to memories of China and to fading traces of their ancestral culture, and they eventually establish stable new lives for themselves.

In contrast with their mothers, the daughters have had good lives—with plenty to eat, comfortable homes, intact families, music lessons, and college educations. Nevertheless, the daughters are discontented and unhappy: Jing-mei is single and aimless, Rose is separated from her husband, Waverly is already divorced, and Lena has summoned up the courage to examine her dysfunctional marriage. Each daughter feels detached from herself, her family, and her community; none of them knows how to reconnect.

The novel traces the evolution of understanding between the mothers and daughters, who are, at the end, finally able to articulate the depth of their caring for each other. The novel concludes when Jing-mei travels to China to meet her two half sisters—the women who were the infants that Suyuan lost in wartime China.

The Kitchen God's Wife • *The Kitchen God's Wife* also explores dynamics of the mother-daughter relationship in the context of cultural and ethnic disjunctions, albeit in less detail than does *The Joy Luck Club*. Instead, *The Kitchen God's Wife* focuses on a woman's journey to wholeness after an eventful life that replicates the Chinese immigrant experience in microcosm. The novel's title refers to Winnie Louie's version of the story of the Kitchen God who achieves deity status when he proves to be capable of shame upon discovering that the wife he has mistreated still cares about his welfare. Unfortunately, according to Winnie, the Kitchen God's wife is denied membership in the Chinese pantheon of deities despite her fidelity.

The novel tells two stories: the sketchy framing narrative that involves the widening rift between Winnie and her daughter, Pearl; and the fully developed chronicle of Winnie's life in China. Through her story, Pearl contextualizes Winnie's reminiscences, describing a series of events and revelations that ultimately changes their relationship. Required by family obligations to attend the funeral of an ancient "aunt" and the engagement party of a "cousin," Pearl spends more time with Winnie than she has in many months, and the enforced companionship prompts the younger woman to examine the roots of their estrangement. Winnie, goaded to action by a letter from China that closes a painful chapter in her past, decides to tell Pearl about her life in China.

Save for the early chapters in which Pearl speaks, and the epilogue in which Winnie and Pearl deify the Kitchen God's wife as Lady Sorrowfree, the novel chronicles the eventful life of Jiang Weili—Winnie's Chinese name—as she negotiates the difficult journey from a privileged childhood through an abusive marriage and the tragedy of war, and ultimately to a secure life in the United States.

The daughter of a wealthy Shanghai merchant, Jiang Weili marries the dashing Wen Fu, only to discover after the wedding that he has misrepresented his family's wealth and status. Worse yet, he turns out to be an adulterer, abuser, and pathological liar. Forced to follow her pilot husband as he is posted to different cities during the war, Weili tries to be a good wife and mother, laboring to establish a home wherever they happen to be assigned. She must spend her dowry for family expenses when Wen Fu gambles away his pay or squanders it on a mistress. After silently enduring her miserable existence and the deaths of her two children, Winnie finally escapes to America and a new life with Jimmy Louie.

The Hundred Secret Senses • Unlike Tan's first two novels, which examine the dynamics of the mother-daughter dyad, *The Hundred Secret Senses* explores the psychological and emotional bonds between sisters. Nevertheless, the novel displays several characteristics common to Tan's fiction: conflict between generations in immigrant families, multiple points of view, a strong grounding in Chinese culture and history, and compelling narratives.

Although *The Hundred Secret Senses* is Olivia's story, Kwan is central to every narrative in the novel. One of Tan's most stunningly original creations, Kwan is an energetic woman who is Chinese at the core despite having adopted Western dress and American slang. Kwan claims to have *yin* eyes, which she describes as an ability to see and converse with the dead, whom she calls "*yin* people."

Central to the novel is the uncomfortable relationship between American-born

Olivia and her Chinese sister, Kwan, who arrived in San Francisco at the age of eighteen. Although sharing a father, the two women are markedly different: Olivia, whose mother is American, is completely Westernized; Kwan, born to a Chinese first wife, never completely assimilates, remaining predominantly Chinese. Embarrassed by Kwan's exuberant Chineseness, Olivia resists her sister's attempts to form a close relationship. She declines invitations, evades contact, and refuses all overtures of friendship. Despite Olivia's coolness, Kwan continues her friendly attempts to be a real sister to Olivia, whose unhappiness is palpable. Maneuvering Olivia and Olivia's estranged husband, Simon, into a trip to the hills beyond Guilin in China, Kwan engineers a situation that forces Olivia and Simon to reassess their relationship and take tentative steps toward reconciliation.

Paralleling Olivia's story and embedded in the novel are Kwan's narratives about a previous life when she was Nunumu, a Chinese servant to a group of missionaries. In that household, Nunumu was befriended by Nelly Banner, a young American woman whose passion for a deceitful adventurer imperils the group, and whose love for a half-breed leads to death for herself and Nunumu. The story of Nunumu and Nelly Banner is set against the backdrop of the nineteenth century Taiping Rebellion, led by a charismatic leader who claimed to be Jesus's younger brother.

As in her first two novels, Tan establishes clear parallels between past and present, between historical events and contemporary problems. Constantly relaying messages from her *yin* friends, who seem inordinately interested in Olivia's marital problems, Kwan brings Olivia to the brink of believing that she, Olivia, has somehow participated in Nunumu's life, has experienced fear of approaching rebel soldiers, has faced death on a rainy hillside. Whether Olivia truly once was Nelly Banner is never certain—what is certain at the end of the novel is Olivia's understanding of the unbreakable ties of love that exist between sisters, friends, and lovers.

The Bonesetter's Daughter • Tan's fourth novel focuses on ghostwriter Ruth Young, her present life with an almost invisible lover, and the ongoing struggle with her mercurial Chinese mother, LuLing. Fully professional as she rewrites her clients' books, Ruth is otherwise hesitant. After LuLing fries eggs with the shells on and prowls the neighborhood in her nightgown, she is diagnosed with Alzheimer's disease and cannot live alone safely. Reluctantly, Ruth moves in. LuLing, a fine calligrapher, presents her with a manuscript of her life in China, but Ruth resists reading it.

Narrated in the voice of LuLing, the manuscript reveals her story. Her nursemaid, Precious Auntie, was the daughter of a famous bonesetter, a healer who showed her a secret cave of "dragon bones" that, when powdered, would cure any pain or could be sold for profit. Liu Hu Sen, a gentle inkmaker from a neighboring village, sought the bonesetter's aid after an accident and was soon betrothed to Precious Auntie. Coffinmaker Chang, a fellow suitor, was rejected.

En route to Hu Sen's village, the wedding party was attacked by Chang, who coveted the valuable dowry of bones and left Precious Auntie's father and bridegroom dead. Because the Lius refused to believe that Chang had murdered their son, Precious Auntie, grief-stricken and already pregnant, attempted to commit suicide by drinking boiling ink. She survived, but her lower face was severely disfigured, and she could no longer speak. Protected by matriarch Great-Granny Liu, she gave birth to a daughter, LuLing, and was kept on as the baby's nursemaid. LuLing was not told that Precious Auntie was her real mother.

Eventually Chang, learning that LuLing knew the location of the secret cave, sought to gain control of it by arranging her marriage to his son. Precious Auntie was helpless to intervene; LuLing alone could read her messages and understand her gestures. After writing a letter to Chang's family, threatening to haunt them forever if the marriage took place, she killed herself to protect her daughter. Only then did LuLing learn the truth. She was sent to an orphanage, where she later met her first husband, a scientist excavating nearby caves for the bones of Peking Man. When Japan invaded China, she escaped to the United States.

As Ruth reads her mother's manuscript, she understands better the bonds that connect her to her mother and grandmother. Accepting her obligation and her love for her mother, she prepares to care for LuLing.

Tan uses silence as a metaphor for loss of power. Although Ruth provides an effective voice for her clients, she frequently loses her own. LuLing briefly loses her voice at the orphanage and later forgets words, even her family name. Most significant is Precious Auntie, who speaks only with hands, eyes, and chalkboard, yet in death bequeaths her strength to her daughter and granddaughter.

The excavation of bones, as scientists come to dig for Peking Man, provides another metaphor for uncovering the past, revealing its hidden truths of identity, parentage, and name. Ruth's discovery of her heritage brings her understanding and reconciliation, allowing her to become whole.

E. D. Huntley
Updated by Joanne McCarthy

Other major works

NONFICTION: "The Language of Discretion," 1990 (in *The State of the Language,* Christopher Ricks and Leonard Michaels, editors); *The Opposite of Fate: A Book of Musings,* 2003.

CHILDREN'S LITERATURE: *The Moon Lady,* 1992; *The Chinese Siamese Cat,* 1994.

Bibliography

Benanni, Ben, ed. *Paintbrush: A Journal of Poetry and Translation* 22 (Autumn, 1995). This is a special issue of the journal focusing on Tan and on *The Joy Luck Club* in particular. It includes articles on mothers and daughters, memory and forgetting.

Bloom, Harold, ed. *Amy Tan.* Philadelphia: Chelsea House, 2000. Bloom also provides an introduction to the installment in the Modern Critical Views series. Pulls together the comments of contemporary critics.

Cheung, King-Kok. *An Interethnic Companion to Asian American Literature.* New York: Cambridge University Press, 1997. An essay collection with a critical overview of Asian American literary studies. Most interesting to readers of Tan's novels are essays by Sau-ling Cynthia Wong, Shirley Geok-lin Lim, Jinqi Ling, and Donald Geollnicht.

Cooperman, Jeannette Batz. *The Broom Closet: Secret Meanings of Domesticity in Postfeminist Novels by Louise Erdrich, Mary Gordan, Toni Morrison, Marge Piercy, Jane Smiley, and Amy Tan.* New York: Peter Lang, 1999. A study of the role of traditionally feminine concerns, such as marriage and family, in the works of these postfeminist writers.

Gee, Alison Singh. "A Life on the Brink." *People Weekly* 55, no. 18 (May 7, 2001): 85-88. Review of Tan's work at the time she published *The Bonesetter's Daughter.*

Gray, Paul. "The Joys and Sorrows of Amy Tan." *Time* 157, no. 7 (February 19, 2001): 72-75. Another review of Tan's work at the time she published *The Bonesetter's Daughter.*

Ho, Wendy. *In Her Mother's House: The Politics of Asian American Mother-Daughter Writing.* Walnut Creek, Calif.: AltaMira Press, 1999. Includes two chapters dedicated specifically to Tan, "Losing Your Innocence But Not Your Hope: Amy Tan's Joy Luck Mothers and Coca-Cola Daughters," and "The Heart Never Travels: The Incorporation of Fathers in the Mother-Daughter Stories of Maxine Hong Kingston, Amy Tan, and Fae Myenne Ng."

Huh, Joonok. *Interconnected Mothers and Daughters in Amy Tan's 'The Joy Luck Club.'* Tucson, Ariz.: Southwest Institute for Research on Women, 1992. Examines the mother and adult-child relationship in Tan's novel. Includes a bibliography.

Huntley, E. D. *Amy Tan: A Critical Companion.* Westport, Conn.: Greenwood Press, 1998. Discusses Tan's biography and analyzes her novels in the context of Asian American literature. Analyzes major themes such as the crone figure, food, clothing, language, biculturalism, mothers and daughters. Includes useful bibliography.

Pearlman, Mickey, and Katherine Usher Henderson. "Amy Tan." *Inter/View: Talks with America's Writing Women.* Lexington: University Press of Kentucky, 1990. Provides biographical information on Tan, revealing the sources of some of the stories in *The Joy Luck Club.*

Snodgrass, Mary Ellen. *Amy Tan: A Literary Companion.* Jefferson, N.C.: McFarland, 2004. Replete with tools for further research, including study questions, an extensive bibliography, and a glossary of Chinese terms found in Tan's works, Snodgrass presents a readable, engaging introduction to both Tan's life and works.

Tan, Amy. "Amy Tan." Interview by Barbara Somogyi and David Stanton. *Poets and Writers* 19, no. 5 (September 1, 1991): 24-32. One of the best interviews with Tan. Tan speaks about her childhood and her early career as a business writer, her decision to write fiction, her success with *The Joy Luck Club*, and some of its autobiographical elements.

Paul Theroux

Born: Medford, Massachusetts; April 10, 1941

Principal long fiction • *Waldo*, 1967; *Fong and the Indians*, 1968; *Girls at Play*, 1969; *Murder in Mount Holly*, 1969; *Jungle Lovers*, 1971; *Saint Jack*, 1973; *The Black House*, 1974; *The Family Arsenal*, 1976; *Picture Palace*, 1978; *The Mosquito Coast*, 1981; *Half Moon Street: Two Short Novels*, 1984; *O-Zone*, 1986; *My Secret History*, 1989; *Chicago Loop*, 1990; *Millroy the Magician*, 1994; *My Other Life*, 1996; *On the Edge of the Great Rift: Three Novels of Africa*, 1996 (includes *Fong and the Indians*, *Girl at Play*, and *Jungle Lovers*); *Kowloon Tong*, 1997; *The Collected Short Novels*, 1999; *Hotel Honolulu*, 2001; *Blinding Light*, 2005.

Other literary forms • In addition to a steady stream of novels, Paul Theroux has published several collections of short stories, *Sinning with Annie, and Other Stories* (1972), *The Consul's File* (1977), *World's End* (1980), *The Collected Stories* (1997), and *The Stranger at the Palazzo d'Oro, and Other Stories* (2003); a volume of criticism, *V. S. Naipaul: An Introduction to His Work* (1972); and a memoir, *Sir Vidia's Shadow: A Friendship Across Five Continents* (1998). He is also well known for his travel books, *The Great Railway Bazaar: By Train Through Asia* (1975) and *The Old Patagonian Express: By Train Through the Americas* (1979), *Fresh-Air Fiend: Travel Writings, 1985-2000* (2000), *Sir Vidia's Shadow: A Friendship Across Five Continents* (2000), and *Dark Star Safari: Overland from Cairo to Cape Town* (2002). In addition, he has published collections of children's stories, *A Christmas Card* (1978) and *London Snow: A Christmas Story* (1979).

In addition to his books, Theroux has written numerous reviews and articles, many of them based on his perceptions of events in the non-Western world. These are to be found in newspapers and periodicals such as *The New York Times Magazine*, the *Sunday Times* (of London), *Harper's*, and *Encounter*.

Achievements • It is in the quirky nature of fame that Theroux, a prolific writer of novels, should be better known for his travel writing than for his fiction. *The Great Railway Bazaar* became a best-seller in 1975, gaining for Theroux both popular and commercial success. A second travel book, *The Old Patagonian Express*, published four years later, firmly established his popular reputation. Both offer the reader elegant and humane examples of a genre widely practiced between the world wars but not commonly seen today.

In the long run, however, Theroux's achievements will most likely rest upon his fiction. He has won a small share of awards for his work, including four Playboy Editorial Awards for fiction (1972, 1976, 1977, and 1979), the Literature Award from the American Academy of Arts and Letters (1977), and the Whitbread Prize for fiction (for *Picture Palace*, 1978). In 1982, he won the James Tait Black Memorial Prize and the *Yorkshire Post* Best Novel of the Year Award for *The Mosquito Coast*. In 1984, Theroux was inducted into the American Academy and Institute of Arts and Letters. *The Mosquito Coast* was released as a motion picture, starring Harrison Ford, in 1986; *Half Moon Street* was also turned into a film in 1986, starring Sigourney Weaver and Michael Caine.

Theroux writes in the best tradition of English literature, demonstrating a mastery of fictional conventions as well as a willingness to grapple with some of the thornier issues of modern life. Critics have compared him to, among others, Charles Dickens, Joseph Conrad, W. Somerset Maugham, Graham Greene, and Evelyn Waugh. Interested in neither the splashy innovations of a Donald Barthelme nor the lurid headline material of a Norman Mailer, Theroux is nevertheless a novelist to follow.

Biography • Paul Edward Theroux was born of French Canadian and Italian parentage in Medford, Massachusetts, in 1941, the third of the seven children of Albert and Anne Theroux. Literature and writing were important aspects of his early life. Albert Theroux, a leather salesman, read daily to the family from the classics and encouraged the publication of family newspapers. For his efforts, he was rewarded with two novelists: Paul, and his brother Alexander.

After conventional public schooling and a bachelor's degree in English from the University of Massachusetts, Theroux volunteered for the Peace Corps in 1963 to escape the draft. He taught English in Malawi for two years until he was expelled for his unwitting involvement in the convolutions of African politics. From Malawi, Theroux went to Makerere University in Kampala, Uganda, where he lectured on seventeenth century English literature and maintained a careful political stance during the beginnings of Idi Amin's rise to power. At Makerere, Theroux met V. S. Naipaul, who became for a time his literary mentor. Theroux left Uganda in 1968 after being trapped in a street riot and went to Singapore, where he spent the next three years lecturing at the university.

© 1996 Newsday

Throughout this period, Theroux was writing prodigiously, both fiction and reportage, which he published in a variety of journals, both African and European. In 1967, he married Anne Castle, then also a teacher, and fathered two sons, Louis and Marcel. In 1972, judging himself able to earn his living by his pen alone, Theroux gave up teaching and moved his family to London. After he and his wife divorced, he returned to the United States, making his home in Massachusetts.

The Roman Catholic background, the leftish political interests, the ten years in Africa and Asia, the friendship with V. S. Naipaul—these heterogeneous influences all left their mark on Theroux's fiction. At the same time, one notes how Theroux secularizes, liberalizes, and makes contemporary the Catholic ethic, turns the African experience into a metaphor for all social experience, and absorbs and makes his own the lessons of Naipaul.

Analysis • Paul Theroux approaches his major theme—the ethical behavior of people in society—by way of postcolonial Africa and Southeast Asia, in stories that explore cultural interaction and the meaning of civilization. The three early African novels, *Fong and the Indians, Girls at Play*, and *Jungle Lovers*, set the scene, as it were, and suggest the terms for nearly all of his later fiction. These African novels offer not only a fictional portrait of the undeveloped world struggling toward independence but also a metaphor for all modern society and social ethics. In the apparently simpler world of East Africa, where white expatriate confronts black African, where Chinese meets Indian meets German meets American meets Australian, Theroux explores the ways individuals interact to form a social unit and the results, often absurd, of attempts to impose foreign values and ideas of civilization upon the primitive life of the jungle.

Although the later novels leave behind the specifically African setting, they continue to explore the theme of civilization versus jungle, expanding in particular upon the moral and ethical implications of certain kinds of social behavior. *The Family Arsenal* and *Saint Jack* provide instructive examples. In the former, Valentine Hood, an American ex-diplomat from Vietnam living in London, is struck by the domesticity displayed by the members of the terrorist band with which he lives: It is like a family. From this insight develop both the central theme of that novel and its plot structure. In *Saint Jack*, Jack Flowers creates a secular religion out of "giving people what they want." In *The Black House* and *The Mosquito Coast*, Theroux separates his protagonists from society to explore the meaning of exile, foreignness, and individualism. However, underlying all of these fictions will be found the basic assumption that every human experience, from death to redemption, from fear to loneliness, from love to murder, must be understood in a social context.

Fong and the Indians • *Fong and the Indians*, the first of Theroux's African novels, is the witty tale of the business partnership between Sam Fong, a Chinese grocer, and Hassanali Fakhru, the Indian entrepreneur who rents him the store, supplies his goods, and, when business is poor, even becomes his customer. Fakhru dominates Fong's economic life, manipulating it for his own benefit by taking advantage of Fong's innocent incompetence as a businessman. However, as the plot unfolds, it becomes clear the the relationship between Fong and Fakhru is far from one-sided. Moreover, it also becomes clear that this relationship is representative of all social and economic relationships. Each individual in a society suffers limitations of understanding that arise both from his own prejudices and from his cultural heritage.

When two people meet to do business, they may well be speaking different languages, either literally or metaphorically. Misunderstandings are unavoidable, and the outcome of any action is unpredictable: Good intentions may or may not result in good consequences; the same is true of bad intentions. Chaos and absurdity reign when no one quite understands what anyone else is doing.

The plot of *Fong and the Indians* is an intricate comedy of errors involving Fong, the unwilling grocer; Fakhru, the capitalist swindler; and two CIA agents on a mission to convert suspected communists. The fiction works as both a satirical portrait of modern African society and an allegory in which the grocery business, the swindles, and the "good will" mission—artifices of civilization—are, in the context of African reality, revealed to be absurd. In *Fong and the Indians*, Theroux explores "civilization"; in later books, *Jungle Lovers, Girls at Play, The Black House,* and *The Mosquito Coast,* he explores the meaning of "Africa"—the reality of the jungle. At no time does Theroux become an apologist for the Third World, elevating primitive civilization over modern. Rather, he turns "jungle" into a metaphor for humanity's natural environment: The jungle is both dangerous and nurturing; it demands that its inhabitants concentrate upon basic human needs. Although the metaphor is most easily understood when Theroux sets his story in the literal jungle of Africa or Central America, there is "jungle" too in South London, in an English village, even in Florida.

In *Fong and the Indians*, Fakhru swindles Sam Fong by convincing him that canned milk represents a victory of civilization. In Africa, however, canned milk makes no sense. Africans do not need it; Europeans prefer the fresh milk from Nairobi. Fong's only hope of becoming rich rests upon the wild improbability that the milk train will one day be wrecked. Aware of the absurdity, Fong accepts both the hope and the improbability of its fulfillment. Fong triumphs because he learns to love what he does not understand. He has the patience to submit, to accommodate his life to the requirements of survival. His change of diet, from the traditional Chinese cuisine he has maintained for all his thirty-seven years in Africa to a free, native one based on bananas and fried locusts, is at once a measure of his economic decline and an assurance of his ultimate triumph.

Saint Jack • Theroux's ethic, then, appears to be based upon the virtue of inaction. Because human understanding is limited, all events appear ambiguous. Even innocently motivated attempts to improve the lot of humanity may prove unexpectedly destructive, such as Marais's attempt to bring revolutionary ideals to Malawi in *Jungle Lovers,* Valentine Hood's murder to rid the world of Ron Weech in *The Family Arsenal,* or even Maud Coffin Pratt's photographs of the pig feast and of her brother and sister in the mill in *Picture Palace.* Because all events are ambiguous, it is impossible to predict which actions will prove evil and which actions will prove good. Therefore, the only possible moral strategy is to take no action at all, to be patient and accommodate oneself to the unknowable mystery of the jungle.

Inaction, however, should not be confused with selfish laziness; rather it is an active, morally motivated inaction akin to the traditional Christian virtue of patience. Patience redeems the absurdity of the modern world, protecting humankind from despair and leading ultimately to a triumph of innocence and virtue that will in turn redeem society. This is the lesson of *Saint Jack.*

A middle-aged, balding, American expatriate, full of muddle, fear, and loneliness, Jack Flowers jumps ship in Singapore. A stranger and a misfit, Jack sees no hope of rescue; he does not believe in miracles. He is a modern man making a realistic appraisal of his chances in an unfriendly and dangerous world. However, Jack wrests from this vision of despair an ad-lib ethic based upon fulfilling the desires of others. He becomes what others would have him be. Condemning no one, pardoning all, Jack participates in each person's unique fantasy. In the public world, he is called a pimp—he may even be a spy—but in his own private world, Jack is a saint: thoroughly reliable and incapable of cultural misunderstanding. He gives to each what everyone needs—pleasure, security, and forgiveness—and stands ready with whatever is needed to meet even an unexpected desire—be it pornographic pictures, the kind attentions of a good girl, or a game of squash. Jack shapes his own needs to match his companion's: He is the perfect friend and protector.

Jack's tattooed arms, emblazoned with Chinese obscenities and curses disguised as flowers, symbolize the way he eases the pain of human loneliness and fear by providing an illusion of hope and friendship and the reality of a temporary pleasure taken in safety. Pity, compassion, and a stubbornly innocent vision of human needs save Jack himself from doing evil and redeem the actions of all those he takes care of, even General Maddox himself.

The terms of this novel are coyly religious—Saint Jack, the manager of Paradise Gardens—but God is not really present in Singapore. What might in a Christian fiction be termed *grace* is here good luck, and even Jack's redeeming power itself results, in the end, from his own fantasy. The effect is, on one hand, tongue-in-cheek, and on the other, quite serious. Theroux appears to be walking the delicate line between a modern recognition that, in this absurd world, good and evil are meaningless categories and a commonsense realization that people need moral categories and at least an illusion of meaning in order to survive relatively sane.

The Family Arsenal • The search for meaning and moral categories provides both the theme and the structure of *The Family Arsenal*. When the story opens, Valentine Hood has come to live with a group of unrelated people in South London. Their domesticity makes them a parody of the typical middle-class family: Mayo, the mother, a thief; Valentine, the father, a murderer; and Murf and Brodie, the teenage children, terrorist bombers. Early in the novel, many odd characters are introduced: Ralph Gawber, an accountant with a fondness for puzzles and a doomsday foreboding; Araba Nightwing, a radical woman actor who plays Peter Pan; Ron Weech, the hoodlum whom Hood chases and murders; Lorna Weech, his wife; Rutter, a gunrunner; and Lady Arrow. Initially, the relationships among these characters appear obscure if not irrelevant; yet as the plot develops, groupings take shape until the reader discovers, with Valentine Hood, that all are inextricably bound together by all sorts of dirty secrets, making them, in the words of one character, like one big family no one can quit.

The puzzlelike structure of this novel parodies the conventional thriller plot. Its purpose is, however, not action-packed adventure but rather the slow revelation that, as Hood has suspected all along, inaction is best because all events (be they murder, theft, or bombing) are morally ambiguous. Thus, Hood changes from social avenger to listener. He develops an innocent vision of pity and love akin to Jack Flowers's that not only reveals the human bonds among all members and classes of society but also redeems his own guilt and saves at least some from the dangers and death that threaten them. By the end of the story, all is discovered and characters are regrouped into more pleasing families based on love rather than convenience.

Paralleling the revelation of relationships in the plot of *The Family Arsenal* is

Hood's changing perception of the artistic organization of the stolen Van der Weyden that hangs in Mayo's closet. Mayo stole the painting believing that its theft would signal the beginning of social revolution. It does not: The world cares little about stolen artworks except as an interesting excuse for a headline. Yet, in an unexpected and very personal way, the painting does, in the end, play a revolutionary role in the story: It becomes the symbolic focus for the way art can organize seemingly disparate shapes and colors into a single beautiful whole. The Van der Weyden, like the tattoos on Jack's arms, suggests the resemblance between the personal vision of innocence that can redeem through pity and love and the vision of the artist that can change brutal reality into beauty.

Picture Palace • The most extensive development of this theme occurs in *Picture Palace*, which becomes less a song of triumph for the artist's vision than a warning of the danger that arises when that vision becomes separated (as it necessarily must) from its real social context. Civilization versus the jungle, art versus reality—in Theroux's fiction these themes become almost versions of each other. The ethical effects of efforts by either art or civilization to improve human society are always unclear, dependent as much upon luck as fantasy. Instinctively, Maud Coffin Pratt seems to realize this tenet and locks away her photograph of Phoebe and Orlando in an incestuous embrace: To her, the picture represented love and innocent fulfillment, but when her brother and sister find it, they see only their own guilt and death. Unlike Jack Flowers (who can grab back his photographs of General Maddox) or Valentine Hood (whose revelations of family secrets save them in the end), Maud's personal vision of innocence redeems no one; indeed, it backfires completely, and she is left alone at the end of her life, famous but anonymous.

The Mosquito Coast • In *The Mosquito Coast*, Theroux returns to the jungle milieu to explore further the consequences of extreme individualism, the separation of self from society and environment. With his perpetual motion ice machine, Allie Fox expends a mad energy trying to produce icebergs in order to impress the Indians with the superiority of his civilized genius. Needless to say, whether he floats the ice downstream to a village or carries it by sledge across the mountains, the ice melts: The impressiveness of civilization disappears in the heat of the sun. Relying completely upon his own creativity, Fox, the Yankee inventor, may be seen as a type of the artist. His attempt to impose his personal vision of utopia upon the brutal reality of the jungle fails utterly; his story reads as a warning of the danger of art without social context.

Like Sam Fong's canned milk in *Fong and the Indians*, Fox's ice machine in *The Mosquito Coast* represents an absurd attempt to civilize the jungle; yet Fong is rewarded with riches (the milk train does wreck), while Fox dies mad and beaten on the beach of Central America. Both may be seen as emblems of the modern world, alone in a strange land, possessing nothing, trying to shape a life out of events that are mysterious, ambiguous, possibly dangerous, and probably absurd. Their differing responses to the jungle environment determine their different ends and provide the reader with the key to Theroux's view of social ethics.

Allie Fox rejects patience and accommodation; he rejects the mystery and the ambiguity of the jungle. He will build a bugless outpost of civilization; he would rather starve than eat a banana. In Theroux's world, it is poetic justice that Fox should misinterpret events and bring about the ruin of all that he has built. With true tragic irony, Fox learns from his failure not the value of accommodation, but only the need for an increased purity, an increased separation from the jungle, a separation doomed to failure. If Fong is the comic face of humanity, then Fox must be the tragic face.

O-Zone • With *O-Zone*, Theroux fashions a future in which major American cities are sealed off from one another and aliens stalk the now-deserted outside. Despite Theroux's descriptive skills, however, critics disliked *O-Zone*—mainly because it had very little plot, which they believed had been sacrificed for Theroux's love of narrative (turned to better use in his travel writing).

My Secret History • About *My Secret History*, on the other hand, critics complained because the narrative takes the first third of the book to really begin. A long novel that is really six novellas grouped together, it follows a young man from Massachusetts who moves to Africa and, from there, to England. Andrew Parent (who changes his first name to "Andre" while in college) starts out as an altar boy in Boston, becoming first a Peace Corps volunteer in one African country, then a teacher in another African country, before finally deciding to become a writer, ultimately moving to London.

Ultimately, Andre becomes an international womanizer, as well as a successful writer, and the last chapter/novella concentrates on his facing the consequences of what he has done to his life. Theroux's cosmopolitan experiences are what fuel his characters, and that he draws from his own life is only natural for a writer. Some critics have believed that his work is too self-referential—that it is thinly disguised autobiography. Pointing to his mentor V. S. Naipaul's 1987 autobiographical novel *The Enigma of Arrival*, they have wondered whether *My Secret History* is a midlife crisis roman à clef.

Theroux's work, however, cannot be so easily categorized or dismissed. The progression of Theroux's novels demonstrates a marked coherence of interest and an increasing complexity of thematic and structural development. Although Theroux draws freely from the modern storehouse of pornography, violence, and antiheroism, he displays at the same time a real if not profound interest in some of the classic themes of Western literature—the source of good and evil, the use of pity and love in society, art, and reality. Technically, his work shows a similar melding of popular fiction (the gothic horror story, the thriller) with the structure and conventions of the classic novelists.

My Other Life • Just as he resists any preconceived notions of a foreign culture he is about to enter, Theroux expects the same of readers who immerse themselves in his writings. "My secret is safe," he states in his introduction to *The Collected Stories*. The secret is his identity as a writer. To assign him to a category is to overlook the sense of separation that drives him in all directions in life. He is the consummate explorer who not only delights in discovery but also observes and records in imaginative detail. However, as Theroux asks readers not to label him, he also reminds them that "My stories are the rest of me," and "I inhabit every sentence I write," statements that could be directed to his novel *My Other Life*. Written as a companion piece to *My Secret History*, the novel reflects what the author considers his "need to invent." In this case it is an "imaginary memoir" designed to portray his life as a series of short stories, a device that led one critic to refer to the work as another example of a Theroux novel being better for its parts than its whole.

Theroux's later novels • The "other life" is a common theme throughout Theroux's works. He utilizes it to reveal the darker side of human nature, as exemplified in *Chi-*

cago Loop. In *Kowloon Tong* Theroux resurrects the sense of separation and belonging that permeates earlier works such as *The Mosquito Coast.* He also returns to the Far East for his setting, specifically Hong Kong at the time Great Britain's rule over the colony was coming to a close. The central figure, Neville "Bunt" Mullard, symbolizes the internal conflicts and contradictions that invariably arise between colonists and the colonized. Among the latter is Mr. Hung, a mysterious Chinese figure whose efforts to take over Mullard's business expose the less appealing aspects of the two competing cultures.

Linda Howe
Updated by William Hoffman

Other major works

SHORT FICTION: *Sinning with Annie, and Other Stories,* 1972; *The Consul's File,* 1977; *World's End,* 1980; *The London Embassy,* 1982; *The Collected Stories,* 1997; *The Stranger at the Palazzo d'Oro, and Other Stories,* 2003.

PLAY: *The Autumn Dog,* pr. 1981.

SCREENPLAY: *Saint Jack,* 1979 (with Peter Bogdanovich and Howard Sackler).

NONFICTION: *V. S. Naipaul: An Introduction to His Work,* 1972; *The Great Railway Bazaar: By Train Through Asia,* 1975; *The Old Patagonian Express: By Train Through the Americas,* 1979; *Sailing Through China,* 1983; *The Kingdom by the Sea: A Journey Around Great Britain,* 1983; *Patagonia Revisited,* 1985 (with Bruce Chatwin); *Sunrise with Seamonsters: Travels and Discoveries, 1964-1984,* 1985; *The Imperial Way,* 1985 (with Steve McCurry); *Riding the Iron Rooster: By Train Through China,* 1988; *To the Ends of the Earth: The Selected Travels of Paul Theroux,* 1990; *The Happy Isles of Oceania: Paddling the Pacific,* 1992; *Travelling the World: The Illustrated Travels of Paul Theroux,* 1992; *The Pillars of Hercules: A Grand Tour of the Mediterranean,* 1995; *Fresh-Air Fiend: Travel Writings, 1985-2000,* 2000; *Sir Vidia's Shadow: A Friendship Across Five Continents,* 2000; *Nurse Wolf and Dr. Sacks,* 2001; *Dark Star Safari: Overland from Cairo to Cape Town,* 2002.

CHILDREN'S LITERATURE: *A Christmas Card,* 1978; *London Snow: A Christmas Story,* 1979.

Bibliography

Barth, Ilene. "A Rake's Progress on Four Continents." *Newsday* June 1, 1989. This review of *My Secret History* gives a detailed plot summary of this lengthy novel. Barth compares it to Theroux's "prickly travelogues," noting the similarities between his fiction and his life.

Baumgold, Julie. "Fellow Traveler." *Esquire* 126 (September, 1996): 184. This informal conversation with Theroux provides some insight into the author's method of blending fact and fiction as part of his creative process.

Beecroft, Simon. "*Sir Vidia's Shadow:* V. S. Naipaul, the Writer, and *The Enigma of Arrival.*" *Journal of Commonwealth Literature* 35, no. 1 (2000): 71-85. Presents a structural analysis of Theroux's book on the breakdown of his long friendship with Naipaul, comparing it with Naipaul's own book *The Enigma of Arrival.*

Bell, Robert F. "Metamorphoses and Missing Halves: Allusions in Paul Theroux's *Picture Palace.*" *Critique: Studies in Modern Fiction* 22, no. 3 (1981): 17-30. Discusses concepts of the interchangeability of identities, the double image, and the gap existing between art and life.

Burns, Jim. "The Travels of Theroux: Seventeen Books Pay for a Lot of Train

Tickets." *Herald Examiner* (Los Angeles), May, 1988. This interview with Theroux provides a good sketch of what motivates him to write, to travel, and to write about traveling. Some biographical information is also included.

Coale, Samuel. *Paul Theroux*. Boston: Twayne, 1987. Part of Twayne's United States Authors series, this book provides a comprehensive look at Theroux's work as well as providing a chronology of events in the author's life. Includes references for each chapter and a bibliography of both primary and secondary sources and an index.

Glaser, E. "The Self-Reflexive Traveler: Paul Theroux on the Art of Travel and Travel Writing." *Centennial Review* 33 (Summer, 1989): 193-206. This article provides more insight into what motivates Theroux's writing and traveling. This penetrating profile and interview of Theroux is invaluable in the light of the scarcity of book-length works about him; includes some references.

Kerr, Douglas. "A Passage to *Kowloon Tong*: Paul Theroux and Hong Kong, 1997." *Journal of Commonwealth Literature* 34, no. 2 (1999): 75-84. Discusses Theroux's representation in his novel of the transfer of power over Hong Kong from Britain to China, and the response to the novel in Hong Kong and China.

O'Connor, Teresa F. "Jean Rhys, Paul Theroux, and the Imperial Road." *Twentieth Century Literature* 38 (Winter, 1992): 404-414. Considers the possible influence of Rhys's unpublished manuscript "Imperial Road" on Theroux's work.

Mark Twain

Born: Florida, Missouri; November 30, 1835
Died: Redding, Connecticut; April 21, 1910

Principal long fiction • *The Gilded Age*, 1873 (with Charles Dudley Warner); *The Adventures of Tom Sawyer*, 1876; *The Prince and the Pauper*, 1881; *Adventures of Huckleberry Finn*, 1884; *A Connecticut Yankee in King Arthur's Court*, 1889; *The American Claimant*, 1892; *Pudd'nhead Wilson*, 1894; *Tom Sawyer Abroad*, 1894; *Personal Recollections of Joan of Arc*, 1896; *Tom Sawyer, Detective*, 1896; *A Double-Barrelled Detective Story*, 1902; *Extracts from Adam's Diary*, 1904; *A Horse's Tale*, 1906; *Eve's Diary, Translated from the Original Ms*, 1906; *Extract from Captain Stormfield's Visit to Heaven*, 1909; *Report from Paradise*, 1952 (Dixon Wecter, editor); *Simon Wheeler, Detective*, 1963; *Mark Twain's Mysterious Stranger Manuscripts*, 1969 (William M. Gibson, editor).

Other literary forms • In addition to his novels, Mark Twain wrote a great deal of short fiction, which can be divided, although often only very arbitrarily, into short stories, tales, and humorous sketches. One of the best examples of his short stories is "The Man That Corrupted Hadleyburg," and one of the best examples of his humorous sketches is the jumping frog story. Somewhere between the story and the sketch are tales such as "Captain Stormfield's Visit to Heaven." Twain also wrote speeches and essays, both humorous and critical. Representative of his best satiric essays, which range from the very funny to the very sober, are "Fenimore Cooper's Literary Offenses" and "To the Person Sitting in Darkness." The first of these is a hilarious broadside against James Fenimore Cooper's style and invention in which Twain is obviously enjoying himself while at the same time continuing his ongoing war against the romanticizing of the past. "To the Person Sitting in Darkness," considered by some to be his finest piece of invective, is his attack upon what he saw as the exploitation of the Philippines following the Spanish-American War by, in his words, "The Blessings-of-Civilization Trust." Early in his career, he wrote the travel sketches and impressions, *The Innocents Abroad* (1869), *Roughing It* (1872), and *A Tramp Abroad* (1880), and later, *Following the Equator* (1897). Two of his most important books are autobiographical, *Life on the Mississippi* (1883) and *Mark Twain's Autobiography*, published after his death in various editions in 1924.

Achievements • The coincidental appearance of Halley's comet in the years of Twain's birth and death, 1835 and 1910, has been much remarked. A historical event, however, in contrast to the cosmic one, occurring very near the midpoint of his life, provides a better symbol for his career and his achievement than does the mysterious, fiery comet. In 1869, at Promontory Point, Utah, a golden spike was driven to complete the first North American transcontinental railroad. The subsequent settling of the great midwestern center of the continent and the resulting transformation of a frontier society into a civilized one, a process people thought would take hundreds of years, was to be effected in several decades. Twain's life spanned the two Americas, the frontier America that produced so much of the national mythology and the emerging urban, industrial giant of the twentieth century. At the heart of Twain's

Library of Congress

achievement is his creation of Tom Sawyer and Huck Finn, who embody that mythic America, midway between the wilderness and the modern super-state.

Tom and Huck, two of the nation's most enduring characters, give particular focus to Twain's turbulent, sprawling, complex career as journalist, humorist, entrepreneur, and novelist. The focus is dramatic because the two characters have made their way into the popular imagination with the abiding vitality of legend or folklore. They have been kept before generations of Americans in motion pictures, television, cartoons, and other popular art forms as well as in their original form in the novels. The focus is also symbolic because of the fundamental dualism that the two characters can be seen to represent on the personal, the literary, and the cultural planes.

On the personal plane, Tom and Huck represent aspirations so fundamental to Twain's life as to make them seem rather the two halves of his psyche. Like good and bad angels, they have been taken to represent the contending desires in his life: a strong desire for the security and status of material success on the one hand, set against the deeply ingrained desire for freedom from conventional social and moral restraints on the other. It has been conjectured that steamboat piloting was perhaps the most satisfying of Twain's occupations because it offered him high degrees of both respectability and freedom. Although the character of Tom, the symbol of perennial boyhood, can be easily overburdened by this perspective, there is in him the clear outline of the successful, settled, influential man-of-affairs-to-be. If Tom had grown up, he—like Twain himself—might well have made and lost a fortune in the publishing business and through investments in the Paige typesetter. He almost certainly would have been a successful professional or businessman. He would most likely have traveled abroad and would have been eager to associate with nobility at every opportunity. It is relatively easy to imagine Tom growing up. It is instructive to realize that it is almost impossible to imagine Huck's doing so.

On the literary plane, the two may also be seen as representing contending forces, those of the two principal literary schools of the period, the Romantic and the realistic. Surely, Twain's pervasive attacks upon Romantic literature are somewhat compulsive, reminiscent of Nathaniel Hawthorne's preoccupation with the Puritans. Both protest too much. Twain is one of America's foremost Romantics, even if he did see himself as a realist, and even if he did engage much of his time in puncturing the sentimental balloons of the disciples of Sir Walter Scott, Cooper, and the graveyard poets. He was both Romantic and realist, and Tom and Huck emerge almost allegorically as symbols of the two major literary schools of the late nineteenth century.

Tom as the embodiment of socially conforming respectability and as a disciple of Romantic literature contrasts illustratively with Huck as the embodiment of the naturally free spirit, who is "realistic" in part because of his adolescent honesty about such things as art, royalty, and the efficacy of prayer. It is the symbolic dualism on the historical plane, however, that brings into sharpest focus the nature of Twain's central and most enduring achievement. On the historical plane, his two central characters reflect most clearly Twain's principal legacy to posterity: the embodiment in fiction of that moment in time, a moment both real and imaginary, given some historical particularity by the driving of the golden spike at Promontory Point in 1869, when America was poised between the wilderness and the modern, technological state. In this context, Tom represents the settlements that were to become the towns and cities of the new century, and Huck represents the human spirit, freer, at least in the imagination, in the wilderness out of which the settlements were springing. At the end of *Adventures of Huckleberry Finn*, Twain sends Huck on that impossible mission that has been central to the American experience for centuries, when he has him decide to "light out for the territory" before Aunt Sally can "adopt" and "civilize" him.

Twain the humorist and satirist, Twain the silver-mining, typesetting entrepreneur, Twain the journalist, the family man, the anguished, skeptical seeker after religious faith—all must be taken into consideration in accounts of the nature of his achievements. Without Tom Sawyer and Huck Finn, he would have made his mark as a man of his time, a man of various and rich talents. Most likely, his reputation would rest today largely upon his talents as a humorist and satirist, and that reputation still figures largely in assessment of his overall achievement. With Tom and Huck, however, his achievement is given the depth and dramatic focus of a central contribution to the national mythology. Huck's "voice" is frequently compared to the voice of Walt Whitman's "Song of Myself" (1855). Such comparisons rest in part upon rhetorical similarities between the two voices, similarities in what has been called the "vernacular mode." More significantly, they derive from the similarities of the achievements of the poet and the novelist in the establishing of historically and culturally distinctive American "voices" in poetry and fiction. Tom Sawyer and Huck Finn loom large on the nineteenth century literary horizon. They stand, along with Cooper's Natty Bumppo and Chingachgook, Hawthorne's Hester Prynne and Arthur Dimmesdale, and Whitman's persona in "Song of Myself," as the principal characters of the emerging national literature. Twain's contribution to that body of literature is at the deepest center of his achievement as a major American writer.

Biography • Mark Twain was born Samuel Langhorne Clemens in Florida, Missouri, in 1835. He first used the pen name "Mark Twain," taken from the leadsman's cry for two fathoms of water, in 1862.

Twain's father was a Virginia lawyer, and the family was of poor but respectable southern stock. In 1839, the family moved to Hannibal, Missouri, the Mississippi River town that provided the source material and background of some of Twain's best-known fiction. After his father died in 1847, Twain left school to become an apprentice in the printing shop of his brother Orion. From 1853 to 1856, Twain worked as a journeyman printer in St. Louis, New York, Philadelphia, Keokuk, and Cincinnati. Between 1857 and 1860, he acquired much of his knowledge of the Mississippi River as a pilot, beginning that short though richly productive career under the tutelage of a senior pilot, Horace Bixby. He was a Missouri state militia volunteer for several weeks after the Civil War began. In 1861, he left Missouri for the West with his brother Orion, who had been appointed secretary of the new Nevada Territory. In Nevada, Twain drifted into prospecting and journalism, beginning his career as a reporter with the *Virginia City Territorial Enterprise* and continuing it with the San Francisco *Morning Call.*

Twain's literary career and the beginning of his fame might be said to have begun in 1865 with the publication in the New York *Saturday Press* of "Jim Smiley and His Jumping Frog" (later known as "The Celebrated Jumping Frog of Calaveras County"). As a journalist, he went to the Sandwich Islands in 1866 and to Europe and the Holy Land in 1867. The latter journey provided him with the experiences that he shaped into his first book, *The Innocents Abroad. Roughing It*, his narrative of prospectors and speculators striving to get rich on the frontier, appeared in 1872, and his first novel-length fiction, written with Charles Dudley Warner, *The Gilded Age*, came in 1873.

In 1870, Twain married Olivia Langdon. After beginning their married life in Buffalo, New York, they resettled in Hartford, Connecticut, in 1871. Their infant son, Langdon, died in 1872, the year Susy, their first daughter, was born. Two more daughters, Clara and Jean, were born in 1874 and 1880. Twain's most productive years as a novelist came during this middle period when his daughters were young and he was prospering. *The Adventures of Tom Sawyer, The Prince and the Pauper, Adventures of Huckleberry Finn,* and *A Connecticut Yankee in King Arthur's Court*, were all written during this highly productive period.

By 1890, Twain's financial fortunes were crumbling, mostly owing to bad investment in his own publishing firm and in the Paige typesetter. In 1891, he and his wife closed their Hartford mansion and went to Europe to economize. In 1896, after Twain completed a round-the-world lecture tour, his daughter Susy died, and his wife, Livy, shortly afterward suffered a nervous collapse from which she never recovered. Twain blamed himself for bringing on his beloved family the circumstances that led to both tragedies. His abiding skepticism about human nature deepened to cynicism and found expression in those dark stories of his last years, such as "The Man That Corrupted Hadleyburg," his unfinished "Mysterious Stranger" stories, and his Socratic dialogue, *What Is Man?* In 1910, he died at the age of seventy-four in Redding, Connecticut.

Analysis • It is instructive to note that the most pervasive structural characteristic of Mark Twain's work, of his nonfiction as well as his fiction, is dualistic. That observation is not worth much without detailed application to specific aspects of particular works, but even before turning to particulars, it is useful to consider how many "pairs" of contending, conflicting, complementary, or contrasting characters, situations, states of being, ideas, and values run through Twain's work. One thinks immediately of Tom and Huck, of Huck and Jim, of Huck and Pap, of the Widow Douglas and Miss Watson, of the prince and the pauper, of the two sets of twins in *Pudd'nhead Wilson*, and of Mark Twain and Samuel Clemens. One also thinks of boys testing themselves against adults, of youth and adulthood, of the free life on the river contrasted with the settled life of the river towns, of the wilderness and civilization, of the promises of industrial progress against the backdrop of the humbler, traditional rural setting, of Eden and everything east of Eden, and, finally, of good and evil.

The tonal quality of Twain's works is also dualistic. The jumping frog story is almost pure fun. The "Mysterious Stranger" stories, one of which was first published in bowdlerized form after Twain's death, are almost pure gloom. Most of Twain's fiction comes between the two, both chronologically and thematically. Except for *The Gilded Age*, which he wrote with Charles Dudley Warner, the novels, from *The Adven-*

tures of Tom Sawyer to the final two, *Pudd'nhead Wilson* and *Personal Recollections of Joan of Arc*, fall within the thematic and tonal extremes established by the short fiction. That is, Tom's adventures take place in the hallowed light of innocence and virtue beyond the reach of any truly effective evil forces, while Roxy's adventures in *Pudd'nhead Wilson* are of almost unrelieved gloom. *Adventures of Huckleberry Finn* is midway between the extremes, with its blending of the light and affirmation that shine so brightly in Twain's childhood idyll with the darkened vision of the later years.

The Adventures of Tom Sawyer • Nearly everyone agrees that *The Adventures of Tom Sawyer*, Twain's second novel, is an American classic, and many also agree that there is no accounting for its success. It is at the same time a novel of the utmost simplicity and of deep complexity. The novel is a marvelous boy's adventure story, a fact given perspective by Twain's observation that "it will be read only by adults." That is, the essence of childhood can be savored only after the fact, only after one has passed through it and can look back upon it. Popularizations of Tom's adventures are produced for children, but the continuing vitality of the novel depends upon the adult sensibility and its capacity and need for nostalgic recollection. Twain plays on all the strings of that sensibility as he guides the reader through Tom's encounters with the adult world, represented by Aunt Polly and Judge Thatcher, through Tom's romance with Becky, and finally to the adventurous triumph over evil in the person of Injun Joe.

Aunt Polly is the perfect adult foil for a perfect boyhood. Not only does she provide the emotional security that comes from being loved in one's place, but she also serves as an adult Tom can challenge through his wits, thereby deepening his self-confidence about his place in the adult world. The fence whitewashing episode is surely one of the best known in American literature. In it, Tom not only outwits his friends, whom he persuades to whitewash the fence for him, but also successfully challenges the adult world that, through Aunt Polly, assigned the "boy's chore" to him in the first place. The episode also provides Twain an opportunity to exercise his irony, which, in contrast to much that was to come in the later fiction, is serenely gentle here. Judge Thatcher represents the secure, if somewhat pompous, authority of the adult world beyond the domestic circle. The much desired recognition of that authority is achieved with decisive pomp when the Judge makes the treasure found in the cave legally Tom's and Huck's.

The romance with Becky is almost pure idyll, although the young lovers' descent into the cave almost inevitably raises speculations about deeper implications. Although Injun Joe as evil incarnate is believable enough to raise the hair along the back of the necks of adults as well as children, especially when the last candle burns out in the cave, there is never any doubt that Tom and Becky will be saved, that good will triumph—never any doubt, that is, for the adult sensibility, secure beyond the trials and tribulations of adolescent infatuation and terror.

The book as childhood idyll is really a simple matter, but that does not diminish the significance of that dimension of the work. Rather, it affirms an understanding of the book's success on that level. There is more to be considered, however, especially in terms of the companion piece to come, *Adventures of Huckleberry Finn*. The poignance of *The Adventures of Tom Sawyer* is attributable in part to the fact that it is an imaginative reconstruction of youthful experience from the perspective of early middle age. The actual historical frame of the re-creation adds its own deeply poignant dimension to the book. The American national experience was clearly in the transitional state between frontier and modern society when the novel was published in 1876. Twain's idyll of boyhood is set in a time and place in history calculated to deepen the significance of the adult's backward recollection of a time of innocence and joy. The American wilderness was never Eden, but that image has haunted the American imagination from at least the time of James Fenimore Cooper's creation of his frontiersman Natty Bumppo down to at least the time of Robert Frost's creation of his travelers through the dark, lonely woods.

Finally, in part because it is one of those many pairings of characters so pervasive in Twain's work, Tom's relationship with his half brother, Sid, should be noted. The relationship is instructive in that it foreshadows that of the later Tom-Huck relationship. Sid is the "model" boy who serves as Twain's foil for Tom's adventuresome independence. Although Tom is never good in the subservient, lap-dog sense that Sid is, there is a kind of lateral movement of his character from the early to the later novel; in *The Adventures of Tom Sawyer,* Tom plays off the foil of Sid's pious "respectability," while in *Adventures of Huckleberry Finn,* Tom, himself, has moved over to provide a similar foil for Huck's freedom.

The Prince and the Pauper • Unlike its predecessor, *The Prince and the Pauper* is a "children's book" that has remained simply that, a book for children. Twain professed to have taken great joy in the writing of it, probably in part because of the relief he felt upon completing the troublesome *A Tramp Abroad*. His wife and children admired the book, as did William Dean Howells and the reviewers for the New York *Herald*, the Boston *Transcript, The Atlantic Monthly,* and the *Century*. Nevertheless, the novel holds little interest for the mature reader except in terms of its relationship to the two superior novels that preceded and followed it.

Its plot hinges upon one of Twain's most explicit pairings, that of Prince Edward with the pauper Tom Cantry. The switching of these look-alike adolescents in the England of Henry VIII allows the Prince to learn what poverty and hardship are like in the alleyways of his kingdom and the pauper to satirize, through his innocence, the foibles of royalty and court life. Neither the satire nor the compassion, however, ring true. It is almost as if Twain were finding his way from his first classic to his second through this experiment, set in a time and place far removed from his native Mississippi River valley.

With that contrast in mind, it is perhaps reasonable to see the prince and the pauper as another Sid and Tom, another Tom and Huck, all of the sets representing at various removes those two basic drives of Twain's nature for respectability and freedom. Huck and Tom Cantry, the pauper, are "freer" than are Tom and Prince Edward, although the relationships are not that simple, since the members of each pair are attracted like magnetic opposites to their mates. This attraction is made most explicit in *The Prince and the Pauper,* where the two actually exchange places. Later in his career, in *Pudd'nhead Wilson,* Twain made a comparably explicit exchange with wholly tragic consequences. In *The Prince and the Pauper,* it is all play with little consequence at all except for the exigencies of a contrived, melodramatic plot. Twain's truest pairing, that of Huck and Jim, was yet ahead of him.

Adventures of Huckleberry Finn • *Adventures of Huckleberry Finn* is almost universally hailed as Twain's best book, as well as one of the half dozen or so American classics of the nineteenth century. This is not to say that the novel is without defects. The ending, in particular, presents some very real problems, structurally, thematically, and rhetorically. The very high place of the novel, however, is generally conceded. This success depends upon several considerations. In the first place, the novel continues the mythic idyll of American boyhood begun with *The Adventures of Tom Sawyer.* That connection and that continuation by itself would have ensured the book a place in the national archives if not the national heart. Most agree, however, that its success derives from even deeper currents. *Adventures of Huckleberry Finn* is Twain's best book because, for whatever reasons, he brought together in it, with the highest degree of artistic balance, those most fundamental dualities running through his work and life from start to finish. The potentially destructive dualities of youth and age, of the need for both security and freedom, of the wilderness and civilization, of innocence and corruption, all are reconciled by means of an aesthetic transformation. Historical, realistic dualities as well as psychological and moral dualities are brought into an artistic synthesis, into a novel, the most distinctive feature of which, finally, is its own modal duality, played out in the terms of a delicate balance between lyricism and satire.

Huck's relationship with Jim, the runaway slave, is central to the novel's narrative, to its structure, and to its theme. Escaping "down" the river, a cruel irony in itself, provides the episodic structure, which is the narrative thread that holds together the developing relationship between the two runaways on the raft. The escape, the quest for freedom, is literal for both Huck and Jim as they flee from Pap and Jim's owner, Miss Watson. It may also be seen as symbolic on several planes: historical, philosophical, and moral. The historical setting of the novel is that pivotal era in American history when the new nation was being carved out of the wilderness. The flight down the river is a flight from the complexities of the ever-expanding, westward-moving settlements of the new civilization. The continuing vitality of the novel depends in part upon the survival in the twentieth century of the need for that imaginative escape. Like Henry David Thoreau's Walden Pond, Huck's Mississippi River, originally an escape from what may now seem some of the simpler strictures of society, continues to serve the American psyche as an imaginative alternative to modern civilization.

The philosophical dimensions of the rapidly disappearing frontier are those of nineteenth century Romanticism. Celebrating their freedom on the raft from the legal and social strictures of the town along the river, Huck and Jim are at the same time affirming the central Romantic thesis concerning people's need to return to nature and to the natural self. There are two kinds of Romanticism in the novel: that which Tom espouses in his adolescent preoccupation with adventure, and that which Huck practices on the river under the stars and, most significantly, in the final resolution of the problem of Jim as a runaway slave. Twain holds up Tom's bookish Romanticism as childish at best and, for the most part, as silly. This attack on Romanticism—a secondary theme in *Adventures of Huckleberry Finn*, where Twain sends the derelict steamer, the *Walter Scott*, to its destruction on a rock—was one of Twain's lifelong preoccupations. It was continued with a vehemence later in *A Connecticut Yankee in King Arthur's Court*, but its deep-running, destructive potential for Twain is harnessed in *Adventures of Huckleberry Finn.* The satire is there, but it is in the largely playful terms of the antics of the King and the Duke, their mangling of William Shakespeare, and the funeral art and poetry of Emmeline Grangerford. This playful treatment of one of his serious themes results in part from the fact that Twain is here working a deeper vein of Romanticism in the person of his supreme fictional creation, Huck.

The moral climax of the novel comes in chapter 31, when Huck decides that he will "go to hell" rather than turn in Jim. The difficulties with the ending of the book derive largely from that relatively early resolution of its central theme. Shortly thereafter, Huck is reunited with Tom, who is responsible for all the preposterous plans to save Jim, who, ironically, no longer needs to be saved. There are real problems here with the plot, with motivation, and with the prose itself, which is no longer sustained by the lyricism of Huck's accounts of life on the raft. The artistic achievement of the climax, however, makes such problems pale into relative insignificance. Twain embodies in Huck and dramatizes in his decision a principal line of American political and moral thought that has its roots in Thomas Jefferson and Thomas Paine, its "philosophical" development in Ralph Waldo Emerson and Thoreau, and its aesthetic transformation at the hands of Twain and Whitman. Huck is the embodiment of both the political and the Romantic ideals of common humanity, with no past or roots, whose principal guide is experience rather than tradition. He is one of the principal literary symbols of that fundamental American mythical dream of moral rejuvenation in the Edenic wilderness of the "new" continent. He stands at the center of nineteenth century American literature and at the center of Twain's achievements.

A Connecticut Yankee in King Arthur's Court • In *Adventures of Huckleberry Finn*, Twain's attack upon the Romantic glorification of the past is a peripheral theme. In *A Connecticut Yankee in King Arthur's Court*, it is central and devastating, both in the novel itself and in its signaling of the direction in which Twain's thought and creative energies were heading. Although this too is a boy's book of a kind, there is about it none of the idyllic radiance of *Adventures of Tom Sawyer* nor the harmonious balancing of opposites of *The Adventures of Huckleberry Finn*. Rather, there is finally outright war between the forces of the feudal past and those of the progressive present, with considerable ambiguity about which is to be considered the good and which the evil.

There is no doubt that the reader's sympathies at the outset are with the Yankee mechanic, Hank Morgan, who, after a blow on the head, wakes up in King Arthur's England of 528 c.e. After saving himself from execution as a witch by "commanding" a total eclipse of the sun, he vies successfully with Merlin for power and prestige at court. He is like Huck in his commonsense responses to life in general, and in particular to the romantic claims of the feudal society in which he finds himself. He is unlike Huck in his vigorous progressivism, in his determination to bring the fruits of nineteenth century democracy and technology to feudal England. He introduces explosives, sets up schools to train workmen in the mechanical arts, gives instruction in journalism to his page with an eye to a national press, and stretches telephone lines haphazardly across the countryside. His talents, taken for magic for the most part, earn for him the title "the Boss," and the abiding enmity of Merlin, whom he replaces at court. He plans to declare a republic after Arthur's death, and the sixth century kingdom enjoys all the fruits of progress: schools, trains, factories, newspapers, the telephone and telegraph. The end of the story, however, just before Hank returns to his own century, pictures anything but the envisioned utopia. Arthur dies in a battle with Lancelot, Camelot is reduced to shambles, and Hank fortifies himself in a cave against the surviving chivalry of England. One of his final concerns is with the pollution caused by the dead bodies piled in the trenches around his fortress. The repressive, superstitious nightmare of feudal society has been compounded by the fearful efficiency of nineteenth century technology.

The ambiguity of the ending of the novel is symptomatic. The artistic balance of *Adventures of Huckleberry Finn* is no longer in evidence. Twain, always something of an allegorist, was by 1889 becoming more and more a polemicist, increasingly more interested in conflicts between abstract ideas and values than in the development and portrayal of human characters in all their complexities. Hank can be identified with Huck in terms of their common sense and their human values, but the big difference between them is that Huck's chief concern is with another human being, while Hank's is with an abstraction called feudalism.

Pudd'nhead Wilson • Twain was to do some of his most important writing in the last two decades of his life, including short fiction and social and moral criticism. His best novels, however, were completed in 1875 and during the 1880's. Of those coming after 1889, *Pudd'nhead Wilson* (also known as *The Tragedy of Pudd'nhead Wilson*) is the most readable and the most consistent with the principal direction of his deepening cynicism about the "damned human race." The novel's only really interesting character is Roxy, a slave woman who switches her son with that of her owner Percy Driscoll to save her child from eventually being sold "down river." The whole of the dark tale that follows indicates, in Maxwell Geismar's words, how much "irony and tragedy have taken over the center stage in [Twain's] comic proscenium of life."

Lloyd N. Dendinger

Other major works

SHORT FICTION: *The Celebrated Jumping Frog of Calaveras County, and Other Sketches,* 1867; *Mark Twain's (Burlesque) Autobiography and First Romance,* 1871; *Mark Twain's Sketches: New and Old,* 1875; *Punch, Brothers, Punch! and Other Sketches,* 1878; *The Stolen White Elephant, and Other Stories,* 1882; *Merry Tales,* 1892; *The £1,000,000 Bank-Note, and Other New Stories,* 1893; *The Man That Corrupted Hadleyburg, and Other Stories and Essays,* 1900; *King Leopold's Soliloquy: A Defense of His Congo Rule,* 1905; *The $30,000 Bequest, and Other Stories,* 1906; *The Curious Republic of Gondour, and Other Whimsical Sketches,* 1919; *The Complete Short Stories of Mark Twain,* 1957 (Charles Neider, editor); *Letters from the Earth,* 1962; *Selected Shorter Writings of Mark Twain,* 1962; *Mark Twain's Satires and Burlesques,* 1967 (Franklin R. Rogers, editor); *Mark Twains's Which Was the Dream? and Other Symbolic Writings of the Later Years,* 1967 (John S. Tuckey, editor); *Mark Twain's Hannibal, Huck and Tom,* 1969 (Walter Blair, editor); *Mark Twain's Fables of Man,* 1972 (Tuckey, editor); *Life as I Find It,* 1977 (Neider, editor); *Early Tales and Sketches,* 1979-1981 (2 volumes; Edgar Marquess Branch and Robert H. Hirst, editors); *A Murder, a Mystery, and a Marriage,* 2001 (Roy Blount, Jr., editor).

PLAYS: *Colonel Sellers,* pr., pb. 1874 (adaptation of his novel *The Gilded Age*); *Ah Sin,* pr. 1877 (with Bret Harte); *Is He Dead?: A Comedy in Three Acts,* pb. 2003 (Shelley Fisher Fishkin, editor).

NONFICTION: *The Innocents Abroad,* 1869; *Roughing It,* 1872; *A Tramp Abroad,* 1880; *Life on the Mississippi,* 1883; *Following the Equator,* 1897 (also known as *More Tramp Abroad*); *How to Tell a Story, and Other Essays,* 1897; *My Début as a Literary Person,* 1903; *What Is Man?,* 1906; *Christian Science,* 1907; *Is Shakespeare Dead?,* 1909; *Mark Twain's Speeches,* 1910 (Albert Bigelow Paine, editor); *Europe and Elsewhere,* 1923 (Paine, editor); *Mark Twain's Autobiography,* 1924 (2 volumes; Paine, editor); *Mark Twain's Notebook,* 1935 (Paine, editor); *Letters from the Sandwich Islands, Written for the Sacramento Union,* 1937 (G. Ezra Dane, editor); *Mark Twain in Eruption,* 1940 (Bernard DeVoto, editor); *Mark Twain's Travels with Mr. Brown,* 1940 (Franklin Walker and G. Ezra Dane, editors); *Mark Twain to Mrs. Fairbanks,* 1949 (Wecter, editor); *The Love Letters of Mark Twain,* 1949 (Dixon Wecter, editor); *Mark Twain of the Enterprise: Newspaper Articles and Other Documents, 1862-1864,* 1957 (Henry Nash Smith and Frederick Anderson, editors); *Traveling with the Innocents Abroad: Mark Twain's Original Reports from Europe and the Holy Land,* 1958 (Daniel Morley McKeithan, editor; letters); *Mark Twain-Howells Letters: The Correspondence of Samuel L. Clemens and William D. Howells, 1872-1910,* 1960 (Smith and William M. Gibson, editors); *The Autobiography of Mark Twain,* 1961 (Neider, editor); *Mark Twain's Letters to His Publishers, 1867-1894,* 1967 (Hamlin Hill, editor); *Clemens of the Call: Mark Twain in San Francisco,* 1969 (Edgar M. Branch, editor); *Mark Twain's Correspondence with Henry Huttleston Rogers, 1893-1909,* 1969 (Lewis Leary, editor); *A Pen Warmed-Up in Hell: Mark Twain in Protest,* 1972; *Mark Twain's Notebooks and Journals,* 1975-1979 (3 volumes); *Mark Twain Speaking,* 1976 (Paul Fatout, editor); *Mark Twain Speaks for Himself,* 1978 (Fatout, editor); *Mark Twain's Letters,* 1988-2002 (6 volumes; Edgar Marquess Branch, et al, editors); *Mark Twain's Own Autobiography: The Chapters from the "North American Review,"* 1990 (Michael J. Kiskis, editor); *Mark Twain's Aquarium: The Samuel Clemens Angelfish Correspondence, 1905-1910,* 1991 (John Cooley, editor); *Mark Twain: The Complete Interviews,* 2006 (Gary Scharnhorst, editor).

MISCELLANEOUS: *The Writings of Mark Twain,* 1922-1925 (37 volumes); *The Portable Mark Twain,* 1946 (Bernard DeVoto, editor); *Collected Tales, Sketches, Speeches, and Essays, 1853-1891,* 1992 (Louis J. Budd, editor); *Collected Tales, Sketches, Speeches, and Essays, 1891-1910,* 1992 (Budd, editor).

Bibliography

Camfield, Gregg. *The Oxford Companion to Mark Twain.* New York: Oxford University Press, 2003. Collection of original essays, including several by other scholars, on diverse aspects of Twain's life and writing, with encyclopedia reference features.

Emerson, Everett. *Mark Twain: A Literary Life.* Philadelphia: University of Pennsylvania Press, 2000. A complete revision of Emerson's *The Authentic Mark Twain* (1984), this masterful study traces the development of Twain's writing against the events in his life and provides illuminating discussions of many individual works.

Fishkin, Shelley Fisher. *Lighting Out for the Territory: Reflections on Mark Twain and American Culture.* New York: Oxford University Press, 1996. A broad survey of Mark Twain's influence on modern culture, including the many writers who have acknowledged their indebtedness to him; discusses Twain's use of Hannibal, Missouri, in his writings; charts his transformation from a southern racist to a committed antiracist.

_____,ed. *A Historical Guide to Mark Twain.* New York: Oxford University Press, 2002. Collection of original articles by scholars on a wide variety of subjects pertaining to Mark Twain; includes a bibliographical essay by the editor.

Horn, Jason Gary. *Mark Twain: A Descriptive Guide to Biographical Sources.* Lanham, Md.: Scarecrow Press, 1999. Richly annotated bibliography of nearly three hundred books and other sources on Mark Twain, including many works of literary criticism

Kaplan, Justin. *Mr. Clemens and Mark Twain.* New York: Simon & Schuster, 1966. Pulitzer Prize-winning biography is a superior general work on Twain's life after 1861. Many reprint editions are available.

LeMaster, J. R., and James D. Wilson, eds. *The Mark Twain Encyclopedia.* New York: Garland, 1993. Comprehensive reference work broadly similar in organization to Rasmussen's *Critical Companion to Mark Twain,* differing in devoting most of its space to literary analysis.

Leonard, James. S., ed. *Making Mark Twain Work in the Classroom.* Durham, N.C.: Duke University Press, 1999. Collection of essays by leading Twain scholars designed for students and teachers. Special attention is given to *A Connecticut Yankee in King Arthur's Court, Joan of Arc, Innocents Abroad,* and *Adventures of Huckleberry Finn.*

Messent, Peter B. *Mark Twain.* New York: St. Martin's Press, 1997. A standard introduction to Twain's life and works. Provides bibliographical references and an index.

Rasmussen, R. Kent. *Bloom's How to Write About Mark Twain.* New York: Chelsea House, 2008. Practical guide to writing student essays on Mark Twain, with numerous general and specific suggestions on his major novels. Includes a general introduction to writing on Mark Twain and chapters on ten individual works. Each chapter has a lengthy bibliography.

_____. *Critical Companion to Mark Twain.* New York: Facts On File, 2007. Revised and much expanded edition of Rasmussen's *Mark Twain A to Z* (1995), which covered virtually every character, theme, place, and biographical fact relating to Mark Twain and contained perhaps the most complete chronology ever compiled. Among new features in this retitled edition are lengthy critical essays on Twain's major works; an extensive, annotated bibliography; and a glossary of unusual words in Twain's writings. Indexed.

Sloane, David E. E. *Student Companion to Mark Twain.* New York: Greenwood Press, 2001. Essays on aspects of Twain's life, with special chapters on individual books.

Ward, Geoffrey C., and Dayton Duncan. *Mark Twain: An Illustrated Biography.* New York: Alfred A. Knopf, 2001. A heavily illustrated companion to the PBS television documentary. More than a picture book, however, this volume provides ample biographical information that is well researched and thoughtfully presented.

Anne Tyler

Born: Minneapolis, Minnesota; October 25, 1941

Principal long fiction • *If Morning Ever Comes*, 1964; *The Tin Can Tree*, 1965; *A Slipping-Down Life*, 1970; *The Clock Winder*, 1972; *Celestial Navigation*, 1974; *Searching for Caleb*, 1976; *Earthly Possessions*, 1977; *Morgan's Passing*, 1980; *Dinner at the Homesick Restaurant*, 1982; *The Accidental Tourist*, 1985; *Breathing Lessons*, 1988; *Saint Maybe*, 1991; *Ladder of Years*, 1995; *A Patchwork Planet*, 1998; *Back When We Were Grownups*, 2001; *The Amateur Marriage*, 2004; *Digging to America*, 2006.

Other literary forms • In addition to her novels, Anne Tyler published more than forty short stories, including several in *Harper's*, *Mademoiselle*, *The New Yorker*, *Seventeen*, and the *Southern Review*. There is no collection to date, although two stories appeared in the O. Henry Prize volumes for 1969 and 1972 and others in the first edition of the Pushcart Prize anthology (1976), *Best American Short Stories* (1977), *Stories of the Modern South* (1978, 1981), *The Editor's Choice: New American Stories* (1985), *New Women and New Fiction* (1986), *Louder than Words* (1989), and several anthologies of American literature published by major publishing houses for use in college and university courses. Tyler also wrote several autobiographical and personal essays, one for *The Washington Post* in 1976 and another for *The Writer on Her Work* (1980), edited by Janet Sternburg. In 1975, her reviews of current fiction, criticism, and biography began appearing in major newspapers and magazines, including the *Boston Globe*, the *Chicago Sun-Times* and the *Chicago Tribune*, the *Detroit News*, *The New Republic*, *The New York Times Book Review*, *USA Today*, and *The Washington Post*.

Achievements • Despite praise for the truth of her characterizations and her eye for details, Tyler did not receive much national recognition for her fiction until the publication of her sixth novel, *Searching for Caleb*. Prior to 1976, the largest segment of her audience was in the South, although her short stories appeared in prestigious national magazines throughout the 1960's and 1970's. All of her novels except *A Slipping-Down Life* have been published abroad. Besides English editions, translations into Danish, French, German, Italian, and Swedish have appeared. Nevertheless, the American academic and critical communities were slow to appreciate Tyler's work. Her strong supporters include John Updike, who favorably reviewed her novels for *The New Yorker*, beginning with *Searching for Caleb*, and Reynolds Price, Tyler's professor at Duke University, who also reviewed her work.

In 1976, Tyler began to receive increasing recognition. In 1977, the American Academy and Institute of Arts and Letters cited her as a novelist of excellence and promise. *Earthly Possessions* and *Morgan's Passing* also received largely favorable national reviews. Although a few critics, including Updike, expressed some disappointment in *Morgan's Passing*, the Writers Workshop of the University of Rochester awarded it the sixth annual Janet Heidinger Kafka prize for fiction by an American woman.

With the publication of *Dinner at the Homesick Restaurant*, her first novel to make the best-sellers list, Tyler at last acquired full national stature. Benjamin DeMott's front-page notice in *The New York Times Book Review* pointed to the novel's wit and the depth of Tyler's psychological insight and characterizations. DeMott saw the book as clear evidence of Tyler's having joined the ranks of major novelists. Updike reiterated this praise, citing *Dinner at the Homesick Restaurant* as a work of considerable power. As a result of this increasing recognition and praise, scholarly studies of Tyler's work, including her early novels, began to appear. Tyler's reputation as a major modern American novelist was fixed with the publication of The Accidental Tourist, which won the 1985/1986 National Book Critics Circle Award for fiction. The successful film version of the novel increased Tyler's popularity with the reading public. *Breathing Lessons* was nominated for the National Book Award and won the 1989 Pulitzer Prize for fiction.

© Diana Walker

Biography • Anne Tyler was born in Minneapolis, Minnesota, on October 25, 1941, to Phyllis Mahon, a social worker, and Lloyd Parry Tyler, an industrial chemist. She was the oldest of four children, the only girl. Both parents were Quakers dedicated to finding an ideal community, a quest that produced the theme of frustrated idealism in Tyler's fiction. As a consequence of her parents' idealism, Tyler spent most of her early years, from infancy until age eleven, in various rural Quaker communes scattered throughout the midwestern and southern United States. When she was six, the family was settled in Celo, North Carolina—a large, isolated valley commune virtually independent of the outside world and unquestionably the setting for Tyler's short story "Outside," which appeared in the *Southern Review* in 1971.

Tyler later wrote of the impact of her early years on her fiction. Unable to sleep at night and needing to amuse herself, she began telling herself stories at the age of three. Her isolation in the rural communes in which she lived as a child contributed to the themes of isolation and community dominant in her novels. Additionally, growing up in North Carolina, where she spent summers tying tobacco, she listened carefully to the stories of the tobacco handlers and tenant farmers. Later, she was able to capture the cadences of everyday speech in her fiction, realizing that the stories these workers told could form the basis for literature. She was also to rely heavily on the North Carolina tobacco country as the setting for her early novels, especially *The Tin Can Tree* and *A Slipping-Down Life*.

When Tyler was eleven, she and her family moved to Raleigh, where they finally settled into an "ordinary" middle-class existence. There, Tyler attended Broughton

High School and received encouragement in her writing. She also discovered the work of Eudora Welty, which was to have great influence on Tyler's own fiction.

In September, 1958, Tyler entered Duke University as an Angier Duke Scholar majoring in Russian. She was encouraged by Reynolds Price, who taught her freshman composition and later introduced her to his agent. At Duke, Tyler helped edit the *Archive* (the student literary magazine), published three early stories there, acted in several productions of the Wesley Players, and learned a great deal about the craft of fiction from reading Leo Tolstoy and the other major Russian novelists. She twice received the Anne Flexner award for creative writing at Duke and graduated Phi Beta Kappa, just three years after entering, in 1961.

In September, 1961, Tyler began work on a master's degree in Russian at Columbia University, an experience that provides some of the background for *If Morning Ever Comes*. She completed the coursework for the degree but quit before writing her thesis. The following summer she spent in Maine, supporting herself by working on a schooner and proofreading for a local newspaper.

In 1962, Tyler returned to Duke University as the library's Russian bibliographer. That fall, she met her future husband, Taghi Modarressi, an Iranian child-psychiatry student at the Duke Medical Center. The couple married in May, 1963, three months after the publication of Tyler's first short story in a national magazine. They moved to Montreal, Canada, that spring; during their four years there, Tyler wrote her first novel, taught herself Persian in anticipation of living in Iran, and worked as a librarian at the McGill University law library. In September, 1965, she gave birth to her first child, Tezh, a girl. The publication of *The Tin Can Tree* followed the next month.

In June, 1967, the Modarressis moved to Baltimore, Maryland. Although Tyler's short stories continued to appear frequently in national publications between 1965 and 1970, her third novel was not published until January, 1970, first in condensed form in *Redbook* and later that same year in its entirety by Alfred A. Knopf. Between *The Tin Can Tree* and *A Slipping-Down Life* came one other book—*Winter Birds, Winter Apples*—which was not published. A second daughter, Mitra, was born in November, 1967, in Baltimore. A dedicated mother and a productive, organized writer, Tyler managed her dual careers for years by writing in the mornings while her children were at school. Although Tezh moved to New York and Mitra to San Francisco, Tyler and her husband continued to live in Baltimore. Taghi Modarressi died there of lymphoma in April, 1997, at the age of sixty-five. Tyler continued to reside in, and set her fiction in, Baltimore.

Analysis • In *The Writer on Her Work*, Anne Tyler discusses the importance of her having lived as a child in "an experimental Quaker community in the wilderness." For her, this early experience of isolation and her later effort "to fit into the outside world" provided the "kind of setting-apart situation" the writer requires for aesthetic distancing. Tyler's early isolation and struggle to belong also provided both the style and material for her fiction: the ironic distance characteristic of her prose as well as the subject of the individual's relationship to the community, particularly to other members of one's own household and family. Most of Tyler's short fiction and all of her novels published to date, from *If Morning Ever Comes* to *A Patchwork Planet*, concern the intricacies of family relationships and the isolation of the individual within the family. For Tyler, families clearly provided not only her major source for learning about the world as a child, but also fertile ground for studying how people endure the pain of loss and disappointment of life, adjust to living with others, and yet continue to love. All of the major conflicts and central themes of her novels evolve from this concern with the family and the individual's relationship to the community.

In this regard, Tyler falls clearly within the southern literary tradition with its emphasis on family life and history. As Paul Binding points out in *Separate Country: A Literary Journey Through the American South* (1979), Tyler, like her mentor Reynolds Price, relies on interaction and "badinage between members of a family or between people who know one another well in order to illuminate personality." Tyler does not, however, evoke or write of a regional past. She focuses on the present, narrating the past to provide a personal or familial, not a regional, history. Her characters and families are not symbolic figures. They are, instead, idiosyncratic personalities, truthfully depicted, memorable yet atypical. In all but her first three novels and, to an extent, *Ladder of Years*, Tyler's setting is not the small towns and rural landscapes so often considered synonymous with southern life. Rather, her terrain is the border city of Baltimore and the decay and transience of modern urban life. Price, in fact, has said that she is the closest thing the South has to an urban novelist, indicating Tyler's somewhat unusual position among late twentieth century American writers: a southerner with a traditional interest in family, community, and the past; a modern woman fascinated with change and drawn to urban life; a writer with faith in humankind's ability to love and endure yet keenly aware of the difficulties of modern life, particularly the failure of communication within the family.

In her concern for familial relationships, Tyler's novels raise the existential issues of freedom and commitment. Significantly, hers is a compassionate art without explicit moral judgment—an absence of judgment for which some critics have faulted her. The effect of this gentle portrayal of serious themes is ironic: The disturbing failure of Tyler's characters to understand fully and to be understood by those they love is counterbalanced by a witty, carefully detailed style. Violence is usually absent from her work as well, and so are the grotesques found in the fiction of Flannery O'Connor and Carson McCullers. The most disfigured character in Tyler's work— Evie Decker, the fat teenager in *A Slipping-Down Life* who carves a local rock singer's name in her forehead—is compassionately portrayed. Like Eudora Welty, Tyler populates her novels with ordinary people, all of whom, she comments in *The Writer on Her Work*, are mildly eccentric in some way and "have something unusual" at their centers, something "funny and strange" and "touching in unexpected ways." From Ben Joe Hawkes in *If Morning Ever Comes*, who reads upside down to relieve boredom, to the elusive and difficult black sheep of her fictional families—Caleb and Duncan Peck, Morgan Gower, Cody Tull, and Barnaby Gaitlin—Tyler warmly and humorously portrays a wide spectrum of fascinating yet ordinary human beings.

Additionally, with Reynolds Price as her teacher and Eudora Welty as a model, Tyler saw early in her career the rich source of literary materials offered by commonplace experience. Paul Binding also cites the influence of Tyler's study of the Russian masters, particularly Ivan Turgenev and Anton Chekhov, as a basis for her tolerant and warm portrayal of multiple generations of entangled and eccentric families. Finally, perhaps most prominent is Tyler's own witness to her parents' idealism, their quest for a perfect community throughout her youth, and later their apparently easy adjustment to an ordinary existence in a middle-sized southern city. Like her own father, whom she describes in *The Writer on Her Work*, the heroes of Tyler's novels are those who are "infinitely adapting" and always "looking around . . . with a smile to say, 'Oh! So this is where I am!'" They are complex people, enriched and deepened by experience—Elizabeth Abbott in *The Clock Winder*, Justine Peck in *Searching for Caleb*,

Charlotte Emory in *Earthly Possessions,* Jenny Tull in *Dinner at the Homesick Restaurant,* Maggie Moran in *Breathing Lessons,* and Delia Grinstead in *Ladder of Years* best represent the type—able to enjoy life because they view themselves and others with tolerance and wit.

In an interview with Clifford Ridley for the *National Observer,* Tyler commented that she did not particularly like either of her first two books because "they seem so bland." Ben Joe Hawkes, the hero of *If Morning Ever Comes,* is "a likable guy; that's all you can say about him." Although it is true that Ben Joe lacks the zaniness and interest that some of Tyler's later characters exhibit, his struggle to deal with his family, to recognize both his own independence and theirs, and to come to terms with the past and the psychological distance that isolates people even within an intimate group provides a basis for understanding Tyler's later work and her place within the southern literary tradition. *If Morning Ever Comes* had its origins in two short stories: "I Never Saw Morning," which appeared in the April, 1961, *Archive* and was later collected in *Under Twenty-five: Duke Narrative and Verse, 1945-1962* (1963), edited by William Blackburn; and "Nobody Answers the Door," which appeared in the fall, 1964, issue of the *Antioch Review.* Both involve incidents suggested by the novel but occurring prior to the time of its opening. With the novel, they indicate Tyler's strong sense of the continuity of her characters' lives.

If Morning Ever Comes • As in later novels, the plot and subject of *If Morning Ever Comes,* Ben Joe's five-day journey home to Sandhill, North Carolina, from Columbia University, where he is a law student, evolve from family conflict. The family of women Ben Joe has left behind—six strikingly independent sisters, a proud mother, and a spry, seventy-eight-year-old grandmother, the first of Tyler's zanies—fail to tell him what is happening at home. Jenny, the family letter-writer, is all business. No one mentions the illegitimate son whom Ben Joe's father left behind with a mistress when he died, nor the support payments Ben Joe personally delivered for years before he left for New York. The family treats lightly even the fact that Ben Joe's oldest sister, Joanne, has taken her child, left her husband, and returned home after seven years. Their behavior and their failure to understand Ben Joe's concern and worry point clearly to the theme of the individual's isolation within the family, here a male in an entire family of women.

On the surface, *If Morning Ever Comes* is a simply structured novel covering less than a week in the life of its hero. As one critic has observed, however, going home is "only partly a spatial relocation." Ben Joe, like other southern literary heroes, "from Quentin Compson to Jack Burden," must return home "to embrace the spiritual crisis" created by an unsettled past and attempt to forge a future shaped by that very past. In this regard, *If Morning Ever Comes* is clearly a southern novel. The fact that it draws on a sharp contrast between the peaceful North Carolina setting and the briskness of New York, as well as the hero's discomfort and sense of dislocation in the North, is also suggestive of Tyler's southern literary roots.

The Tin Can Tree • Although not widely reviewed nor acclaimed, *The Tin Can Tree* is a moving novel that expands and deepens Tyler's treatment of family relationships and the individual's struggle to remain committed in the face of significant loss and change. Just as Ben Joe Hawkes in *If Morning Ever Comes* remained committed to his family despite their pride and reticence, and to his father's memory despite the elder Hawkes's unfaithfulness, so also the characters in *The Tin Can Tree,* the members of three separate families sharing one house—the Pikes, the Greens, and the Potters—must deal with the commonly experienced grief at the death of the Pikes' six-year-old daughter, Janie Rose, adjust, and resume the task of living. Tyler's achievement here is that she captures eight different characters' varying responses to grief while avoiding the sentimental and maudlin. She opens the novel with the close of the funeral service, thus deliberately focusing on life, rather than death, and the resumption of the tasks of everyday living.

In addition to this theme of grief, *The Tin Can Tree* explores the background and interactions of James and Ansel Green and Joan Pike, Janie Rose's cousin. The study of James's commitment to his ailing brother Ansel, the two brothers' alienation from their family, and Joan's distance from her own elderly parents as well as her unresolved romantic involvement with James, give the novel a depth lacking in *If Morning Ever Comes*, with its heavy focus on one central character. As one reviewer noted, *The Tin Can Tree* illustrates Tyler's talent for bringing "into focus a remarkable range of human traits and emotions." Lou Pike's depressive withdrawal and immobility after her daughter's death, her husband's worried yet practical concern, their son Simon's sense of rejection and neglect, Joan's uncertainty and anger at James and his brother Ansel—all acquire full portraiture. A love of detail permeates the book, from the Potter sisters' eccentric way of wearing hats and gloves even when visiting only at the other end of the porch to the details of Janie Rose's behavior, her "tin can tree" made in honor of God during a religious period and her wearing layer upon layer of underwear on "her bad days." Such details make the characters real and Janie Rose's death more immediate and painful.

The Tin Can Tree is also the first Tyler novel to draw explicitly on the author's tobacco-field experience. Joan Pike, a school secretary, spends part of her summers handling tobacco in the warehouses, as Tyler herself did as a teenager. Besides providing elements of plot and characterization, the Tobacco Road landscape mirrors the sterility of the characters' lives following Janie Rose's death and provides a voice for the novel's theme. "Bravest thing about people, Miss Joan," one of the tobacco tiers says, "is how they go on loving mortal beings after finding out there's such a thing as dying." Unlike Erskine Caldwell, whose stereotypical white trash characters are often farcical grotesques, Tyler deepens the Tobacco Road landscape by a compassionate, detailed account of the grief of several families at the death of a child. Hers is a fiction of psychological insight, not a document for social change. *The Tin Can Tree*, as one critic observed, is "a novel rich in incident that details the closing of a family wound and the resumption of life among people stunned by the proof of mortality."

A Slipping-Down Life • In her third novel, *A Slipping-Down Life*, Tyler returned to the existential themes of the individual's isolation, the struggle for identity, and the lack of understanding and meaningful communication among people living closely together. Set in the fictional towns of Pulqua and Farinia, North Carolina—suspiciously similar to the actual town of Fuquay-Varina near Raleigh—it was the last of the Tyler's books set entirely in North Carolina but also the first to portray the barrenness of familial relationships in a clearly modern setting. Although most of *If Morning Ever Comes* and all of *The Tin Can Tree* are set in peaceful, remote areas where family life, though troubled, seems unaffected by distinctly modern problems, *A Slipping-Down Life* draws heavily on the impact of modern American culture and media on family life. Also, where Tyler's first two novels covered only a few days in the lives of the principal characters, *A Slipping-Down Life* chronicles one full year in the life of its heroine—a fat, dowdy, teenage girl named Evie Decker—indicating a development in Tyler's ability to handle character over an extended period of time.

Originating in a "newspaper story about a fifteen-year-old girl in Texas who'd slashed 'Elvis' in her forehead," the novel traces Evie's barren interaction with her father, her only living relative, as well as the development and dissolution of a relationship with a local rock singer named Bertram "Drumstrings" Casey, the first of Tyler's unadmirable yet likable antiheroes—exploitative and selfish yet touchingly shy and dependent on his parents and Evie. Evie's entanglement with Drum, leading eventually to their marriage, is initiated by her carving the name "Casey" in her forehead with a pair of nail scissors, and ends with the couple's separation, the death of Evie's family, and her discovery of Casey in bed with another woman. Throughout, Evie thinks of herself as though she were acting on a stage set, taking her cues from the soap operas she watches daily with Clotelia, the Deckers' sullen maid and Evie's sometime chiding surrogate mother. Like Joan Pike in *The Tin Can Tree* and later Tyler heroines—Justine Peck in *Searching for Caleb* and Charlotte Emory in *Earthly Possessions*—Evie is an only child faced with growing up alone in a dark, stifling household and creating an identity without the companionship and aid of siblings or understanding parents.

Besides its characterizations, *A Slipping-Down Life* is also noteworthy for capturing at least part of the American experience during the 1960's: the lonely world of teenagers, the generation gap, the high school student's unending quest for popularity and romance, as well as a small town's tawdry local rock scene, featuring the chilled air in a roadside house, painfully loud music, necking couples, and the smell of stale beer. As one reviewer observed, *A Slipping-Down Life* captures "a *way* of life, a way that is tacked upon teenage bulletin boards, sewn to dresses 'decorated with poodles on loops of real chain,' enclosed in high-school notebooks containing *Silver Screen* magazine."

The Clock Winder • Tyler's first three novels all involve some type of journey home during which a central character confronts both the distance between himself and his family and the difficulties of unresolved past conflicts. Ben Joe's journey from New York to Sandhill in *If Morning Ever Comes* fits this pattern, as do James Green's trip to Caraway, North Carolina, in *The Tin Can Tree* and, in *A Slipping-Down Life*, Evie Decker's return to her father's house following his death. A similar trip occurs in *The Clock Winder*. A novel characterized by Sarah Blackburn as having all the "virtues" of southern writing—"an easy, almost confidential directness, fine skill at quick characterization, a sure eye for atmosphere, and a special nostalgic humor"—*The Clock Winder* was at the time of its publication Tyler's most ambitious work, tracing the intricate relationships of a large cast of characters over an entire decade. It was also her first novel set in Baltimore.

The diverse, eccentric, eight-member Emerson family of Baltimore and their one adopted member, Elizabeth Abbott, clearly form one of those huge, "loving-bickering" southern families Tyler told Clifford Ridley she hoped to create in writing *If Morning Ever Comes*. Mrs. Emerson—a skinny, fragile widow—is unrelenting in nagging her children about their neglected duties to her. She is, consequently, estranged from all but one: Timothy, a pressured medical student who, with his twin, Andrew, is one of the most neurotic and disturbed characters in Tyler's novels. Into this entangled, crisis-prone family, Elizabeth Abbott brings the very skills she is unable to practice with her own family in Ellington, North Carolina. Tolerant, practical, dextrous, and witty—the first of Tyler's "infinitely adapting" heroines based on her own father—Elizabeth is a godsend for the nervous Mrs. Emerson. In Ellington, she is a bumbler, a rebellious college dropout, and a painful reminder of failure to her minister father. Her life at home is bleak, ordinary, and restricted. Commitment to the Emersons, despite their family feuds, offers interest and freedom from the Abbott family's dicta, an opportunity to form a new identity and life free of reminders of past mistakes.

Besides expanding character, setting, and time frame, *The Clock Winder* is unusual among Tyler's first four works for its use of violence and its experimentation with point of view. Timothy Emerson commits suicide by shooting himself in Elizabeth's presence, sending her home to her family for several years. Later, after her return to Baltimore, his twin shoots her, though he causes only a flesh wound. Also, where earlier Tyler novels used omniscient point of view focusing largely on one major character—the exception is *The Tin Can Tree*, in which Joan Pike and James Green serve alternately as centers of consciousness—*The Clock Winder* shifts perspective among many characters, some of them minor. In one chapter, the reader witnesses the succession of disconnected thoughts, the confusion of physical sensations, and the temporal disorientation accompanying Mrs. Emerson's stroke. Another presents the views of the youngest Emerson, Peter, who appears only in the final chapter of the novel. These shifts in point of view result in an intimate portrait not only of the novel's central character, Elizabeth, but also of the Emersons—a varied, contrasting family of idiosyncratic individuals.

Celestial Navigation • With *Celestial Navigation*, Tyler moved her novels to a totally urban landscape. Eight months after the novel's publication, she told a Duke University audience that she "could no longer write a southern novel" since she had lived away from the South too long to capture realistically the "voices" and behavior of the people who live there. Set almost exclusively in a seedy Baltimore boardinghouse "smack in the middle" of a deteriorating inner-city neighborhood, *Celestial Navigation* is Tyler's portrait of the artist. It covers thirteen years in the central character's life, expanding the study of character development found in earlier novels and illustrating her increasing skill in handling point of view. The various boarders narrate firsthand their experiences and relationships to other residents. Additionally, since it focuses largely on boarders rather than kin, somewhat like *The Tin Can Tree* with its three families unrelated by blood, and because it includes the common-law marriage of its hero, *Celestial Navigation* redefines the meaning of family ties as characterized in Tyler's novels. It also intensifies the isolation of the protagonist. Jeremy Pauling, the artist-hero of the novel and the owner of the rooming house, is so reclusive that for years he has not left the city block where he lives. His principal ties are not with his two sisters in Richmond, neither very understanding of his peculiar artistic temperament, but with the boarders with whom he lives.

The caring family of boarders the novel studies, however, are essentially isolated strangers living in private rooms. They are mostly older people with severed family connections or no remaining kin. Ironically, they exhibit more tolerance and unquestioning respect for the peculiarities and privacy of one another than do many blood-related members. Mrs. Vinton, an aged spinster who works in a bookstore, stays on to care for Jeremy years after the others move or die, yet she never interrupts his trancelike states or work. With the other boarders—the elegant widow Mrs.

Jarrett, the nubile Mary Tell, the young Olivia, and the fractious old Mrs. Somerset shuffling about in slippers—Mrs. Vinton is a testament to Tyler's talent for realistically capturing a gallery of idiosyncratic yet identifiably ordinary people.

The real achievement of *Celestial Navigation*, though, is Jeremy Pauling. He is one of Tyler's minor grotesques. A pale, pudgy sculptor, he rarely speaks and withdraws for days at a time to his secluded bedroom-studio. The novel works as Jeremy's story, however, partly because Tyler gives him a full range of emotions—including sexual attraction to several female boarders and a love for the children he has by his common-law marriage. She also views him with both compassion and humor and lets the reader see him from several points of view. Tyler shifts to third-person point of view to narrate Jeremy's chapters, since Jeremy himself is incapable of communicating his impressions in the coherent manner of the other characters. Tyler has said that the character of Jeremy is based in part on a shy, easily flustered little man she helped one day in the library where she worked, but she added several of her own traits to the character: a dread of telephones and doorbells (something retained from her isolated childhood) and, most important, her own artistic vision, an eye for the "smallest and most unnoticed scenes on earth," very much like those details Tyler captures in *Celestial Navigation*.

Searching for Caleb • *Searching for Caleb* marked a turning point in Tyler's career. It was her first novel to receive national recognition, at a time when Tyler's own reviews began to appear in national publications. As Walter Sullivan commented in 1977 when reviewing *Searching for Caleb* for the *Sewanee Review*, Tyler "retained" in her work "a kind of innocence . . . a sense of wonder at all the crazy things in the world and an abiding affection for her own flaky characters." *Searching for Caleb* was also evidence that Tyler had retained her southern literary roots and her delight in huge families and the range of human characters those families produce. Something of a combined family history and detective story, the novel is one of Tyler's most ambitious works, tracing five generations of one large, dichotomous, and extremely long-lived clan, the Pecks of Baltimore, from the 1880's through 1973. As in *The Clock Winder* and *Celestial Navigation*, Tyler shows her strong fascination with urban life, a result perhaps of her own early life in remote areas. She also returns to Roland Park, one of Baltimore's oldest residential neighborhoods and the main setting of *The Clock Winder.*

As the title suggests, *Searching for Caleb* involves a quest for the vanished Caleb, the great uncle of the novel's protagonists, Duncan and Justine Peck, and the half brother of their grandfather, Daniel Peck. Representing one side of the family, Caleb, Justine, and Duncan are outcasts of a sort: spirited, talented, imaginative, and free individuals unable or unwilling to live as family rules dictate. Caleb becomes a musician, Justine a fortune-teller. Duncan, her husband and first cousin, leads an unsettled life as a mechanic and jack-of-all-trades, foreshadowing Morgan Gower, the hero of *Morgan's Passing*. Like Morgan and, later, Barnaby Gaitlin of *A Patchwork Planet*, Duncan dismays his family.

The other side of the family, the Pecks of Roland Park, headed by Daniel, are uniformly humorless and restricted. The women, though educated, are unthreatening; the men, all attorneys educated at Johns Hopkins, drive black Fords and dress in Brooks Brothers suits. They are, above all, clannish, living side by side in similar Roland Park houses. For them, family tradition and training—in effect, the past—are inescapable. Even Daniel's late-life quest for his half brother evolves from his ties to family and an unsettled conflict. It represents a delayed response to the question frequently asked in his childhood: "Daniel, have you seen Caleb?"

Searching for Caleb, like Tyler's earlier novels, also illustrates the author's belief in the need for human adaptability, tolerance, and love. Justine epitomizes the philosophy. She weathers a dark and uncertain childhood with a depressive mother, frequent moves with her restless husband, the death of both parents and her grandfather, and the loss of her one daughter in marriage to a milquetoast minister. Yet, she remains spirited and continues to love her family. She insists on visiting Roland Park, a longing Duncan cannot understand, and she is committed to finding Caleb, not only out of a love of travel and adventure but also to share the experiences with her grandfather and to find her own roots. With its focus on community and family and its delineation of the unsettled conflicts of the past affecting the present, *Searching for Caleb* indicates Tyler's own roots in the family of southern literature.

Earthly Possessions • When it appeared in 1977, *Earthly Possessions* was Tyler's most unfavorably received novel. Among disapproving reviewers, Roger Sale in *The New York Times Review of Books* saw the book as "a cartoon" of sorts, with the life of Charlotte Emory, the protagonist, "reduced . . . by her own hand" until all "possible anguish is . . . lost." The reason for this response is no doubt the sardonic nature of Charlotte herself, an entrapped housewife who sets out to leave her husband but gets kidnapped instead in a bungled bank robbery. Such reversals characterize Charlotte's life and have led her to "loosen" her hold so that she sees everything from an ironic distance. Charlotte, moreover, is the novel's only narrator, and she tells her life story in chapters alternating perfectly with those narrating her experiences with Jake Simms, her kidnapper, on their trip south from Clarion, Maryland, Charlotte's hometown. Along the way, Tyler captures the fragmentation and transience of modern life, reflected in a string of drive-in restaurants, banks, and films. The triumph of the novel is not, as in earlier Tyler works, characterization, but the panorama of contemporary American life that the book captures during this journey of hostage and kidnapper.

With its contrapuntal chapters, *Earthly Possessions* is Tyler's most highly structured novel, the first to be told entirely in the first person by one narrator. The result is an artificial temporal arrangement and a restricted focus, one lifetime as compared with those of eight or nine Emersons, five generations of Pecks. Also, the reader is always in the presence of two somewhat unsavory characters: a nail-biting, minor-league criminal and a stoical, cynical woman. All might have come from the pen of Flannery O'Connor but for the touchingly human flaws Tyler draws. Neither Jake nor Charlotte, despite their failings, is morally culpable. What they share is a common, impractical desire for freedom from the entanglements of life: for Charlotte, marriage complete with a house full of relatives and in-laws, rooms of furniture (earthly possessions), even sinners from the mourner's bench at her husband's church; for Jake jail for a petty crime and a pregnant girlfriend. Heading south to rescue Jake's Kewpie-doll girlfriend from a home for unwed mothers, Charlotte realizes that Jake is, like herself, "criss-crossed by strings of love and need and worry." Even Charlotte and Jake's relationship grows into a type of commitment. Eventually the two share the driving as well as their troubles. Any "relationship," Tyler told Marguerite Michaels in an interview for *The New York Times Book Review*, even one "as bizarre as" that of "a bank robber and hostage could become . . . bickering [and] familiar. . . . Anything done gradually enough becomes ordinary."

Earthly Possessions, despite its problems, shares with *The Tin Can Tree* and *Celestial Navigation* a redefinition of family ties. With Tyler's other novels, it also illuminates the problems and conflicts of the individual within a close relationship, whether familial or not, and focuses on the eccentric nature of ordinary lives, the ordinariness of the bizarre.

Morgan's Passing • In her eighth novel, Tyler returned to the heart of Baltimore for her setting and to a central character, Morgan Gower, who is strikingly eccentric. Reviewers compared him with Saul Bellow's Henderson and Joseph Heller's Major Major. He also resembles Duncan Peck as well as other Tyler protagonists. Like those heroes, Morgan is in conflict with his family: seven daughters who find him embarrassing, a slovenly though good-natured wife, a senile mother, and a depressed, inert sister. Like Ben Joe Hawkes, Morgan feels trapped and misunderstood in a house cluttered with "the particles of related people's unrelated worlds" and full of women with whom he is unable to communicate satisfactorily. Although his family insists on going about life unconsciously, Morgan, spirited and highly inventive, faces a midlife crisis that calls for a change. He must also come to terms with his past, the consequences of marrying Bonny for her money as well as his father's inexplicable suicide when Morgan was a teenager. Like Duncan Peck, Morgan is a kind of mechanical genius who takes up various projects, then drops them—"a tinkering, puttering, hardware sort of man." Like the renegade Pecks, he eventually abandons his Baltimore family to take up a new life and identity with a traveling amusement company.

Despite these resemblances to other Tyler heroes, Morgan is a unique creation, the product of Tyler's maturing vision of life. Her understanding of his sexual attraction to a young puppeteer and her portrayal of his frustration with his wife suggest a depth of insight into the problems of marriage, a depth lacking in the early *If Morning Ever Comes*. Morgan is also a complex character, an impostor who tries on identities complete with matching costumes. At times he is "Father Morgan, the street priest of Baltimore"; at other times, he is an immigrant with family still abroad, a doctor who delivers a baby in the backseat of a car—any role in which people will accept him. Though most of this role-playing is harmless, Morgan is an antihero lacking a firm identity, a modern eccentric who revels in the anonymity and emptiness of decaying city neighborhoods and a man who assumes a false identity to take up life with another man's wife without benefit of divorce. Not surprisingly, reviewers found it difficult to like Morgan, but few found him unbelievable.

Tyler's increasing skill in capturing and making believable such a character testifies to her maturation as a writer. As John Leonard commented in *The New York Times* when reviewing the novel, readers "are obliged to care" about Tyler's "odd people" "because their oddities are what we see at an angle in the mirror in the middle of a bad night." Drawing from selected everyday scenes covering twelve years in Morgan's life, Tyler roots her novel firmly in the here and now. Morgan becomes believable because he is not always posing. He reads the morning paper over coffee, affectionately slaps his wife on her rear end, smokes too much, attends a daughter's wedding, despairs over a quarrel-filled family vacation, works in a hardware store, and comes down with a terrible cold. Tyler's is a realistic art illuminating family conflict and solidly based in the ordinary details of life.

Dinner at the Homesick Restaurant • Of all Tyler's novels, *Dinner at the Homesick Restaurant* most inspires comparison with the work of Flannery O'Connor. The title is reminiscent of O'Connor's wit and irony, and the mood of the novel, as one reviewer noted, is that of "O'Connor's Gothic South" with its "sullen, psychic menace." At her best, as in *Celestial Navigation*, Tyler captures the pain, anxiety, and isolation beneath the surface of ordinary lives. At times, however, particularly in *Earthly Possessions* but also *Morgan's Passing*, she treats this pain lightly, thus denying a sense of genuine struggle. In *Earthly Possessions*, Charlotte is flippant and ironic; in *Morgan's Passing*, Morgan is a zany, the mood quick and light. *Dinner at the Homesick Restaurant*, representing what John Updike called a "darkening" of Tyler's art, presents the other side of the coin from *Morgan's Passing*, not only in mood but also in story line. Its focus is not the husband who abandons his family to find a new life, but the family he left behind. It is a stunning psychological portrait of the Tulls, Pearl and her three children, and the anger, guilt, hurt, and anxiety they feel growing up in an uncertain world without a father. All carry their pain through life, illustrating more profoundly than any of Tyler's earlier books the past's haunting influence on the present.

Covering thirty-five years, three generations of Tulls, the novel opens with Pearl on her deathbed. This first chapter, reminiscent of Katherine Anne Porter's short story "The Jilting of Granny Weatherall," depicts Pearl as a stoical, frightened woman who has weathered a youth filled with dread of being an old maid, a quick marriage, and a lonely struggle to rear three "flawed" children: Cody, the oldest boy, a troublemaker from childhood, "prone to unreasonable rages"; Jenny, the only girl, "flippant" and "opaque"; Ezra, his mother's favorite, a gentle man who has not "lived up to his potential" but instead has become the ambitionless owner of the Homesick Restaurant. Not one of Pearl's children has turned out as she wished. Consequently, she, like other Tyler characters, feels "closed off" from her family, the very children to whom she has devoted her life. Later chapters reveal why, focusing on each of the children in turn and tracing the evolution of their lives as well as their fear of their mother's rages. All, like their mother, end up in some way "destroyed by love."

Tyler's compassionate portrayal of her characters and her characteristic humor do mitigate the darkness of this novel. Although Pearl, her forehead permanently creased from worry, verbally and physically abuses her children, Tyler lets the reader understand the reasons for Pearl's behavior and shows a far mellower Pearl in old age. Jenny, after struggling through medical school, two marriages, and a nervous breakdown, is nursed back to health by her mother. Cody spares no expense in caring for his family, even though he is unable to forgive Pearl for mistreating him as a child. The teenager Cody plays cruel but funny tricks on his brother, Ezra—partly out of resentment of Ezra's being the favorite but also from Cody's own pain and sense of rejection. Taking slats from Ezra's bed, Cody strews the floor with pornographic magazines so Pearl will think Ezra the kind of disappointment she finds Cody to be. Later, after stealing Ezra's sweetheart, he recognizes not only his guilt but also his love for his brother. These tales fill out the dark psychological portrait Tyler draws, making *Dinner at the Homesick Restaurant*, like many of Tyler's earlier books, a confirmation of life's difficulty as well as of the value of love.

The Accidental Tourist • A mood of dark comedy pervades *The Accidental Tourist*. It is the only Tyler work in which a murder occurs, and a sense of the inexplicable, tragic nature of reality moves the plot and forms a backdrop for the novel. The book opens with Macon and Sarah Leary returning from a truncated beach vacation and the sudden announcement by Sarah that she wants a divorce. Macon, the central character, is a forty-four-year-old writer of guidebooks for travellers who find themselves in foreign places but prefer the familiarity of home. The logo for the series, titled Accidental Tourist, is a winged armchair, a motif suggesting Macon's attitude toward the disruptions of travel. In the opening pages of *The Accidental Tourist*, the reader learns of the death of Macon and Sarah's twelve-year-old son, Ethan, who was killed in a robbery at a burger stand. Besides their grief at the death of their son, Macon and Sarah must confront the permanent jarring of their world by the random nature of the crime: The robber shot Ethan as an afterthought; Ethan and his friend had impulsively stolen away from a summer camp. With Sarah's leaving, Macon's life crumbles, yet he strives desperately to maintain control, to reduce life to its simplest terms. He sleeps in one sheet sewn together like a body bag and showers in his shirt to save on laundry. In a spirit of fun, Tyler gives Macon an alter ego, a Welsh corgi, Edward, who becomes increasingly surly as Macon's life disintegrates. Through Edward, Tyler introduces the unpredictable Muriel Pritchett, a dog trainer set on finding a father for her sickly son, Alexander.

Told from a limited third-person point of view, *The Accidental Tourist* displays Tyler's art at its best: her eye for idiosyncratic behavior and the accidental quality of reality, her focus on family as the center of life's triumphs and tragedies. The family here is not only Macon and Sarah but also Macon's siblings: his sister Rose, whose romance with Julian Edge, Macon's publisher, forms a dual plot to Macon's romance with Muriel, and his two brothers, Charles and Porter. For part of the novel, Tyler centers on the Leary siblings, all marred by their mother's carefree abandonment of them. Both Charles and Porter are divorced, and Rose now maintains her grandparents' home for her brothers. What is striking about the house is its orderliness—every item in the kitchen is shelved in alphabetical order—and its changelessness. When Macon breaks a leg in a freak accident, he returns to his siblings and resumes life just as if he had never been married, had a child, and lived away for years. The characteristics of families, Tyler suggests, are permanently etched. It is the occurrences of life that constantly shift.

Breathing Lessons • In *The Accidental Tourist*, Tyler depicted the dissolution of a twenty-year marriage following the violent death of the Learys' son. In *Breathing Lessons*, she presents the opposite: the duration of Ira and Maggie Moran's marriage for twenty-eight years. Told primarily through flashbacks as the couple journeys to the funeral of a friend, the novel covers nearly thirty years in one September day and contrasts the Morans' courtship and marriage with the relationship of their son, Jesse, and his former wife, Fiona. From its beginning, *Breathing Lessons* concerns not only Ira and Maggie's bickering, love, and tolerance for each other but also Maggie's struggle to reconcile Jesse and Fiona.

Set in Pennsylvania and Baltimore, the novel has three principal divisions, each told from a restricted third-person point of view. The first and third sections focus on Maggie's consciousness, while the middle section, which constitutes something of an interlude, centers on Ira's thoughts. The first section wittily depicts the music and mores of the 1950's. The second part depicts a side trip in which Ira and Maggie temporarily become involved with an elderly black man who has separated from his wife of more than fifty years. This section also provides Ira's family history and his response to his wife and children. Tyler reveals here a masterful handling of exposition through internal thought sequences and flashbacks. The novel's third section, which introduces the characters of Fiona and Leroy, her daughter, returns to Maggie's thoughts and her memories of Jesse and Fiona's relationship. A return to Baltimore with Fiona and Leroy completes the section, suggesting the cyclical nature of experience, a central theme in the novel.

In *Breathing Lessons,* Tyler continues to balance a lighthearted view of human nature with a depth of insight into the darker side of marriage. Maggie and Ira's marriage, while offering a sound balance of two contrasting personality types who can bicker and then reconcile, has its dark side also: a "helpless, angry, confined feeling" that Maggie experiences "from time to time." Ira, too, realizes that marriage involves "the same old arguments, . . . the same old resentments dragged up year after year." The joyful side of Tyler's fiction is her fondness for zany characters, her keen eye for the bizarre in human behavior, which she observes with amused detachment, and her finely tuned ear for human speech. *Breathing Lessons* offers many examples, beginning with the zesty, lowerclass names of her characters: Serena, Fiona, Duluth. Maggie herself belongs to a long line of lively, unpredictable Tyler heroines—most expert caretakers—beginning with Granny Hawkes in *If Morning Ever Comes,* Tyler's first novel. In fact, in both her acute observations of others and her repeated attempts "to alter people's lives," Maggie resembles her creator, the fiction writer who manipulates the lives of her characters to fill her plot.

Saint Maybe • The "darkening" of Tyler's work continues in *Saint Maybe* despite its lovably offbeat characters and unambiguously happy ending. Possible marital infidelity, child neglect, and suicide set the novel moving. The Bedloes are an "ideal, apple-pie" family, determined to be happy and "normal." Trouble invades their Eden in the form of Lucy, a sexy single mother who marries the elder son, Danny, bringing along two young children and, most likely, another she is carrying when she meets her new groom. She also brings an insatiable restlessness. The Bedloes welcome the addition to the fold, proclaiming their son fortunate to have found "a ready-made family." It is the seventeen-year-old protagonist Ian, Danny's younger brother, who questions Lucy's virtue, a query with lethal consequences: Danny's suicide when he sees himself a cuckold and Lucy's when she forfeits a bleak future with an overdose of pills.

Guilt over the tragedy he believes he has caused drives Ian to join the Church of the Second Chance, a congregation of born-again Christians who pursue active atonement for their failings. Obsessively seeking forgiveness, Ian drops out of college at the age of nineteen to raise his brother's orphaned stepchildren. Christlike, he forswears sexual activity and pursues carpentry. He leads a martyred though by no means solitary existence over the next twenty-three years. As with many Tyler heroes, Ian lacks self-awareness: He cannot recognize his own goodness, does not understand that he has paid any debt in full. However, when at forty-two he marries Rita diCarlo, a character reminiscent of Muriel Pritchett, Macon Leary's freewheeling lifeline in *The Accidental Tourist,* Ian is delightfully surprised to realize that he has not spent his years paying a penance but leading a rich—if unorthodox—life.

Ladder of Years • *Ladder of Years* tells the story of forty-year-old Cordelia Grinstead's circular flight from her upper-middle-class life in Baltimore. Until she simply walks away from her husband and teenage children during their vacation, Delia has never left home. Having passively married her father's assistant, who chose her as a helpmate in assuming the family medical practice, Delia lives her married life in her girlhood home, where she suffocates under the weight of domesticity. Her presence is defined by the demands of the family she nurtures, yet her children's increasing self-sufficiency threatens her with obsolescence. Fleeing home, Delia embarks on a journey toward self-discovery, a quest reminiscent of Charlotte Emory's in *Earthly Possessions*. She initially revels in her spare new existence in a small Maryland town, but as with other of Tyler's would-be renegades from the hearth, the caregiver's habits of heart and mind reassert themselves. Realizing that she has re-created the very role she believed she had shed, Delia embraces her identity as a nurturer and returns home, aware finally of her family's genuine yet unvoiced appreciation.

A Patchwork Planet • *A Patchwork Planet* revisits *Saint Maybe*'s theme of debt and repayment. Black sheep Barnaby Gaitlin is a former juvenile delinquent who, to the shame of his affluent parents, was arrested in his youth for breaking into the homes of their wealthy Guilford neighbors. To keep her son out of jail, Margot Gaitlin (born Margo Kazmerow, "just a Polish girl from Canton") swallowed her pride to beg and buy her neighbors' silence. Barnaby's freedom cost $8,700, a sum his embittered mother continually holds over him. Though Barnaby eventually repays this debt, he learns that self-respect cannot be purchased.

A handyman who performs odd jobs for an assortment of crotchety yet colorful senior citizens, Barnaby stumbles across a client's "Twinform" while tidying her attic. The mannequin—shaped and painted to resemble the owner—was invented by his great-grandfather as an aid to foolproof dressing: By first modeling an outfit on a "double," one could gauge and adjust the effect of the intended apparel. Barnaby is intrigued by this premise of the trial run, and he imputes his many mistakes to his failure to hold metaphoric dress rehearsals for his life. He is convinced that he lacks necessary information for successful living, a need that prompted the boyhood burglaries during which he would examine his victims' photographs and diaries for clues to how they managed their lives. He remains rudderless at the age of thirty, wavering between intentionally disappointing his parents through exaggerated irresponsibility and straining to please them, nearly marrying the unsuitably staid Sophia Maynard because she lends him the respectability he lacks.

Barnaby sinks to an emotional low when he is wrongly accused of theft, a crime Sophia believes him guilty of and a charge that he feels he vicariously deserves. However, in the homemade blanket alluded to in the novel's title, Barnaby finds the expansive perspective from which to accept the love and faith that his clients rightly place in him. On an elderly woman's quilt he sees that Earth is "makeshift and haphazard, clumsily cobbled together, overlapping and crowded and likely to fall into pieces at any moment." He is moved to accept and forgive his own failings as a universal condition of his humanity. The novel ends with his resolute goodbye to the girlfriend who doubted his goodness: "Sophia, you never did realize. I am a man you can trust."

Stella A. Nesanovich
Updated by Theresa M. Kanoza

Other major works

SHORT FICTION: "The Common Courtesies," 1968; "Who Would Want a Little Boy?," 1968; "With All Flags Flying," 1971; "The Bride in the Boatyard," 1972; "Spending," 1973; "The Base-Metal Egg," 1973; "Half-Truths and Semi-Miracles," 1974; "A Knack for Languages," 1975; "Some Sign That I Ever Made You Happy,"

1975; "The Geologist's Maid," 1975; "Your Place Is Empty," 1976; "Average Waves in Unprotected Waters," 1977; "Foot-Footing On," 1977; "Holding Things Together," 1977; "Uncle Ahmad," 1977; "Under the Bosom Tree," 1977; "Linguistics," 1978; "Laps," 1981; "The Country Cook," 1982; "Teenage Wasteland," 1983; "Rerun," 1988; "A Woman Like a Fieldstone House," 1989; "People Who Don't Know the Answers," 1991.

CHILDREN'S LITERATURE: *Tumble Tower,* 1993 (illustrations by Mitra Modarressi).

Bibliography

Bail, Paul. *Anne Tyler: A Critical Companion.* Westport, Conn.: Greenwood Press, 1998. Part of a series of reference books about popular contemporary writers, this book contains a biography and individual chapters that discuss twelve of Tyler's novels. General analysis includes how her novels fit into southern regional literature, women's literature, and popular culture, as well as critiques from feminist and multicultural points of view. Bail also discusses plot, characters, themes, literary devices, historical settings, and narrative points of view as they apply to individual novels. Extensive bibliography.

Croft, Robert W. *Anne Tyler: A Bio-Bibliography.* Westport, Conn.: Greenwood Press, 1995. Part of a series focusing on American authors, this book is divided into two parts: a biography that includes four chapters, each followed by endnotes. It concludes with an extensive bibliography, divided into primary and secondary sources, with a list of Anne Tyler's papers at Duke University.

_____. *An Anne Tyler Companion.* Westport, Conn.: Greenwood Press, 1998. General handbook covering all aspects of Tyler's fiction.

Evans, Elizabeth. *Anne Tyler.* New York: Twayne, 1993. Contains biography and an overview of Tyler's works. Includes a useful bibliography of primary and secondary sources.

Petry, Alice Hall. "Bright Books of Life: The Black Norm in Anne Tyler's Novels." *The Southern Quarterly* 31, no. 1 (Fall, 1992): 7-13. A study of Tyler's favorable portrayals of African Americans as wise and knowing characters.

Ravenel, Shannon, ed. *Best of the South.* Chapel Hill, N.C.: Algonquin Books, 1996. The introduction, by Anne Tyler, discusses the importance of settings and how they change over time. To illustrate, she describes the southern town, where she spent her teens: its tree-lined square, statue of a Confederate soldier, the movie theater, dime store with a snack bar, and the department store where Miss Mildred clerked. She compares it to today's scene in Raleigh, North Carolina, with its malls lined with salad bars, maxi-movie theaters, music video stores, fast-food restaurants, and the Gap. She discusses the "yeasty prose" of southern writing with its musical quality and conversational tone, characters who are just as important as what happens, and the narrative point of view and dialogue with which southerners identify.

Salwak, Dale, ed. *Anne Tyler as Novelist.* Iowa City: University of Iowa Press, 1994. A collection of essays addressing Tyler's development, attainments, and literary reputation.

Stephens, C. Ralph, ed. *The Fiction of Anne Tyler.* Jackson: University Press of Mississippi, 1990. A collection of essays selected from papers given in 1989 at the Anne Tyler Symposium in Baltimore and representing a range of interests and approaches.

Sweeney, Susan Elizabeth. "Anne Tyler." In *The History of Southern Women's Literature,* edited by Carolyn Perry and Mary Louise Weaks. Baton Rouge: Louisiana State University Press, 2002. Brief examination of Tyler's fiction in the context of southern women's writing.

Tyler, Anne. "Still Just Writing." In *The Writer on Her Work: Contemporary Women Writers Reflect on Their Art and Situation.* Edited by Janet Sternberg. New York: W. W. Norton, 1980. Tyler's personal essay explains how she keeps her life balanced.

Voelker, Joseph C. *Art and the Accidental in Anne Tyler.* Columbia: University of Missouri Press, 1989. The first book-length study of Anne Tyler's fiction, this volume focuses on the development of Tyler's aesthetics and her treatment of character, particularly her view of selfhood as mystery and of experience as accidental.

John Updike

Born: Shillington, Pennsylvania; March 18, 1932

Principal long fiction • *The Poorhouse Fair*, 1959; *Rabbit, Run*, 1960; *The Centaur*, 1963; *Of the Farm*, 1965; *Couples*, 1968; *Bech: A Book*, 1970; *Rabbit Redux*, 1971; *A Month of Sundays*, 1975; *Marry Me: A Romance*, 1976; *The Coup*, 1978; *Rabbit Is Rich*, 1981; *The Witches of Eastwick*, 1984; *Roger's Version*, 1986; *S.*, 1988; *Rabbit at Rest*, 1990; *Memories of the Ford Administration*, 1992; *Brazil*, 1994; *In the Beauty of the Lilies*, 1996; *Toward the End of Time*, 1997; *Bech at Bay: A Quasi-Novel*, 1998; *Gertrude and Claudius*, 2000; *Seek My Face*, 2002; *Villages*, 2004; *Terrorist*, 2006.

Other literary forms • Since publishing his first story in *The New Yorker* in 1954, Updike has truly become a man of letters, publishing in virtually every literary genre—poetry, short fiction, novel, essay, drama, art criticism, and autobiography. His first short-story collection, *The Same Door*, appeared in 1959; many more followed, including *The Afterlife, and Other Stories* in 1994 and and *Licks of Love: Short Stories and a Sequel, "Rabbit Remembered"* in 2000. In 2000, he coedited *The Best American Short Stories of the Century*, with Katrina Kenison.

Updike's play *Buchanan Dying* was published in 1974. His poetry has appeared in many volumes of his own, ranging from *The Carpentered Hen, and Other Tame Creatures* in 1958 to *Americana, and Other Poems* in 2001. He has also published many poems in anthologies. Updike published his first nonfiction prose collection in 1965; most of his nonfiction works are collections of essays and criticism, but the autobiographical *Self-Consciousness: Memoirs* appeared in 1989, and the single-themed *Golf Dreams: Writings on Golf* was published in 1996. Updike's essays on art have been collected in *Just Looking: Essays on Art* (1989) and *Still Looking: Essays on American Art* (2005).

Achievements • One of the major figures to emerge in American fiction after World War II, John Updike is widely acclaimed as one of the most accomplished stylists and prolific writers of his generation. Showing remarkable versatility and range, his fiction represents a penetrating chronicle in the realist mode of the changing morals and manners of American society. Updike's work has met with both critical and popular success. His first novel, *The Poorhouse Fair*, was awarded the Rosenthal Award of the National Institute of Arts and Letters in 1960. In 1964, he received the National Book Award for *The Centaur*. He was elected the same year to the National Institute of Arts and Letters. A number of his short stories have won the O. Henry Prize for best short story of the year and have been included in the yearly volumes of *Best American Short Stories*. In 1977, he was elected to the prestigious American Academy of Arts and Letters. In 1981, his novel *Rabbit Is Rich* won the Pulitzer Prize in fiction and the American Book Award. During that same year, he was awarded the Edward MacDowell Medal for literature.

Although Updike's novels continue the long national debate on the American civilization and its discontents, perhaps more significant is their depiction of restless and aspiring spirits struggling within the constraints of flesh, of time and gravity—lovers and battlers all. For Updike (writing about the novel in an essay), "Not to be in

© Davis Freeman

love, the capital N novel whispers to capital W western man, is to be dying."

Biography • The only child of Wesley and Linda Grace (née Hoyer) Updike, John Updike spent the first thirteen years of his life living with his parents and grandparents in his maternal grandparents' home in Shillington, Pennsylvania, in rather strained economic conditions. In 1945, the Updikes had to move to the family farm in Plainville, ten miles away from Shillington. Updike's father supported the family on his meager salary as a mathematics teacher at the high school. His mother had literary aspirations of her own and later became a freelance writer. A number of short stories, such as "Flight," and the novels *The Centaur* and *Of the Farm* drew upon this experience. As a youth, Updike dreamed of drawing cartoons and writing for *The New Yorker*, an ambition he fulfilled in 1955. Updike went to Harvard University in 1950 on a full scholarship, majoring in English. He was editor of *The Harvard Lampoon* and graduated in 1954 with highest honors. In 1953, he married Radcliffe student Mary Pennington, the daughter of a Unitarian minister; they were to have four children.

After a year in Oxford, England, where Updike studied at the Ruskin School of Drawing and Fine Art, he returned to the United States to a job offered him by E. B. White as a staff writer with *The New Yorker*, for which he wrote the "Talk of the Town" column. In April of 1957, fearing the city scene would disturb his development as a writer, Updike and his family left New York for Ipswich, Massachusetts, where he would live for the next seventeen years and that would serve as the model for the settings of a number of stories and novels. During this time, Updike was active in Ipswich community life and regularly attended the Congregational Church. In 1974, the Updikes were divorced. In 1977, Updike remarried, and he and his new wife, Martha Bernhard, settled in Georgetown, Massachusetts.

During the late 1950's and early 1960's, Updike faced a crisis of faith prompted by his acute consciousness of death's inevitability. The works of such writers as Søren Kierkegaard and, especially, Karl Barth, the Swiss orthodox theologian, helped Updike come to grips with this fear and to find a basis for faith. Religious and theological concerns pervade Updike's fiction. In a real sense, like Nathaniel Hawthorne's writing more than one hundred years earlier, Updike's fiction explores for his time the great issues of sin, guilt, and grace—of spiritual yearnings amid the entanglements of the flesh.

Updike's success as a writer enabled him to travel under government auspices. In 1964-1965, Updike traveled to Russia, Romania, Bulgaria, and Czechoslovakia as part of the U.S.S.R.-U.S. Cultural Exchange Program. In 1973, he traveled and lectured as a Fulbright lecturer in Ghana, Nigeria, Tanzania, Kenya, and Ethiopia. Updike's Bech novels and *The Coup* reflect those journeys.

Analysis • A writer with John Updike's versatility and range, whose fiction reveals a virtual symphonic richness and complexity, offers readers a variety of keys or themes with which to explore his work. The growing and already substantial body of criticism Updike's work has engendered, therefore, reflects a variety of approaches. Alice and Kenneth Hamilton were among the first critics to give extensive treatment to the religious and theological elements in Updike's fiction. Rachel Burchard explores Updike's fiction in terms of its presentations of authentic quests for meaning in modern times, for answers to age-old questions about humanity and God, and of its affirmation of human worth and hope despite the social and natural forces threatening defeat of the human enterprise. Considering technique as well as theme, Larry Taylor treats the function of the pastoral and antipastoral in Updike's fiction and places that treatment within a long tradition in American literature. British critic Tony Tanner discusses Updike's fiction as depicting the "compromised environment" of New England suburbia—the fear and dread of decay, of death and nothingness, and the dream of escaping from the complications of such a world. Edward Vargo focuses upon the recurrence of ritualistic patterns in Updike's fiction, the struggle to wrest something social from an increasingly secularized culture. Joyce Markle's thematic study of Updike's fiction sees a conflict between "Lovers," or Life-givers, and the embodied forces of convention, dehumanizing belief, and death.

In a 1962 memoir titled "The Dogwood Tree: A Boyhood," Updike discusses his boyhood fascination with what he called the "Three Great Secret Things: Sex, Religion, and Art." Critic George W. Hunt contends that "these three secret things also characterize the predominant subject matter, thematic concerns, and central questions found throughout his adult fiction." Detailing Updike's reliance upon the ideas of Søren Kierkegaard and Karl Barth, Hunt's study is interested in the religious implications of Updike's work. A more sociological interest informs Philip Vaughan's study of Updike's fiction, which, to Vaughan, provides readers with valid depictions of the social conditions—loneliness, isolation, aging, and morality—of modern times. David Galloway sees Updike's fiction in existential terms, seeing Updike's protagonists as "absurd heroes" seeking meaning in an inhospitable universe. More impressionistic but quite suggestive is Elizabeth Tallent's short study of the fate of Eros in several of Updike's novels. Believing that a thesis or thematic approach does not do full justice to Updike's work, Donald J. Greiner examines Updike's novels more formalistically in order to "discuss the qualities that make Updike a great writer."

Using a comparative approach, George Searles discusses Philip Roth and Updike as important social realists whose work gives a true sense of life in the last half of the twentieth century. To Searles, Updike's overriding theme is cultural disintegration—questing but alienated protagonists confronting crises caused by a breakdown of the established order. Jeff Campbell uses Updike's long poem *Midpoint* (1969) as a key to an analysis of Updike's fiction. Seeing Updike as an "ironist of the spiritual life," Ralph C. Wood discusses Updike's fiction—along with the fiction of Flannery O'Connor, Walker Percy, and Peter De Vries—as depicting the "comedy of redemption," a study deeply indebted to the theology of Karl Barth.

In a compendious study of American fiction since 1940, Frederick R. Karl offers a useful overview of Updike:

> Updike's fiction is founded on a vision of a compromised, tentative, teetering American, living in suburban New England or in rural Pennsylvania; an American who has broken with his more disciplined forebears and drifted free, seeking self-fulfillment but uncertain what it is and how to obtain it.

Although this rather global description fairly represents the recurring condition in most of Updike's novels, it does not do justice to the complex particularities of each work. Nevertheless, it does point to the basic predicament of nearly all of Updike's protagonists—that sense of doubleness, of the ironic discrepancy of the fallen creature who yet senses, or yearns for, something transcendent. Updike's people are spiritual amphibians—creatures in concert with two realms, yet not fully at home in either. Updike employs an analogous image in his novel *The Centaur*—here is a creature that embodies the godly with the bestial, a fitting image of the human predicament in Updike's fiction. His fiction depicts the ambiguity of the "yes-but" stance toward the world, similar to the paradox of the "already and the not-yet." In his fine story "The Bulgarian Poetess" (1966), Updike writes: "Actuality is a running impoverishment of possibility." Again there is a sense of duplicity, of incompleteness. In such a world, problems are not always solved; they are more often endured, if not fully understood. However, even the curtains of actuality occasionally part, unexpectedly, to offer gifts, as Updike avers in his preface to *Olinger Stories: A Selection* (1964)—such gifts as keep alive a vision of wholeness in an often lost and fragmented world.

The Poorhouse Fair • Updike's first novel, *The Poorhouse Fair*, may seem anomalous in comparison with the rest of his work. In fact, the novel depicts a collision of values that runs throughout Updike's work. As in so much of Updike's fiction, the novel is concerned with decay, disintegration, a loss or abandonment of vital traditions, of values, of connection to a nurturing past. This opposition is embodied in the two principal characters: ninety-four-year-old John Hook, former teacher and resident of the poorhouse, and Stephen Conner, the poorhouse's prefect. The novel is set in the future, sometime during the late 1970's, when want and misery have virtually been eliminated by a kind of humanistic socialism. Such progress has been made at a price: sterility, dehumanization, spiritual emptiness, and regimentation. In a world totally run by the head, the heart dies. Hook tells Conner, in response to the prefect's avowed atheism: "There is no goodness, without belief." Conner's earthly paradise is a false one, destroying what it would save. The former prefect, Mendelssohn, sought, as his name would suggest, to fulfill the old people's spiritual needs in rituals and hymn singing.

Out of frustration with Conner's soulless administration, the old people break into a spontaneous "stoning" of Conner in the novel's climax. In effect, Conner is a corrupt or perverted martyr to the new "religion" of godless rationalism. The incident symbolizes the inherent desire and need for self-assertion and individualism. Conner's rationalized system is ultimately entropic. The annual fair is symbolic of an antientropic spirit in its celebration of the fruits of individual self-expression—patchwork quilts and peach-pit sculptures. In its depiction of an older America—its values of individuality, personal dignity, and pride—being swallowed up by material progress and bureaucratic efficiency, the novel is an "old" and somber book for a young author to write. In effect, Updike depicts an America become a spiritual "poorhouse," though materially rich. It is Hook, one of the last links to that lost America, who struggles at the end for some word to leave with Conner as a kind of testament, but he cannot find it.

The Centaur • In a number of stories and the novels *The Centaur* and *Of the Farm*, Updike draws heavily upon his experiences growing up in Shillington, Pennsylvania. Both novels—though very different from each other—concern the reckoning of a son with a parent, in the case of *The Centaur* with his father and in *Of the Farm* with his mother, before he can proceed with his life. This is emotional and spiritual "homework" necessary for the son's passage to maturity, to freedom from the past, yet also to a new sense of responsibility. As in all Updike's fiction, this passage is difficult, complex, and ambiguous in its resolution.

The Centaur is arguably Updike's most complex novel, involving as it does the complicated interweaving of the myth of Chiron the centaur with the story of an adolescent boy and his father one winter in 1947. Although the novel won the National Book Award, its reception was quite mixed. A number of reviewers thought the use of myth to be pretentious and not fully realized, while others praised the author's achievement. The novel is part *Bildungsroman*, a novel of moral education, and part *Künstlerroman*, a novel of an artist seeking his identity in conflict with society or his past. Operating on different levels, temporally and spatially, the nine chapters of the novel are a virtual collage, quite appropriate for the painter-narrator, nearly thirty, self-described as a "second-rate abstract expressionist," who is trying to recover from his past some understanding that might clarify and motivate his artistic vocation. Peter Caldwell, the narrator, reminisces to his black mistress in a Manhattan loft about a three-day period in the winter of 1947, fourteen years earlier. On the realistic level, Peter tells the story of his self-conscious adolescence growing up an only child, living on a farm with his parents and Pop Kramer, his grandfather. His father is the high school biology teacher and swim coach, whose acts of compassion and charity embarrass the boy. On the mythic level, the father is depicted as Chiron the centaur, part man and part stallion, who serves as mentor to the youthful Greek heroes. As such, he suffers for his charges. By moving back and forth between the mythic and the realistic levels, Peter is able to move to an understanding of his father's life and death and to a clarification of his own vocation.

Just as Chiron sacrifices his immortality—he accepts death—so that Prometheus may be free to live, so too does George give his life for his son. Although George is obsessed with death, it is doubtful that his sacrifice takes the form of death. Rather, his sacrifice is his willingness to go on fulfilling his obligations to his family. In reflecting upon this sacrifice by his father, Peter, feeling a failure in his art, asks: *"Was it for this that my father gave up his life?"* In the harsh reappraisal his memory provides, Peter is learning what he could not know as an adolescent. Love, guilt, and sacrifice are somehow inherent in the very structure of life. It is this that his mythicized father reveals to him in the very act of his narrating the story. For many critics, George Caldwell's sacrificial act frees the son to resume his artistic vocation with courage. For others, the novel is a mock epic showing in Peter the artist, the son of a scientist father and the grandson of a preacher, a loss of the metaphoric realm that makes great art possible and that leaves Peter diminished by his confinement to the earth alone. However the end is taken, the mythic element of the narrative richly captures the doubleness of human existence so pervasive in Updike's fictions.

Of the Farm • A short novel, *Of the Farm* is another tale of the intricacy of love, guilt, sacrifice, and betrayal. In *The Centaur,* Peter Caldwell, stalled and failing in his artistic vocation, goes home through a creative act of the memory and imagination to recover his lost vision, a basis to continue his work. Peter can fulfill his Promethean charge because his father was Chiron. In contrast, *Of the Farm*'s Joey Robinson goes home to get his mother's blessing on his recent remarriage. Joey seeks forgiveness of the guilt he bears for the acts of betrayal that have constituted his life. He betrays his poetic aspirations by becoming an advertising executive and betrays his marriage to Joan and his three children through adultery and divorce. Bringing home for his domineering mother's approval his sensuous new wife, Peggy, sets the stage for more betrayals and recriminations. As the weekend progresses, Peggy and Joey's mother vie for Joey's soul. Joey cannot please both women or heal the wounds of his past betrayals. For Joey, Peggy is the "farm" he wishes to husband. At the end, failing to win his mother's blessing, Joey and Peggy return to their lives in the city, leaving Joey's mother to die amid the memorials of her own unrealized dreams. If the novel is an exploration of human freedom, as the epigraph from Jean-Paul Sartre would suggest, the reader sees that freedom escapes all the characters, bound as they are by conflicting desires, guilt, and obligation.

Rabbit, Run • When Updike published *Rabbit, Run* in 1960, a story of an ex-basketball player and his floundering marriage set during the late 1950's, he had no intention of writing a sequel. Yet, Updike returned to Harry "Rabbit" Angstrom once every ten years for four novels—*Rabbit Redux* (1971), *Rabbit Is Rich* (1981), and *Rabbit at Rest* (1990)—as a kind of gauge of the changes occuring in American culture. This series of novels is among the most popular of his work.

For *Rabbit, Run*, Updike uses a quote from Pascal for an epigraph: "The motions of Grace, the hardness of heart; external circumstances." Updike has commented that those three things describe human lives. In a real sense, those things also describe the basic movements and conflicts in the Rabbit novels. From *Rabbit, Run* to *Rabbit at Rest*, as the titles themselves suggest, Rabbit's life has been characterized by a series of zigzag movements and resistances and yearnings, colliding, often ineffectually, with the external circumstances of a fast-paced and changing world. *Rabbit, Run* takes place during the late 1950's, when Harry Angstrom, a former high school basketball great nicknamed Rabbit, at the age of twenty-six finds himself in a dead-end life, with a job selling items in a dime store and a marriage to a careless and boozy woman. Wounded by the stifling boredom of everyday life and the cloying pressures of conforming and adapting to his environment, so characteristic of the 1950's, Harry wonders, confusedly, what has happened to his life. The disgust he feels about his present life is aggravated by his memories of when he was "first-rate at something" as a high school basketball great. Out of frustration, Rabbit bolts from his life-stifling existence, feeling that something out there wants him to find it.

Updike's novel is the study of this nonhero's quest for a nonexistent grail. Rabbit's zigzagging or boomeranging movements from wife Janice to mistress Ruth, the part-time prostitute, wreaks havoc: Janice accidentally drowns the baby; Ruth is impregnated and seeks an abortion. Pursued by the weak-faithed, do-gooder minister Eccles and failed by his old coach Tothero, Rabbit has no one to whom he can turn for help. Rabbit, like so many of Updike's protagonists, is enmeshed in the highly compromised environment of America, locked in the horizontal dimension yet yearning for something transcendent, the recovery of the vertical dimension. For

Rabbit, the closest he can come to that missing feeling is sex, the deep mysteries of the woman's body replacing the old revelations of religion. Rabbit, though irresponsible, registers his refusal to succumb to such a world through movement, his running replacing the lost territories of innocent escape.

Rabbit Redux • Ten years later, in *Rabbit Redux*, Rabbit has stopped running. He is back home with Janice and works as a typesetter. It is the end of the 1960's, and Rabbit watches the Moon landing on television as well as the upheavals of the civil rights movement, campus demonstrations, and the Vietnam War. Rabbit feels that the whole country is doing what he did ten years earlier. As Janice moves out to live with her lover Stavros, Rabbit and his son Nelson end up as hosts to Jill, a runaway flower child, and a bail-jumping Vietnam veteran and black radical named Skeeter. This unlikely combination allows Updike to explore the major cultural and political clashes of the 1960's. This time Rabbit is more a passive listener-observer than an activist searcher. Skeeter's charismatic critiques of the American way of life challenge Rabbit's unquestioning patriotism and mesmerize him. As a result, Rabbit is helpless when disaster comes—his house is set on fire, and Jill dies inside. Rabbit helps Skeeter escape. Fearing for her lover's heart, Janice returns to Rabbit. Unlike the restless figure of the first novel, Rabbit now seems to have capitulated or resigned himself to those powerful "external circumstances" from which he once sought escape. Rabbit bears witness, numbingly, to a disintegrating America, even as it puts a man on the Moon. America's spiritual landscape is as barren as that on the Moon. The novel ends with Rabbit and Janice asleep together. Perhaps they can awake to a new maturity and sense of responsibility for what they do in the world.

Rabbit Is Rich and **Rabbit at Rest** • In the first two Rabbit novels, Rabbit was out of step with the times—running in the placid 1950's, sitting in the frenetic 1960's. In *Rabbit Is Rich*, he is running again, but this time in tune with the rhythms of the 1970's. Rabbit now jogs, which is in keeping with the fitness craze that began during the 1970's. He and Janice are prospering during the decade of inflation and energy crises. They own a car dealership and are members of a country club. Rabbit plays golf and goes to Rotary Club lunches. Instead of newspapers, as in *Rabbit Redux*, he reads *Consumer Reports*, the bible of his new status. The ghosts of his past haunt him, however: the drowned baby, the child he did or did not have with Ruth, memories of Jill and Skeeter. The chief reminder of the sins of his past is his son Nelson, returning home, like something repressed, to wreak havoc on the family's new affluent complacency. Like his father of old but lacking Rabbit's conscience and vision, Nelson has a quest for attention that practically wrecks everything that he touches: his father's cars, his relationships. Rabbit can see himself in Nelson's behavior and tries to help him avoid recapitulating Rabbit's mistakes, but communication is difficult between them. With Skylab falling and America held hostage by Iranians, the present is uneasy and anxious, the future uncertain. Characteristically, Rabbit turns to sex to fill the spiritual void. He and Janice make love on top of their gold Krugerrands. Rabbit lusts for the lovely Cindy, but in the wife-swapping escapade during their Caribbean holiday, Rabbit gets Thelma Harrison instead and is introduced to anal sex—a fitting image of the sense of nothingness pervading American culture at the end of the "Me Decade." Updike does not end there. He leaves Rabbit holding his granddaughter, "another nail in his coffin," but also another chance for renewal, perhaps even a motion of grace, a richness unearned.

The sense of exhaustion—of a world "running out of gas" in so many ways—that pervades *Rabbit Is Rich* becomes more serious, even terminal, in *Rabbit at Rest*. The fuzzy emptiness and mindlessness of the 1980's pervade the novel, even as so much is described in such vivid detail. Rabbit and Janice now winter in Florida, and Nelson runs the car dealership. Rabbit sustains himself on junk food and endless television viewing, images of the emptiness of American life under Ronald Reagan. He suffers a heart attack and undergoes an angioplasty procedure. His son's cocaine addiction and embezzlement of $200,000 from the business shock the family. However, this often coarse and unsympathetic man continues to compel the reader's interest. He wonders about the Dalai Lama then in the news. As the Cold War dissipates, Rabbit asks: "If there's no Cold War, what's the point of being an American?" The man called "Mr. Death" in *Rabbit, Run* now must face death in his own overblown body and contemplate it in relation to a world he has always known but that now is no more. Can such a man find peace, an acceptance and understanding of a life lived in such struggle and perplexity? In *Rabbit Is Rich*, Harry confesses to Janice the paradox of their lives: "Too much of it and not enough. The fear that it will end some day, and the fear that tomorrow will be the same as yesterday." In intensive care in Florida, at the end of *Rabbit at Rest*, Rabbit says, "Enough." Is this the realization and acceptance of life's sufficiency or its surplus? A confession of his own excesses and indulgences, or a command of sorts that he has had enough? These are only a few of the questions raised by the Rabbit novels.

Marry Me • Many critics praise Updike for being the premier American novelist of marriage. Nearly all of his fiction displays the mysterious as well as commonplace but ineluctable complexities and conflicts of marriage. It is one of Updike's major concerns to explore the conditions of love in modern times. His fiction is his updating and reworking of the Tristan and Isolde myth, about which Updike had commented in his review of Denis de Rougement's book *Love in the Western World* (1956)—lovers whose passion is enhanced by the obstacles needed to be overcome to fulfill it; the quest for an ideal lover who will assuage the fear of death and the longing for the infinite; the confusions of eros and the death wish. Many of Updike's male protagonists are aspects of both Tristan and Don Juan in their quest for a life-enhancing or death-denying passion. Such are the ingredients in the novels *Couples, Marry Me: A Romance* and *The Witches of Eastwick*. All the novels are set during the 1960's—the spring of 1962 to the spring of 1963 in *Marry Me*, the spring of 1963 to the spring of 1964 in *Couples*, and probably 1969 for *The Witches of Eastwick*. In their various ways, each novel tries to answer the question, "After Christianity, what?" Human sexuality is liturgy and sacrament of the new religion emerging in America during the 1960's—a new end of innocence in a "post-pill paradise." The three novels make an interesting grouping because all deal with marriages in various states of deterioration, and all explore the implications of "sex as the emergent religion, as the only thing left," Updike said. Although not published until 1976, *Marry Me* was actually written before *Couples*. In fact, one story seems to lead right into the other. *The Witches of Eastwick* explores the theme from a woman's perspective.

Both Jerry Conant of *Marry Me* and Piet Hanema of *Couples* are educated professionals, married with children, and live in upper-middle-class suburbs of great cities. They are both suffering spiritually, longing for an affirmation from outside their selves, for some sort of blessing and certainty. As Jerry says, "Maybe our trouble is that we live in the twilight of the old morality, and there's just enough to torment us, and not enough to hold us in." The mortal fear that such an insight inspires leads both men to desperate quests for a love that will mend or heal their spiritual brokenness or emptiness. *Marry Me* takes place during the second year of the Kennedy administration, when the charm of the Camelot myth still captivated the United States. Significantly, Updike calls *Marry Me* a "romance" rather than a novel, in order to suggest an attempt to use the freer form to explore the ambiguities of love, marriage, and adultery. The novel ends in ambiguity, with no clear resolution. In fact, there are three possible endings: Jerry with his lover Sally in Wyoming, Jerry with his wife, Ruth, in France, and Jerry in the Virgin Islands alone, on the island of St. Croix, symbolizing perhaps Jerry's self-immolation.

Couples • *Couples* is set during the last year of the Kennedy presidency, including Kennedy's assassination, and is thus a much more cynical book, harsher and darker than *Marry Me*. A certain light has gone out in the land; death and decay haunt the imagination. In contrast to *Marry Me*, choices are made and lives reconstitute themselves in a kind of cyclical way at the end of *Couples*. These two rather weak men fail at their quest to find in the flesh what they have lost in the spirit. Both men are believers and churchgoers, and both face a crisis in their faith. The church, committed to secularity and worldliness, fails them. Their respective wives are naturalistic and feel at home on earth and offer them little surcease to their anxiety. In *Marry Me*, Jerry must contend with Sally's husband, Richard, an atheist with one blind eye, who insists on clear-cut decisions. For Jerry, however, every choice involves a loss that he cannot tolerate.

In *Couples*, Piet is pitted against Freddy Thorne, the self-proclaimed priest of the new religion of sensuality. To Freddy, it is their fate to be "suspended in . . . one of those dark ages that visits mankind between millennia, between the death and rebirth of gods, when there is nothing to steer by but sex and stoicism and the stars." The many adulteries among the ten couples of *Couples* lead finally to divorce and disintegration of the secular paradise of Tarbox, the fictional suburb of the novel. Piet leaves his unattainable but earthbound wife, fittingly named Angela, for the sensuous Foxy Whitman, whose abortion of Piet's child Freddy arranges. When his church is destroyed by fire, Piet is freed from his old morality and guilt and the tension inherent in his sense of fallenness. However, the satisfaction obtained with Foxy is a foreclosure of the vertical hope and is a kind of death. Both novels depict the failure of sex as a religion as well as the profound disappointments with love in its romantic or secular forms. Such may be Updike's answer to the question he posed: "After Christianity, what?"

The Witches of Eastwick • The setting of *The Witches of Eastwick* is a small town in Rhode Island during the first year or so of Richard Nixon's presidency, an era of protest and discontent. Three divorcés, Alexandra Spofford, Jane Smart, and Sukie Rougemont, discover the power of sisterhood and femininity and become witchlike in their powers. The delicate balance of their friendship is upset by the entrance of the apparently demoniac Darryl Van Horne, who takes them all as his lovers. The novel's three parts, "The Coven," "Malefica," and "Guilt," suggest a progression from their newfound power and independence through an encounter with the demoniac to a rediscovery of responsibility through an awareness of guilt. Like Updike's many male protagonists, the three women must come to grips with death before they can reconstitute a meaningful life. Van Horne is a satanic figure whose machinations lead to a dissipation of the women's powers. When he chooses the young Jennifer Gabriel for his wife, the women employ their powers to create a curse to bring about Jennifer's death. When she does die, the women feel guilt, even though it is not clear that their curse caused the woman's cancer. Van Horne preaches a sermon on the evilness of a creation saturated with disease and leaves town with Jennifer's brother, Christopher. The three women disband and find their way into suitable marriages. Such use of witchcraft allows Updike to explore the nature of evil and its connections with nature, history, and technology. The ambiguities of feminism are examined in the context of the moral and social confusions of the late 1960's in an effort to break down the destructive and outmoded polarities of the patriarchical tradition.

Bech* and *The Coup • The first two Bech books—*Bech: A Book* and *Bech Is Back*—and *The Coup* are novels and stories resulting from Updike's travels to Eastern Europe and to Africa. Each work offers the author an opportunity to develop a very different persona from those of his domestic novels, as well as the chance to explore another aspect of "otherness" and "difference." *Bech: A Book* is a collection of seven stories about a middle-aged and very successful Jewish novelist, Henry Bech, and his various experiences both abroad and in America. The collection is framed by the fiction of Updike writing about an actual person contemporary with him. The book has a foreword by the putative author as well as two appendices. Such devices afford Updike an opportunity for humorous satire of the literary life in America. Bech emerges as a strong and believable character struggling with the failure of his success as a writer in a success-plagued culture. In *Bech Is Back*, Updike creates seven more stories about Bech's travels and his wrestling with the ambiguities of fame, fortune, and human worth, the protagonist's success with women an index of his success and worth as a writer. He must struggle with the question of whether he has sold out his talent for the marketplace, defiling both.

Felix Ellellou, the protagonist of *The Coup*, is a bold creation for Updike, a black Islamic Marxist whose memoirs constitute the novel. Now in exile, the former president of the fictional sub-Saharan nation of Kush recounts the story of his rise and fall and of his perpetual struggle to avoid the ambiguous gifts of American aid. He fears not only the junk food but also the forces of secularity and materialism that will ultimately make of his beloved Kush a spiritual wasteland. He virtually stands alone in his resistance to the so-called benefits of American civilization, toward which he admits ambivalence. In Ellellou, one can see an African version of Updike's body-spirit conflict so prevalent in his fiction. For Ellellou, freedom must be freedom from material possessions, yet he anguishes over his people's poverty-stricken plight. He believes that it is better to die in poverty than from spiritual loss. In privation, he believes, the spirit will soar. Despite Ellellou's stoicism, his faith is plagued by doubts. He suspects that the new world religion will be godless and entropic. Updike's African novel is a replay of the author's critical interrogation of the moral and spiritual failures of the West.

A Month of Sundays, Roger's Version,* and *S. • Updike's concern with love, marriage, and adultery in so much of his fiction links him to Nathaniel Hawthorne's great novel *The Scarlet Letter* (1850), America's first great treatment of the complex social and religious consequences of adulterous love. Three novels in particular treat different dimensions of that adulterous triangle of Hawthorne's novel—*A Month of Sundays, Roger's Version,* and *S.* Hawthorne's Dimmesdale is updated in the figure of the

Reverend Tom Marshfield, the exiled protagonist of *A Month of Sundays*. Roger Lambert of *Roger's Version*, the professor of theology specializing in heresies, is Updike's treatment of Hawthorne's Roger Chillingworth. Sarah Worth of *S.* is a contemporary depiction of Hawthorne's Hester, the truly noble and strong character of *The Scarlet Letter.* Hawthorne's Dimmesdale is crushed by his inability to integrate the body-and-soul division. So, too, does Updike's Marshfield suffer from this split in a novel with many allusions to *The Scarlet Letter.* Marshfield marries the former Jane Chillingworth, whose father was Marshfield's ethics instructor. The retreat center is managed by Ms. Prynne, who reads the diary entries of Marshfield and his fellow clerical exiles.

The novel traces Marshfield's integration of body and spirit, a mending of Marshfield's fragmented self, enabling him to return to his ministry as a true helper to the faithful. Roger Chillingworth in *The Scarlet Letter* was the cuckolded husband seeking revenge for his wife's adultery. In *Roger's Version*, Roger Lambert imagines that his wife, Esther, is having an affair with Dale, the computer science graduate student trying to prove God's existence by computer. Dale is a kind of innocent, a fundamentalist seeking technological support for his faith. By the end, Dale's project has failed, as Roger believed it would, and Dale returns to Ohio, his faith demolished. Yet, Dale's project provoked Roger to revivify his own faith and to engage his world more responsibly than he has. Updike's Sarah Worth of *S.* is certainly one possible version of a late twentieth century Hester Prynne. Sarah is a woman who has taken her life fully into her own hands without shame or illusion. After bolting from her faithless but wealthy physician husband, Sarah goes to an ashram in Arizona for spiritual renewal. That proves to be a false endeavor, but Sarah survives intact (and with much of the cult's money). Loving and compassionate yet willful and worldly, Sarah Worth dares to follow her own path.

Toward the End of Time • Ever the chronicler of societal obsessions, Updike in 1997 provided his readers with a millennial book, *Toward the End of Time*. In this, his twentieth novel, the year is 2020, and the Sino-American nuclear war has recently destroyed the North American infrastructure and the U.S. government. In a universe of two moons and new life-forms, the "metallobioforms" that rose up out of the nuclear slime, the normal order of things seems to have come undone. Updike's protagonist, Ben Turnbull, seems at times to assume the identities of such disparate entities as an ancient Egyptian tomb robber and a medieval monk, and he is having an affair with a dark-eyed young woman whom he suspects is also a doe. Updike spends considerable time mulling over the mysteries of quantum mechanics and string theory, implying that such abstractions may contain the key to the enigma of time. In the end, though, the drama of Ben's post-millennial existence seems an elaboration of the sublunary obsessions of other Updike protagonists. The story of this sixty-six-year-old retired financial adviser could almost serve as a coda to the Rabbit books.

Bech at Bay • With *Bech at Bay: A Quasi-Novel*, Updike ended the saga of another of his favorite alter egos, the now-septuagenarian Henry Bech. Like its predecessors, this "quasi-novel" consists of a series of linked stories concerning the crabbed but accomplished—and now superannuated—Jewish novelist. *Bech at Bay* finds Bech at the heart of late twentieth century American literary life; however, that life, like Bech himself, seems to have lost nearly all its vitality. The mood is set in the book's opening section, "Bech in Czech," in which Bech finds himself on a book tour in the gloom of Prague, haunted by the uneasy feeling that he is no more than a character in someone else's book. In another episode, Bech is tapped to head an elite artistic organization called "The Forty"—a group not unlike the American Academy of Art and Letters, which Updike served as chancellor—but finds himself presiding over its demise when the elderly existing members refuse to admit any new blood.

Nonetheless, Bech has not lost all his imaginative powers. In "Bech Noir," he fantasizes the murders of critics who have abused him. Then, in the volume's finale, Bech is awarded the Nobel Prize. Delivering his acceptance speech before the Swedish Academy, Bech asserts his vitality by holding aloft his newborn daughter for the audience's edification. The gesture is, if nothing else, life affirming. Exactly how Bech—a "semi-obscure" writer with a slim body of work—arrived at this pinnacle of literary recognition is no clearer than the import of Bech's entire literary saga. Updike may be saying that for his fictional counterpart, this jaded urban Jew with writer's block, life and sex trump art. As the title of the book tells the reader, this last installment of the Bech series is a quasi-novel, and Henry Bech seems often to be merely a mask for his creator. The epigraph, "Something of the unreal is necessary to fecundate the real," which Updike borrows from Wallace Stevens, points to the correspondence between creator and creation.

With the astonishing variety and richness of his narratives, John Updike's fiction constitutes a serious exploration and probing of the spiritual conditions of American culture in the late twentieth century. The fate of American civilization is seen in the condition of love—its risks and dangers as well as its possibility for gracious transformation.

John G. Parks
Updated by Lisa Paddock

Other major works

SHORT FICTION: *The Same Door,* 1959; *Pigeon Feathers, and Other Stories,* 1962; *Olinger Stories: A Selection,* 1964; *The Music School,* 1966; *Museums and Women, and Other Stories,* 1972; *Problems, and Other Stories,* 1979; *Three Illuminations in the Life of an American Author,* 1979; *Too Far to Go: The Maples Stories,* 1979; *The Chaste Planet,* 1980; *Bech Is Back,* 1982; *The Beloved,* 1982; *Trust Me,* 1987; *Brother Grasshopper,* 1990 (limited edition); *The Afterlife, and Other Stories,* 1994; *Licks of Love: Short Stories and a Sequel, "Rabbit Remembered",* 2000; *The Complete Henry Bech: Twenty Stories,* 2001; *The Early Stories, 1953-1975,* 2003.

PLAYS: *Three Texts from Early Ipswich: A Pageant,* pb. 1968; *Buchanan Dying,* pb. 1974, pr. 1976.

POETRY: *The Carpentered Hen, and Other Tame Creatures,* 1958; *Telephone Poles, and Other Poems,* 1963; *Dog's Death,* 1965; *Verse,* 1965; *Bath After Sailing,* 1968; *The Angels,* 1968; *Midpoint, and Other Poems,* 1969; *Seventy Poems,* 1972; *Six Poems,* 1973; *Cunts (Upon Receiving the Swingers Life Club Membership Solicitation),* 1974; *Query,* 1974; *Tossing and Turning,* 1977; *Sixteen Sonnets,* 1979; *Five Poems,* 1980; *Jester's Dozen,* 1984; *Facing Nature,* 1985; *Mites, and Other Poems in Miniature,* 1990; *A Helpful Alphabet of Friendly Objects,* 1995; *Americana, and Other Poems,* 2001.

NONFICTION: *Assorted Prose,* 1965; *Picked-Up Pieces,* 1975; *Hugging the Shore: Essays and Criticism,* 1983; *Just Looking: Essays on Art,* 1989; *Self-Consciousness: Memoirs,* 1989; *Odd Jobs: Essays and Criticism,* 1991; *Golf Dreams: Writings on Golf,* 1996; *More Matter: Essays and Criticism,* 1999; *Still Looking: Essays on American Art,* 2005.

EDITED TEXTS: *The Best American Short Stories of the Century,* 2000.

Bibliography

Boswell, Marshall. *John Updike's Rabbit Tetralogy: Mastered Irony in Motion.* Columbia: University of Missouri Press, 2001. A study of Harry Angstrom's literary journey through life.

Broer, Lawrence R., ed. *Rabbit Tales: Poetry and Politics in John Updike's Rabbit Novels.* Tuscaloosa: University of Alabama Press, 1998. Twelve essays that demonstrate that Updike's Rabbit novels are a carefully crafted fabric of changing hues and textures, of social realism and something of grandeur. Includes bibliographical references and index.

De Bellis, Jack, ed. *John Updike: The Critical Responses to the "Rabbit" Saga.* Westport, Conn.: Praeger, 2005. A collection of thirty-four scholarly essays examining Updike's Rabbit novels.

Miller, D. Quentin. *John Updike and the Cold War: Drawing the Iron Curtain.* Columbia: University of Missouri Press, 2001. Studies the influence of Cold War society and politics in forming Updike's worldview.

Newman, Judie. *John Updike.* New York: St. Martin's Press, 1988. A part of the Modern Novelists series, Newman covers the long fiction with facility and insight and offers a solid foundation for understanding Updike's primary concerns throughout his writing. Contains a good, comprehensive introduction and a judicious bibliography.

O'Connell, Mary. *Updike and the Patriarchal Dilemma: Masculinity in the Rabbit Novels.* Carbondale: Southern Illinois University Press, 1996. Examines the themes of men, masculinity, and patriarchy in Updike's Rabbit series. Includes an index and bibliography.

Pinsker, Sanford. "The Art of Fiction: A Conversation with John Updike." *The Sewanee Review* 104 (Summer, 1996): 423-433. Updike discusses the visual artists who have inspired him, how his academic experiences helped to shape his writing, and how he regards criticism of his work.

Pritchard, William H. *Updike: America's Man of Letters.* South Royalton, Vt.: Steerforth Press, 2000. A biography of the novelist, whom Pritchard sees as the heir to such American storytellers as William Dean Howells and Henry James, alone in a sea of metafiction.

Rogers, Michael. "The Gospel of the Book: *LJ* Talks to John Updike." *Library Journal* 124, no. 3 (February 15, 1999): 114-116. Updike expounds on books, contemporary writers, and the state of publishing at the end of the twentieth century.

Schiff, James A. *John Updike Revisited.* New York: Twayne, 1998. A general introduction surveying all of Updike's work but focusing on his fiction during the late 1990's. The chapter on the short story is relatively brief, with short analyses of such stories as "A & P" and "Separating."

_____. *Updike's Version: Rewriting "The Scarlet Letter."* Columbia: University of Missouri Press, 1992. Schiff explores the influence of Hawthorne's novel on Updike's oeuvre. Contains an index and bibliography.

Trachtenberg, Stanley, ed. *New Essays on "Rabbit, Run."* New York: Cambridge University Press, 1993. Essays in this collection address Updike's notable novel and such themes as middle-class men in literature. With bibliographical references.

Gore Vidal

Born: West Point, New York; October 3, 1925

Principal long fiction • *Williwaw*, 1946; *In a Yellow Wood*, 1947; *The City and the Pillar*, 1948, revised 1965; *The Season of Comfort*, 1949; *A Search for the King: A Twelfth Century Legend*, 1950; *Dark Green, Bright Red*, 1950; *Death in the Fifth Position*, 1952 (as Edgar Box); *The Judgment of Paris*, 1952, revised 1965; *Death Before Bedtime*, 1953 (as Box); *Death Likes It Hot*, 1954 (as Box); *Messiah*, 1954, revised 1965; *Julian*, 1964; *Washington, D.C.*, 1967; *Myra Breckinridge*, 1968; *Two Sisters: A Memoir in the Form of a Novel*, 1970; *Burr*, 1973; *Myron*, 1974; *1876*, 1976; *Kalki*, 1978; *Creation*, 1981; *Duluth*, 1983; *Lincoln*, 1984; *Empire*, 1987; *Hollywood: A Novel of America in the 1920's*, 1990; *Live from Golgotha*, 1992; *The Smithsonian Institution*, 1998; *The Golden Age*, 2000.

Other literary forms • Gore Vidal wrote short stories as well as novels, and he is known as a master essayist, having regularly published collections of essays. Vidal also wrote or adapted plays during the so-called golden age of television, and he wrote screenplays during the last days of the Hollywood studio system.

Achievements • Gore Vidal is considered a leading American literary figure. Although primarily a novelist, he has mastered almost every genre, except poetry. He won success in films, in television, and on Broadway. Many readers consider him a better essayist than novelist, though Vidal emphatically rejects that judgment.

Although many of his contemporaries focused their writings on mundane details of everyday life, Vidal continued to write the novel of ideas. He maintained his focus on the largest questions: What is the nature of Western civilization? What flaws have prevented the United States from achieving its democratic promise? How does a free individual live an intellectually fulfilling and ethically proper life in a corrupt society? These concerns are reflected not only in his writing but also in his political activities, including a bid for the U.S. Senate in 1982. Vidal won a National Book Award in 1993 for his collection of essays *United States: Essays, 1952-1992*, and his books are routinely included in "best" lists and course syllabi.

Biography • Eugene Luther Vidal was born on October 3, 1925 (he took the name Gore when he was fourteen). He was born at West Point, where his father, Eugene, taught aeronautics at the military academy. Eugene Vidal helped establish civil aviation in the United States and later became the director of air commerce in the administration of Franklin D. Roosevelt. Gore's mother, Nina, was a beautiful socialite, the daughter of powerful Oklahoma senator Thomas P. Gore. Soon after Gore's birth, the family moved to Senator Gore's mansion in Washington, D.C. Gore Vidal, one of the most learned of contemporary writers, never went to college. His education began at the home of Senator Gore: The senator, who was blind, used his grandson as a reader and in return gave him free run of his huge library. In 1935, the Vidals were divorced, and Nina married Hugh D. Auchincloss, a member of a prominent family of bankers and lawyers. Gore Vidal then moved to the Auchincloss estate on the Potomac River in Virginia. Here his education included rubbing shoulders with the nation's political, economic, and journalistic elite.

Vidal was brought up removed from real life, he says, protected from such unpleasant realities as the effects of the Great Depression. He joined other patrician sons at St. Albans School, after which he toured Europe in 1939, then spent one year at Los Alamos School in New Mexico, before finishing his formal education with three years at Phillips Exeter Academy in New Hampshire.

In 1943, Vidal joined the Army and served on a transport ship in the Aleutian Islands. His military service gave him subject matter and time to write his first novel, *Williwaw.* He finished his second book, *In a Yellow Wood,* before he left the Army. In 1946, he went to work as an editor for E. P. Dutton and soon published

© Jane Bown

The City and the Pillar. Good critical and popular response brought him recognition as one of the nation's best young authors. He used Guatemala as his home base from 1947 to 1949 and then bought an old estate, Edgewater, on the Hudson River in New York. He wrote five more novels before he was thirty years old.

Meanwhile, a controversy engulfed him and shifted his life and career. *The City and the Pillar* had dealt with homosexuality; because of this, the literary establishment removed him from its list of "approved" writers, and critics largely ignored his next few novels. To earn money during the 1950's, he wrote mysteries under the name Edgar Box and wrote scripts for the major live television dramatic series. He also became a successful screenwriter, with such films as *The Catered Affair* (1956) and *Suddenly Last Summer* (1959, with Tennessee Williams). In addition, he wrote plays. He achieved major Broadway successes with *Visit to a Small Planet: A Comedy Akin to a Vaudeville* (1957) and *The Best Man: A Play About Politics* (1960).

These were his years of "piracy," Vidal says, aimed at gaining enough financial security to allow him to return to his first love, novels. His years in Hollywood and on Broadway established Vidal's public reputation for sophisticated wit and intelligence. He ran for Congress in 1960, supported by such famous friends as Eleanor Roosevelt, Joanne Woodward, and Paul Newman. Although he was defeated, he ran better in his district than did the Democratic presidential candidate, John F. Kennedy. Vidal shared a stepfather with Jacqueline Kennedy and had become friends with the Kennedy family; this connection pulled him further into public affairs.

In 1964, Vidal published *Julian,* his first novel in ten years. It was a major critical and public success. Many best-sellers followed, including *Myra Breckinridge, Burr, Creation,* and *Lincoln.*

Conflict over civil rights, the Vietnam War, and the Watergate scandal made the 1960's and 1970's one of the most tumultuous periods in American political history.

Vidal's essays, published in major journals, established his reputation as an astute and hard-hitting social critic. His acid-tongued social commentary brought him to many television guest shows, where he made many friends and enemies. He had spectacular public feuds with members of the Kennedy family and with such fellow celebrities and authors as William F. Buckley, Jr., Norman Mailer, and Truman Capote. In 1968 he was a cofounder of the New Party, and in 1970-1972 he was cochair of the People's Party. In 1982, he ran for the U.S. Senate in California, and, out of a field of eleven in the Democratic primary, came in second, behind Governor Jerry Brown, who lost the general election.

The range and breadth of Vidal's interests showed in *United States*, a thousand-page collection of his essays that won the National Book Award for 1993. Here one finds literary discussions ranging from readings of Henry James and William Dean Howells to attacks on those of his contemporaries (John Barth, Thomas Pynchon) whom he calls "the academic hacks," novelists writing only for an audience of literature professors. He also attacks what he calls the "heterosexual dictatorship" and the increasingly grandiose and imperial self-image of the United States.

Palimpsest: A Memoir (1995) was a book that Vidal said he had sworn never to write, a personal memoir. He revealed his family background and told of his struggles with establishments literary and political, concluding with his view of his quarrel with the Kennedy family. In a lyrical passage, he spoke of the great love of his teenage years, a classmate named Jimmie Trimble who died in World War II. During the 1990's, Vidal added a new aspect to his public persona by appearing as a character actor in several films, including *Bob Roberts* (1992), *With Honors* (1994), *The Shadow Conspiracy* (1996), and *Gattaca* (1997).

In 1998 Vidal was embroiled in further public debate as a member of the committee that selected the Modern Library's one hundred best twentieth century English-language novels. One of many controversial aspects of the list was the absence of those writers he called academic hacks. Vidal insisted that his role was only to make recommendations and that he bore no responsibility for the final selections.

Analysis • In an age and country that have little room for the traditional man of letters, Gore Vidal has established that role for himself by the force of his writing and intelligence and by his public prominence. He is a classicist in writing style, emphasizing plot, clarity, and order. Iconoclastic wit and cool, detached intelligence characterize his elegant style.

Because Vidal knows most contemporary public figures—including jet-setters, Wall Street insiders, and Washington wheeler-dealers—many readers comb his writing to glean intriguing bits of gossip. *Two Sisters: A Memoir in the Form of a Novel*, for example, is often read as an account of the lives and loves of Jacqueline Kennedy Onassis and her sister, Lee Bouvier. Some people search Vidal's writing for clues to his own life and sexuality.

Vidal draws from his own rich experience as he creates his fictional world, yet he is a very private person, and he resists people's urge to reduce everyone to a known quantity. Vidal refracts real people and events through his delightfully perverse imagination. The unwary gossipmonger can easily fall into Vidal's many traps.

If one can with certainty learn little from Vidal's fiction about such famous people as the Kennedys, readers can learn much about his major concern, the nature of Western civilization and the individual's role within it. He is interested in politics—how people make society work—and religion, the proper perspective on life as one faces death. In his early novels, one can see Vidal's interest in ideas. Vidal's young male protagonists find themselves entering a relativistic world in which all gods are dead. A "heterosexual dictatorship" and a life-numbing Christian establishment try to impose false moral absolutes. Society tempts the unwary by offering comfort and security and then removes the life-sustaining freedom of those who succumb to the temptation.

The City and the Pillar • In writing his third novel, Vidal probed the boundaries of society's sexual tolerance. The result, *The City and the Pillar,* affected the rest of his career. To Vidal, the book is a study of obsession; to many guardians of moral purity, it seems to glorify homosexuality. In American fiction, either homosexuality had been barely implied or the homosexual characters had been presented as bizarre or doomed figures. In contrast, Vidal's protagonist is an average young American man, confused by his homosexual proclivities and obsessed with the memory of a weekend encounter with another young man, Bob Ford. Although Bob regards the weekend as a diversion to be enjoyed and forgotten, Jim enters the homosexual world. If he is doomed, it is not because he prefers men to women, but because he is obsessed with the past. When he finally meets Bob again and tries to revive the affair, Bob rejects him. Enraged and humiliated, Jim kills Bob. Vidal later issued a revised edition in which Jim forces Bob to submit sexually; in the emotional backwash from the confrontation, Jim realizes the sterility of his obsession.

Vidal later said that he could have been president had it not been for the homosexual label applied to him. Readers assumed that Vidal must be the character he invented. Vidal is a sexual libertarian who believes that sex in any form between consenting adults is a gift to be enjoyed. He believes, furthermore, that a "heterosexual dictatorship" has distorted human sexuality. "There is no such thing as a homosexual or a heterosexual person," Vidal says. "There are only homo- or heterosexual acts. Most people are a mixture of impulses if not practices, and what anyone does with a willing partner is of no social or cosmic significance." In 1948, people were not ready for that message. Although the book was a best-seller, such powerful establishment journals as *The New York Times* eliminated him from the list of "approved" writers. His next few books were failures, critically and financially.

The Judgment of Paris • Two of the books ignored after *The City and the Pillar, The Judgment of Paris* and *Messiah,* later found admirers. In these novels Vidal began to develop the style that is so recognizably his own. Moreover, it is in these two books that Vidal fully expresses his philosophy of life: "I have put nearly everything that I feel into *The Judgment of Paris,* a comedic version, and *Messiah,* a tragic version of my sense of man's curious estate."

In *The Judgment of Paris,* Vidal retells the ancient myth of Paris, who was asked by Zeus to choose the most beautiful of three goddesses: Hera (power), Athena (knowledge), and Aphrodite (love). In the novel, Philip Warren, an American innocent, meets Regina Durham (Hera) in Rome, Sophia Oliver (Athena) in Egypt, and Anna Morris (Aphrodite) in Paris. Regina and Sophia offer him, respectively, political power and life of the intellect. To Philip, political power rests on manipulation of people, and intellectual life requires the seclusion of the scholar from humanity. He chooses love, but he also leaves Anna Morris. His choice implies that one must accept no absolutes; nothing is permanent, not even love. One must open oneself to love and friendship and prepare to accept change as one moves through life.

Messiah • Many readers consider *Messiah* an undiscovered masterpiece. Religion, the human response to death and nothingness, has been a major concern in Vidal's fiction, especially in *Messiah, Kalki*, and *Creation*. *Messiah* is narrated by Eugene Luther, an old man secluded in Egypt. He is a founding member of a new religion that has displaced Christianity and is spreading over the world. Luther, who has broken with the church he helped build, scribbles his memoirs as he awaits death. The movement was built around John Cave, but Cave was killed by his disciples, and Cave's word was spread by an organization using modern advertising techniques. One can readily find in *Messiah* characters representing Jesus Christ, Saint Paul, Mother Mary, and Martin Luther. The process by which religious movements are formed interests Vidal. *Messiah* shows, by analogy, how the early Church fathers manipulated the Gospels and the Christ figure for their own selfish needs.

Julian • With *Julian*, Vidal again examines the formation of a religious movement, this time looking directly at Christianity. Julian the Apostate, Roman emperor from 361 to 363 C.E., had long been the object of hatred in the West, because he had tried to reverse the Christianization of the empire. In the nineteenth and twentieth centuries, Julian began to attract admirers who saw him as a symbol of wisdom and of religious toleration.

Julian, reared as a Christian, lived in an age when the modern Christian Church was taking shape. Warring prelates conducted abstract debates that robbed religion of its mystery and engaged in persecutions that ignored Jesus' message of love and peace. Julian was trained as a philosopher. His study of ancient wisdom awakened in him love and respect for the gods of the ancient world and for the Eastern mystery religions then being suppressed by Christianity. When he became emperor, Julian proclaimed religious toleration and tried to revive "paganism."

Like Paris before him and Philip Warren after, Julian was offered the worlds of intellect, love, and power. Julian chose power, but he tempered the absolute authority of emperor with love and wisdom. He was also a military genius who, like Alexander the Great, was tempted by the dream of world conquest. He was killed during an invasion of Persia.

Vidal constructs his novel as a fictive memoir written by Julian and presenting Julian's own view of himself and his world. The novel opens in 380 C.E., seventeen years after Julian's death. Two friends of Julian, the philosophers Libanius of Antioch and Priscus of Athens, correspond as they prepare Julian's memoirs for publication. Their letters and comments on the manuscript provide two other views of the events described by Julian. Because they are writing as Emperor Theodosius is moving to destroy the ancient religions, Julian's life takes on a special poignancy. Vidal's major point, says biographer Ray Lewis White, is that modern people of the West are the descendants of the barbarians who destroyed the classical world, and that the modern world has yet to be civilized. If Julian had lived, Vidal believes, Christianity might well have remained only one of several Western religions, and Western civilization might now be healthier and more tolerant than it is.

Creation • In 1981 Vidal took readers even further back into history in *Creation*. In 445 B.C.E., Cyrus Spitama, an elderly Persian diplomat to Athens and grandson of the Persian prophet Zoroaster, begins to dictate his memoirs to his nephew, the philosopher Democritus. Cyrus is angry after hearing the historian Herodotus give his account of the Persian-Greek war, and he decides to set down the truth.

Here Vidal traces the earliest foundations of Western civilization and the formation of major world religions. Cyrus, a diplomatic troubleshooter for the Persian court, takes the reader on a tour of the ancient world. He knows Persian emperors Darius and Xerxes; as a traveler to China and India, he meets the Buddha and Confucius, and he remembers his own grandfather, Zoroaster. In Athens he talks with such famous figures as Anaxagoras and Pericles and hires Socrates to repair his wall. In *Creation*, Vidal shows the global interaction of cultures that goes back to the ancient world. He rejects the provincialism that has allowed historians to wall Western civilization off from its Asian and African sources.

Burr • This master of historical fiction also turned his attention to the United States. Starting with *Washington, D.C.*, Vidal began a sequence of novels covering United States history from its beginning to the post-World War II era. In chronological sequence, the novels are *Burr, Lincoln, 1876, Empire, Hollywood,* and *Washington, D.C.* Vidal's iconoclastic view of the past may have shocked some readers, but in the turmoil of the Vietnam and Watergate era, many people were ready to reexamine United States history. At a time when many Americans held that the old truths had failed, Vidal said that those truths had been hollow from the start.

Burr is one of the most widely admired of Vidal's novels. Aaron Burr, the preeminent American maverick, appealed to Vidal personally. *Burr* is narrated by Charlie Schuyler, who in 1833 is a twenty-five-year-old clerk in Burr's law office. He is an aspiring author who writes for William Leggett and William Cullen Bryant, editors of the *New York Evening Post.* Disliking Martin Van Buren, President Andrew Jackson's heir apparent, Leggett and Bryant set Charlie to work running down the rumor that Van Buren is the illegitimate son of Burr; if the rumor is true, they can use the information to destroy Van Buren. The seventy-seven-year-old Burr responds warmly to Charlie's overtures to write about his life. In the next few years, Burr gives the young writer copies of his journal and dictates to him his memories of the past.

Although Vidal's portrait of the Founders shocks some readers, his interpretation is in line with that of many of the nation's best historians. Vidal reminds the reader that Burr was one of the most able and intelligent of the Founders. Vidal allows Burr, from an insider's viewpoint, to demystify the founders of the republic. George Washington, Alexander Hamilton, Thomas Jefferson, and the other Founders created the republic, Burr says, because it satisfied their personal economic and political interests to do so.

Burr admires some of his contemporaries, especially James Madison and Andrew Jackson, but he detests Thomas Jefferson. Jefferson is a ruthless man who wants to create a nation "dominated by independent farmers each living on his own rich land, supported by slaves." What Burr cannot excuse is Jefferson's cant and hypocrisy:

> Had Jefferson not been a hypocrite I might have admired him. After all, he was the most successful empire-builder of our century, succeeding where Bonaparte failed. But then Bonaparte was always candid when it came to motive and Jefferson was always dishonest.

What are the motives of the Founders? Burr tells Alexander Hamilton: "I sense nothing more than the ordinary busy-ness of men wanting to make a place for themselves. . . . But it is no different here from what it is in London or what it was in Caesar's Rome." The Founders write the Constitution because it suits their purposes, and they subvert it when it suits their purposes.

Burr makes no secret of his opportunism, although he does regret his mistakes. He should have realized that the world is big enough for both Hamilton and himself, he says. Instead, Vice President Aaron Burr kills Hamilton in a duel and is then accused by Jefferson of heading a plot to break up the United States and establish himself as the king in a new Western empire.

Charlie does find evidence that Van Buren is Burr's son, but Charlie, having come to love the old man, refuses to use it. Van Buren rewards him with a government position overseas.

Lincoln and *1876* • With *Lincoln*, Vidal surprised those who expected him to subject the Great Emancipator to the same ridicule he had directed at Washington and Jefferson. Vidal's Lincoln is a cold, remote, intelligent man who creates a unified, centralized republic that is far different from the one envisioned by the Founders. In *1876*, Charlie Schuyler returns to the United States from Europe, where he has lived since 1837. He left in the age of Jackson and returns in the age of Ulysses S. Grant to a booming industrializing, urbanizing nation. He watches, in the American centennial year, as the politicians steal the presidential election from Democrat Samuel J. Tilden. He sees members of the ruling class using the rhetoric of democracy but practicing it as little as they had in the days of Washington and Jefferson.

Empire • In *Empire*, Vidal paints wonderful word portraits of Henry Adams, Henry James, William Randolph Hearst, John Hay, and Theodore Roosevelt, along with the fictional characters of newspaper publishers Caroline and Blaise Sanford and Congressman James Burden Day. The creation of the internal empire, begun by Jefferson's Louisiana Purchase, had already made a shambles of the American democratic promise. Now Roosevelt and other American leaders begin to look overseas for new areas to dominate. Their creation of the overseas empire lays the groundwork for the increasingly militarized republic that emerges in the twentieth century.

Hollywood • Many of these same figures appear in *Hollywood*, set a few years later, in the administrations of Woodrow Wilson and Warren Harding. Although the forging of the American empire continues, Vidal turns his gaze on a new force that is corrupting the democratic promise, the mass media. Newspaper publisher Hearst and the Sanfords have long understood the power of the press, but Hearst and Caroline Sanford see that the new medium of film has potential power beyond the printed page. Instead of reporting events, film could create a new reality, within which newspapers and politicians would have to work.

Washington, D.C. • In *Washington, D.C.*, Blaise Sanford, his son Peter, Senator James Burden Day, and his assistant, Clay Overbury, are locked in a political and moral drama. Senator Day, a southern conservative, much like Senator Gore, opposes the new republic being created by Franklin Delano Roosevelt, Harry Truman, and Dwight D. Eisenhower. He has a chance to be president but lacks money. Burden Day gives in to temptation and takes a bribe; his presidential bid fails, and later Clay Overbury, using his knowledge of the bribe, forces Day out of the Senate and takes his seat. Overbury is a young man who cares nothing for friends or ideas or issues. Winning personal power is the only thing that interests this politician, who is modeled on John F. Kennedy.

As Day is dying, he says to the spirit of his unreconstructed southern father: "You were right. . . . It has all gone wrong." Aaron Burr would have understood what he meant.

Myra Breckinridge • If most scholars approved of Vidal's well-researched historical fiction, many readers were shocked at *Myra Breckinridge*. Myra opens her book with the proud proclamation: "I am Myra Breckinridge whom no man will ever possess." She maintains her verve as she takes readers on a romp through popular culture. Because the novel is dead, she says, there is no point in writing made-up stories; the film of the 1940's is the high point of Western artistic creation, although it is being superseded by a higher art form, the television commercial. Myra has arrived in Hollywood to fulfill her destiny of reconstructing the sexes. She has a lesson to teach young would-be stars such as Rusty Godowsky and old cowboy stars such as Buck Loner:

> To be a man in a society of machines is to be an expendable, soft auxiliary to what is useful and hard. Today there is nothing left for the old-fashioned male to do, . . . no physical struggle to survive or mate. . . . [O]nly in travesty can he act out the classic hero who was a law unto himself, moving at ease through a landscape filled with admiring women. Mercifully, that age is finished. . . . [W]e now live at the dawn of the age of Women Triumphant, of Myra Breckinridge!

Beneath the gaiety of Myra's campy narrative, a serious purpose emerges. Her dead homosexual husband, Myron, had been abused and humiliated by many men. Myra carries out her plan to avenge Myron, and to revive the Female Principle, by forcing Buck Loner to submit to her demands to take over his acting studio, and by raping with a dildo the macho, all-American stud Rusty.

Myra is brought down by an automobile accident, which upsets her hormonal balance. Her breasts vanish, and she sprouts a beard; she is, in fact, Myron, after a sexchange operation. As the book ends, Rusty is a homosexual, and Myron/Myra is married and living happily with Rusty's former girlfriend. In a sequel, *Myron*, Myron and Myra struggle for domination of the single body and again have much to say about popular culture, the mass media, and human sexuality.

Perhaps as respites from the scrupulous historicity of the American history novels, Vidal interspersed them with fantasies in which reality was plastic and ever changing. In *Myron*, characters were likely to find themselves in the midst of the old films they were watching. *Duluth* represented a deliberately postmodernist interpenetration of an actual Duluth with a serial television show also called *Duluth*.

Live from Golgotha • *Live from Golgotha* continued the motif of a reality subject to random change. It is set in 96 C.E., but the first century is being manipulated by forces from the twentieth, operating through psychic channelers and the Hacker, whose computer manipulations apparently can destroy not only records of the past but even memories of those records. Indeed, there is a plan afoot to return to the Crucifixion, televise it live, and perhaps even change the events.

Timothy, the narrator, is the biblical Timothy to whom Saint Paul wrote epistles. He has been chosen to preserve the Gospel story in the face of these computerized depredations, though his knowledge of the event is at best secondhand, coming from Paul, who knows it only through a vision. The story departs radically from the standard biblical story. Timothy and Paul are actively bisexual, as are most of the first century people depicted. Jesus is thought to have been morbidly obese. Anachronistic terms such as "Mossad" and "intifada" abound. Future figures such as Mary Baker Eddy and Shirley MacLaine make appearances.

Timothy eventually learns that the actual Jesus was a Zealot, a political revolutionary. With electronic assistance, Jesus framed Judas, the fat man Paul saw in the vision, and fled to the twentieth century. There he became the Hacker in order to clear out images of "gentle Jesus meek and mild." He plans to start Armageddon through a nuclear attack on Arab capitals. Timothy uses more advanced technology to prevent Jesus' escape from arrest. The Crucifixion takes place, with the real Jesus, but Japanese technicians add to the image a rising sun and the mother goddess Amaterasu. *Live from Golgotha* was condemned for its irreverence and blasphemy, as well as for the outlandishness of its central conceit, but many readers nevertheless enjoyed its wit and its lusty portrayal of the first century Roman world.

The Smithsonian Institution • Vidal's next novel, *The Smithsonian Institution*, also dealt with retroactive time change, but of a political rather than a theological sort. T., a thirteen-year-old mathematics prodigy in 1939, is summoned to the Smithsonian Institution to take part in a secret scientific experiment. He soon learns that the apparent wax dummies that are part of the project are actually living people. Indeed, T. is seduced by Mrs. Grover Cleveland. T. has an Einstein-like ability to visualize equations dealing with time. Anxious to ward off the coming of World War II because it would lead to the development of terrifying new weapons, the scientists secretly in charge of the Smithsonian (with the assistance of the supposed wax dummies of political leaders) plan to use T.'s ideas to construct a time machine and change the past so that the war will not occur. After one trip that only makes things worse, T. returns to a war in which he saves an alternate version of himself and enables the war to be concluded more quickly, without the weapons development.

Some commentators have said that the audience Vidal created for himself with his highly regarded historical novels was destroyed by *Myra Breckinridge* and *Myron* and by his later campy fantasies *Kalki* and *Duluth*. However, Vidal continued to write one best-seller after another, and his books have steadily gained critical admirers. Vidal's books, essays, and television appearances stimulated, intrigued, and angered a large part of his audience, yet his appeal as a writer and public figure remained compelling. As long ago as 1948, with *The City and the Pillar*, Vidal made a decision to live his life and conduct his artistic career in his own way. To many admirers, he is a symbol of freedom. The turmoil of the modern age makes his civilized voice of reason seem more necessary than ever before. Often accused of cynicism, Vidal responded that he is a pessimist and a realist who also believes that people can, or must act as if they can, take action to make the world better.

The Golden Age • Caroline Sanford provides the central focus of *The Golden Age* as it begins in 1939, but she soon gives way as protagonist to her young nephew and heir, Peter Sanford. Peter meets President Franklin D. Roosevelt and Harry Truman and most of the other political insiders of his time, as well as such cultural figures as playwright Tennessee Williams, composer Leonard Bernstein, and even a young novelist named Gore Vidal.

Sanford family relationships are tangled, although death simplifies matters as the years pass. Peter's father, Blaise Sanford, champions the ruthlessly ambitious Clay Overbury in his relentless drive for power. Overbury forces his benefactor, Senator James Burden Day, into retirement so that Overbury can take Day's Senate seat.

However, the Sanford domestic entanglements take a backseat to the geopolitical maneuvers that begin in 1939. Caroline observes the drama firsthand, through her friendship with Harry Hopkins, Roosevelt's alter ego. Hopkins mocks the blindness of isolationists who oppose Roosevelt's attempts to support France and Great Britain, under assault from Nazi dictator Adolf Hitler. Hopkins says that the unspoken reality is that Americans have a world empire and that Great Britain is America's client state, which must be protected for American self-interest. Peter and his friend Gore Vidal later speculate about Roosevelt's role in the Japanese attack on Pearl Harbor. They believe that Roosevelt deliberately provoked Japan into an attack, allowing the United States to enter World War II and establish itself as the dominant global power.

After World War II, Peter and his friend Aeneas Duncan publish a journal, *American Idea*, which becomes a major force in American intellectual and cultural life, and marks the beginning, they believe, of a postwar golden age, in literature, dance, music, and art.

The American renaissance flared and then quickly dimmed. Everything takes a backseat to the Cold War. The two wartime allies, the United States and Soviet Union, divide the world between them and face off in a potentially deadly confrontation. President Truman puts the finishing touches on the American empire. He uses the people's fear of the Soviet Union to build a national security state, creating the Department of Defense, Central Intelligence Agency, and the National Security Council. His newly militarized national government then inaugurates a loyalty program that quashes dissent and ends the brief golden age.

The book skips ahead to the millennium. On New Years Day, 2000, Peter meets a young man, Aaron Burr Decker, Caroline's great-grandson. Aaron asked Peter to participate in a televised dialogue with Peter's friend, Vidal, which takes place in Vidal's home in Italy. The two old men, Gore and Peter, try to make sense of the era in which they had lived. Peter finally reminds Gore that he, Peter, is only a made-up character in a Vidal novel. Why, he asks, did you not give me a better world in which to live?

William E. Pemberton
Updated by Arthur D. Hlavaty

Other major works

SHORT FICTION: *A Thirsty Evil: Seven Short Stories*, 1956; *Clouds and Eclipses: The Collected Short Stories*, 2006.

PLAYS: *Visit to a Small Planet: A Comedy Akin to a Vaudeville*, pr. 1957; *The Best Man: A Play About Politics*, pr., pb. 1960; *Romulus: A New Comedy*, pr., pb. 1962; *An Evening with Richard Nixon*, pr. 1972.

SCREENPLAYS: *The Catered Affair*, 1956; *Suddenly Last Summer*, 1959 (with Tennessee Williams); *The Best Man*, 1964 (adaptation of his play); *Last of the Mobile Hot-Shots*, 1969; *Caligula*, 1977.

TELEPLAYS: *Visit to a Small Planet, and Other Television Plays*, 1956; *Dress Gray*, 1986.

NONFICTION: *Rocking the Boat*, 1962; *Reflections upon a Sinking Ship*, 1969; *Homage to Daniel Shays: Collected Essays, 1952-1972*, 1972; *Matters of Fact and of Fiction: Essays, 1973-1976*, 1977; *The Second American Revolution, and Other Essays, 1976-1982*, 1982; *At Home: Essays, 1982-1988*, 1988; *Screening History*, 1992; *The Decline and Fall of the American Empire*, 1992; *United States: Essays, 1952-1992*, 1993; *Palimpsest: A Memoir*, 1995; *Virgin Islands, A Dependency of United States: Essays, 1992-1997*, 1997; *Gore Vidal, Sexually*

Speaking: Collected Sex Writings, 1999; *The Last Empire: Essays, 1992-2000,* 2000; *Dreaming War: Blood for Oil and the Cheney-Bush Junta,* 2002; *Perpetual War for Perpetual Peace: How We Got to Be So Hated,* 2002; *Imperial America,* 2004; *Point to Point Navigation: A Memoir, 1964 to 2006,* 2006.

MISCELLANEOUS: *The Essential Gore Vidal,* 1999 (Fred Kaplan, editor); *Inventing a Nation: Washington, Adams, Jefferson,* 2003; *Conversatons with Gore Vidal,* 2005 (Richard Peabody and Lucinda Ebersole, editors).

Bibliography

Baker, Susan, and Curtis S. Gibson. *Gore Vidal: A Critical Companion.* Westport, Conn.: Greenwood Press, 1997. A helpful book of criticism and interpretation of Vidal's work. Includes bibliographical references and index.

Dick, Bernard F. *The Apostate Angel: A Critical Study of Gore Vidal.* New York: Random House, 1974. An entertaining and perceptive study, based on interviews with Vidal and on his papers at the University of Wisconsin at Madison. Dick focuses on Vidal's work rather than on his biography. The book contains footnotes and a bibliography.

Ebersole, Lucinda, and Richard Peabody, eds. *Conversations with Gore Vidal.* Jackson: University Press of Mississippi, 2005. Collection of interviews with Vidal.

Harris, Stephen. *The Fiction of Gore Vidal and E. L. Doctorow: Writing the Historical Self.* New York: P. Lang, 2002. Discusses Vidal's strong identification with history as reflected in his writing.

Kaplan, Fred. *Gore Vidal: A Biography.* New York: Doubleday, 1999. A comprehensive biography of the novelist, playwright, scriptwriter, essayist, and political activist who helped shape American letters during the second half of the twentieth century.

Kiernan, Robert F. *Gore Vidal.* New York: Frederick Ungar, 1982. This study of Vidal's major writings tries to assess his place in American literature and gives astute descriptions of the Vidalian style and manner. The book, which uses Vidal's manuscript collection, contains a brief note and bibliography section.

Parini, Jay, ed. *Gore Vidal: Writer Against the Grain.* New York: Columbia University Press, 1992. Vidal's distaste for much of the academic study of contemporary fiction has been mirrored in a lack of academic study of his work. Jay Parini sought to redress the balance by compiling this work, which deals with both Vidal's fiction and nonfiction.

Stanton, Robert J., and Gore Vidal, eds. *Views from a Window: Conversations with Gore Vidal.* Secaucus, N.J.: Lyle Stuart, 1980. A compilation of interviews excerpted and arranged along themes. Vidal comments on his and other authors' works, on sexuality, and on politics. Vidal edited the manuscript and made corrections, with changes noted in the text.

Kurt Vonnegut

Born: Indianapolis, Indiana; November 11, 1922
Died: New York, New York; April 11, 2007

Principal long fiction • *Player Piano*, 1952; *The Sirens of Titan*, 1959; *Mother Night*, 1961; *Cat's Cradle*, 1963; *God Bless You, Mr. Rosewater: Or, Pearls Before Swine*, 1965; *Slaughterhouse-Five: Or, The Children's Crusade, a Duty-Dance with Death*, 1969; *Breakfast of Champions: Or, Goodbye Blue Monday*, 1973; *Slapstick: Or, Lonesome No More!*, 1976; *Jailbird*, 1979; *Deadeye Dick*, 1982; *Galápagos*, 1985; *Bluebeard*, 1987; *Hocus Pocus*, 1990; *Timequake*, 1997; *God Bless You, Dr. Kevorkian*, 1999 (novella).

Other literary forms • Although known primarily for his novels, Kurt Vonnegut also wrote for Broadway and television and published a children's book and wrote essays for many different publications. His essays have been collected in *Wampeters, Foma, and Granfalloons (Opinions)* (1974), *Palm Sunday: An Autobiographical Collage* (1981), *Conversations with Kurt Vonnegut* (1988), *Fates Worse than Death: An Autobiographical Collage of the 1980's* (1991), *Like Shaking Hands with God: A Conversation About Writing* (1999, with Lee Stringer); and *A Man Without a Country* (2005). He began writing short stories for both pulp and mainstream magazines during the early 1950's, and many of his stories are collected in *Canary in a Cat House* (1961), *Welcome to the Monkey House* (1968), and *Bagombo Snuff Box: Uncollected Short Fiction* (1999).

Achievements • Critical acclaim eluded Vonnegut until *Slaughterhouse-Five* was published in 1969. An immediate best-seller, it earned for Vonnegut respect from critics who had previously dismissed him as a mediocre science-fiction writer. Vonnegut has been honored as the Briggs-Copeland Lecturer at Harvard University, as a member of the National Institute of Arts and Letters, and as the Distinguished Professor of English Prose at the City University of New York. Through his insightful and sympathetic treatment of the psychologically and morally disabled victims of the modern world, Vonnegut earned a reputation as one of the greatest humanist writers of his time.

Biography • Kurt Vonnegut, Jr., was born in Indianapolis, Indiana, in 1922. Both the location and the era of his birth helped shape his distinctive worldview. Growing up in the American heartland in the calm interval between the world wars, Vonnegut had a brief vision of a middle-class world that embraced the values of honesty, decency, and human dignity. For Vonnegut, this was the world as it should be, a world unravaged by violence and war, a world untouched by technology. This period of childhood happiness was, however, merely the calm before the storm in this life that would be rocked by a series of personal and national disasters: the suicide of his mother on Mother's Day; his prisoner-of-war experience in World War II; the deaths of his sister and brother-in-law; the dissolution of his first marriage; the bombings of Dresden and Hiroshima; the assassinations of President John F. Kennedy and the Reverend Martin Luther King, Jr.; the Vietnam War; the death of his first wife, with whom he had maintained a close friendship; and the death of his brother Bernard. All the heartaches of his family and his nation reverberate through Vonnegut's work, while the artist, through his fiction, stands as advocate for a saner, calmer world.

During the Great Depression years, Vonnegut's family suffered emotional and financial setbacks. When Vonnegut entered Cornell University in 1940, his father forbade him to study the arts and chose instead for his son a career in science, a career with guaranteed job security. In 1943 Vonnegut left Cornell to enlist in the Army, despite his own public opposition to the war. Less than one year later, he was captured by the Germans and, in 1945, survived one of the greatest massacres of the war, the Allied firebombing of Dresden. This horror pursued Vonnegut for twenty-three years, until he worked through the pain by writing *Slaughterhouse-Five.*

After the war, Vonnegut married and began studies in anthropology at the University of Chicago. After three years, he left college and took a job as a publicist with General Electric (GE), where his brother worked as a physicist. Vonnegut's background in science and his disillusionment at GE influenced his first two novels, *Player Piano* and *The Sirens of Titan*, both parables of dehumanization in a technological society.

Between 1952 and 1998, Vonnegut wrote more than a dozen novels, numerous essays, a Broadway play, and a musical work, *Requiem*, which was performed by the Buffalo Symphony. He and Joe Petro III had a showing of twenty-six of their silk-screen prints in Denver in 1996. Despite his varied artistic talents, however, Vonnegut has always been known for his fiction. Vonnegut remarried in 1978; he and his wife, Jill Krementz, settled in New York.

When Vonnegut published his short novel *Timequake* in 1997, he declared that it would be his last book. Two years later, however, he published a volume of previously uncollected stories, *Bagombo Snuff Box*; a volume on his ideas about writing, *Like Shaking Hands with God*; and the novella *God Bless You, Dr. Kevorkian*. In 2005, he published *A Man Without a Country*, a collection of essays he had published over the previous five years; most expressed his random thoughts on writing.

Analysis • In his novels, Kurt Vonnegut coaxes the reader toward greater sympathy for humanity and deeper understanding of the human condition. His genre is satire—sometimes biting, sometimes tender, always funny. His arena is as expansive as the whole universe and as tiny as a single human soul. Part philosopher, part poet, Vonnegut, in his fictive world, tackles the core problem of modern life: How can the individual maintain dignity and exercise free will in a world overrun by death and destruction, a world in which both science and religion are powerless to provide a solution? The reader will find no ready answers in Vonnegut, only a friendly guide along the questioning path.

Vonnegut himself, behaved with a commendable sense of responsibility, dignity, and decency: He labored to show humankind its ailments and to wake it to the work it has to do. He admitted to having lived comfortably while so many of the world's population suffered, but in quoting the words of American socialist Eugene Debs in his dedication to *Hocus Pocus*, he seemed to define the position that he himself took as human being and as author and public figure for half of the twentieth century: "While there is a lower class I am in it. While there is a criminal element I am of it. While there is a soul in prison I am not free." He spoke out in many forums for many causes and for all of humankind, and his has been a wide audience.

Player Piano • Ilium, New York, sometime in the near future, provides the setting for Vonnegut's first dystopian novel, *Player Piano*. Ilium is a divided city. On one side of the river live the important people, the engineers and managers who program and run the computers and machines that run people's lives. On the other side of the river, Homestead, live the down trodden inhabitants of the city, those locked into menial, dehumanizing jobs assigned to them by the central computer.

Paul Proteus, the protagonist, is the brilliant young manager of the Ilium Works, a man being groomed for even greater success. However, just as Ilium is a divided city, so is Paul divided about his life and his future. Paul suffers a growing discontent with his job at the Ilium Works, where people have been replaced by machines, and machines are supervised by computers. Outwardly, Paul has no reason for worry or doubt. He has the best job and the most beautiful wife in Ilium, he is being considered for the highest

© Jill Krementz

post in his company, and he is climbing the ladder of success. Nevertheless, Paul's uneasiness increases. At first he seeks escape, settling on a farm in an attempt to get back to nature and free himself from his automatic life. He finds, however, that he has become an automaton, completely out of touch with the natural world, and his attempt at escape fails.

Finally, Paul is drawn to the other side of the river. His sympathy for the dehumanized masses and his acknowledgment of complicity in their plight drive Paul to join the masses in armed revolution. The fighters take to the streets, frantically and indiscriminately destroying all machines. The revolution fails, leaving Paul disillusioned and defeated, realizing that he has been manipulated by leaders on both sides of the conflict. Now he must surrender and face execution.

Paul's manipulation, first by those who would replace person with machine and then by those who would destroy the machines, is symbolized by the "player piano" of the title. The simplest of machines, the player piano creates its music without the aid of human beings, neatly rendering the skilled musician obsolete. Paul is entranced by the music of the player piano, in his fascination manipulated by the machine just as it manipulates its ivory keys.

The most striking symbol of the story, however, is the small black cat befriended by Paul as it wanders aimlessly through the Ilium Works. The cat, symbol of all that is natural and pure, despises the monstrous factory machines. The doomed animal is helplessly sucked into an automated sweeper, which spits it down a chute and ejects it outside the factory. Miraculously, it survives, but as Paul races to its rescue, the cat is roasted on the factory's electric fence, symbolizing humanity's destruction by the forces of technology. With characteristic Vonnegut irony, however, *Player Piano* ends on an affirmative note. Although the price of escape is its life, the cat does escape the Ilium Works. Near the end of the novel, Paul sees beautiful flowers growing outside the factory—flowers rooted in cat excrement, signifying ultimate rebirth and a glimmer of hope for Paul and his world.

Mother Night • In his third novel, *Mother Night,* Vonnegut peers even more deeply into the human soul, exploring the roots of human alienation, probing an individual's search for his "real" identity, and uncovering the thin veil that separates reality from illusion. The story is told as the memoirs of Howard W. Campbell, Jr., a self-proclaimed "citizen of nowhere." A successful writer and producer of medieval romance plays, Campbell sees himself as a sensitive *artiste.* Nevertheless, he allows himself to be recruited by Major Frank Wirtanen to be an American double agent posing as a Nazi radio propagandist in Germany. Secretly, Campbell sends coded American messages in his propaganda broadcasts, but he does not understand the code and never comprehends the messages he transmits. Still unaware, he even transmits the news of his beloved wife's death.

Publicly, Campbell is reviled as a traitorous Nazi hatemonger, but he does not mind, because he enjoys being on the radio. Eventually, though, he begins to lose touch with his "real" self. Is he the sensitive artist, the cruel Nazi, or the American patriot? Like Paul Proteus, Campbell allows himself to be manipulated by those around him. With no will or identity of his own, Campbell is easy prey for those who would use him for their own ends.

Two of Campbell's manipulators are his postwar friend George Kraft and his sister-in-law Resi, who poses as Campbell's long-lost wife, Helga. George and Resi are actually Russian spies plotting to capture Campbell and transport him to Russia. They abandon this plan, however, when they realize their love for Campbell, and they finally attempt to escape to freedom with him. Before the three can flee together, however, the Russians are arrested by American agents. Campbell is arrested as well but is soon freed by his friend Frank Wirtanen.

Gripped by existential fear at finding himself a free man, Campbell appeals to a Jewish couple in his apartment building, a doctor and his mother, both survivors of Auschwitz. Campbell begs to be tried for his crimes against the Jews and soon finds himself awaiting trial in a Jerusalem prison. Before Campbell goes to trial, Frank Wirtanen sends a letter on his behalf, explaining how he had recruited Campbell and honoring him as an American patriot. However, Campbell can never be a truly free man until he purges his conscience. Upon his release from prison, he is nauseated by the prospect of his freedom, knowing that he is one of the many people "who served evil too openly and good too secretly." In his failure to resist evil and his openness to manipulation by others, Campbell had given up his free will and lost his ability to choose. Coming to this realization, he finally asserts his will to choose and ironically chooses to die, vowing to hang himself "for crimes against himself."

Cat's Cradle • Equally dark is Vonnegut's fourth novel, *Cat's Cradle.* In addition to its broad parody of science and religion, *Cat's Cradle* expands on Vonnegut's earlier themes of the dangerous misuse of science and technology, humans' moral responsibility in an immoral world, and the importance of distinguishing reality from illusion. The parodic tone is set in the very first line, "Call me Jonah," bringing to mind the Old Testament Book of Jonah. Like that Jonah, this protagonist (really named John) faithfully pursues God's directives but never truly comprehends the order behind God's plan. Continuing the parody, John encounters the Bokononist religion, whose bible, The Books of Bokonon, proclaims in its first line, "All of the true things I am about to tell you are shameless lies," an obvious inversion of the Johannine maxim "You will know the truth, and the truth will make you free" (John 8:32). In the world John inhabits, the only real freedom is the ultimate freedom—death.

John is writing a book, "The Day the World Ended," an account of the bombing of Hiroshima. His obsession with the destruction of Hiroshima foreshadows his involvement in the eventual destruction of the world by "ice-nine," a substance that converts liquid into frozen crystals. In *Cat's Cradle*, the atomic bomb and ice-nine are both the doomsday toys of an amoral scientist, Dr. Felix Hoenikker. Hoenikker pursues his work so intensely that he has little time for his three children, who grow up to be emotionally warped and twisted Products of Science. Hoenikker's only legacy to his children is the ice-nine he was brewing in the kitchen before his sudden death on Christmas Eve. After their father's death, the three children—Angela, Frank, and Newt—divide the ice-nine among themselves, knowing that it is their ticket to a better future. Newt, a midget, barters his ice-nine for an affair with a Russian ballerina. The homely Angela uses her portion to buy herself a husband. Frank gives his to Miguel "Papa" Monzano, dictator of the Caribbean Republic of San Lorenzo, in exchange for the title of general and the hand of Monzano's beautiful adopted daughter, Mona.

Pursuing information on the Hoenikker family, John finds himself in San Lorenzo, where he is introduced to Bokononism. The people of San Lorenzo are desperately poor, for the soil of the island is as unproductive as the Sahara. The island's teeming, malnourished masses find their only comfort in Bokononism, which urges them to love and console one another. John finds that, ironically, the religion started as a game by the island's founders. Knowing no way to lift the country from its destitution, they decided to give the people hope by inventing a religion based on *foma*, or comforting lies. The religion encouraged people to find strength in their *karass*, groups of people with whom they are joined to do God's mysterious will. To strengthen the faith of the people, Bokononism was outlawed, its founder banished on pain of death. As the people's faith grew, so did their happiness and their dependence on *foma*, until all the inhabitants of the island were "employed full time as actors in a play." For the inhabitants of San Lorenzo, illusion had become reality.

Soon after his arrival on the island, John finds that Papa Monzano is critically ill; it is expected that "General" Frank Hoenikker will succeed Papa and take the beautiful Mona as his bride. Secretly, though, Frank has no desire to rule the island or marry Mona. He is a simpering mass of insecurities, hiding behind his fake title. Frank's life, like everything around him, has been a lie: He has bought a false sense of dignity, which he wears like a military uniform, but inside he is gripped with fear, the same fear that pulses through the veins of the dying dictator. Papa and Frank become symbols for all people, running scared and grasping at false comforts as they confront brutal reality. Faced with the horror of an agonizing death, Papa clutches his vial of ice-nine, his last illusion of security and power. Uttering the desperate cry, "Now I will destroy the whole world," he swallows the poison and turns himself into an ice-blue popsicle. Papa's power proves illusory, however, as John and the Hoenikker children clean up the mess and seal off Papa's bedroom.

John, Frank, Angela, and Newt inform the staff that Papa is "feeling much better" and go downstairs to watch a military celebration. Despite their success at covering up Papa's death and hiding their secret, John and the Hoenikker children sense impending doom. As all the islanders watch the military air show, a bomber careens out of control and bursts into flame, setting off a massive explosion and landslide. As his castle disintegrates, Papa Monzano's body is propelled from the bedroom closet, plunging into the waiting sea, infecting all with ice-nine.

As the story ends, only John, Newt, and Bokonon remain, awaiting their imminent death. John recalls Angela's heroic end, remembering how she had clutched her clarinet bravely and played in the face of death, music mocking terror. John dreams of climbing the highest mountain and planting some magnificent symbol. As his heart swells with the vision of being the last man on the highest mountain, Newt mocks him and brings him back to earth. The story concludes with the last verse of The Books of Bokonon, in which Bokonon mourns human stupidity, thumbs his nose at God, and kills himself with ice-nine.

Like many of Vonnegut's satirical writings, *Cat's Cradle* functions as humanity's wake-up call. For Vonnegut, heroism is not a dream; dignity is not an illusion. Nevertheless, he understands all too well the fear that grips a person on the brink of action, the torpor that invades the soul. In his frustration, all the artist can do is plod on, calling out his warnings as he goes.

Slaughterhouse-Five • Vonnegut's efforts to touch the soul of humanity are most fully realized in his sixth novel, *Slaughterhouse-Five*, his most touching and brilliant work. Incorporating all Vonnegut's common themes—the nature of reality and illusion, the question of free will and determinism, the horror of humankind's cruelty to itself, the vision of life as an ironic construct—*Slaughterhouse-Five* produces "an image of life that is beautiful and surprising and deep." This often-misunderstood novel leads the reader on a time-warped journey, as popular films say, "to hell and back." Emotionally suffocated by his experience in World War II, Vonnegut waited twenty-three years to tell the story of his capture by the Germans and his survival of the Allied firebombing of Dresden, the calculated annihilation of a quarter of a million refugees and civilians in an unguarded city.

As befits a tale of such distorted experience, *Slaughterhouse-Five* breaks all novelistic conventions. The story is divided into ten sections, spanning the years from 1944 to 1968. Opening with a simple, first-person narrative, Vonnegut describes his return to Dresden in 1967. He recounts his life after the war, discusses his wife and children, and relives a conversation with his old war buddy Bernard V. O'Hare, in which he reveals why *Slaughterhouse-Five* is subtitled *The Children's Crusade*. In the original Children's Crusade of 1213, Roman Catholic monks raised a volunteer army of thirty thousand children who were intent on traveling to Palestine but instead were sent to North Africa to be sold as slaves. In the end, half the children drowned en route and the others were sold. For Vonnegut, this incident provides the perfect metaphor for all wars: hopeless ventures fought by deluded children. Thus Vonnegut prepares the reader for this personal statement about the tragedy of war. Nevertheless, the reader finds himself unprepared for the narrative shape of the tale.

Breaking from his reverie, Vonnegut reads from a Gideon Bible the story of Lot's wife, turned to a pillar of salt for looking back on Sodom and Gomorrah. To Vonnegut, her reaction was tender, instinctively human, looking back on all those lives that had touched hers, and he adopts Lot's wife as a metaphor for his narrative stance. *Slaughterhouse-Five* will be a tale told by a "pillar of salt." Vonnegut assumes the role of a masked narrator, a disinterested party, allowing himself the aesthetic distance he needs to continue his painful journey. Yet, when the reader turns to chapter 2, he finds another surprise, as chapter 2 begins, "Listen: Billy Pilgrim has come unstuck in time."

To increase his emotional distance from the story, Vonnegut, the masked narrator, tells not his own story but the story of pathetic Billy Pilgrim, Vonnegut's mythical fellow soldier. Through time travel over which he has no control, Billy is forced to relive the chapters of his life, in seemingly random order. For Billy, as for Vonnegut, his war chronology is too unsettling to confront head-on. Instead of assimilating his life experiences, Billy unconsciously tries to escape the memory of them by bouncing back and forth in time from one experience to another. Not until the end of the tale can he face the crucial moment, the horror of Dresden.

The reader first sees Billy as a forty-six-year-old retired optometrist living in Ilium, New York. Billy's daughter, Barbara, thinks that he has lost his mind. Billy has given up interest in business and devotes all of his energies to telling the world about his travels to the planet Tralfamadore. Two years earlier, Billy had been captured by aliens from Tralfamadore and had spent six months on their planet. Billy's belief in Tralfamadorian philosophy is the great comfort of his life, and he is eager to share this philosophy with the world. The aliens taught Billy, the optometrist, a better way to "see." On Tralfamadore, time is not linear; all moments are structured and permanent, and death is merely one moment out of many moments in a person's life. The Tralfamadorians do not mourn the dead, for even though one may be dead in one moment, he or she is alive and happy in many others. The Tralfamadorians respond to life's temporary bad moments with a verbal shrug, "So it goes." Their world is a world without free will, without human responsibility, without human sorrow. On an intellectual level, Billy hungrily embraces their philosophy, yet deep inside him (as inside Vonnegut) stirs the need to reconstruct his life, to reconcile his past. So, armed with Tralfamadorian detachment, Billy steps back in time to where it all began.

It is 1944, and Billy, a night student at the Ilium School of Optometry, is drafted into action during World War II. No soldier is more unsuited to war than is Billy. Timid and friendless, he is a chaplain's assistant, a hapless soul with a "meek faith in a loving Jesus which most soldiers found putrid." Billy's marching companion is Roland Weary, a savage young man, even by military standards. Weary's father collects ancient instruments of torture, and Weary regales Billy with gruesome tales of cruelty, giving the gentle boy an unwanted view of a monstrous world. Weary, a callous, stupid killing machine, is the natural result of humanity's barbarity. Although physically robust, he is morally depleted, a symbol of the spiritually bankrupt world into which poor Billy has been thrust. Billy—kind, sensitive, tenderhearted—has no natural defenses against the barbarity that surrounds him, so he becomes unstuck in time.

After a brief respite of time travel, Billy returns to the war. He and Weary have been captured behind German lines, taken prisoner by two toothless old men and two young boys. The Germans are accompanied by a guard dog, a female German shepherd named Princess who had been stolen from a farmer. Princess and Billy are confused and shivering from the cold. Of the whole motley group, only the barbarous Weary belongs at war. Billy, Princess, the old men, and the young boys symbolize helpless humanity in the grip of military madness.

Billy and his fellow prisoners, including Vonnegut and Bernard V. O'Hare, are taken to a prisoner-of-war camp before their transport to Dresden. As Billy recalls these moments of his life, he is moved to time travel many times. He flashes forward to 1948, when, emotionally shattered by his war experience, he checks himself into a veterans' hospital for mental patients. Here the reader is introduced to Valencia Merble, Billy's unlovely fiancé, and Eliot Rosewater, his fellow mental patient. In the hospital, Eliot and Billy devour the science-fiction novels of Kilgore Trout. They are drawn to Trout's work for the same reason Billy is drawn to the philosophy of Tralfamadore: Human experience on earth has been too disturbing; life seems meaningless. Escaping to the world of science fiction relieves the pressure, enabling Eliot and Billy to "reinvent" themselves in a kinder universe.

Before Billy returns to his war story, he again relives his adventures on the planet Tralfamadore, where he spends six months in the Tralfamadore Zoo, displayed in a glass cage. Here Billy learns of his own death in 1976. He will be murdered by Paul Lazarro, a former inmate in Billy's prisoner-of-war camp. The maniacal Lazarro, incorrectly blaming Billy for the death of Roland Weary, has plotted revenge since 1944. Naturally, Billy's innocence makes his meaningless death doubly absurd. At this time, Billy also learns of the eventual destruction of the world by the Tralfamadorians. While testing a new rocket fuel for their spacecraft, they accidentally blow up the universe. "So it goes."

When Billy returns to his war story, he and his fellow American soldiers are in Dresden, working in a factory producing vitamin syrup for pregnant women. However, soon there will be no pregnant women in Dresden. The American soldiers are quartered underground in a former pig butchery—slaughterhouse number five. On the night of February 13, 1945, Billy (and Vonnegut) nestles safely in the shelter while the city is flattened by British and American firebombs. The next morning, the prisoners go aboveground, finding the city as lifeless as the surface of the moon. Only the one hundred American prisoners and their guards had survived.

In chapter 10, Vonnegut himself returns as narrator. It is 1968. In the intervening years, Billy has survived an airplane crash in which all of his fellow passengers have died. Valencia, frantically hurrying to see Billy in the hospital, has died of accidental carbon-monoxide poisoning. Robert Kennedy and Martin Luther King, Jr., have been assassinated. The Vietnam War is raging.

Finally, Vonnegut takes the reader back to Dresden. He and Billy are there, where the prisoners of war are digging for bodies, mining for corpses. Billy's digging companion dies of the dry heaves, unable to face the slaughter. Billy's friend Edgar Derby is executed for stealing a teapot. When the corpse mines are closed down, Billy, Vonnegut, and their companions are locked up in the suburbs to await the end of the war. When the war is over, the freed soldiers wander out into the street. The trees are blooming, and the birds are singing; springtime has finally arrived for Kurt Vonnegut.

Looking back on the novel, the reader realizes that Billy's time travels have been more than simply a coping device; they provide a learning tool as well. The jumble of events to which Vonnegut subjects Billy are not random and meaningless. Even if Billy remains blankly ignorant of the connections between events in his life, both the reader and the author learn about emotional survival in the modern world. For Vonnegut, who has called himself "the canary in the coal mine," Billy's story is a parable and a warning to all humankind: a warning that men and women must resist the temptation to abandon their free will, as Billy had, and an exhortation to keep one's dignity in the face of modern dehumanization.

The fact that *Slaughterhouse-Five* is a story of survival may seem contradictory or ironic, but that is always Vonnegut's approach. It would be hard for the reader to imagine more death than he witnesses here—the slaughter in Dresden and the deaths of Billy, his wife, his father, and assorted soldiers, all culminating in the foretelling of the destruction of the universe by the Tralfamadorians. However, the reader comes to understand that everything about Vonnegut's tale is ironic. Edgar Derby is executed, amid the Dresden corpse mines, for stealing a teapot; Billy, sitting in a slaughterhouse, is saved from destruction. No wonder Billy sees himself as the plaything of uncontrollable forces. However, Vonnegut knows better. Billy, comfortably numbed by Tralfamadorian philosophy, never reinvents himself—but Vonnegut does. Writing this book enabled the author to face his past, his present, and his future. In fact, after writing *Slaughterhouse-Five*, Vonnegut proclaimed that he would never *need* to write another book. *Slaughterhouse-Five* embodied for Vonnegut the spirit of the phoenix: his soul, through his art, rising from the ashes.

After the spiritual and psychological rejuvenation wrought by *Slaughterhouse-Five*, Vonnegut became a totally unfettered artist in his next two books, *Breakfast of Champions* and *Slapstick*. In *Breakfast of Champions*, he sets all of his characters free, disdaining his role as puppeteer. Admitting that, in English poet John Keats's words, he had been "half in love with easeful Death," he asserts that he has rid himself of this dangerous fascination. In *Slapstick*, he becomes frankly autobiographical, abandoning his aesthetic distance, eschewing all masks, facing his uncertain future and painful past with calm equanimity.

Galápagos • In *Galápagos*, called by Vonnegut himself his best novel, the ghost of Leon Trotsky Trout, son of Kilgore Trout, calmly tells the story of humankind from 1986 to a point one million years in the future. He tells of the end of humankind as known by its "big-brained" twentieth century readers and of the new Adam and Eves and their new Eden. Satirist and atheist that he is, Vonnegut idealizes no part of or party to his story. Knowledge is still the poisoned apple, but naturalist Charles Darwin, not God, is the featured figure of this final record of human life as known to its recorder.

Leon Trout died in the construction of the luxury liner the *Bahia de Darwin*, the launching of which is advertised as "the nature cruise of the century." Worldwide crises, however, cause all but a paltry few to withdraw their names from the list of passengers and crew. The cruise itself is begun by accident, and Mary Hepburn, not the figurehead captain, Adolf von Kleist, guides it to its destination. This unaware Adam and sterile-but-godlike Eve, with six Kanka-bono girls "from the Stone Age," begin the new race according to Darwin's (and God's?) dictum: Having eaten of the rotten apple, humankind, with its big, self-destructive brain, is no longer fit to survive; it is a matter of shrink and swim or die. Humankind thus becomes small-brained fisherkind as witnessed by the curious ghost of Leon Trout—who can now, having so witnessed, travel through the blue tunnel into the Afterlife.

Satirist, moralist, and spokesman for humankind that he is, Vonnegut, as Jonathan Swift before him, has offered in *Galápagos* his modest proposal to a humankind bent on its own destruction. He has also offered as epigraph to his tome the words of Anne Frank: "In spite of everything, I still believe people are really good at heart."

Timequake • In *Timequake* Vonnegut has humankind, because of a glitch in time, replay years 1991 to 2001 "on automatic pilot." He speaks as failed author of a ten-year project, *Timequake One*. Kilgore Trout, whom he personally identifies as his alter ego and as look-alike to his father, plays a crucial role in this novel. Vonnegut reprises his authorial roles as science-fiction writer, fiction writer, autobiographer, and spokesman for humankind.

Vonnegut's fictional story shows characters living and dying, living and dying again, and then waking and reeling from the reintroduction of free will. When humanity is roused from its ten years on automatic pilot, Trout becomes its hero. Because people have had no free will for ten years, they have forgotten how to use it, and Trout shows them the path to readjustment. Trout's words, for which he is celebrated, are: "You were sick, but now you're well again, and there's work to do."

Vonnegut's epilogue honoring his "big brother Bernie," who died toward the end of *Timequake*'s composition, calls to mind his prior references to saints he has known who, in an indecent society, behave decently. His references throughout *Timequake* and this final tribute to Bernard Vonnegut seem a recommendation of that gentle man to the status of saint.

Karen Priest
Updated by Judith K. Taylor

Other major works

SHORT FICTION: *Canary in a Cat House*, 1961; *Welcome to the Monkey House*, 1968; *Bagombo Snuff Box: Uncollected Short Fiction*, 1999.

PLAY: *Penelope*, pr. 1960, revised pr., pb. 1970 (as *Happy Birthday, Wanda June*).

TELEPLAY: *Between Time and Timbuktu: Or, Prometheus-5, a Space Fantasy*, 1972.

NONFICTION: *Wampeters, Foma, and Granfalloons (Opinions)*, 1974; *Palm Sunday: An Autobiographical Collage*, 1981; *Conversations with Kurt Vonnegut*, 1988; *Fates Worse than Death: An Autobiographical Collage of the 1980's*, 1991; *Like Shaking Hands with God: A Conversation About Writing*, 1999 (with Lee Stringer); *A Man Without a Country*, 2005.

CHILDREN'S LITERATURE: *Sun Moon Star*, 1980 (with Ivan Chermayeff).

Bibliography

Allen, William Rodney. *Understanding Kurt Vonnegut*. Columbia: University of South Carolina Press, 1991. Allen's study, part of the Understanding Contemporary American Literature series, places Vonnegut, and especially *Slaughterhouse-Five*, in the literary canon. Contains an annotated bibliography and an index.

Bloom, Harold, ed. *Kurt Vonnegut*. Philadelphia: Chelsea House, 2000. Collection of critical essays about Vonnegut that have been assembled for student use.

Boon, Kevin A., ed. *At Millennium's End: New Essays on the Work of Kurt Vonnegut*. Albany: State University of New York Press, 2001. A collection of eleven essays examining the novelist's moral vision.

Klinkowitz, Jerome. *The Vonnegut Effect*. Columbia: University of South Carolina Press, 2004. Evaluation of Vonnegut's contributions to literature by the author of several books on him.

Klinkowitz, Jerome, Julie Huffman-Klinkowitz, and Asa B. Pieratt, Jr. *Kurt Vonnegut, Jr.: A Comprehensive Bibliography*. Hamden, Conn.: Archon Books, 1987. An authoritative bibliography of works by and about Vonnegut. Lists Vonnegut's works in all their editions, including the short stories in their original places of publication, dramatic and cinematic adaptations, interviews, reviews, secondary sources, and dissertations.

_____. *"Slaughterhouse-Five": Reforming the Novel and the World.* Boston: Twayne, 1990. This book contains the most thorough and most modern treatment available of *Slaughterhouse-Five.* With care and insight, Klinkowitz debunks earlier, fatalistic interpretations of the novel. Features a comprehensive chronology, a thorough bibliography, and an index.

_____. *Vonnegut in Fact: The Public Spokesmanship of Personal Fiction.* Columbia: University of South Carolina Press, 1998. Klinkowitz makes a case for Vonnegut as a sort of redeemer of the novelistic form, after writers such as Philip Roth declared it dead. He traces Vonnegut's successful integration of autobiography and fiction in his body of work. Provides an extensive bibliography and an index.

Leeds, Marc. *The Vonnegut Encyclopedia: An Authorized Compendium.* Westport, Conn.: Greenwood Press, 1995. A concordance and encyclopedia identifying Vonnegut's most frequently recurring images and all his characters; indispensable for serious students of Vonnegut.

Merrill, Robert, ed. *Critical Essays on Kurt Vonnegut.* Boston: G. K. Hall, 1990. A comprehensive collection of essays on Vonnegut's works and career, which includes reviews, previously published essays, and articles commissioned for this work. The extensive introduction traces in detail Vonnegut's career and critical reception from the beginnings to 1990.

Morse, Donald E. *The Novels of Kurt Vonnegut: Imagining Being an American.* Westport, Conn.: Praeger, 2003. This analysis examines Vonnegut's novels against the framework of American history and literature of the twentieth century.

Mustazza, Leonard, ed. *The Critical Response to Kurt Vonnegut.* Westport, Conn.: Greenwood Press, 1994. Presents a brief history of the critical response to Vonnegut and critical reviews.

Rasmussen, R. Kent. *"Timequake."* In *Magill's Literary Annual 1998,* edited by John D. Wilson. Pasadena, Calif.: Salem Press, 1998. Lengthy review of *Timequake* that places the book's characters, events, and themes within the context of Vonnegut's other fiction and argues that the novel was Vonnegut's attempt to exorcise the demons of his traumatic experiences in World War II.

Reed, Peter J., and Marc Leeds, eds. *The Vonnegut Chronicles: Interviews and Essays.* Westport, Conn.: Greenwood Press, 1996. Vonnegut discusses, among other topics, postmodernism and experimental fiction. Includes a bibliography and an index.

Stone, Brad. "Vonnegut's Last Stand." *Newsweek* 130 (September 29, 1997): 78. A biographical sketch that focuses on *Timequake,* which Vonnegut has called his last book.

Tomedi, John. *Kurt Vonnegut.* Philadelphia: Chelsea House, 2004. Collection of critical essays on Vonnegut's works.

Alice Walker

Born: Eatonton, Georgia; February 9, 1944

Principal long fiction • *The Third Life of Grange Copeland*, 1970; *Meridian*, 1976; *The Color Purple*, 1982; *The Temple of My Familiar*, 1989; *Possessing the Secret of Joy*, 1992; *By the Light of My Father's Smile*, 1998; *Now Is the Time to Open Your Heart*, 2004.

Other literary forms • Alice Walker published her first volume of poetry during the late 1960's. She published three more volumes during the 1970's, one volume during the 1980's, and one during the early 1990's. After a ten-year hiatus, she returned to poetry again with two new volumes in 2003, *A Poem Traveled Down My Arm* and *Absolute Trust in the Goodness of the Earth: New Poems*. She was one of the first editors of *Ms.* magazine, which Gloria Steinem founded in 1971. Early on, Walker wrote many essays for that magazine. She has published eight volumes of essays and other nonfiction writings, including *In Search of Our Mothers' Gardens: Womanist Prose* (1983), *Living by the Word: Selected Writings, 1973-1987* (1988), *Warrior Marks: Female Genital Mutilation and the Sexual Blinding of Women* (1993, with Pratibha Parmar), and *We Are the Ones We Have Been Waiting For: Inner Light in a Time of Darkness—Meditations* (2006). Her writings for children include *Langston Hughes: American Poet* (1974), *To Hell with Dying* (1988), *Finding the Green Stone* (1991), and *There Is a Flower at the Tip of My Nose Smelling Me,* (2006).

Walker's interest in the then-little-known writer Zora Neale Hurston led to her pilgrimage to Florida to place a tombstone on Hurston's unmarked grave, to Walker's editing of *I Love Myself When I Am Laughing . . . and Then Again When I Am Looking Mean and Impressive: A Zora Neale Hurston Reader* (1979), and to her introduction to Robert Hemenway's *Zora Neale Hurston: A Literary Biography* (1977).

Achievements • Walker's literary reputation is based primarily on her fiction, although her second book of poetry, *Revolutionary Petunias, and Other Poems* (1973), received the Lillian Smith Award and a nomination for a National Book Award. Her first short-story collection, *In Love and Trouble: Stories of Black Women* (1973), won the Rosenthal Award of the National Institute of Arts and Letters. In addition, she received a Charles Merrill writing fellowship, an award for fiction from the National Endowment for the Arts, and a Guggenheim Fellowship. She was also a Bread Loaf Scholar and a fellow at the Radcliffe Institute. *The Third Life of Grange Copeland* was widely and enthusiastically reviewed in publications as varied as *The New Yorker, The New Republic,* and *The New York Times Book Review,* although journals aimed primarily at a black readership were often silent or critical of the violence and graphic depiction of rural black life. With the publication of *Meridian*, Walker's second novel, her work as a poet, novelist, essayist, editor, teacher, scholar, and political activist came together. *Meridian* was universally praised in scholarly journals, literary magazines, popular magazines, and black-oriented journals. Some critics, mainly black male reviewers, objected again to the honest, straightforward portrayals of black life in the South and to Walker's growing feminism, which they saw as being in conflict with her commitment to her race.

Walker's third novel, *The Color Purple*, was widely acclaimed; Steinem wrote that this novel "could be the kind of popular and literary event that transforms an intense reputation into a national one," and Peter Prescott's review in *Newsweek* began by saying "I want to say at once that *The Color Purple* is an American novel of permanent importance." These accolades were substantiated when Walker received both the American Book Award and the 1983 Pulitzer Prize for fiction.

Biography • Alice Walker was born in Eatonton, Georgia, on February 9, 1944, the last of eight children of Willie Lee and Minnie Lou Grant Walker, sharecroppers in rural Georgia. Her relationship with her father, at first strong and valuable, became strained as she became involved in the Civil Rights and women's movements. A moving depiction of her estrangement from her father occurs in her essay "My Father's Country Is the Poor," which appeared in *The New York Times* in 1977. For Walker, a loving and healthy mother-daughter relationship has endured over the years. An account of that relationship is central to her essays "In Search of Our Mothers' Gardens" and "Lulls—A Native Daughter Returns to the Black South" and in Mary Helen Washington's article "Her Mother's Gifts," in which Walker acknowledges that she often writes with her mother's voice—"Just as you have certain physical characteristics of your mother . . . when you're compelled to write her stories, it's because you recognize and prize those qualities of her in yourself."

One of the central events in Walker's childhood was a BB gun accident that left her, at the age of eight, blind in one eye. Scar tissue from that wound, both physical and psychological, seems to have left her with a compensating acuteness of vision, despite the conviction that she was permanently disfigured. Walker was affected enough by the accident to say in a 1974 interview with John O'Brien,

> I have always been a solitary person, and since I was eight years old (and the recipient of a disfiguring scar, since corrected, somewhat), I have daydreamed—not of fairy-tales—but of falling on swords, of putting guns to my heart or head, and of slashing my wrists with a razor.

Walker's partial blindness allowed her to attend Spelman College in Atlanta on a scholarship for students with disabilities, following her graduation from Butler-Baker High School in 1961. She left Spelman after two years—which included summer trips to the Soviet Union and to Africa as part of a group called Experiment in International Living—for Sarah Lawrence College, from which she graduated in 1965.

Walker's political activity governed her movements during the years immediately following her college graduation: She spent the summer of 1965 in the Soviet Union and also worked for civil rights in Liberty County, Georgia. The next year she was a case worker for New York City's Department of Social Services, and then a voter-registration worker in Mississippi. In 1967, she married Melvyn Leventhal, a civil rights lawyer, and moved to Jackson, Mississippi, where she continued her civil rights work, lived in the heart of the South as part of an interracial couple, and taught at Jackson State University, while continuing to write stories, poems, and essays. She taught at Tougaloo College in Mississippi for a year before returning to the East, where she was a lecturer in writing and literature at Wellesley College, an editor at *Ms.* magazine, and an instructor at the University of Massachusetts at Boston. By 1977, she had divorced her husband, accepted a position as associate professor of English at Yale University, and written six books.

Courtesy, The Eatonton Messenger

After *The Color Purple* won critical acclaim in 1986, Walker and her family shared the success with Eatonton. Walker's sister established The Color Purple Educational Scholarship Fund, and Walker adopted three elementary schools to help provide needed supplies for students who maintained above-average grades. Walker continued her activities in political forums as well, working for civil rights and protesting against nuclear weapons. She became an avid objector to female genital mutilation ("female circumcision") in Africa through public speaking and through her novel *Possessing the Secret of Joy* and her nonfiction book *Warrior Marks: Female Genital Mutilation and the Sexual Blinding of Women* (1993), which focus on the horrors and scars of this practice. *Possessing the Secret of Joy* explores female sexuality, a subject that Walker also treats in *By the Light of My Father's Smile*. In 2004, she returned to prose fiction with *Now Is the Time to Open Your Heart*, the story about an aging woman novelist searching for meaning.

Walker also used her success to help other female writers. She advocated women's literature classes and helped promote neglected female and black writers. In 1984, Walker began her own publishing company, Wild Trees Press. Throughout the 1980's and 1990's she lived in Northern California, where she continued to write stories, essays, poems, and novels.

Analysis • The story of Alice Walker's childhood scar provides the most basic metaphor of her novels: the idea that radical change is possible even under the worst conditions. Although she was never able to regain the sight in one eye, Walker's disfigurement was considerably lessened:

> I used to pray every night that I would wake up and somehow it would be gone. I couldn't look at people directly because I thought I was ugly. . . . Then when I was fourteen, I visited my brother Bill [who] took me to a hospital where they removed most of the scar tissue—and I was a *changed person*. I promptly went home, scooped up the best-looking guy, and by the time I graduated from high school, I was valedictorian, voted "Most Popular," and crowned queen!

The idea that change and personal triumph are possible despite the odds is central to all of Walker's writing. Her work focuses directly or indirectly on the ways of survival adopted by black women, usually in the South, and is presented in a prose style characterized by a distinctive combination of lyricism and unflinching realism. Walker's women attempt not merely to survive, but to survive completely with some sense of stability, despite the constant thread of family violence, physical and mental abuse, and a lack of responsibility on the part of the men in their lives. Walker is simultaneously a feminist and a supporter of civil rights, not only for black Americans but also for minorities everywhere.

Walker's vision was shaped in part by a work from the first flowering of black writing in America: Jean Toomer's *Cane* (1923). She said in 1974 about Toomer's book that "it has been reverberating in me to an astonishing degree. *I love it passionately*; could not possibly exist without it." Like *Cane*, the first part of which centers mainly on women in the South, Walker's novels are made up of nearly equal parts of poetry, portraiture, and drama, broken up into a series of sections and subsections. Other important literary influences on Walker include Zora Neale Hurston, from whom she inherited a love of black folklore; Flannery O'Connor, who wrote of southern violence and grotesqueries from her home in Milledgeville, Georgia, fewer than ten miles from Walker's childhood home; and Albert Camus, whose existentialism speaks to the struggle for survival and dignity in which Walker's characters are engaged. Walker herself defined her "preoccupations" as a novelist: "The survival, the survival *whole* of my people. But beyond that I am committed to exploring the oppressions, the insanities, the loyalties, and the triumphs of black women."

The Third Life of Grange Copeland, on the surface a novel about the cycle of rage and violence torturing the lives of a father and his son, is as much about the recipients of that rage—the women and children whose lives are directly affected. Although the novel is unremitting in its picture of desperate poverty's legacy of hatred, hopelessness, and cruelty, it concludes optimistically with Ruth Copeland's hope for a release from sorrow through the redemption promised by the early days of the Civil Rights movement and by the knowledge and love inherited at the sacrifical death of her grandfather.

The Third Life of Grange Copeland • Writing in 1973, Walker observed that her first novel, *The Third Life of Grange Copeland*, "though sometimes humorous and celebrative of life, is a grave book in which the characters see the world as almost entirely menacing." This dark view of life is common to Grange Copeland, the patriarch of a family farming on shares in rural Georgia, his son Brownfield, and the wives and daughters of both men. For all these characters, the world is menacing because of the socioeconomic position they occupy at the bottom of the scale of the sharecropping system. Father and son menace each other in this novel because they are in turn menaced by rage born out of the frustration of the system. Although the white people of the book are nearly always vague, nameless, and impersonal, they and the system they represent have the ability to render both Grange and Brownfield powerless.

It is not accidental that these characters' names have agricultural connotations. "Grange" suggests a late nineteenth century association of farmers, a feudal farm and grain storage building, and a combination of graze and range, while "Brownfield" and "Copeland" are self-explanatory—for the inability to cope with the land is what leads both male characters along virtually parallel paths. For the father, the mere appearance of the white farm boss's truck is enough to turn his face "into a unnaturally bland mask, curious and unsettling to see." The appearance of the truck causes the son to be "filled with terror of this man who could, by his presence alone, turn his father into something that might as well have been a pebble or a post or a piece of dirt." Although Grange is, in this same image, literally a piece of land, he eventually returns to the South and learns to live self-sufficiently, farming a section of soil he tricked his second wife into giving to him. Brownfield, in contrast, is never able to escape from the sharecropping system, although he sees that, like his father, he is "destined to be no more than overseer, on the white man's plantation, of his own children." Brownfield is able to live obliviously on a farm in Georgia, content to blame all of his problems on others. The poor rural black workers of this novel are themselves little more than a crop, rotated from farm to farm, producing a harvest of shame and hunger, cruelty and violence.

Unlike the men of the novel, the women are menaced by both black and white people, by both the agricultural system and the "strange fruit" it produces. Margaret, Grange's first wife, is both physically and mentally degraded by her husband and then sexually exploited by a white truck driver, resulting in her second pregnancy. Unable to cope with this situation, Grange deserts his family, after which his wife poisons both her child and herself. Following his father's pattern, Brownfield marries and begins to work the land, but after "a year when endless sunup to sundown work on fifty rich bottom acres of cotton land and a good crop brought them two diseased shoats for winter meat." he too begins to abuse his wife. Although Brownfield's wife, Mem, is a schoolteacher intelligent enough to try to break the cycle of raising other people's crops, her brief rebellion against her husband's malevolent beatings and mental tortures is a failure: He is able to subjugate her through repeated pregnancies that sap her rebellion as they turn her once rich and strong body into a virtual wasteland of emaciation. Because her body, which represents the land of the South, is still able to produce children despite its depleted condition, Brownfield is enraged enough to murder her in retaliation for her physical shape: "he had murdered his wife because she had become skinny and had not, with much irritation to him, reverted, even when well-fed, to her former plumpness. . . . Plumpness and freedom from the land, from cows and skinniness, went all together in his mind." Despite his irrational abuse of her, Mem is not ashamed "of being black though, no matter what he said. . . . Color was something the ground did to the flowers, and that was an end to it."

What the ground did to these generations of southern black people is the subject of Walker's novel—the whole lurid history of violence, hatred, and guilt that she chronicles in this story of one family's griefs. By the book's end, Brownfield Copeland has murdered his wife and an unnamed albino baby, while Grange Copeland has murdered his son Brownfield—first spiritually, then physically—and indirectly has killed his first wife and her infant.

Walker's characters are allegorical representations of the classic modes of survival historically adopted by black Americans in dealing with their oppression. Brownfield identifies with whites by daydreaming of himself on a southern plantation, sipping mint juleps, and then by bargaining for his freedom with the sexual favors of black women. Both of Grange's wives attempt to be true to the white stereotype of black women as promiscuous sexual beings, free of any moral restraints. Brownfield's wife, Mem, attempts the passive resistance advocated by Martin Luther King, Jr., but she is destroyed by what her husband calls "her weakness . . . forgiveness, a stupid belief that kindness can convert the enemy." Brownfield's daughter, Daphne, who calls herself the Copeland Family Secret Keeper, tries the strategy of inventing a falsely romantic history of the past, of the good old days when her father was kind, echoing those historical revisionists who try to argue that slavery was not that bad. Brownfield's other daughters try to stay away from their father altogether, regarding him "as a human devil" of whom they were afraid "in a more distant, impersonal way. He was like bad weather, a toothache, daily bad news."

Each of the title character's three lives (at home in the South as a sharecropper married to Margaret; in the North as a hustler of alcohol, drugs, and women; and finally back in the South as a farmer married to Josie and rearing his granddaughter Ruth) parallels a traditional survival strategy, which Grange summarizes as follows, "The white folks hated me and I hated myself until I started hating them in return and loving myself. Then I tried just loving me, and then you, and *ignoring* them much as I could." To put it another way, Grange tries at first to adapt to the system by believing what whites say about black people; then he turns to the classic escape of the runaway slave—heading North to freedom; finally, he tries the technique of praising black life while ignoring whites altogether. A large part of the novel's devastation is caused by the repeated use of these techniques, not against whites, but against other members of the Copeland family. Only Ruth, the granddaughter through whom Grange seeks redemption, is able to deal with whites in an intelligent, balanced, nondestructive yet independent way. She has learned from her grandfather, and from her family history, that pure hatred becomes self-hatred, and violence begets self-violence; she therefore becomes the novel's symbol of the new black woman, ready to assume her place in black history as a courageous worker in the Civil Rights movement that the rest of her family has been groping to discover.

Meridian • Walker's second novel, *Meridian*, picks up chronologically and thematically at the point where her first novel ended. *Meridian* describes the struggles of a young black woman, Meridian Hill, about the same age as Ruth Copeland, who comes to an awareness of power and feminism during the Civil Rights movement, and whose whole life's meaning is centered in the cycles of guilt, violence, hope, and change characteristic of that dramatic time. Thematically, *Meridian* picks up the first novel's theme of self-sacrificial murder as a way out of desperate political oppression in the form of the constant question that drives Meridian Hill—"Will you kill for the Revolution?" Meridian's lifelong attempt to answer that question affirmatively (as her college friends so easily do), while remaining true to her sense of responsibility to the past, her sense of ethics, and her sense of guilt of having given to her mother the child of her teenage pregnancy, constitutes the section of the novel titled "Meridian." The second third of the novel, "Truman Held," is named for the major male character in the narrative.

The third major section of the novel, "Ending," looks back at the turmoil of the Civil Rights movement from the perspective of the 1970's. Long after others have given up intellectual arguments about the morality of killing for revolution, Meridian is still debating the question, still actively involved in voter registration, political activism, and civil rights organization, as though the movement had never lost momentum. Worrying that her actions, now seen as eccentric rather than revolutionary, will cause her "to be left, listening to the old music, beside the highway," Meridian achieves release and atonement through the realization that her role will be to "come forward and sing from memory songs they will need once more to hear. For it is the song of the people, transformed by the experiences of each generation, that holds them together."

In 1978, Walker described *Meridian* as "a book 'about' the Civil Rights movement, feminism, socialism, the shakiness of revolutionaries and the radicalization of saints." Her word "about" is exact, for all of these topics revolve not chronologically but thematically around a central point—the protagonist, Meridian Hill. In some ways, Meridian *is* a saint; by the book's end she has sustained her belief in the Civil Rights movement without losing faith in feminism and socialism, despite family pressures, guilt, literally paralyzing self-doubts, the history of the movement, and the sexism of many of its leaders. In contrast, Truman Held represents those men who were reported to have said that "the only position for a woman in the movement is prone." Although Truman Held is Meridian's initial teacher in the movement, she eventually leaves him behind because of his inability to sustain his initial revolutionary fervor, and because of his misogyny. Unlike Brownfield Copeland, Truman argues that women are of less value than they should be, not because of skinniness, but because "Black women let themselves go . . . they are so fat." Later in the novel, Truman marries a white civil rights worker whose rape by another black man produces disgust in him, as much at his wife as at his friend. When Truman seeks Meridian out in a series of small southern hamlets where she continues to persuade black people to register to vote and to struggle for civil rights, he tells her that the movement is ended and that he grieves in a different way than she. Meridian answers, "I know how you grieve by running away. By pretending you were never there." Like Grange Copeland, Truman Held refuses to take responsibility for his own problems, preferring to run away to the North.

Meridian's sacrificial dedication to the movement becomes a model for atonement and release, words that once formed the working title of the book. *Meridian* could also have been called "The Third Life of Meridian Hill" because of similarities between Meridian's life and Grange Copeland's. Meridian leads three lives: as an uneducated child in rural Georgia who follows the traditional pattern of early pregnancy and aimless marriage, as a college student actively participating in political demonstrations, and as an eccentric agitator—a performer, she calls herself—unaware that the movement is ended. Like Grange Copeland in another sense, Meridian Hill is solid proof of the ability of any human to change dramatically by sheer will and desire.

Meridian is always different from her friends, who, filled with angry rhetoric, ask her repeatedly if she is willing to kill for the revolution, the same question that Grange asked himself when he lived in the North. This question haunts Meridian, because she does not know if she can or if she should kill, and because it reminds her of a similar request, posed in a similar way by her mother: "Say it now, Meridian, and be saved. All He asks is that we acknowledge Him as our Master. Say you believe in Him . . . don't go against your heart." In neither case is Meridian able to answer yes without going against her heart. Unlike her college friends and Truman Held, who see the movement only in terms of future gains for themselves, Meridian is involved with militancy because of her past: "But what none of them seemed to understand was that she felt herself to be, not holding on to something from the past, but *held* by something in the past."

Part of the past's hold on her is the sense of guilt she feels about her relationships with her parents. Although her father taught her the nature of the oppression of minorities through his knowledge of American Indians, her strongest source of guilt comes from her mother, who argues, like Brownfield Copeland, that the responsibility for *all* problems stems from outside oneself: "The answer to everything," said Meridian's mother, "is we live in America and we're not rich." Meridian's strongest sense of past guilt comes from the knowledge she gains when she becomes pregnant: "it was for stealing her mother's serenity, for shattering her mother's emerging self, that Meridian felt guilty from the very first, though she was unable to understand how this could possibly be her fault."

Meridian takes the form of a series of nonchronological sections, some consisting of only a paragraph, some four or five pages long, that circle around the events of Meridian's life. The writing is clear, powerful, violent, lyrical, and often symbolic. Spelman College, for example, is here called Saxon College. The large magnolia tree in the center of the campus, described with specific folkloric detail, is destroyed by angry students during a demonstration: "Though Meridian begged them to dismantle the president's house instead, in a fury of confusion and frustration they worked all night, and chopped and sawed down, level to the ground, that mighty, ancient, sheltering music tree." This tree (named The Sojourner, perhaps for Sojourner Truth) expands symbolically to suggest both the senseless destruction of black ghettos by African Americans during the turmoil of the 1960's, and also Meridian Hill herself, who receives a photograph years later of The Sojourner, now "a gigantic tree stump" with "a tiny branch, no larger than a finger, growing out of one side." That picture, suggesting as it does the rebirth of hope despite despair, also evokes the last vision of Meridian expressed by the now-shamed Truman Held:

> He would never see 'his' Meridian again. The new part had grown out of the old, though, and that was reassuring. This part of her, new, sure and ready, even eager, for the world, he knew he must meet again and recognize for its true value at some future time.

The Color Purple • Like Walker's first two novels, *The Color Purple* has an unusual form. *The Color Purple* presents the author's familiar and yet fresh themes—survival and redemption—in epistolary form. Most of the novel's letters are written by Celie, an uneducated, unloved, black woman living in rural Georgia during the 1920's; Celie's letters are written in what Walker calls "black folk English," a language of wit, strength, and natural humor. Ashamed of having been raped by her stepfather, a man whom Celie thinks at the time is her father, she begins to send letters to God, in the way that children send letters to Santa Claus, because her rapist told her to tell nobody but God. Although her early letters tell of rape, degradation, and pain, of her stepfather's getting rid of the two children born of his cruelty, the tone is nevertheless captivating, ironic, and even humorous. Soon the despair turns into acceptance, then into understanding, anger, rebellion, and finally triumph and loving forgiveness as the fourteen-year-old Celie continues to write until she reaches an audience, some thirty years later. Like the author, who began writing at the age of eight, and who has turned her childhood experience in rural Georgia into three novels of violence, hatred, understanding, love, and profound hope for the future, Celie is a writer, a listener, a thinker, and a promoter of Walker's constant theme: "Love redeems, meanness kills."

Like Meridian Hill, Celie compares herself to a tree. After her stepfather's repeated rapes, Celie is sold into a virtual state of slavery to a man who beats her, a man she neither knows, loves, nor talks to, a man she can never call anything but Mr. —, an ironic throwback to the eighteenth century English epistolary novel. Celie tries to endure by withholding all emotion: "I make myself wood. I say to myself, Celie, you a tree. That's how come I know trees fear man." Like The Sojourner, or like the kudzu vine of the deep South that thrives despite repeated attempts to beat it back, Celie continues to express her fears and hopes in a series of letters written in a form of black English that is anything but wooden. The contrast between the richly eccentric prose of Celie's letters and the educated yet often lifeless sentences of her sister Nettie's return letters supports Walker's statement that "writing

The Color Purple was writing in my first language." The language of the letters is at first awkward, but never difficult to follow. As Celie grows in experience, in contact with the outside world, and in confidence, her writing gradually becomes more sophisticated and more like standard written English, but it never loses its originality of rhythm and phrase.

Based on Walker's great-grandmother, a slave who was raped at the age of twelve by her owner, Celie works her way from ignorance about her body and her living situation all the way through to an awakening of her self-worth, as well as to an understanding of the existence of God, the relations between men and women, and the power of forgiveness in uniting family and friends. Much of this transformation is brought about through the magic of a blues singer named Shug Avery, who guides Celie in understanding sexuality, men, and religion without causing her to lose her own fresh insights, naïve though they are.

The letters that make up the novel are something like the missives that the protagonist of Saul Bellow's novel *Herzog* (1964) writes but never sends, in that they are often addressed to God and written in an ironic but not self-conscious manner. Because of the combination of dark humor and despair, the letters also evoke memories of the desperate letters from the physically and spiritually maimed addressed to the hero of Nathanael West's *Miss Lonelyhearts* (1933). Although Celie is unlettered in a traditional sense, her ability to carry the complicated plot forward and to continue to write—first without an earthly audience, and then to her sister, whom she has not seen for more than twenty years—testifies to the human potential for self-transformation.

Discussing Celie's attempts to confirm her existence by writing to someone she is not certain exists, Gloria Steinem says, "Clearly, the author is telling us something about the origin of Gods: about when we need to invent them and when we don't." In a sense, Shug Avery becomes a god for Celie because of her ability to control the evil in the world and her power to change the sordid conditions of Celie's life. Early in the book, when Celie is worrying about survival, about rape, incest, beatings, and the murder of her children, her only source of hope is the name "Shug Avery," a name with a magical power to control her husband. Not even aware that Shug is a person, Celie writes "I ast our new mammy bout Shug Avery. What it is?" Finding a picture of Shug, Celie transfers her prayers to what is at that point only an image:

> I see her there in furs. Her face rouge. Her hair like somethin tail. She grinning with her foot up on somebody motocar. Her eyes serious tho. Sad some. . . . An all night long I stare at it. An now when I dream, I dream of Shug Avery. She be dress to kill, whirling an laughing.

Shug Avery becomes a god to Celie not only because she is pictured in the first photograph Celie has ever seen, but also because she is dressed in a style that shows a sense of pride and freedom.

After Celie's sister's letters begin to appear, mailed from Africa, where Nettie is a missionary, the ironic connection between the primitive animism of the Africans and Celie's equally primitive reaction to Shug's picture becomes clear. Although Nettie has crossed the ocean to minister to a tribe of primitive people, her own sister is living in inhuman conditions in Georgia: ignorance, disease, sexism, lack of control of the environment, and the ever-increasing march of white people. When Shug explains her own animistic religious beliefs—which include the notion that God is not a he or a she, but an it (just as Celie once thought Shug Avery was an it)—Celie is converted to a pantheistic worship that makes her early identification with trees seem less naïve.

When the narrator of Herman Melville's "Bartleby the Scrivener" tries to explain Bartleby's withdrawal from life, he thinks of the dead letter office in which the scrivener was rumored to have worked, and says, "On errands of life, these letters speed to death." In contrast, Celie's and Nettie's letters, ostensibly written to people long thought to be dead, speed across the ocean on errands of life, where they grow to sustain not merely the sisters in the book but all those lucky enough to read them. As the author says of *The Color Purple*, "It's my happiest book . . . I had to do all the other writing to get to this point." For the reader who has gotten to this point in Walker's career by reading all of her other books, there is no question that Alice Walker's name could be substituted for Celie's in the author's statement about her most recent novel: "Let's hope people can hear Celie's voice. There are so many people like Celie who make it, who come out of nothing. People who triumph."

Possessing the Secret of Joy • The novels *By the Light of My Father's Smile* and *Possessing the Secret of Joy* share strong characters whose sexual identities suffer in order to conform to the society in which they live. Only through death can Tashi and Mad Dog become complete and escape the male-dominated world and its restrictions.

Walker combines fact and fiction in *Possessing the Secret of Joy* to illustrate the effects that female genital mutilation has on the women who are subjected to the procedure. The main character, Tashi, an African tribal woman, willingly undergoes the tribal ritual of genital mutilation in a desire to conform to her culture and feel complete. This procedure leaves her physically and mentally scarred. Tashi realizes that the procedure destroyed her emotionally and made her feel as if she were something other than her true self. After her mutilation, she marries Adam Johnson and moves to America. She is renamed Evelyn Johnson, and her chapter headings shift from "Tashi" to "Evelyn" in order to demonstrate the conflict within her as she struggles to find her true identity. The conflict leads her to madness.

Tashi strives to understand her insanity and to interpret her recurring nightmares of a tower. With the help of her therapists, Mzee and Raye, and the members of her family, Tashi realizes the reasons for her insanity and gradually becomes stronger and able to face her nightmares and what they represent. The chapters are told through the eyes of all the main characters, a technique that provides insight into the effect that Tashi has on those around her. Through its main characters, Tashi, Olivia, and Adam, *Possessing the Secret of Joy* is connected to, but is not a sequel to, Walker's previous novels *The Color Purple* and *The Temple of My Familiar.*

By the Light of My Father's Smile • Walker's sixth novel, *By the Light of My Father's Smile*, follows the Johnson family on a journey through life, and to rebirth through death. Magdalena, referred to as Mad Dog, discovers her sensuality and its connection with her spirituality while living with her parents in Mexico. Her parents are pretending to be missionaries in order to do an anthropological study of the Mundo people. Magdalena is acutely aware of her emotions and sensuality, but she is severely beaten by her father when he discovers her sexual activity.

Magdalena's sister Susannah, shadowed by Magdalena's anger and frustration, is awakened to her true desires by her friend Irene, who is able to survive and accept life on her own terms despite the restrictions placed on her by her society. Susannah realizes that her unhappiness is the result of having been "sucked into the black cloth" and hypocrisy of the world. Each member of the Johnson family suffers through life searching for true love and happiness, which they find only in death. The story moves between the spiritual world and physical world as the father watches his two daughters come to terms with their anger and their true spirits. As characters pass into the spiritual world, they are enlightened to their failings in the physical world and make amends with those they have injured. Only when acceptance of each soul is obtained can the four family members cross the river and live in eternity.

Timothy Dow Adams
Updated by Mary A. Blackmon

Other major works

SHORT FICTION: *In Love and Trouble: Stories of Black Women*, 1973; *You Can't Keep a Good Woman Down*, 1981; *The Complete Stories*, 1994; *Alice Walker Banned*, 1996 (stories and commentary).

POETRY: *Once: Poems*, 1968; *Five Poems*, 1972; *Revolutionary Petunias, and Other Poems*, 1973; *Goodnight, Willie Lee, I'll See You in the Morning: Poems*, 1979; *Horses Make a Landscape Look More Beautiful*, 1984; *Her Blue Body Everything We Know: Earthling Poems, 1965-1990 Complete*, 1991; *A Poem Traveled Down My Arm*, 2003; *Absolute Trust in the Goodness of the Earth: New Poems*, 2003.

NONFICTION: *In Search of Our Mothers' Gardens: Womanist Prose*, 1983; *Living by the Word: Selected Writings, 1973-1987*, 1988; *Warrior Marks: Female Genital Mutilation and the Sexual Blinding of Women*, 1993 (with Pratibha Parmar); *The Same River Twice: Honoring the Difficult*, 1996; *Anything We Love Can Be Saved: A Writer's Activism*, 1997; *The Way Forward Is with a Broken Heart*, 2000; *Sent by Earth: A Message from the Grandmother Spirit After the Attacks on the World Trade Center and Pentagon*, 2001; *We Are the Ones We Have Been Waiting For: Inner Light in a Time of Darkness—Meditations*, 2006.

CHILDREN'S LITERATURE: *Langston Hughes: American Poet*, 1974; *To Hell with Dying*, 1988; *Finding the Green Stone*, 1991; *There Is a Flower at the Tip of My Nose Smelling Me*, 2006.

EDITED TEXTS: *I Love Myself When I Am Laughing . . . and Then Again When I Am Looking Mean and Impressive: A Zora Neale Hurston Reader*, 1979.

Bibliography

Banks, Erma Davis, and Keith Byerman. *Alice Walker: An Annotated Bibliography, 1968-1986*. New York: Garland, 1989. Very useful bibliography of works by and about Walker.

Bates, Gerri. *Alice Walker: A Critical Companion*. Westport, Conn.: Greenwood Press, 2005. A well-crafted biography that discussed Walker's major works, tracing the themes of her novels to her life.

Bloom, Harold, ed. *Alice Walker*. New York: Chelsea House, 1989. An important collection of critical essays examining the fiction, poetry, and essays of Walker from a variety of perspectives. The fourteen essays, including Bloom's brief introduction, are arranged chronologically. Contains useful discussions of the first three novels, brief analyses of individual short stories, poems, and essays, and assessments of Walker's social and political views in connection with her works and other African American female authors. A chronology of Walker's life and a bibliography may be of assistance to the beginner.

Dieke, Ikenna, ed. *Critical Essays on Alice Walker*. New York: Greenwood Press, 1999.

Especially well-suited for use in college literature classrooms, this collection gives particular attention to Walker's poetry and her developing ecofeminism.

Gates, Henry Louis, Jr., and K. A. Appiah, eds. *Alice Walker: Critical Perspectives Past and Present*. New York: Amistad, 1993. Contains reviews of Walker's first five novels and critical analyses of several of her works of short and long fiction. Also includes two interviews with Walker, a chronology of her works, and an extensive bibliography of essays and texts.

Lauret, Maria. *Alice Walker*. New York: St. Martin's Press, 2000. Provocative discussions of Walker's ideas on politics, race, feminism, and literary theory. Of special interest is the exploration of Walker's literary debt to Zora Neale Hurston, Virginia Woolf, and even Bessie Smith.

Montelaro, Janet J. *Producing a Womanist Text: The Maternal as Signifier in Alice Walker's "The Color Purple."* Victoria, B.C.: English Literary Studies, University of Victoria, 1996. Examines themes of feminism, motherhood, and African American women in literature.

Wade-Gayles, Gloria. "Black, Southern, Womanist: The Genius of Alice Walker." In *Southern Women Writers: The New Generation*, edited by Tonette Bond Inge. Tuscaloosa: University of Alabama Press, 1990. An excellent, thorough introduction to the life and literary career of Walker. Placing emphasis on Walker's voice as a black, southern woman throughout her works and arguing that Walker's commitment is to the spiritual wholeness of her people, Wade-Gayles examines several essays that are important to an understanding of her fiction and beliefs, her first three novels, both collections of short stories, and her collections of poetry. Supplemented by a bibliography of Walker's works, endnotes, and a useful secondary bibliography.

Walker, Melissa. *Down from the Mountaintop: Black Women's Novels in the Wake of the Civil Rights Movement, 1966-1989*. New Haven, Conn.: Yale University Press, 1991. Places Walker beside other African American women whose fiction mirrored the racial plight that called forth the Civil Rights movement.

Walker, Rebecca. *Black, White, and Jewish: Autobiography of a Shifting Self*. New York: Riverhead, 2001. A self-indulgent but nevertheless insightful memoir by Alice Walker's daughter. Rebecca Walker, who describes herself as "a movement child," grew up torn between two families, two races, and two traditions, always in the shadow of an increasingly famous mother.

White, Evelyn C. *Alice Walker: A Life*. New York: W. W. Norton, 2004. The life and accomplishments of Walker are chronicled in this biography through interviews with Walker, her family and friends.

Winchell, Donna Haisty. *Alice Walker*. New York: Twayne, 1992. Provides a comprehensive analysis of Walker's short and long fiction. A brief biography and chronology precede the main text of the book. Each chapter refers to specific ideas and themes within Walker's works and focuses on how Walker's own experiences define her characters and themes. Following the narrative is a useful annotated bibliography.

Robert Penn Warren

Born: Guthrie, Kentucky; April 24, 1905
Died: West Wardsboro, near Stratton, Vermont; September 15, 1989

Principal long fiction • *Night Rider*, 1939; *At Heaven's Gate*, 1943; *All the King's Men*, 1946; *World Enough and Time: A Romantic Novel*, 1950; *Band of Angels*, 1955; *The Cave*, 1959; *Wilderness: A Tale of the Civil War*, 1961; *Flood: A Romance of Our Time*, 1964; *Meet Me in the Green Glen*, 1971; *A Place to Come To*, 1977.

Other literary forms • Robert Penn Warren wrote successfully in so many genres that Charles Bohner called him "the pentathlon champion of American literature." In addition to his novels, he published short stories, numerous volumes of poetry, and a considerable amount of nonfiction. Warren's fiction and his poetry often consider the same philosophical themes: the meaning of history, the loss of innocence and the recognition of evil in the fallen world, and the difficulty of finding a moral balance in a world in which traditional Christian values seem to be faltering. For example, in his book-length poem *Brother to Dragons: A Tale in Verse and Voices* (1953), Warren begins with a historical event—a brutal murder of a slave by Thomas Jefferson's nephew, Lilburne Lewis—and creates a philosophical examination of people's fallen nature. Warren does something very similar in his novel *World Enough and Time*. The story is based on a murder that occurred in 1825, but the novel, like the poem, becomes an examination of people's fall from innocence and the difficulty of establishing moral ideals in a fallen world.

Warren's concerns over history and morality are also evident in his earliest, nonfiction works. In his first book, a biography, *John Brown: The Making of a Martyr* (1929), Warren contends that Brown did not tread the path of morality quite so righteously as Ralph Waldo Emerson had thought he had; in his fallen condition, Brown mistook his own egotism for pure idealism. Warren's neo-orthodox insistence on people's fallen nature and his skepticism about the possibilities of pure idealism, both of which are reflected in his novels, led him to accept the traditionalist attitudes of the southern intellectuals who made up the "Fugitive Group," and he contributed to the agrarian manifesto *I'll Take My Stand* (1930). Warren did, however, espouse a more liberal attitude toward racial matters in his later nonfiction works *Segregation: The Inner Conflict in the South* (1956) and *Who Speaks for the Negro?* (1965).

Warren's social criticism ultimately proved less influential than his literary criticism. His *Selected Essays* (1958) contains perceptive studies of Samuel Taylor Coleridge's *The Rime of the Ancient Mariner* (1798), Joseph Conrad's *Nostromo* (1904), William Faulkner, Ernest Hemingway, and Katherine Anne Porter. These essays are important not only for what they say about these authors but also for what they reveal about Warren's own work. Even more important than these essays, however, was Warren's collaboration with Cleanth Brooks. Their textbooks, *Understanding Fiction* (1943) and *Understanding Poetry* (1938), helped to change substantially the way literature was taught in the United States.

Warren continued to publish literary criticism at intervals throughout his life; indeed, *New and Selected Essays* appeared in the year of his death, 1989. However, with a poetry-writing career that spanned fifty years, he was at least equally well known as a craftsman in that genre. His poems have been widely anthologized, and he is recognized as one of the foremost twentieth century American poets.

Achievements • For most readers Warren's name is probably most associated with his novel *All the King's Men*, for which he won both the Pulitzer Prize for fiction and the National Book Award. He also won the Robert Meltzer Award from the Screen Writers Guild for the play based on that novel. Warren's short story "Blackberry Winter" has also been highly acclaimed and widely anthologized. Other readers think of Warren primarily as a poet, and with good reason; he won the Pulitzer Prize for poetry twice, first for *Promises: Poems 1954-1956* (1957), which also won the Edna St. Vincent Millay Prize and the National Book Award for Poetry, and a sec-

Robert A. Ballard, Jr.

ond time for *Now and Then: Poems 1976-1978* (1978). *Selected Poems: New and Old, 1923-1966* (1966) won the Bollingen Prize from Yale University, and *Audubon: A Vision* (1969) won the Van Wyck Brooks Award and the National Medal for Literature. Warren was elected to the American Philosophical Society in 1952 and to the American Academy of Arts and Sciences in 1959. He was named first poet laureate of the United States in 1986.

Biography • Robert Penn Warren's background and experience had a tremendous impact upon the thematic concerns of his fiction. He demonstrated the need, common to so many southern writers, to cope with the burden of the past. He also wrote out of a scholar's familiarity with and devotion to certain prominent literary artists, past and present, particularly the Elizabethan and Jacobean dramatists, Joseph Conrad, William Faulkner, and T. S. Eliot. His academic studies, pursued in a long career as an English professor, may have had a great deal to do with the structure of his works and their typically tragic mode. His recurring subject, however, was the peculiar experience of the South; a love-hate relationship with a dying heritage runs throughout his work.

Born to Robert Franklin and Anna Ruth Penn Warren on April 24, 1905, in the tiny Kentucky town of Guthrie, Warren grew up in an almost classic southern situation. His father, a banker and businessman struggling to support a large family, did not initially fire the young Warren's imagination as his grandfather did. The emotional bond between Warren and his maternal grandfather, Gabriel Thomas Penn, ripened during long summers spent on his grandfather's tobacco farm. Here, Warren experienced the pastoral charms of agrarian life, soaked up the nostalgic glow of the American Civil War from his grandfather, and absorbed the rhetoric and humor that permeates the southern storytelling.

Gabriel Thomas Penn had been a cavalryman during the Civil War, and many an afternoon with his grandson was spent reliving the legendary time. It is not surprising that the boy looked upon the Civil War as America's great epic, as imbued with nobility and tragedy as Homer's *Iliad* (c. 800 B.C.E.) He was not blind, however, to the irony and ambiguity of his grandfather, as representative of the values of the aristocratic horse soldier. Warren has commemorated his realization that the romantic image of the Confederate cavalryman had its darker side in the poem "Court Martial" in *Promises: Poems 1954-1956*, which is about his grandfather's hanging of bushwhackers without benefit of legal trial. Because this poem was written much later, however, it is possible that the ambiguous view of the grandfather was partially constructed from a more mature understanding. The event, however, was a true one that evidently made a deep impression on the young Warren. In any case, Warren was absorbing background for a number of later novels, such as *Wilderness: A Tale of the Civil War* and *Band of Angels*. In neither of these does he write as an apologist for the Old South, but he does expose the moral shortcomings of northerners, much as he does in his early biography of John Brown.

Warren was also absorbing the local tales of tobacco war, when the growers of dark-fired tobacco banded together to boycott the tobacco company that regulated prices. Warren's first novel, *Night Rider*, was written from childhood memories of such local stories. Warren's brother Thomas, who became a grain dealer, knew all the farmers of the region and was adept at repeating such tales.

The young Warren loved nature; collected butterflies, snakes, rocks, and leaves; and aspired to paint animals (an interest reflected in his poem about John Audubon). Later, he hunted with his brother and learned taxidermy. These experiences were more important, perhaps, to the content of his poetry than to his fiction. In spite of his persistent affinity for nature, he usually recognized in his fiction its essential amorality: "The blank cup of nature," he calls it in *World Enough and Time*.

In spite of the contribution to his early imaginative development by his grandfather and his agrarian milieu, the influence of Warren's father was subtle and pervasive, perhaps more significant in the long run to the human relationships explored in his novels. Ambiguous father-son relationships appear over and over in such novels as *All the King's Men*, *The Cave*, *At Heaven's Gate*, and *A Place to Come To*. None is modeled after Warren's actual relationship to his own father, but they reflect a combination of admiration, guilt, and mystery that suggests some deep personal involvement in the issues they raise.

Warren often admitted to an odd sense of guilt about "stealing his father's life." Robert Franklin Warren had wanted to be a lawyer and a poet but had become a businessman instead, because of financial responsibilities not only to his own family but also to a family of half brothers and sisters left without a provider when his father died. One of Warren's favorite reminiscences was about finding a book with some poems written by his father in it and carrying it with delight to him. His father summarily confiscated the book, and his son never saw it again. Warren thought perhaps his father had been embarrassed or pained at this reminder of a goal long since set aside. According to Warren, his father never regretted the obligations that dictated the terms of his life. Indeed, he took joy in them. Warren speaks with an admiration bordering on awe of the seemingly effortless rectitude of his father and of the ideal relationship between his father and mother.

As the result of an accident when he was fifteen years old, Warren lost the sight of one eye and was thus prevented from pursuing a career as a naval officer, as he had planned. Warren went, instead, to Vanderbilt University and came under the influence of John Crowe Ransom and the Fugitives, a group of academics and townspeople who met regularly to discuss philosophy and poetry. Ransom soon recognized Warren's unusual ability and encouraged him to write poetry.

Warren graduated summa cum laude from Vanderbilt in 1926 and pursued a master's degree at the University of California at Berkeley. While there, he became an ardent student of Elizabethan and Jacobean drama, which perhaps struck a responsive chord in an imagination already steeped in the violence and melodrama of southern history. He started to work on a doctorate at Yale University but left as a Rhodes scholar for Oxford, England, where he received a Bachelor of Letters degree in 1930.

During this period, Warren wrote his first book, *John Brown: The Making of a Martyr.* To some extent, this book grew out of an impulse shared with a number of his Vanderbilt friends and other writers of the so-called Southern Renaissance. They were concerned about the exclusively northern bias of most historians dealing with events leading up to and during the Civil War and its aftermath. Certainly, Warren presents a jaundiced view of the radical abolitionist. Brown seems to have provided a nucleus for Warren's meditations about the effects of power and the misuses of altruism that were to be explored in a number of later novels, especially *Night Rider* and *All the King's Men.* He also wrote his first fiction while at Oxford, a short story called "Prime Leaf," about the impact of the Kentucky tobacco war on an old man, his son, and his grandson. The old man has a role similar to that of the elder Todd in *Night Rider,* the wise man who bows out of the organization when it resorts to vigilante tactics.

Warren taught at a number of universities, including Louisiana State, where he lived in the legendary ambience of the southern demagogue Huey Long, whose presence lies behind the fictional Willie Stark of *All the King's Men.* Warren later said that he knew nothing about the real Huey Long, but the mythical Huey was on everyone's lips. Even casual conversations often dwelt upon questions of power and ethics, of means and ends, of "historical costs." In an essay titled "All the King's Men: The Matrix of Experience," in John Lewis Longley's *Robert Penn Warren: A Collection of Critical Essays* (1965), Warren writes:

> Melodrama was the breath of life. There had been melodrama in the life I had known in Tennessee, but with a difference; in Tennessee the melodrama seemed to be different from the stuff of life, something superimposed upon life, but in Louisiana people lived melodrama, seemed to live, in fact, for it, for this strange combination of philosophy, humor and violence. Life was a tale that you happened to be living—and that "Huey" happened to be living before your eyes.

These remarks demonstrate that Warren was not primarily a historical novelist but rather a classicist, fascinated with the universal patterns in particular experience. Thus, he discouraged close comparisons between Willie Stark and Huey Long, pointing out that he wrote the first version of the story as a verse drama in Italy, as he watched Benito Mussolini, another man of the people, consolidate his power.

In Warren's writing career, the years from 1943 to 1950, though a dry period for poetry, were productive ones for fiction and literary criticism. Besides *All the King's*

Men, he produced *At Heaven's Gate*, about the unscrupulous liaison between government and industry, and *World Enough and Time*, about a nineteenth century murder case. When Warren was poetry consultant for the Library of Congress in 1944-1945, Katherine Anne Porter, who was fiction consultant that year, threw on his desk the confession of Jeroboam Beauchamp, hanged for murder in Kentucky in 1826. Porter announced cryptically that she was giving him a novel. This was, indeed, the germ for his most complex novel, *World Enough and Time*.

Warren's dry period in poetry eventually ended after he divorced his first wife, Emma Brescia, married the writer Eleanor Clark, and fathered two children. He began writing excellent poetry and produced several more novels. A long association with Yale University began in 1950.

In 1986 Warren was named the first poet laureate of the United States, a post he held for two years. He died of cancer in 1989, at his summer home near Stratton, Vermont.

Analysis • Often, what Robert Penn Warren said about other writers provides an important insight into his own works. This is especially true of Warren's perceptive essay "The Great Mirage: Conrad and *Nostromo*" in *Selected Essays*, in which he discusses the enigmatic speech of Stein in Joseph Conrad's *Lord Jim* (1900):

> A man that is born falls into a dream like a man who falls into the sea. If he tries to climb out into the air as inexperienced people endeavor to do, he drowns—*nicht wahr?* ... No! I tell you! The way is to the destructive element submit yourself, and with the exertions of your hands and feet in the water make the deep, deep sea keep you up.

Warren interprets the dream here as "man's necessity to justify himself and his actions into moral significance of some order, to find sanctions." The destructiveness of the dream arises from humans' nature as egotistical animals with savage impulses, not completely adapted to the dream-sea of ideas. The one who learns to swim instead of drowning in the unnatural sea of ideas is he who realizes that the values he creates are illusion, but that "the illusion is necessary, is infinitely precious, is the mark of his human achievement, and is, in the end, his only truth." Warren calls *Nostromo* "a study in the definition and necessity of illusion." This phrase could also describe most of Warren's works of fiction.

Warren's classification of thematic elements in Conrad's stories could also be applied to his own. Warren writes that Conrad is concerned with the person who lacks imagination but clings to fidelity and duty (like the old captain in *Youth*, 1902), the sinner against human solidarity and the human mission (like Kurtz in *Heart of Darkness*, 1902, and Decoud in *Nostromo*), and the redeemed individual (Jim in *Lord Jim* and Dr. Monygham in *Nostromo*). Warren says that Conrad is most interested in the latter—"the crisis of this story comes when the hero recognizes the terms on which he may be saved, the moment, to take Morton Zabel's phrase, of the 'terror of the awakening.'"

One might note that in Warren's novel *At Heaven's Gate*, Jerry's dirt-farmer father fits the pattern of natural rectitude, while Slim Sarrett, the nihilistic, cynical artist, is certainly the sinner against human solidarity. No one seems to be redeemed in *At Heaven's Gate*, though Jerry might have a chance in a hypothetical future, since he has acquired considerable self-knowledge. Mr. Munn in *Night Rider* has also stripped away his own illusions, but he dies, like William Shakespeare's Macbeth, without redemption. In other novels of this period, however, Burden in *All the King's Men*, and perhaps even the murderer in *World Enough and Time*, achieve some kind of absolution. Warren and Conrad share this deep obsession with the need for redemption, and though the sentiment is religious and may be expressed in Christian imagery, it is consistently humanistic in emphasis. The world they both recognize is a naturalistic one, but people must live in two worlds, the world of facts and the world of ideas, which they create themselves. Warren's notion of submission to the realm of ideas is analogous, perhaps, to Ernest Hemingway's code of the hunter, the fisherman, the bullfighter, or the soldier, which provides existential meaning in a meaningless world.

Warren's early novels, particularly *Night Rider, All the King's Men,* and *World Enough and Time,* which critics generally agree are his best, trace a pattern of increasing complexity in the theme of people's vacillation between the fantasy of dreams and the reality of facts. After *World Enough and Time,* which is almost too densely packed and convoluted in theme, Warren relaxed his insistence that everything must be said on the subject of illusion and reality in one novel. Later works, such as *Meet Me in the Green Glen* and *Wilderness: A Tale of the Civil War,* though not conspicuously different in theme, concentrate on a particular manifestation of the problem—on the nature of love in *Meet Me in the Green Glen,* and on the nature of altruism in *Wilderness.*

Actually, Warren's examination of the apposition between the world of ideas and the world of facts begins in his first book, *John Brown: The Making of a Martyr.* Warren portrays the militant abolitionist as not so much obsessed with freeing slaves as with starring in his own myth. Brown is encouraged in this role by the unqualified praise of Ralph Waldo Emerson, whom Warren believed to be a writer of empty words, with little perception of the real world; Warren quotes Emerson as saying of Brown, "He is a man to make friends wherever on earth courage and integrity are esteemed—the rarest of heroes, a pure idealist, with no by-ends of his own." Warren did not for a moment believe that Brown was a "pure idealist"; moreover, Warren had a continuing distrust of "pure idealists," whoever they might be. In his fiction, Warren was inclined to show abstract idealists as lacking in self-knowledge, capable of self-righteous violence because they refuse to acknowledge their own irrational impulses. The best example of this personality type in Warren's fiction is Adam Stanton, in *All the King's Men,* who assassinates Willie Stark because Willie, the man of fact, seduced Adam's sister.

John Brown, however, as a man who uses exalted ideas to inflate his own self-image, is more akin to Warren's Professor Ball, Dr. MacDonald, and Mr. Munn of *Night Rider;* Bogan Murdock, the industrialist, and Slim Sarett, of *At Heaven's Gate;* and Wilkie Barron, the manipulative false friend of Jeremiah Beaumont, in *World Enough and Time.* Willie Stark, though categorized by Jack Burden as the "man of fact," in contrast to Adam Stanton, the "man of idea," has his own idealistic dream of the people's hospital, free to anyone who needs it. Whether that dream was truly altruistic, however, or tinged by the secret need for a personal monument to his existence, is ambiguous.

Night Rider • Warren suggests that the self is itself part of the dream-sea of ideas. Warren's protagonists are often initially passive persons whose emptiness is filled by other more dynamic personalities. Having acquired a somewhat fictitious self under such influence, they proceed to act in the real world as though that dream were true—often with tragic results. Thus, Mr. Munn seems an innocuous, ordinary young lawyer when he first appears in *Night Rider*, but he is drawn irresistibly to his more dynamic friend, Mr. Christian, who has a legitimate concern for the plight of the tobacco growers at the mercy of the price-controlling tobacco company. Munn learns to savor his new role as labor leader. He is ripe, then, for indoctrination by more conniving, professional agitators, Professor Ball and Dr. MacDonald, who preach a secret society that will scrape the fields of uncooperative growers and punish backsliders who dare to violate the embargo. What begins as a lawful strike by the downtrodden majority becomes lawless action by a vigilante group that destroys crops, burns warehouses, and commits murder.

In the case of Munn, the crisis of this psychic change in direction comes when he realizes that his assigned task to assassinate the tobacco farmer Bunk Trevelyon, whom he once defended in court on a murder charge, is not only his "duty" to the group; it also satisfies something very personal in himself that he has not yet recognized. Trevelyon had committed the murder of which he was once accused, and the African American who was hanged for that murder was innocent. Trevelyon thus becomes the symbol for Munn's half-conscious cooperation in framing the African American, or, to use another favorite term of Warren, Munn's original sin. In this ritual of retribution, the shared myth of community justice fuses with Munn's private myth of killing the shadow-self, an act of both self-condemnation and deliberate concealment of a secret crime.

After this private confrontation and ritual killing of his shadow-self, Munn makes no more moral objections to anything Ball and MacDonald want to do. The three lead a concerted assault on the company warehouses, which results in a number of casualties. One person who dies is young Benton Todd, who had been an ardent admirer of Munn. Moreover, Todd hoped to marry Mr. Christian's daughter, Lucille, who has been having a secret affair with Munn. If Trevelyon symbolizes the murderous shadow-self that Munn has hated to acknowledge, Benton Todd suggests the lost idealism, the better dream that Munn has betrayed.

Munn's subsequent flight to the West to escape prosecution for a murder he did not commit might have resulted in redemption, but it does not. The pattern of redemption is presented to him obliquely by the story of Proudfit, the impoverished farmer who is sheltering Munn. Proudfit tells of his own checkered career in the West, as a buffalo hunter and hide-tanner, with companions as rough and wild as himself. Eventually, however, he lives in peace among American Indians. When he becomes ill, the Native Americans care for him, using all their resources of natural healing and religious ritual. In his fever, he eventually has a vision of Kentucky, where he was reared, and a young woman waiting beside a stream. His strength then begins to return, so he leaves the Native American friends and goes back to find the very woman he saw in his vision, now his wife, and the very hill he saw, which is now his farm.

Proudfit's story is both an engrossing dialect narrative and a unique version of the underlying myth of death and resurrection. Proudfit's humble redemption contrasts with the myth of sin and damnation implied in Munn's career. Both Proudfit and Munn have a period of withdrawal (Proudfit, among the American Indians; Munn, on Proudfit's remote farm), time to rethink their past lives and future goals. This experience is analogous, perhaps, to the withdrawal and contemplation that the mythic hero undergoes before he returns to his homeland as a new man. Munn, however, is not transformed. He does become mildly obsessed with the innocent African American who died in Trevelyon's stead, but he cannot even remember the man's name.

Perhaps his inability to name the scapegoat is intended to suggest Munn's distance from the redemption offered by Christ's sacrifice. This does not mean that Warren was advocating Christianity; he was admitting, at least, a moral vacuum where traditional values have been eliminated in a society concerned primarily with power and wealth.

All the King's Men • The polarity of idea and fact receives more explicit development in *All the King's Men*. Again, an essentially passive person, Jack Burden, feeds emotionally on a more dynamic personality, Willie Stark. Burden calls himself—somewhat cynically—an idealist, but his idealism consists mostly of a fastidious preference for not getting his hands dirty with some of Stark's more questionable political maneuvers. Stark is good-naturedly tolerant of Burden's moral preferences, since he has Tiny Duffy to do his dirty work.

Burden considers himself a good judge of character and motives, but when a cherished image about the purity and goodness of his old girlfriend, Anne Stanton, is proven to be false, he is devastated and lost in self-doubt. Anne, who is quite a passive, unfulfilled person herself, has become Stark's mistress. Burden's first impulse is to flee, to escape, to drown, to fall into what he calls the Great Sleep. From this symbolic death, Burden is born again into a bleak but emotionally insulating belief in the Great Twitch—an understanding of the world as completely amoral and mechanistic, wherein no one has any responsibility for what happens. Here, indeed, Burden has stepped out of the fantasy of dreams into the reality of facts.

Burden can now consent to let Stark use the information he has uncovered concerning Judge Irwin's long-forgotten political crime. Burden soon discovers how brutal the world of fact can be, when Judge Irwin's suicide reveals that the judge was actually Burden's own father. Hardly recovered from this blow, Burden recognizes a measure of responsibility for the deaths of Willie Stark and his best friend, Adam Stanton, who is shot by Willie's bodyguard after the assassination. Through his passivity and noninvolvement, Jack Burden had virtually handed over Anne Stanton to his more dynamic boss, and thus set the stage for assassination.

The novel is a fascinating study of symbiotic relationships, of which the most striking is that between Willie Stark, the practical politician, and Adam Stanton, the puritanical idealist and perfectionist. Warren also suggests a politically symbiotic relationship between the demagogue and the people he represents. In social terms, the world of *All the King's Men* is more complex than that of *Night Rider*. Munn's career is essentially that of the tragic hero, the good but not exclusively good man who is corrupted by power. Willie Stark, however, is sustained not only by his own drive for power but also by the concerted will of his constituency, who feel themselves to be socially and politically helpless. He is probably more significant as an antidote to their depression than as an answer to their physical needs. Even though Willie wants to change the world of facts for their benefit—build roads, bridges, a free hospital—it is for his psychological impact, exemplifying the triumph of the common person over the privileged elite, that he is beloved. Thus, even the man of facts floats in the symbolic sea of ideas.

World Enough and Time • If the relationship between dream and reality is complicated in *All the King's Men*, in *World Enough and Time* it becomes intricately complex. Seldom have human aspirations been so relentlessly exposed, one after another, as frail illusions. Though it might be termed a historical novel, because it is based loosely on an actual event, or a philosophical novel, because it comments repeatedly on the abstract meaning of human behavior and aspiration, *World Enough and Time* is better termed a psychological novel, or more precisely, perhaps, an examination of the psychological motivations for philosophizing. It is certainly not, like Andrew Marvell's poem "To His Coy Mistress," to which the title ironically alludes, a neat argument for seizing pleasures while one may. It is not a neat argument for any philosophical position, but it illuminates the sequential confusion of a reasonably thoughful, well-meaning person trying to identify himself and justify his actions.

Jeremiah Beaumont, the orphaned son of an unsuccessful Kentucky farmer in the early nineteenth century, becomes the loved protégé of Colonel Cassius Fort, a well-known lawyer and statesman of the region. Jerry's exalted view of Colonel Fort receives a cruel blow from his dashing friend Wilkie Barron, a popular man-about-town and dabbler in politics. Wilkie tells Jerry of a beautiful woman he once loved in vain, who was seduced by an older man who had come to console her when her father died. When the young woman, Rachel Jordan, had a stillborn child, the older man abandoned her. The knave who wronged her was the unimpeachable Colonel Fort.

The persuasive Wilkie succeeds in promoting in a somewhat passive Jerry a romantic vision of wronged womanhood. From this point on, Jerry creates his own drama of love and revenge, though Wilkie continues to manipulate him in ways he never understands until near the end of his life. Jerry repudiates Colonel Fort, his surrogate father, and woos and eventually wins the lovely Rachel, who is in a neurotic state of depression, not because of the supposed perfidy of Colonel Fort but because of her baby's death. Jerry, blind to the real source of her despondency, hounds her into commanding him to defend her honor. Fort refuses a duel with Jerry, however, and the honorable vengeance seems destined to fizzle. Rachel is again pregnant, and Jerry is fitting into the comfortable role of country squire. An unknown messenger brings to Rachel a slanderous handbill in which Colonel Fort, presumably denying to his political opponents his affair with Rachel, claims that Rachel had slept with a slave. Fort had gallantly claimed paternity of the child as a chivalric gesture. This shocking document, which is actually a forgery written by Wilkie Barron, precipitates Rachel's labor, and Jerry's child is also born dead. Jerry, in remorse, kills Fort—not openly in a duel, as he had planned, but secretly, letting it appear to be a political assassination.

Jerry's trial is a bewildering process in which deceit and truth become inextricably mixed. Wilkie Barron appears, however, and reveals Jerry's vow to kill Fort, the reaction Wilkie had himself orchestrated even before Jerry had met the wronged lady. All is lost, and Jerry is sentenced to hang. Rachel comes and stays with him in his basement jail cell, where they indulge in a passionate interlude—a veritable frenzy of love in the face of imminent death.

The unpredictable Wilkie appears at the last minute, after the lovers have unsuccessfully tried to commit suicide by drinking laudanum. Wilkie rescues them and sends them west to live in the desolate island refuge of a notorious bandit. This is a return to nature, but a nature devoid of its original innocence, incapable of healing the scars of "civilization." Jerry sinks into a bestial pattern and Rachel into insanity, eventually killing herself. Jerry, who finds out that the slanderous handbill came from Wilkie Barron, is himself murdered as he seeks to find his way back to the hangman, resigned now to the most austere prize of all—neither love nor honor, but simply knowledge.

The flight to the West seems an almost gratuitous extension of suffering, especially since the real Jereboam Beauchamp, who murdered Colonel Solomon Sharp in 1825, did hang for his crime. The real trial and death of Beauchamp and his wife, Ann Cook, were only slightly less miserable, however, than Warren's fictional account.

Warren's extension to allow further demoralization of the lovers does help to explore all possible approaches to the problem of reconciling the ideal and the real. At first, Jerry believes that the idea must redeem the world: The mental context defines the object. However, this route leads to an idealism divorced from action and allows a further evil to develop in the world—the death of his child. Then he believes that the world will redeem the idea—that is, the act of killing Fort will vindicate the idea of honor. In his flight to the West, he commits a third error, the opposite to his first: to deny the idea completely and embrace the physical world—"to seek communion only in the blank cup of nature."

Perhaps this tortured journey through innocence and experience should arrive at some reconciliation of opposites, but, if so, that too seems more dream than reality. "There must be a way whereby the word becomes flesh," muses Jerry in his last days. Even so, "I no longer seek to justify. I seek only to suffer." If this is not a particularly lucid analysis of philosophical possibilities, it may nevertheless be true psychologically to the mental and moral confusion in which people live. Perhaps it is intended to represent that "terror of the awakening" that Warren finds in Conrad's *Lord Jim* when the "hero recognizes the terms on which he may be saved."

In his later novels, Warren continued to deal with the tension between the ideal and the real. The central mystery is usually the self, which the protagonist does not know except through a painful dialectic between exalted idea and gross fact. The protagonist also suffers from an inability to identify his real father or the real home where he belongs. Jack Burden and Jeremiah Beaumont both have several surrogate fathers, but they are responsible for the deaths of those to whom they owe the greatest filial loyalty. In *At Heaven's Gate*, Jerry Calhoun rejects his real father, the man of natural rectitude and love, and gives his devotion to Bogan Murdock, who, in Conrad's phrase, is hollow at the core.

A Place to Come To • Even in Warren's last novel, *A Place to Come To*, the protagonist's first act is to despise his father and flee from his homeland; his last is to return to his hometown and make peace with the gentle stepfather he had never wanted to meet and the deaf father who had humiliated him as a child. As Warren wrote in "The Ballad of Billie Potts," the son must always return to the father, who often represents the flawed and fallen world that is his heritage.

Wilderness • The struggle between the ideal and the real in Warren's later novels is most explicit in *Wilderness: A Tale of the Civil War*, about an idealistic young Jew from Bavaria who comes to the United States to fight for the freedom of the slaves. When his father, a political prisoner in Berlin, dies, Adam Rosenzweig realizes that he has "lived only in the dream of his father's life, the father's manhood, the father's heroism." The trip to America is a way to star in his own heroic story. Adam's career in America is a progress in disillusionment; the telltale symbol of the compromising world of physical fact is his clubfoot, which he has desperately sought to hide in a specially constructed boot. If *World Enough and Time* is Warren's most complex treatment of idealism, *Wilderness* is his most direct treatment of this recurring subject, uncluttered by secondary themes or plots. Some critics prefer it for that reason, though it lacks the depth and humanity of Warren's earlier epic treatment of romantic idealism.

Meet Me in the Green Glen • *Meet Me in the Green Glen* is a pastoral novel about the nature of love. The love of a homeless young Italian immigrant for a dowdy country wife begins with carnal passion devoid of any attempt to idealize sexual attraction. The ironically named Angelo has distinct similarities to Conrad's "natural man," Nostromo, who lives in the physical world with little thought of any other. In fact, Angelo protects himself from any really serious bond with Cassie, the frustrated wife of a paralyzed man, casting her in the more tawdry dream of "scarlet woman" with gifts of a tight red dress and cosmetics. Only at the last, when she pleads for his life in court by confessing to the murder of her husband, of which Angelo is accused, does he recognize a love that transcends the merely physical. Just as Adam in *Wilderness* becomes more human when he admits the strength of flawed reality, so Angelo becomes more human when he recognizes the strength of dreams. In spite of Cassie's confession, Angelo is condemned to die, because, in his ignorance of the racial situation, he violates the mores of the community. Cassie, unable to save her lover, drifts off in the dream-sea of ideas, forgetting the sordid elements of their affair and only retaining the dream that transcends the body's need.

In these and other episodes in his fiction, Warren showed his fascination with what he called, in his Conrad essay, "the Great Mirage." It is a dark vision which sees all human values as illusions, yet insists—with the passion that fueled six decades of creative work—that such illusions are necessary, and that humanity must continue to invent itself.

Katherine Snipes

Other major works

SHORT FICTION: *Blackberry Winter*, 1946; *The Circus in the Attic, and Other Stories*, 1947.

PLAYS: *Proud Flesh*, pr. 1947; *All the King's Men*, pr. 1958 (adaptation of his novel).

POETRY: *Thirty-six Poems*, 1935; *Eleven Poems on the Same Theme*, 1942; *Selected Poems, 1923-1943*, 1944; *Brother to Dragons: A Tale in Verse and Voices*, 1953; *Promises: Poems, 1954-1956*, 1957; *You, Emperors, and Others: Poems, 1957-1960*, 1960; *Selected Poems: New and Old, 1923-1966*, 1966; *Incarnations: Poems, 1966-1968*, 1968; *Audubon: A Vision*, 1969; *Or Else—Poem/Poems, 1968-1974*, 1974; *Selected Poems 1923-1975*, 1976; *Now and Then: Poems, 1976-1978*, 1978; *Brother to Dragons: A New Version*, 1979; *Ballad of a Sweet Dream of Peace*, 1980 (with Bill Komodore); *Being Here: Poetry 1977-1980*, 1980; *Rumor Verified: Poems, 1979-1980*, 1981; *Chief Joseph of the Nez Percé*, 1983; *New and Selected Poems, 1923-1985*, 1985; *The Collected Poems of Robert Penn Warren*, 1998 (John Burt, editor).

NONFICTION: *John Brown: The Making of a Martyr*, 1929; *Modern Rhetoric*, 1949 (with Cleanth Brooks); *Segregation: The Inner Conflict in the South*, 1956; *Selected Essays*, 1958; *The Legacy of the Civil War: Meditations on the Centennial*, 1961; *Who Speaks for the Negro?*, 1965; *Democracy and Poetry*, 1975; *Portrait of a Father*, 1988; *New and Selected Essays*, 1989; *Cleanth Brooks and Robert Penn Warren: A Literary Correspondence*, 1998 (James A. Grimshaw, Jr., editor); *Selected Lettes of Robert Penn Warren*, 2000-2001 (2 volumes; William Bedford Clark, editor).

EDITED TEXTS: *An Approach to Literature,* 1936 (with Cleanth Brooks and John Thibault Purser); *Understanding Poetry: An Anthology for College Students,* 1938 (with Brooks); *Understanding Fiction,* 1943 (with Brooks); *Faulkner: A Collection of Critical Essays,* 1966; *Randall Jarrell, 1914-1965,* 1967 (with Robert Lowell and Peter Taylor); *American Literature: The Makers and the Making,* 1973 (with R. W. B. Lewis).

Bibliography

Bloom, Harold, ed. *Robert Penn Warren.* New York: Chelsea House, 1986. This collection of essays on Warren's work considers both the poetry and the fiction.

Blotner, Joseph. *Robert Penn Warren: A Biography.* New York: Random House, 1997. Blotner began his biography while Warren was still alive and had the good fortune to have the cooperation not only of his subject but also of the larger Warren family. Blotner's book is straightforward and chronological; it makes a good beginning.

Burt, John. *Robert Penn Warren and American Idealism.* New Haven, Conn.: Yale University Press, 1988. Burt describes his work as traversing "regions" of Warren's work: the elegies, the narrative poems, and three major novels—*Night Rider, All the King's Men,* and *World Enough and Time.* What unifies these works, Burt maintains, is Warren's ambivalence about experience, an ambivalence endemic to American idealism.

Clark, William Bedford, ed. *Critical Essays on Robert Penn Warren.* Boston: G. K. Hall, 1981. A comprehensive collection of criticism by leading literary scholars of Warren's major work as novelist, poet, biographer, and essayist. Among the contributors are Harold Bloom, Malcolm Cowley, Carlos Baker, John Crowe Ransom, and Randall Jarrell. The collection includes a valuable 1969 interview with Warren by Richard Sale.

Cutrer, Thomas W. *Parnassus on the Mississippi: The Southern Review and the Baton Rouge Literary Community.* Baton Rouge: Louisiana State University Press, 1984. Cutrer provides a history of the literary circle around the influential *Southern Review* at the time that Warren and Cleanth Brooks were the journal's editors.

Grimshaw, James A. *Understanding Robert Penn Warren.* Columbia: University of South Carolina Press, 2001. An introduction to Warren's novels, poems, and plays.

Justus, James H. *The Achievement of Robert Penn Warren.* Baton Rouge: Louisiana State University Press, 1981. A cogent study of Warren's work from the premise that the latter largely derives from the cultural circumstances of time and place in his career. The book is divided into four sections dealing, respectively, with Warren's themes, poetry, nonfiction prose, and novels.

Madden, David, ed. *The Legacy of Robert Penn Warren.* Baton Rouge: Louisiana State University Press, 2000. A collection of critical and biographical essays on Warren's life and work. Includes bibliographical references and an index.

Nakadate, Neil. *Robert Penn Warren: A Reference Guide.* Boston: G. K. Hall, 1977. This helpfully annotated reference guide to significant scholarship on Warren and his work encompasses writings by Warren from 1929 to 1977, and about him from 1925 to 1975. A checklist of doctoral dissertations and master's theses on Warren is also included.

Ruppersburg, Hugh. *Robert Penn Warren and the American Imagination.* Athens: University of Georgia Press, 1990. Ruppersburg considers the Warren opus an attempt to define a national identity. He focuses, in particular, on *Brother to Dragons, Audubon: A Vision,* and *Chief Joseph of the Nez Percé.* Subscribing to Warren's notion that he was

not a historical writer, Ruppersburg also attempts to place Warren in a contemporary context, emphasizing such modern American concerns as civil rights and nuclear warfare.

Warren, Robert Penn. *Robert Penn Warren Talking: Interviews 1950-1978.* Edited by
Floyd C. Watkins and John T. Hiers. New York: Random House, 1980. A collection
of eighteen interviews conducted in a variety of modes and settings over a period
of nearly thirty years, ranging from a session with students at Vanderbilt to a Bill
Moyers transcript. Gives insights not only into Warren's thought and development
during the period but also into the personality of the man as it emerges in the give-
and-take of live discourse.

_____. Edited by Floyd C. Watkins, John T. Hiers, and Mary Louise Weaks.
Talking with Robert Penn Warren. Athens: University of Georgia Press, 1990. A collection of twenty-four interviews, extending from 1953 to 1985, in which Warren talks
about his work with characteristic honesty, openness, folksiness, and wit from the
joint perspective of writer, interpreter, and critic. The group of interviewers includes Ralph Ellison, Marshall Walker, Bill Moyers, Edwin Harold Newman, Floyd
C. Watkins, and Eleanor Clark.

Yarborough, Jane, and Robert Penn Warren. *Robert Penn Warren's All the King's Men.*
New York: Barron's Educational Books, 1985. This guide to reading Warren's best-
known work contains analyses of the novel's plot, style, form, and structure, and
information about the author and his times.

Eudora Welty

Born: Jackson, Mississippi; April 13, 1909
Died: Jackson, Mississippi; July 23, 2001

Principal long fiction • *The Robber Bridegroom*, 1942; *Delta Wedding*, 1946; *The Ponder Heart*, 1954; *Losing Battles*, 1970; *The Optimist's Daughter*, 1972.

Other literary forms • In spite of her success and acclaim as a novelist, Eudora Welty always regarded herself as essentially a writer of short stories. In an interview that appeared in the fall, 1972, issue of the *Paris Review*, she said, "I'm a short-story writer who writes novels the hard way, and by accident." In 1980, all of her previously collected short fiction and two uncollected stories were published in one volume, *The Collected Stories of Eudora Welty*. Another new collection, *Moon Lake, and Other Stories*, was published in the same year, and *Retreat* was released in 1981. Prior to that, some had appeared in *Short Stories* (1950) and in *Selected Stories of Eudora Welty* (1954). Other early short-story collections are *A Curtain of Green, and Other Stories* (1941); *The Wide Net, and Other Stories* (1943); *The Golden Apples* (1949), regarded by some as a loosely structured novel, but considered by Welty to be a group of interconnected stories; and *The Bride of the Innisfallen, and Other Stories* (1955). Welty also published numerous essays and reviews, some of which were collected in *The Eye of the Story: Selected Essays and Reviews* (1978). In addition, she published a book for children, *The Shoe Bird* (1964), and books of her own photographs, *One Time, One Place* (1971) and *Eudora Welty: Photographs* (1989). A memoir, *One Writer's Beginnings*, appeared in 1984. Two posthumous works have also been published, *On Writing* (2002), which collects seven essays about literature, and *Some Notes on River Country* (2003).

Achievements • Although it was not until she wrote *Losing Battles* and *The Optimist's Daughter* that Welty's name began to appear on the best seller lists, her work had long been recognized and appreciated by discerning readers. In five decades of writing and publishing, she received nearly every major award for fiction offered in the United States. Among them are the prestigious William Dean Howells Medal of the Academy of Arts and Letters for "the most distinguished work of American fiction" for the years 1950 through 1955, the National Institute of Arts and Letters Gold Medal for the Novel in 1972, the Pulitzer Prize for Fiction in 1973, and the National Medal for Literature at the American Book Awards ceremony in 1980. In addition, she was awarded several honorary doctorates, Guggenheim Fellowships, special professorships, and membership in the National Institute of Arts and Letters.

Interested in neither fame nor fortune, Welty simply wanted the opportunity to write and the assurance that there are readers who enjoy her work. She repeatedly expressed gratitude to such writers and editors as Robert Penn Warren, Cleanth Brooks, Albert Erskine, Ford Madox Ford, and Katherine Anne Porter, who were among the first persons of influence to recognize her ability and to promote interest in her early stories. Warren, Brooks, and Erskine accepted some of her first stories for *The Southern Review* and thus opened the door for subsequent publication in such magazines as *The Atlantic Monthly*, *Harper's Bazaar*, and *The New Yorker*. This exposure

Frank Hains/Courtesy,
Mississippi Department of Archives and History

to a national audience also facilitated the publication of her first volume of stories.

**Biography • **On April 13, 1909, Eudora Alice Welty was born in Jackson, Mississippi, where she would spend most of her life. She was the only daughter of Christian Webb Welty and Mary Chestina Andrews Welty; she had two younger brothers. Soon after their marriage in 1904, Welty's parents had moved to Jackson. Her father, who came from Ohio, where his father owned a farm, was president of the well-established Lamar Life Insurance Company. Her mother, a West Virginian, was descended from pre-Revolutionary War Virginia stock, engendered by country preachers, teachers, and lawyers. Welty, who claimed that she would feel "shy, and discouraged at the very thought" of a biography about her, felt that a "private life should be kept private." Nevertheless, though she insisted that it is the writer's work, not his or her life, that is important, she did finally write a memoir of her family history and her early years, *One Writer's Beginnings*, which was published in 1984 and received positive critical comment.

Perhaps one reason that Welty suggested that her own biography would not "particularly interest anybody" is that she lived for the most part in the mainstream of American society. As Katherine Anne Porter aptly observes in her introduction to *A Curtain of Green*, Welty is not the "spiritual and intellectual exile" that typifies the modern artist. She attended Central High School in Jackson, then went for two years to Mississippi State College for Women, in Columbus, before transferring to the University of Wisconsin in 1927. After graduating with a bachelor of arts degree in English in 1929, she enrolled in the School of Business at Columbia University, where she studied advertising for a year. By then, the country was in the throes of the Great Depression, and she returned to Jackson to seek work.

During the next several years, Welty held a variety of jobs in advertising, radio scriptwriting, and part-time newspaper work. She also began writing stories. Possibly the most important of those early jobs was the position of "Junior Publicity Agent" with the Works Progress Administration (WPA) from 1933 to 1936. In this position, Welty was required to travel extensively through Mississippi doing newspaper stories on various WPA projects. Her work involved taking photographs, talking with a great variety of people, and, perhaps most important, listening to them. As Welty herself confessed, she had a "good ear" and a visual imagination, qualities that enabled her to hear and observe things and people during those three years that she would use in her fiction throughout her life.

A number of the photographs that Welty took while on her WPA assignment were displayed for a month in the Lugene Gallery in New York, a small camera shop. Later, some of them appeared in her published collection of photographs *One Time, One Place*. Only after several years of discouraging rejection slips did Welty finally publish a story, "Death of a Traveling Salesman," in a small magazine called *Manuscript* in 1936. Soon after that, her talent was discovered by Robert Penn Warren, Albert Erskine, and Cleanth Brooks. Then, John Woodburn of Doubleday, Doran, and Company became interested in her work, and with his support, her first collection of short stories, *A Curtain of Green, and Other Stories*, was published in 1941. The next year, her first novel, *The Robber Bridegroom*, appeared. Two of her books have been successfully adapted for the stage, *The Ponder Heart* as a New York stage play in 1956 and *The Robber Bridegroom* as a Broadway musical in 1974.

Humane, thoughtful, and generous, Welty was modest in her acceptance of the many honors that came to her. Scarcely a year would pass after 1940 in which she would not receive a major award of some kind. She also gave abundantly of her time to schoolchildren, scholars, interviewers, and aspiring writers. She was active in community causes in Jackson, gave scores of lectures and readings, assisted numerous charities, and even provided recipes for cookbooks.

Welty asserted in a famous article, "Place in Fiction," in *The South Atlantic Quarterly* (1956), that a deep sense of place is vital to a writer's development. She herself spent her entire adult life in the neo-Tudor house her father built in 1926 across the street from the campus of Belhaven College in Jackson. In fact, as a young woman she would listen, through the open window of her bedroom, to the melodious sounds emanating from the music building on the Belhaven campus. Music, as well as the visual arts, became an important motif in her fiction. Welty said that aspects of two women characters in her fiction most greatly illustrate qualities of her own life—the high regard for art held by Miss Eckhart, the piano teacher in "June Recital" (in *The Golden Apples*), and the great concern of Laurel McKelva Hand (*The Optimist's Daughter*) with her family's past. However, Laurel, unlike Miss Eckhart, is able to deal with her conflicts and achieves "a separate peace."

During the years of severe unrest over civil rights issues, Welty's critics attacked her for not actively taking up that cause in her fiction. She answered those critics eloquently in a 1965 *Atlantic Monthly* essay titled "Must the Novelist Crusade?" However, in *The New Yorker* the next year, Welty published a short story, "Where Is the Voice Coming From?," attacking the ugly racism of the South that had resulted in the murder of a black civil rights leader.

In her introduction to *The Collected Stories of Eudora Welty*, Welty expresses characteristic gratitude for the help and encouragement she received during her career. In her memoir she speaks of her good fortune in being reared in a family that encouraged the reading of books. She had a particular love for myths, fairy tales, and legends, and she believed it her good fortune to have grown up in a region where, as she said, people love talking and delight in a good yarn. Even though she was teased as a child for having a "Yankee" father, her work is deeply rooted, like its creator, in the South as a place. Nevertheless, neither she nor her fiction could be called "regional" in any narrow sense of the term. In fact, she balked at the regionalist title. Her work, for all its down-home southern flavor, attests the universality of her vision and the capacity of her art to elude easy labels. Her subject was not the South, but humanity. She died of pneumonia in the place of her birth, Jackson, Mississippi, on July 23, 2001, at the age of ninety-two.

**Analysis • ** Paramount in Welty's work is the sense of what "community," or group membership, means in the South and how it is expressed through manners, attitudes, and dialogue. Clearly, it provides a special way of seeing and responding. In Welty's published essays and interviews, certain concerns keep surfacing—the relationship between time and place and the artistic endeavor; the importance of human relationships in a work of fiction; the necessity for the artist to be grounded in real life and yet be aware of life's "mystery"; the value of the imagination; and the function of memory. These concerns find expression in her work principally in the tension between what is actual, what is seen and heard in a specific time and place, and what is felt or known intuitively. Welty uses the sometimes conflicting demands of the community and the self, the surface life and the interior life, to describe this tension in her novels. On one hand is the need for community and order; on the other is the need for the separate individual life that often works against community and order.

Typically, a Welty novel swings between overt action, including dialogue, and individual contemplation. This is especially evident in *Delta Wedding*, where Welty almost rhythmically alternates dialogue and action with the inner musings of her principal female characters. In *The Optimist's Daughter*, only Laurel Hand's thoughts are set against the exterior action, but it becomes apparent that her father, as he lies unmoving in his hospital bed, is silently contemplating the mystery of life and human relationships for perhaps the first time in his life. Her mother, too, near the end of her life, had begun speaking out the painful things she must have harbored for many years in her dark soul. Even Edna Earle Ponder in *The Ponder Heart* seems to talk incessantly to keep the inner life from raising itself into consciousness. In *Losing Battles*, where Welty says she consciously tried to tell everything through speech and action—she had been accused of obscurantism in previous works—the pattern still emerges. Instead of swinging between action and cerebration, however, this novel swings between action and description. Nevertheless, the effect is surprisingly similar, though the pages of action and dialogue far outnumber the pages of description and the transitions between the two modes of narration are very abrupt. Even so, the young schoolteacher who chooses love and marriage against her mentor's advice slips occasionally into Welty's meditative mode. The alternation of thought and action is also the basic structural pattern of the stories in *The Golden Apples*.

Thus, in Welty's novels, external order is established through speech and action that sustain community, either the social or family group. In fact, the novels are often structured around community rituals that reinforce the group entity against outside intrusions and shore up its defenses against its most insidious foe, the impulse to separateness in its individual members. *Delta Wedding* is set entirely in the framework of one of these community-perpetuating rituals. For the moment, the wedding is everything, and members of the group pay it homage by gathering, giving gifts, feasting, and burying their individual lives in its demands. *Losing Battles* is also framed by a community ritual, the family reunion. The threat from individual outsiders is felt constantly, and the family takes sometimes extreme measures to ward off influences that might undermine its solidarity. There are at least two rituals that provide structure for *The Ponder Heart*, the funeral and the courtroom trial. The first of these is conducted in enemy territory, outside the acceptable group domain; the second is conducted in home territory, and acquittal for the accused member of the group is a foregone conclusion. A funeral is also the major external event of *The Optimist's Daughter* and becomes the battleground in a contest for supremacy between two opposing groups or communities. Several of the stories or chapters in *The Golden Apples* are also structured around community rituals, including the June piano recital, the girls' summer camp, and the funeral.

In addition to these large, highly structured observances, there are the multitude of unwritten laws that govern the group. Welty's community members attach great importance to certain objects and practices: a treasured lamp given to the bride, a handcrafted breadboard made for a mother-in-law, the establishment of family pedigrees, the selection of one male member of the community for special reverence and heroic expectation, the protection of the past from intrusion or reassessment, and, perhaps most important of all, the telling of stories as an attestation of the vitality and endurance of the group.

Underlying all of this attention to ritual and group expectation, however, is the unspoken acknowledgment that much of it is a game the participants have agreed to play, for their own sake and for the sake of the community. Some of the participants may be fooled, but many are not. Aware but fearful, they go through the motions of fulfilling community requirements in an effort to hold back the dark, to avoid facing the mystery, to keep their individual selves from emerging and crying for existence. They sense themselves to be at what Welty called "the jumping off place" and are afraid to make the leap in the dark. They agree to pretend to be fooled. They tell stories instead of rehearsing their fears and uncertainties. The bolder ones defy the group and either leave it or live on its periphery. In every book, there are moments when a character confronts or consciously evades the dark underside of human personality and experience, and memory becomes a device for dealing with the effects of that confrontation or for evading it.

Paradoxically, storytelling, an important ritual for securing the past and bolstering community against passion, disorder, the intimations of mystery, and the erosive effects of individual impulses and yearnings, assists in the breakdown of the very group it was intended to support. The risk of indulging in rituals is that they sometimes set people to thinking and reevaluating their own individual lives and the lives of others close to them. The ritual is performed by the group, but it may stir the solitary inner being to life and to the kind of probing contemplation that jeopardizes the group's authority. Such a countereffect may be triggered by the storytelling ritual even though that ritual is meant to seal up the past for ready reference whenever the group needs reinforcement. Because storytelling relies on memory, it can become an exercise of the individual imagination. It tends to lapse, as one commentator observes, "into the memory of a memory" and thus shifts sides from the group's activities into the realm of mystery. The community's habit of setting up straw men for heroes can similarly erode community solidarity because it too relies upon imagination and memory. It glorifies the individual rather than the group spirit.

As Welty presents this conflict, then, between the self and the group, and between the intuitive and the actual, she writes into her work a sense of foreboding. The community, especially the traditional southern community, is doomed. It cannot forever maintain itself on the old terms, for it is dependent upon the acquiescence of separate individuals who seem increasingly impervious to the efforts of the group to contain them. Welty's work also suggests that some of the things the community prizes and perpetuates are merely gestures and artifacts with little intrinsic value or meaning. When the meanings behind what a community treasures have been lost or forgotten, that community cannot long endure. In actively laboring to exclude others, the group works against its own best nature, its capacity for loving and caring. Threats to order and community may indeed come from the outside, but Welty insists that the more serious threats come from the inside, from that part of the human heart and mind that seeks to go its own way.

The Robber Bridegroom • Welty's first novel, *The Robber Bridegroom*, is quite unlike her later work. Its most noticeable differences are its setting in a much older South, on the old Natchez Trace in the days of bandits and Native Americans, and its fairy-tale style and manner. Even with these differences, Welty establishes what becomes her basic fictional stance. She achieves tension between the actual and the imaginary by freighting this very real setting with fabulous characters and events. The legendary characters are transformed by Welty's imagination and deftly made to share the territory with figures from the Brothers Grimm. Welty indicated the double nature of her novel, or novella, when in an address to the Mississippi Historical Society she called it a "Fairy Tale of the Natchez Trace." A favorite of William Faulkner, the book is a masterpiece, a delightful blend of legend, myth, folklore, and fairy tale that swings from rollicking surface comedy and lyrical style to painful, soul-searching explorations of the ambiguities of human experience.

Although it deals with love and separateness—Robert Penn Warren's terms for the conflicting needs of communities and individuals in Welty's work—it does not deal with them in the same way that the later novels do. Clement Musgrove, a planter whose innocence leads him into marriage with the greedy Salome and an excursion into humanity's heart of darkness, learns what it is like to face the cold, dark nights of despair comfortless and alone. His daughter, Rosamond, is beautiful and loving, but she is also an inveterate liar who betrays her husband's trust in order to learn his "real" identity. Jamie Lockhart, who leads a double life as both bandit and gentleman, keeps his true identity hidden even from her whom he loves. Thus, like so many Welty characters, the principal actors in *The Robber Bridegroom* have interior lives that threaten the equilibrium of their exterior worlds.

In another sense, too, *The Robber Bridegroom* is closely linked with Welty's other novels. In writing the book, Welty testifies to the value of stories and the storytelling ritual that buttresses community, a theme that reappears in all of her novels. She finds common ground with her readers in this novel by spinning a yarn full of their favorite childhood fairy tales. Then, too, fairy-tale worlds, imaginative though they are, sustain surface order, for they are worlds of sure answers, of clear good and evil, of one-dimensional characters, and of predictable rewards and punishments. As such, they confirm what the community collectively believes and perpetuates. Just as imagination, intuition, and the ponderings of the individual human soul jeopardize the codes a community lives by in other Welty novels, so do they undercut the basic assumptions of the fairy tale in this novel. Here, answers are sometimes permanently withheld, people are complex and unpredictable, the richest prize is found in human relationships rather than in kingdoms and gold, appearances are deceiving, and evil may lie in unexpected places. It is worthy of note that Welty began her novelwriting career with a book that delights in the fairy tale at the same time that it questions community assumptions about fairy-tale morality.

Delta Wedding • The tension between community expectations and individual yearnings and apprehensions is central to *Delta Wedding*. The narrative takes place in the Mississippi delta country, during the week of Dabney Fairchild's wedding. The Fairchild family, after whom the nearby town is named, is of the social elite and has moderate wealth, mostly in property. The wedding provides an occasion for the family to gather and exercise the rituals and traditions that bind them together and strengthen their sense of community. The wedding itself is the principal ritual with its attendant food preparation, dress making, rehearsal, and home and yard decorating. Welty's eye for manners and ear for speech are flawless as the Fairchilds deliberate over the consequences of George Fairchild's having married beneath him and Dabney's seemingly unfortunate repetition of her father's mistake. The Fairchilds still claim George, however, even though they have little use for his wife, Robbie Reid, and they will continue to embrace Dabney in spite of her choosing to marry an outsider, Troy Flavin. It is the habit of community to maintain order by defining and placing people and things in relation to itself. A person either does or does not have legitimate ties to the group.

The Fairchilds also repeat family stories in order to keep the past secure and give stability to the present. Their current favorite story is also one that makes a hero out of the male heir-apparent. George's dead brother was apparently more remarkable than he, but George is the one survivor, and the family's hopes rest with him. At least a dozen times in the book, some version is told of George's staying on the railroad track with his mentally disabled niece whose foot was caught in the rails. Instead of leaping to safety with the others, he stayed to face the oncoming train. Luckily, the engineer of the Yellow Dog was able to stop the train in time. By choosing to stay with Maureen instead of answering his wife's plea to save himself, George made a reflexive choice for honor and blood over marital obligation. Later, he again chooses family over wife when he comes for the prewedding activities instead of looking for his absent, heartbroken wife.

Running counter to the speech and actions that affirm order and community, however, is an undercurrent of threat to that order. Welty intersperses the overt actions and attitudes of the family, especially of the aunts, whose sole desire is to perpetuate the clan structure, with individual ruminations of other female characters who are part of that structure and yet somewhat peripheral to it. Ellen, who married into the Fairchilds and has never dared resist them, has moments of personal doubt that would be regarded as treasonous were they known by her aunts. Dabney also wonders, in a brief honest moment, about the homage paid to the wedding ritual for its own sake. Further, she accidentally breaks a treasured lamp, a family heirloom given her by the aunts as a wedding present. Little Laura, having lost her mother, has also lost her basic tie to the family. From her position on the edge of the Fairchild clan, she questions the community tenets that exclude her. Even George seems ready to violate community expectations by his apparent willingness to deprive two of the aunts of their home.

The novel's essential statement, then, is that the community is losing its hold. In an interview published in 1972 by *The Southern Review*, Welty is asked the question: "Is Shellmound [the home of the Fairchilds] with its way of life and its values doomed?" She replies, "Oh, yes. I think that was implicit in the novel: that this was all such a fragile, temporary thing. At least I hope it was." She adds, "Well, you're living in a very precarious world without knowing it, always." The community's position is inexorably altered in the face of individual yearning and independent action.

The Ponder Heart • There are two large community rituals in *The Ponder Heart*: the funeral of Bonnie Dee Peacock and the trial of Uncle Daniel Ponder for her murder. Such narrative matter sounds ominous enough to one unfamiliar with Welty's capacity for comedy, but to the initiated, it promises a hilarious display of southern talk and manners. Nevertheless, *The Ponder Heart* is troubled, as Welty's other novels are, by an ominous current running beneath its surface action. Like the Fairchilds of *Delta Wedding*, the Ponders have social position and wealth—perhaps greater than that of the Fairchilds. They are on the decline, however, in spite of the efforts of Edna Earle Ponder, Welty's first-person narrator, to maintain the family and its image. Symbolic of the failing family or community image that Edna Earle seeks to perpetuate and protect are two buildings that the family owns, the Beulah Hotel, run by Edna Earle, and the Ponder home a few miles out of town. In the end, both buildings are virtually empty. The family has shrunk to two members, and the future holds no promise.

The storyline tells of middle-aged Uncle Daniel's taking to wife young Bonnie Dee Peacock, losing her, regaining her, losing her again, reclaiming her, and then finally losing her by tickling her to death in the aftermath of an electric storm. Uncle Daniel's mental age is considerably lower than his chronological age, but he is blessed with a generous nature. He gives away everything he can get his hands on, and has to be watched continually. Not that Edna Earle cares to restrain him very much, for he is the revered scion, like George in *Delta Wedding*, without whose approbation and presence the community would totter. Her duty is to protect and sustain Daniel, and she will not even permit herself private doubts over what that duty requires. The entire novel is the report of her conversation about Uncle Daniel with a visitor who is stranded at the Beulah. Clearly, Edna Earle's talk and actions are designed to maintain order and community as she has known them all her life. She believes that if she relaxes her vigil, the structure will collapse.

The ritual of the Peacock funeral is important because it is grossly inferior to the Ponder notion of what constitutes a funeral. The Peacocks are what the Ponders (except Daniel, who in his innocence would not know the difference) would call "country"; in other words, they are regarded as comically inferior beings who have no business marrying into the Ponder family. The trial is more to Edna Earle's liking, though it is threatened by the presence of the low-bred Peacocks and a prosecuting shyster lawyer who is an outsider. Edna Earle gets caught in a lie designed to protect Daniel, but the day is saved when Daniel begins passing out greenbacks in the courtroom. The jury votes for acquittal in record time, and Daniel cheerily dispenses the whole family fortune. He discovers to his sorrow afterward, however, that people who have taken his money can no longer face him. Thus, in the end, Daniel, who wanted nothing more than company and an audience for his stories, is left lonely and friendless. Though Edna Earle tries to inject new hope through the promise of a new audience—her captive guest at the Beulah—doom is on the horizon for the Ponders even more surely than it was for the Fairchilds. The collapse of community structure in this novel, as in *Delta Wedding*, can be laid partly to the failure of the community's rather artificial system of supports—rituals, traditions, family stories, pedigrees, and a family "hero." It must also be laid, however, to the fact that Uncle Daniel, in his innocence, breaks away and acts as an individual. He is not capable of the contemplation that undermines community in *Delta Wedding*, but neither can he be restrained to act as a member of the group instead of as himself.

Losing Battles • In *Losing Battles*, Welty partially turns the tables on what she had done with the conflict between community and self in her previous two novels and in *The Golden Apples*. Here, she shows that community, though mildly ruffled by individual needs and doubts, can prevail when it is sustained by strong individuals who are also loyal group members. Welty indicates in a *Southern Review* interview that she de-liberately chose as her setting the poorest section of Mississippi during the time of the Depression, so that her characters would be shown on a bare stage with them-selves as their only resource, without "props to their lives." Thus, the artificial struc-tures built of money and status that support community in *Delta Wedding* and *The Pon-der Heart* are not available to the Vaughn-Beecham-Renfro clan in *Losing Battles.* Perhaps that is one reason for their greater durability.

The story is told almost entirely through dialogue and action, interlaced with oc-casional lyrical descriptions of setting and even less frequent ruminations of the story's principal outsider, Gloria Renfro, the hero's wife. The action takes place en-tirely in one day and the following morning, with details of the past filled in through family storytelling. Jack Renfro, the young grandson who has been exalted by family hope and expectations, bears some resemblance to George Fairchild and Daniel Ponder. On him lies the chief burden of sustaining the family, of guaranteeing its sur-vival as a unit. He returns home from the state penitentiary to the waiting family re-union that is celebrating old Granny Vaughn's birthday. He finds there not only his bride, but a baby daughter he has never seen. The family has believed, has had to be-lieve, that things will be better once Jack has returned home. Jack himself believes it, and, as Welty indicates, the others take their faith from him. Through a series of wild, funny episodes—and more than a few tender moments—the family prevails. Welty said that in this comic novel she intended to portray the indomitability, the un-quenchable spirit of human beings. Folks such as these may be losing the battles, but they are still fighting them, and that is what counts.

Welty described "the solidity of the family" as "the strongest thing in the book." She also recognized that, in a clan such as this, a character sometimes has to be him-self or herself before he or she can reinforce the unity of the group. Welty said that such a "sticking together" as is seen in *Losing Battles* "involves both a submerging and a triumph of the individual, because you can't really conceive of the whole unless you *are* an identity." The extended family of *Losing Battles* engages in rituals to maintain it-self just as the Fairchild family does in *Delta Wedding*. It acknowledges milestones reached by its members, milestones such as weddings and ninetieth birthdays; it tells stories; it creates a hero; and it works painstakingly to establish and affirm blood rela-tionships with any who might seek entrance into the group. All is done with the honor of the clan—or the individual as member of the clan—in mind, whether it is going to jail or rescuing a car from a cliff on Banner Top.

In spite of the prevailing unity and the optimistic conclusion to the novel's events, there are small rumblings of individual assertion against community. Gloria loves Jack, but she does not want to be a member of his family. She envisions a smaller com-munity, made up of just her, Jack, and their baby, Lady May. The group, however, will not allow her to build a community of her own. Against her will, it tries to reconstruct a parentage for her that would make her a blood relation. The relatives perform a rather cruel ritual of pouncing on her and forcing her to eat watermelon, but she re-mains adamant. She also remains steadfast in her admiration for Miss Julia Mortimer, the schoolteacher who picked Gloria as her successor and who fought a losing battle all her life against the joyful ignorance of the likes of Jack's family.

Thus, there are several influences in the book that threaten, though not seriously, the sense of community. Gloria and her child, and Miss Julia, are the most obvious ones. It becomes apparent, though, in the very style of the narration, which repeat-edly turns from family action and talk to brief imaginative description, that the ordering of the actual and the real according to community necessity does not entirely carry the day. There is another side to experience, the imaginative, the intuitive—a part of the individual soul that resists allegiance.

The Optimist's Daughter • In *The Optimist's Daughter,* Welty returns to a more balanced combination of action and contemplation. The book's perceiving eye is Laurel Hand, daughter of Becky and Judge McKelva. The abiding question for Laurel is why, after the death of the intelligent, sensitive Becky, the Judge took for a wife a crass, tasteless woman half his age. Laurel helplessly watches her father's still form as he silently reviews his life in a hospital room, ironically set against the backdrop of the Mardi Gras festival. She repeats her helpless watch as he lies in his coffin at Mount Salus while his wife, Wanda Fay Chisom, performs her gnashing, wailing ritual of bereavement and his old friends perform their ritual of eulogy. The Chisom family, who nod appreciatively as Fay grossly mourns, are the same breed as the Peacocks in *The Ponder Heart,* entirely out of context in the McKelva home. Laurel, however, is equally uncomfortable with her own group's rites of community preservation— telling stories about the Judge that make a hero of him, despising the intrusive outsider, urging Laurel to stay and bolster the old relationship. Laurel's husband Phil was killed in military service many years ago, and Laurel herself is working in Chicago, but the women who were bridesmaids at her wedding have kept that group intact and still refer to themselves as "the bridesmaids."

Laurel's last night at home is spent in anguish. Trapped by an invading chimney swift in rooms full of memories, she is caught hopelessly in the past. In the course of the night, she is forced to examine the protective structure she had built around her parents' marriage and her own. In doing so, she must allow memory and imagination to reinterpret the past that she had wanted to keep sealed away in the perfection of her own making, and she must relinquish her old idea of what constitutes group unity and loyalty. The Wanda Fays of the world will always claim their space, will always intrude. The secret for surviving their intrusion, Laurel discovers, is to withdraw one's protective walls so that the Fays have nothing to knock down. Laurel at last allows truth to dismantle the edifice of community as she had conceived it, and she finds, through the imagination and the heart, a new source of strength in watching the artificial construct tumble. Thus, the foreboding and pessimism arising from the impending doom of community in *Delta Wedding* and *The Ponder Heart,* diverted for a time in the paradoxical optimism of *Losing Battles,* are to some extent reversed in Laurel's final acceptance in *The Optimist's Daughter. The Golden Apples* had foretold such an outcome, for a number of its characters must also deal with the relationship between their individual lives and the group life.

The miracle of Welty's work is the skill with which her imagination bears on the actual and makes a reconciliation out of the conflicting demands of the community and the private life, out of that which can be perceived by the senses and that which can be known only intuitively. For Welty, the actual was mainly the realities of Mississippi life. In her work, however, the reality of Mississippi became a springboard rich with possibilities for an imagination that knew how to use time and place as doorways to the human heart.

Marilyn Arnold
Updated by Philip A. Tapley

Other major works

SHORT FICTION: *A Curtain of Green, and Other Stories*, 1941; *The Wide Net, and Other Stories*, 1943; *The Golden Apples*, 1949; *Short Stories*, 1950; *Selected Stories of Eudora Welty*, 1954; *The Bride of the Innisfallen, and Other Stories*, 1955; *Moon Lake, and Other Stories*, 1980; *The Collected Stories of Eudora Welty*, 1980; *Retreat*, 1981.

NONFICTION: *Music from Spain*, 1948; *The Reading and Writing of Short Stories*, 1949; *Place in Fiction*, 1957; *Three Papers on Fiction*, 1962; *One Time, One Place: Mississippi in the Depression, a Snapshot Album*, 1971; *A Pageant of Birds*, 1974; *The Eye of the Story: Selected Essays and Reviews*, 1978; *Ida M'Toy*, 1979; *Miracles of Perception: The Art of Willa Cather*, 1980 (with Alfred Knopf and Yehudi Menuhin); *Conversations with Eudora Welty*, 1984 (Peggy Whitman Prenshaw, editor); *One Writer's Beginnings*, 1984; *Eudora Welty: Photographs*, 1989; *A Writer's Eye: Collected Book Reviews*, 1994 (Pearl Amelia McHaney, editor); *More Conversations with Eudora Welty*, 1996 (Prenshaw, editor); *Country Churchyards*, 2000; *On William Hollingsworth, Jr.*, 2002; *On Writing*, 2002 (includes essays originally pb. in *The Eye of the Story*); *Some Notes on River Country*, 2003.

CHILDREN'S LITERATURE: *The Shoe Bird*, 1964.

MISCELLANEOUS: *Stories, Essays, and Memoir*, 1998.

Bibliography

Champion, Laurie, ed. *The Critical Response to Eudora Welty's Fiction*. Westport, Conn.: Greenwood Press, 1994. Useful collection of critical essays on Welty's writing.

Georgia Review 53 (Spring, 1999). A special issue on Welty celebrating her ninetieth birthday, with articles by a number of writers, including Doris Betts, as well as a number of critics and admirers of Welty.

Gretlund, Jan Nordby, and Karl-Heinz Westarp, eds. *The Late Novels of Eudora Welty*. Columbia: University of South Carolina Press, 1998. Collection of essays on Welty's last works of long fiction.

Kreyling, Michael. *Understanding Eudora Welty*. Columbia: University of South Carolina Press, 1999. General appreciation of Welty's themes and writing style.

Manning, Carol S. *With Ears Opening Like Morning Glories: Eudora Welty and the Love of Storytelling*. Westport, Conn.: Greenwood Press, 1985. An advanced book offering a critical interpretation of Welty's writing. Manning believes that the root of Welty's creativity is the southern love of storytelling. Offers a select bibliography.

Marrs, Suzanne. *Eudora Welty: A Biography*. Orlando, Fla.: Harcourt, 2005. Literary biography provides insight into Welty's life and writing and serves to refute some popular conceptions of the writer.

_____. *One Writer's Imagination: The Fiction of Eudora Welty*. Baton Rouge: Louisiana State University Press, 2002. A combination of critical analysis and memoir, written by a long-time friend of Welty who is also a scholar and the archivist of Welty's papers. Discusses the effects of both close personal relationships and social and political events on Welty's imagination and writing.

Mississippi Quarterly 50 (Fall, 1997). Special issue on Welty, with essays comparing Welty to William Faulkner, Edgar Allan Poe, and Nathaniel Hawthorne, and discussions of the women in Welty's stories, her political thought, her treatment of race and history.

Montgomery, Marion. *Eudora Welty and Walker Percy: The Concept of Home in Their Lives and Literature*. Jefferson, N.C.: McFarland, 2004. Comparative study of domestic themes in the writings of Welty and Walker Percy, another southern writer who was her contemporary.

Prenshaw, Peggy Whitman, ed. *Conversations with Eudora Welty.* Jackson: University Press of Mississippi, 1984. A collection of interviews with Welty spanning the years 1942-1982. Welty talks frankly and revealingly with interviewers such as William F. Buckley, Jr., and Alice Walker about her fiction and her life, addressing such topics as her methods of writing, her southern background, her love of reading, and her admiration for the works of writers such as William Faulkner, Elizabeth Bowen, and Katherine Anne Porter.

Thornton, Naoko Fuwa. *Strange Felicity: Eudora Welty's Subtexts on Fiction and Society.* Westport, Conn.: Praeger, 2003. An analysis of Welty's major works that uncover her views about the role of her fiction in the social and literary worlds.

Waldron, Ann. *Eudora Welty: A Writer's Life.* New York: Doubleday, 1998. The first full-length biography of Welty, but one that was done without her authorization or permission; provides a great deal of detail about Welty's life and literary career but derives commentary about Welty's work from reviews and other previous criticism.

Westling, Louise. *Sacred Groves and Ravaged Gardens: The Fiction of Eudora Welty, Carson McCullers, and Flannery O'Connor.* Athens: University of Georgia Press, 1985. Westling examines Welty's fiction, along with the work of other eminent female southern writers, as part of a tradition of southern women's writing. Westling brings a feminist perspective to bear on such aspects of southern women's writing as myth, sexuality, and the symbolic power of place. Welty's fiction is analyzed as a feminine celebration of a matriarchal society in which women can find freedom and fulfillment outside the social strictures of traditional southern life.

Nathanael West

Born: New York, New York; October 17, 1903
Died: El Centro, California; December 22, 1940

Principal long fiction • *The Dream Life of Balso Snell*, 1931; *Miss Lonelyhearts*, 1933; *A Cool Million: The Dismantling of Lemuel Pitkin*, 1934; *The Day of the Locust*, 1939.

Other literary forms • Nathanael West often used the short-story form for preliminary sketches of characters and themes that later appeared in his novels. Between 1930 and 1933 especially, he wrote stories with a broader focus and in a more sophisticated style than his first work, *The Dream Life of Balso Snell*. The stories include "The Adventurer," "Mr. Potts of Pottstown," "Tibetan Night," and "The Sun, the Lady, and the Gas Station," all unpublished. After the publication of *Miss Lonelyhearts* in 1933, West also worked as a scriptwriter in Hollywood for several years, producing such works as *Born to Be Wild* (1938) and *Men Against the Sky* (1940).

Achievements • Since West's death in an automobile accident in 1940, his work has steadily gained critical attention. His characters' hysterical pitch of loneliness, their frustration, and their inability to find a source of relief have gradually interested a wide audience, especially since World War II. Stripped of their professional masks, the people in West's novels reveal a talent for cruelty. They tease, exploit, or murder to ensure their own survival in a world reminiscent of T. S. Eliot's *The Waste Land* (1922), but their world is without Eliot's hint of redemption or spirituality. In *Miss Lonelyhearts*, the world is dead; in *The Day of the Locust*, it is corrupt and jaded, a modern Sodom that West symbolically destroys. This last novel was made into a film during the 1970's; although it never became a box-office hit, West would have approved of its powerful treatment of dreamers and misfits.

Biography • Nathanael West was born Nathan Weinstein in New York City on October 17, 1903. His father's and mother's families had known one another before they immigrated to the United States from Russia. His father's side used construction skills learned in the old world to become successful contractors in the new country, taking advantage of the building boom of the turn of the century. His mother's side was well educated, and Anna Wallenstein Weinstein wanted her son Nathan and her two daughters to have all the perquisites of an upwardly mobile, middle-class life. Soon after settling in New York City, the Weinsteins learned to enjoy their comforts and to value them highly. They also assumed that their son would receive the finest possible education, pursue a professional career, or at least join the family business. West was an avid reader but a much less ambitious student. He attended a variety of grammar schools before his parents placed him in DeWitt Clinton High School. West, however, preferred exploring Central Park during the day and the theater district in the evenings. He was particularly attracted to the vaudeville shows, his first exposure to techniques such as slapstick and stereotypes that he later used in his fiction.

West was not very disciplined, but his clever and adventurous nature helped to get him into Tufts University without a high school diploma. After one unsuccessful year there, he attended Brown University. West's biographer attributes Brown's acceptance of West to a complicated mismatching of transcripts with another student whose name was also Weinstein, though whether this was planned or accidental is not absolutely certain. Whatever the case, West graduated from Brown in 1924 with a degree in philosophy, which he earned in only two and a half years.

Neither West nor his parents had much nostalgia for their Jewish Lithuanian roots; instead, they concentrated on rapid assimilation. In 1926, he legally changed his name to Nathanael West. Even so, the subject of roots still appears in most of his work. The degree of corruption in Lemuel Pitkin's hometown in *A Cool Million* is nothing compared to what he finds elsewhere in the country. The protagonist in *Miss Lonelyhearts* suffers from acute isolation despite his efforts to communicate, and this seems to stem from his earliest memories of childhood; he is estranged from his Baptist upbringing and has only a single comforting memory of his youth. Tod Hackett in *The Day of the Locust* leaves the East Coast, where he was an undergraduate at the Yale School of Fine Arts, for Hollywood. He observes other new arrivals and decides that they have come to California to die in one way or another. Although he does not include himself in this category, it is clear that he too succumbs to the superficial glitter and wastefulness.

West's parents encouraged him to pursue a dependable career, but their son was not interested, and he persuaded them to send him to Paris in 1926. He enjoyed the artistic and literary circles there, but signs of the coming Depression were being felt in the construction industry and West had to return to New York after three months. Relatives managed to find him a job as a night manager of a midtown hotel, providing West with an income, a place to write, and a steady flow of guests to watch. West found these people fascinating, and so it is not surprising that seedy hotels and their transient occupants find their way into *The Day of the Locust*. Working as a night manager also gave West time to revise *The Dream Life of Balso Snell*, which he had begun while in college. William Carlos Williams liked the manuscript and recommended that Moss and Kamin publish it; five hundred copies were printed in 1931. S. J. Perelman, also a student at Brown, married West's sister Laura. Through Perelman, who worked at *The New Yorker*, West met other writers and artists. It was also through his brother-in-law that West conceived of the controlling idea for *Miss Lonelyhearts*. Perelman knew a writer named Susan Chester who gave advice to readers of *The Brooklyn Eagle*. The three of them met one evening in 1939, and she read samples of the letters. West was moved by them and eventually used an advice-to-the-lovelorn column and a tormented newspaper columnist for what is probably his most famous novel. *Miss Lonelyhearts* was published by Liveright in 1933.

West soon went to Southern California to work on film scripts. His experience with the less glamorous aspects of Hollywood and the film industry, with the masses of aspiring actors, and with people who had little talent to begin with, but compensated for that with their dreams, helped provide the themes, landscapes, and characters of West's final novel, *The Day of the Locust*. In 1940, West married Eileen McKenney, the sister of Ruth McKenney, who worked with Perelman at *The New Yorker*. West's careless driving was known to all his friends, and a few months after his marriage, he and his wife were killed in an automobile crash.

Analysis • Although all of West's fiction is concerned with certain recurring themes, it gradually matures in tone, style, and subject. *The Dream Life of Balso Snell*, his first novel, has a clever but sarcastic and ugly adolescent tone. *The Day of the Locust*, his last novel, is also satirical and sarcastic, but its greater maturity and empathetic tone make it both disturbing and profoundly moving.

West's Miss Lonelyhearts dreams that he is a magician who does tricks with doorknobs: He is able to make them speak, bleed, and flower. In a sense, this conceit explains all of West's work. His protagonists travel across dead landscapes that they try to revivify. In *The Dream Life of Balso Snell*, the landscape is mechanical, wooden, purely farcical; in *A Cool Million*, West shows one American town after another, all equally corrupt. *Miss Lonelyhearts* is set in the dirt and concrete of New York City, and *The Day of the Locust* is set in the sordid but irresistible Southern California landscape. West's typical protagonist is a quester, intent on

Courtesy, New Directions Publishing

bringing life wherever he travels; Miss Lonelyhearts especially is obsessed with the challenges of a savior. The task of making a dead world bloom, however, seems hopeless. Life may surface in a moment of communication or lovemaking, but something is likely to go awry, as the moment reverses itself into an unnatural distortion. For example, as Miss Lonelyhearts tries to comfort an old man he meets in Central Park, he suddenly has the urge to crush and destroy him. Shrike, his employer at the newspaper office, compares making love to his wife with sleeping with a knife in his groin. This dichotomy is at the heart of West's vision. Characters driven by benevolent ambitions are thwarted—by themselves, by those in need of their help, by cosmic and divine indifference—until they become grotesque parodies of their original selves. Innocence and success can be recalled only through dreams. At best, the world is passively dead; at worst, it is aggressively violent.

The Dream Life of Balso Snell • The quester of *The Dream Life of Balso Snell* does not take himself seriously, and the novel itself seems to be an extended literary joke. Balso Snell describes a dream in which he encounters the famous wooden horse of the Greeks in ancient Troy. A brash and distinctly modern tour guide leads him through the interiors of the horse, which quickly become the subject of numerous adolescent witticisms. The inside of the horse expands to a landscape that Balso explores for the rest of his dream. West's purpose is humor and parody, which he accomplishes mercilessly although unpleasantly, beginning even with the title of this first book. Following his "path," Balso meets a Roman Catholic mystic, and West has the opportunity to mock the literary lives of saints. Then Balso meets a schoolboy who has just hidden his journal in the trunk of a nearby tree. Balso reads its entries, which serve as a parody of the nineteenth century Russian novel. Balso then meets the boy's teacher, Miss McGeeny, who has been busily writing a biography of a biographer's biographer; West parodies another literary genre.

The Dream Life of Balso Snell is not a significant work of fiction, but it is useful for readers to appreciate how quickly West's style and perspective deepened. His later novels have the same piercing quality, and West never lost his tendency to satirize, but the later novels are finely and precisely directed. West's later fiction also has the same motifs—quester, mechanical or obsessive journeys, dreams, and suffering humanity—but West examines them much more seriously in the later novels.

Miss Lonelyhearts • West is in superb control of his material in *Miss Lonelyhearts*, published only two years after *The Dream Life of Balso Snell*. The vituperative tone of the earlier work is balanced by greater development of plot and diversity of character. Following his preference for fast action and exaggeration, West uses comic-strip stereotypes: the meek husband and the bullying wife, Mr. and Mrs. Doyle; the bullish employer, Shrike, and his castrating wife Mary; and Miss Lonelyhearts's innocent but dumb girlfriend Betty. Miss Lonelyhearts himself is only somewhat more developed, primarily because he is in almost every episode and because the third-person voice sardonically presents his private thoughts.

As in *The Dream Life of Balso Snell*, a central quester travels a barren landscape. Between the newspaper office and the local speakeasy is Central Park. As Miss Lonelyhearts walks across it, he realizes that there should be signs of spring but, in fact, there are none to be seen. Then he recalls that last year, new life seemed wrenched from the soil only in July. Miss Lonelyhearts's job as a newspaper columnist thrusts him into the position of a quester, and he makes a highly unlikely candidate. Simultaneously attracted to and repelled by his mission to assuage the grief of his readers, he makes attempts to get close to some of them, such as Mr. and Mrs. Doyle, but he then suddenly feels a compulsion to keep separate from them. This dichotomy keeps him in motion, reeling him like a puppet from one person's apartment to another, building a pressure that is released only when Miss Lonelyhearts has a final breakdown.

In each new location, the newspaperman tries to make a meaningful connection with another human being. Strict chronology becomes vague as the protagonist's state of mind becomes increasingly disturbed. He reaches toward Betty when they are sitting on the couch in her apartment but suddenly has no interest in her. He does remain sexually interested in Mary Shrike, but she refuses his advances as long as they stay in her apartment, and in the restaurant she teases him sadistically. He telephones Mrs. Doyle, a letterwriter, saying he will advise her in person. He exploits her unhappiness to satisfy his own need but, not surprisingly, is disappointed in the results. Rather than help others, the quester of this novel uses them as targets for venting his own anger. As he is increasingly frustrated in his task of bringing beauty and gentleness into the world, Miss Lonelyhearts takes to the isolation of his own room.

Another kind of quest occurs here, one that parodies the earlier quest. Rather than embark on further quests from one location to another in New York City, Miss Lonelyhearts hallucinates a journey; his bed serves as his mode of transportation. It appears to him a perfect world and a perfect journey, sanctioned by God, who finally communicates to him that he has chosen the right conclusion to his quest. Miss Lonelyhearts feels that he has become a rock, perfect in its design not because God has helped to create it, but because it is impenetrable to all but its own existence. It is ironic that the driven quester actually drives himself into a blissful delusion of isolation.

Reality intrudes. Mr. Doyle, incensed at being cuckolded, rushes up the stairs to the apartment. Miss Lonelyhearts rushes down the stairs, hoping to meet him and welcome what he assumes is Doyle's conversion. Instead, there is a scuffle and

Doyle's gun fires. Only in dreams do doorknobs blossom and human beings turn into gentle and compassionate creatures—at least in West's novels. Miss Lonelyhearts dies, a victim of his own miscalculation.

A Cool Million • The protagonist of *A Cool Million: The Dismantling of Lemuel Pitkin*, is another miscalculating quester. Pitkin is an idealistic young man who leaves his hometown to seek his fortune. The fact that the immediate cause of his departure from Ottsville, Vermont, is the dishonest foreclosing of his mother's mortgage does not dampen his enthusiastic belief that his nation is the land of limitless possibilities. He has faith in himself and in those who insist they are using him for his own good.

Mr. Shagpole Whipple, ex-president of the United States and now director of the Rat River National Bank in Ottsville, becomes Lemuel's earliest supporter. He advises his young friend that America "is the land of opportunity," a land that "takes care of the honest and the industrious." Lemuel is inspired and sets out in what becomes a parody of the Horatio Alger myth. On the train to New York City, he enjoys a conversation with a Mr. Mape, who was left "a cool million" by his father. Lemuel is impressed, especially since, he explains, he must make his fortune starting with only the thirty dollars in his pocket. By the end of the trip, he has been divested of that thirty dollars. Lemuel is the fall guy for another scheme, so that he, and not the thief, is apprehended by the police, brought to trial, and declared guilty. Being sent to prison is only the first of a long series of misfortunes. Lemuel is always someone's dupe or prey, but he bounces back to try again, although he repeatedly gets nothing out of his adventures. In fact, the more he travels, the less he has. Lemuel loses his teeth, his scalp, his eye, part of a hand, one leg; each time there is someone close by who can benefit from his new loss. Lemuel is used by entrepreneurs and thieves of all varieties.

A Cool Million is fast-paced and episodic. Its characters are pure stereotypes—the ingenuous dupe, the patriot, the innocent young girl, the deceitful villain. Everyone and everything is satirized: midwesterners, Jews, southerners, capitalists, and socialists. *A Cool Million* shows how West was beginning to use his material for clearly defined purposes and to control his sharp-edged humor and black comedy in order to make a point. This novel, however, remains a minor work in comparison to *Miss Lonelyhearts* and *The Day of the Locust*. In these works, pathos emerges from West's stereotypes and seems all the more powerful because of its sources. *A Cool Million* is clever and biting but not poignant or profound.

The Day of the Locust • West is at his best in *The Day of the Locust*. Tod Hackett, the central quester, comes to Hollywood from the East Coast to learn set and costume designing. The people he gets to know are desperately in need of beauty, romance, and renewal, but, as in *Miss Lonelyhearts*, the harder they struggle to achieve these goals, the farther away they are.

The story is about dreamers who have traveled to what they believe is the dream capital of America, which West portrays as the wasteland of America. In addition to Tod, there is Faye Greener, beautiful but exploitative, making up in vanity what she lacks in intelligence. Homer Simpson is a thickheaded but sincere middle-aged bachelor from the Midwest. He has run from his one attempt to break through his dull-witted loneliness because the memory of failure is too painful. Characters such as Faye and Homer are particularly successful; although they are stereotypes, they still have something unpredictable about them. This quality usually manifests itself involuntarily by a spasm or quirk. For example, Faye is obviously a second-rate actor, but Tod sees through her tawdry facade to a deep archetypal beauty. Faye is unaware of any such quality; even if she knew, she would not appreciate it, because it has almost nothing in common with the self she has created. Homer has difficulty controlling parts of his body. He does not fall asleep easily because waking up is so arduous. His hands seem disassociated from his psyche; he has to put them under cold running water to rouse them, after which his fingers seem to follow their own rhythms. Like Faye, he has a structural purity without means to express it. Like Miss Lonelyhearts, his emotions swell in intensity, causing pressure that eventually must find release.

Faye becomes Tod's obsession. If he is a quester, she is his grail, and a most difficult challenge. Tod can neither support her nor further her acting career. Instead, he becomes a voyeur, watching her tease Earle Shoop, the cowboy from Arizona, and Miguel, the Mexican. He settles for simply painting Faye in a mural he calls "The Burning of Los Angeles." Tod observes that people come to California to die, despite their ambitions, and the mural reflects their disappointments. In the mural, a mob chases Faye, who seems oblivious to imminent danger and maintains a calm, detached expression. Those who realize they have failed need to express their anger, and those who think they have succeeded exist in a state of happy but dangerous ignorance. As in all of West's fiction, the challenge is as impossible as turning doorknobs into flowers. As the dreamers recognize the gap between their desires and accomplishments, thwarted ambition leads to frustration, and frustration to violence. The power of *The Day of the Locust* derives from the last few chapters, which describe the mindless and destructive product of such frustrated dreams.

It is the evening of a motion-picture premiere; violet lights run across the sky, and crowds of fans are kept under control by police barricades. The premiere provides the opportunity for fans to see face-to-face the "stars," the ones who have made it. The tension is too great, however, and the control too tenuous. The crowd begins to charge toward the theater, and Tod is caught in the pressure. *The Day of the Locust* is a tight, "pressured" novel, but all gives way at the end. As the crowd surges, it builds up strength from the people whose lives are filled with boredom and mistakes. There is mass pandemonium. Homer, moving like a robot, mechanically and swiftly murders a child who has been teasing him. Tod, submerged in the crowd, is hurt, but steadies himself at the base of a rail. In agony, he begins to think about his mural, "The Burning of Los Angeles," until reality and his thoughts merge. He thinks of the burning city, of mobs of people running into the foreground with baseball bats, and he and his friends fleeing from the mob. He actually believes he is painting the flames when policemen grab him from the rail and lift him into a police car. When the siren begins, Tod is not sure whether he or the siren has been making the noise. In effect, he succumbs to the chaos around him.

The Day of the Locust is a bleak novel, reflecting West's belief that recognizing limitations is difficult for humanity, which prefers to think that all things are possible. West shows limitations to be everywhere: within the masses; within the questers trying to save them; within the arid landscape itself. As the limitations prove insurmountable, natural ambitions and desires for harmony are inverted. Love becomes pantomime and compassion a veil for selfish and sadistic purposes. West's characters and settings desperately need to be renewed, but the job of salvation is difficult, one that West's protagonists fail to achieve.

Miriam Fuchs

Other major works

SHORT FICTION: *Follow Your Heart,* 1936 (with Lester Cole and Samuel Ornitz); *The President's Mystery,* 1936 (with Cole); *Ticket to Paradise,* 1936 (with Jack Natteford); *It Could Happen to You,* 1937 (with Ornitz); *Born to Be Wild,* 1938; *Five Came Back,* 1939 (with Jerry Cady and Dalton Trumbo); *I Stole a Million,* 1939; *Men Against the Sky,* 1940.

MISCELLANEOUS: *Novels and Other Writings,* 1997 (includes long fiction, letters, and unpublished writings).

Bibliography

Bloom, Harold, ed. *Nathanael West.* New York: Chelsea House, 1986. This useful collection includes essays on all of West's work in a representative selection. S. E. Hyman's essay is a valuable introduction to West. Contains bibliography.

_____. *Nathanael West's "Miss Lonelyhearts."* New York: Chelsea House, 1987. This valuable collection offers nine essays from a variety of viewpoints on *Miss Lonelyhearts.* Includes a chronology and a bibliography.

Martin, Jay, ed. *Nathanael West: A Collection of Critical Essays.* Englewood Cliffs, N.J.: Prentice-Hall, 1971. This collection contains some brief critical commentaries by West himself as well as analyses by others. Martin's introductory essay is a useful summary. Some of the others presuppose a fairly sophisticated reader. Includes bibliography.

Siegel, Ben, ed. *Critical Essays on Nathanael West.* New York: G. K. Hall, 1994. Divided into two sections—reviews and essays. In addition to the comprehensive introduction surveying West's life and career, the essay section provides studies of individual novels and of West's work as a whole. Includes notes and index but no bibliography.

Veitch, Jonathan. *American Superrealism: Nathanael West and the Politics of Representation in the 1930's.* Madison: University of Wisconsin Press, 1997. Contains separate chapters on each novel as well as an introduction discussing the "crisis of representation during the 1930's." Includes detailed notes but no bibliography.

Widmer, Kingsley. *Nathanael West.* Boston: Twayne, 1982. Widmer's general introduction concentrates on "West as the prophet of modern masquerading, role-playing, and its significance" while offering useful analyses of West's work. Lengthy notes and an annotated bibliography are provided.

Wisker, Alistair. *The Writing of Nathanael West.* New York: St. Martin's Press, 1990. Chapters on each novel and a series of appendixes on various aspects of West's work, including his handling of violence, his unpublished fiction, and revisions of his work. Includes notes and bibliography.

Edith Wharton

Born: New York, New York; January 24, 1862
Died: St.-Brice-sous-Forêt, France; August 11, 1937

Principal long fiction • *The Touchstone*, 1900; *The Valley of Decision*, 1902; *Sanctuary*, 1903; *The House of Mirth*, 1905; *Madame de Treymes*, 1907; *The Fruit of the Tree*, 1907; *Ethan Frome*, 1911; *The Reef*, 1912; *The Custom of the Country*, 1913; *Summer*, 1917; *The Marne*, 1918; *The Age of Innocence*, 1920; *The Glimpses of the Moon*, 1922; *A Son at the Front*, 1923; *Old New York*, 1924 (4 volumes; includes *False Dawn*, *The Old Maid*, *The Spark*, and *New Year's Day*); *The Mother's Recompense*, 1925; *Twilight Sleep*, 1927; *The Children*, 1928; *Hudson River Bracketed*, 1929; *The Gods Arrive*, 1932; *The Buccaneers*, 1938.

Other literary forms • In addition to her novels, of which several had appeared serially in *Scribners*, *The Delineator*, and *The Pictorial Review*, Edith Wharton published eleven collections of short stories and three volumes of poetry as well as a variety of nonfiction works. She wrote an early and influential book on interior decorating, *The Decoration of Houses* (1897, in collaboration with architect Ogden Codman, Jr.), a short book on the art of narrative, *The Writing of Fiction* (1925) published originally in *Scribner's Magazine*, and a delightful if highly selective autobiography, *A Backward Glance* (1934), which includes among other things an amusing account of Henry James's circumlocutory manner of speech. Wharton, an indefatigable traveler, recorded accounts of her travels in *Italian Villas and Their Gardens* (1904), *Italian Backgrounds* (1905), *A Motor-Flight Through France* (1908), and *In Morocco* (1920). During World War I, she wrote numerous pamphlets and letters to inform Americans about French and Belgian suffering and to enlist sympathy and support. Articles she wrote to explain the French people to American soldiers were later collected in the volume *French Ways and Their Meaning* (1919), and accounts of her five tours of the front lines were published under the title *Fighting France from Dunkerque to Belfort* (1915). Wharton also published a great many short stories, articles, and reviews that have never been collected. A number of her stories and novels have been adapted for the stage, motion pictures, and television, and have also been translated into French, Italian, Spanish, German, Danish, Finnish, and Japanese.

Achievements • Unlike Henry James, whose readership was small and intensely discriminating, Wharton managed to attract a large audience of general readers and at the same time command the interest of critics and fellow writers as well. Among her admirers were Sinclair Lewis and F. Scott Fitzgerald; Bernard Berenson, the art critic; and Percy Lubbock. Wharton's popularity remained high almost to the end of her career during the 1930's, but critical enthusiasm began to diminish after 1920, when the quality of her fiction declined. Even in the early years, 1905 to 1920, when Wharton's best fiction was being published, there were reservations expressed or implied by those who thought her a follower of and to some extent a lesser James, a charge easier to disprove than to eradicate. The truth is, that, though Warton learned from James— and a few of her novels, particularly *Madame de Treymes*, reflect Jamesian themes as well as techniques—Wharton had her own manner as well as her own subject, and as she grew older, she continued to discover differences between her fiction and James's. It should also be pointed out (whether in praise or blame will depend on the critic) that James was a more dedicated artist than Wharton; his fiction had a finish and a coherence to be found in only a half-dozen of her novels; moreover, Wharton sometimes skated on the thin ice of superficiality, and in one novel, *The Glimpses of the Moon*, plunged through. Toward the end of her career, she also grew increasingly out of touch with life in the postwar world, much of which offended her. Her long residence in France, moreover, not only cut her off from the life of her fellow countrymen, but also—since she spoke French or Italian almost exclusively—loosened her grasp of English, so much so that a critic such as the young Edmund Wilson could complain that there were awkward phrases even in her masterpiece *The Age of Innocence.*

Wharton's major talent was for social observation. Unlike James, whose interest was ultimately metaphysical and whose novels were often invented from the slightest hints and employed few details, she filled her novels with precise accounts of the decoration of houses, of dress and of dinner parties, describing them often down to the cut of a waistcoat and the contents of the soup tureen. This is not to say that such details were signs of superficiality, but rather that Wharton's fiction depended heavily on the notation of manners and were the result of direct observation. Wharton tended to write—again, unlike James—out of her own direct experience. Even novels such as *Ethan Frome* and *Summer*—both set in provincial New England, and so different from the world she inhabited in New York and Paris—were created with remarkable attention to surface details, of which the famous cut glass, red pickle dish of Zeena's in *Ethan Frome* is a familiar example.

Wharton's fiction, it now appears, was (again, unlike James's) significantly autobiographical. Even the novels of provincial life, so different on the surface, treated issues that came out of the tensions of her own restricted upbringing and her unhappy marriage. Marriage was one of Wharton's principal subjects and provided her with a way of exploring and dramatizing her two main themes: the entrapment of an individual, as R. W. B. Lewis puts it in his *Edith Wharton: A Biography* (1975), and the attempt by an outsider, often a vulgar lower-class individual, to break into an old, aristocratic society. There is a sense in which these two themes are contradictory; the first one implies a point of view that identifies with the individual rather than with society; the second one judges from the point of view of society. The apparent contradiction, however, merely points up the range and boundaries of the author's sensibility. In some novels, *Ethan Frome* and *The House of Mirth*, for example, Wharton writes with sympathy of the trapped individual; in others, *The Custom of the Country*, and *The Children*, she writes from the standpoint of a traditional society. In her best novels, there is both sympathy for the trapped individual and the invocation of an outside claim—marriage vows, moral code, traditional manners—with the balance of sympathy tipped to the individual.

Wharton's major work was written between 1905, the year *The House of Mirth* was published, and 1920, when *The Age of Innocence* appeared. Interesting novels were still to come: *The Mother's Recompense*, *The Children*, and *The Buccaneers*, which has the best qualities of her earlier fiction; but the major works of the late 1920's and early 1930's, *Hudson River Bracketed* and *The Gods Arrive*, betray a serious falling off of energy and of talent. In these novels, Wharton was attempting to judge the contemporary world by the values of the past, but was so out of sympathy with the life around her and so out of touch with its manners that her representation of it in these later books can hardly be taken seriously.

Library of Congress

Despite this later decline, however, and despite the undeniable influence of James on some of her early work, Wharton produced a considerable body of original fiction, high in quality and superior to most of what was being published at the time. Her fiction also influenced other, younger American writers, notably Sinclair Lewis and F. Scott Fitzgerald. After a long decline in readership and a period of critical indifference, there now appears to be a renewal of interest in her writing, both by critics and scholars of the American novel and by feminist scholars interested in extraliterary issues.

Biography • Edith Wharton was born Edith Newbold Jones on January 24, 1862, in New York City. Her parents, George Frederic and Lucretia Rhinelander Jones, were descendants of early English and Dutch settlers and belonged to the pre-Civil War New York aristocracy, families whose wealth consisted largely of Manhattan real estate and who constituted in their common ancestry, landed wealth, and traditional manners a tightly knit, closed society. With the industrial expansion that occurred during and immediately after the Civil War, the old society was "invaded" by a new class of self-made rich men such as John Jacob Astor and Cornelius Vanderbilt. Whereas the old society had lived unostentatiously, observing, outwardly at least, a strict code of manners—the women presiding over a well-regulated social life and the men making perfunctory gestures at pursuing a profession—the new rich spent lavishly, built expensive, vulgar houses, and behaved in ways the old order found shockingly reprehensible. With its energy, its money, and its easier morality, the new order almost inevitably triumphed over the old, and this displacement of New York society constituted one of the chief subjects of Wharton's fiction, particularly in *The House of Mirth* and *The Custom of the Country.*

Wharton was educated at home by governesses, and later, tutors, and it was expected that she would assume the role young women of her class were educated to play, that of wife, mother, a gracious hostess. From an early age, however, Wharton showed intellectual and literary talents that, along with an acute shyness, kept her at the edge of conventional social life and later threatened to consign her at the age of twenty-three to a life of spinsterhood—the worst fate, so it was thought, that could befall a young woman of her class. After one engagement had been called off (because the young man's mother opposed it), and a promising relationship with a young lawyer, Walter Berry (who later became a close friend), had failed to develop romantically, Wharton married a man twelve years her senior,

Edward ("Teddy") Robbins Wharton, a friend of her favorite brother.

Teddy Wharton was a socially prominent Bostonian without a profession or money of his own; Henry James and other friends in England were later incredulous that Wharton could marry a man so obviously her intellectual inferior and so incompatible in his interests; nevertheless, the marriage in the beginning must have been a liberation, both from the social pressure to marry and from her mother's domination. Wharton was close to her father, but there was a coolness between her and her mother that is frequently reflected in her fiction in the portrayal of mother-daughter relationships. By marrying Teddy, she was at last free to come and go as she pleased, to establish her own residence, which she did on a grand scale at Lenox, Massachusetts, and to travel abroad as often as she liked. In time, however, the marriage to Teddy became irksome, partly from lack of deep affection for him, but also because of his increasing bouts of depression and, later, his financial and sexual irresponsibilities. After revelations of his mismanagement of her estate and his adulterous affairs, she divorced Teddy in 1913. In his research for the biography of Wharton, Lewis uncovered the fact that she herself had had a brief but intense affair in 1908 with an American journalist named Morton Fullerton, and that that relationship had a profound influence on her fiction.

Wharton had lived and traveled in Europe as a child with her parents and after her marriage had visited abroad as often as possible, alternating the seasons between her house at Lenox and an apartment in Paris, with shorter visits to England and rural France. In 1903, when she met James in England, there began an important friendship, with frequent visits and exchanges of letters and motor trips in Wharton's powerful automobile. The Whartons always traveled in luxury, and their style and Edith's energy quite overwhelmed James at the same time he delighted in them. Like James, and for somewhat the same reasons, Wharton became in time an expatriate, giving up the newer, rawer life of America for the rich, deeply rooted culture of Europe. She felt at home in the salons and drawing rooms of Paris and London, where art and literature and ideas were discussed freely, where women were treated by men as equals, and where life itself was more pleasing to the senses and to the contemplative mind. Wharton also felt that in Europe, respect for the family, for manners, for learning, and for culture, even among the poorer classes, was very much alive.

Even before the final break with Teddy, Wharton had lengthened her frequent stays abroad and, finally, in 1911, allowed the house at Lenox to be sold. When World War I broke out, she remained in Paris and devoted her time, energy, and money to the relief of French and Belgian refugees; in 1916, she was officially recognized for her services to her adopted country by being made a Chevalier of the Legion of Honor. After the war, she bought a house just north of Paris and, later, another in the south of France. She made only one more trip home, in 1923, to receive an honorary degree at Yale. The remainder of her life was spent abroad.

According to those who knew her well, Wharton was a highly intelligent, well-read, brilliant conversationalist, somewhat remote at first, though the grand manner that many complained of was apparently a way of covering up her deep shyness. She read and spoke Italian and French fluently, and her salons in both Paris and Saint Claire were gathering places for literary, artistic, and social luminaries of the time, including such well-known figures as F. Scott Fitzgerald, Bernard Berenson, Jean Cocteau, Aldous Huxley, and Kenneth Clark. Despite the hectic pace of her social life and her frequent travels, Wharton continued to write regularly, turning out novels and short stories and articles, most of which sold well and brought her a great deal of money. She suffered a slight stroke in 1935, which for a time curtailed her activities; two years later, she was fatally stricken. After a short illness, she died at her home in St.-Brice-sous-Forêt, August 11, 1937. Her body was buried in a cemetery at Versailles, beside the grave where the ashes of her old friend Walter Berry had been buried earlier.

Analysis • On a surface level, there is a surprising variety in the kinds of characters and the aspects of life with which Wharton was familiar. In *The House of Mirth*, for example, one of her best novels, she was able to create characters such as the Trenors and the Van Osburghs, who belong to opposite ends of the upper level of old New York society, as well as Nettie Struther, the poor working-class girl who befriends Lily Bart when she has sunk from the glittering world of Fifth Avenue social life to a seedy, boardinghouse existence. In *The Fruit of the Tree*, she created not only the world of the fashionable Westmores, but also the factory milieu in which the foreman John Amherst attempts to bring industrial reform. In *The Reef*, she could treat life in a French chateau, as well as in a sordid hotel in Paris, and in her two brilliant short novels, *Ethan Frome* and *Summer*, she managed to depict a life in rural Massachusetts that she could only have known by observation, rather than by direct experience.

It must be admitted, however, that Wharton is at times less than convincing. Some critics consider her attempt to deal with factory life in *The Fruit of the Tree* inept, even ludicrous, though others believe it entirely adequate; and certainly the life of impoverished Nettie Struther is delineated with nothing like the thoroughness of Lily Bart's, whose upper-class milieu Wharton knew at firsthand. The extent of Wharton's social range and her ability to create realistic characters from a background quite different from her own is nevertheless impressive, unrivaled in American fiction of the time.

As for variety of character types, one might cite in particular those to be found in *The House of Mirth*, in the range of male characters—from the fastidious Selden to the rapacious Gus Trenor and the socially ambiguous and vulgar Simon Rosedale, all of them suitors for Lily's attention. Both *Ethan Frome* and *Summer* present a more limited range, but both contain sharply realized and distinctly differentiated characters, including the powerful Ethan, the pretty young Mattie, and Zeena, the neurasthenic wife of Ethan. In *Summer*, Charity Royall, the mountain girl, is vividly created, as is her feckless young lover and her elderly guardian and attempted seducer, Lawyer Royall.

Despite this surface breadth, this impressive range of social observation, Wharton's novels have a rather narrow thematic focus. It has been said that Edith Wharton's chief theme is entrapment. Blake Nevius, in *Edith Wharton: A Study of Her Fiction* (1953), points out how this theme is implicit in the principal relationships among characters in many of the novels, in which a superior nature is caught in a wasteful and baffling submission to an inferior nature. It was a situation that Wharton herself must have experienced, not only with a mother who was obsessed with fashion and propriety, but also in a society narrowly given up to the pursuit of pleasure. It was a situation in which she later found herself in her marriage to Teddy, who disliked and resented her interest in social and intellectual life. In novel after novel, one sees this same situation treated—superior individuals trapped in relationships with their inferiors and prevented from extricating themselves by a finer sensibility.

The House of Mirth • In *The House of Mirth*, Lily Bart is impoverished by the bankruptcy and later the death of her father and is obliged to recoup her fortune in the only way open to her, by attempting to marry a rich man. Lily's situation was not Wharton's, but the social pressures on her must have been similar: to make a suitable marriage, with social position certainly, and, if possible, money as well. In the novel, Lily is given a choice that Wharton apparently did not have: an offer of marriage from an emancipated young lawyer of her own class (though Walter Berry, a lawyer, was thought at one time to have been Wharton's suitor). Wharton chose a passionless marriage with Teddy; Lily was not allowed that solution. Selden deserts her at the crucial moment, and she dies of an overdose of sleeping medicine.

In her autobiography *A Backward Glance*, Wharton stated that her subject in *The House of Mirth* was to be the tragic power of New York society in "debasing people and ideas," and Lily Bart was created in order to give that power dramatic scope. Lily's entrapment by society and her eventual destruction are not the final story. Lily overcomes the limitations of her upbringing and aspirations and acts on principle. She has in her possession a packet of letters that could be used to regain her social position, but the letters would involve the reputation of Selden. She also has a ten-thousand-dollar inheritance that could be used to establish herself in a profitable business, but she burns the letters and uses the money to repay a debt of honor. Lily dies, but in choosing death rather than dishonor, she has escaped entrapment.

The Age of Innocence • In *The Age of Innocence*, published fifteen years after *The House of Mirth*, the underlying conflict is the same, though the tone of the novel and the nature of the entrapment are somewhat different. Here, the trapped individual is a man, Newland Archer, a young lawyer who is engaged to marry May Welland, a pretty and shallow young woman of respectable old New York society of the late nineteeth century. This is the world of Wharton's young womanhood, a society that is narrow and rigid and socially proper. Into this limited and self-contained world, she brings Ellen Olenska, a cousin of May, who belongs to this world by birth but left it years before and has since married a Polish count. Ellen has now separated from her husband, who has been notoriously unfaithful, and has returned to the bosom of her family for support and comfort. Archer is engaged by the family to help her in her quest for a divorce settlement. The inevitable happens. Archer and Ellen fall in love. Archer is attracted by Ellen's European sophistication, her freedom of thought and manners, and her refusal to take seriously the small taboos of New York society. Archer considers breaking with May and marrying Ellen. The family, sensing his defection, contrive with other members of the society to separate the lovers and reunite Archer with May, his conventional fiancé. Social pressure forces Ellen to return to Europe, and Archer is again thinking of pursuing Ellen; then May announces that she is expecting a baby. Archer is finally and permanently trapped.

As though to drive home the extent to which Archer has been defeated, Wharton takes him to Paris years later. His son is grown, his wife dead, and Ellen Olenska is now a widow living alone. Archer makes an appointment to see Ellen but gets only as far as a park bench near her apartment. At the last minute, he decides to send his son to see her, while he remains seated on the bench, telling himself that it would be more real for him to remain there than to go himself to see Ellen. The trap has done its work.

Although one can see resemblances between Ellen and Wharton—the expatriation, the charm, the liberated views, perhaps even the slight French accent with which Ellen speaks—Archer is also Wharton, or that side of her that could never entirely escape the past. *The Age of Innocence* was thought by some reviewers to be a glorification of the past, which it clearly is not. Wharton does evoke with some nostalgia the old New York of her youth, but she also sets forth with delicate but cutting irony that society's limitations and its destructive narrowness. Archer has led an exemplary life, one is led to believe, but the happiness he might have had was gently but firmly denied him. Whereas a more popular novelist might have allowed Archer to be reunited with Ellen at the end of the novel, Wharton insists that that would be unreal; for her, personal happiness in the real world is the exception rather than the rule.

Ethan Frome • Two of Wharton's best novels—also two of her shortest—both deal with protagonists trapped by passionless marriages. The earliest of these, *Ethan Frome*, is about a Massachusetts farmer married to an older, neurasthenic wife, whose pretty young cousin has come to work for her. The inevitable again happens. Ethan falls in love with Mattie and dreams about running away with her. Ethan's jealous wife, however, arranges for Mattie to be sent away, and Ethan is obliged to escort her to the train station. It is winter, and the lovers stop for a brief time together. They embrace, realize the inevitability of separation, and decide to kill themselves by coasting down a steep hill into a great elm tree. During the ride down the steep hill, Ethan accidentally swerves the sled; a crash occurs, in which the lovers are seriously injured but survive. Mattie becomes a whining invalid, while Zeena, the neurotic wife, takes over the running of the household, and Ethan, who is severely disfigured, feels himself like a handcuffed convict, a prisoner for life.

As Lewis has pointed out, the situation in *Ethan Frome* is very much like the situation in Wharton's own life at the time. If one shifts the sexes, Frome is Wharton trapped in a loveless marriage with the neurasthenic Teddy and passionately in love with a younger man who shared her interests and feelings, Morton Fullerton. The violent ending may be seen as Wharton's passionate statement about her own desperate situation. The success of *Ethan Frome*, however, does not depend on making such biographical connections; the book is a brilliantly realized work of realistic fiction that owes its power not to some abstractly conceived pessimistic philosophy of life, but to Wharton's successful transposition of her own emotional life into the language of fiction.

Summer • *Summer* was published six years after *Ethan Frome* and was called by Wharton and her friends the "hot Ethan." As in *Ethan Frome*, there is a triangle: Lawyer Royall, elderly guardian of Charity, a pretty young mountain girl, and a visiting architecture student, Lucius Harney. During the idyllic summer months, an intense and passionate affair takes place between Charity and Harney. Harney returns to Boston, and Charity is left to face her guardian, who is also in love with her, and the prospect of an illegal abortion. The novel concludes with a reconciliation between Charity and her guardian and a secure if passionless marriage with him. Although it would be a mistake to overemphasize biographical parallels, they are unmistakable. The affair of Charity and Harney suggests Wharton's earlier affair with Fullerton, while the intrusive presence of the fatherly Lawyer Royall suggests Teddy's irksome claims on Wharton's loyalties. An interesting alteration of chronology is in making the marriage with the older man follow the affair rather than precede it, as it had in Wharton's own life. *Summer* was written four years after the Whartons were divorced, and by then, she may have had time to view her marriage to Teddy more dispassionately, as the practical solution it must originally have been. Like Lily's death, the surrender to marriage is a defeat as well as a moral triumph.

Summer is one of Wharton's finest novels, written according to her own testimony, in a state of "creative joy" and reflecting in its characters, scenes, and symbolic structures, the deep well of the unconscious that seems to nourish the most powerful works of American fiction.

The Reef • *The Reef*, published the year before the Whartons' divorce, and commonly acknowledged to be Wharton's most Jamesian novel, again deals with conflicts between the individual and society and the problems of marriage. In this novel, however, the society is remote; the inheritor of the society's standards, Anna Leath, an American widow of a French nobleman, is reunited with an old friend, George Darrow, also an American, a lawyer, living in Europe. Anna and Darrow become engaged and are about to be married when Anna discovers that Darrow has had an affair with Sophy Viner, her daughter's governess, a girl of a lower class, and that Sophy, who is also her stepson's fiancé, is still in love with Darrow. For Darrow, the situation is a matter of diplomatic maneuvering, of steering his way between the two women and the stepson, but for Anna, it presents a moral dilemma involving, on one hand, an inherited code of conduct, which tells her that Darrow must be abandoned, and a personal one, which tells her not to give him up.

The moral complexities of the novel are a good deal more complicated than any summary can indicate. Indeed, they are so ambiguous that one is hard pressed to decide where the author stands. It is possible, however, to see in this novel situations parallel to Wharton's earlier involvement with Fullerton, and a possible moral dilemma over her own infidelity. In a sense, Wharton is Sophy Viner, but Sophy (and Wharton's affair with Fullerton) seen in the light of a later moral judgment; Wharton is also Anna, attempting to accept the break with conventional morality that led to Darrow's affair with Sophy. The trap in which Anna finds herself is doubly baited, and no matter which way she turns, she must fall, either morally or emotionally. The fact that Anna chooses Darrow after all suggests the same kind of compromise other Wharton protagonists have made, Justine of *The Fruit of the Tree* and Charity Royall of *Summer* especially, both of whom were betrayed by the weakness of the men they loved but settled for what was finally available.

The Custom of the Country • *The Custom of the Country* is a different sort of work, influenced by the French realist Honoré de Balzac rather than by Henry James; it attempts to deal, as did Balzac, with the destruction of an aristocracy by the invasion of uncivilized materialists. The protagonist of the novel, Undine Spragg, is a handsome young woman from Apex, a city in the American Middle West. Undine's father made a great deal of money in Apex and now has come East to try his hand in New York City. The Spraggs move into an expensive, vulgar hotel, and the parents would be content to exist on the fringes of New York society, but Undine, who is as ambitious as she is vulgar, manages to meet and then marry Ralph Marvel, an ineffectual member of old New York society. When life with Marvel grows boring, Undine becomes the mistress of a richer and more aggressive New York aristocrat, Peter Van Degen; when Van Degen drops her, she manages to snare the son of an old aristocratic French family, the Marquis de Chelles. Undine marries de Chelles, but she has learned nothing, being without taste, manners, or ideas; her sole interest is in amusing and gratifying herself. As soon as she gets what she thinks she wants, she becomes dissatisfied with it and wants something she decides is better. She grows tired of having to fit herself into the demands of the feudal aristocracy into which she has married; when she attempts to sell family heirlooms, whose value she does not understand, her husband divorces her. Her third husband is a perfect match, a hard-driving vulgar materialist from Apex, Elmer Moffat, whose chief interest is in buying up European art. Moffat also aspires to an ambassadorial post, but is barred because he is married to Undine, a divorced woman.

The Custom of the Country is regarded by some critics as among Wharton's best fiction, but, as Blake Nevius has observed, during the course of the novel, Undine ceases to be a credible character and becomes an "inhuman abstraction." Clearly, she came to represent everything that Wharton detested in the America of 1912, and, at a deeper and vaguer level, perhaps also expressed Wharton's fear and resentment at the displacement of her own class by more energetic and less cultivated outsiders. The fact that such fears were real enough and the implicit social criticisms valid, does nothing to alter the fact that, measured against books such as *The House of Mirth*, *Ethan Frome*, *Summer*, and *The Reef*, *The Custom of the Country* is crude and unconvincing. James had been right years earlier in advising Wharton to write about that part of the world she knew best, for in attempting to deal with the Middle West in *The Custom of the Country*, and later, in *Hudson River Bracketed* and *The Gods Arrive*, with bohemian circles about which she knew very little, she condemned herself to superficiality and caricature. It is difficult to take seriously Undine Spragg of *The Custom of the Country* or Advance Weston, the protagonist of *Hudson River Bracketed* and *The Gods Arrive*, who is said to be from Pruneville, Nebraska, and later Hallelujah, Missouri, and Euphoria, Illinois. Caricature is an expression of outrage, not understanding.

The Buccaneers • The last of Wharton's novels, *The Buccaneers*, published the year after her death, was a return to the territory of her earlier fiction, old New York of the 1870's. The novel was unfinished at her death and lacks the coherence of her best early work, but she could still write with the sharpness and scenic fullness that had characterized *The House of Mirth* and *The Age of Innocence*.

Wharton was a novelist of manners, then, not a chronicler of large social movements, and her real subject was the entrapment of superior individuals who keenly feel the pull of moral responsibility. Her talents for social observation, for noting subtleties of dress and decoration, for nuance of voice and phrase, and for language—precise and yet expressive—were essential instruments in the creation of her novels. Wharton has been unduly charged with pessimism; her characteristic tone is ironic, the product of a sensibility able to see and feel the claims on both sides of a human dilemma. If her voice faltered in her later years and she conceded too much to the popular taste for which she increasingly wrote, she nevertheless produced some of the finest American fiction published in the first two decades of the century, and her name deserves to stand with those of James and F. Scott Fitzgerald, who outrank her only at their best.

W. J. Stuckey

Other major works

SHORT FICTION: *The Greater Inclination*, 1899; *Crucial Instances*, 1901; *The Descent of Man*, 1904; *The Hermit and the Wild Woman*, 1908; *Tales of Men and Ghosts*, 1910; *Xingu, and Other Stories*, 1916; *Here and Beyond*, 1926; *Certain People*, 1930; *Human Nature*, 1933; *The World Over*, 1936; *Ghosts*, 1937; *The Collected Short Stories of Edith Wharton*, 1968; *Collected Stories, 1891-1910*, 2001 (Maureen Howard, editor); *Collected Stories, 1911-1937*, 2001 (Howard, editor).

POETRY: *Verses*, 1878; *Artemis to Actæon*, 1909; *Twelve Poems*, 1926.

NONFICTION: *The Decoration of Houses*, 1897 (with Ogden Codman, Jr.); *Italian Villas and Their Gardens*, 1904; *Italian Backgrounds*, 1905; *A Motor-Flight Through France*, 1908; *Fighting France from Dunkerque to Belfort*, 1915; *French Ways and Their Meaning*, 1919; *In Morocco*, 1920; *The Writing of Fiction*, 1925; *A Backward Glance*, 1934; *The Letters of Edith Wharton*, 1988; *The Uncollected Critical Writings*, 1997 (Frederick Wegener, editor); *Yrs. Ever Affly: The Correspondence of Edith Wharton and Louis Bromfield*, 2000 (Daniel Bratton, editor).

Bibliography

Banta, Martha. "The Ghostly Gothic of Wharton's Everyday World." *American Literary Realism: 1870-1910* 27 (Fall, 1994): 1-10. An analysis of Wharton's ghost story "Afterward" and her novella *Ethan Frome* as illustrative of the nineteenth century craving for a circumscribed experience of the bizarre.

Bell, Millicent, ed. *The Cambridge Companion to Edith Wharton*. Cambridge, England: Cambridge University Press, 1995. Essays on *The Age of Innocence, Summer, The House of Mirth, The Fruit of the Tree*, and *The Valley of Decision*, as well as on Wharton's handling of manners and race. Bell gives a critical history of Wharton's fiction in her introduction. Includes a chronology of Wharton's life and publications and a bibliography.

Bendixen, Alfred, and Annette Zilversmit, eds. *Edith Wharton: New Critical Essays*. New York: Garland, 1992. Studies of *The House of Mirth, The Fruit of the Tree, Summer, The Age of Innocence, Hudson River Bracketed*, and *The Gods Arrive*, as well as on Wharton's treatment of female sexuality, modernism, language, and gothic borrowings. There is an introduction and concluding essay on future directions for criticism. No bibliography.

Benstock, Shari. *No Gifts from Chance: A Biography of Edith Wharton*. 1994. Reprint. Austin: University of Texas Press, 2004. As the first substantial biography of Wharton to appear in nearly two decades, Benstock's study is informed by her investigation of a variety of primary sources that have become available in recent years.

Dwight, Eleanor. *Edith Wharton: An Extraordinary Life*. New York: Abrams, 1994. A lively succinct biography, copiously illustrated. Includes detailed notes, chronology, and bibliography.

Gimbel, Wendy. *Edith Wharton: Orphancy and Survival*. New York: Praeger, 1984. Drawing upon psychoanalytic theories and feminist perspectives, Gimbel analyzes the four works that she sees as key to understanding Wharton: *The House of Mirth, Ethan Frome, Summer*, and *The Age of Innocence*. The analyses of these works, with their deeply psychological overtones, are well worth reading.

Lindberg, Gary H. *Edith Wharton and the Novel of Manners*. Charlottesville: University Press of Virginia, 1975. Presents Wharton's style with a keen understanding of the ritualism of the social scenes in her work. Strong analytical criticism with a good grasp of Wharton's use of irony.

Overton, Grant M. *The Women Who Make Our Novels.* New York: Moffat, 1922. Written while Edith Wharton was still alive, Overton's book pronounces Wharton's overall literary achievement brilliant but lifeless, but he exempts *Ethan Frome, The House of Mirth,* and *Summer* from this verdict.

Pennel, Melissa McFarland. *Student Companion to Edith Wharton.* Westport, Conn.: Greenwood Press, 2003. A handy student guide to Wharton's writings that includes bibliographical references and an index.

Singley, Carol J., ed. *Edith Wharton's "The House of Mirth": A Casebook.* New York: Oxford University Press, 2003. Collection of critical essays on Wharton's novel *The House of Mirth.*

_____. *A Historical Guide to Edith Wharton.* New York: Oxford University Press, 2003. Collection of original articles by scholars on a wide variety of subjects pertaining to Wharton; includes a bibliographical essay.

Elie Wiesel

Born: Sighet, Transylvania, Romania; September 30, 1928

Principal long fiction • *L'Aube*, 1960 (novella; *Dawn*, 1961); *Le Jour*, 1961 (novella; *The Accident*, 1962); *La Ville de la chance*, 1962 (*The Town Beyond the Wall*, 1964); *Les Portes de la forêt*, 1964 (*The Gates of the Forest*, 1966); *Le Mendiant de Jérusalem*, 1968 (*A Beggar in Jerusalem*, 1970); *Le Serment de Kolvillàg*, 1973 (*The Oath*, 1973); *Le Testament d'un poète juif assassiné*, 1980 (*The Testament*, 1981); *Le Cinquième Fils*, 1983 (*The Fifth Son*, 1985); *Le Crépuscule, au loin*, 1987 (*Twilight*, 1988); *L'Oublié*, 1989 (*The Forgotten*, 1992); *Les Juges*, 1999 (*The Judges*, 2002); *Le Temps des déracinés*, 2003 (*The Time of the Uprooted*, 2005).

Other literary forms • After the appearance in 1956 of *Un di Velt hot geshvign* (in French as *La Nuit*; *Night*, 1960), Elie Wiesel published more than a dozen volumes of essays and nonfiction works. Other works include *Les Juifs de silence* (1966; *The Jews of Silence*, 1966), a personal testimony of his trip to Russia; *Le Chant des morts* (1966; *Legends of Our Time*, 1968), *Entre deux soleils* (1970; *One Generation After*, 1970), *Un Juif aujourd'hui* (1977; *A Jew Today*, 1978), and *After the Darkness: Reflections on the Holocaust* (2002). He also published collections of short stories, several volumes of biblical portraits and Hasidic tales; plays, such as *Zalmen: Ou, La Folie de Dieu* (1968; *Zalmen: Or, The Madness of God*, 1974) and *Le Procès de Shamgorod tel qu'il se déroula le 25 février 1649* (1979; *The Trial of God: As It Was Held on February 25, 1649, in Shamgorod*, 1979); and a cantata, *Ani Maamin: Un Chant perdu et retrouvé* (1973; *Ani Maamin: A Song Lost and Found Again*, 1973). Some of his later works, the biblical portraits and Hasidic tales, although written in French, were originally published in the English translation by his wife, Marion Wiesel.

Achievements • Wiesel is one of the most important figures in the genre known as "the literature of the Holocaust." He brings to literature a new literary vocabulary, rooted in the Bible, that is at once mystical, legalistic, theological, and historical. As a survivor of the Holocaust, he considers himself to be a messenger from the dead to the living, and, as a witness, he bears testimony both to the unfathomable events of the death camps and to the current, unfolding history of his people. Wiesel's work, parochial in context, is universal in perception. It speaks to all humankind, for all participated, either actively or silently, in the supreme trial of their humanity. He views the Holocaust as touching upon every facet of one's life and interests, and he perceives humanity's major problem to be survival in the post-Holocaust world.

As a writer, Wiesel is preoccupied with the inadequacy of language, but not in the abstract manner of many contemporary writers. Language affirms a belief in humankind and attests its grandeur. The Holocaust negates humanity. It represents a misuse of language; the failure of imagination; the rule of the depraved; the suspension of the senses, of beliefs, of time; the inversion of order. To capture the Holocaust in language is to impose upon it a decorum that in itself is a betrayal of those victimized by this satanic maelstrom. Wiesel believed, when he began to write, that the tale nevertheless must be told, because the murderer murders not only his victim but also

himself. He says, "At Auschwitz, not only man died, but also the idea of man." Awareness of the Holocaust may save the world from self-obliteration.

Wiesel raises questions that are unanswerable, questions intended to arouse the
consciousness of a people, the progeny of the indifferent observers of the decade of
the 1940's. He also vies with God, not as a defiant disbeliever, but as a believer in the
biblical tradition of the prophets who have challenged God, remonstrated with Him,
and protested heavenly decrees. There is no gaiety in Wiesel's works. There is laughter, but it is not a joyous laughter. It is the laughter of a madman defying his creator.
Writers, theologians, and humanists of all faiths are attempting to come to terms with
the problems he presents.

Writing, for Wiesel, is not simply intended as a moral lesson for the post-Holocaust generations. It is also, and perhaps primarily—as he explains in the essay "Mes
Maîtres" ("My Teachers"), in *Legends of Our Time*—a monument to the unburied
dead, to the millions whose celestial cemeteries are bereft of tombstones.

Wiesel's first publication, *Night*, is in the form of a memoir of his Holocaust experiences. Wiesel did not have an easy time publishing his initial work. It originally appeared in 1956 as an eight-hundred-page manuscript in Yiddish titled *Un di Velt hot
geshvign* (and the world was silent) and was published in Argentina by a Yiddish press.
It was then condensed to a little more than one hundred pages, translated into
French, given the title *La Nuit*, and, with the help of Wiesel's close friend François
Mauriac, published in France in 1958. It was an instant success. Stella Rodway translated the French version into English, but major publishing houses in the United
States rejected the manuscript because the subject matter was "too sad" to appeal to
the general public. Finally, in 1960, Hill and Wang accepted the manuscript for publication. Wiesel would continue to write in French; his later books were translated
into English by his wife, Marion. The exception is his eyewitness account of his trip to
Russia, *The Jews of Silence*, which was originally written in Hebrew as a series of journalistic articles for an Israeli newspaper. It was thereafter put together in its present
form. Some of Wiesel's essays first appeared in various magazines prior to their appearance in *Legends of Our Time* and *A Jew Today*.

Wiesel is a celebrated lecturer sought after by various organizations, conferences,
and campuses; he served on the boards of numerous national and international organizations; he holds honorary doctoral degrees from more than forty colleges and
universities and has received awards for literary, academic, and humanitarian contributions from thirty-five organizations. In 1983 he won the Belgian International
Peace prize, and in 1986 he received the Nobel Peace Prize.

Biography • Eliezer Wiesel, the third child and only son of Shlomo and Sarah Wiesel, was born in the village of Sighet, in Transylvania, Romania, on September 30,
1928. He had two older sisters, Bea and Hilda, and one younger one, Tzipporah. His
parents were Orthodox Jews. As a child, Eliezer was a profound believer in God and
spent his days in religous studies. His father, though religious, was a man of culture
and a rational humanist. He taught his son to believe in humanity and saw to it that he
learned secular subjects, such as Latin, mathematics, and physics, as well as religious
ones. His mother was more spiritual. She taught her son a love of God. The constant
argument in the Wiesel home was whether their son should be a professor or a rabbi.
Wiesel's maternal grandfather, Dodye Feig, was a Hasid. The young boy would visit
with his grandfather to listen to the tales of the Hasidim and the miracles wrought by
the rabbis. Eliezer's talent as a storyteller had its beginnings in the stories told to him

by his grandfather. He also evinced an appreciation for music and took violin lessons at an early age. After the war, he earned his keep as a choirmaster. His cantata, *Ani Maamin*, with a musical score by Darius Milhaud, is one of the most moving works to be produced about the Holocaust. At the age of twelve, he studied the Kabbala under the tutelage of his master, Moshe. Wiesel's first work, *Night*, commences with the serenity of his youth. The portrait of his grandfather and the conflicting attitudes of his parents are subjects of essays to be found in *Legends of Our Time* and *A Jew Today*.

The tranquillity of Wiesel's life was disturbed in the spring of 1944. Although the war in Europe had been going on since 1939, Hungary was one of the last countries to be invaded by the Germans. The inhabitants of the town of Sighet, protected as they were by the Carpathian Mountains and isolated from the events taking place, did not recognize or believe that disaster was imminent. Immigration, when it was still possible, had never been seriously considered. Sud-

Copyright Washington Post, reprinted by permission of the Washington, D.C., Public Library

denly, in a matter of weeks, ten thousand Jews were first placed in ghettos and then deported to Auschwitz. For Wiesel, one of the most bizarre aspects of the deportation was the apathy and indifference of the general public. Friends and neighbors turned their backs on the people who had lived with them for generations. Wiesel deals with this in his novel *The Town Beyond the Wall* and also in various essays and lectures.

The four-day ride in the sealed boxcar, the arrival at Auschwitz, the separation of families, his last glimpse of his mother and younger sister, the concentration camp experience (including the loss of faith), the stripping away of his humanity, the march to Buchenwald, the death of his father, and finally liberation by the Americans in April, 1945, are tersely rendered in *Night*. Various aspects of this experience are reflected upon by some of the characters of his other novels and by Wiesel directly in some of his essays. The Holocaust itself, while it remains the impetus and muted background of all his writings, does not appear again as the bulk of any particular work. Instead, Wiesel turns from the memoir to the novel form, from fact to fiction, as his protagonists search, as he has done, for a way to live in the post-Holocaust world with the burden of the unimaginable behind them and with the guilt of living confronting them.

When Wiesel was liberated, at the age of sixteen and a half, he refused to be repatriated to the town that had evicted its Jews one year earlier. Instead, he joined a transport of children that was going to France at the invitation of Charles de Gaulle. Upon his arrival in France, he made the decision that he must testify to what he had experienced, but not until he understood it fully himself. He knew it would take time to prepare himself for that testimony, perhaps ten years. He realized that he needed better communication skills and a keener understanding of what had happened. Meanwhile, he vowed not to speak of his experience of the Holocaust. (This vow of silence later became the subject matter for his novel *The Oath*.)

In France, Wiesel learned that his two older sisters were alive. At Versailles, he became acquainted with François Wahl, a young philosopher at the Sorbonne, who taught him French by having Wiesel read French classical literature and classics translated into French. Wiesel moved to Paris in 1946. There, he earned his livelihood as a choir director and as a teacher of the Bible. In 1948, he enrolled at the Sorbonne to study philosophy, the humanities, and literature, hoping to find the answers to the theological, philosophical, and humanistic questions that were plaguing him. His studies broadened his horizons but did not present him with solutions, and he was becoming restless. However, he landed a job as Paris correspondent for the Israeli newspaper *Yediot Aharonot*, and the next few years were spent traveling in North America, South America, Europe, North Africa, Asia, and the Middle East. As a journalist, Wiesel covered the Israeli War of Independence, which forms the background of his novella *Dawn*. In 1952, Wiesel traveled to India on an assignment. While in India, he wrote a dissertation comparing the Hindu, Christian, and Jewish religions. He also decided to teach himself English at that time.

One of Wiesel's assignments brought him back to Paris, where he met François Mauriac, who convinced him that he must break his vow and start telling his story. The result of this meeting was *Night*, a memoir in the form of a novella. The years after his liberation and the meeting with Mauriac are reflected in his essay "An Interview Unlike Any Other," in *A Jew Today*.

In 1956, Wiesel was sent to New York to cover the United Nations. He also began writing articles in Yiddish for the *Jewish Daily Forward*. During his first summer in New York, he was almost killed by a taxicab while crossing Times Square. He required weeks of hospitalization and months of recuperation. He could move about only with the help of a wheelchair. This experience became the subject of the novella *The Accident*, which he wrote while he was housebound. During that time, his French visa expired, and he applied for American citizenship.

Wiesel returned to Sighet in 1965. He arrived in the middle of the night. It was an unbearable experience for him, poignantly and searingly related in an essay titled "Le Dernier Retour" ("The Last Return"). The retelling of this incident also appears in the collection *Legends of Our Time* and in "The Watch," in *One Generation After*, and it is recorded with great accuracy in his novel *The Town Beyond the Wall*. Wiesel could not bring himself to spend more than twenty-four hours in the city he had left so abruptly some twenty years before.

Wiesel's first visit to Russia, in 1965, resulted in three works, each in a different form: *The Jews of Silence*, a compilation of newspaper articles concerning this trip; *Zalmen*, a play dealing with the anguish of the rabbi of the Moscow synagogue; and *The Testament*, a novel begun during his trip but set against the background of the Stalinist purge of Jewish writers and poets in 1952. Wiesel returned to Russia again in 1979, as chairman of the President's Commission on the Holocaust.

After 1948, Wiesel made several trips to Israel in his capacity as correspondent for *Yediot Aharonot*. His participation in the June, 1967, war provided the impetus for the novel *A Beggar in Jerusalem*. He returned to Israel in 1968, this time to be married in Jerusalem, to Marion Erster Rose, a Viennese, a concentration camp survivor also, and a linguist.

Wiesel joined the faculty at City College of New York in 1972, first as a visiting professor teaching courses on Jewish literature, the Holocaust, and Hasidism, and then, in 1973, as Distinguished Professor. Thereafter, he would teach at Boston University, as an Andrew Mellon professor of the humanities.

Analysis • Wiesel said that all his works are "commentary" on *Night*, his one work that deals directly with the Holocaust. His novels are odysseys of a soul fragmented by the Holocaust, in quest of tranquillity, an attempt to move away from the night reaching the shores of day. The key to understanding Wiesel, then, is his memoir in the form of a novella, *Night*. It is a slim volume that records his childhood memories of his hometown and his experiences in the concentration camp. It also contains the themes, images, and devices that recur throughout his work.

Night • The opening chapter of *Night* begins with the social setting of Wiesel's native village of Sighet in Transylvania—its inhabitants, their customs, their beliefs—and his first meeting with Moché, the beadle, a character who forms a link to all his other works. Events occur rapidly. The disruption of normalcy with the invasion of the Germans, the forcing of the Jews into ghettos, their deportation, and the obliteration of the Jewish community are recorded tersely but accurately.

From the moment the Jews of Sighet leave the tranquil setting of their native village until they are liberated, time is suspended. The concentration camp is a universe like no other. There, every day is a waking nightmare. Each day is a repetition of deprivation, starvation, cremation; death, either by torture, gunshot, or fire, is the only certainty. The boys look like old men; the men cry like children. Existence depends upon endurance, regardless of age.

Not only is the town obliterated and time obliterated, but also the individual is transformed into an unrecognizable substance. The bestial inhumanity of the victimizers, the divorce from social, moral, and humanistic constraints, marks their apotheosis in the kingdom of Hell. The inmates of the concentration camp's universe are metamorphosed also. The tattooing of numbers on their arms indelibly brands them as objects of inventory, to be used as long as they work well and to be disposed of when they malfunction. *Night* describes this transformation. Early in the work, Wiesel says of himself that he "had become a completely different person." The work ends after the war. He has survived and has been liberated; he looks into the mirror and sees a corpse staring back at him. The corpse becomes part of his life, and the tension of his works rests upon separating himself from the corpse, which means finding a place for himself among the living and giving the corpse a proper burial in the form of a literary monument. Separating himself from the corpse is not an easy task. It involves personal, social, and theological issues: assuaging his own guilt for having survived and coming to terms with an indifferent society and an indifferent God, who allowed the Holocaust to take place.

Wiesel's later works chart his attempt at reconciliation with life, reintegration into society, rediscovery of his religious heritage, and reaffirmation of his belief in God, in spite of everything. This is accomplished by the use of a dual character or alter ego. In each novel, the personality of the protagonist, a survivor of the Holocaust, is complemented by that of the antagonist, usually someone who was not directly involved in the war. They lead separate lives until their paths cross and their souls fuse. The antagonist then disappears; his existence is no longer necessary.

Within the biographical-historical-psychological framework of Wiesel's works are recurring metaphors, characters, and themes. The Holocaust, the overriding presence in Wiesel's oeuvre, is metaphorically night. The sealed, unlit boxcar bearing Wiesel and his townspeople arrived at Auschwitz at midnight. For the victims, night describes the abyss to which they were consigned; for the oppressors, it indicates the depravity of the soul; for the world, it represents the failure of enlightenment, the blackness in which the world was engulfed during the Holocaust period. For Wiesel, night is a physical and psychological condition. As a victim, he moved like a shadow through the kingdom of Death, communicating with corpses. As a survivor, the corpses still haunt him. In Auschwitz, time lost its significance, and night became the only frame of reference. Night continues to circumscribe the parameters of confinement for the protagonists in *The Town Beyond the Wall, The Gates of the Forest, A Beggar in Jerusalem, The Oath,* and *The Testament.*

The lasting effects of the devastation on the psyche are summed up by Wiesel in an incantatory paragraph that appears early in *Night*:

> Never shall I forget that night, the first night in camp which has turned my life into one long night, seven times cursed and seven times sealed. Never shall I forget that smoke. Never shall I forget the little faces of the children, whose bodies I saw turned into wreaths of smoke beneath a silent blue sky.

Having pledged never to forget, Wiesel makes memory an important aspect of all his writings. His characters, especially his protagonists, are haunted by their memories. Memory controls their lives and motivates their actions. It is also a bridge to their future.

Moché, the beadle of *Night*, survives the massacre of the first roundup of Jews and returns to Sighet to tell the tale and warn the others concerning their impending doom. The townspeople, however, refuse to believe him and think he has gone mad. Moché appears in every book; his role is usually that of messenger in the tale he tells. Madness is an essential element in all Wiesel's works. On one hand, it is indicative of the malady that struck the world during the Holocaust years. Wiesel, however, treats his madmen sympathetically. Their madness is not clinical but mystical. They are visionaries, saints, or messengers, endowed with the task of saving the world. As such, they become one with humankind, God, and creation. Wiesel's point is that madness can be a force of evil or good. Adolf Hitler and his Nazis were mad. Their madness was employed to destroy the world. Most of Wiesel's madmen want to bring about the Messiah; they want to redeem the world.

Another theme that is paramount in Wiesel's works is that of silence. Wiesel's ten years of silence after his liberation afforded him the opportunity for reflection and meditation on past events and future actions. He followed a carefully conceived plan not to speak. It was not that he had nothing to say or that he was indifferent; his decision was prompted by the knowledge that no words could describe what had taken place. His silence was intended as an "eloquent silence, a screaming silence, a shouting silence." Wiesel broke his silence when he decided to write, and in each of his novels, excepting *The Town Beyond the Wall*, the protagonist is confronted with a similar problem and makes a similar decision. Related to the theme of silence is the theme of responsibility, which is expressed in breaking the silence.

To evoke accurately the ravaged soul of the survivor in the post-Holocaust world,

Wiesel creates a society of characters different from those one is used to meeting in novels. The characters are beggars, witnesses, messengers, storytellers, and chroniclers.

The Town Beyond the Wall • *The Town Beyond the Wall,* Wiesel's first novel after his three novellas, depicts his attempt to go home again. After his liberation from Buchenwald, Wiesel refused to return to his native town. He became, like the beggars or messengers in his stories, a *navenadnik,* a wanderer, a lost soul traveling throughout the world to find an inner peace and a place that he could call home. He traveled for ten years and finally, albeit accidentally, settled in the United States. It became home for him, however, only when he could totally and irrevocably sever his ties with his hometown. No matter where he went, he was drawn to the memories of his childhood, the familiarity and tranquillity of those days. He had to return at least once in order to realize that the Sighet of his youth no longer existed. It was a journey, as Wiesel says, to "nothingness."

The Town Beyond the Wall is divided into four parts and is presented in a series of reveries that help the protagonist cope with the torture imposed upon him by his captors during his confinement in prison. Michael, a survivor of the Holocaust, has returned to his hometown of Szerencseváros with the aid of his friend, Pedro. The town is now under communist rule, and he has entered it illegally. He is betrayed, imprisoned, and—because he remains silent and will not inform on his friend—is given the standard treatment, a torture called "The Prayer," which consists of keeping a prisoner on his feet facing a wall until he speaks or loses consciousness. In order to surmount the pain, Michael devises a method of transcending time by moving back and forth in his consciousness so that the present recedes to his subconscious level and the past moves forward into his consciousness. The reflections relating to his hometown are twice filtered, first as they are told to Pedro and then as he recalls them during his "prayers."

The pendular movement between different levels of consciousness, so that time is obliterated, is suggestive of Wiesel's imprisonment in the concentration camp. It is as if Wiesel is saying that time exists only in society. After being removed from society, people are also removed from time. In fact, they have no need for it. Time stops for them, but because time continues to move on for the world beyond their confinement, they will never be able to retrieve it.

Night hovers over *The Town Beyond the Wall,* as it hovered over Wiesel's first work. The protagonist is enveloped in a physical and psychological darkness. With his eyes closed, shutting out all light and consciousness, he evokes the nightmare world of his past, the fears of his childhood, his reflections on the Holocaust, the death of those who influenced him—Moché, the madman; Varady, his neighbor; Kalman, his teacher; his father; Yankel, his friend from the concentration camp—and the bleakness of life in France. An aspect of this nightmare world is his divided consciousness. This is suggested by the time and place in which he meets Pedro: in Tangiers, an hour before midnight in a dimly lit café, which is under a sign of a black cat. Pedro is his antagonist. He is what Saul Bellow would call "the Spirit of Alternatives." They walk the city together late at night. Pedro listens to Michael, providing him with alternatives to his dilemmas, answers to his questions, and a *modus vivendi.* He is a good friend. Their identities, at the conclusion, fuse, and when Michael is imprisoned, Pedro disappears, living only in Michael's memory in the form of an attitude toward life.

Through his relationship with Pedro, Michael comes to realize that silence in the form of indifference is destructive. People affirm their humanity when they involve themselves with or share in the anguish of humankind. To be a spectator of life is to deny life. That was the reason for Michael's return to Szerencseváros. He wanted to confront the spectator, the man who watched his Jewish neighbors being humiliated, looked on as the children cried of thirst, and then turned his back without any expression of emotion. That is why, at the end of the novel, he decides that he must reach out to his cellmate, who has rejected the world and now exists as a mute on the periphery of life. Michael knows that by restoring an interest in existence to his silent companion, he is also asserting his own essence, giving meaning to his own life. Wiesel later expands on this theme in *The Oath*.

In *The Town Beyond the Wall*, silence is viewed as detrimental. In the opening section, when Michael reflects upon his childhood friendship with the renegade Varady, he notes that the community expresses its hatred for him through silence. In the next chapter, Michael's failure to respond to his friend's need results in Yankel's committing suicide. In the third section, Michael tells the tale of a mother and child who attempt to flee the Germans by hiding in the wagon of hay owned by a friendly neighbor who offers to take them to safety. He tells them that their lives depend on their being silent. Silence, however, did not help them; they were killed when the Hungarian officers repeatedly stuck their bayonets through the hay. In the conclusion, Michael's silence, while it may have saved the life of Pedro, may also have cost him his own life.

Wiesel expresses his own equivocation regarding silence in this novel. Words may betray, words may deceive, but speech remains the only expression of civilized people. Language, when properly used and properly understood, is instructive and a means of creating a bond between people. It may not save the world, but it may save one human being. This is the lesson Wiesel learned from Mauriac, which caused him to break his vow.

Madness is presented as the opposite of silence. One takes refuge in being mute, the other in being vocal. The silent one sees without responding; the madman sees and reacts, usually through the use of words that other characters cannot comprehend or that they refuse to comprehend. Wiesel elaborates on this theme in the scene at the insane asylum in *A Beggar in Jerusalem*. In *The Town Beyond the Wall*, Pedro prevents Michael from joining the cadre of madmen. He tells him, "To see liberty only in madness is wrong." Madness is seen as a force of evil in this work. Michael's cellmate is mad; he sees things that are not there and says things that do not make sense, and he finally attempts to kill a third cellmate, Menachem.

It is significant that *The Town Beyond the Wall* ends in the cell. Michael is still a prisoner of his past. He is reaching out toward others, attempting to find his own identity, but he has not yet been able to do so. Wiesel's next novel deals with this problem; each of his novels, excluding *The Testament*, charts his journey away from *Night*.

The Gates of the Forest • Although *The Town Beyond the Wall* examines the possibility of going home and acknowledges the impossibility of doing so, *The Gates of the Forest* concentrates on retrieving a lost name and the identity that goes with it. This novel also begins with night and imprisonment. The opening setting is not a cell but a cave in the forest. It is springtime, with its intimations of rebirth and regeneration, but the war once again casts its shadowy reflection over the entire work. Gavriel, a seventeen-year-old Jewish youth, has escaped deportation and is hiding from the German and

Hungarian police. He has assumed the name of Gregor to increase his chances of remaining alive. His father was with him in hiding but had gone in search of food three days earlier, and he has not returned. Prior to his leaving, he had admonished his son not to break his silence and betray his whereabouts. A stranger, another Jew, makes his way to Gregor's hideout. The man has no name, and Gregor gives him his. The entire work is devoted to searching out the efficacy of silence and its relationship to an individual's identity.

The Gates of the Forest is also divided into four sections, alternating between the forest and the city. The first two sections establish the protagonist as a man of various masks. In the first section, he gives his name to a stranger who first jeopardizes and then saves his life. In section 2, he assumes two guises: that of a deaf-mute bastard child and that of the betrayer of Christ. After escaping from the forest, Gregor seeks refuge with Martha, the peasant woman who used to work for them. It is her idea that he disguise his identity and become the child of her wayward sister, Ileana. He assumes yet another identity in this village, when the school principal decides to stage a Passion play and bestows upon him the part of Judas. Section 2 concludes with Gregor proclaiming his true self—Gavriel. Now that he has pronounced his name, he has to labor at reclaiming his identity. The second half of the work is devoted to transforming the personality of Gregor into that of Gavriel: the estranged individual into a man of God. He does this by intimately relating to his own people and by refusing to be other than what he is. He joins a Jewish partisan group in the forest. When the war is ended, he meets Clara, who was also a partisan, and marries her. In New York, Gregor joins in a Hasidic celebration and gains an audience with a Hasidic rebbe. He confronts him with all the problems that have afflicted him since the war, especially his inability to believe in God after what has happened. The rebbe's answers provide him with a "gate" to the future. It is in the synagogue after his meeting with the rebbe that Gavriel reclaims his name and his identity as a man of God.

The rebbe and the stranger are Gregor's antagonists. The stranger at the beginning of the novel has the name Gavriel—"Man of God"; the rebbe, at the end of the work, *is* the man of God. The stranger disappears early in the work, and Gregor's search for him proves futile. He thinks he sees Gavriel at the rebbe's house of study, but it is an illusion, a dream. He sees, or dreams that he sees, only another stranger. He insists that the stranger listen to his story. The act of telling the story restores Gavriel's identity. He awakens from his dream knowing what he has to do: help Clara lay her ghosts to rest and restore his relationship with God. The work ends with his recitation of Kaddish, which, while it is a prayer for the dead, affirms the greatness of God. Once again, Wiesel concludes that silence is not a solution. Through the use of words, people not only speak to God but also become "messengers to heaven."

There is in this novel, as in all Wiesel's novels, much autobiographical detail. Wiesel, as Gavriel-Gregor, the storyteller, presents his attitude toward the Germans, the Christians, and Europe itself, as well as the humanism of his father, the mysticism of his childhood, the isolation and ignorance of the Jews of Transylvania regarding their fate, his inability to cry, his guilt as a survivor, his going to France immediately after the war, his becoming a journalist and traveling to North Africa, the Far East, and the United States, his refusal to say Kaddish upon the death of his father, and his inability to believe in a God who remained silent during the Holocaust. Above all, this work charts the author's slow but certain return to religion and the Hasidism of his childhood. The visits to the Hasidic rebbe are autobiographical, as is the search for a master or teacher. Wiesel continues to study with a Talmudic master and maintains a close relationship with a Hasidic rebbe in Brooklyn, New York.

Night, in this work, is significant as a general obfuscation of identity. The novel begins at night, in the cave with the protagonist who bears an assumed name, and it concludes in the morning, as Gavriel finds himself. Madness is a force of evil. It connotes the failure of rationality and describes the malady of the times, the frenzy of the mob. It is a condition from which one must be saved. Clara is on the verge of madness, and Gregor attempts to rescue her. The masters (or teachers), the stranger Gavriel, and the rebbe are storytellers, and storytellers always bear messages. Gregor is both witness and messenger. In his role as Judas, he is witness to the madness of the peasants. Upon entering the partisan camp, he is a messenger bearing news from the outside, telling the group about the massacre of the townspeople. Later, he brings word of the death of Leib, leader of the partisans.

The work concludes in the season of winter with the ushering in of a new day. In its reconciliation with the past, the "gates of the forest" open onto a new life for Wiesel and his protagonists while not fully closing upon the darkened phase of his youth.

A Beggar in Jerusalem • *A Beggar in Jerusalem* is a difficult novel. It is lyric, mystical, sensitive, yet powerful. Written in a mood of ecstasy, the seven-hundred-page first draft was condensed to its present length of slightly more than two hundred pages.

A Beggar in Jerusalem was galvanized by two crucial events in Wiesel's post-Holocaust life: a trip to Israel in 1967 and his marriage in 1968. At the outbreak of the Six-Day War in 1967, between the Arabs and Israelis, with its threat of extermination of the Jews once again, Wiesel went to Israel as a journalist. This work captures and records a victorious moment in Jewish history, the reunification of Jerusalem and, with it, the securing of the Wailing Wall. It also transmits the texture of this experience, the significance that Jerusalem embodies for Wiesel and the Jewish people. It is an emotional presentation, communicating the yearning of a people, the fulfillment of dreams, the "returning" home to Jerusalem. Wiesel was married in 1968 in a synagogue near the Wall. The novel is also a dedication to his wife, Marion. As such, it looks backward into his past and forward into the future. Like *The Town Beyond the Wall* and *The Gates of the Forest*, it, too, is a quest. In this novel, the search is for a new being. Wiesel does not want to rid himself of his past; it becomes an integral part of his life. The new being has to integrate his past experiences with his present identity and his future with his wife.

Silence is not a major issue in this work. It is the telling of tales and memory that are paramount. *A Beggar in Jerusalem* shifts between time periods, suggesting that contemporary events are meaningful only in the perspective of history. The joy of conquest is tempered with the sadness of two millennia of Jewish suffering. As in all Wiesel's works, the Holocaust forms the background and molds and shapes the events of this hauntingly beautiful novel. It is a paean to Jerusalem, but it does not extol the victors. There is no gaiety, no victory celebration. It is a somber novel that concentrates on the anticipation and fear that precede war, acknowledges the human torment that follows war, and focuses on the collective responsibility of humankind.

The aftermath of war is not glorious; instead of heroes, the novel offers a strange array of beggars, vagabonds, madmen, and storytellers. All are Holocaust survivors who left the camps with nothing, had no home to which to go, were unwanted by everyone, and were treated like beggars everywhere—displaced persons whose lives take on meaning in the sharing of experiences. The beggars—Moché, the madman, among them—meet at night. They exchange tales of anguish as they debate God's justice and their own human condition.

David, the narrator of the work, is also a survivor of the Holocaust. As a representative of the past, he is the witness and the teller of tales. He interrupts the present tale of the Six-Day War with memories, the collective experiences of his people, and stories he has heard from others. He is a beggar and seeks out the company of other beggars, survivors like himself. This narrator-beggar ironically bears the name of the king of Israel, David. David's antagonist, Katriel, is an Israeli officer. He represents the present, a new generation which believes that it can alter its destiny. The work begins as a search for Katriel, who disappears after the war. David's and Katriel's stories move along separate lines, yet they are related. They meet during the war in the army camp and enter into a pact whereby they will remain together, each helping the other to conquer his fear. The survivor will bear witness for the other. They remain together for the war and the victory. They are together at the Wailing Wall, and both observe the custom of writing a wish on a piece of paper that is slipped into a crack in the wall. The destiny of the antagonists of *The Town Beyond the Wall* and *The Gates of the Forest* befalls Katriel: He vanishes. No one knows what has happened to him. Actually, the personalities of Katriel and David have fused at the Wall in Jerusalem. The present has joined the past to create a new being. The fact that David and Katriel are now one is suggested when David repeats to Malka, Katriel's wife, a story about a beggar told to him by Katriel. He then asks her, "But do you know who the beggar was? Sometimes I tell myself he was Katriel, he was I."

In this novel, Wiesel ends his quest. He no longer searches for a home. He has come to realize the validity of the words of a wandering preacher whom he met as a young boy—that all roads lead to Jerusalem. He also recalls the words of Katriel: "One doesn't go to Jerusalem, one returns to it." He no longer searches for identity or a new being; it has been reshaped by Jerusalem, "the city which miraculously transforms man into pilgrim; no one can enter it and go away unchanged." At the conclusion of *A Beggar in Jerusalem*, both the protagonist and his creator find that Jerusalem, the city of peace, is a concept one carries within oneself.

In *The Town Beyond the Wall* and *The Gates of the Forest*, the protagonists learn of the necessity to involve themselves in the life of other human beings. In *A Beggar in Jerusalem*, Wiesel moves from the single individual to the community: The beggars are comforted by the others in their group, Jewish people everywhere offer their support to the threatened Jewish state, and Israel wins the war, as the narrator states, with the aid of the six million who died.

The Oath • Responsibility, both individual and collective, is the major theme of *The Oath*. In the works that preceded *The Oath*, especially *The Town Beyond the Wall* and *The Gates of the Forest*, the dramatic tension created by the desire for silence gave way to the practical need to speak, yet Wiesel continued to question his decision to speak. In *One Generation After*, he suggests that the horrors of the Holocaust might have been transmitted more eloquently and consequently more effectively by the abjuration of speech. Had the survivors "remained mute, their accumulated silences would have been unbearable: the impact would have deafened the world." *The Oath* addresses itself to this issue. It, too, is a personal statement in which Wiesel works out his own problems regarding his decision to break his vow of silence. *The Oath* seems to resolve the tensions created in the desire for silence, recognizing the futility of explanation and the need for speech. It does not, however, conclude Wiesel's concern with the issue, which he takes up once again in *The Testament*.

The Testament • The Holocaust marked the destruction of East European Jewish life and culture. Not long after World War II, another area of Jewish culture was liquidated. On August 19, 1952, Joseph Stalin climaxed his infamous purge of Yiddish artists in the Soviet Union. On that day, thirty Yiddish writers were executed simply because they were Jewish. Hundreds more had been murdered earlier or were killed shortly afterward. These artists were consigned to oblivion, but Wiesel commemorates their achievements and bemoans their loss in *The Testament*. In so doing, he helps "the dead vanquish death."

Like Wiesel's earlier novels, *The Testament* is animated by the dramatic and dialectical tension between silence, or the "futility of all explanation," and the need to recount or bear witness. In this work, father and son are in opposition to each other. The father, Paltiel Kossover, an obscure poet, has substituted the god of communism for the God of his forefathers, only to realize, too late, that his zeal is misdirected, that the new god has rejected him, and that his destiny is linked to his own people. This is the legacy he transmits to his son, in the form of a testament written in jail prior to his execution. The son, Grisha, a mute—he bit off his tongue so that he would not be able to testify against his father—reads the father's testament in an apartment in Jerusalem, to which he has come in 1972. The document was saved by a witness to the execution, Zupanev, a jailer who is determined not to allow Paltiel Kossover's memory to be obliterated.

The testament binds the present to the past, links the current tragedy to its historical predecessors. Zupanev says that Grisha, as a mute, is an "ideal messenger"—ideal because no one suspects him—who will be able to assimilate the events of the document into his consciousness and then recount them to future generations. Grisha's role as an effective witness is diminished, nevertheless, by his inability to speak.

Among Wiesel's novels, *The Testament* is the harshest in outlook and the darkest in vision. All his other works end on a note of optimism. This one does not. Only the setting of Jerusalem illuminates the night of the novel. The work begins in hope, at the Lod airport, with the ingathering of the Russian exiles. It ends in death and in memory and indicates that Wiesel has little faith in the writer's ability to change humanity and human nature. It is his testament that "mankind didn't change." Nevertheless, Wiesel continues to write. One explanation for his persistence is suggested by the prologue to *The Testament*, which recounts an anecdote concerning a Just Man and his desire to correct injustice. He says: "In the beginning, I thought I could change man. Today, I know I cannot. If I still shout today, if I still scream, it is to prevent man from ultimately changing me."

The Forgotten • The Holocaust and its aftermath would remain powerful themes in Wiesel's writings, as he shows again in *The Forgotten*. The forgotten of the title refers to that which is forgotten as well as to he who is forgotten, for memory, remembrance, and mental and psychological forgetting are all important leitmotifs.

Professor Elhanan Rosenbaum, Malkiel's increasingly sick and senile father, is rapidly losing his memory. To hold on to his dissolving past, he sends Malkiel to his native Carpathian village to retrace the family origins, a mission for which the son is highly qualified. As a *New York Times* reporter, Malkiel specializes in the dead, whether the victims of the Cambodian killing fields or the mighty of the obituary page. In President Nicolae Ceauşescu's Romania the reporter meets a philosophical Jewish gravedigger, who, through his tales told in the style of Hebraic storytellers, is both a witness of Nazi horrors and Jewish heroism and a repository of Jewish folklore and memory. Malkiel learns of his grandfather's self-sacrifice and of his father's courage and also of the fact that, as in so many German-occupied countries, most people actively participated in tracking and killing Jews or did nothing to save them. He also learns that the young Elhanan did not speak out while a comrade took revenge on their worst enemy by raping his widow, a silence that would haunt his father forever.

During lucid moments the father tells the son of his illegal entry into Palestine with Talia, his future wife, and of the intoxicating first days of Israel's independence, which symbolically and dramatically coincide with Malkiel's birth and Talia's death. Woven with the moving and passionate plea not to forget the dead are Malkiel's torturing liaisons with Inge the German and Leila the Arab, each of whom revives a special memory of hatred and pain. On the other hand, Tamar, his Jewish colleague and lover, presents him with a more difficult dilemma when she questions conduct and ethics of modern-day Israel.

Only through legends, stories, eyewitness accounts—in short, words—can one hope to triumph over forgetfulness and ultimately death itself. From the power of words the spinner of tales survives, and so does his message, however incomplete and lost in the fog of memory. To seize and reassemble those shattered fragments of Elhanan's failing memory, Wiesel uses various narrative devices—letters, flashbacks, journal entries, tape recordings, prayers, unspoken dialogues—complemented by parables taken from Hasidic and Talmudic scholars.

Beginning with the publication of *Night* in 1956, Wiesel established himself as the bard of the Holocaust. *The Forgotten*, though, shines with a luminosity that was often absent from his earlier works, as if Wiesel had come out of his own Night Kingdom, scathed but also full of hope and optimism. All is remembered; nothing is forgotten: "Thanks to him [Elhanan's grandson yet to be born], I shall live on; thanks to you, Abraham lives."

L. H. Goldman
Updated by Pierre L. Horn

Other major works

SHORT FICTION: *Le Chant des Morts*, 1966 (essays and short stories; *Legends of Our Time*, 1968); *Entre deux soleils*, 1970 (essays and short stories; *One Generation After*, 1970); *Un Juif aujourd'hui*, 1977 (essays and short stories; *A Jew Today*, 1978).

PLAYS: *Zalmen: Ou, La Folie de Dieu*, pb. 1968 (*Zalmen: Or, The Madness of God*, 1974); *Le Procès de Shamgorod tel qu'il se déroula le 25 février 1649*, pb. 1979 (*The Trial of God: As It Was Held on February 25, 1649, in Shamgorod*, 1979).

NONFICTION: *Un di Velt hot geshvign*, 1956 ((in Yiddish), 1958, in French as *La Nuit*; *Night*, 1960); *Les Juifs du silence*, 1966 (travel sketch; *The Jews of Silence*, 1966); *Discours d'Oslo*, 1987; *Le mal et l'exil: Reconte avec Élie Wiesel*, 1988 (*Evil and Exile*, 1990); *A Journey of Faith*, 1990 (with John Cardinal O'Connor); *From the Kingdom of Memory: Reminiscences*, 1990; *Tous les fleuves vont á la mer*, 1994 (memoir; *All Rivers Run to the Sea*, 1995); *Et la mer n'est pas remplie*, 1996 (*And the Sea Is Never Full: Memoirs*, 1999); *Le Mal et l'exil: Dix ans après*, 1999; *Conversations with Elie Wiesel*, 2001 (Thomas J. Vinciguerra, editor); *After the Darkness: Reflections on the Holocaust*, 2002; *Elie Wiesel: Conversations*,

2002 (Robert Franciosi, editor); *Wise Men and Their Tales: Potraits of Biblical, Talmudic, and Hasidic Masters*, 2003.

CHILDREN'S LITERATURE: *King Solomon and His Magic Ring*, 1999.

MISCELLANEOUS: *Célébration hassidique*, 1972-1981 (2 volumes; biographical sketches and stories; volume 1 *Souls on Fire*, 1972; volume 2 *Somewhere a Master: Further Hasidic Portraits and Legends*, 1982); *Ani Maamin: Un Chant perdu et retrouvé*, 1973 (cantata; *Ani Maamin: A Song Lost and Found Again*, 1973); *Célébration biblique*, 1975 (biographical sketches and stories; *Messengers of God: Biblical Portraits and Legends*, 1976); *Four Hasidic Masters and Their Struggle Against Melancholy*, 1978 (biographical sketches and stories); *Images from the Bible*, 1980 (biographical sketches and stories); *Five Biblical Portraits*, 1981 (biographical sketches and stories); *Paroles d'étranger*, 1982 (biographical sketches and stories); *Somewhere a Master*, 1982 (biographical sketches and stories); *The Six Days of Destruction: Meditations Towards Hope*, 1988 (with Albert H. Friedlander); *Silences et mémoire d'hommes: Essais, histoires, dialogues*, 1989; *Célébration talmudique: Portraits et légendes*, 1991; *Sages and Dreamers: Biblical, Talmudic, and Hasidic Portraits and Legends*, 1991; *Célébration prophétique: Portraits et légendes*, 1998; *Celebrating Elie Wiesel: Stories, Essays, Reflections*, 1998 (Alan Rosen, editor).

Bibliography

Bloom, Harold, ed. *Elie Wiesel's "Night."* New York: Chelsea House, 2001. A collection of critical essays representing a broad spectrum of responses to Wiesel's memoir.

Brown, Robert McAfee. *Elie Wiesel: Messenger to All Humanity.* Rev. ed. Notre Dame, Ind.: University of Notre Dame Press, 1989. A leading Christian theologian provides an important overview and interpretation of Wiesel's multifaceted writing.

Cargas, Harry James. *Conversations with Elie Wiesel.* South Bend, Ind.: Justice Books, 1992. An updated and expanded edition of Cargas's 1976 interviews with Wiesel, this important book features Wiesel speaking not only about the Holocaust but also about his audience, craft, and mission as a witness and writer.

Horowitz, Sara. *Voicing the Void: Muteness and Memory in Holocaust Fiction.* Albany: State University of New York Press, 1997. Contains a helpful discussion of Wiesel's emphasis on the importance of memory.

Kolbert, Jack. *The Worlds of Elie Wiesel: An Overview of His Career and His Major Themes.* Selinsgrove, Pa.: Susquehanna University Press, 2001. A useful starting point for Wiesel's work. Combines biography with literary and philosophical analysis.

Mass, Wendy, ed. *Readings on "Night."* New York: Greenhaven Press, 2000. Includes biographical chapters, a summary of the plot and characters of Wiesel's book, and discussion of major themes, the author's art, relationships in the novel, literary interpretation, and the legacy of the book.

Patterson, David. *In Dialogue and Dilemma with Elie Wiesel.* Wakefield, N.H.: Longwood Academic, 1991. In a series of fascinating interviews, Wiesel speaks not only about the Holocaust but also about his audience, his craft, and his mission as a writer and witness.

_____. *The Shriek of Silence: A Phenomenology of the Holocaust Novel.* Lexington: University Press of Kentucky, 1992. Patterson's book explores the distinctive ways in which Wiesel wrestles with the theme of silence as a feature of the Holocaust and its aftermath.

Rittner, Carol, ed. *Elie Wiesel: Between Memory and Hope.* New York: New York University Press, 1990. A balanced collection of provocative essays, written by scholars from different disciplines.

Rosen, Alan, ed. *Celebrating Elie Wiesel: Stories, Essays, Reflections.* Notre Dame, Ind.: University of Notre Dame Press, 1998. Distinguished scholars reflect on the ethical and religious dimensions of Wiesel's essays and novels.

Rosenfeld, Alvin H., and Irving Greenberg, eds. *Confronting the Holocaust: The Impact of Elie Wiesel.* Bloomington: Indiana University Press, 1978. Including "Why I Write," a significant essay by Wiesel, this volume contains a balanced collection of worthwhile essays written by scholars from varied disciplines.

Roth, John K., and Frederick Sontag. *The Questions of Philosophy.* Belmont, Calif.: Wadsworth, 1988. Wiesel's perspectives on the relationships among God, evil, and human responsibility are discussed in a chapter titled "How Should I Deal with Evil and Death?"

Sibelman, Simon P. *Silence in the Novels of Elie Wiesel.* New York: St. Martin's Press, 1995. This study of a dominant theme in Wiesel is thorough, intelligent, and stimulating.

Wiesel, Elie, and Richard D. Heffner. *Conversations with Elie Wiesel.* Edited by Thomas J. Vinciguerra. New York: Schocken, 2001. A dialog between Wiesel and his interviewer. Offers the reader a wide-ranging discussion in which Wiesel touches on tolerance, nationalism, and state-endorsed killing.

Thornton Wilder

Born: Madison, Wisconsin; April 17, 1897
Died: Hamden, Connecticut; December 7, 1975

Principal long fiction • *The Cabala*, 1926; *The Bridge of San Luis Rey*, 1927; *The Woman of Andros*, 1930; *Heaven's My Destination*, 1934; *The Ides of March*, 1948; *The Eighth Day*, 1967; *Theophilus North*, 1973.

Other literary forms • Thornton Wilder is as well known for his plays as for his fiction. *Our Town* (1938), *The Merchant of Yonkers* (1938, revised as *The Matchmaker*, 1954), and *The Skin of Our Teeth* (1942) are some of his best known. Collections of his short plays were published in *The Angel That Troubled the Waters, and Other Plays* (1928) and *The Long Christmas Dinner, and Other Plays in One Act* (1931). *A Life in the Sun*, commonly known as *The Alcestiad*, was published in 1955, and a collection of his essays, *American Characteristics, and Other Essays*, was published in 1979. A set of cullings from his diaries, *The Journals of Thornton Wilder, 1939-1961*, was released in 1985.

Achievements • Wilder began his career as a teacher and in a sense never gave up the practice of that profession. He attempted to persuade generations of readers of the power of love, the need for individual integrity, the importance of maintaining faith in people's essential goodness. His clear style and straightforward narrative earned for him a broad readership, transcending categories of age, class, or education. Though detractors have labeled him middle class and middlebrow, he received enthusiastic praise throughout his career from such critics as Edmund Wilson, Malcolm Cowley, Edmund Fuller, Henry Seidel Canby, and John Updike. Wilder has been less a subject of scholarly research than some of his contemporaries—F. Scott Fitzgerald and Ernest Hemingway, for example—yet he has remained widely read since his first novel was published in 1926, and his versatility as a writer—of two Pulitzer-Prize-winning full-length plays and dozens of short plays—has brought him worldwide recognition.

Wilder won a Pulitzer Prize for fiction in 1928, the first National Medal for Literature in 1964, and a National Book Award in 1967, besides being the recipient of several honorary doctorates.

Biography • Thornton Niven Wilder was born in Madison, Wisconsin, on April 17, 1897, the son of Amos Parker Wilder and Isabella Thornton Niven Wilder. His father, a newspaper editor, moved the family to Hong Kong in 1906 when he was assigned a diplomatic post there. The young Wilder attended the Kaiser Wilhelm School, then the China Inland Mission Boys' School, where he harbored a brief desire to become a missionary himself. When his family returned to the United States, settling in California, he continued his education at the Thacher School in Ojai, then Berkeley High School, where he first began to write plays and act in class productions. In 1915, he entered Oberlin, a school his father chose because it was less socially elite than his own alma mater, Yale. At Oberlin, Wilder continued his involvement in theatrical productions and contributed prolifically to the college's literary magazine. After two years there, Wilder was allowed by his father to enroll at Yale, where, after a period of home-sickness for Oberlin, he again proved himself, in the words of professor and literary critic William Lyon Phelps, to be "a star of the first magnitude . . . unusually versatile, original, and clever."

Wilder graduated with no specific career goals in mind. His father, believing a European experience would be broadening, sent him to study at the American Academy in Rome for a summer. Meanwhile, he searched for a suitable job for his son and found one at Lawrenceville, a preparatory school in New Jersey. There, when his French classes were over, Wilder began a novel with the working title *Memoirs of a Roman Student,* to be published as *The Cabala* in 1926. In the same year, Wilder took advantage of Lawrenceville's proximity to Princeton to earn his master of arts degree. He took a year's leave of absence from teaching and began work on a new novel, *The Bridge of San Luis Rey,* published to enormous acclaim in 1927, and earning Wilder his first Pulitzer Prize.

In 1929, Wilder was invited to teach at the University of Chicago by an Oberlin classmate, Robert Hutchins, who had just been named president of the prestigious Illinois university. Wilder was writing intensely: *The Woman of Andros* was published in 1930, a collection of short plays in 1931, and *Heaven's My Destination* in 1934. He remained at the University of Chicago until the mid-1930's, teaching one semester and writing during the next. More and more, he was drawn to the theater. He completed *The Merchant of Yonkers,* later revised as *The Matchmaker* (and still later transformed into the Broadway musical *Hello, Dolly!*) in 1937 and then turned to a more serious play, *Our Village,* soon retitled *Our Town.* This play was met with great enthusiasm when it opened in New York in 1938 and earned Wilder his second Pulitzer Prize.

The political upheaval in Europe, soon to involve America, found its way into Wilder's next play, *The Skin of Our Teeth,* which evoked a deep response in audiences both in the United States and abroad; the play was awarded a Pulitzer Prize in 1943. Wilder served in the U.S. Army during World War II, and emerged with his optimism intact and his faith in humanity unshaken.

During the late 1940's, Wilder again turned to fiction, dealing with the problem of authority and dictatorship in *The Ides of March.* This novel reflected his talks with Gertrude Stein, whom Wilder had met in 1934 when Stein was lecturing at the University of Chicago. They shared ideas on the problem of identity and the creation of a believable reality for readers. Stein attempted to deal with these problems in her own book, *Ida, a Novel* (1941); Wilder took as his subject Julius Caesar.

In 1950, Wilder delivered the Charles Eliot Norton lectures at Harvard, then traveled—always a stimulation and joy for him—and worked on *The Alcestiad,* his retelling of the Greek legend of Alcestis. During the early 1960's, he retreated to Arizona to write *The Eighth Day.* By the end of the decade, his pace had slowed. He worked on short plays and completed his quasi-autobiographical *Theophilus North.* He died in his sleep on December 7, 1975.

Analysis • Wilder's seven novels, written over nearly fifty years, show a remarkable consistency in theme and tone. His early books, contemporaneous with Theodore Dreiser's *An American Tragedy* (1925) and Sinclair Lewis's *Arrowsmith* (1925), are far from the realism and naturalism that dominated American literature during the 1920's and 1930's. Though he joined groups active in civil rights and social justice, these themes did not find their way into his works in the manner of John Dos Passos or John Steinbeck. His later works, similarly, show none of the interest in psychoanalysis

Thornton Wilder Society

that may be found in the works of Sherwood Anderson, for example, none of the angry intensity of a Norman Mailer.

Wilder chose not to comment on contemporary politics, social problems, psychological angst, or cultural changes, preferring instead to mine those themes he considered of utmost importance: love, brotherhood, tolerance, and faith. His faith was expressed not in strictly Judeo-Christian terms, but in humanistic convictions that incorporated diverse religious beliefs. Without being didactic, Wilder wished to educate, to inspire, to allow his readers to move beyond an obsession with the individual case to a consideration of humankind and its history. His second novel, *The Bridge of San Luis Rey*, is representative of the themes that recur throughout his works, and his final statement in that book well expresses his one abiding conviction: "There is a land of the living and a land of the dead and the bridge is love, the only survival, the only meaning."

The Cabala • Though Wilder drew on his memories of Rome for his first novel, *The Cabala*, the book is a fantasy, only incidentally autobiographical. The "Cabala" is an aristocratic social circle in which two Americans find themselves involved. These two, Samuele and James Blair, represent Wilder's interest in duality of personality that recurs in later works and results in part from his having been born a twin (his sibling was stillborn). Samuele is a typical Wilder character: innocent, sensitive, stable, with a deep strain of common sense. Blair is the dry intellectual so obsessed by books that he fears real life.

Samuele is the vehicle by which a number of episodes are linked, since he is asked by various members of the Cabala to intervene in the lives of others. First, he is called in to restrain the impetuous and licentious Marcantonio, but fails: The young man engages in incest and then kills himself. Then, Samuele must console the lovely young Alix, unfortunate enough to fall in love with James Blair. Finally, he must deal with the royalist Astrée-Luce in her plot to "prop up" and empower cynical Cardinal Vaini. Samuele is baffled by these obsessed and decadent characters, and is hardly satisfied by an explanation offered to him that the group is possessed by ancient gods who have passed on their power to unsuspecting mortals. Finally, on advice from Vergil's ghost, Samuele returns to America. For Wilder, Europe, for all its richness of culture, was too deeply mired in the past to allow the spirit to grow. Samuele could thrive only in America, a country of youth and intellectual freedom.

The Bridge of San Luis Rey • In his second novel, *The Bridge of San Luis Rey*, Wilder again uses a structure of separate episodes linked by one thread, this time the collapse of an ancient bridge over a chasm in Peru. Again, he offers a religious figure, but instead of the jaded Cardinal, there is the sympathetic brother Juniper, who searches for meaning in the deaths of those who perished: the Marquesa de Montemayor; Pepita, her maid; Esteban, a young Indian; Uncle Pio, an aging actor, and his ward Jaime. Brother Juniper finds that the five were victims of love, and those who survive are forced to a change of consciousness by the deaths of those they spurned or misjudged.

As in *The Cabala*, Wilder explores twinness in the tale of Esteban and his twin brother Manuel. The two are extraordinarily close, and when Manuel falls in love with a woman, Esteban becomes despondent. However, he nurses his brother faithfully after Manuel is injured, suffering his delirious ravings until Manuel dies. Nearly mad with grief, Esteban first assumes his dead brother's identity, then attempts suicide, only to die when the bridge collapses. A sea captain, Alvarado, had offered to sign him on his crew, and tried to console him by reminding him, "We do what we can. We push on, Esteban, as best we can. It isn't for long, you know. Time keeps going by. You'll be surprised at the way time passes." Wilder was always conscious of the brevity of life and the need, therefore, to cling to love where one finds it. In *The Bridge of San Luis Rey*, he urges the celebration and fulfillment of love as the only meaning in the world.

The Woman of Andros • From eighteenth century Peru, Wilder moved to pre-Christian Greece in his third novel, *The Woman of Andros*, again dealing with love; its theme, as in *The Bridge of San Luis Rey*, is "How does one live? . . . What does one do first?" Society on the island of Brynos was not essentially different, according to Wilder, from that of his own America. When Chrysis, the central character, says "Lift every roof, and you will find seven puzzled hearts," she speaks of people's bewilderment in the face of the unknown, their search for communion, their need for love—basic human struggles that are not rooted in any particular time or place.

In 1930, however, a number of critics were disappointed with this message. In a time of economic and social crisis, Wilder seemed to retreat into yet another esoteric setting, far removed from the urgencies of the day. One critic writing in *The New Republic* dubbed Wilder a "Prophet of the Genteel Christ" who wrote for a wealthy elite not interested in social problems. The article touched off a month of debate, with letters supporting or attacking Wilder appearing in each issue of the journal. At the end of December, Wilder finally received his greatest support when Sinclair Lewis, accepting the Nobel Prize for Literature, praised his fellow writer "who in an age of realism dreams the old and lovely dreams of the eternal romantic."

Heaven's My Destination • Throughout the controversy, Wilder remained silent. He was sensitive to the criticism, however, and in his next novel attempted to find a setting and characters that would appear relevant to his own time. *Heaven's My Destination* concerns the misadventures of George Marvin Brush, a salesman of religious textbooks, who travels across Depression-ridden America preaching, moralizing, and interfering in the lives of ordinary citizens. Converted to Bible Belt Christianity by a woman evangelist at Shiloh Baptist College, he has proceeded to spread his own fundamentalist version of the Gospel wherever he goes. Wilder returned to the episodic structure of his first two novels in presenting George's adventures in picaresque form. Unlike Don Quixote, however, with whom George has been compared, Wilder's protagonist is rarely endearing, more often exasperating.

George is different from the "normal" Americans with whom he interacts, yet Wilder is satirizing not only his earnest hero, but also those who spurn him. George, after a while, becomes depressed by his society and exclaims, "It's the world that's crazy. Everybody's crazy except me; that's what's the matter. The whole world's nuts." Why, asks this ardent believer, is God "so slow" in changing things?

For all his misconceptions, George does act upon truly humanistic beliefs. He takes a vow of poverty and occasionally of silence, refuses his interest from the bank and dislikes raises in pay. "I think everybody ought to be hit by the depression equally," he says, as he gives away his money. Like Samuele, George maintains his integrity in an environment that threatens to corrupt him and is selfless in his efforts to aid those who need him—even if they protest against his interference.

George Brush was Wilder's answer to the critics who dismissed his previous works, and in a sense, he gave them what he thought they deserved—a priggish, monomaniacal American overreacting to mundane occurrences. Even with such a cartoon-strip character, however, Wilder could not help but imbue him with gentleness and humility, and for Edmund Wilson, George Brush emerged as a "type of saint . . . and therefore a universal character."

In part, it was George's earnestness, his reluctance to see evil and his determination to do good, that caused Wilder to exclaim, "I'm George Brush." Certainly his persistent faith in humanity unites him with his character, but there is further correspondence in Brush's essential isolation, the loneliness that causes him to reach out for companionship. For Wilder, such isolation was characteristically American; solitude was to be treasured, but loneliness was threatening. He once noted an adage that he thought well expressed the American spirit: "If you can see the smoke from your neighbor's chimney, you're too near." In his next novel, fourteen years later, he created yet another lonely, questing character, but this time Wilder eschewed satire and humor to deal seriously with people powerful before the world, yet powerless before death.

The Ides of March • *The Ides of March*, written just after World War II, deals with an archetypal dictator, Julius Caesar. Here, Wilder aimed to revive the spirit of the man from a palimpsest of historical and fictional treatments. The novel, therefore, becomes a study in identity and a technical challenge in creating for readers a believable reality. In structure, *The Ides of March* differs sharply from Wilder's previous work. He assembles fictionalized letters, diary entries, messages, and documents in an effort to offer a vibrant picture of Roman life. Caesar himself is a man obsessed not only with power but also with death, and he must learn how to celebrate life faced with a dark world and an uncaring universe.

Wilder contrasts Caesar with his friend and counselor Lucius Turrinus, who offers a philosophy that was by then familiar to Wilder's readers: "The universe is not aware that we are here," Lucius tells Caesar. "Hope has never changed tomorrow's weather." However, love could change the world, and Caesar comes to exclaim, "I wish to cry out to all the living and all the dead that there is not part of the universe that is untouched by bliss."

Caesar's urge to seize life and live it to the fullest causes his companions to label him rash and irreverent; but he feels himself to be above them because he has clearly envisioned his own death, and in so doing believes himself "capable of praising the sunlight." Wilder transfers to the Roman dictator much of the sentiment expressed in his play *Our Town*, where Emily Webb dies and is allowed to return to Earth for one day. Only then does she realize how wonderful life is, how desperately she wants to live, and how foolish most people are in squandering their brief existence.

Caesar refuses to be foolish; perhaps he will be ruthless, impetuous, temperamental, passionate—but he will live each moment.

The Ides of March had two major inspirations: the war itself, with its focus on the use and misuse of power, the character of a dictator, and the death of innocents; and a personal confrontation with death—first that of Wilder's friend and mentor Edward Sheldon, a playwright whose character informs Lucius Turrinus, and upon whose wisdom Wilder often relied; then, and most important, the death of his mother, his most ardent supporter and admirer.

The Eighth Day • After *The Ides of March* was published, Wilder devoted nearly two decades to his plays; not until 1967 would he write another novel. In *The Eighth Day*, Wilder returned to an American setting, the turn-of-the-century Midwest, and to traditional narrative. He carefully unfolds the tale of John Barrington Ashley, tried for the murder of his neighbor, Breckenridge Lansing, and found guilty. Five days after being sentenced to death, he escapes with the help of an unknown accomplice. Five years later, Ashley is found innocent on the basis of new evidence. Ashley's flight, which takes him to Chile, is contrasted with the life of his wife and children in a small town that barely tolerates the outlaw's family.

Wilder's concern, however, is not with one family's history, but with the archetypal family, and Ashley represents not one wronged citizen, but the man of the Eighth Day, a new man with faith in humanity and a strong commitment to working toward a better future. Wilder tells his readers that faith and action can bring about a better life. Throughout the novel, he assigns several characters to speak for him, most notably Dr. Gillies, a country physician, who observes:

> Nature never sleeps. The process of life never stands still. The creation has not come to an end. The Bible says that God created people on the sixth day and rested, but each of those days was many millions of years long. That day of rest must have been a short one. Man is not an end but a beginning. We are at the beginning of the second week. We are children of the eighth day.

On the eighth day, people must begin to forge their own futures, and though Dr. Gillies knows that there will be "no Golden Ages and no Dark Ages," still he believes in the power of each individual to work toward the collective fate of humankind.

Because the novel is concerned essentially with imparting a message, the characters—as in *The Cabala* and *Heaven's My Destination*—are not fully realized individuals, but instead are one-dimensional representations of predictable types. The Ashley family, ignored and rebuffed by their neighbors, never lose their aristocratic elegance. They persist in their nightly reading of William Shakespeare even when economic problems would seem severe enough to lower their morale. Here, Wilder pleads for art as the true salvation of humankind, its highest achievement, "the only satisfactory products of civilization."

Through Dr. Gillies, who echoes the sentiments of Chrysis in *The Woman of Andros* and Lucius in *The Ides of March*, Wilder reminds his readers that they occupy only a brief span of time when contrasted with eternity and so must exhibit proper humility. They are small specks in a vast universe, and their duty is not to enhance their own egos, but to work together toward a higher good. "We keep saying that 'we live our lives,'" Dr. Gillies exclaims. "Shucks! Life lives us." Wilder had sent this message for forty years; he insisted again, in the turbulent, self-conscious, self-indulgent late 1960's, on attempting to awaken his readers to his own values.

Theophilus North • Wilder was seventy when *The Eighth Day* was published, the time of a writer's life when he might consider writing his autobiography or memoirs. Wilder, however, chose not to reveal his memories or bare his soul; instead, he wrote a last novel, *Theophilus North*, with a protagonist, he once told an interviewer, who was what his twin brother might have been if he had lived.

Theophilus may be Wilder's imaginary brother, but his life bears striking similarities to that of Wilder himself. He has lived in China, attended Yale, and spent a summer in Rome; after teaching at a boys' preparatory school in New Jersey, he leaves his job to explore life and goes to Newport, Rhode Island—a town where Wilder often vacationed—to set his new course. Like Samuele, Theophilus is gentle, well mannered, polite, helpful. These traits endear him to the Newport natives, and he is asked to intervene in several lives. The structure here, as in many previous Wilder novels, is one of loosely linked episodes.

Theophilus succeeds in such tasks as separating mismatched lovers, liberating an aging man from the manipulation of his daughter, allowing a shrewish wife to mend her ways, extricating one man from his unwitting involvement with criminals, bringing home a wayward husband, finding a lover for a maimed young man, and impregnating a woman whose husband is sterile. Throughout, Theophilus is a typical Wilder hero—a man of good will, of faith, of sincerity.

Theophilus North is Wilder's only novel in which sexuality is of central importance. The sexual episodes are conducted offstage and seem unbelievable and strained. Theophilus, in his seductions and in his everyday relationships with his neighbors, is curiously unaffected and uninvolved. Though he displays emotion, he seems to lack passion.

Wilder's characters, from Samuele to John Ashley, from the circle of Roman aristocrats to Newport society, remain thin and superficial, emblems rather than specific, rounded human beings. Such characterization was in keeping with Wilder's conviction that each individual was, in the long history of the human race, of but little importance. His trials, anguish, suffering, and joy were not significant when placed in the context of all human suffering and all human joy. Rather than writing about individual human beings, Wilder chose to write about humanity; rather than dealing with the intricacies of individual lives, he chose to compress those lives into brief episodes to demonstrate the multiplicity of life.

Wilder, deeply philosophical and reflective, was always the teacher, the educator, with an abiding concern for the future of humanity. "Hope," he wrote in *Theophilus North*, "is a projection of the imagination; so is despair. Despair all too readily embraces the ills it foresees; hope is an energy and arouses the mind to explore every possibility to combat them." In all his works, he exuded hope and, even in dark times, urged his readers to work together in faith and in love.

Linda Simon

Other major works

PLAYS: *The Trumpet Shall Sound*, pb. 1920, pr. 1927; *The Angel That Troubled the Waters, and Other Plays*, pb. 1928 (includes 16 plays); *The Happy Journey to Trenton and Camden*, pr., pb. 1931 (one act); *The Long Christmas Dinner, and Other Plays in One Act*, pb. 1931 (includes *Queens of France, Pullman Car Hiawatha, Love and How to Cure It, Such Things Only Happen in Books,* and *The Happy Journey to Trenton and Camden*); *The Long Christmas Dinner*, pr., pb. 1931 (one act; as libretto in German, 1961; translation and music by Paul Hindemith); *Lucrece*, pr. 1932, pb. 1933 (adaptation of André Obey's *Le Viol de Lucrèce*); *A Doll's House*, pr. 1937 (adaptation of Henrik Ibsen's play); *Our Town*, pr., pb. 1938; *The Merchant of Yonkers*, pr. 1938, pb. 1939 (adaptation of Johann Nestroy's *Einen Jux will er sich machen*); *The Skin of Our Teeth*, pr., pb. 1942; *Our Century*, pr., pb. 1947; *The Matchmaker*, pr. 1954, pb. 1956 (revision of *The Merchant of Yonkers*); *A Life in the Sun*, pr. 1955, pb. 1960 (in German), pb. 1977 (in English; commonly known as *The Alcestiad*; act 4 pb. as *The Drunken Sisters*); *Plays for Bleecker Street*, pr. 1962 (3 one-acts: *Someone from Assissi*; *Infancy*, pb. 1961; and *Childhood*, pb. 1960); *The Collected Short Plays of Thornton Wilder*, pb. 1997-1998 (2 volumes).

SCREENPLAYS: *Our Town*, 1940 (with Frank Craven and Harry Chantlee); *Shadow of a Doubt*, 1943 (with Sally Benson and Alma Revelle).

NONFICTION: *The Intent of the Artist*, 1941; *American Characteristics, and Other Essays*, 1979; *The Journals of Thornton Wilder, 1939-1961*, 1985.

TRANSLATION: *The Victors*, 1948 (of Jean-Paul Sartre's play *Morts sans sépulture*).

Bibliography

Blank, Martin, ed. *Critical Essays on Thornton Wilder.* New York: G. K. Hall, 1996. A solid collection of criticism on Wilder. Includes bibliographical references and an index.

Blank, Martin, Dalma Hunyadi Brunauer, and David Garrett Izzo, eds. *Thornton Wilder: New Essays.* West Cornwall, Conn.: Locust Hill Press, 1999. A contemporary look at Wilder and his oeuvre.

Bloom, Harold, ed. *Thornton Wilder.* Philadelphia: Chelsea House, 2003. Collection of critical essays about Wilder that have been assembled for student use.

Bryer, Jackson R., ed. *Conversations with Thornton Wilder.* Jackson: University Press of Mississippi, 1992. A collection of interviews with Wilder, presenting interesting perspectives on the man and his literary works. Index.

Burbank, Rex J. *Thornton Wilder.* 2d ed. Boston: Twayne, 1978. In this updated version of the 1962 edition, Burbank traces the history of critical controversy surrounding Wilder's work, offers insights into his methods of fictional and dramatic composition, and assesses his work's relative merits. Chronology, bibliography.

Castronovo, David. *Thornton Wilder.* New York: Ungar, 1986. A useful introductory study of Wilder's works, both novels and plays, including chronology, notes, and bibliography.

Goldstone, Richard H. *Thornton Wilder: An Intimate Portrait.* New York: Saturday Review Press, 1975. An intimate portrait of Wilder by a close friend who had written previous studies on the subject, had access to personal documents, and interviewed family and friends. Includes notes, a selected bibliography, and an index.

Harrison, Gilbert A. *The Enthusiast: A Life of Thornton Wilder.* New York: Ticknor and Fields, 1983. A chatty biographical study of Wilder by a biographer who was provided access to Wilder's notes, letters, and photographs. Harrison successfully recreates Wilder's life and the influences, both good and bad, that shaped him.

Simon, Linda. *Thornton Wilder: His World.* Garden City, N.Y.: Doubleday, 1979. A solid biographical study of Wilder that includes examinations of his published works and photographs, notes, a bibliography, and an index.

Walsh, Claudette. *Thornton Wilder: A Reference Guide, 1926-1990.* New York: G. K. Hall, 1993. A complete guide to Wilder and his works. Includes bibliographical references and an index.

Ethel Wilson

Born: Port Elizabeth, South Africa; January 20, 1888
Died: Vancouver, British Columbia, Canada; December 22, 1980

Principal long fiction • *Hetty Dorval,* 1947; *The Innocent Traveller,* 1949; *The Equations of Love,* 1952; *Lilly's Story,* 1953; *Swamp Angel,* 1954; *Love and Salt Water,* 1956.

Other literary forms • Eleven short stories and eight essays by Ethel Wilson were published in magazines between 1937 and 1964. Two of the stories, "Hurry, Hurry!" and "Mrs. Golightly and the First Convention," were later anthologized, and two others, "I Just Love Dogs" and "The Window," were selected for *Best British Short Stories of 1938* and *Best American Short Stories: 1959,* respectively. These four stories, three of the others, and one of the essays, along with nine stories and an essay not previously published, were collected in *Mrs. Golightly, and Other Stories* (1961). Besides the stories and essays, seven excerpts from novels also appeared separately as short stories in magazines. One of these, "Miss Tritt," from *The Equations of Love,* was anthologized as a short story.

Achievements • Wilson was among the Canadian authors of the 1930's who broke away from the frontier tradition of provincial and didactic romances. She adapted to Canadian backgrounds the universal themes and methods of the realistic and psychological novel. She was one of the first Canadians to achieve a critical reputation abroad, not indeed as a major novelist, but certainly as an important minor one. Her novels are in the main current of the British and French realistic tradition, especially that of the early twentieth century, showing affinities with the works of E. M. Forster, Virginia Woolf, Arnold Bennett, Ivy Compton-Burnett, and Marcel Proust. Nevertheless, she maintained strong individuality in both theme and form. She wrote that authors can be "endangered by the mould or formula becoming apparent, and then the story has no life." Without being innovative, therefore, her novels have a great deal of variety of theme and approach, so that they are difficult to classify.

Perhaps because Wilson did not attempt to follow literary trends, and perhaps also because she began publishing relatively late in her life, when she was nearly fifty, her works did not have a dramatic impact on Canadian letters. She was publishing out of her generation, and her realism and understatement seemed somewhat old-fashioned to those authors of the 1930's who were following naturalistic trends. Nevertheless, she was influential in raising the quality of the art in Canada and in quietly introducing the theme of women "finding themselves" in some sense, well before the theme became popular among feminists. Her heroines are not necessarily strong or aggressive but they mature, meet the vicissitudes of their lives with determination and ingenuity, and for the most part succeed in small but important ways. Wilson's treatment of this theme and her impeccable craftsmanship contributed significantly to the maturing of the novel in Canada.

Biography • Ethel Davis Wilson was born in Port Elizabeth, South Africa, on January 20, 1888, to Robert William Bryant and Lila (Malkin) Bryant. Her mother died when she was only two, and her father took her to Staffordshire, England, to be reared by her maternal grandmother and successive aunts and uncles. Her family members were involved in a number of literary activities, including reading, journalism, and translation, and were acquainted with Matthew Arnold and Arnold Bennett. This literary atmosphere no doubt stimulated her interest in letters, and the literary allusions and quotations in her works demonstrate a comprehensive familiarity with the English tradition. Her father died when she was ten, and she went to Vancouver, British Columbia, to join her grandmother, who had moved there. Many of these family and early personal experiences are recounted in *The Innocent Traveller*, the semi-biographical novel based on the life of her aunt.

In Vancouver, Wilson attended Miss Gordon's School, but she was sent to Trinity Hall School in Southport, England, for her secondary education. In 1907, she graduated from Vancouver Normal School with a Second Class Teacher's Certificate. Between 1907 and 1920, she taught in Vancouver elementary schools.

On January 4, 1921, Wilson married Dr. Wallace Wilson. Their marriage was a happy one, marked by a good deal of traveling in Canada, Europe, and around the Mediterranean, and the successful development of both their careers. Dr. Wilson became a respected physician; he studied internal medicine in Vienna in 1930, represented Canada at the British Medical Association's convention in 1938 and at the World Health Organization in Paris in 1947, and was president of the Canadian Medical Association in 1946 and 1947. The relationship between the Wilsons may have provided details for the happy marriages and the deepening love relationships in *Hetty Dorval*, *Lilly's Story*, and *Love and Salt Water*. The love of travel is also obvious in her work; travel is healing, broadening, and sensitizing to her characters, and Wilson's ability to describe the essential atmosphere of various locales is one of her strongest attributes.

Wilson published her first short story in 1937, and another in 1939 before her career was interrupted by World War II. Although Dr. Wilson was in the Canadian Army and Wilson herself served by editing a Red Cross magazine between 1940 and 1945, she made little use of wartime experiences in her novels, except tangentially in *The Innocent Traveller* and *Love and Salt Water*. Only the short story "We Have to Sit Opposite" deals specifically with wartime problems.

It is likely that Wilson's career in writing was encouraged by ill health. She was a victim of arthritis, which by 1956 had become so severe that she could not walk around in London, as she described in her essay "To Keep the Memory of So Worthy a Friend." She wrote, "One of the advantages of being lame is that one can sit and think. . . . And so I often think and think." In her last three novels, several major characters suffer handicaps, either physical or psychological, which affect their relationships with others in various ways and that must be transcended. No doubt her own disability enabled her to interpret this theme sympathetically.

The late 1940's and the 1950's were Wilson's most productive years, all of her novels and most of her short stories and essays being written or published during that period. At the peak of her success, after the publication of *Swamp Angel*, she received three awards: an honorary doctorate from the University of British Columbia in 1955, a special medal from the Canada Council in 1961 for contributions to Canadian Literature, and the Lorne Pierce Gold Medal from the Royal Society of Canada in 1964.

Dr. Wilson died in 1966, and Ethel Wilson lived in retirement in Vancouver until her death in 1980.

Analysis • Although Wilson's canon is small, it is of high quality. The writing style is direct, simple, and expressive. Only occasionally, in the early books, does the diction or syntax call attention to itself as excellent. In general, only if one should try to paraphrase a passage or change a word would he become aware of that rightness of style that is typical of an artist. Passages describing the beauty of nature are most immediately impressive. Wilson's account of the train journey of the Edgeworths across Canada to Vancouver, in *The Innocent Traveller*, offers a vivid impression of the countryside and evokes the haunting vastness of the plains and forests stretching northward from the train track to the arctic circle. Magnificent descriptions of the northern lights occur in more than one book, and the mist-shrouded or sun-brightened mountains of the Vancouver area are sketched with a sensitive pen.

Less frequent but equally impressive are descriptions of unsightly scenes, such as the interior of the slovenly Johnson apartment in *Tuesday and Wednesday* (published in *The Equations of Love*). It is not only in description, however, that Wilson excels; her humor is deft, ironic, and humane in passages such as the chapter "Nuts and Figs," from *The Innocent Traveller*, in which Great-Grandfather Edgeworth, in his declining days, proposes to two worthy lady friends in one afternoon and is refused, to the gratification of all three. Thoughtful and philosophical passages are also subtly presented, so that except for a few intrusive statements in the early, less integrated books, the concepts are suggested through economical language and apt symbols.

For Wilson, nature is not only a major inspiration for description, but also a method of characterization. Most of her protagonists are close to nature. Their ability to love and the essential civilization of their emotions are measured by their appreciation of the beauties and dangers of the Canadian mountains, forests, and waters. One notable exception is the garrulous Topaz Edgeworth, who exists in her human relationships rather than in nature, and the other is Hetty Dorval, an antagonist, whose appreciation of nature is one of the deceptive charms of her evil. Wilson's characters are firmly rooted in their environments and grow out of them. Her attitude toward them is dispassionately empathetic; they are clearly and humorously drawn, with subtle complexities. All are believable, and the best of them are memorable. She develops understanding of even her most unsympathetic characters, to the extent that plot is often weakened because she is drawn into digressions about the characters, about whom she cares more than she cares about careful plot structure. Topaz Edgeworth, Nell Severance, Lilly Hughes, and Maggie Lloyd are her most convincing creations, and it is the success of their characterization which causes *The Innocent Traveller*, *Lilly's Story*, and *Swamp Angel* to be her best novels.

If style and characterization are what make Wilson's novels outstanding, the plots are what keep them from being great. Plotting appears always to have been difficult for Wilson. Her admirers defend the inconsequentiality of her plots as true to life, expressing a philosophy about the fortuitous connections, or lack of connections, between the events in a person's history. Wilson minimizes suspense as a plot device; in fact, she often uses a technique of revealing future events, since causality interests her more than suspense. Nevertheless, the novels that are most effectively plotted, *Lilly's Story* and *Swamp Angel*, are recognized to be her best.

The Equations of Love • The title of Wilson's third book, *The Equations of Love*, suggests her recurring themes as a novelist. The typical protagonist of a Wilson novel is orphaned or otherwise separated from her family, as Wilson herself was as a child.

Deprived of parental love, she becomes independent but lonely. This typical protagonist usually takes a journey, which is both a literal "trip"—aboard ship or into the Canadian wilderness—and an interior voyage of self-discovery. She is both soothed and awed by her insignificance in the natural world, which is beautiful but indifferent. Out of her new self-awareness, she learns to give of herself and to build a relationship, usually but not necessarily marriage, that brings new meaning to her life, either happiness or philosophical maturity. Love is the solution to this symbolic orphanhood, yet love, too, is imperfect. Orphanhood leaves its mark, and people make do with various "equations of love." This sense of irrevocable loss, of necessary compromise, saves Wilson's love-stories from sentimentality without veering toward cynicism. There is nobility in the aspiration toward love and self-subordination, triumph in even the flawed achievement of those graces. Wilson is impressed by the human ability to transcend egotism through whatever equation of love is possible to each individual.

Hetty Dorval • For a first novel, *Hetty Dorval* is exceptionally good, although a melodramatic climax undercuts the subtleties of its characterization. It introduces Wilson's recurring themes: orphanhood, egotism, and love; the tempering of the ego by nature or travel; the lasting impact of momentary impressions or casual coincidences; the emotional maturation of a young woman. It is the story of Frances Burnaby, and the influence of Hetty Dorval on her maturation. Hetty crosses Frankie's path only a half-dozen times, but the temptation that she represents is very strong. The two are parallel in certain important respects: Both are only children, and both are reared with considerable protection and privilege. Both are attracted by elements of wildness, such as the turbulent Thompson River and the flight of wild geese. Frankie, however, has been reared by her parents with friends and loving discipline.

By contrast, illegitimate Hetty's mother, Mrs. Broom, has hidden her maternal role, and with it her model of a loving relationship, to give Hetty a superior social standing: She has pretended to be Hetty's nurse and later her lady's maid, so that Hetty has learned tyranny and self-indulgence. Hetty is seraphically beautiful, with selfish charm, concerned only with her own pleasures. Frankie's mother calls her "The Menace" even before she knows Hetty's full story. Hetty's beauty and charm and her elemental wildness attract Frankie as a child. Even though the younger girl gives up the older woman's friendship, in obedience to her parents' orders, she does not understand the evil in Hetty's character. As she grows up and gains experience, however, in each subsequent contact with Hetty she learns more and comprehends more fully the destructiveness of Hetty's egotism. Frankie's full comprehension of what is morally wrong with Hetty's way of life comes when Richard Tretheway, the man she loves, falls in love with Hetty, and she has to decide what action she should take.

Three of the major characters in the story are orphaned: Frankie loses her father during the course of the story; Richard has lost his mother before Frankie meets him; and Hetty is a psychological orphan, having no publicly acknowledged father or mother. Each has dealt with the problems of isolation in a different way. Frankie grows to love the Tretheway family and builds new familial relationships with them; Richard has tried to substitute as a mother to his younger sister Molly; and Hetty has turned to self-indulgence and the collection and abandonment of men. Each of these compensatory behaviors is one possible equation of love, but Hetty's is not honest or giving. The traits in Frankie's character that are similar to Hetty's are finally subordinated in Frankie as she learns to love. Although Hetty comments near the end of the book about their kinship, Frankie has moved beyond Hetty in self-control and compassion, and has thus ended her egocentric solitude.

The Innocent Traveller • Wilson's second novel, *The Innocent Traveller,* is a radical departure from her archetypal plot line. Topaz Edgeworth is not a solitary orphan, but a beloved child in a large and close family. Family is an all-pervasive concept throughout the book; characters are designated according to their role in the family, which changes as they age. Father becomes Grandfather and finally Great-Grandfather Edgeworth. Topaz herself is defined successively in terms of child, daughter, sister, aunt, and great-aunt. Topaz does lose her mother when she is young, but Father marries Mother's sister, and the family continues with virtually imperceptible interruption. Topaz continues to live with her father until she is middle-aged, and after his death, she lives with her older sister in much the same role of dependent daughter. Even with the death of the sister, she lives with her niece in virtually the same role, as if she were daughter to her niece. Although she moves to Canada, the wilderness does not impress her, nor does the new environment broaden her sympathies. *The Innocent Traveller* is a happy book, Topaz a happy woman, with a sense of warmth and security very different from the solitary mood of the other novels. Complementing this happy mood are glowing descriptions of the English and Canadian landscapes and sensitive expressions of a generous, witty, and perceptive philosophy.

What this book contributes to analysis of Wilson's thematic development is the contrast it provides with her recurring story of orphanhood and reconciliation. Topaz is never orphaned; she also never matures. Topaz is characterized as a delightfully irrepressible child, a lovable nonconformist, but gradually (and only between the lines), an irresponsible eccentric, and finally an irritating, futile burden on her family. She is loved, but she does not love deeply in return; she is an affectionate family member, but she does not feel the needs and tragedies of others. She remains childishly egocentric to the last of her life. After her death, "there is no mark of her that I know, no more than the dimpling of the water caused by the wind . . . and when we met together . . . perhaps no one remembers, until afterwards, to mention her name." The contrast between Topaz and Wilson's typical orphaned protagonists is striking. Topaz is never independent and never feels solitary; therefore, she never comes to value loving relationships. She never goes off alone to come to terms with herself and her universe; therefore, she never comes to terms with society. She never feels insignificant in nature; therefore, she never feels the need to establish significance through commitment and love. Having realized these themes from the converse and happy side, Wilson was prepared to use them more powerfully in *The Equations of Love* and *Swamp Angel.*

Tuesday and Wednesday • *Tuesday and Wednesday,* a novella, the first part of *The Equations of Love,* deals with grotesque and pitiable "equations" in a mood of dark humor or satire. It is the story of the marital relationship of Myrt and Mort Johnson, no longer a marriage of love, but an equation of shared resentment and frustration, lightened by moments of sensuality and a habitual tender impulse. Mort is shiftless, envious, self-deceived, but good-natured and capable of friendship. Myrt is self-pitying, domineering, lazy, sporadically sensual, often spiteful, but kind when it is no trouble to be kind. They live apart from most human contacts; Mort is too feckless and Myrt too lazy to entertain. They have no family except one aunt and one orphaned cousin, Victoria May Tritt, to whom they are indifferently kind because she is even more lonely and repressed than they are. This kindness passes in her mind as beneficence, and her gratitude constitutes a kind of love for them. Mort has a friend, Eddie, whom Myrt dislikes because of his drinking and brawling, but the two men share a bond of camaraderie and wishful thinking. These are the relationships that pass for love in the seedy near-slums of the city.

One evening, Mort meets Eddie, drunk; during a search in the dark for Eddie's lost suitcase, the inebriated Eddie falls off a pier and drowns. Mort, in his efforts to save his friend, falls into the water and is dragged under by Eddie to his death. Witnesses testify to Eddie's drunkenness, and the police conclude that both men were drunk, reporting the accident to Myrt in those terms. In her typical spite and self-pity, Myrt is not grieved, but affronted by Mort's drinking, abandoning her, and damaging her reputation by his association with the brawling Eddie. To salvage her self-esteem, she bitterly adopts the role of martyr. Victoria May has seen the meeting of Eddie and Mort, however, and knows that Mort was not drunk. In her love for both Myrt and Mort, she tells not only that part of the story but also the fiction that Mort dived after Eddie in a heroic attempt to save his friend. Thus, in her love for this unlikely pair, she both redeems Mort and comforts his wife by recalling Myrt's love for Mort, restoring her self-esteem, and establishing her right to grieve.

Even though *Tuesday and Wednesday* is darkly satirical, the story is in some ways the clearest of Wilson's statements about the success, however flawed, of the human drive for love as a solution to loneliness. Antagonistic though they may be, Myrt and Mort nevertheless love each other in their own way and cling together against their isolation. Mort's love for Myrt, with so little to thrive on, is sad and admirable. Myrt's need for Mort to pierce the shell of her egotism is believable and moving. Victoria May is almost heroic in her lie for Mort. Such unsatisfactory substitutes for love are pitiable, but they transcend the dingy and uninspiring atmosphere in which these characters live.

Lilly's Story • *Lilly's Story*, the second half of *The Equations of Love*, approaches the equations in a more positive way, although the heroine begins even more unpromisingly than Myrt and Mort. Lilly is an abandoned child, growing up like an alley cat. Never having experienced love, she expects none, and her first equation of love is the lust she excites to acquire food and stockings from men. Running away from the police, she gets a job as a waitress in a small town some distance from Vancouver and finds another equation of love, a man who provides her some temporary security, like "a kennel into which a bitch crawls." When this man leaves, and she finds she is pregnant, she goes to another small town farther into the wilderness and gets a job as a maid.

In this new environment, Lilly knows love for the first time, her love for her baby; and for her baby's sake, she invents a dead husband and behaves with such circumspection that she earns the respect of the couple whom she serves. Respect is a new equation of love. In this wilderness location, she also learns a new identification with nature that she could not have known in the slums of Vancouver. She lets Eleanor grow up in touch with this natural environment. Lilly also admires the pretty home and gentle manners of her employers, and she allows Eleanor, her child, to receive training from Mrs. Butler, determined that Eleanor will have a better life than her own. Eventually, Lilly leaves the Butlers and finds employment as housekeeper in a hospital. She and the Matron become close friends, and Lilly begins to build relationships that are overcoming her circle of self-protection. Eleanor grows into a lady and goes to nursing school, where she meets and marries a young lawyer. It is from this marriage that Lilly learns what love can be and what she has missed, when she sees Eleanor

> come up to her husband with her face raised, and on her face a revealed look that Lilly had never seen on Eleanor's face nor on any face. . . . She had lived for nearly fifty years, and she had never seen this thing before. So this was love, each for each, and she had never known it.

Soon after this, a threat from Lilly's past drives her to Toronto, where she meets a widower and marries him, not with the passion that she has observed in Eleanor, but at least with "the perfect satisfaction which is one equation of love."

Lilly could be another Mrs. Broom (*Hetty Dorval*), but instead of hiding her motherhood and spoiling her child, Lilly drags herself out of that egocentric circle in order to prevent egocentrism in Eleanor, and in so doing, she finds loving relationships that almost transform her. Lilly starts off too badly and is too warped by her orphanhood ever to be totally transformed by love, but at least her story is a triumph of the power of love over egocentrism.

Swamp Angel • Maggie Lloyd, is triply solitary: Her mother died when she was a baby, her young husband in the war, and her baby and her father shortly thereafter. Maggie, unlike Wilson's other orphaned heroines, is never trapped in egocentrism by her loneliness. She has too much giving in her nature, and makes a second marriage out of compassion. Her story opens when she leaves that mistaken equation of marriage and goes into the wilderness, not to find but to reestablish herself. She finds a job as cook and assistant manager to a fishing lodge owner who has been lamed and can no longer manage alone. His wife, Vera, is the orphan in this story who has been warped and damaged by her loneliness. Vera finds no comfort in the beauty of the wilderness that restores Maggie after her separation. Vera, to the contrary, longs to return to the city from which she came, and instead of building new relationships that might redeem her, she nags at her husband and grows jealous of his admiration for Maggie.

Maggie eventually tries to commit suicide but cannot, and the story ends with Maggie trying to think how to break through Vera's egocentrism to help her. Another pair of "orphans" in this story are Maggie's friends Nell Severance and her daughter Hilda. Although their story constitutes a subplot, in some ways they are more important to the theme than is Vera. Nell is a widow who has had more than her share of excitement and romance. She used to be a juggler on the stage, and she met and married a man she loved deeply. Because of her career and eventful marriage, however, she neglected Hilda to the extent that Hilda has always felt a degree of isolation and alienation from her mother. Nell's loved memento from her past life is a small revolver, the Swamp Angel, which was part of her juggling act. Hilda has always resented the revolver, as it reminds her of her neglect as a child, but she has never told her mother of her feelings: This is her gift of love to her mother. Nell is aware of Hilda's aversion to the gun, although she does not know the reason; one day she boxes it and sends it to Maggie: This is her gift of love to her daughter. Hilda goes away on a vacation, and comes back with new self-knowledge and recognition of her love for Albert Cousins, whom she marries not long before Nell dies. Thus, she builds new relationships to end her sense of solitude. These are very loving relationships, successful resolutions to the problems of isolation.

Swamp Angel makes use of two important symbols that specify more clearly than any of Wilson's earlier books the meanings of wilderness/egotism and orphanhood/ love. While in the wilderness, Maggie goes swimming. She feels happy, strong, elemental, and in control of her movements. She can swim wherever she wishes; she is alone and completely independent. She also realizes, however, that this feeling is an illusion: She is not a god. The water is sensual and comforting, but it could drown her as impartially as it now buoys her. She swims back to her boat and returns to the lodge, to the things of civilization and the friends she serves in her job. The other key symbol is the Swamp Angel itself. It is a symbol of Nell's past, and she clings to it until she realizes that it makes Hilda uncomfortable. She gives it to Maggie to discard, reflecting that the symbol is less important than the reality, which cannot be taken away, but which grows less important as she grows nearer to death. Like the water in which Maggie swims, the gun symbolizes independence and control, but it also symbolizes egotism. In giving it away, Nell severs herself from the past in order to build a better relationship with her daughter. Unlike Maggie and Nell, Vera clings to her past, cannot find herself in nature, and so cannot build loving relationships with her husband and son. She tries to drown herself in the same lake where Maggie swims and where she throws Nell's gun.

Ethel Wilson's books can be summed up as minor masterpieces of style, insightful, witty, believable, and intelligent. They are prevented from being major works by faults in plotting, and they have not had a great influence upon literary trends. Nevertheless, they are all readable and entertaining, and the best are compelling. They deserve renewed attention in this age of increased receptivity to literature by and about women.

Carol I. Croxton

Other major works

SHORT FICTION: *Mrs. Golightly, and Other Stories*, 1961.

MISCELLANEOUS: *Ethel Wilson: Stories, Essays, and Letters*, 1987 (David Stouck, editor).

Bibliography

Bhelande, Anjali. *Self Beyond Self: Ethel Wilson and Indian Philosophical Thought.* Mumbaim, India: S.N.D.T. Women's University, Bharatiya Vidya Bhavan, 1996. Examines the Indic influences on Wilson and her philosophy.

McAlpine, Mary. *The Other Side of Silence: A Life of Ethel Wilson.* Madeira Park, B.C.: Harbour, 1989. The first full biography about Wilson to be published.

McMullan, Lorraine, ed. *The Ethel Wilson Symposium.* Ottawa: University of Ottowa Press, 1982. Papers presented at a conference held April 24-26, 1981, at the University of Ottawa, Canada. McMullan's introduction is especially useful.

McPherson, Hugo. "Fiction: 1940-1960." In *Literary History of Canada: Canadian Literature in English*, edited by Carl Frederick Klinck. 2d ed. Vol. 2. Toronto: University of Toronto Press, 1976. Wilson's fiction is discussed in the context of a supposed "search for identity" thought to infuse Canadian literature's development in the mid-twentieth century. McPherson notes a contrary individuality in Wilson's writing that transcends her failure at times to reconcile her creative impulses as both "artist and sibyl."

Mitchell, Beverley. "Ethel Wilson." In *Canadian Writers and Their Works: Fiction Series*, edited by Robert Lecker, Jack David, and Ellen Quigley. Vol. 6. Toronto: ECW Press, 1985. Wilson's life and complete works are thoroughly examined. An exhaustive bibliography follows Mitchell's straightforward, readable analysis, making this study a must for Wilson readers.

Pacey, Desmond. *Ethel Wilson*. New York: Twayne, 1967. This thorough, readable overview of Wilson's long and short fiction is not deeply analytical, but it does consider Wilson's lightly ironic vision and her valuable contribution to Canadian literature despite her relatively short publishing history. Despite its age, the book still contains some useful insights. A selected bibliography and an index are included.

Stouck, David. *Ethel Wilson: A Critical Biography*. Toronto: University of Toronto Press, 2003. Biography of Wilson that examines her life in the context of her writings and seeks to resolve contradictions between her public and private personas.

Woodcock, George. "Innocence and Solitude: The Fictions of Ethel Wilson." In *Modern Times*. Vol. 3. in *The Canadian Novel*, edited by John Moss. Toronto: NC Press, 1982. Woodcock discusses Wilson's originality and vision as they are expressed in her novels and novellas.

_____. "On Ethel Wilson." In *The World of Canadian Writing: Critiques and Recollections*. Vancouver, B.C.: Douglas and McIntyre, 1980. Slightly revised since its 1974 publication, this reflective personal essay enumerates the strengths of Wilson's personality and her unique works. This volume contains an index of the names of authors mentioned or treated in the book.

Larry Woiwode

Born: Carrington, North Dakota; October 30, 1941

Principal long fiction • *What I'm Going to Do, I Think*, 1969; *Beyond the Bedroom Wall: A Family Album*, 1975; *Poppa John*, 1981; *Born Brothers*, 1988; *Indian Affairs*, 1992.

Other literary forms • Larry Woiwode is known primarily for his longer fiction, but he also frequently published short stories in such prominent literary periodicals as *The Atlantic Monthly* and *The New Yorker*; several of his stories were chosen for anthologies of the year's best. He has written book reviews and essays for many newspapers, including *The New York Times*. His collections of essays include *Aristocrat of the West: The Story of Harold Schafer* (2000) and *What I Think I Did: A Season of Survival in Two Acts* (2000). His collections of short fiction include *The Neumiller Stories* (1989), which contains thirteen previously uncollected stories, including three penned during the 1980's, expands the "family album" of narratives about the Neumiller clan that Woiwode began in his novels *Beyond the Bedroom Wall* and *Born Brothers*. He also published a well-received book of poetry, *Even Tide* (1977).

Achievements • Woiwode's first novel, *What I'm Going to Do, I Think*, won for him the prestigious William Faulkner Foundation Award for the "most notable first novel" of 1969 and the American Library Association Notable Book award in 1970 and brought him immediate critical attention. It was a best seller and was translated into several foreign languages. His second novel, *Beyond the Bedroom Wall*, actually begun before *What I'm Going to Do, I Think*, was nominated for both the National Book Award and the National Book Critics Circle Award, and it won the American Library Association Notable Book award in 1976. It became an even bigger commercial and critical success than his first novel. Woiwode's third novel, *Poppa John*, however, was much less successful commercially and critically. The novel's premise and protagonist indeed represented a departure from the regional narrative Woiwode had successfully employed in his previous fiction, but it did earn the Cornerstone Best Book of the Year Award in 1982.

    Poppa John notwithstanding, critics are quick to credit Woiwode's idiosyncratic, family-centered narratives with helping indirectly to rehabilitate the family chronicle, a genre long considered out of fashion. After nearly a decade of relative publishing silence, Woiwode returned to this narrative genre in *Born Brothers* and *The Neumiller Stories*. Woiwode's evolving canon of Neumiller narratives depicts prodigal sons and daughters who, no matter where they tread, fulfill their destiny in rediscovering their roots and the family relationships that nurtured them early in their lives. Woiwode unabashedly admires the traditional nuclear family, and his fiction underscores the value of finding one's way by retracing one's steps. His narrative strength is thus seen in the fact that, even among readers accustomed to despondent, "lost" protagonists preoccupied with discovering the mysteries of life in the squalor of the city or some illicit relationship, Woiwode can make such old-fashioned premises seem startlingly fresh and appealing.

    In the ebb and flow of many a writer's career, an acclaimed "first novel" often permanently overshadows subsequent efforts, and the disappointment with—and apparent dearth of fresh ideas that followed after—the publication of *Poppa John* provoked many critics and readers to wonder if Woiwode had lost his narrative vision. Such concerns were answered with the publication of *Born Brothers* and *The Neumiller Stories*.

Biography • Larry Alfred Woiwode (pronounced "why-wood-ee") was born in Carrington, North Dakota, October 30, 1941, and spent his early years in nearby Sykeston, a predominantly German settlement amid the rugged, often forbidding north-midwestern terrain. No doubt the beauty as well as the stark loneliness of this landscape heightened the author's appreciation for the effect of nature upon individual character. At the age of ten, he moved with his family to Manito, Illinois, another evocatively midwestern environment capable of nurturing the descriptive powers of a budding fiction writer.

Woiwode attended the University of Illinois for five years but failed to complete a bachelor's degree, leaving the university in 1964 with an associate of arts in rhetoric. He met his future wife, Carol Ann Patterson, during this period and married her on May 21, 1965. After leaving Illinois, Woiwode moved to New York City and supported his family with freelance writing, publishing in *The New Yorker* and other prestigious periodicals while working on two novels.

Woiwode was a writer-in-residence at the University of Wisconsin, Madison, and had extended teaching posts at Wheaton College (Illinois) and at the State University of New York at Binghamton, where he served as a faculty member (intermittently) beginning in 1983. In 1977, he was awarded the Doctor of Letters degree from North Dakota State University. He and his family returned to North Dakota in 1978 to maintain an organic farm.

Analysis • To understand Woiwode's craft and achievement, one must finally recognize the essentially religious character of his narratives and their thematic structure. He is an advocate for restoring a moral, even religious voice to modern letters. Although believing that the most important human questions are, in fact, religious ones, Woiwode rejects the notion that there can be legitimate, compelling "novels of ideas"; for him, such fiction connotes mere propagandizing. Woiwode handles such questions not by placing philosophical soliloquies in the mouths of sophisticated, worldly protagonists, but by creating authentically ordinary characters, and settling them comfortably into the concrete and utterly mundane world of daily life.

In achieving this effective depiction of what might be called heightened normality, Woiwode's prose is consistently active, alive, and unassuming, approaching at times the crisp clarity of Ernest Hemingway but touched with a finely tuned lyricism. Although Woiwode has sometimes been criticized for lapsing too easily into didacticism or marring an otherwise evocative scene with excessive detail, his keen eye for the extraordinary ordinariness of life makes his narrative vision compelling and believable.

As a novelist, Woiwode stands apart from most of his contemporaries in refusing to drown his characters in the angst-ridden excesses that have become so conventional in the modern American novel. His characters are not helpless victims of their times but participants in them; they are accountable not so much for what has happened to them but for what they do in response to their circumstances. Their conflicts, from Chris Van Eenanam's enigmatic search for manhood in *What I'm*

Going to Do, I Think to Poppa John's drive to recover his self-identity, are not merely contrived psychological dramas played out inside their own consciousness, but compelling confrontations with the very concrete world of everyday life. This is a world that registers as authentic to the reader precisely because of Woiwode's gift for realism.

Woiwode's characters eventually recognize that the answers to their dilemmas are only partly in themselves. In the reestablishment of personal trust in friendships and the nostalgia of forgotten familial relationships, they recover a sense of balance and worth in themselves. However obliquely, each major Woiwode character finds himself in a quest for a transcendent moral order, a renewed trust in God and humanity that would give him a reference point for his life. This quest animates their rejection of narcissism and a search for a love and security that only marital and familial relationships can foster.

© Nancy Crampton

Woiwode's willingness to affirm that these relationships are central to self-fulfillment and to the stability of American culture makes him unique among a generation of writers whose thematic concerns tend to focus on their characters' dehumanization in society and alienation from family life and marital fidelity. Woiwode thus belongs in the company of self-consciously moralistic writers such as Walker Percy and Saul Bellow, who are more interested in the ways human beings survive and thrive in a fallen world than in the ways they capitulate to it.

When compared with other writers of his caliber, Woiwode cannot be considered a particularly prolific author. However, two of his novels were critically acclaimed, national best sellers, and they are among the best American novels written after 1960. The publication in consecutive years of *Born Brothers* and *The Neumiller Stories* seems to have redeemed Woiwode from the ambivalent response to *Poppa John*, and Woiwode's reputation as an important American writer in the second half of the twentieth century seems secure.

What I'm Going to Do, I Think • Woiwode's first novel, *What I'm Going to Do, I Think*, is an absorbing character study of two newlyweds, each of whom is originally drawn to the other as opposites proverbially attract. Chris Van Eenanam, the protagonist, is a listless mathematics graduate student, an unhappy agnostic unsure of his calling in life. The novel's title accentuates his self-doubt and indecision, echoing something Chris's father once said in observing his accident-prone son, "What I'm going to do, I think, is get a new kid." Ellen Strohe, his pregnant bride, is a tortured young woman, dominated by the overbearing grandparents who reared her after her parents' accidental death. Neither she nor Chris can abide their interference and meddling.

Despite the fact that little action takes place "live" before the reader, the psychological realism in Woiwode's use of compacted action and flashbacks and the patterned repetition of certain incidents carry the reader along as effortlessly as might a conventionally chronological narrative. The reader learns "what happens" primarily as events filter through the conversations and consciousness of Chris and Ellen Van Eenanam during their extended honeymoon at her grandparents' cabin near the northwestern shore of Lake Michigan.

In this retreat from the decisions Chris elects not to face, the couple, now intimate, now isolated, confront a grim modern world, which has lost its faith in a supreme being fully in control of his created universe. This loss is exemplified most dramatically in the lives of Chris and Ellen as they try to sort out the meaning of affection and fidelity in their new relationship as husband and wife and as potential parents. Ellen's pregnancy is at first a sign of a beneficent nature's approval of their union, but later, as each has a premonition of their unborn child's death, it becomes a symbol of an ambivalent world's indifference to their marriage and its apparent fruitlessness.

In the absence of a compensatory faith even in humankind itself, a secondary faith arguably derived from faith in God, Chris and Ellen come to realize that they have lost their ability to navigate a hostile world with lasting, meaningful relationships. Neither mathematics nor nature can fill the vacuum left by an impotent faith whose incessant call is to fidelity and perseverance without passion or understanding. In a suspenseful epilogue that closes the novel with an explanation of what has happened to them in the seven years following their marriage, Chris and Ellen return to their honeymoon cabin. Chris retrieves the rifle he has not touched in many years, and, as the action builds toward what will apparently be his suicide, he repeats to himself the beginning of a letter (suicide note?) that he could not complete: *"Dear El, my wife. You're the only person I've ever been able to talk to and this is something I can't say. . . . "*

As he makes his way to the lake, he fires a round of ammunition into a plastic bleach container half-buried in the sand. In the novel's enigmatic final lines, Chris fires "the last round from his waist, sending the bullet out over the open lake." This curious ending seems intended by Woiwode to announce Chris's end of indecision—a recognition that his life can have transcendent meaning only in embracing fully his marriage commitment to Ellen.

Beyond the Bedroom Wall • The expansiveness and comic vitality of Woiwode's second novel, *Beyond the Bedroom Wall*, offer a marked contrast to *What I'm Going to Do, I Think*. In *Beyond the Bedroom Wall*, Woiwode parades sixty-three characters before the reader by the beginning of chapter 3. True to its subtitle, *A Family Album*, *Beyond the Bedroom Wall* is a sprawling, gangly work of loosely connected snapshots of the Neumiller family. An engaging homage to the seemingly evaporating family unit at the end of the twentieth century, the novel's "plot" is nearly impossible to paraphrase, consisting as it does of some narrative, some diary entries, and even its protagonist Martin Neumiller's job application for a teaching position. Because Woiwode published nearly a third of the forty-four chapters of *Beyond the Bedroom Wall* as self-contained short stories in *The New Yorker*, it is no surprise that the book reads as a discontinuous montage of events, images, and personalities.

The novel opens in part 1 with the funeral of Charles Neumiller, a German immigrant farmer who had brought his family to America before the war, and it continues, to part 5, closing with stories of the third generation of Neumillers in 1970, bringing the Neumiller family full circle from birth to life to death. However, it is Martin Neumiller, Charles's son, a god-fearing, devoutly Roman Catholic man and proud son of North Dakota, whose adventures and misadventures give the novel any unity it possesses. "My life is like a book," he says at one point. "There is one chapter, there is one story after another." The eccentric folks he encounters in and out of his extended family form a burlesque troupe of characters who boisterously sample both the joys and the sorrows of life on Earth. In the Neumiller "family album," Woiwode lends concreteness to his notion that reality is a fragile construction, one that sometimes cannot bear scrutiny "beyond the bedroom wall," that is, beyond the dreamy world of sleep, of its visions of what might be. Woiwode intimates that whatever hope there may be for fulfilling one's dreams, it is anchored in "walking by faith, and not by sight," by trusting in and actively nurturing family intimacy.

The rather sentimental, "old-fashioned" quality Woiwode achieves in this family chronicle, his evocation of once-embraced, now-lamented values, prompted critic and novelist John Gardner to place Woiwode in the company of literature's greatest epic novelists:

> When self-doubt, alienation, and fashionable pessimism become a bore and, what's worse, a patent delusion, how does one get back to the big emotions, the large and fairly confident life affirmations of an Arnold Bennett, a Dickens, a Dostoevski? *Beyond the Bedroom Wall* is a brilliant solution.

Woiwode's eye for the rich details of daily life enables him to move through vast stretches of time and space in executing the episodic structure in this novel. His appreciation for the cadences of midwestern speech and his understanding of the distinctiveness of prairie life and landscape and its impact on the worldviews of its inhabitants recall other regional writers such as Rudy Wiebe and Garrison Keillor at their best.

Poppa John • *Poppa John* is shockingly short when compared with the massive *Beyond the Bedroom Wall,* and is more a novella than a novel. The book takes its title from the character Ned Daley played for many years on a popular television soap opera. His immense popularity beginning to overshadow the show itself, he is abruptly written out of the show in a dramatic "death." Ned thus finds himself suddenly unable to recover a sense of purpose, so long has he lived within the disguise of Poppa John, the fiery father figure, who often quoted Scripture to his television family. Now close to seventy, outspoken and Falstaffian in appearance and behavior, he seeks his deeply lost identity. Ned to his wife, but Poppa John to everyone else, he is lost in the malevolent nostalgia of growing old without self, or self-respect.

The novel opens two days before Christmas, a few months after Poppa John's television "death." Facing the Christmas season with wife, Celia, broke, broken, and without prospects for the future, the couple wander New York City, squandering their savings on gifts they had always wanted to buy for each other. Forced to "be himself," he finds he has leaned too heavily on the preacherlike Poppa John character, and his life begins to unravel. He is finally forced to face his own inconsistencies, his doubts, and even his sins, as Ned, an "elderly boy," is incapable of trusting in a life beyond the present. Speeding to a climax in its closing pages, the novel depicts Poppa John "coming to himself" on Christmas Day, realizing that he, after all these years, does believe in God, and therefore can come to believe in himself.

Poppa John perhaps deserved a better critical reception than it received; as a more than interesting attempt to portray an elderly actor's disintegrating life, it contains some of Woiwode's most lyrical scenes. In the end, however, it remains an unsatisfying chronicle—in part because the complexity apparent in Poppa John's character is never fully realized, presented as it is in a very compressed time frame. Although Poppa John emerges as a potentially authentic character in the early parts of the novella, Woiwode gives the reader little insight into the motivations that would prompt his sudden conversion experience at the climax of the story.

Born Brothers • In *Born Brothers*, Woiwode returns to the characters, setting, and moral center that brought him his greatest and most uniformly favorable critical attention. Woiwode begins what he calls not a sequel but a "companion volume" to *Beyond the Bedroom Wall* in the middle of the twentieth century, the narration filtered through the consciousness of Charles Neumiller, a lost soul searching his memories for a meaning to life and a purpose for living it. He finds both in exploring his relationship with his brother Jerome. Charles's fragmentary childhood memories in fact become the narrative building blocks for the often elliptical and multiperspective chronicle that unravels before the reader in an even more challenging sequence than that of *Beyond the Bedroom Wall*. *Born Brothers* contains less a plot than a chain of remembrances; as family members and their ahistorical interactions with Charles are paraded before the reader in a kind of visual patchwork, one is compelled to enter Charles's consciousness and see the world through his convoluted epistemology.

Despite his outward sophistication and sense of being, Charles is obsessed with suicide; he seems incapable of conceiving of a meaningful order outside the family structure that had shaped his life and has now dissipated with the death of his mother and the collapse of his marriage. In part, it is Woiwode's intent to explain American society's apparent moral disintegration—rampant promiscuity, unwanted pregnancy, and divorce—by reference to the absence of strong family ties. Charles longs for the bond of brotherhood he once shared—or thinks he shared—with elder brother Jerome. That idyllic childhood in North Dakota, free from the cares and stresses modern, industrial life, allows to impinge without provocation upon Charles's consciousness. Charles's strange career as a "radio personality" who is both the interviewer and the interviewee is somehow emblematic of his need for conversion, for freedom from self. He needs an "outside," a reference point, which, Woiwode hints, will come only from faith in the transcendent God whose eternal family Charles is invited to join.

Woiwode makes few compromises for the reader unwilling to attend to—or, perhaps eavesdrop upon—Charles Neumiller's open-ended musings. To refer to his ramblings as stream-of-consciousness narration is to give too precise a labeling, for not merely a consciousness is under consideration here but the history of a mind and a life as well. The journey to and through that history is not one that the casual reader will be inclined to take, which underscores the main criticism of Woiwode's prose shared even by critics sympathetic to his family chronicle: his apparent inattention to the toll his often exhaustive detail takes on both his characters and his readers. Jonathan Yardley's judgment seems most apt:

It's a pity to see a writer of Woiwode's talent and humanity stuck, at mid-career, in the endless exploration and reexploration of material that has yielded its last fresh insight if not its last lovely sentence.

Indian Affairs • With its broken sequence of scenes and lack of exposition or resolution of conflicts, *Indian Affairs* has elements of a postmodern novel. Woiwode uses this style to reflect the inner turmoil of Chris Van Eenanam, the main character of *What I'm Going to Do, I Think.* Chris and his wife Ellen return to an isolated cabin in the Michigan woods so that he can write his doctoral dissertation on American poet Theodore Roethke's natural philosophy and poetry. Mundane interruptions such as cutting firewood, installing a water pump, shopping, and tavern hopping distract him. A gang of drunken Native American teenagers threatens him when he does not supply them with beer, and a mysterious stalker forces him to keep a loaded gun. On a deeper level, Chris undergoes an identity crisis—a need to affirm his masculinity, to cope with religious and moral dilemmas, and to resolve the conflict of whether his roots are Caucasian or American Indian.

Chris and Ellen's childless seven-year marriage has brought them no sense of permanence or hope for the future. Although they are thirty years old, Chris is still a graduate student, and they are dependent upon Ellen's wealthy grandparents for use of the cabin. Ellen's previous miscarriage and her ensuing barrenness symbolize the status of their marriage. Ellen resolves her unhappiness by recording her thoughts in a journal. Meanwhile, she joins a feminist discussion group, goes to a bar without an escort, and tries the hallucinogen peyote to ease her feelings of emptiness. Her conflicts disappear when she becomes pregnant again.

Chris spends much time with his bachelor friend Beau Nagoosa, a Chippewa Indian who has dropped out of white culture to build his own cabin. He supports himself as a woodcutter and justifies stealing wood on absentee landowners' property by telling himself it was once Native American land. Beau resents the invasion of white real-estate promoters, who claim to represent Volunteers in Service to America (VISTA), yet he accommodates them and compromises his ideals.

Chris and Beau discuss humanity's role within the spiritual harmony of the natural world. For Chris, Roethke's claim that objects in nature are sentient is synonymous with Native American beliefs. Beau introduces Chris to peyote, which stimulates vivid sensory perceptions and fantasies but renders both Chris and Beau unable to cope with their real problems. Frustrated by chaotic events in his life and dissatisfied with the prospect of returning to academe in New York, Chris is overcome with depression. Feeling that nothing can guide him now except his own instincts, Chris decides to adhere to a line from one of Roethke's poems, "I'll be an Indian." Chris's future role as a teacher or leader is ambiguous.

As Chris begins to identify more strongly with his own Blackfoot Indian heritage and feel reverence for the natural world, conflicts escalate between the segregated white and Native American communities. The natural environment shrinks as urban development expands. Tribal leadership does not extend beyond exhibition dancing at powwows. American Indian families disintegrate, alcoholism and drug use destroy lives, and teenage youths engage in threat-making and violence. Woiwode's realistic and tragic portrayal of Native American life offers no solution to the problems.

To fully appreciate Woiwode's book, readers should have read *What I'm Going to Do, I Think* and have more than a passing acquaintance with the philosophies and writings of Theodore Roethke and Vine Deloria, an American Indian cultural nationalist. Woiwode's underlying theme is that modern Native Americans lack effective leaders to guide them.

Bruce L. Edwards, Jr.
Updated by Martha E. Rhynes

Other major works

SHORT FICTION: *The Neumiller Stories*, 1989; *Silent Passengers: Stories*, 1993.

POETRY: *Poetry North: Five North Dakota Poets*, 1970 (with Richard Lyons, Thomas McGrath, John R. Milton, and Antony Oldknow); *Even Tide*, 1977.

NONFICTION: *Acts*, 1993; *Aristocrat of the West: The Story of Harold Schafer*, 2000; *What I Think I Did: A Season of Survival in Two Acts*, 2000.

Bibliography

Chappell, F. "American Gothic." *National Review*, March 24, 1989, 45-46. A favorable review of *Born Brothers* that explores the book's American roots.

Connaughton, Michael E. "Larry Woiwode." In *American Novelists Since World War II, Second Series*. Vol. 6 in *Dictionary of Literary Biography*, edited by James E. Kibler, Jr. Detroit: Gale Research, 1980. An assessment of Woiwode's gift for regional fiction that explores the themes and narrative style of his first two novels.

Freise, Kathy. "Home Again on the Prairie." *North Dakota Horizons* 23 (Summer, 1993): 19-23. Details Woiwode's connections with the state and its role in his books dealing with the Neumiller family.

Gardner, John. Review of *Beyond the Bedroom Wall*, by Larry Woiwode. *The New York Times Book Review* 125 (September 28, 1975): 1-2. An enthusiastic review of what most critics believe is Woiwode's best novel; Gardner's plaudits won a wide audience for Woiwode beyond the small circle of intellectuals who had hailed his first novel.

Jones, Timothy. "The Reforming of a Novelist." *Christianity Today*, October 26, 1992, 86-89. In this interview, Woiwode discusses his view of the nonreligious, humanistic approach of the East Coast literary establishment and the fact that his most recent writing at the time included a greater emphasis on a religious view of such issues as belief and doubt.

Moritz, Charles. *Current Biography Yearbook*. New York: H. W. Wilson, 1989. The essay on Woiwode traces his life and literary work and reviews critical responses to his novels. For the most part, the novels are discussed in terms of their autobiographical content, especially of the characters, including those who most resemble Woiwode himself. Although it does not contain much criticism about Woiwode's work, this essay is particularly helpful, since it identifies and evaluates the available secondary sources. Includes a bibliography.

Nelson, Shirley. "Stewards of the Imagination: Ron Hanson, Larry Woiwode, and Sue Miller." *Christian Century*, January 25, 1995, 82-86. An interview with three novelists in which they discuss their works and careers as well as the role of religion in their lives and writing. Includes an excerpt from Woiwode's *Poppa John*.

Scheick, William J. "Memory in Larry Woiwode's Novels." *North Dakota Quarterly* 53, no. 3 (1985): 29-40. Scheick discusses the importance of memory in *What I'm Going to Do, I Think*, *Beyond the Bedroom Wall*, and *Poppa John*. He identifies two types of memories, those that make a character feel guilt and long for death and those that develop a sense of connection to one's family. The ability to order these allows Woiwode's characters to achieve a balance between them.

Woiwode, Larry. Interview by Michele Field. *Publishers Weekly* 234 (August 5, 1988): 67-68. Woiwode discusses his life, his career, and the relationship between biographical fact and fiction.

_____. "An Interview with Larry Woiwode." *Christianity and Literature* 29 (Winter, 1979): 11-18. Woiwode discusses the autobiographical nature of his work, the Jacob/Esau biblical framework of *Born Brothers*, the "mechanics of memory," his religious rebirth, the influence of William Maxwell, and his future writing plans. This frank, informative interview contains a considerable amount of biographical information, most of which is applied to Woiwode's writing, and some perceptive comments about the Christian themes of *Born Brothers*.

_____. "The Reforming of a Novelist." Interview by Timothy K. Jones. *Christianity Today* 36 (October 26, 1992): 86-88. In this interview Woiwode discusses his conversion experience, his church service, the role of faith in his writing, and reactions to his books.

_____. *What I Think I Did: A Season of Survival in Two Acts.* New York: Basic Books, 2000. In this memoir, Woiwode tells the story of his growing up and of his early adventures in the literary world.

Thomas Wolfe

Born: Asheville, North Carolina; October 3, 1900
Died: Baltimore, Maryland; September 15, 1938

Principal long fiction • *Look Homeward, Angel*, 1929; *Of Time and the River*, 1935; *The Web and the Rock*, 1939; *You Can't Go Home Again*, 1940; *The Short Novels of Thomas Wolfe*, 1961 (C. Hugh Holman, editor).

Other literary forms • During his lifetime Thomas Wolfe published four major works: two novels, *Look Homeward, Angel* and *Of Time and the River*; a collection of short stories, *From Death to Morning* (1935); and his description of his life as a creative artist, *The Story of a Novel* (1936). In addition to his major works, he also sold a few lengthy stories to magazines; *Scribner's Magazine* published "A Portrait of Bascom Hawke" (April, 1932) and "The Web of Earth" (July, 1939). Both of these have since been republished as short novels in *The Short Novels of Thomas Wolfe* (1961), a collection edited by C. Hugh Holman. Because Wolfe viewed each piece of his writing as only a part of some larger design, he frequently adapted past material to meet a present need. For example, he modified "A Portrait of Bascom Hawke" for later inclusion in *Of Time and the River*, and "The Child by Tiger" (1937), a short story he published in *The Saturday Evening Post*, appeared two years later with changes in point of view in *The Web and the Rock*. After his death, Wolfe's editor at Harper's, Edward Aswell, put together three posthumous books from two large packing cases of unfinished manuscript that Wolfe left behind. Two of these books—*The Web and the Rock* and *You Can't Go Home Again*—are novels; the third is a volume of stories, titled *The Hills Beyond* (1941). Wolfe began his career (unsuccessfully) as a playwright with *The Mountains*, which he wrote in 1920 but which was not published until 1970 by the University of North Carolina at Chapel Hill, Wolfe's alma mater. Wolfe's letters and notebooks have also been published, allowing for firsthand insight into his personal and creative life.

Achievements • Wolfe captured the essence of what it meant to be young in his time with the publication of *Look Homeward, Angel*. He further influenced readers of the Great Depression-plagued 1930's with stories he published in magazines such as *The New Yorker*, *Harper's Bazaar*, *Redbook*, *Scribner's Magazine*, and *The Saturday Evening Post*. Widely read in America and abroad, Wolfe was a well-respected author during his lifetime, a man who in a very real sense lived the part of the driven artist. Wolfe is still read, even if not to the extent of his more significant contemporaries, Ernest Hemingway, William Faulkner, and F. Scott Fitzgerald. In retrospect, Wolfe's achievement is especially remarkable when one considers that his literary life spanned little more than a decade. In 1957, Faulkner ranked Wolfe above all of his contemporaries: "My admiration for Wolfe is that he tried the best to get it all said; he was willing to throw away style, coherence, all the rules of preciseness to try to put all the experience of the human heart on the head of a pin." Wolfe's weaknesses are now recognized, but he is still praised for his strengths. A balanced view of his work has emerged, and his reputation as an important figure in twentieth century American literature is secure.

Biography • Born on October 3, 1900, in Asheville, North Carolina, Thomas Wolfe was the youngest of the seven surviving children of Julia Elizabeth Westall and William Oliver Wolfe. Of Pennsylvania Dutch-German stock, Wolfe's father was a man of intense vitality, a stone-cutter who instilled in Wolfe a love of language, whether it be the high rhetoric of Elizabethan poetry or the low vernacular of the mountain people surrounding Asheville. Wolfe's mother was more attuned to the values of commerce than her husband (she was forever speculating in real estate). In fact, one biographer has termed the match an "epic misalliance." Domestic relations in the Wolfe household were often strained; young Wolfe grew up a witness to his father's drunken rampages and his mother's ensuing resentment. From this family cauldron came much of the autobiographical material Wolfe poured forth in *Look Homeward, Angel.*

Library of Congress

In September of 1912, Wolfe entered the North State Fitting School, where he came under the influence of his teacher, Margaret Roberts (Margaret Leonard in *Look Homeward, Angel*). Roberts encouraged Wolfe's voracious appetite for reading by introducing him to the best of English literature. In 1916, at the precocious age of fifteen, Wolfe entered the University of North Carolina at Chapel Hill. Six feet tall and still growing (he would eventually reach six feet six inches), Wolfe was a skinny, long-legged youth, sensitive to the criticism of his older classmates. Wolfe's first year at Chapel Hill was unremarkable, but he eventually made a name for himself as an excellent student and a campus literary figure. In March of 1919, *The Return of Buck Garvin*, a play Wolfe had written in a dramatic writing course, was performed by the Carolina Playmakers, with Wolfe performing in the title role.

After graduating in 1920, Wolfe entered Harvard University to pursue his interests as a playwright. He was especially attracted by the famous workshop given by playwright George Pierce Baker (whom he would later depict as Professor Hatcher in *Of Time and the River*). Wolfe hoped to make a literary name for himself, but after a series of setbacks, he accepted an appointment as an instructor in English at the Washington Square College of New York University and began teaching in February of 1924, continuing to do so intermittently until 1930.

In October of 1924, Wolfe made his first trip to Europe. Many of his experiences there he later incorporated into *Of Time and the River.* Returning to New York in August of 1925, Wolfe met Aline Bernstein, a wealthy married woman who was involved in the theater world of New York. For the next seven years, Wolfe participated in a stormy on-and-off again affair with Bernstein, who was seventeen years his elder. She was the mother-mistress Wolfe seemed to need; certainly, she inspired *Look Homeward, Angel*, which he commenced while abroad with Bernstein in July of 1926.

The popular image of Wolfe as a literary lion is in part caused by the critical success he achieved with *Look Homeward, Angel* but is based mostly on his personal appearance and habits. Often dressed in shabby clothes, he was known to prowl the streets of Brooklyn, where he had settled after another trip abroad in 1931. One night while wandering the streets he was overheard to say, "I wrote ten thousand words today! I wrote ten thousand words today!" Although Wolfe resented efforts to publicize his eccentricities, it was almost inevitable that his behavior and fame would make him a legendary figure.

In December of 1933, Wolfe began work on what was to become *Of Time and the River*. It was also during this period that Maxwell Perkins, Wolfe's editor at Scribner's, worked closely with the author on the formation of the novel. Wolfe incorporated his experiences at Harvard, in Europe, and with Bernstein into *Of Time and the River*, which picks up the Eugene Gant story where *Look Homeward, Angel* concludes. In 1937, after critics had raised questions concerning Perkins's influence on his work, Wolfe left Scribner's for Harper and Brothers. His editor at Harper's was Edward C. Aswell, and Wolfe left two large crates containing nearly a million words of manuscript with him before leaving on a tour of the West in May of 1938. In July, Wolfe fell ill with pneumonia and was hospitalized near Seattle. In September, having been transferred to Johns Hopkins Hospital in Baltimore, he underwent brain surgery for complications he suffered from tuberculosis. He died on September 15, 1938.

Analysis • Throughout Wolfe's fiction there is evidence of a powerful but sometimes uncontrolled mind at work. Few would argue Wolfe's genius, but many have questioned how well he directed it. Part of the difficulty may have come from his self-professed intention to create an American mythology. The result would be the record of an individual, lonely and lost in the flux of time, forever exploring the diversity of American life. Partly because of his early death and partly because of his own difficulties in giving form to ideas, Wolfe never managed to unify the vast body of his work. Add to this the considerable amount of influence his editors exerted upon his manuscripts, and some intriguing questions still remain about the interrelationships of segments in the writings and the final form of his novels.

Wolfe wrote with passionate intensity, producing vast quantities of manuscript. His central themes focus on a lonely individual, the isolated artist, in search of self-discovery and the true meaning of the American experience. In *Look Homeward, Angel*, the first of these themes is most pronounced, for this is autobiography very thinly veiled. The story of Eugene Gant is in many ways the story of Thomas Wolfe. After the publication of *Look Homeward, Angel*, which was generally well received, some critics began to raise questions concerning the novel's weaknesses, especially the obvious attempt by Wolfe to capture experience at the expense of artistic control. It was not until 1936, however, that the landmark case against Wolfe would be launched with the publication in the *Saturday Review* of "Genius Is Not Enough," Bernard DeVoto's indictment of Wolfe and his fiction.

De Voto was responding to *The Story of a Novel*, Wolfe's extremely frank account of his own life as a writer and the work that went into *Of Time and the River*. For Wolfe, writing was a chaotic experience, something done with great pain and toil. DeVoto acknowledged that Wolfe was a genius "of the good old-fashioned, romantic kind, possessed by a demon, driven by the gales of his own fury, helpless before the lava-flood of his own passion"; he further argued, however, that such genius was in and of itself not enough. Today the legacy of DeVoto's remarks remains manifest in a series of stereotypes: By some readers (especially academics), Wolfe is still thought of as one who never controlled his rhetoric, as one who was unable to organize his work, and as one who sometimes pushed autobiography to the limits of reporting.

To illustrate Wolfe's lack of rhetorical restraint, DeVoto pointed to *Of Time and the River*, commenting that Wolfe invested each experience he described with so much raw emotion that a midnight snack took on the same importance as the death of Oliver Gant. As DeVoto stated, "If the death of one's father comes out emotionally even with ham-on-rye, then the art of fiction is cockeyed." As for the charge that Wolfe was a writer who never exerted sufficient control over his material, DeVoto and others have cited the sprawling sections of his mammoth novels where there is supportive evidence that episodes stand by themselves rather than in relation to others. The extent of Wolfe's involvement with his editors (Maxwell Perkins at Scribners from 1928 to 1937; Edward Aswell at Harper's from 1937 to 1938) also raises questions about his own ability to revise and organize his novels.

Perhaps the most revealing example of editorial influence on Wolfe's fiction concerns *Of Time and the River*. While Wolfe was working on the novel, Perkins met with him day and night for more than a year in an attempt to help him gain control over the voluminous amount of material he had written. Often Perkins would ask Wolfe to go home and cut a section, only to find that he would return with an episode thousands of words longer. In one of the most dramatic decisions any editor has made with a figure as significant as Wolfe, Perkins, without Wolfe's final approval, sent the manuscript of *Of Time and the River* to the printer in September of 1934. Perkins made the decision because he believed the novel was as complete as Wolfe could make it and that Wolfe needed to get on with other work. Whatever the reasons, the ultimate responsibility for the publication of any book rests squarely upon the writer. Because Wolfe was so deferential to his editor and because he was unable or unwilling to see his novel through to the end, he opened himself to questions concerning his craftsmanship, questions that are still being asked today.

Finally, there remains the issue of autobiography in Wolfe's novels. Wolfe himself claimed that autobiography was a part of any serious creative work, but there are in his novels, especially *Look Homeward, Angel*, sections that read like a mere diary. There is also a great deal of artistic invention in his novels, and certainly almost all writers use material based on their own experiences; nevertheless, many of Wolfe's depictions were so thinly fictionalized that individuals were easily recognized, and many were hurt and embarrassed by what they thought were the unflattering portraits Wolfe rendered of them. Wolfe's use of autobiography pushed to journalistic limits raises more questions about his fictional method.

Although Wolfe's rhetoric, his conception of structure, and the autobiographical element within his work have been discussed as weaknesses, these three elements can also be cited as the strengths of his writing. For example, it is true there is ample evidence to support DeVoto's claim that Wolfe's rhetoric is often artificially heightened, but at the same time, one of his most compelling attributes is his ability to depict something as insignificant as a "ham-on-rye" so clearly that readers may suddenly find themselves hungry. More to the point, however, are passages such as the Laura James sections of *Look Homeward, Angel*, where Wolfe manages to capture as well as any writer what it means to be young and in love. There are also numerous passages

sages within his other novels that stand as some of the most poetic set pieces to be found in prose. In large measure, Wolfe is still read today because of the magnificence of his style, however extravagant it may be at times.

Wolfe held to an organic theory of art, one in which content dictates form. He was constantly searching for new ways to communicate experience; in this sense, the criticism directed at him for being a "formless" writer may in some ways be unfair. Certainly there is no doubt that in his attempts to depart from traditional formats he sometimes lost control of his material—*Of Time and the River*, for example, is marred by this flaw. On the other hand, he did manage to find an effective structure in "The Web of Earth," his lengthy story written under the influence of James Joyce. The entire work is filtered through the consciousness of an old woman engaged in reminiscence, and it is the finest example of artistic unity in Wolfe's work. In *Look Homeward, Angel*, Wolfe modified a traditional novelistic form, the *Bildungsroman* (the story of a youth initiated by experience into maturity), organizing the novel not around a unified sequence of events but instead around a series of sense impressions. In this way, the loose structure serves to complement the rhapsodic style. The result is a powerful rendering of the book's central theme—that of an artistic youth lost and in search of self-knowledge and self-definition.

As for the contention that Wolfe is too highly autobiographical, that his writing too often approaches mere reportage, there can be no denying that on occasion, he is guilty as charged. In most instances, however, he was by no means a mere reporter of events. His fiction is memorable because he was such an apt interpreter of human beings and everyday experiences. He was able to synthesize experience into art; he himself claimed that everything in a work of art is changed, that nothing is a literal representation of actual experience. Whether he always achieved this transmutation, it can safely be said that Wolfe is still read today because his novels stand as a testimony to human experience artistically rendered from a unique and personal vision.

Look Homeward, Angel • *Look Homeward, Angel*, Wolfe's first and most significant novel, made use of extensive autobiographical material. In many ways, it is the story of his own life, the life of his family, his neighbors, and the region in which he lived. For those who know something of Wolfe's background, there are unmistakable connections between the fictional characters in *Look Homeward, Angel* and the real people among whom Wolfe grew up in Asheville, North Carolina. After the novel's publication, many from his hometown—and indeed many in his own family—were angered by what they took to be unflattering depictions of themselves in the novel. Wolfe's own account of the reaction to his novel can be found in *The Story of a Novel*, wherein he describes the uproar in Asheville and provides his own defense of his fictional method. Essentially, Wolfe believed that the people he described, whatever their faults, were magnificent. As magnificent as he thought his characters were, however, he often described them (no doubt truthfully) with all their faults made highly visible.

The ethics of his method can be questioned when one considers how it must have been to have lived in Asheville at the time the novel was published, to have opened its pages and to have found the characters so thinly fictionalized that their real counterparts could be easily identified. The ethical issue is not so much whether Wolfe was accurate in his depictions of the whole range of humanity he described, but rather how one would feel if he were identified as the model for the town drunk or as the counterpart of the unscrupulous businessman. It did not take long for the people of

Asheville to start pointing fingers at one another after figuring out who was who in the novel. Perhaps with some justification, all fingers eventually pointed toward Wolfe himself; the controversy over what he had done to his town and the people in it was so pronounced that he was unable to return to Asheville until seven years after the publication of *Look Homeward, Angel.*

Wolfe departed from the development of a traditional plot in *Look Homeward, Angel* and instead made use of impressionistic realism to tie events and characters together. The narrator moves in and out of the consciousness of the principal characters, giving readers impressions of their inner feelings and motivations. As much as anything else, *Look Homeward, Angel* is the story of a quest, a search for self-knowledge and for lasting human interaction. The subtitle of the novel is *A Story of the Buried Life,* and much of what Wolfe depicts concerns itself with the inner lives of the characters in the novel—what they really think and feel as well as how isolated and alienated they are from one another. In this sense, the novel explores the relationship of time, change, and death as elements that will always frustrate the human desire for happiness and fulfillment.

Look Homeward, Angel was initially titled *O Lost* and then *Alone, Alone.* The title on which Wolfe finally settled comes from "Lycidas," John Milton's poem in which the archangel Michael is asked to look back toward England to mourn a young man's death and all the unfulfilled potential it signifies. Eugene Gant, is, like most of Wolfe's protagonists, the isolated and sensitive artist in search of meaning and companionship in a hostile world. Given this theme, it is ironic that some of Wolfe's least effective passages are the results of his attempts to describe Eugene's feelings of loneliness and despair. In such segments (which recur in almost all of Wolfe's works), he often lapses into contrived language; rather than arising from natural consequences or from the interplay between one character and another, feelings seem forced by authorial intervention. On the other hand, the novel does contain some of his finest writing, especially when he describes people, places, and things with visionary intensity.

Look Homeward, Angel covers the first twenty years of Eugene Gant's life—his adolescence, his four years at the private school of Margaret Leonard, and his four years at the university. A pattern of potential fulfillment destroyed by frustration is personified in Eugene's parents, Eliza and Oliver, who are modeled after Wolfe's own mother and father. Oliver Gant is a stonecutter who passionately desires to create something beautiful, to carve an angel's head. He is an unfulfilled artist, a man of intense vitality who desires a full and sensuous life. His intensity, his capacity for life, is checked by his wife, Eliza, who is his antithesis: parsimonious, cold, and materialistic. This pattern of frustrated potential recurs throughout the novel. In one example, after spending his first year at the university and losing his innocence in a brothel, Eugene returns home to spend the summer at Dixieland, his mother's boardinghouse. There he meets and falls in love with Laura James (based on his own first love, Clara Paul). In his descriptions of the young, passionate love that develops between them, Wolfe's prose becomes a lyrical celebration that turns to tragic frustration as Eugene learns that Laura is engaged to marry another young man back home, that she will never be a part of his life again. Thus, potential (in this example, physical and spiritual union between Eugene and Laura) is checked by reality (separation and isolation). This pattern manifests itself in varying ways throughout the novel. The story of a youth coming of age by initiation into experience, *Look Homeward, Angel* is a comprehensive account of the inner life of a sensitive and artistic youth.

With the publication of *Look Homeward, Angel*, Wolfe was thrust (not unwillingly) into the limelight as a legend, a novelist who demonstrated enormous potential. His success was spectacular, but because he was a driven artist (much like his fictional counterpart, Eugene Gant), his initial success created a good many subsequent problems. He immediately felt the burden to surpass his first effort with an even better second novel. At the same time, he ran into difficulty giving form to his expansive ideas (a problem with which he would grapple for the remainder of his life). During this same period, he also began leading a turbulent private life. He was involved with Aline Bernstein (the "A. B." to whom *Look Homeward, Angel* is dedicated), and their relationship—as tempestuous as any could conceivably be—would figure heavily in the remainder of his life and work.

Of Time and the River • Comprising eight sections, each of which is named after some epic or mythic figure, *Of Time and the River* exceeds nine hundred pages in length and spans two continents, continuing the story of Thomas Wolfe as personified in the character of Eugene Gant. Wolfe continues the story with Eugene's departure from Altamont for study at Harvard. He stated his ambitious theme for *Of Time and the River* in *The Story of a Novel*; his central idea was to depict the search for a father, not only in a literal but also in a figurative sense. While trying to exemplify his theme, Wolfe also struggled to form *Of Time and the River* out of the vast amount of manuscript he had written (a detailed discussion of that struggle is related in *The Story of a Novel*). The struggle reached its peak when his editor, Maxwell Perkins, sent the novel to press without Wolfe's knowledge. In one of his letters to Perkins, Wolfe claimed that another six months' work would have allowed him to complete the necessary revisions that would have made the book less episodic.

There can be no doubt that had Wolfe written *Of Time and the River* without Perkins's influence, it would have been a very different novel—perhaps a better one than it is. As it stands, it is, as Wolfe himself noted, episodic; its parts are not always aligned to form a unified plot. Even so, there are fine passages throughout that more than compensate for its ponderous pace and meandering plot. In *The Story of a Novel*, Wolfe describes how he wrote one scene that ran to eighty thousand words (about two hundred pages). He was attempting to capture "the full flood and fabric" of four people simply talking to one another for four continuous hours. This scene, as good as he thought it was, eventually was cut, but it illustrates the massive amount of writing he did for the novel as well as the extensive amount of cutting he did to get it into publishable form.

Perhaps the novel's most magnificent scene is that which describes the death of Eugene's father, who has been slowly dying of cancer. Gant, the paternal figure whose presence was so unforgettable in *Look Homeward, Angel*, is now old and enfeebled. His death, which comes in a final moment of tranquillity, stands in stark contrast to his life, which was lived with violent gestures and howling protests. Often drunk, sometimes violent, he was a hard man to live with, but his death comes as a reminder that life lived intensely—however excessively—is life worth living. The death of his wife, Eliza, would not begin to elicit the intensity of emotion aroused by his final moments, for she stands as a testimony to all that opposes the force and fury of his life.

Other memorable scenes in the novel include those that take place in Boston with Eugene's uncle, Bascom Pentland. Uncle Bascom and his demented wife are two of the more finely drawn eccentrics in the novel. These segments as well as others involving Eugene's dreams to become a playwright, his time spent as an English instructor at a city university in New York, and his eventual travel to Europe, all contribute to Wolfe's attempt to describe the vast array of people, places, and things unique to the American experience.

While working out his central theme of a search for a father, Wolfe developed a three-part vision of time: time present, time past, and time eternal. The first, time present, is the time in which the actual events in the novel take place, the time of reality. The second, time past, represents all of the accumulated experience that affects time present. The third, time eternal, stands for the lasting time of oceans, forests, and rivers, of things that form the permanent backdrop for people's experiences. These three levels of time allow Wolfe to contrast, in a vast and symbolic scale, the relationship of past, present, and eternal experience with the experience of Eugene Gant. The result is an intensely personal search for meaning, an attempt to reconcile opposites, to find something lasting and meaningful.

Throughout the novel, a scene that takes place in the present may be linked with past scenes and eternal scenes. In this way, all three levels of time are united. For example, a train ride taking place in present time provides Eugene with the opportunity to recall the travelers of earlier days, their epic searching, their longing for discovery, for movement. During the same segment, Eugene speculates that other people in the future (eternal time) will also travel the earth in search of one another. The novel frequently develops itself in this way, and it is these segments that give the novel its mysterious, almost haunting, quality. At the same time, however, these same passages become repetitious (if not tedious), and illustrate once again the lack of restraint so evident throughout Wolfe's work. In contrast to these overwritten segments are a good many specific characterizations as well as a variety of satiric passages aimed at mediocre people, middle-class values, and intellectual pretenders. This is a vast and comprehensive book that ends when Eugene sets sail back to the United States. Aboard ship he meets Esther Jack (Aline Bernstein), who, although certainly not the father for whom he is searching, is nevertheless someone who can help him transcend the tormented youth he has endured to this point in his life.

Both *The Web and the Rock* and *You Can't Go Home Again* were put together by Edward Aswell, Wolfe's editor at Harper's, and published posthumously as novels. It was not until 1962, when Richard S. Kennedy published *The Window of Memory: The Literary Career of Thomas Wolfe*, that the extent of Aswell's influence on the two novels became fully known. Just before his death, Wolfe left a large packing crate of manuscript with Aswell. From that collection of manuscript, it was generally assumed that Aswell found two separate narratives, which he then published as the two posthumous novels. Surprisingly, however, Professor Kennedy discovered, after an extensive study of Wolfe's papers and manuscripts at Harvard University, that Aswell constructed *The Web and the Rock* and *You Can't Go Home Again* from what was a massive—but fragmentary—amount of manuscript that Wolfe apparently intended to condense into a single narrative. Had Wolfe lived, he most certainly would not have published the two novels as Aswell published them. In a very real way, they are as much the product of Aswell's editorializing as they are a product of Wolfe's imagination. Even so, the two novels represent a significant part of Wolfe's creative output, and analysis of them can help put his entire achievement into a clearer perspective.

The Web and the Rock • Wolfe claimed that he was turning away from the books he had previously written, that *The Web and the Rock* would be his most "objective" work to date. It should be noted that at that time, Wolfe had become particularly sensitive about the criticism he had received from DeVoto and others concerning his alleged inability to exert artistic control over his material. As a result, not only did he claim his new novel to be objective, but also he abandoned his previous protagonist, Eugene Gant, in favor of a new one, George "Monk" Webber. The change was more in name than in substance, however, for Webber, like Eugene Gant, bears a close resemblance to Wolfe himself. Indeed, *The Web and the Rock* is quite similar to Wolfe's earlier works: Its first half parallels *Look Homeward, Angel*, while its second half stands as a sequel to *Of Time and the River.*

One of the strongest chapters in the novel is enlightening insofar as it illustrates how Wolfe continually reshaped past material. "The Child by Tiger" was first published in 1937 as a short story, but in the eighth chapter of *The Web and the Rock*, Wolfe reworks the story with changes in character and point of view. It is a moving story about the nature of good and evil, innocence and experience. Dick Prosser, a black man of ability and potential, is the object of the racial prejudice that was so pronounced in the South during the early part of the twentieth century. He is a man who befriends several young white boys; he teaches them how to throw a football, how to box, and how to make a fire. In short, he becomes a kindly father figure who initiates them into experience. There is, however, another side to Prosser. Driven to the point of madness by prejudicial treatment, by his own apocalyptic brand of religion, and by his involvement with a woman, he goes on a shooting spree one night, killing black and white people alike. Eventually shot by the mob formed to hunt him down, his bullet-riddled body is hung up for display in the window of the undertaker's parlor. In the course of these events, the young men who were Prosser's friends are initiated into a world full of violence and death. For the first time in their lives, they experience profound loss, and they witness evil as it is personified in the bloodthirsty mob. Woven within the story are stanzas from William Blake's poem "The Tyger," from which the chapter title is derived.

In what makes up the second half of the novel, Wolfe deals with his own experiences in New York City. He explores his relationship with Bernstein, depicting her as a sophisticated mistress and himself as a brilliant but egocentric genius. Their relationship is described in detail—from their lovemaking and eating to their quarrels and reconciliations. These segments are remarkable for their candor and intriguing because of the insight they provide into the tempestuous relationship between the two. Webber's past experiences, the environment in which he was reared, and his ancestry symbolically form the web in which he is snared, and, as Esther Jack becomes a part of that web, he escapes to Germany. His search for the rock, the strength and beauty of vision that is represented by the father figure for whom he longs, is interrupted by his realization at the end of the novel that "you can't go home again." In short, he knows that he must look to the future to escape the past.

You Can't Go Home Again • Continuing the chronicle of George Webber's life and artistic development, *You Can't Go Home Again* metaphorically develops the theme that Webber cannot go "home," cannot return to past places, old ideas, and former experiences because time and change have corrupted them. In this sense, "home" is an idealized vision of the United States as it appeared to George in his youth. These youthful visions come into abrupt contact with reality, and the resulting clash allows Wolfe to explore the very fabric of American society.

The novel begins approximately six months after *The Web and the Rock* ends. Webber has returned home to the United States, and, against his better judgment, he decides to resume his relationship with Esther Jack. He also resumes work on his novel *Home to Our Mountains (Look Homeward, Angel)* and finds a publisher, James Rodney (Scribner's), as well as a sympathetic editor and father figure, Foxhall Edwards (Maxwell Perkins). Before his book is published, however, he returns home for the first time in years to attend the funeral of his Aunt Maw. Home in this novel is Libya Hill (like the Altamont of *Look Homeward, Angel*, the locale still represents Asheville, North Carolina). On the train trip home, he meets his childhood friend Nebraska Crane, a onetime big-league baseball star. A Cherokee Indian, Crane is now satisfied to lead the simple life of a family man and part-time tobacco farmer, standing in contrast to Webber, whose intellectual drive and literary ambition make him a driven "city" man.

Also on the train is Judge Rumford Bland, a blind syphilitic whose corruption serves to symbolize the corruption in Libya Hill toward which Webber is traveling. Upon his arrival, Webber finds that his quiet boyhood town has become crazed from a land-boom mentality that has everyone making huge paper fortunes in real estate (these events parallel those immediately preceding the Great Depression). Thus, his idealized expectations of home are shattered by the corruption and madness running rampant throughout Libya Hill.

After the publication of his novel, Webber receives abusive letters from the residents of Libya Hill. Typically, Wolfe incorporated his own experiences into his fiction. In this instance, he drew upon his unpleasant memories of what happened after he published *Look Homeward, Angel*. An entire book in the novel ("The World That Jack Built") is devoted to the wealthy lives of Esther and Frederick Jack (the Bernsteins). Writing about his own breakup with Aline Bernstein, Wolfe describes Webber's move to Brooklyn and the end of his relationship with Esther Jack. In Brooklyn, Webber learns to love the low-life characters who inhabit the streets—the prostitutes, the derelicts, and the petty criminals—for they are very much a part of the American experience. To ignore them—or worse yet, to explain them away somehow—would be to deny the underbelly of America that Webber (and Wolfe) found so compelling.

After his years in Brooklyn (with scenes devoted to his relationship with Foxhall Edwards, his editor), Webber tires of New York and sails for Europe. In Germany, he is welcomed with the fame and notoriety he has sought for so long, but he also witnesses the darker side of Nazi Germany. The novel is the story of one man's pilgrimage, a search for a faith that will endure within a society so corrupt that each individual is destroyed by it. *You Can't Go Home Again* is not an entirely cynical book, however, for it concludes with a sense of hope and faith in the future.

Throughout his novels, Wolfe explored isolation, death, and the changes wrought by time—themes that exemplify his interest in the darker elements of life. In his attempts to capture the essence of a moment, he often overlooked the artistic demands that the novel imposes upon any writer. He was not a craftsman of the novel because he often sacrificed form, unity, and coherence to capture experience. His reputation is linked directly to his ambitious attempts to say it all, and *Look Homeward, Angel*, although only the beginning of the story Wolfe desired to tell, stands as his most satisfying and fully realized work.

Philip A. Luther

Other major works

SHORT FICTION: *From Death to Morning*, 1935; *The Hills Beyond*, 1941; *The Complete Short Stories of Thomas Wolfe*, 1987.

PLAYS: *The Mountains*, pr. 1921, pb. 1970; *Welcome to Our City*, pr. 1923 (pb. only in Germany as *Willkommen in Altamont*, 1962); *Mannerhouse*, pb. 1948.

POETRY: *The Face of a Nation: Poetical Passages from the Writings of Thomas Wolfe*, 1939; *A Stone, a Leaf, a Door: Poems by Thomas Wolfe*, 1945.

NONFICTION: *The Story of a Novel*, 1936; *Thomas Wolfe's Letters to His Mother*, 1943 (John Skally, editor); *The Portable Thomas Wolfe*, 1946 (Maxwell Geisman, editor); *The Letters of Thomas Wolfe*, 1956 (Elizabeth Nowell, editor); *The Notebooks of Thomas Wolfe*, 1970 (Richard S. Kennedy and Paschal Reeves, editors); *The Thomas Wolfe Reader*, 1982 (C. Hugh Holman, editor); *Beyond Love and Loyalty: The Letters of Thomas Wolfe and Elizabeth Nowell*, 1983 (Kennedy, editor); *My Other Loneliness: Letters of Thomas Wolfe and Aline Bernstein*, 1983 (Suzanne Stutman, editor); *The Autobiography of an American Novelist: Thomas Wolfe*, 1983; *To Loot My Life Clean: The Thomas Wolfe-Maxwell Perkins Correspondence*, 2000 (Matthew J. Bruccoli and Park Bucker, editors).

Bibliography

Bassett, John Earl. *Thomas Wolfe: An Annotated Critical Bibliography*. Lanham, Md.: Scarecrow Press, 1996. A helpful tool for the student of Wolfe. Indexed.

Bloom, Harold, ed. *Thomas Wolfe*. New York: Chelsea House, 2000. A compendium of critical essays on Wolfe's oeuvre. Introduction, chronology, and bibliography.

Donald, David Herbert. *Look Homeward: A Life of Thomas Wolfe*. 1987. Reprint. Cambridge, Mass.: Harvard University Press, 2003. Donald's fine biography stresses Wolfe's accomplishment as a social historian and his novels as "a barometer of American culture." Like others, Donald admits the presence of much bad writing but confesses to responding enthusiastically to the good. Makes full use of Wolfe's letters to his mistress, Aline Bernstein.

Evans, Elizabeth. *Thomas Wolfe*. New York: Frederick Ungar, 1984. Provides an excellent shorter introduction to Wolfe for both the beginning and the advanced student. Economical and accurate, it is keyed clearly to Wolfe scholarship and is rich in unpretentious literary allusion. Though Evans is cautious in her admiration of Wolfe's fiction, she is appreciative of it as well. Contains a chronology and a good short bibliography.

Holman, C. Hugh. *The World of Thomas Wolfe*. New York: Charles Scribner's Sons, 1962. An older text, an example of the "controlled research" concept popular during the 1960's, this book is specifically designed for high school and college students. A good cross section of Wolfe criticism is offered, with practical information for further study. Topics for library research and term papers are suggested.

Idol, John Lane. *Literary Masters: Thomas Wolfe*. Detroit: Gale, 2001. General survey of Wolfe's major writings.

_____. *A Thomas Wolfe Companion*. New York: Greenwood Press, 1987. An expression of the resurgence of interest in Wolfe by an unabashed devotee, this handy book is a potpourri of Wolfeana with glossaries of characters and places, genealogical charts of Wolfe's fictional families, a descriptive and "analytic" bibliography of primary works, and an annotated bibliography of secondary materials.

Johnston, Carol Ingalls. *Of Time and the Artist: Thomas Wolfe, His Novels, and the Critics*. Columbia, S.C.: Camden House, 1996. Looks at Wolfe's autobiographical fiction and the critical response to it.

McElderry, Bruce R. *Thomas Wolfe*. New York: Twayne, 1964. An excellent basic intro-duction to Wolfe's life and work, McElderry's study provides lucid analysis well supported by standard critical opinion, including a chapter on the shorter fiction. Contains a useful chronology and annotated select bibliographies of primary and secondary sources.

Phillipson, John S., ed. *Critical Essays on Thomas Wolfe*. Boston: G. K. Hall, 1985. Con-tains twenty-three essays, most formerly published, written between 1970 and the early 1980's. Arranged by genre, the book contains seven essays on Wolfe's short fiction.

Rubin, Louis D., Jr., ed. *Thomas Wolfe: A Collection of Critical Essays*. Englewood Cliffs, N.J.: Prentice-Hall, 1973. A collection, with an introduction by Rubin, of a dozen stimulating essays by a variety of critics, scholars, and writers ranging from the im-pressionistic—a mode that Wolfe almost inevitably inspires—to the scholarly. Contains the notorious Bernard DeVoto review (1936) of *The Story of a Novel* titled "Genius Is Not Enough."

Herman Wouk

Born: New York, New York; May 27, 1915

Principal long fiction • *Aurora Dawn*, 1947; *The City Boy*, 1948; *The Caine Mutiny*, 1951; *Marjorie Morningstar*, 1955; *Slattery's Hurricane*, 1956; *Youngblood Hawke*, 1962; *Don't Stop the Carnival*, 1965; *The Lomokome Papers*, 1968; *The Winds of War*, 1971; *War and Remembrance*, 1978; *Inside, Outside*, 1985; *The Hope*, 1993; *The Glory*, 1994; *A Hole in Texas*, 2004.

Other literary forms • Herman Wouk wrote several plays; the first, *The Traitor*, was produced on Broadway in 1949 and was published by Samuel French the same year. His most successful theatrical work, *The Caine Mutiny Court-Martial* (based upon the novel published in 1951), appeared on Broadway in 1954 and was published by Doubleday the same year. *Nature's Way* was produced on Broadway in 1957 and was published by Doubleday the following year. Eric Bentley, speaking of *The Caine Mutiny Court-Martial*, said that Wouk showed a gift for crisp dialogue that no other regular writer for the American theater could rival. The musical *Don't Stop the Carnival*, a collaboration with pop musician Jimmy Buffett, was produced in 1998. Wouk collaborated with Richard Murphy in writing the screenplay for *Slattery's Hurricane* (1949), which he later adapted as a novel. Wouk also wrote teleplays, for *The Winds of War* (1983) and *War and Remembrance* (1988). *This Is My God*, which Wouk first published in 1959 and followed with a revised edition in 1973, is a description and explanation of Orthodox Judaism, especially as it is practiced in America. The volume was a Reader's Digest Condensed Book Club selection and an alternate selection for the Book-of-the-Month Club in 1959.

Achievements • It is a peculiarity of American criticism to denigrate popular success in literature. Almost from the outset of his career, Wouk was a very popular writer; putting aside prejudicial presuppositions, this can be acknowledged as a genuine achievement, for Wouk did not attain his popular status by catering to the baser tastes of his readers. Beginning with *The Caine Mutiny*, his books appeared regularly on best-seller lists. Several of his titles were selections of major book clubs. Wouk was awarded the Pulitzer Prize for Fiction in 1952 for *The Caine Mutiny*. During that same year, Columbia University presented him the Medal of Excellence, an honor extended to distinguished alumni. Several universities awarded him honorary doctoral degrees.

Wouk might be described as a traditional novelist, in that his writing does not reflect the experimental qualities that are to be found in so much twentieth century American fiction. Like John Updike, he gives primacy of place to the narrative element in fiction; he brings to the novel his own peculiar brand of rough-hewn vigor. At a time when conventional wisdom judged it bad form for a novelist to take a clear stand on moral issues—as if ambiguity itself were a virtue—Wouk consistently declared his moral position in his writings. This was not always to the benefit of his fiction, but by and large, his novels are stronger for his conviction that literary art does not subsist in a vacuum but is part of a larger moral universe.

Biography • Herman Wouk was born in New York City on May 27, 1915, the son of Abraham Isaac and Esther (Levine) Wouk. Wouk's father, an industrialist in the power laundry field, started out as an immigrant laundry worker earning three dollars a week. Wouk was educated at Townsend Harris Hall and at Columbia University, where he graduated with honors in 1934. While at Columbia, he studied philosophy and comparative literature and was editor of the *Columbia Jester*. From 1934 to 1935, he worked as a gag writer for radio comedians, and from 1936 to 1941, he was a scriptwriter for Fred Allen. In 1941, Wouk moved to Washington, D.C., following his appointment to the United States Treasury Department as a dollar-a-year man; his job was to write and produce radio shows to sell war bonds. He left this work to join the Navy. After completing Officer Candidate School, he was commissioned an ensign and assigned to mine sweeper duty in the Pacific fleet. He served in the Navy from 1942 to 1945, first aboard the U.S.S. *Zane* and then aboard the destroyer-minesweeper U.S.S. *Southard*; eventually he was to be promoted to the position of Executive Officer of that ship. He was decorated with four campaign stars during the war, and received a Unit Citation as well. When Wouk was processed out of the Navy in 1945, he held the rank of lieutenant. Wouk married Betty Sarah Brown in December, 1945. They had three sons, Abraham Isaac (who died before reaching his fifth birthday), Nathaniel, and Joseph.

Wouk began his career as a serious writer while he was in the Navy; before his release from the service, he had completed a good portion of his first novel. That novel, *Aurora Dawn*, was published by Simon and Schuster in 1947. The following year, his second novel, *The City Boy*, was published. Neither of these works gained a great deal of attention for Wouk, but with the publication of *The Caine Mutiny* in 1951 (awarded the Pulitzer Prize the following year), he was quickly established as a writer of consequence. His play, *The Caine Mutiny Court-Martial*, began its successful run on Broadway in 1954. *Marjorie Morningstar* appeared in 1955 and his nonfiction work on Jewish culture and religion, *This Is My God*, in 1959. The 1960's saw the publication of *Youngblood Hawke* and *Don't Stop the Carnival*. Wouk's sprawling two-volume fictional account of World War II, which he began writing in 1962, was published during the 1970's; the first volume, *The Winds of War*, appeared in 1971, and the second, *War and Remembrance*, in 1978. Wouk wrote the teleplay for the eighteen-hour television film based on *The Winds of War*, which was broadcast during the week of February 6-13, 1983. He was coauthor of the teleplay for the television adaptation of *War and Remembrance*, which appeared in 1988.

Unlike many contemporary popular novelists, Wouk shunned the public spotlight throughout his career. Though the Wouks spent more than a decade after they were married in New York, they moved to the Virgin Islands in 1958, partly so that Wouk could find a place to write free of interruptions. In 1964, the family moved to Georgetown, a Washington, D.C., suburb, so that he could be closer to archival materials he needed to consult in order to write *The Winds of War* and *War and Remembrance*. During the next three decades, Wouk divided his time between his home in the nation's capital and one in Palm Springs, California, occasionally appearing at public events to accept awards or participate in fund-raising or religious events. In 1995, Wouk entered into an agreement with popular singer Jimmy Buffett to write the book for a musical based on *Don't Stop the Carnival*. Featuring a number of Caribbean songs composed by Buffett, the musical opened in Florida in 1997 and moved to Broadway in 1998.

Wouk's great popular success enabled him to devote his full time to his craft, but on occasion he took academic or semiacademic positions. From 1953 to 1957, he was a visiting professor of English at Yeshiva University, and during 1973-1974, he was scholar-in-residence at the Aspen Institute for Humanistic Studies. A member of the Authors Guild and the Dramatists Guild, he served on the board of directors for institutions and organizations such as the College of the Virgin Islands, the Washington National Symphony, and Kennedy Center Productions.

Analysis • Wouk is a novelist in the tradition of the great English novelists of the nineteenth century; he is also a spiritual descendant of such American writers as James Fenimore Cooper, William Dean Howells, Theodore Dreiser, and James T. Farrell. What he has in common with these writers is narrative prowess, a commitment to realism, and a lively moral consciousness. Furthermore, like these writers, Wouk addresses himself to the population at large. Since World War II, there has been detectable in American fiction a distinction between writers who seem to be inclined to write primarily for other writers or for academic critics, and those inclined to write for a general audience. The fact that Wouk is numbered among the latter would appear to be traceable to a definite decision on his part. His first novel, *Aurora Dawn*, has the flavor of the experimental fiction that began to proliferate in the postwar period.

If one were to have speculated in 1946 upon the course that Wouk's literary career was going to take, it would have been a safe guess to say that he would probably continue down the road of experimentation, that he would become more and more concerned with language as an end in itself, and that eventually, he would be writing books destined to be read only in upper-division English courses in universities. This was not what happened, however; in his second novel, *The City Boy*, Wouk followed a

National Archives

conventional narrative pattern and told his story in language that was not constantly calling attention to itself.

In *Aurora Dawn* and *The City Boy*, Wouk was still stretching his muscles and attempting to find his proper level as a writer. He came into his own with *The Caine Mutiny*. In that novel, and in every novel that followed for the next four decades, there is the presence of a central theme, treated in various ways and from varying perspectives. The theme is the conflict between traditional values and a modern consciousness that is either indifferent to those values or flatly antipathetic toward them. The conflict is not treated in abstract terms, but in terms of individuals who are caught up in it, and how the individual fares is in great part determined by the side with which he chooses to ally himself.

Aurora Dawn • Wouk's first novel, *Aurora Dawn*, which he began while serving as an officer in the Navy, is an effort at satire. The butt of the satire is the advertising industry and, more generally, the foolishness of anyone in business whose ethical consciousness is dimmed by avarice. The moral of the story is explicit: Greed is the root of all evil. Andrew Reale, the novel's young protagonist, is bright, energetic, and imaginative, but until he undergoes a conversion at novel's end, his primary concern is getting ahead. He wants to be successful above all else, and to him, success means money. In his scramble to get to the top as quickly as possible, his myopia becomes acute and his values are severely twisted. He is willing to make compromises where compromises should not be made. A connection is intimated between Reale's moral weakness and his failure to continue to adhere to the religious principles according to which he was reared, a recurring theme in Wouk's fiction.

Reale's obsessive pursuit of success leads him to jilt his fiancé, the beautiful and innocent Laura Beaton, so that he can take up with the beautiful but frivolous Carol Marquis, daughter of the despicable but very rich Talmadge Marquis. It leads him to be crassly manipulative in his dealings with the Reverend Calvin Stanfield, who is simple, straightforward, and a good man. Finally, it leads him, in a move of pure expediency, to quit an employer who has been generous with him so that he can join forces with Talmadge Marquis. All Reale's machinations, however, are to no avail. The hastily courted Carol Marquis runs off with an eccentric painter, and Laura Beaton, brokenhearted at Reale's rejection of her, marries an older man. In the end, Reale gets better than he deserves. His thwarted attempt to blackmail Father Stanfield proves to be the occasion of a conversion experience for him. He suddenly sees the wickedness of his ways and decides to alter his course. Laura Beaton is miraculously released from her unconsummated marriage, so that Reale is able to get the woman of his dreams after all. Fleeing the wicked city, the bride and groom go off to live together in New Mexico.

The novel is not realistic and cannot be judged according to the criterion of verisimilitude. It is a light, playful work in which humor plays an important part. Despite several brilliant passages, however, the novel does not come across as successful satire, and that would seem to be attributable to the fact that Wouk is vacillating and hesitant in what he wants to say. What he takes with one hand, he gives back with the other. The novel is clever, in both good and bad senses. Although its language is often lively, it can as well be pretentious and self-conscious at times. The anachronistic devices of addressing the reader directly, inserting explicit authorial commentary on the action, and interspersing the narrative with short philosophical asides do not always work to maximize the effect. The humor of the novel is capable of being right on the mark, but for the most part it is a bit forced; Wouk, the radio gagman, is too much in evidence. The flaws to be found in *Aurora Dawn* are flaws that are not uncommon in a first novel. Despite its weaknesses, however, already in evidence in this work are the two traits that have subsequently become the chief strengths of Wouk's fiction: a vigorous talent for narrative and a lively sensitivity to moral issues.

The City Boy • Perhaps the most striking thing about Wouk's second novel, *The City Boy*, is that, stylistically, it represents a marked departure from the standards he had established in his first novel. The language of the work does not call attention to itself; it is clear, straightforward, and unpretentious. The novel is humorous in tone, and its plot structure is loose. It revolves around the adventures—most of which take place in an upstate summer camp—of a New York City boy, Herbie Bookbinder. John P. Marquand's comparison of this novel with Mark Twain's *The Adventures of Tom Sawyer* (1876) is well founded. In many respects, Herbie is an urban version of the scamp from the midwestern frontier. He is a bright and enterprising lad, and if he is mischievous at times, it is seldom with malice. Much of what he does is calculated to impress Lucille Glass, the object of his single-minded puppy love. Herbie is unlike Tom Sawyer in that he is an outsider as far as other boys are concerned, largely because of his poor athletic skills and his penchant for things intellectual. A goodly number of Herbie's efforts in the novel are given over to his attempts to gain the status of a regular guy. He succeeds, finally, and as a result is welcomed into the full fellowship of his peers. *The City Boy* is a light novel—in some respects a boy's book—but in it, Wouk's moral consciousness is manifested by his underscoring the difference between good and evil in the actions of the characters.

The Caine Mutiny • *The Caine Mutiny* is Wouk's best novel, the work on which his reputation rests. The novel takes place against the backdrop of war, but it cannot be regarded as a "war story" in any simplistic sense. It is a story about the subtle and complicated relationships that exist among men who are part of the enclosed world that constitutes the military establishment. One of its central themes concerns the matter of authority—how it is exercised within a military context, and how it is abused. The novel explores the manner in which various personality types act and react within a hierarchical, authoritarian structure. In addition, it examines the ways in which the lives of those caught up in the trauma of war are altered, sometimes profoundly. Other themes that the novel treats are loyalty and disloyalty, patriotism, doers versus sayers, personal integrity, and the process by which young men are tested in stressful situations.

   The Caine Mutiny can easily be misread. One might conclude that its chief concern is the everlasting battle between despotism and democracy, that Captain Queeg therefore is clearly the villain of the piece, and that its heroes are Lieutenant Maryk, Willie Keith, Tom Keefer, and the others who were involved in the mutiny. It is not that simple. If it were, *The Caine Mutiny* would be little more than a melodrama. Captain Queeg is not a hero, but neither is he a diabolical type. He is a sorry human being; he has serious personal problems (his eccentricity is not amusing—he is, in fact, a sick man); and, perhaps most serious, given his status as a commanding officer, he is incompetent professionally. For all that, he is consistent in trying to do his job to the best of his ability. Queeg's problem is that he is a man who is in over his head; he can at times scarcely cope with situations that are his duty to control. The circumstances surrounding the event that lead to the mutiny are sufficiently ambiguous as to render doubtful the claim of the mutineers that, had they not relieved Queeg of command when they did, the ship would have been lost.

Wouk's assessment of the situation seems to be communicated most directly through the character of Lieutenant Greenwald, the young aviator-lawyer who defends Maryk at the court-martial. Greenwald is not sympathetic with the mutineers, but he decides to defend Maryk because he respects the Executive Officer's personal integrity and because he is convinced that Maryk, in assuming command of the *Caine* during the typhoon, was acting in good faith. Greenwald succeeds in having Maryk acquitted of the charge of mutiny, mainly by drawing out of Queeg in the courtroom telltale signs of his emotional instability, but he takes no joy in his victory. After the trial, he puts the damper on the victory celebration being staged by the *Caine*'s officers when he gives them a stinging tongue-lashing. His ire is directed particularly at Tom Keefer, whom he perceives correctly as being the chief instigator of the mutiny, but one who refused, when the matter came to a head, to put himself on the line. Greenwald's position seems to be that, while the *Caine*'s officers are legally innocent, they are morally guilty. However sophisticated a rationale they might provide for their actions, what was at the bottom of those actions, in his view, was disloyalty, and disloyalty, for a military officer, is an unforgivable sin. One might say that the trial does not prove either clear-cut guilt or innocence. If anything, it demonstrates the complexity and ambiguity of all human situations. Greenwald's position is that, given the ambiguity, it is always better not to second-guess legitimately constituted authority. It is the chief responsibility of the naval officer to do his duty through thick and thin.

If there is a clear villain in *The Caine Mutiny*, Keefer would appear to be the most likely candidate for the role. Keefer is, in many respects, a preeminently modern man. He is committed to what he presumably regards as the absolute truths of Freudian psychology, which he employs in a reductionist way, as weapons against those who do not share his worldview. He is in the Navy, but not of it, and, in fact, he rather enjoys and exploits his position as an iconoclastic outsider. He maintains an attitude of supercilious superiority toward people such as Queeg, and toward everything that the Navy represents. His view is narrow, restricted by the dictates of his overriding egotism. Keefer is a carping critic of the Navy, but he does not hesitate to take selfish advantage of what the Navy can offer him at every turn. His hypocrisy allows him to talk a big game, but when the pressure is on and when circumstances call for words to be translated into action, he invariably backs off. Perhaps the most damning thing that could be said of Keefer is that he is a coward, as he demonstrates when he is captain of the *Caine* and precipitously abandons ship. By the novel's end, however, Keefer seem to have arrived at a degree of self-awareness that hitherto had eluded him; he confesses to Willie Keith, who succeeds him as commanding officer, that Keith is a better man than he. He is right.

Keith is the central character of the novel; his moral education is the real subject of *The Caine Mutiny*. Willie is an aristocratic rich kid from New York who comes to learn, among other things, the value of democracy. His relationship with Maria Minotti, alias May Wynn, can be interpreted in this way. The bulk of Keith's education, however, takes place in the Navy. When he first comes aboard the *Caine*, he is very much under the influence of Keefer, and he accepts Keefer's cynical interpretation of things as the correct one. Eventually, Keith realizes that the Navy, though imperfect, is not a bad organization. What is more, given the realities of the modern world, it is a necessary organization. Unlike Keefer, Keith is prepared to acknowledge that the Navy in World War II is contributing toward the preservation of the way of life into which both men have been born and to which they are devoted, and that, excepting a total transformation of human nature, navies will probably always be needed to ensure the protection of people's freedom. Keith is not changed into a mindless patriot and militarist, but his criticism of the Navy and its personnel becomes more discriminate, more intelligent, more responsible. He learns to judge matters according to criteria that are not self-centered, and develops an appreciation for the larger scheme of things. He takes pride in his work, and as he rises in rank, his conscientiousness increases; he tries to be the best officer he can.

The world of the Navy, in *The Caine Mutiny*, is in certain respects a microcosm of the world at large. It is beset by all sorts of problems, but there is no perfect alternative somewhere to which one might flee. A person's maturity is measured by his or her ability to establish standards of excellence and to work assiduously to achieve them in spite of various limitations, sometimes severe—limitations in him- or herself, in others, and in the situation.

Marjorie Morningstar • On the surface, Wouk's fourth novel, *Marjorie Morningstar*, would seem to lead nowhere. It is the story of a young Jewish woman, the daughter of immigrants established comfortably in the middle class of New York, who has been sufficiently Americanized as to have for her chief ambition the desire to become a famous actor, a star. Marjorie Morningstar (née Morgenstern) is a beautiful woman whose theatrical talent, while not scintillating, is probably sufficient to underwrite the realization of her dream, given a lucky break here and there. She is willing to make the sacrifices, within certain bounds, and to invest the hard work that the ascent to stardom almost inevitably entails. If Marjorie is determined about anything, it is that she is not going to allow herself to lapse into the staid, conventional life that is the destiny of the vast majority of nice, middle-class Jewish girls. She is going to be different; she is going to break out of the mold. After several fruitless efforts to break into the theater and to make it big, after a sequence of adventures with an assortment of men, chiefly with Noel Airman, she ends up doing what she vowed she would never do. She marries a Jew, a successful lawyer by the name of Milton Schwartz, and she retires to a plush suburb to live the most conventional of conventional lives. The novel, then, would seem to end on an almost laughably anticlimactic note, but only if one fails to perceive the kind of statement that it is attempting to make.

If *The Caine Mutiny* delineates the education of Willie Keith, the education of Marjorie Morningstar is the primary concern of the novel that bears her name. If Marjorie comes full circle, as it were, and ends by embracing the conventional, it is because she discovers that the conventional is worthy of being embraced, the conventional not only as representing middle-class morality, but also, and much more important, as embodying traditional cultural and religious values. The glamorous life to which Marjorie aspired, whether or not she was always fully conscious of the fact, was a life that repudiated traditional values. As a teenager and young woman, she fought her own tradition, particularly as manifested in the Jewish religion; she looked upon it as crude and superstitious, a carry-over from humankind's primitive past. This tradition, however, was more deeply embedded in her, was more integral a part of her identity than she was willing to admit, and throughout her various experiences it guided her actions more than she knew.

Marjorie's failure to realize her dream of becoming a star actually represents the triumph of her better, truer self. Her concern shifts from thin, superficial values to those with substance and depth. The drama of her quest for self-realization is played out principally around her long and erratic affair with Noel Airman. When she first meets Airman, who is some ten years her senior, she is scarcely more than a girl, and she is completely enamored of him. He is handsome, intelligent, urbane, and witty, a talented composer of popular songs who shows promise of becoming a success in the theater. Noel represents much of what she wants to become, and all of what she has decided is most valuable in life, which is emphasized by the fact that she throws decorum to the winds and pursues him actively. When she finally catches him, however, she realizes that she does not really want him. The man who was once her ideal, her hero, the man whom she wanted to marry more than anyone else, is at last perceived, albeit faintly, as a god with clay feet.

Who is this Noel Airman? He is Saul Ehrmann, a man who has actively repudiated his Jewish identity and its associated traditions, but who has failed to come up with a practical substitute for either. He is a rootless vagabond, a shameless Casanova, a man who eschews commitment as a matter of principle, and who tries hard to make a profession of cynicism. It would be wrong, however, to think of him entirely in negative terms. He is not a character lacking in complexity, and he is not devoid of critical self-knowledge, which at times can be acute and penetrating. Nevertheless, this self-awareness serves only to accentuate the pathetic quality of the man, for in the final analysis, he is impotent to act upon his better impulses. He does not have the moral stamina to follow through, and this is so, Wouk implies, precisely because he has cut himself off from his tradition.

The fact that Marjorie arrives at a new state of consciousness that allows her to see Airman for what he is, and accordingly to reject him, is attributable in part to her brief but fateful acquaintance with Michael Eden. Eden, like Airman, is a Jew, but, unlike Airman, he is not in flight from the fact. He is a strong, taciturn man whose personal sufferings have led him to dedicate himself to a melancholy but determined altruism. He is involved in the very risky business of rescuing Jews from Nazi Germany. Here is a man who is every bit as bright and talented as Airman but who has what Airman lacks—integrity and a sense of purpose in life. Although it is not Marjorie's destiny to marry Eden, meeting him has the effect of altering her perception of Airman. Milton Schwartz, the man she marries, has in common with Eden a fundamental decency.

Youngblood Hawke • Wouk's sixth novel, *Youngblood Hawke*, based to some extent on the life of Thomas Wolfe, could be the story of many a young American writer of the twentieth century, and for that reason, the novel, besides its intrinsic worth as a work of fiction, has considerable value as a historical document. The story of Arthur Youngblood Hawke is a success story, but it is a story of failure as well. Indeed, Hawke's case is in many respects a tragic one. Hawke is a lanky, down-home Kentuckian who, after being released from the Navy at the end of World War II, moves to New York to conquer the city and the country, by his pen. He comes to his task with a spotty education, with an explosive imagination, and with a seemingly boundless store of energy. Writing is his life, and his engagement in it is passionate. There is much about Hawke that smacks of the all-American boy. He is crude and unpolished, but straightforward and gentle in his dealings with people—except with those who deserve otherwise. He is an honest man, in his way, and an assiduous worker. He wants to be a success as a writer. He wants to become a millionaire, not so that he can give up writing but so that, freed from financial worries, he can devote himself to it without distractions. Hawke is in the mold of the rustic innocent who has long played a part in American literature.

Hawke's early success works against him in the long run. His first novel, though receiving rough treatment at the hands of the critics, gains a large popular audience; his second novel wins the Pulitzer Prize and increasing respect from the critics. He is associated with a solid, respectable publishing house whose head values his work, has faith in his future, and is willing to be very generous in making contractual arrangements with him. Hawke's obsessional longing for financial independence, however, prompts him to break ties with his publisher and begin publishing his own books; he also makes some risky investments. His luck turns, and in a matter of months he finds himself on the threshold of bankruptcy. He determines that he is going to write his way out of his debts; leaving behind the plush life that he enjoyed only too briefly in New York, he returns to Kentucky, and there, living in a cabin in the woods, he works furiously to complete what proves to be his final novel. In fact, he overworks, devoting himself not only to the novel but also, earlier, to a theatrical production which he hopes will strike it rich. The strain brought about by his frenetic activities exacerbates an old head injury, and, after a wild chase to South America made in a state of delirium, he ends up back in New York. He is hospitalized there and dies at the age of thirty-three.

As Youngblood Hawke lies dying, his vaguely addressed prayer is that he might be given more time so that he can work. Everything that he has done he considers as only preparatory exercises to his great multivolume *Comedy*. The fact that his magnum opus was never written is not simply attributable to the fact that Hawke showed poor business sense or that he was careless of his health. There is evidence in the novel to warrant the conclusion that Hawke's failure to fulfill his chief artistic ambition amounts to an exacting payment he has had to make for his sins. There have been two principal women in his life, but, by his own admission, there should have been only one. In the beginning of the novel, before he bursts upon the American literary scene, he meets a young editor, Jeanne Green, who subsequently becomes for him what Maxwell Perkins was for Thomas Wolfe. Jeanne, besides being a very talented editor, is, like Hawke, essentially a small-town person. She is simple, unpretentious, genuine. Hawke falls in love with Jeanne almost immediately—his better self tells him that this is the woman in his life, the woman he should marry—but he becomes involved in a torrid affair with a wealthy, sophisticated, fundamentally selfish New Yorker, Frieda Winters. Frieda is older than he; she is married, has three children, and is no stranger to adulterous affairs. Hawke is honest enough with himself to admit that he is involved in adultery; the reader is told that he hates both the word and the fact. He does not have the moral courage, however, to extricate himself from the affair—not until, as it turns out, it is too late. His relationship with Frieda proves to be an enervating experience; if it does not exactly destroy him, it contributes substantially toward his destruction.

What allowed Hawke to become involved in an affair that he knew to be wrong? One explanation is that he failed to be true to the basic religious principles that he had been taught as a boy but that in his impetuous youth he attempted to reject. Unlike Marjorie Morningstar, whose roots in a religious tradition were sufficiently deep and tenacious to carry her through the hard times, Hawke succumbs to the facile moral standards of a secularized society.

Don't Stop the Carnival • Wouk's next novel, *Don't Stop the Carnival*, is the weakest of his entire corpus. It is a comic novel and it would seem to have some kind of satiric intent, but the humor, instead of carrying the moral import of the tale, more often than not obstructs it. The work's humor is hampered by obtrusive, heavy-handed moralizing, and its seriousness is trivialized by a humor that too often degenerates into tedious slapstick. Most damaging for the novel is the fact that Wouk's narrative talent, which is his forte, serves him poorly here. The plot is too often based upon contrivance, and in some instances blatant authorial manipulation is very much in evidence. Add to this fact that characterization is unconvincing, and the sum total is a generally undistinguished piece of fiction that holds the reader's attention only by an adamant act of will. It is not that the novel is completely lacking in substance, but the detectably substantive elements are not allowed to emerge fully. There is, for example, a statement being made about the haplessness of "liberal" types who are awash in a world that in many respects is the result of their own brand of thinking, but the message is befuddled by static of various kinds and one must strain to detect it.

The Winds of War* and *War and Remembrance • Wouk's impressive companion novels, *The Winds of War* and *War and Remembrance*, published in 1971 and 1978, respectively, are in effect a single, sustained work of fiction, and therefore can be discussed together. Wouk spent sixteen years in completing the work, and it seems likely that he regards it as his magnum opus. *The Winds of War* is focused primarily on the European theater, beginning with the German invasion of Czechoslovakia and Poland, putting special emphasis upon the latter. The Battle of Britain is also treated at close range. The book ends with the bombing of Pearl Harbor, the point at which *War and Remembrance* takes up the story. This book, while continuing to trace the course of events in Europe, especially those events having to do with the systematic extermination of the Jews by the Nazis, shifts attention to the Pacific theater and provides poignant descriptions of the major naval battles fought there. The book ends with the dropping of the atomic bombs and the Japanese acceptance of unconditional surrender. In these two massive volumes that constitute a single work, an ambitious fictional history of World War II, Wouk once again shows himself to be a master of narrative. This is not a mere chronicle of events; rather, major events of the war are given dramatic immediacy by the tactic of having one of the many key characters in the narrative involved in those events. One is even provided access to the Axis point of view through excerpts from the analytic histories of the German General Armin von Roon, interspersed throughout the work.

The key character in the work is Victor "Pug" Henry, a naval officer who has given thirty years of his life to military service. He is a staid, conservative man, a patriot but not a jingoist, dedicated to professional excellence and quietly guided by deeply embedded religious principles. Following his various adventures in Europe and in the Pacific, one is not only brought into direct contact with important historical personages but treated to his thoughtful reactions to them as well. Wouk is the type of artist who likes to paint on a large canvas, but the canvas he is covering in this work is of mammoth proportions. All the more remarkable, then, is the control he exercises here; nothing gets away from him. There is a satisfying unity and completeness about this wide-ranging tour de force. It is thickly peopled with a vast array of characters, and their attitudes toward the war run the full gamut from self-sacrificing heroism to cold-blooded murderousness.

One of the most interesting characters in the work is Aaron Jastrow, a Jewish-American, world-renowned scholar and former Yale professor who at the outbreak of the war is living in active retirement in Italy. In tracing the story of Aaron Jastrow, and that of his Polish cousin Berel, Wouk recounts in moving fashion the sickening circumstances of the infamous "final solution." Aaron himself was born in Poland and reared in a strict Orthodox tradition. As he reached young manhood, he put aside his religion and settled into a benevolent agnosticism. Accompanied by his niece Natalie, he is hounded by the Nazis throughout Europe for years, until he finally ends up in the land of his birth, in a death camp. His life is choked out in the gas chambers. He speaks to the reader directly through *A Jew's Journey*. What one learns from this document is that the most significant journey in the waning months of Jastrow's life is a spiritual one. His personal confrontation with the horrors of Nazism has the effect of returning him to the religion of his birth. When he comes to die, he is possessed of an inner peace his murderers could never know, and he represents a basic human dignity that they have chosen to abandon for themselves and to attempt to destroy in others.

The Winds of War and *War and Remembrance* are about a specific war, but they are about war in general as well. Wouk does not romanticize World War II, but he suggests that it was absolutely essential that the Allied forces emerge as victorious. It was an unspeakably grim yet nevertheless necessary struggle. The bombs that ended the war, however, changed the nature of war forever. If humankind were capable before Hiroshima and Nagasaki of arguing that all-out war, however cruel and crude, was a workable solution to human problems, that argument proved no longer tenable. World War II was perhaps the most gruesome war that human beings have ever inflicted upon themselves. Wouk's thesis is that wars in the future will not be avoided simply by proclaiming them to be unthinkable. One must think about them; one must think especially about the most gruesome of wars. Through memory, perhaps a pathway to peace can be found.

Inside, Outside • Wouk's *Inside, Outside* appeared in 1985. *The Caine Mutiny* is by consensus Wouk's single best work of fiction, but *Inside, Outside* could arguably be offered as a legitimate contender for that honor. Here one finds all Wouk's considerable skill in operation: his commanding ability to create characters that live and breathe and convince, telling their interesting and interlocking stories within the context of a fictional world that, while complex, never degenerates into incoherence. Wouk's characters move and make their marks in a world that can be as confused and disorienting as that created by any other modern fictionist, but the core, the center, of Wouk's world, although subjected to great strain, always manages to hold; that is, although Wouk's characters live in an extremely difficult and demanding world, that world preserves its essential meaningfulness. Wouk does not burden himself with the absurd task of attempting to populate an absurd universe.

It is difficult to specify what makes for the peculiar success of this novel, but certainly at work is Wouk's uncanny ability—which is singularly devoid of self-advertising and therefore easy to overlook—to create what one might call fictional immediacy. Wouk can effect the magic of bringing into being a fictional world that more than half persuades the reader that it is not fictional at all. In other words, he is a maker of art.

Inside, Outside revolves around the life and times of one Israel David Goodkind. It is principally his story, and he tells it with verve. The novel is interestingly structured.

The time frame of the narration is 1973. In that year, Goodkind, a successful New York lawyer, finds himself in the rather unusual position—given the fact that he has been a lifelong Democrat—of serving in Washington as a special assistant to President Richard M. Nixon. The job, though flattering in its way, is anything but exacting, and Goodkind begins to expend his considerable free time in writing; however, this activity is not simply an idle exercise with which to fill the gaps in his undemanding day. He takes his writing quite seriously, and he intends to produce something of real literary worth. He endeavors to fulfill an ambition he has harbored since his youth, but which thus far he has not managed to accomplish. He writes about his own life, which takes him back to the turn of the century and the stories of his parents, two Jewish emigrants from Russia. They both arrive in New York; there they meet and marry, and there their children, Israel and Lee, are born. The reader follows the entire course of Goodkind's life as he recounts its developments, its delays, its assorted dramatic and melodramatic reversals, with meticulous and loving detail. The reader is brought into the very center of Goodkind's world and discovers it to be a world that is at once intensely provincial and intensely cosmopolitan—the kind of combination which is possible perhaps only in New York City. It is a wide world, thickly populated with a rich variety of relatives and friends. The reader is given the opportunity to meet them all, and, with differing degrees of completeness, to come to know their stories, too.

Such is the main strand of the novel's narrative. Its secondary strand is no less compelling. Goodkind is interrupted periodically in his recounting of his past by the pressing events that take place around him in 1973 as he continues his writing project. Two significant historical events mark that time period. One is the Israeli-Egyptian War; the other is the resignation of President Nixon in the wake of the Watergate scandal. The first event takes place within the time frame of the novel, and Goodkind reports on it as he writes. The second event draws closer and closer, but the novel ends without the president's resignation having yet taken place. The Israeli-Egyptian War plays an important symbolic role in the narrative because one of the central themes of the novel is the situation of the Jew in the modern world.

The "inside" of the novel's title refers to the somewhat self-enclosed, clearly identifiable, but far from homogeneous world of Jewish religion and culture, whereas the "outside" refers to the world at large. Wouk is something of an oddity among contemporary American novelists because of his open and unapologetic commitment to his religious convictions. This fact largely explains the decided and persistent moral tone of his fiction. One can find expressions, more or less strong, more or less developed, of his commitment to Judaism throughout his fiction, but in no other novel, it seems, does his religious faith play so central and integral a part than in *Inside, Outside*.

What Wouk gives the reader in this novel, along with much else, is a dynamic and dramatic picture of the manifold consciousness that constitutes late twentieth century Judaism. The picture he presents is intricate, complicated, and in some respects even contradictory. Wouk deals with the rich reality that is Judaism in a manner that is—variously—intensely objective and intensely subjective. He seems to leave nothing out of the picture; negative elements are treated with as much thoroughness as are positive elements. Nevertheless, Wouk does not treat the heart of his subject matter, the essential identity of Judaism, with anything but respect and reverence.

If by novel's end one cannot identify its protagonist as a typical modern Jew, that is only because one has come to understand that there is no such thing. I. David

Goodkind is a representative modern Jew, but so are many who are quite different from him, and Goodkind himself is far from simple. On one hand, Goodkind reflects the "inside" component of his world, but a distinct "outside" dimension to his personality exists as well. Both together, "inside" and "outside," make up who he is. Goodkind is a religious Jew who faithfully practices his religion. He is also a political Jew who sympathizes with the Zionist tradition and takes great patriotic pride in the state of Israel. At the same time, Goodkind is a thorough American. In a larger sense, he is an eminently modern man, one who, even in spite of himself at times, reflects the consciousness of the contemporary Western intellectual, with all the limitations peculiar to it. His judgments on the major issues that impinge upon his life have to them a ring of confident cosmopolitanism, which disguises their lack of substantial metaphysical foundations. For example, although he is in many respects exemplary for his perspicacity and sensitivity, he is obtuse in response to some of the clear signs of decadence in modern culture.

Mention might be made of the unorthodox manner in which the novel deals with the character of President Nixon. Wouk goes beyond the crude journalistic stereotypes to discover in Nixon not merely a caricature but a real human being. Finally, *Inside, Outside* is simultaneously a serious and a humorous work, and both of these faces complement each other, helping to bring each into greater relief. In some of his other novels, Wouk has demonstrated his facility in handling humor, but that skill is especially in evidence in *Inside, Outside*.

The Hope and The Glory • Wouk was not able to sustain in his next two novels the high level of artistry he achieved in *Inside, Outside*. In *The Hope* and *The Glory* he continues to exploit his interest in Judaic issues, using the techniques that proved successful in *The Winds of War* and *War and Remembrance*. Though published separately, *The Hope* and *The Glory* are much like Wouk's two-volume romance about World War II; collectively they provide a portrait of the early years of the state of Israel, depicting the struggles of the Jewish people to establish a new independent country in their ancestral homeland.

The Hope is set in the years immediately following World War II, when a small but determined group of Zionist freedom fighters ousted the British from Palestine and declared the foundation of the new state of Israel. As he did in *The Winds of War* and *War and Remembrance*, Wouk creates a number of fictional characters whose lives intersect with the real-life heroes and heroines of the new Jewish nation. Wouk offers a vivid account of the 1948 War of Independence, focusing on the struggles of leaders such as David Ben-Gurion and Moshe Dayan to unite the disparate political and paramilitary groups in the region. The climax of the novel is the stunning victory of the Israelis over their Arab enemies in the Six-Day War of 1967. *The Glory* is a sequel, containing many of the same characters. In recounting the tale of the Jewish nation from 1967 to the announcement of the Camp David Peace Accords, Wouk has his fictional characters support the likes of Golda Meir and Menachem Begin.

Though with less success than he realized in his World War II novels, Wouk gives his narrative a sense of immediacy by concentrating his attention on the effects of the Israelis' struggle on the lives of common men and women. To accomplish this, he creates four families whose fortunes are intertwined not only with historical personages of note but also with each other: the Baraks, the Blumenthals, the Pasternaks, and the Luries. Among them are fighters, local politicians, businessmen, and even ambassadors who represent Israel in the United States and at the United Nations. Political issues are paralleled by small acts of love and vengeance, bringing a certain degree of humanity to the large historical canvas on which Wouk depicts the nation he loves.

Like most novels published by Wouk since the appearance of *The Caine Mutiny,* both *The Hope* and *The Glory* attracted a large readership, but neither received praise from critics. The negative critical reaction seems justified. Although the historical accounts are accurate and presented with a strong sense of control, at least one reviewer found this extremely complex political subject treated with "only slightly more subtlety than a grade-school Thanksgiving pageant." Knowing that he would be open to criticism because of his strong partisan views, Wouk was careful to offer a note in *The Hope* that he worked hard not to present a caricature of the Arabs. However, there is a general laxity in dealing with both major and minor Jewish figures. Instead of striving for complexity, Wouk often resorts to stereotypes that create heroes and villains more commonly found in melodrama or popular romances. His men are almost all superhuman, his women submissive handmaids. What could have been a wonderful final performance in a distinguished career as a popular novelist seems to have emerged as little more than a drifting away into contemporary cliché.

Despite his broad popular appeal, Wouk has generally not found favor with the critics, especially academic critics. The common response of the latter has been simply to ignore him. It is difficult to explain precisely why this is so. Perhaps Wouk's very popularity militates against him, as if there existed a necessary relationship between popularity and artistic worth: The more popular a writer, the poorer the quality of what he writes. Perhaps Wouk's traditionalist worldview and forthright advocacy of Judeo-Christian moral principles, to which many critics today are hostile, account in part for the critical neglect of his work.

In any case, Wouk deserves more critical attention than he has received. He is not the greatest among the many fine novelists to appear in the United States since World War II, but neither is he an inconsequential figure. His prose is solid and vigorous, eschewing preciosity and self-indulgence. Writing with intelligence and sensitivity, he appeals neither to a small clique of literary aesthetes nor to the lowest common denominator of a general audience. His attitude toward fiction is that shared by all the major novelists of literary history; his fiction is not concerned with itself but with the world at large. His fiction does not attempt the irrelevant task of creating a moral universe from scratch, but accepts and responds to the moral universe that is already in place.

Dennis Q. McInerny
Updated by Laurence W. Mazzeno

Other major works

PLAYS: *The Traitor,* pr., pb. 1949; *The Caine Mutiny Court-Martial,* pr., pb. 1954; *Nature's Way,* pr. 1957; *Don't Stop the Carnival,* pr. 1998 (adaptation of his novel; musical, with Jimmy Buffett).

SCREENPLAY: *Slattery's Hurricane,* 1949 (with Richard Murphy).

TELEPLAYS: *The Winds of War,* 1983; *War and Remembrance,* 1988.

NONFICTION: *This Is My God,* 1959; *The Will to Live On: This Is Our Heritage,* 2000.

Bibliography

Beichman, Arnold. *Herman Wouk: The Novelist as Social Historian*. New Brunswick, N.J.: Transaction Books, 1984. A lifelong friend of Wouk, Beichman offers a strident defense of the novelist against those who fault him for both his conservative political stance and his decision to stress narrative and action over complex characterization.

Darby, William. *Necessary American Fictions: Popular Literature of the 1950's*. Bowling Green, Ohio: Bowling Green State University Press, 1987. Examines *The Caine Mutiny* as a mirror of 1950's popular values.

Gerard, Philip. "The Great American War Novels." *World and I* 10 (June, 1995): 54-63. Gerard notes that World War II was "the last public event that defined a generation of novelists." In this essay, he looks at the works of many of them, including Wouk's *The Caine Mutiny*.

Mazzeno, Laurence W. *Herman Wouk*. New York: Twayne, 1994. Offers a brief biographical sketch and analyses of the major novels through *Inside, Outside*. The book contains excerpts from hundreds of reviews of Wouk's fiction, providing a sense of the contemporary reaction to each of Wouk's major works.

Shapiro, Edward S. "The Jew as Patriot: Herman Wouk and American Jewish Identity." *American Jewish History* 84 (December, 1996): 333-351. Shapiro provides a retrospective review of Wouk's career, arguing persuasively that Wouk is concerned principally with defining American Jewish identity.

Shatzky, Joel, and Michael Taub, eds. *Contemporary Jewish-American Novelists: A Biocritical Sourcebook*. Westport, Conn.: Greenwood Press, 1997. Includes an entry on Wouk's life, major works, and themes, with an overview of his critical reception and a bibliography of primary and secondary sources.

Wouk, Herman. *The Will to Live On: This Is Our Heritage*. New York: Harper Perennial, 2000. An updating of Wouk's *This Is My God* (1959), this book restates Wouk's devotion to Judiasm and surveys the condition of Jews and belief in Judaism at the end of the twentieth century. Pays particular attention to the state of Israel.

Richard Wright

Born: Roxie, Mississippi; September 4, 1908
Died: Paris, France; November 28, 1960

Principal long fiction • *Native Son*, 1940; *The Outsider*, 1953; *Savage Holiday*, 1954; *The Long Dream*, 1958; *Lawd Today*, 1963.

Other literary forms • In addition to his five novels, Richard Wright published collections of essays and short stories and two autobiographical volumes. Two collections of short stories, the early *Uncle Tom's Children* (1938,) and the posthumously collected *Eight Men* (1961), represent some of Wright's finest fiction. Wright himself believed that the characters in *Uncle Tom's Children* were too easily pitied and that they elicited from readers a sympathy that was unlike the tough intellectual judgment he desired. Wright later wrote that his creation of Bigger Thomas in *Native Son* was an attempt to stiffen that portrayal so that readers could not leniently dismiss his characters with simple compassion, but would have to accept them as free, fully human adults, whose actions required assessment. Nevertheless, the stories of *Uncle Tom's Children* are carefully written, and the characters, though sometimes defeated, embody the kind of independence and intractability that Wright valued in his fiction.

Two stories from *Eight Men* reveal the themes to which Wright gave sustained development in his novels. In "The Man Who Was Almos' a Man," the main character learns that power means freedom, and although he first bungles his attempt to shoot a gun, his symbol of power, he lies to his family, keeps the gun, and at the conclusion of the story leaves home to grow into manhood elsewhere. In "The Man Who Lived Underground," the main character, nameless at first, is accused of a crime he did not commit. Fleeing underground to the sewers of the city, he becomes a voyeur of life, seen now from a new perspective. The values that served him badly above ground do not serve him at all below. By the end of the story, he has come to understand that all men are guilty; his name is revealed, and with his new values, he ascends once more to accept responsibility for the crime. Because all men are guilty, it is less important to him that the crime is not his own than that he acknowledge freely that he shares in human guilt.

Even more important than these two collections is the first volume of Wright's autobiography, *Black Boy* (1945), which opens up a world of experience to the reader. It traces the first seventeen years of Wright's life—from his birth in Mississippi and the desertion of the family by his father, through years of displacement as he travels from one relative to another with his ill mother and religious grandmother. The early years find Wright, like his later protagonists, an outsider, cut off from family, from friends, from culture. He is as out of place among black people as among white people, baffled by those black people who play the roles whites expect of them, himself unable to dissimulate his feelings and thoughts.

Although the work is nonfiction, it is united by powerful metaphors: fire, hunger, and blindness. Wright's inner fire is mirrored throughout the work by actual fires; indeed, his first act is to set afire the curtains in his home. His physical hunger, a constant companion, is an image of his hunger for knowledge and connection, and his two jobs in optical factories suggest the blindness of society, a blindness given further representation in *Native Son*.

What Wright learns in *Black Boy* is the power of words. His early life is marked by physical violence: He witnesses murders and beatings, but it is the violence of words that offers liberation from his suffocating environment. Whether it is the profanity with which he shocks his grandmother, the literalness with which he takes his father's words, or the crude expressions with which he taunts Jewish shopkeepers, he discovers that words have a power that makes him an equal to those around him. When he feels unequal, as in his early school experiences, he is speechless. The culmination of this theme occurs when Wright acquires a library card and discovers through his readings in the American social critics of the early part of the twentieth century, such as H. L. Mencken and Sinclair Lewis, that he is not alone in his feelings and that there are others who share his alienation and discontent.

When Wright finally sees his father many years after his desertion, his hatred dissolves: He realizes that his father, trapped by his surroundings, with neither a cultural past nor an individual future, speaks a different language from his own, holds different thoughts, and is truly a victim and therefore not worthy even of his hatred. Wright's characters must never be victims, for as such they hold no interest. At the end of the book, he goes north, first to Memphis and, when that fails, north again to Chicago, pursuing the dream, having now the power of words to articulate it and to define himself.

The record of his years in Chicago is found in the posthumously published second autobiographical volume, *American Hunger* (written in 1944, published in 1977). Largely a record of his involvement and later disillusionment with the Communist Party, this book is interesting for its view of a later, mature Wright who is still struggling with institutions that would limit his freedom.

Achievements • In his best work, Wright gives American literature its strongest statement of the existential theme of alienated people defining themselves. Wright's use of the black American as archetypal outsider gives his work a double edge. On one hand, no American writer so carefully illuminates the black experience in America: The ambivalence of black feeling, the hypocrisies of the dominant culture, and the tension between them find concrete and original manifestation in Wright's work, a manifestation at once revealing and terrifying.

It is not only in his revelation of black life, however, that Wright's power lies, for as much as his writing is social and political, it is also personal and philosophical. The story of alienated people is a universal one; because the concrete experiences of the outsider are so vividly rendered in Wright's fiction, his books have an immediate accessibility. Because they also reveal deeper patterns, they have further claims to attention. Much of Wright's later fiction seems self-conscious and studied, but it cannot diminish the greatness of his finest work.

Biography • Born in Mississippi of sharecropper parents, Richard Wright had a lonely and troubled childhood. His father deserted the family early, and after his mother suffered a stroke, Wright was forced at a young age to work to help support the family, which moved frequently from one relative to another. His portrayal of his mother is of a stern but loving parent, unable to contend with the stronger personality of his extremely religious grandmother. Wright's grandmother believed that all fiction was "the devil's lies"; her chief goal was to force Wright into a religious conversion, a goal in which she was singularly unsuccessful.

Wright moved from school to school, attempting to make friends and make his talents known. Though both tasks were difficult, he became valedictorian of his class. Even this accomplishment was spoiled when the principal insisted that Wright read a speech that the principal himself had written, and Wright refused. An uncle told Richard, "They're going to break you," and society, both black and white, seemed intent on doing so. Wright was determined to resist, not to be claimed by his environment as he believed so many black people around him were.

Wright left Mississippi for Memphis, Tennessee, had little luck there, and—with money stolen from the film theater where he worked—moved to Chicago. When others stole, Wright disapproved—not for moral reasons, but because he believed stealing did not change the fundamental relationship of a person to his environment.

Library of Congress

When it offered a chance to change that environment, Wright accepted it.

In Chicago, Wright became involved with others who viewed the country as he did, first in a federal theater project and then with the communist John Reed Club, which supported his writing until Wright's goals differed from their own. In 1937, he moved to New York City to become the editor of the *Daily Worker*. A year later, he published his first important work, *Uncle Tom's Children*, after which he won a Guggenheim Fellowship, which provided him with the time and funds to write *Native Son*. The novel was published to great acclaim and was followed by a second major work, *Black Boy*. Although his writing career was a success, Wright was arguing more frequently with the Communist Party, with which he finally broke in 1944, and was becoming less optimistic about the hope of racial progress in the United States.

In 1946, Wright moved to France, where he spent the rest of his life. Although he wrote a great deal there, nothing in his later work, with the possible exception of *The Outsider*, approaches the strength of *Native Son* and *Black Boy*. The existentialism that was always implicit in his work became the dominant theme, but—displaced from his native environment—Wright never again found a convincing dramatic situation in which to work out his preoccupations.

Wright died in France of a heart attack on November 28, 1960. After his death, three more works, *Eight Men*, *Lawd Today*, and *American Hunger*, were published.

Analysis • Wright's best work is always the story of one man's struggle to define himself and by so doing make himself free and responsible, fully human, a character worthy not of pity but of admiration and horror simultaneously. Typically, the character is an outsider, and Wright uses blackness as a representation of that alienation, though his characters are never as interested in defining their blackness as in defining their humanity. Although many characters in Wright's works are outsiders without being aware of their condition, Wright is never interested in them except as foils. Many of them avoid confronting themselves by fleeing to dreams; religion and liquor are two avoidance mechanisms for Wright's characters, narcotics that blind them to their surrounding world, to what they are and what they might be.

Even Wright's main characters must not think about that world too often: To let it touch them is to risk insanity or violence, and so his characters strive to keep the fire within in check, to keep the physical hunger satisfied. Thus, all of Wright's protagonists are initially trapped by desire and by fear—fear of what might happen to them, what they may do, if they risk venturing outside the confines of black life in America—and the desire to do so. The life outside may be glimpsed in films; Bigger Thomas, for example, goes to a film and watches contrasting and artificial views of black and white society. However, as untruthful as both views are, they remind Bigger of a reality beyond his present situation. Desire is often symbolized by flight; Bigger, like other Wright characters, dreams of flying above the world, unchained from its limitations.

Most of Wright's stories and novels examine what happens when the protagonist's fear is mastered for a moment when desires are met. The manifestation of desire in Wright is almost always through violence (and it is here, perhaps, that he is most pessimistic, for other, more positive, manifestations of desire, such as love, can come only later, after the protagonists have violently acted out their longings). Violence is central to Wright's fiction, for as important as sex may be to his characters, power is much more so, and power is often achieved through violence; in Wright's world, beatings and murders are frequent acts—central and occasionally creative.

After the character acts, he finds himself trapped again in a new set of oppositions, for in acting, he has left the old sureties behind, has made himself free, and has begun to define and create himself. With that new freedom comes a new awareness of responsibility. He is without excuses, and that awareness is as terrifying as—though more liberating than—the fears he has previously known. Although Wright does not always elaborate on what may follow, the characters open up new possibilities for themselves. If one may create one's self by violence, perhaps, Wright sometimes suggests, there are other, less destructive ways as well.

Some of Wright's novels end on this note of optimism, the characters tragically happy: tragic because they have committed violent and repulsive acts, but happy because for the first time they have *chosen* to commit them; they have freed themselves from their constraints, and the future, however short it may be, lies open. Others end simply with tragedy, the destruction achieving no purpose, the characters attaining no illumination.

Lawd Today • *Lawd Today*, written before *Native Son*, but not published until after Wright's death, tells the story of Jake Jackson from his awakening on the morning of February 12, 1936, to that day's violent conclusion. Jackson is Wright's most inarticulate protagonist: He has a banal life, undefined dreams, and a vague sense of discontent that he is unable to explain. Violent and prejudiced, he speaks in clichés, a language as meaningless as his life.

Technically, the book incorporates a montage of radio broadcasts, newspaper articles, and religious and political pamphlets into the narration of Jake's day. Divided into three sections, *Lawd Today* opens with Jake's dream of running up an endless staircase after a disappearing voice. That dream gives way to the reality of his life: hunger, anger, and recrimination. Tricked by Jake into an abortion for which Jake still owes five hundred dollars and now claiming to have a tumor that will cost another five hundred dollars to remove, Jake's wife represents his entrapment. In the first section, "Commonplace," Jake reveals his brutish and trivial character: his anger at his wife, a jealousy and resentment that lead him to bait her so he can hit her, a mock battle straightening his hair, and a meeting with friends who work with him at the post office. As they play bridge to pass the time until work, Wright presents without comment their stupid, cliché-ridden conversation.

Section 2, "Squirrel Cage," shows the men at work. They are all alienated in meaningless, routine jobs, but Jake's position is the most desperate, for his wife has been to see his boss, and he is now threatened with the loss of his job. Falling deeper into debt by borrowing more money and making mistakes on the job, Jake is trapped by his work—despite his own protestations, as a self-proclaimed Republican and capitalist, that work is liberating. This section, too, ends with a long, rambling, and banal conversation among the men at work.

In the concluding section, "Rat's Alley," the men go to a brothel for a good time on some of Jake's borrowed money. There, Jake is robbed and then beaten for his threats of revenge. Finally, Jake stumbles homeward, his day nearing an end. The February weather, pleasant when the book began, has turned bad. All of Jake's frustration and anger finally erupt; he beats his wife, whom he finds kneeling asleep by the bed in an attitude of prayer. As they struggle, he throws objects through the window. She grabs a shard of broken glass and slashes him three times. The book ends with Jake lying in a drunken stupor, bleeding, while his wife is on her knees, also bleeding, praying for death. Outside, the wind blows mercilessly.

Although some of the experimentalism of *Lawd Today* seems artificial, and although the protagonist is too limited to sustain the reader's interest, this early work is powerful and economical. The situation, if not the character, is typical of Wright's work, and the reader understands Jake's violent frustration. *Lawd Today* has its flaws, but it foreshadows the strengths of Wright's best work and in its own right is a daring and fascinating novel.

Native Son • Along with *Black Boy, Native Son* is one of Wright's finest achievements: a brilliant portrayal of, as Wright put it, the way the environment provides the instrumentalities through which one expresses oneself and the way that self becomes whole despite the environment's conspiring to keep it divided.

The book parallels Theodore Dreiser's *An American Tragedy* (1925): Both are three-part novels in which there is a murder, in part accidental, in part willed; an attempted flight; and a long concluding trial, in both cases somewhat anticlimactic. Both novels are concerned with the interplay of environment and heredity, of fate and accident, and both have protagonists who rebel against the world that would hold them back.

In the first part of *Native Son*, Bigger Thomas is a black man cut off from family and peers. Superficially like his friends, he is in fact possessed of a different consciousness. To think about that consciousness is for him to risk insanity or violence, so Bigger endeavors to keep his fears and uncertainty at a preconscious level. On the day of the first section, however, he is required by the welfare agency to apply for a job as a menial at the home of the rich Dalton family. Mr. Dalton is a ghetto landlord who soothes his conscience by donating sums of money for recreational purposes. The fact that it is a minuscule part of the money he is deriving from black people is an irony he overlooks. Mrs. Dalton is blind, a fact that is necessary to the plot as well as being symbolic. Their daughter, Mary, is a member of the Communist Party, and from the moment she sees Bigger, who wants nothing more than to be left alone, she begins to enlist his support.

The first evening, Bigger is to drive Mary to a university class. In reality, she is going with Jan Erlone, her communist boyfriend, to a party meeting. Afterward, they insist that Bigger take them to a bar in the black part of town. Jan and Mary are at this point satirized, for their attitudes toward black people are as limited and stereotyped as any in the novel. Bigger does not want to be seen by his friends with whites, but that fact does not occur to Mary. After much drinking, Bigger must carry the drunken Mary to her bedroom. He puts her to bed, stands over her, attracted to the woman he sees. The door opens and Mrs. Dalton enters. When Mary makes drunken noises, Bigger becomes frightened that Mrs. Dalton will come close enough to discover him, so he puts a pillow over Mary's face to quiet her. By the time Mrs. Dalton leaves, Mary is dead.

Wright wanted to make Bigger a character it would be impossible to pity, and what follows is extremely grisly. Bigger tries to put Mary's body in the furnace and saws off her head to make her fit. However accidental Mary's death may appear to the reader, Bigger himself does not regard it as such. He has, he thinks, many times wanted to kill whites without ever having the opportunity to do so. This time there was the act without the desire, but rather than seeing himself as the victim of a chance occurrence, Bigger prefers to unite the earlier desire with the present act, to make himself whole by accepting responsibility for the killing. Indeed, he not only accepts the act but also determines to capitalize on it by sending a ransom note. Later, accused of raping Mary as well, an act he considered but did not commit, he reverses the process, accepting responsibility for this, too, even though here there was desire but no act. His only sign of conscience is that he cannot bring himself to shake the ashes in the furnace; this guilt is not redemptive, but his undoing, for, in an implausible scene in the Dalton basement, the room fills with smoke, the murder is revealed to newspaper reporters gathered there, and Bigger is forced to flee.

Bigger runs with his girlfriend, Bessie Mears. She, like Bigger, has a hunger for sensation, which has initially attracted him to her. Now, however, as they flee together, she becomes a threat and a burden; huddled with her in an abandoned tenement, Bigger wants only to be rid of her. He picks up a brick and smashes her face, dumping her body down an airshaft. His only regret is not that he has killed her, but that he has forgotten to remove their money from her body.

The rest of the plot moves quickly: Bigger is soon arrested, the trial is turned into a political farce, and Bigger is convicted and sentenced to death. In the last part of the novel, after Bigger's arrest, the implications of the action are developed, largely through Bigger's relations to other characters. Some of the characters are worthy only of contempt, particularly the district attorney, who, in an attempt at reelection, is turning the trial into political capital. Bigger's mother relies on religion. In a scene in the jail cell, she falls on her knees in apology before Mrs. Dalton and urges Bigger to pray, but toughness is Bigger's code. He is embarrassed by his mother's self-abasement, and although he agrees to pray simply to end his discomfort, his attitude toward religion is shown when he throws away a cross a minister has given him and throws a cup of coffee in a priest's face. In his view, they want only to avoid the world and to force him to accept guilt without responsibility.

Bigger learns from two characters. The first is Boris Max, the lawyer the Communist Party provides. Max listens to Bigger, and for the first time in his life, Bigger exposes his ideas and feelings to another human. Max's plea to the court is that, just as Bigger must accept responsibility for what he has done, so must the society around him understand its responsibility for what Bigger has become and, if the court chooses to execute Bigger, understand the consequences that must flow from that action. He does not argue—nor does Wright believe—that Bigger is a victim of injustice. There is no injustice, because that would presume a world in which Bigger could hope for justice, and such a world does not exist; more important, Bigger is not a victim, for he has chosen his own fate. Max argues rather that all men are titled to happiness. Like all of Wright's protagonists, Bigger has earlier been torn between the poles of dread and ecstasy. His ecstasy, his happiness, comes from the meaningfulness he creates in his existence, a product of self-realization. Unhappily for Bigger, he realizes himself through murder: It was, he feels, his highest creative act.

If Max articulates the intellectual presentation of Wright's beliefs about Bigger, it is Jan, Mary's lover, who is its dramatic representation. He visits Bigger in his cell and, having at last understood the futility and paucity of his own stereotypes, admits to Bigger that he too shares in the responsibility for what has happened. He, too, addresses Bigger as a human being, but from the unique position of being the one who is alive to remind Bigger of the consequences of his actions, for Bigger learns that Jan has suffered loss through what he has done and that, while Bigger has created himself, he has also destroyed another.

Native Son ends with the failure of Max's appeals on Bigger's behalf. He comes to the cell to confront Bigger before his execution, and the novel closes with Bigger Thomas smiling at Max as the prison door clangs shut. He will die happy because he will die fulfilled, having, however terribly, created a self. *Native Son* is Wright's most powerful work, because his theme, universal in nature, is given its fullest and most evocative embodiment. In the characterization of Bigger, alienated man at his least abstract and most genuine, of Bigger's exactly rendered mind and milieu, and of Bigger's working out of his destiny, *Native Son* is Wright's masterpiece.

The Outsider • Wright's next novel, *The Outsider*, written in France and published thirteen years after *Native Son*, suffers from a surfeit of internal explanation and a failure to provide a setting as rich as that of *Native Son*. Nevertheless, its portrayal of Cross Damon and his struggle to define himself, while too self-conscious, adds new dimensions to Wright's myth.

As the novel opens, Damon is trapped by his life. His post office job is unfulfilling, his wife is threatening, and his underage mistress is pregnant. He "desires desire," but there is no way for that desire to be completed. "A man creates himself," he has told his wife, but the self Damon has created is a nightmare. He broods, his brooding as close as he comes to religion. Another underground man, Damon gets his chance for new life on the subway. Thought dead after his identification papers are found near the mangled body of another, Damon gets a chance to create himself anew. He must invent, he thinks, not only his future, but also a past to fit with his present; this new opportunity brings with it a different and more potent sense of dread.

From the beginning of this new life, Damon is remarkably successful at the mechanics of creating a past. He easily obtains a birth certificate and a draft card. At a deeper level, however, he traps himself as surely as he has been trapped in his old life, so that his new one becomes a continuous act of bad faith. Even before he leaves Chicago, he hides in a brothel where he encounters a coworker who recognizes him. Damon murders the man and throws his body out a window. The pattern of violence, so typical of Wright's characters, begins in earnest for Damon.

Taking a train to New York, Damon meets two people who will influence his new life, a black waiter who introduces him to the world of communist politics in New York City, and Ely Houston, the district attorney, who is the most articulate person in the novel and the only one fully to understand Damon. Houston asks Damon why, when all black people are outsiders, so few seem conscious of this fact. Wright suggests that being human is too much to be borne by people, that the struggle to define oneself is too difficult; the novel is a testament to that suggestion.

The Communist Party members, too, are outsiders, and there is nothing unified about their company. Each one that Damon meets is playing god, hoping to protect and extend his personal power. Their awareness of their motives varies, but they are a threat to Damon, and the action of the book is propelled by a series of murders: Damon himself wants to act like a god. Near the end of the book, Houston comes to understand that Damon is the killer, but—rather than indicting and punishing him legally—Houston allows him to go free, alone with his knowledge of what he is. Damon is horrified by his fate, but he is robbed of even that when he is killed by two Communist Party members who fear him.

The Outsider is both an extension and a modification of Wright's earlier views; it is far more pessimistic than *Native Son*, and the influence of the French existentialists is more pervasive. Like earlier Wright heroes, Damon is engaged in defining the world and himself. "The moment we act 'as if' it's true, then it's true," he thinks, because each person, in the absence of a god, is able to create the world and its truth. From Fyodor Dostoevski, Wright again borrows the notion of the underground man and the idea that without a god, all is permitted. However, as each man plays god, as each becomes criminal, policeman, judge, and executioner, there are no longer limits. People desire everything, and desire is described as a floating demon. People are jealous gods here—the worlds they create are petty, their jealousy destructive. Damon is loved in the novel, but that love, unlike the love in *Native Son*, which is held up as potentially meaningful, is here without promise. Although he creates himself and his world in *The Outsider*, all that is made is violent and brutal, a world without redemption even in the act of self-realization.

At the end of the novel, Cross Damon dies, not with Bigger Thomas's smile, but with the knowledge that alone, people are nothing. Searching in his last moments of freedom for a clean, well-lighted place in which to rest before he confronts the world again, Cross finds only death. Before he dies, he admits his final act of bad faith: He has thought that he could create a world and be different from other men, that he could remain innocent. Like Joseph Conrad's Kurtz in *Heart of Darkness* (1902), Damon dies realizing the futility of that hope; having looked into his own heart of darkness, he dies with the word *horror* on his lips.

It is Wright's bleakest conclusion, the book his most relentless examination of the consequences of his own philosophy. If *The Outsider* lacks the narrative drive of *Native Son*, it remains a strongly conceived and troubling piece of fiction.

The Long Dream • Wright's last novel, *The Long Dream*, despite some effective scenes, is one of his weakest. The story of Rex "Fishbelly" Tucker's growing up and coming to terms with his environment is a pale repetition of earlier themes. The first section describes Tucker's youth. His father, an undertaker, is the richest black man in town, but his money comes also from a brothel he runs on the side. Tucker admires his father's success while detesting his obsequiousness with whites. When, however, Fishbelly is arrested, he twice faints at the white world's threats. Having presented himself as a victim, he becomes one. Walking home after his father has arranged his freedom, Fishbelly sees an injured dog, which he puts out of its misery. Fishbelly then comes upon a white man, pinned to the ground with a car door on his body. When the white man calls out to Fishbelly, using the term "nigger," Fishbelly walks on, leaving the man to die.

In the second section, Fishbelly finds a woman, but she and forty-one others are burned to death in a fire at the bar. The rest of the novel is an unconvincing story of the police who want the return of the canceled checks that Fishbelly's father has used to pay them off, the police's arranged murder of the father, the subsequent framing and imprisoning of Fishbelly for rape, and Fishbelly's keeping the checks for his future use. All of this is seriously contrived. At the end, Fishbelly is on a plane leaving for France, where his childhood friends are stationed in the army, which they describe as exciting. He is talking to an Italian whose father has come to America and found a dream, where Fishbelly himself has known only a nightmare. France, he dreams, will offer him what America has not.

In Fishbelly's attempt to understand himself and his environment, he is a typical Wright protagonist. He is weaker than Wright's usual characters, however, and that shallowness, coupled with an implausible plot, prevents Wright's last work of long fiction from succeeding.

Unlike many highly acclaimed books of the 1940's, *Native Son* and *Black Boy* have not dated. They are a lacerating challenge to contemporary readers and writers—a challenge to share the relentless integrity of Richard Wright's vision.

Howard Faulkner

Other major works

SHORT FICTION: *Uncle Tom's Children: Four Novellas*, 1938 (expanded as *Uncle Tom's Children: Five Long Stories*, 1938); *Eight Men*, 1961.

PLAY: *Native Son: The Biography of a Young American*, pr. 1941 (with Paul Green).

POETRY: *Haiku: This Other World*, 1998 (Yoshinobu Hakutani and Robert L. Tener, editors).

NONFICTION: *Twelve Million Black Voices: A Folk History of the Negro in the United States*, 1941 (photographs by Edwin Rosskam); *Black Boy: A Record of Childhood and Youth*, 1945; *Black Power: A Record of Reactions in a Land of Pathos*, 1954; *The Color Curtain*, 1956; *Pagan Spain*, 1957; *White Man, Listen!*, 1957; *American Hunger*, 1977; *Richard Wright Reader*, 1978 (Ellen Wright and Michel Fabre, editors); *Conversations with Richard Wright*, 1993 (Keneth Kinnamon and Michel Fabre, editors).

MISCELLANEOUS: *Works*, 1991 (2 volumes).

Bibliography

Baldwin, James. *The Price of the Ticket: Collected Nonfiction, 1948-1985*. New York: St. Martin's Press/Marek, 1985. The essays "Everybody's Protest Novel" and "Alas, Poor Richard" provide important and provocative insights into Wright and his art.

Bloom, Harold, ed. *Richard Wright*. New York: Chelsea House, 1987. Essays on various aspects of Wright's work and career, with an introduction by Bloom.

Butler, Robert. *"Native Son": The Emergence of a New Black Hero.* Boston: Twayne, 1991. An accessible critical look at the seminal novel. Includes bibliographical references and index.

Fabre, Michel. *The Unfinished Quest of Richard Wright.* New York: William Morrow, 1973. Although this volume is one of the most important and authoritative biographies available on Wright, readers interested in Wright's life should consult Margaret Walker's biography as well (see below).

_____. *The World of Richard Wright.* Jackson: University Press of Mississippi, 1985. A collection of Fabre's essays on Wright. A valuable resource, though not a sustained, full-length study. It contains two chapters on individual short stories by Wright, including the short story "Superstition." Supplemented by an appendix.

Felgar, Robert. *Richard Wright.* Boston: Twayne, 1980. A general biographical and critical source, this work devotes two chapters to the short fiction of Wright.

Hakutani, Yoshinobu. *Richard Wright and Racial Discourse.* Columbia: University of Missouri Press, 1996. This study of Wright's fiction as racial discourse and the product of diverse cultures devotes one chapter to Wright's *Uncle Tom's Children,* focusing primarily on racial and cultural contexts of "Big Boy Leaves Home."

JanMohamed, Abdul R. *The Death-Bound-Subject: Richard Wright's Archaeology of Death.* Durham, N.C.: Duke University Press, 2005. Probing exploration of the theme of violence in Wright's writings and the anticipation of death by African Americans.

Kinnamon, Keneth. *The Emergence of Richard Wright.* Urbana: University of Illinois Press, 1972. A study of Wright's background and development as a writer, up until the publication of *Native Son.*

_____, comp. *A Richard Wright Bibliography: Fifty Years of Criticism and Commentary, 1933-1982.* Westport, Conn.: Greenwood Press, 1988. A mammoth annotated bibliography (one of the largest annotated bibliographies ever assembled on an American writer), which traces the history of Wright criticism. This bibliography is invaluable as a research tool.

_____, ed. *Critical Essays on Richard Wright's "Native Son."* New York: Twayne, 1997. Divided into sections of reviews, reprinted essays, and new essays. Includes discussions of Wright's handling of race, voice, tone, novelistic structure, the city, and literary influences. Index but no bibliography.

Rowley, Hazel. *Richard Wright: The Life and Times.* New York: Henry Holt, 2001. Full biography of Wright that examines his life in the context of the African American experience in America.

Walker, Margaret. *Richard Wright: Daemonic Genius.* New York: Warner Books, 1988. A critically acclaimed study of Wright's life and work written by a friend and fellow novelist. Not a replacement for Michel Fabre's biography but written with the benefit of several more years of scholarship on issues that include the medical controversy over Wright's death. Walker is especially insightful on Wright's early life, and her comments on Wright's short fiction are short but pithy. Includes a useful bibliographic essay at the end.

TERMS AND TECHNIQUES

Absurdism: Philosophical attitude pervading much of modern drama and fiction, which underlines the isolation and alienation that humans experience, having been thrown into what absurdists see as a godless universe devoid of religious, spiritual, or metaphysical meaning. Conspicuous in its lack of logic, consistency, coherence, intelligibility, and realism, the literature of the absurd depicts the anguish, forlornness, and despair inherent in the human condition. Counter to the rationalist assumptions of traditional humanism, absurdism denies the existence of universal truth or value.

Allegory: Literary mode in which a second level of meaning, wherein characters, events, and settings represent abstractions, is encoded within the surface narrative. The allegorical mode may dominate the entire work, in which case the encoded message is the work's primary excuse for being, or it may be an element in a work otherwise interesting and meaningful for its surface story alone. Elements of allegory may be found in Jonathan Swift's *Gulliver's Travels* (1726) and Thomas Mann's *The Magic Mountain* (1924).

Anatomy: Literally the term means the "cutting up" or "dissection" of a subject into its constituent parts for closer examination. In his *Anatomy of Criticism* (1957), Northrop Frye uses the term to refer to a narrative that deals with mental attitudes rather than people. As opposed to the novel, the anatomy features stylized figures who are mouthpieces for the ideas they represent.

Antagonist: Character in a fictional work who stands as a rival or opponent to the PROTAGONIST.

Antihero: As defined by Seán O'Faoláin, a fictional figure who, deprived of social sanctions and definitions, is always trying to define himself and to establish his own codes. Ahab may be seen as the antihero of Herman Melville's *Moby Dick* (1851).

Archetype: Term that entered literary criticism from the psychology of Carl G. Jung, who defined archetypes as "primordial images" from the "collective unconscious" of humankind. Jung believed that works of art derived much of their power from the unconscious appeal of these images to ancestral memories. In his extremely influential *Anatomy of Criticism* (1957), Northrop Frye gave another sense of the term wide currency, defining the archetype as "a symbol, usually an image, which recurs often enough in literature to be recognizable as an element of one's literary experience as a whole."

Atmosphere: General mood or tone of a work; it is often associated with setting but can also be established by action or dialogue. A classic example of atmosphere is the primitive, fatalistic tone created in the opening description of Egdon Heath in Thomas Hardy's *The Return of the Native* (1878).

Bildungsroman: Sometimes called the "novel of education," the *Bildungsroman* focuses on the growth of a young PROTAGONIST who is learning about the world and finding his or her place in life; typical examples are James Joyce's *A Portrait of the Artist as a Young Man* (serial 1914-1915, book 1916) and Thomas Wolfe's *Look Homeward, Angel* (1929).

Biographical criticism: Criticism that attempts to determine how the events and experiences of an author's life influence his work.

Canon: Authorized or accepted list of books. In modern parlance, the literary canon comprehends the privileged texts, classics, or great books that are thought to belong permanently on university reading lists. Recent theory—especially feminist, Marxist, and poststructuralist—critically examines the process of canon formation and questions the hegemony of white male writers. Such theory sees canon formation as the ideological act of a dominant institution and seeks to undermine the notion of canonicity itself, thereby preventing the exclusion of works by women, minorities, and oppressed peoples.

Character: Characters in fiction can be presented as if they were real people or as stylized functions of the plot. Usually characters are a combination of both factors.

Classicism: Literary stance or value system consciously based on the example of classical Greek and Roman literature. While the term is applied to an enormous diversity of artists in many different periods and in many different national literatures, "classicism" generally denotes a cluster of values including formal discipline, restrained expression, reverence for tradition, and an objective rather than a subjective orientation. As a literary tendency, classicism is often opposed to ROMANTICISM, although many writers combine classical and romantic elements.

Climax/Crisis: Whereas climax refers to the moment of the reader's highest emotional response, crisis refers to a structural element of plot. Crisis refers to a turning point in fiction, a point when a resolution must take place.

Complication: Point in a novel at which the conflict is developed or when the already existing conflict is further intensified.

Conflict: Struggle that develops as a result of the opposition between the PROTAGONIST and another person, the natural world, society, or some force within the self.

Contextualist criticism: Extension of FORMALIST CRITICISM, which assumes that the language of art is constitutive. Rather than referring to preexistent values, the artwork creates values only inchoately realized before. The most important advocates of this position are Eliseo Vivas (*The Artistic Transaction*, 1963) and Murray Krieger (*The Play and Place of Criticism*, 1967).

Conventions: All those devices of stylization, compression, and selection that constitute the necessary differences between art and life. According to the Russian Formalists, these conventions constitute the "literariness" of literature and are the only proper concern of the literary critic.

Deconstruction: Influential modern school of criticism based on the works of the French philosopher Jacques Derrida. Deconstruction treats literary works as unconscious reflections of the reigning myths of Western culture. The primary myth is that there is a meaningful world that language signifies or represents. The deconstructionist critic is most often concerned with showing how a literary text tacitly subverts the very assumptions or myths on which it ostensibly rests.

Detective story: The so-called classic detective story (or mystery) is a highly formalized and logically structured mode of fiction in which the focus is on a crime solved by a detective through interpretation of evidence and ratiocination; the most famous detective in this mode is Arthur Conan Doyle's Sherlock Holmes. Many modern practitioners of the genre, however, such as Dashiell Hammett, Raymond Chandler, and Ross Macdonald, have deemphasized the puzzlelike qualities of the detective story, stressing instead characterization, theme, and other elements of mainstream fiction.

Determinism: Belief that an individual's actions are essentially determined by biological and environmental factors, with free will playing a negligible role. (See NATURALISM.)

Dialogue: The similitude of conversation in fiction, dialogue serves to characterize, to further the plot, to establish conflict, and to express thematic ideas.

Displacement: Popularized in criticism by Northrop Frye, the term refers to the author's attempt to make his story psychologically motivated and realistic, even as the latent structure of the mythical motivation moves relentlessly forward.

Dominant: Term coined by Roman Jakobson to refer to that which "rules, determines, and transforms the remaining components in the work of a single artist, in a poetic canon, or in the work of an epoch." The shifting of the dominant in a GENRE accounts for the creation of new generic forms and new poetic epochs. For example, the rise of realism in the mid-nineteenth century indicates realistic conventions becoming dominant and romance or fantasy conventions becoming secondary.

Doppelgänger: A double or counterpart of a person, sometimes endowed with ghostly qualities. A fictional character's *Doppelgänger* often reflects a suppressed side of his or her personality. One of the classic examples of the *Doppelgänger* motif is found in Fyodor Dostoevski's novella *The Double* (1846); Isaac Bashevis Singer and Jorge Luis Borges, among others, offer striking modern treatments of the *Doppelgänger.*

Epic: Although this term usually refers to a long narrative poem that presents the exploits of a central figure of high position, the term is also used to designate a long novel that has the style or structure usually associated with an epic. In this sense, for example, Herman Melville's *Moby Dick* (1851) and James Joyce's *Ulysses* (1922) may be called epic.

Episodic narrative: Work that is held together primarily by a loose connection of self-sufficient episodes. PICARESQUE NOVELS often have an episodic structure.

Epistolary novel: Novel made up of letters by one or more fictional characters. Samuel Richardson's *Pamela* (1740-1741) is a well-known eighteenth century example. In the nineteenth century, Bram Stoker's *Dracula* (1897) is largely epistolary. The technique allows for several different points of view to be presented.

Existentialism: Philosophical, religious, and literary term, emerging from World War II, for a group of attitudes surrounding the pivotal notion that existence precedes essence. According to Jean-Paul Sartre, "man is nothing else but what he makes himself." Forlornness arises from the death of God and the concomitant death of universal values, of any source of ultimate or a priori standards. Despair arises from the fact that an individual can reckon only with what depends on his or her will, and the sphere of that will is severely limited; the number of things on which he or she can have an impact is pathetically small. Existentialist literature is antideterministic in the extreme and rejects the idea that heredity and environment shape and determine human motivation and behavior.

Exposition: Part or parts of a fictional work that provide necessary background information. Exposition not only provides the time and place of the action but also introduces readers to the fictive world of the story, acquainting them with the ground rules of the work.

Fantastic: In his study *The Fantastic* (1970), Tzvetan Todorov defines the fantastic as a GENRE that lies between the "uncanny" and the "marvelous." All three genres embody the familiar world but present an event that cannot be explained by the laws of the familiar world. Todorov says that the fantastic occupies a twilight zone between the uncanny—when the reader knows that the peculiar event is merely the result of an illusion—and the marvelous—when the reader understands that the event is supposed to take place in a realm controlled by laws unknown to humankind. Thus, the fantastic is essentially unsettling, provocative, even subversive.

Feminist criticism: Criticism advocating equal rights for women in a political, economic, social, psychological, personal, and aesthetic sense. On the thematic level, the feminist reader should identify with female characters and their concerns. The object is to provide a critique of phallocentric assumptions and an analysis of patriarchal ideologies inscribed in a literature that is male-centered and male-dominated. On the ideological level, feminist critics see gender, as well as the stereotypes that go along with it, as a cultural construct. They strive to define a particularly feminine content and to extend the CANON so that it might include works by lesbians, feminists, and women writers in general.

Flashback: Scene in a fictional work that depicts an earlier event; it can be presented as a reminiscence by a character in the story or it can simply be inserted into the narrative.

Foreshadowing: Device to create suspense or dramatic irony by indicating through suggestion what will take place in the future.

Formalist criticism: There were two particularly influential formalist schools of criticism in the twentieth century: the Russian Formalists and the American New Critics. The Russian Formalists were concerned with the conventional devices used in literature to defamiliarize that which habit has made familiar. The New Critics believed that literary criticism is a description and evaluation of its object and that the primary concern of the critic is with the work's unity. Both schools of criticism, at their most extreme, treated literary works as artifacts or constructs divorced from their biographical and social contexts.

Genre: In its most general sense, the term "genre" refers to a group of literary works defined by a common form, style, or purpose. In practice, the term is used in a wide variety of overlapping and, to a degree, contradictory senses. Thus, tragedy and comedy are described as distinct genres; the novel (a form that includes both tragic and comic works) is a genre; and various subspecies of the novel, such as the GOTHIC and the PICARESQUE, are themselves frequently treated as distinct genres. Finally, the term GENRE FICTION refers to forms of popular fiction in which the writer is bound by more or less rigid conventions. Indeed, all these diverse usages have in common an emphasis on the manner in which individual literary works are shaped by the expectations and conventions of a particular genre: This is the subject of genre criticism.

Genre fiction: Categories of popular fiction such as the mystery, the romance, and the Western. Although the term can be used in a neutral sense, "genre fiction" is often pejorative, used dismissively to refer to fiction in which the writer is bound by more or less rigid conventions.

Gothic novel: Form of fiction developed in the eighteenth century that focuses on horror and the supernatural. In his preface to *The Castle of Otranto* (1764), the first gothic novel in English, Horace Walpole claimed that he was trying to combine two kinds of fiction, with events and story typical of the medieval romance and character delineation typical of the realistic novel. Other examples of the form are Matthew Lewis's *The Monk* (1796) and Mary Shelley's *Frankenstein* (1818).

Grotesque: According to Wolfgang Kayser (*The Grotesque in Art and Literature*, 1963), the grotesque is an embodiment in literature of the estranged world. Characterized by a breakup of the everyday world by mysterious forces, the form differs from fantasy in that the reader is not sure whether to react with humor or with horror and in that the exaggeration manifested exists in the familiar world rather than in a purely imaginative world.

Hebraic/Homeric styles: Terms coined by Erich Auerbach in *Mimesis: The Representation of Reality in Western Literature* (1953) to designate two basic fictional styles: the Hebraic, which focuses only on the decisive points of narrative and leaves all else obscure, mysterious, and "fraught with background," and the Homeric, which places the narrative in a definite time and place and externalizes everything in a perpetual foreground.

Historical criticism: In contrast to FORMALIST CRITICISM, which treats literary works to a great extent as self-contained artifacts, historical criticism emphasizes the historical context of literature; these approaches, however, need not be mutually exclusive. Ernst Robert Curtius's *European Literature and the Latin Middle Ages* (1940) is a prominent example of historical criticism.

Historical novel: Novel that depicts past historical events, usually public in nature, and features real as well as fictional people. Sir Walter Scott's *Waverley* novels established the basic type, but the relationship between fiction and history in the form varies greatly depending on the practitioner.

Implied author: According to Wayne Booth (*The Rhetoric of Fiction*, 1961), the novel often creates a kind of second self who tells the story—a self who is wiser, more sensitive, and more perceptive than any real person could be.

Interior monologue: Defined by Édouard Dujardin as the speech of a character designed to introduce the reader directly to the character's internal life, the form differs from other monologues in that it attempts to reproduce thought before any logical organization is imposed upon it. See, for example, Molly Bloom's long interior monologue at the conclusion of James Joyce's *Ulysses* (1922).

Irrealism: Term often used to refer to modern or postmodern fiction that is presented self-consciously as a fiction or a fabulation rather than a mimesis of external reality. The best-known practitioners of irrealism are John Barth, Robert Coover, and Donald Barthelme.

Local colorists: Loose movement of late nineteenth century American writers whose fiction emphasized the distinctive folkways, landscapes, and dialects of various regions. Important local colorists included Bret Harte, Mark Twain, George Washington Cable, Kate Chopin, and Sarah Orne Jewett. (See REGIONAL NOVEL.)

Marxist criticism: Based on the nineteenth century writings of Karl Marx and Friedrich Engels, Marxist criticism views literature as a product of ideological forces determined by the dominant class. However, many Marxists believe that literature operates according to its own autonomous standards of production and reception: It is both a product of ideology and able to determine ideology. As such, literature may overcome the dominant paradigms of its age and play a revolutionary role in society.

Metafiction: Fictional work that manifests a reflexive tendency, such as Vladimir Nabokov's *Pale Fire* (1962) and John Fowles's *The French Lieutenant's Woman* (1969). The emphasis is on the loosening of the work's illusion of reality to expose the reality of its illusion. Such terms as IRREALISM, POSTMODERNIST fiction, "anti-fiction," and "surfiction" are also used to refer to this type of fiction.

Modernism: International movement in the arts that began in the early years of the twentieth century. Although the term is used to describe artists of widely varying persuasions, modernism in general was characterized by its international idiom, by its interest in cultures distant in space or time, by its emphasis on formal experimentation, and by its sense of dislocation and radical change.

Motif: Conventional incident or situation in a fictional work that may serve as the basis for the structure of the narrative itself. The Russian Formalist critic Boris Tomashevsky uses the term to refer to the smallest particle of thematic material in a work.

Motivation: Although this term is usually used in reference to the convention of justifying the action of a character from his or her psychological makeup, the Russian Formalists use the term to refer to the network of devices that justify the introduction of individual MOTIFS or groups of motifs in a work. For example, compositional motivation refers to the principle that every single property in a work contributes to its overall effect; realistic motivation refers to the realistic devices used to make the work plausible and lifelike.

Multiculturalism: Tendency to recognize the perspectives of those traditionally excluded from the canon of Western art and literature. In order to promote multiculturalism, publishers and educators have revised textbooks and school curricula to incorporate material by and about women, minorities, non-Western cultures, and homosexuals.

Myth: Anonymous traditional stories dealing with basic human concepts and antinomies. Claude Lévi-Strauss says that myth is that part of language where the "formula *tradutore, tradittore* reaches its lowest truth value. . . . Its substance does not lie in its style, its original music, or its syntax, but in the story which it tells."

Myth criticism: Northrop Frye says that in myth, "we see the structural principles of literature isolated." Myth criticism is concerned with these basic principles of literature; it is not to be confused with mythological criticism, which is primarily concerned with finding mythological parallels in the surface action of the NARRATIVE.

Narrative: Robert Scholes and Robert Kellogg, in *The Nature of Narrative* (1966), say that by narrative they mean literary works that include both a story and a storyteller. Narrative usually implies a contrast to "enacted" fiction such as drama.

Narratology: Study of the form and functioning of NARRATIVES; it attempts to examine what all narratives have in common and what makes individual narratives different from one another.

Narrator: Character who recounts the NARRATIVE, or story. Wayne Booth describes various dramatized narrators in *The Rhetoric of Fiction* (1961): unacknowledged centers of consciousness, observers, narrator-agents, and self-conscious narrators. Booth suggests that the important elements to consider in narration are the relationships among the narrator, the author, the characters, and the reader.

Naturalism: As developed by Émile Zola in the late nineteenth century, naturalism is the application of the principles of scientific DETERMINISM to fiction. Although it usually refers more to the choice of subject matter than to technical conventions, those conventions associated with the movement center on the author's attempt to be precise and scientifically objective in description and detail, regardless of whether the events described are sordid or shocking.

New Criticism. See FORMALIST CRITICISM.

Novel: Perhaps the most difficult of all fictional forms to define because of its multiplicity of modes. Edouard, in André Gide's *The Counterfeiters* (1926), says the novel is the freest and most lawless of all GENRES: he wonders if fear of that liberty is not the reason the novel has so timidly clung to reality. Most critics seem to agree that the novel's primary area of concern is the social world. Ian Watt (*The Rise of the Novel*, 1957) says that the novel can be distinguished from other fictional forms by the attention it pays to individual characterization and detailed presentation of the environment. Moreover, says Watt, the novel, more than any other fictional form, is interested in the "development of its characters in the course of time."

Novella, novelle, nouvelle, novelette, novela: Although these terms often refer to the short European tale, especially the Renaissance form employed by Giovanni Boccaccio, the terms often refer to that form of fiction that is said to be longer than a short story and shorter than a novel. "Novelette" is the term usually preferred by the British, whereas "novella" is the term usually used to refer to American works in this GENRE. Henry James claimed that the main merit of the form was the "effort to do the complicated thing with a strong brevity and lucidity."

Phenomenological criticism: Although best known as a European school of criticism practiced by Georges Poulet and others, this so-called criticism of consciousness is also propounded in America by such critics as J. Hillis Miller. The focus is less on individual works and GENRES than it is on literature as an act; the work is not seen as an object, but rather as part of a strand of latent impulses in the work of a single author or an epoch.

Picaresque novel: Form of fiction that centers on a central rogue figure or picaro who usually tells his or her own story. The plot structure is normally EPISODIC, and the episodes usually focus on how the picaro lives by his or her wits. Classic examples of the mode are Henry Fielding's *Tom Jones* (1749) and Mark Twain's *Adventures of Huckleberry Finn* (1884).

Plot/Story: Story is a term referring to the full narrative of character and action, whereas plot generally refers to action with little reference to character. A more precise and helpful distinction is made by the Russian Formalists, who suggest that plot refers to the events of a NARRATIVE as they have been artfully arranged in the literary work, subject to chronological displacement, ellipses, and other devices, while story refers to the sum of the same events arranged in simple, causal-chronological order. Thus, story is the raw material for plot. By comparing the two in a given work, the reader is encouraged to see the NARRATIVE as an artifact.

Point of view: Means by which the story is presented to the reader, or, as Percy Lubbock says in *The Craft of Fiction* (1921), "the relation in which the narrator stands to the story"—a relation that Lubbock claims governs the craft of fiction. Some of the questions the critical reader should ask concerning point of view are: Who talks to the reader? From what position does the narrator tell the story? At what distance does he or she place the reader from the story? What kind of person is he or she? How fully is he or she characterized? How reliable is he or she? For further discussion, see Wayne Booth, *The Rhetoric of Fiction* (1961).

Postcolonialism: Postcolonial literature emerged in the mid-twentieth century when colonies in Asia, Africa, and the Caribbean began gaining their independence from the European nations that had long controlled them. Postcolonial authors, such as Salman Rushdie and V. S. Naipaul, tend to focus on both the freedom and the conflict inherent in living in a postcolonial state.

Postmodernism: Ubiquitous but elusive term in contempory criticism, "postmodernism" is loosely applied to the various artistic movements that followed the era of so-called high modernism, represented by such giants as James Joyce and Pablo Picasso. In critical discussions of contemporary fiction, the term "postmodernism" is frequently applied to the works of writers such as Thomas Pynchon, John Barth, and Donald Barthelme, who exhibit a self-conscious awareness of their modernist predecessors as well as a reflexive treatment of fictional form.

Protagonist: Central character in a fictional work, the character whose fortunes most concern the reader.

Psychological criticism: While much modern literary criticism reflects to some degree the impact of Sigmund Freud, Carl Jung, Jacques Lacan, and other psychological theorists, the term "psychological criticism" suggests a strong emphasis on a causal relation between the writer's psychological state, variously interpreted, and his or her works. A notable example of psychological criticism is Norman Fruman's *Coleridge, the Damaged Archangel* (1971).

Psychological novel: Form of fiction in which character, especially the inner life of characters, is the primary focus. The form has been of primary importance, at least since Henry James, and it characterizes much of the work of James Joyce, Virginia Woolf, and William Faulkner. For a detailed discussion, see *The Modern Psychological Novel* (1955) by Leon Edel.

Realism: Literary technique in which the primary convention is to render an illusion of fidelity to external reality. Realism is often identified as the primary method of the novel form: It focuses on surface details, maintains a fidelity to the everyday experiences of middle-class society, and strives for a one-to-one relationship between the fiction and the action imitated. The realist movement in the late nineteenth century coincides with the full development of the novel form.

Reception aesthetics: The best-known American practitioner of reception aesthetics is Stanley Fish. For the reception critic, meaning is an event or process; rather than being embedded in the work, it is created through particular acts of reading. The best-known European practitioner of this criticism, Wolfgang Iser, says indeterminacy is the basic characteristic of literary texts; the reader must "normalize" the text either by projecting his or her standards into it or by revising his or her standards to "fit" the text.

Regional novel: Any novel in which the character of a given geographical region plays a decisive role. Although regional differences persist in America, there has been a considerable leveling in speech and customs, so that the sharp regional distinctions evident in nineteenth century American fiction have all but disappeared. Only in the South has a strong regional tradition persisted to the present. (See LOCAL COLORISTS.)

Rhetorical criticism: Form of criticism concerned with the literary work as a means of communicating ideas and the means by which the work affects or controls the reader. Such criticism seems best suited to didactic works such as satire.

Roman à clef: Fictional work wherein actual people, often celebrities of some sort, are thinly disguised.

Romance: Long fictional form that is usually regarded as differing from the novel form in that its focus is on symbolic events and representational characters rather than on "as-if-real" characters and events. Richard Chase says that in the romance, character is depicted as highly stylized, a function of the plot rather than as someone complexly related to society. The romancer is more likely to be concerned with dreamworlds than with the familiar world, believing that reality cannot be grasped by the traditional novel.

Romanticism: Widespread cultural movement in the late eighteenth and early nineteenth centuries, the influence of which is still felt. As a general literary tendency, Romanticism is frequently contrasted with CLASSICISM. Although there were many varieties of Romanticism indigenous to various national literatures, the term generally suggests an assertion of the preeminence of the imagination. Other values associated with various schools of Romanticism include primitivism, an interest in folklore, a reverence for nature, and a fascination with the demoniac and the macabre.

Scene: Central element of narration; specific actions are narrated or depicted that make the reader feel he or she is participating directly in the action.

Science fiction: Fiction in which certain givens (physical laws, psychological principles, social conditions: any one or all of these) form the basis of an imaginative projection into the future or, less commonly, an extrapolation in the present or even into the past.

Semiotics: Science of signs and sign systems in communication. Roman Jakobson says that semiotics deals with the principles that underlie the structure of signs, their use in language of all kinds, and the specific nature of various sign systems.

Sentimental novel: Form of fiction popular in the eighteenth century in which emotionalism and optimism are the primary characteristics. The best-known examples are Samuel Richardson's *Pamela* (1740-1741) and Oliver Goldsmith's *The Vicar of Wakefield* (1766).

Setting: Setting refers to the circumstances and environment, both temporal and spatial, of a NARRATIVE.

Stream of consciousness: Depiction of the thought processes of a character, insofar as this is possible, without any mediating structures. The metaphor of consciousness as a "stream" suggests a rush of thoughts and images governed by free association rather than by strictly rational development. The term "stream of consciousness" is often used loosely as a synonym for INTERIOR MONOLOGUE. The most celebrated example of stream of consciousness in fiction is the monologue of Molly Bloom in James Joyce's *Ulysses* (1922); other notable practitioners of the stream-of-consciousness technique include Dorothy Richardson, Virginia Woolf, and William Faulkner.

Structuralism: As a movement of thought, structuralism is based on the idea of intrinsic, self-sufficient structures that do not require reference to external elements. A structure is a system of transformations that involves the interplay of laws inherent in the system itself. The study of language is the primary model for contemporary structuralism. The structuralist literary critic attempts to define structural princi-

ples that operate intertextually throughout the whole of literature as well as principles that operate in GENRES and in individual works. The most accessible survey
of structuralism and literature is Jonathan Culler's *Structuralist Poetics* (1975).

Summary: Those parts of a fictional work that do not need to be detailed. In *Tom Jones*
(1749), Henry Fielding says "If whole years should pass without producing anything worthy of . . . notice . . . we shall hasten on to matters of consequence."

Thematics: Northrup Frye says that when a work of fiction is written or interpreted
thematically, it becomes an illustrative fable. Murray Krieger defines thematics as
"the study of the experiential tensions which, dramatically entangled in the literary work, become an existential reflection of that work's aesthetic complexity."

Tone: Tone usually refers to the dominant mood of the work. (See ATMOSPHERE.)

Unreliable narrator: Narrator whose account cannot be fully trusted, obliging readers
to reconstruct—if possible—the true state of affairs themselves. Once an innovative technique, the use of the unreliable narrator has become commonplace
among contemporary writers who wish to suggest the impossibility of a truly "reliable" account of any event. Notable examples of the unreliable narrator can be
found in Ford Madox Ford's *The Good Soldier* (1915) and Vladimir Nabokov's *Lolita*
(1958).

Verisimilitude/Vraisemblance: Tzvetan Todorov defines vraisemblance as "the mask
which conceals the text's own laws, but which we are supposed to take for a relation to reality." When one speaks of vraisemblance, one refers to the work's attempts to make the reader believe that it conforms to reality rather than to its own
laws.

Victorian novel: Although the Victorian period extended from 1837 to 1901, the term
"Victorian novel" does not include the later decades of Queen Victoria's reign.
The term loosely refers to the sprawling works of novelists such as Charles Dickens
and William Makepeace Thackeray—works that frequently appeared first in serial
form and are characterized by a broad social canvas.

Western novel: Like all varieties of GENRE FICTION, the Western novel—generally
known simply as the "Western"—is defined by a relatively predictable combination of conventions, MOTIFS, and recurring themes. These predictable elements,
familiar from the many Western series on television and in film, differentiate the
Western from HISTORICAL NOVELS and idiosyncratic works such as Thomas Berger's *Little Big Man* (1964) that are also set in the Old West. Conversely, some novels set in the contemporary West are regarded as Westerns because they deal with
modern cowboys and with the land itself in the manner characteristic of the
genre.

Charles E. May

Time Line

Date and Place of Birth	Name
September 15, 1789: Burlington, New Jersey	James Fenimore Cooper
July 4, 1804: Salem, Massachusetts	Nathaniel Hawthorne
June 14, 1811: Litchfield, Connecticut	Harriet Beecher Stowe
August 1, 1819: New York, New York	Herman Melville
November 29, 1832: Germantown, Pennsylvania	Louisa May Alcott
November 30, 1835: Florida, Missouri	Mark Twain
March 1, 1837: Martin's Ferry, Ohio	William Dean Howells
April 15, 1843: New York, New York	Henry James
October 12, 1844: New Orleans, Louisiana	George Washington Cable
September 3, 1849: South Berwick, Maine	Sarah Orne Jewett
February 8, 1851: St. Louis, Missouri	Kate Chopin
January 24, 1862: New York, New York	Edith Wharton
March 5, 1870: Chicago, Illinois	Frank Norris
August 27, 1871: Terre Haute, Indiana	Theodore Dreiser
November 1, 1871: Newark, New Jersey	Stephen Crane
April 22, 1873: Richmond, Virginia	Ellen Glasgow
December 7, 1873: Back Creek Valley, Virginia	Willa Cather
February 3, 1874: Allegheny, Pennsylvania	Gertrude Stein
January 12, 1876: San Francisco, California	Jack London
September 13, 1876: Camden, Ohio	Sherwood Anderson
September 20, 1878: Baltimore, Maryland	Upton Sinclair
February 14, 1879: Radomno, Prussia (now in Russia)	Frederick Philip Grove
February 7, 1885: Sauk Centre, Minnesota	Sinclair Lewis
August 15, 1885: Kalamazoo, Michigan	Edna Ferber
January 20, 1888: Port Elizabeth, South Africa	Ethel Wilson
July 23, 1888: Chicago, Illinois	Raymond Chandler
May 15, 1890: Indian Creek, Texas	Katherine Anne Porter
October 13, 1890: Pine Grove, Pennsylvania	Conrad Richter
January 7, 1891: Eatonville, Florida	Zora Neale Hurston
December 26, 1891: New York, New York	Henry Miller
June 26, 1892: Hillsboro, West Virginia	Pearl S. Buck
May 27, 1894: St. Mary's County, Maryland	Dashiell Hammett
January 14, 1896: Chicago, Illinois	John Dos Passos

Date and Place of Birth	Name
August 8, 1896: Washington, D.C.	Marjorie Kinnan Rawlings
September 24, 1896: St. Paul, Minnesota	F. Scott Fitzgerald
April 17, 1897: Madison, Wisconsin	Thornton Wilder
September 25, 1897: New Albany, Mississippi	William Faulkner
April 23, 1899: St. Petersburg, Russia	Vladimir Nabokov
July 21, 1899: Oak Park, Illinois	Ernest Hemingway
October 3, 1900: Asheville, North Carolina	Thomas Wolfe
February 27, 1902: Salinas, California	John Steinbeck
October 13, 1902: Alexandria, Louisiana	Arna Bontemps
February 22, 1903: Toronto, Ontario, Canada	Morley Callaghan
October 17, 1903: New York, New York	Nathanael West
February 27, 1904: Chicago, Illinois	James T. Farrell
July 14 or November 21, 1904: Leoncin, Poland	Isaac Bashevis Singer
January 31, 1905: Pottsville, Pennsylvania	John O'Hara
February 2, 1905: St. Petersburg, Russia	Ayn Rand
April 24, 1905: Guthrie, Kentucky	Robert Penn Warren
February 8, 1906: Tysmenica, Galicia	Henry Roth
February 3, 1907(?): New York, New York(?)	James A. Michener
March 20, 1907: Glace Bay, Nova Scotia, Canada	Hugh MacLennan
January 22, 1908: Shellbrook, Saskatchewan, Canada	Sinclair Ross
August 31, 1908: Fresno,s California	William Saroyan
September 4, 1908: Roxie, Mississippi	Richard Wright
February 18, 1909: Lake Mills, Iowa	Wallace Stegner
April 13, 1909: Jackson, Mississippi	Eudora Welty
November 27, 1909: Knoxville, Tennessee	James Agee
January 6, 1910: Central City, Nebraska	Wright Morris
December 30, 1910: New York, New York	Paul Bowles
May 27, 1912: Quincy, Massachusetts	John Cheever
June 21, 1912: Seattle, Washington	Mary McCarthy
August 28, 1913: Thamesville, Ontario, Canada	Robertson Davies
February 5, 1914: St. Louis, Missouri	William S. Burroughs
March 1, 1914: Oklahoma City, Oklahoma	Ralph Ellison
April 26, 1914: Brooklyn, New York	Bernard Malamud
June 17, 1914: Tianjin, China	John Hersey
May 27, 1915: New York, New York	Herman Wouk
June 10, 1915: Lachine, Quebec, Canada	Saul Bellow
December 13, 1915: Los Gatos, California	Ross Macdonald
May 28, 1916: Birmingham, Alabama	Walker Percy
February 19, 1917: Columbus, Georgia	Carson McCullers
September 27, 1917: Lawrence, New York	Louis Auchincloss
February 26, 1918: Staten Island, New York	Theodore Sturgeon
January 1, 1919: New York, New York	J. D. Salinger
January 2, 1920: Petrovichi, Soviet Union	Isaac Asimov
August 22, 1920: Waukegan, Illinois	Ray Bradbury

Date and Place of Birth	Name
November 6, 1921: Robinson, Illinois	James Jones
March 12, 1922: Lowell, Massachusetts	Jack Kerouac
November 11, 1922: Indianapolis, Indiana	Kurt Vonnegut
December 29, 1922: New York, New York	William Gaddis
January 31, 1923: Long Branch, New Jersey	Norman Mailer
February 2, 1923: Atlanta, Georgia	James Dickey
May 1, 1923: Brooklyn, New York	Joseph Heller
August 2, 1924: New York, New York	James Baldwin
September 30, 1924: New Orleans, Louisiana	Truman Capote
March 25, 1925: Savannah, Georgia	Flannery O'Connor
June 11, 1925: Newport News, Virginia	William Styron
October 3, 1925: West Point, New York	Gore Vidal
October 11, 1925: New Orleans, Louisiana	Elmore Leonard
April 23, 1926: Brooklyn, New York	J. P. Donleavy
April 28, 1926: Monroeville, Alabama	Harper Lee
July 18, 1926: Neepawa, Manitoba, Canada	Margaret Laurence
September 3, 1926: Chicago, Illinois	Alison Lurie
January 16, 1928: Albany, New York	William Kennedy
September 30, 1928: Sighet, Transylvania, Romania	Elie Wiesel
December 16, 1928: Chicago, Illinois	Philip K. Dick
January 21, 1929: Mercedes, Texas	Rolando Hinojosa
February 17, 1929: New York, New York	Chaim Potok
October 21, 1929: Berkeley, California	Ursula K. Le Guin
May 27, 1930: Cambridge, Maryland	John Barth
June 3, 1930: Albany, New York	Marion Zimmer Bradley
January 6, 1931: New York, New York	E. L. Doctorow
January 27, 1931: Montreal, Quebec, Canada	Mordecai Richler
February 18, 1931: Lorain, Ohio	Toni Morrison
February 4, 1932: Charles City, Iowa	Robert Coover
March 18, 1932: Shillington, Pennsylvania	John Updike
February 1, 1933: Macon, North Carolina	Reynolds Price
January 15, 1933: Oscar, Louisiana	Ernest J. Gaines
March 19, 1933: Newark, New Jersey	Philip Roth
June 14, 1933: Lodz, Poland	Jerzy Kosinski
July 20, 1933: Providence, Rhode Island	Cormac McCarthy
July 21, 1933: Batavia, New York	John Gardner
December 5, 1934: Sacramento, California	Joan Didion
January 30, 1935: Tacoma, Washington	Richard Brautigan
September 17, 1935: La Junta, Colorado	Ken Kesey
June 3, 1936: Wichita Falls, Texas	Larry McMurtry
November 20, 1936: New York, New York	Don DeLillo
May 8, 1937: Glen Cove, New York	Thomas Pynchon
October 30, 1937: Pastura, New Mexico	Rudolfo A. Anaya
February 22, 1938: Chattanooga, Tennessee	Ishmael Reed
June 16, 1938: Lockport, New York	Joyce Carol Oates
March 25, 1939: New York, New York	Toni Cade Bambara

Date and Place of Birth	Name
November 18, 1939: Ottawa, Ontario, Canada	Margaret Atwood
December 11, 1939: Wyandotte, Michigan	Thomas McGuane
April 10, 1941: Medford, Massachusetts	Paul Theroux
October 4, 1941: New Orleans, Louisiana	Anne Rice
October 25, 1941: Minneapolis, Minnesota	Anne Tyler
October 30, 1941: Carrington, North Dakota	Larry Woiwode
March 2, 1942: Exeter, New Hampshire	John Irving
April 1, 1942: New York, New York	Samuel R. Delany
February 9, 1944: Eatonton, Georgia	Alice Walker
October 1, 1946: Austin, Minnesota	Tim O'Brien
June 22, 1947: Pasadena, California	Octavia Butler
September 8, 1947: Washington, D.C.	Ann Beattie
September 21, 1947: Portland, Maine	Stephen King
March 5, 1948: Albuquerque, New Mexico	Leslie Marmon Silko
December 2, 1948: Peekskill, New York	T. Coraghessan Boyle
May 25, 1949: Saint Johns, Antigua	Jamaica Kincaid
January 25, 1950: New York, New York	Gloria Naylor
August 24, 1951: New York, New York	Oscar Hijuelos
February 19, 1952: Oakland, California	Amy Tan
June 7, 1954: Little Falls, Minnesota	Louise Erdrich
February 8, 1955: Jonesboro, Arkansas	John Grisham
April 8, 1955: Annapolis, Maryland	Barbara Kingsolver

INDEX

Index

Page references to author essays are boldfaced.

Baker, George Pierce, 1457
Baldwin, James, **64-79**, 414, 416, 1096,
    1275, 1277; and William Styron,
    1269-1270; on *Uncle Tom's Cabin*,
    1251
Ballad of the Sad Café, The (McCullers),
    842
Balzac, Honoré de, 248, 445, 646, 648,
    1411
Bambara, Toni Cade, **80-85**
Baraka, Amiri, 67, 416, 1096
Barbary Shore (Mailer), 892
Barney's Version (Richler), 1117
Barometer Rising (MacLennan), 869
Barren Ground (Glasgow), 524
Barrie, James, 199, 464
Barth, John, **86-100**, 139-140; "The
    Literature of Exhaustion," 293, 299
Barth, Karl, 1326-1328
Barthelme, Donald, 336, 1071, 1289
Barthes, Roland, 293, 299
Bean Trees, The (Kingsolver), 741
Beastly Beatitudes of Balthazar B, The
    (Donleavy), 388
Beat generation, 940; Paul Bowles, 129;
    Richard Brautigan, 164; William
    Burroughs, 179-189; Jack Kerouac,
    693-703; Ken Kesey, 708
Beattie, Ann, **101-107**
Beautiful and Damned, The (Fitzgerald),
    476
Bech (Updike), 1334
Bech at Bay (Updike), 1335
Beckett, Samuel, 86, 110, 385; and John
    Barth, 96; and Robert Coover, 291
Becky and Her Friends (Hinojosa), 607
Beecher, Harriet Elizabeth. *See* Stowe,
    Harriet Beecher
Beet Queen, The (Erdrich), 428
Beggar in Jerusalem, A (Wiesel), 1424
Behan, Brendan, 385
Beiles, Sinclair, 179
Being There (Kosinski), 752
Bell for Adano, A (Hersey), 594
Bellamy, Edward, 326
Bellarosa Connection, The (Bellow), 119
Bellefleur (Oates), 995
Bellow, Saul, **108-122**, 414, 571, 1203,
    1449; *Herzog*, 114, 1368; *Mr. Sammler's*

Planet, 116, 709; "Spirit of
    Alternatives," 1421; and William
    Kennedy, 683
Beloved (Morrison), 962
Benchley, Robert, 1017
Bend Sinister (Nabokov), 970
Benét, Stephen Vincent, 474
Bennett, Arnold, 1438-1439, 1451
Berenson, Bernard, 1407
Berger, Thomas, 140
Bergson, Henri, 1229, 1233
Bernard Carr trilogy (Farrell), 441
Bernstein, Leonard, 838
Berryman, John, 307, 310
Bettelheim, Bruno, 726
Beyond the Bedroom Wall (Woiwode),
    1450
"Bicentennial Man, The" (Asimov), 35
Bierce, Ambrose, 805
Big Money, The (Dos Passos), 400
Big Rock Candy Mountain, The (Stegner),
    1217
Big Sleep, The (Chandler), 246
"Big Two-Hearted River" (Hemingway),
    580
Bildungsroman, 1493; Sherwood
    Anderson, 26; Margaret Atwood, 41;
    Stephen Crane, 305; F. Scott
    Fitzgerald, 474-475; Barbara
    Kingsolver, 740, 743; Jerzy Kosinski,
    750; Jack London, 807; Bernard
    Malamud, 906; Flannery O'Connor,
    1010; Ishmael Reed, 1098; John
    Updike, 1329; Thomas Wolfe, 1460
Billy Bathgate (Doctorow), 378
Billy Budd, Foretopman (Melville), 921
Billy Phelan's Greatest Game (Kennedy),
    687
Bingo Palace, The (Erdrich), 431
Biographical criticism, 1494
Birds of America (McCarthy), 833
Black Mask, 240-241, 243, 542, 545
Black Thunder (Bontemps), 125
Blake, William, 68, 113, 117, 181, 511,
    1073, 1464
Bless Me, Ultima (Anaya), 17
Blind Date (Kosinski), 753
Blithedale Romance, The (Hawthorne),
    561

3 6651 0023